S0-BYJ-491

Acknowledgements from the Author

Fifty percent (50%) of the royalties from this book will be donated to the
Michigan Foundation for Agriculture

MISSION:

The Michigan Foundation for Agriculture focuses on the future of Michigan agriculture through leadership and educational activities

VISION:

To be a charitable source of funding that develops new agricultural leaders and provides educational programs teaching children and consumers how agriculture touches their daily lives

PRIMARY INITIATIVES:

- Educational programs for children and adults
- Leadership programs for future agriculture leaders
- Promotional efforts teaching consumers about modern farming practices
- Scholarship opportunities for students in agricultural studies

First of all, I have to acknowledge the monumental effort of the volunteers and staff of **Michigan Farm Bureau** who worked so hard to obtain many of the pictures for this book and to review the county chapters. Without their efforts there would be no book and no opportunity to raise money for the Michigan Foundation for Agriculture.

Many thanks also to the Convention and Visitors Bureaus and Chambers of Commerce around the state for their review of their county chapter and for providing some of the pictures.

A special thanks goes to my husband who never complained about the 5,000+ hours I spent on the computer at home doing the research (and countless revisions) for the book.

I appreciate the encouragement of my many friends who said the book sounded like a great idea and that they would even purchase it. It meant a lot to me and helped to keep me going even when I never knew if the book would ever get published. As I told many of them, if it was never published, at least I had an interesting hobby for eight years.

I would also like to acknowledge the power of the Internet. Over 95% of this book was researched from reliable online sources. That means that you, too, can find out more about almost any item that is mentioned by just using your favorite search engine.

Neither the publisher nor I had any idea about the time consuming nature of a book laid out in this format. It was a groundbreaking adventure. And Kait, the very competent and sweet lay-out specialist, spent an extraordinary amount of time making the whole thing look so good. Many thanks to you both!

DISCOVERING MICHIGAN COUNTY BY COUNTY: LOWER PENINSULA

YOUR A-Z GUIDE TO EACH OF THE 68 COUNTIES IN MICHIGAN'S LOWER PENINSULA

BY
BARBARA J. VANDERMOLEN

IN COOPERATION WITH
MICHIGAN FOUNDATION FOR AGRICULTURE

Discovering Michigan County by County: LOWER PENINSULA
Your A-Z Guide to Each of the 68 Counties in Michigan's Lower Peninsula.
by Barbara VanderMolen

Published by
Thunder Bay Press
Holt, Michigan 48842

First Thunder Bay Press Edition

18 17 16 15 14 1 2 3 4 5

ISBN: 9781933272467

Library of Congress Control Number: 2014933693

Book Design: Kait Lamphere
Mini Map Design: Julie Taylor
Edited by Denise M. Cauchon-Acevedo, Ed.D.
Cover Images: Benzie Lighthouse (director@benzie.org),
        Missaukee Christmas Tree (Michigan Farm Bureau)
        Ottawa Tulips (Michigan Farm Bureau)
        Mackinac Bridge (NPCR)

Printed in the United States of America

TABLE OF CONTENTS

**Counties are numbered according to their alphabetical
order within the entire state of Michigan.**

Counties found in the Upper Peninsula are included in
*Discovering Michigan County by County: UPPER PENINSULA -
Your A-Z Guide to Each of the 15 Counties in Michigan's Upper Peninsula.*

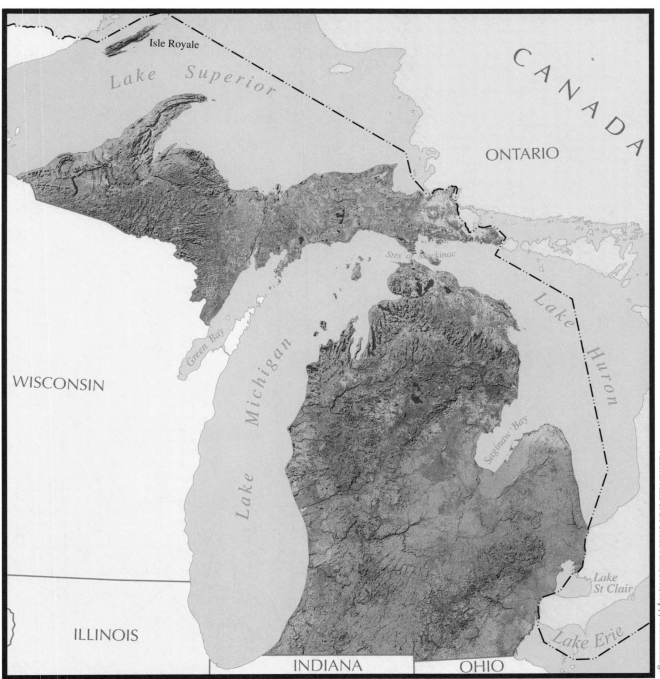

Isle Royale

Lake Superior

CANADA

ONTARIO

Strs. of Mackinac

Lake Huron

WISCONSIN

Green Bay

Lake Michigan

Saginaw Bay

Lake St Clair

ILLINOIS

INDIANA

OHIO

Lake Erie

National Atlas of the United States, 2011, http://nationalatlas.gov

Information on the following counties can be found in the companion book,

Discovering Michigan County by County: UPPER PENINSULA

Your A-Z Guide to Each of the 15 Counties in Michigan's Upper Peninsula.

Discovering Michigan County by County: Upper Peninsula, ISBN: 978-1-933272-47-4, $19.95

A AGRICULTURE

Land in farms: 10% of county
Number of farms: 280
Size of average farm: 160 acres
Market value of all products: #60 of 83 counties
Crops: ...most acres: forage crops
...highest $ sales: other crops and hay
Livestock: ...largest number: cattle & calves
...highest $ sales: milk & dairy products
Dairy, food and meat processing plants: 8
State ranking for harvested trees: #21 of 83 counties
FYI: In 2012, the economic impact of agricultural products sold in Michigan was $91 billion and this industry segment employed one million Michigan residents. That number represents the cumulative impact of the entire agriculture industry and includes on-farm jobs, food processing, agri-business, agri-tourism and all related aspects of the food and farm industry including grocery stores and restaurants.

Michigan's agricultural industry, the original green industry, is the second largest economic block in Michigan. The manufacturing industry is first and the tourism industry is third.

Michigan's agricultural production is divided into the following 14 of the 16 USDA recognized commodity groups and is shown below with the percentage of their market share in Michigan:

- 30% - Grains, oilseeds, dry beans and dry peas
- 22% - Milk & other dairy products
- 11% - Nursery, greenhouse, floriculture and sod
- 8% - Cattle & calves
- 7% - Fruits, tree nuts and berries
- 6% - Hogs & pigs
- 6% - Vegetables, melons, potatoes and sweet potatoes
- 5% - Poultry & eggs
- 4% - Other crops & hay
- <1% - Other animals and animal products
- <1% - Horses, ponies, mules, burros and donkeys
- <1% - Cut Christmas trees and short rotation woody crops
- <1% - Sheep, goats and their products
- <1% - Aquaculture
- 0% - Cotton
- 0% - Tobacco MDA, USDA

B BRIDGE OR BOAT

Tom Garvale

Being on or near the water at sunrise is a popular activity on the Sunrise Side of Michigan. You never know what kind of boat you might see. Sunrise on June 20 is 6:00 a.m. and on January 1 is 8:10 a.m.

C CELEBRATIONS

<u>Glennie</u> *Antique Car Show:* June
<u>Harrisville Harbor</u> *Antique Show:* July
...Wine & Food Festival: July
...Arts & Craft Show: September

D DEMOGRAPHICS

Population: 11,000   **Persons per sq. mile:** 16
Largest city: Harrisville   **Population:** 490
Largest township: Greenbush **Population:** 1,400
Largest village: Lincoln   **Population:** 300
Median household income: $32,600
Owner-occupied median house value: $121,000
Persons affiliated with a religious congregation: 22%
Persons below poverty level: 16%
Students receiving school lunch subsidy: 46%
FYI: Forty-eight percent (5,100) of all housing units in this county are vacation, seasonal, or occasional homes. US Census

E ENVIRONMENT

<u>Huron Greenways</u>, a System of Land and Water Trails for Alcona, Alpena, Cheboygan and Presque Isle Counties, is an effort to preserve, appreciate and connect the unique coastal features of the northern Lake Huron shoreline. Unlike other parts of the state, this shoreline is free and accessible to anyone. This area contains some of the most extensive and significant recreational and ecological sites in the Lower Peninsula. And it is only 40 to 60 miles east from the beaten path of I-75. nemcog.org/greenways

F FLORA & FAUNA

Alice Welch, USDA

The kinnikinick bearberry is a low evergreen that grows on dunes near the water; the bright red berries are a favorite of some birds. American Indians used the plant as part of a mixture that they smoked. It is also common as an herbal remedy for many ailments.

Eric Engbretson/USFWS

The lake sturgeon has no scales but does have bone-like plates on its body. This once common fish can be up to 8' long, weigh 800 lbs. and live 100 years. After over-fishing by early settlers and destruction of their habitat, they are a threatened species. The species has a naturally low reproductive rate, so the DNR works with citizens in the "Sturgeon Patrol" to protect their spawning areas.

G GOVERNMENT

County: ...created: 1840 **...organized:** 1869
...originally part of: Allegan, Cheboygan Counties
Size: 435,000 acres / 674 sq. miles (30 of 83 counties)
The county has 1 city, 1 village, 11 townships, 16 unincorporated communities, 1 Census Designated Place and 1 school district.

Sonya Plude

County seat: Harrisville
...Homestead property tax: 26 mills
Motto: Alcona County: *First of 83*
...Curran: *Black Bear Capital of Michigan*
...Glennie: *The Heart of the Huron National Forest*
...Huron Shores Chamber: *People Loving People*
...Lincoln: *The Village with a Vision*

H HISTORICAL MARKERS 2 of 2

Greenbush School: 1870, a pioneer school that operated until 1947
West Harrisville Depot: 1886, for the Detroit, Bay City and Alpena Railroad that became the Detroit and Mackinaw Railroad; a private home from 1930 to 1996
National Register of Historic Places: 1 listing
State Historic Sites: 5 listings

I INFORMATION

Alcona County, 800-432-2823
Chamber of Commerce: Alcona

J JOKES

You might be an obsessed fisherman if...
...your kids know it's Saturday because the boats are gone.
...your $30,000 bass boat needs new tires so you just "borrow" the ones off the house.
...you are one jerk on one end of the line waiting for a jerk on the other end.
...you named your kids Evinrude and Mercury.
...you think "megabytes" means you had a great day fishing.
...you know the fine line between fishing and standing on the shore looking like an idiot.
...you consider frying up what's left of your bait after a really bad day on the lake.

K KINSMAN

Race	Ancestry
American Indian: <1%	German: 23%
Asian: <1%	English: 14%
Black/African American: <1%	U.S./American: 10%
Hispanic or Latino: 1%	Irish: 9%
Other: 1%	Polish: 7%
White: 98%	French: 7%

L LIGHTHOUSE OR LANDMARK

Michigan State Historic Preservation Office

Built in 1869, the Sturgeon Point Light Station stands 70 feet tall and is still operational today. Its purpose is to warn navigational traffic of a 1½-mile long reef of dangerous rocks and shoals. The keeper's house and tower are open for tours.

M MUSEUMS

Harrisville *Sturgeon Point Lighthouse Museum:* maritime museum; climb the tower; see 1L

Lincoln *Train Depot:* the last remaining depot of its kind in northeastern Michigan

N NATURAL RESOURCES

Elevation: 600 – 1,250 feet
Physiography: hill-lands, lake border plains, plains

Forest type: aspen-birch, oak-hickory, maple-beech-hemlock
Public/private forests: 77% of county

Water in county: 3% of county
    Lakes: 40 ...**largest:** Hubbard (#10-size, MI)
    Rivers: AuSable (au SAHBle), Black, Devils, Pine, West Branch
    Rivers & streams: 360 miles
    Great Lakes shoreline: 27 miles

Growing season, avg.: 131 days (3 temp. zones)
    Last freeze, avg.: May 25 – June 5
    First freeze, avg.: Sept. 15 – Sept. 25
Precipitation, annual avg.: rainfall: 29 inches
               snowfall: 50 inches
Temperature (F), avg.: January: high 29°, low 11°
             July: high 80°, low 58°
    Annual: >90°: 6 days, **<0°:** 23 days
Tornadoes (1930-2010): 12

O ORIGINS

Alcona:[co] (al COE na) from a combination of American Indian words that mean "a beautiful plain;" 1858
Curran:[u] Philip Curran built a lumber camp; 1875
Black River:[u] the name of the river as it empties into Lake Huron at this site; 1849
Glennie:[u] John W. Glennie was killed in 1880 while trying to rescue the crew of a foundering schooner; 1889
Greenbrush:[u] lumber company employee was from Greenbrush, NY; 1848
Harrisville:[c] Benjamin Harris and sons; 1854
Hubbard Lake:[u] pioneer state surveyor, Bela Hubbard, 1878; the lake is in this county, but the village is in Alpena County
Lincoln:[v] probably after Abraham Lincoln; 1885
Lost Lake Woods:[u] a private club with 10,000 acres of wilderness

P PARKS

National: 3   **State:** 6   **County:** 3   **Local:** 8
National: *Huron National Forest:* 120,000 acres, established in 1909 on scattered sites of former "logged out" lands that are now, once again, lush forests.

State Forest: (8,000 acres) AuSable, Oscoda

...Campground: 1
State Park: *Harrisville:* 100 heavily forested acres; a 2-mile nature trail through the "north woods" and 1 mile of sandy beach on Lake Huron

...*Negwegon:* rustic and undeveloped, the least used of all the Michigan State Parks; on Lake Huron

State Scenic Site: *Sturgeon Point:* lighthouse, reef; see 1L, 1M

NPCR

Deb Schmuker

Q QUOTE FROM THE LOCALS

"Alcona County, serving young and old to work, play, to enjoy the surroundings of lake and stream, of forest and fauna. Sunrise, shoreline, woodland creatures - find it all in Alcona County. Offering the best people and places in all Michigan counties...the perfect get-a-way for a vacation." alconacountymi.com

R RECREATION & SPORTS

Golf courses: 3
Great Lakes marinas: 1   **Boat slips:** 100
Hiking/skiing/mountain biking trails: 50 miles
Public access sites: 10
Public recreational land: 27% of county
Rail-trail: (40 miles) Huron Forest Snowmobile Trails
Recreational harbor: Harrisville Municipal Marina
State/federal wild/scenic/natural river: 20 miles of the AuSable River

State-funded snowmobile trails: 40 miles
AuSable River Semi-Primitive Area: 12 miles along the river designated for special management
Hoist Lake Foot Trail System: biologically diverse, varying degrees of challenges
Reid Lake Foot Trail System: 6 miles of gently rolling trails through 3,000 acres

S STATE OF MICHIGAN

Buy Michigan Now

Buy Michigan Now

   Buy Michigan Now is a statewide initiative dedicated to promoting a positive image of the state and its products and revitalizing the local economy. Through the campaign, individuals, families and organizations are encouraged to take an active role in the state's revitalization by learning about Michigan-based businesses and products, and factoring Michigan into their buying decisions. People can visit BuyMichiganNow.com to get involved in the campaign, include a business in the online directory and add their names to the Pledge. Take the Pledge: "I hereby pledge to play an active role in building a strong, vibrant, and diverse Michigan economy. I will be a part of the solution by speaking positively about the state, learning about our products and services, and making a concerted effort to buy from Michigan businesses. I will Think Michigan First!" buymichigannow.com

T TRAVEL

Airports: Flying "M" Ranch, Harrisville City
Bus: Indian Trails
Circle Tour: Lake Huron, US-23
Distance to Lansing: 190 miles
Heritage Route: *Recreational:* Sunrise Side Coastal Highway, see 6T
Lights of Northern Lake Huron Tour: Sturgeon Point Lighthouse
Main roads: US-23, M-65, M-72
Memorial Highway: US-23, *United Spanish War Veteran MH:* to honor those who served and died in the Spanish-American War (1898) where the U.S. gained control of Puerto Rico, Guam and the Philippines

U UNIVERSITIES & COLLEGES

None

V VARIETY

Sonya Plude

The Alcona County Quilt Trail is a community trail throughout the county that is linked to the Appalachian Trail. Large wood blocks are painted to look like a quilt pattern and are placed to denote historical landmarks, nautical presence and unique agricultural buildings. For a map and an explanation of each pattern, go to alconaquilttrail.com.

W WANDERLUST

Agri-tourism: *Cedarbrook Trout Farm*: fee fishing, no license needed
Fall colors: late September to early October
There are many antique and unique stores throughout the county.
The Strawberry Social is held each June at the 1907 restored Bailey School.

X X-TRA STUFF

County Fair: *Alcona:* the best little fair in the north: Aug.
Large employers: Alcona Community Schools, Alcona County, Lincoln Haven Health Care Center, Jamieson Nursing Home, Alcona Tool & Die
From 1876 to 1880, the lumbering firm of Alger Smith and Company, of Black River, was the largest pine timber producer in the world.
There is only one traffic light in this county.

Y YESTERYEAR

THE NORTHLAND IN THE FALL, circa 1934, by R.E. Prescott, was published in the *Alcona County Herald.* "You may call Angelo's art work by its right and proper name, you may have viewed the Rembrandts hanging in the halls of fame, but unless you've seen the Northland in October you can bet you have missed the greatest painting – Folks, you ain't see nuthin' yet.

"With the crimson of the maples banked against the poplar's dun, and the scarlet of the sumac on the hills against the sun, with the azure of the Heavens pierced by green spearpoints of spruce, and etched with "V's" of wild geese, and pastels – but what's the use? – you've just got to live and breathe it, human words won't do at all to describe the gorgeous canvas of the Northland in the Fall.

"In the rooms of royal palace costly tapestry's arrayed; in the grand old world cathedrals master-artist work's displayed; in the art salons of Paris priceless paintings grace the wall. But Dame Nature's greatest picture is the Northland in the fall."

Michelle Maloney

Z ZOO & ANIMAL PLACES

Watchable Wildlife Viewing Areas:[ww] This binocular logo is the national symbol for Wildlife Viewing Sites that can be found throughout Michigan. Along with the possibility of seeing wildlife, be assured that the scenery will also be spectacular. For full descriptions and directions to each of these sites and other state wildlife viewing sites, go online to Michigan DNR Wildlife Viewing Guide or order a printed copy from the State.

Sonya Plude

A AGRICULTURE

Land in farms: 51% of county
Number of farms: 1,600 (#1 of 83 counties)
Size of average farm: 170 acres
Market value of all products: #1 of 83 counties
Crops: ...most acres: corn for grain & silage
...highest $ sales: nursery, greenhouse, floriculture
Livestock: ...largest number: chickens/laying
...highest $ sales: hogs & pigs
Among the top Michigan counties:

- #1- cauliflower, goats, hogs & pigs, market value of all livestock, number of broiler & laying chickens
- #2- celery, corn/silage, mules & burros & don-keys, poultry & eggs, nursery stock, turkeys
- #3- bedding plants acres, blueberries, cucumbers & pickles, cut flowers, nuts, peaches
- #4- floriculture, cut Christmas trees, number of cows and milk production
- #5- forage land
- #6- corn & grain, fruits
- #7- horses, other animals, vegetables

Fennville American Viticulture Area: 75,000 acres, it is part of the Lake Michigan Shore AVA of 1.3 million acres (see 11A); it is a U.S. government designated wine grape-growing area.
Dairy, food and meat processing plants: 28
State ranking for harvested trees: #36 of 83 counties
AgBioResearch Centers (MSU): *Trevor Nichols Research Center:* studies the best ways to keep Michigan's fruit pest-free while preserving the environment and ensuring economic viability for the state's fruit growers
FYI: There are 5,500 farms in Michigan raising chickens and turkeys. Of the 9 million laying hens, 10 farms have 94% of the egg-producing chickens. A laying hen produces about 290 eggs in her 1-year laying career. Michigan  farmers send 680,000 broiling chickens and almost 2 million turkeys to market each year. This county has about one-third of the state production of laying hens and broilers and 15% of the state turkey production. ^{MDA}

B BRIDGE OR BOAT

MDOT Photo Unit

MDOT Historic Bridge: Built in 1879, the New Richmond Swing Bridge at 57th St. and the Kalamazoo River in New Richmond is 429 ft. long and probably the oldest surviving highway swing bridge in the U.S. Owned by Allegan County and fully restored in 2004, it is now a pedestrian bridge in the New Richmond Bridge Park.

C CELEBRATIONS

<u>Fennville</u> *Tuesdays in the Park:* concert series throughout the summer
...*Goose Festival:* wild goose run, gosling run, *Goose Gazette*, talent show, crafts, Oct.
<u>Otsego</u> *Creative Arts Festival:* car show, parade, music, arts & crafts, Sept.
<u>Saugatuck</u> *Waterfront Film Festival:* June

D DEMOGRAPHICS

Population: 111,000	**Persons per sq. mile:** 135
Largest city: Allegan	**Population:** 5,000
Largest township: Dorr	**Population:** 7,440
Largest village: Hopkins	**Population:** 610

Median household income: $50,500
Owner-occupied median house value: $150,000
Persons affiliated with a religious congregation: 38%
Persons below poverty level: 12%
Students receiving school lunch subsidy: 32%

E ENVIRONMENT

"The <u>Stewardship Network</u> builds the capacity of organizations, individuals, and businesses to preserve, restore, and manage Michigan's natural lands and waters. Since its inception, the Network

has collaborated with nonprofits large and small, governmental agencies and units, private business, and dedicated individuals to achieve that goal. The Stewardship Network connects a broad range of groups, rallies volunteers, and fills the gaps in today's preservation efforts. Every day, we're out on the land – making connections, providing hands-on training, building relationships, sharing tools, and passing along new information. Why? So that many groups and individuals that protect our natural areas can become even stronger and more effective." Allegan County is part of the West Michigan Cluster of Allegan, Kent, Muskegon, Newaygo and Ottawa Counties. stewardshipnetwork.org

F FLORA & FAUNA

The wildflower harebell, commonly called bluebell, likes the dry, sandy areas of sand dunes. In folklore, witches used the plant to turn themselves into hares (rabbits).

U.S. Fish and Wildlife Service

Of all the habitats in southern Michigan with Karner blue butterflies, the Allegan State Game Area has the highest population due to the ample supply of wild lupine along with other environmental factors. This nickel-sized butterfly is listed as a Michigan threatened species.

G GOVERNMENT

County: ...created: 1831 **...organized:** 1835
...originally part of: Kalamazoo County
Size: 540,000 acres / 828 sq. miles (19 of 83 counties)
The county has 8 cities, 2 villages, 26 townships with 1 as a charter township, 23 unincorporated communities and 10 school districts.

Jason Jaekel

County seat: Allegan
...Homestead property tax: 43 mills
Motto: <u>Allegan</u>: *All roads lead to Allegan*
...<u>Allegan County</u> Tourist Council: *History Alive*
...<u>Holland</u> Area Convention and Visitors Bureau: *You Don't Need a Passport*
...<u>Otsego</u>: *Come to Work, Come to Play, Come to Stay*
...<u>Plainwell</u>: *Island City*
...<u>Saugatuck-Douglas</u>:[1,000] *The Cape Cod of the Midwest*

...<u>Saugatuck-Douglas</u> Convention and Visitors Bureau: *The Art Coast of Michigan*
...<u>South Haven</u>: *Blueberry Capital of the World*
...<u>Wayland</u>: *Committed to Excellence*

H HISTORICAL MARKERS 8 of 25

All Saints Episcopal Church: 1874, designed by Gordon Lloyd, who was among the Midwest's foremost church architects

Allegan County: 1831, extensive lumbering by the pioneers cleared the way for farm production

Renee McCauley

Douglas Union School: 1866, two teachers taught 129 students that year; Italian Villa style

Dutcher Lodge No. 193: 1875, a rare example of a Masonic lodge still in use a century after its construction

Henika Ladies Library: 1900, Richardsonian style, ashlar fieldstone from a local farm

Old Wing Mission: 1844, Congregational mission for the local American Indians; oldest structure in area

Second Street Bridge: 1886, ornamental wrought iron, 18'x225'; selected by the American Society of Civil Engineers as one the world's greatest civil engineering achievements

NPCR

Singapore: 1830s, a thriving lumber town, but when the lumber ran out, it did too; now a ghost town

National Register of Historic Places: 29 listings
State Historic Sites: 58 listings

I INFORMATION

Chamber of Commerce: Fennville, Otsego, Plainwell, Wayland
Visitor: Allegan County Tourist Council, 888-425-5342, visitallegancounty.com
...Holland Area Convention and Visitors Bureau, 800-506-1299, holland.org
...Saugatuck-Douglas Convention and Visitors Bureau, 269-857-1701, saugatuck.com

J JOKES

For your required laugh-of-the-day, try these silly chicken jokes!

1. Why was the chicken sick? He had the people-pox.
2. Why do hens lay eggs? If they dropped them, they'd break.
3. Why won't a rooster ever get rich? He works for chicken feed.
4. How do chickens bake a cake? From scratch.
5. Did you hear the joke about the broken egg? Yes, it cracked me up.
6. Who tells the best chicken jokes? Comedi-hens.

K KINSMAN

Race		Ancestry	
American Indian: <1%		Dutch: 26% (#2)	
Asian: <1%		German: 18%	
Black/African American: 1%		U.S./American: 10%	
Hispanic or Latino: 7%		English: 8%	
Other: 5%		Irish: 7%	
White: 93%		Polish: 5%	

L LIGHTHOUSE OR LANDMARK

Jason Jaekel

This little "lighthouse" is not really a lighthouse, but just a pretty building on private property that is made to look like a lighthouse. It is a landmark because of its prominent location in the Kalamazoo Lake portion of the Kalamazoo River in Douglas. The ship in the background is the steamship *SS Keewatin*, another landmark that is open for tours.

M MUSEUMS

Allegan County Historical Society

Allegan *Co. Historical Society and Old Jail Museum:* travel back in time

Fennville *Children's Museum:* hands-on learning

Otsego *Area Historical Society Museum:* to illustrate history…by programs, displays and exhibits

Saugatuck-Douglas *Museum:* award winning, in a 1904 "prairie-craftsman style" pumping station

N NATURAL RESOURCES

Elevation: 600 - 900 feet
Physiography: hill-lands, lake border, plains

Forest type: oak, maple-beech, elm-ash-cottonwood
Public/private forests: 33% of county
Legislatively protected sand dunes: 2,500 acres

Water in county: 1% of county
  Lakes: 100   **…largest:** Lake Allegan
  Rivers: Black, Gun, Kalamazoo, Macatawa (mack a TAW wa), Rabbit
  Rivers & streams: 520 miles

Great Lakes shoreline: 24 miles
  Growing season, avg.: 151 days (2 temp. zones)
    Last freeze, avg.: May 5 – May 10
    First freeze, avg.: Oct. 5 – Oct. 15
Precipitation, annual avg.: rainfall: 36 inches (#3/MI)
                 snowfall: 80 inches
Temperature (F), avg.: January: high 31°, low 16°
            July: high 84°, low 60°
  Annual: >90°: 14 days, **<0°:** 8 days
Tornadoes (1930-2010): 29

O ORIGINS

Allegan:[c,co] the Alleghen Indian tribe, meaning "lake of the Algonquin's;" 1833

Dorr:[v] named for Thomas Dorr who led a rebellion against the state of Rhode Island; 1835

Douglas:[c] town of Douglas on Isle of Man in the Irish Sea, or American statesman Stephen A. Douglas; 1851

Fennville:[c] sawmill owner, Elam Fenn; 1860

Gun Lake: Gun Lake appears to be the English translation of the name Chief Penasee; 1836

Holland: see Ottawa County

Hopkins:[v] a signer of the Declaration of Independence, Stephen Hopkins; 1874

Martin:[v] U.S. President, Martin Van Buren; 1836

Otsego:[c] second settler from Otsego Co., NY; American Indian words meaning meeting place and word of greeting; 1831

Plainwell:[c] original name of the township; 1833

Saugatuck:[c] (SAW ga tuck) Pottawatomi for "river's mouth;" 1830

South Haven:[c] see Van Buren County

Wayland:[c] after Wayland, NY; means "the last stop on a railroad line;" 1836

P PARKS

National: 0 **State:** 3 **County:** 9 **Local:** 23
Number of campsites: 4,000
State Game Area: *Allegan:*[wba,ww] 50,000 acres, wild life viewing, oak-pine savannas, wetlands, ponds, open fields, hunting, boating, fishing, camping

Renee McCauley

NPCR

State Park: *Saugatuck Dunes*[wba,ww]*:* 1,000 acres, day use only, 200 ft. high sand dunes, 2½ miles of hiking on the Lake Michigan shoreline

State Underwater Preserve: *Southwest Michigan:* extends 5 miles off shore in Allegan, Berrien, Ottawa and Van Buren counties; contains 17 sites that are shipwrecks or geological formations

County: Bysterveld, Dumont Lake, Ely Lake, Gun Lake, New Richmond Bridge, Pine Point, Silver Creek, West Side

Local: Saugatuck's *Oval Beach:* with Lake Michigan on one side and sand dunes on the other, MTV ranked it as one of the top five beaches in the country. *Conde Naste's Traveler* magazine ranked it as one of the 25 best shorelines in the world. Climb Mount Baldhead sand dune. Oval Beach has a separate gay and lesbian section.

Other: The <u>West Michigan Parks and Recreation Inventory</u> provides "one-stop shopping" for anyone looking to explore a park, trail, or recreation area in Allegan, Barry, Ionia, Kent, Montcalm, Muskegon and Newaygo counties. Go to wm-alliance.org/parks_recreation for more information on 123,000 acres of parkland in the area.

Outdoor Discovery Center Macatawa Greenway: 130 acres with ponds, remnant dunes, wetlands, meadows, remnant prairies and lowland hardwood forests' ecosystems

Silver Creek Park: 320 acres, equestrian park, trails, camping; connected to the Allegan County Equestrian Trail System; see 3R

Q QUOTE FROM THE LOCALS

"The natural beauty of Allegan County has greeted travelers for generations. Its pristine Lake Michigan shoreline and many inland lakes, winding streams and rivers make any stay a memorable experience. Mighty forests, family farms, historic sites and a surprising array of attractions have always welcomed and pleased visitors. Many ways to experience the varied pleasures of nature can be found in Allegan County. As you make your way through… it's easy to see how each of the four seasons provides adventure, activity and entertainment - making Allegan County a great place to visit year-round." visitallegancounty.com

R RECREATION & SPORTS

Auto racing: *U.S. 131 Motorsports Park:* ¼ mile drag strip, Michigan's fastest racetrack
Golf courses: 20
Great Lakes marinas: 24   **Boat slips:** 1,000
Hiking/skiing/mountain biking trails: 40 miles
Horse racing: harness racing at the county fair
Michigan Heritage Water Trail: Kalamazoo Watershed
North Country National Scenic Trail: yes
Public access sites: 28
Public recreational land: 9% of county
Recreational harbor: Saugatuck Harbor of Refuge
State/federal wild/scenic/natural river: 55 miles of the Lower Kalamazoo River
State-funded snowmobile trails: 100 miles
Allegan County Equestrian Trail System: 50+ miles of marked and mapped trails in the Allegan State Game Area

Allegan Wellness and Sports Center: 64 acres, soccer, baseball and football fields, skate park
Bittersweet Ski Resort: 20 runs; learn to ski
Dune rides: Saugatuck, thrills, educational

S STATE OF MICHIGAN

As of 2010, there was a new hunting opportunity for Michigan sportsmen. The <u>Pure Michigan Hunt</u> allows three lucky individuals the opportunity to hunt for elk, bear, wild turkey, antlerless deer and to have first pick of sites at managed waterfowl areas. Michigan is the first state east of the Mississippi to offer this type of multi-species hunt that is popular in the western states. Tickets for the drawing are $4 each and are available at hunting license retailers. cadillacmichigan.com

T TRAVEL

Airports: Padgham, Plainwell Municipal, Tulip City
Bus: Indian Trails
Circle Tour: Lake Michigan, I-196/US-31, A-2/Blue Star Hwy. to the harbor tour at Saugatuck
County road names: …north/south: number Streets …east/west: number Avenues
Distance to Lansing: 90 miles

Renee McCauley

Ferry: the last hand-cranked chain ferry in the U.S. is used to cross the Kalamazoo River in Saugatuck.

Historic Harbortowns: *Douglas:* Keewatin Maritime Museum; *Saugatuck:* Harbor Duck Adventures, Saugatuck Boat Cruises
Main roads: I-96, US-31, US-131, M-40, M-89, M-222
Memorial Highways: US-31, *Blue Star MH:* Blue Star Mothers of America display a flag with a blue star for each family member in the Armed Forces …I-196, *Gerald R. Ford Freeway:* see 41T
Recreational Heritage Route: M-179, Chief Noonday Trail from Wayland to Hastings, heavily wooded gateway to Yankee Springs Recreation Area; recreational and historic activities for the whole family; see 8Q
Scenic Drive: *Allegan County Heritage Trail:* 122 mile

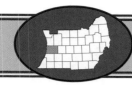

driving tour through farmlands, grasslands, forests, lakes and 1900s ambiance; guidebook and CD are available

...*West Michigan Tourist Association* Fall Scenic Driving Tours: there are 26 driving tours in the state, from 40 to 144 miles each, and two tours are in this county

U UNIVERSITIES & COLLEGES

None

V VARIETY

Erin Ogilvie

The high quality S 2 Yachts, like this 3100 Coronet™, are manufactured in Holland. The company follows Christian principles and works to pursue perfection, delight customers and create customers for life. In addition, they are part of a collaborative effort that developed nautical research stations for coastal and inner-shelf freshwater and saltwater data monitoring.

W WANDERLUST

Agri-tourism: *Bowerman's Blueberries:* raspberries, hydroponic strawberries, veggies

...*Crane Orchards:* U-pick, apples, cherries, peaches, haunted corn maze and cow train ride

...*Dee's Lakeshore:* large variety of fruits and veggies

...*Earl's Farm Market:* asparagus, blackberries, blueberries, raspberries, strawberries, pies

...*Lakeshore Harvest Country:* online information about the areas farms and special events

...*Overhiser Orchards:* apples, apricots, cherries, peaches, plums, market, tours

...*Square Nail Farm:* family farm, orchards, veggies

Brewery: Saugatuck Brewing Company, Inc.

Casino: Gun Lake

Cultural: Lakeshore Jazz Connection, Saugatuck Chamber Music Society

Fall colors: middle October

Live theater: Mason Street Warehouse, Play N Well Players, Red Barn Playhouse, Saugatuck Center for the Arts

...*Allegan Community Players at the Griswold Auditorium:* oldest Michigan theater group, 1929

Wineries: *Fenn Valley:* site selected based on the weather, climate & soil for the very best wines

Allegan Historic District: well preserved homes

Blue Coast Artists:[1,000] travel the scenic Blue Star Hwy. and back roads between South Haven and Saugatuck to experience a behind-the-scenes look at working artists in their studios

Felt Mansion and Estate: the summer home of Dorr Felt, inventor of the first office math-processing machine; private tours available, just call ahead

Renee McCauley

Harbor Duck Adventures: tour Saugatuck & Douglas, the Kalamazoo River and Saugatuck Harbor in a converted WWII Army amphibious vessel

Lakeshore Harvest Country: a driving trail of farms, farm markets and quilt trails between Saugatuck and South Haven

Ox-Bow: 1910, school of art and artists' residency, affiliated with the Art Institute of Chicago; 115 acres of pristine natural forests

Regent Theatre: 1919, restored, Art Deco, still open

Star of Saugatuck: a sternwheeler on the Kalamazoo River and Lake Michigan; cruises available

West Michigan Cultural Trails: "Traveling to experience the place and activities that authentically represent the stories and people of the past and present. It includes historic, cultural and natural resources."

Charter a boat and go fishing on the Big Lake (Michigan).

X X-TRA STUFF

County Fair: *Allegan:* one of the largest fairs in the state; includes the Historical Village, Sept.

Provided by Allegan County Historical Museum

Famous people: …*Entertainment*: Ed Gale, Naranda Michael Walden
…*Sports*: Butch Jones
…*Other*: Dave Coverly, Kevin Van Dam, Dwight Waldo
Hospital: Allegan General
Large employers: Perrigo (makes pharmaceutical, cosmetics), Haworth (makes office furniture), Parker Hannifin (makes bushings, plumbing fixtures, pipefittings), S 2 Yachts (makes fiberglass boats), Venturedyne (makes environment test equipment), Johnson Controls Interiors (makes overhead conveyors)
All of the cities and villages in this county have populations of less than 5,000 people.
Around 1914, less than 100 chain-driven Cornelian automobiles were produced in Allegan.
Fennville's city mascot is the Canada goose. (The Allegan State Game Area is a migratory stop for over 100,000 of these birds a season).
Glenn School is a two-room schoolhouse that still operates a K-5 program.
In 1944, around 250 German soldiers were sent to a P.O.W. camp in Allegan County to assist farmers with their harvest.
Plainwell is known as "Island City" because the downtown is entirely surrounded by water of the Kalamazoo River.
The Old Saugatuck Lighthouse is no longer operational and is a private residence.

Y YESTERYEAR

It can be said that building and house styles are like dogs: some are pure breeds, some are mixed breeds and some are just lovable mutts. There are as many housing designs as there are house designers and architects. But some of the house styles from the 1840s through the 1930s have characteristics that make them unique and identifiable throughout the state. These are the buildings, churches and homes that populate most of the cities and villages around the state and are the ones preserved in the local historic districts (see 13H). They can be large or small, simple with a few key features or elaborate with a lot of features. Many of the smaller older houses you see in cities are very simplified and economical versions of the larger more expensive popular styles.

Presented here is a bare-bones description of the most identifiable features of the thirteen most popular house and building styles in Michigan during its first 100 years after statehood (1837-1940). Don't forget

that many of these houses have been "upgraded" during the past 100 years and have lost some of their original details, but their basic design is still the same.
<small>Baker; McAlester</small>

House styles can be described in terms of their…
…1. *Heyday:* when they were most popular
…2. *Roof:* pitch, style (1. decorative gables, 2. front or side gables, 3. gambrel, 4. hipped, 5. mansard), material

…3. *Windows:* size, shape, ornamentation, placement
…4. *Exterior walls:* material, trim
…5. *Other features:* anything unique to that style
NOTE: the major distinguishing feature(s) of each style is underlined

CARPENTER or CRAFTSMAN
Heyday: 1905-1930
Roof: low-pitched, gabled, exposed roof rafters, unenclosed eave overhang
Windows: standard
Exterior walls: rustic texture of clapboard or wood shingles; front porches had tapered square columns on pedestals
Other features: a whole house kit could be ordered by mail from companies like Sears & Roebuck and delivered by train; it was the most popular smaller house in the country.

COLONIAL REVIVAL (also includes Cape Cod style)
Heyday: 1885-1915
Roof: mostly end gabled, some front gabled, some hipped and gambrel; possible dormers
Windows: symmetrical and rectangular; shutters
Exterior walls: wood or masonry; <u>predominantly flat façade</u>; little or no ornamentation in earliest styles; later styles had more ornamentation
Other features: front door has sidelight or maybe an entry porch with columns

ENGLISH & DUTCH COLONIAL
Heyday: 1890-1930
Roof: English: <u>gambrel</u>
   Dutch: <u>gambrel with gently curving & sloping eaves</u> that may cover a porch; possible dormers
Windows: symmetrical and rectangular; shutters with an ornamental cut-out
Exterior walls: wood or masonry
Other features: considered similar to the Colonial Revival style

English   Dutch

EXOTIC ECLECTIC
Heyday: 1850-1875
Roof: any style
Windows: any style
Exterior walls: any style
Other features: a romance with the past using features considered <u>especially fanciful and bizarre</u>; may have Egyptian or Oriental features such as onion domes or minarets; may have castle-type features

GOTHIC REVIVAL
Heyday: 1840-1880
Roof: steep-pitched; usually with both large front and side gables
Windows: <u>windows may extend into the gable; some may be a pointed arch shape</u>
Exterior walls: wall surface extends to gables without a break
Other features: one-story porch; gables may have decorated verge boards

GREEK REVIVAL

Heyday: 1825-1860

Roof: low-pitched; gabled or hipped

Windows: usually have decorated crown moldings above each

Exterior walls: wood or masonry; wide band of trim at roofline

Other features: there are always <u>columns</u>, either as part of the porch or built-in around the door

ITALIANATE

Heyday: 1840-1885

Roof: <u>low pitched</u>; <u>usually hipped</u>; some are gabled; <u>overhanging eaves with decorative brackets beneath</u>

Windows: tall & narrow; elaborate crown moldings above each

Exterior walls: wood or masonry

Other features: may have cupola on roof; almost always two or more stories; many are almost square; this style was also very popular as a farmhouse

ITALIAN RENAISSANCE

Heyday: 1890-1935

Roof: low-pitched; hipped; many with ceramic tiles

Windows: first story windows may be arched and all will have elaborate crown moldings; <u>second story windows are smaller than first story windows</u>

Exterior walls: smooth limestone or stucco; wide overhanging eaves supported by decorative brackets

Other features: two or more stories; entryway usually has small columns; façade is usually flat and symmetrical

ITALIAN VILLA

Heyday: 1845-1860

Roof: low pitched; side and front gables

Windows: tall; possibly rounded at the top; prominent crown moldings

Exterior walls: usually stucco; wide overhanging eaves supported by decorative brackets

Other features: <u>always has a built-in tower</u>

FYI: Most homes built around the turn of the century had a crawl space beneath the main floor for plumbing and furnaces. A <u>Michigan basement</u> is a term used to describe a crawl space under an older home that was later excavated into a fuller basement. Usually the height was much shorter than current basements and it may have had overhead beams and furnace ducts that made walking around somewhat difficult. It may have had dirt floors or walls, or the dirt floors and walls may have been covered with a thin layer of concrete or bricks to keep the dirt in place. The excavated walls may be slanted and set in from the original crawl space. Many times damp and smelly, they did not offer good storage space for the family's belongings, even though that was the original intent.

QUEEN ANNE

Heyday: 1880-1910

Roof: steeply pitched; irregular shape of hip and/or cross gables; usually a dominant front gable

Windows: anything that is not plain and ordinary; bay; round towers

Exterior walls: aim is to avoid a smooth-walled appearance; some patterned wood shingles; asymmetrical façade; wall inserts & projections

Other features: fanciful appearance; large covered porches or verandas; extensive use of decorative spindle work and decorative woodwork

RICHARDSONIAN ROMANESQUE

Heyday: 1880-1900

Roof: variety of styles; very elaborate

Windows: inset into the masonry wall; round top windows with arches

Exterior walls: masonry or crudely cut blocks of stone; round towers with conical tops; may have two or more colors or textures of stone or brick for decorative purpose

Other features: round arches over porch or entrance; decorative arches; very expensive to build; this style was also very popular for church construction

SECOND EMPIRE

Heyday: 1855-1885

Roof: dual-pitched mansard; may have dormer windows in the roof's steep lower slope; molded cornices both above and below the lower slope with decorative brackets

Windows: generally tall and narrow, some with ornate crown moldings

Exterior walls: many are brick

Other features: this style provided for a usable attic; very popular in commercial buildings also

TUDOR

Heyday: 1890-1940

Roof: steep-pitched; side and large front gable and possibly multiple front gables

Windows: tall and narrow with 3 or more in a group

Exterior walls: primarily stucco, brick, or stone

Other features: massive chimneys; decorative half-timbering

Z   ZOO & ANIMAL PLACES

Watchable Wildlife Viewing Areas:[ww] see 3P

Outdoor Discovery Center: see 3P

Wild West Horseback Riding: hay, sleigh and buggy rides

Equestrian opportunities: see 3P

A AGRICULTURE

Land in farms: 22% of county
Number of farms: 570
Size of average farm: 150 acres
Market value of all products: #49 of 83 counties
Crops: ...most acres: forage crops
...highest $ sales: grains: corn, soybeans, wheat
Livestock: ...largest number: cattle & calves
...highest $ sales: milk & dairy products
Among the top Michigan counties:
• #1- acres of sunflowers
Dairy, food and meat processing plants: 10
State ranking for harvested trees: #28 of 83 counties
FYI: The more than 2,000 acres of <u>sunflowers</u> grown in this county is over $^1/_3$ of state production. Sunflower seeds are used as food for birds and are roasted and salted as a treat for you and me. The oil is used in cooking, in the manufacturing of margarine and even for biodiesel fuel. [MDA]

Michigan Farm Bureau

Just the sight of a field of sunflowers will put a smile on any face.

B BRIDGE OR BOAT

NOAA, Thunder Bay National Marine Sanctuary

This is just one of the 50 shipwrecks in the Thunder Bay National Marine Sanctuary and Underwater Preserve. The sanctuary is 450 sq. miles in Lake Huron that has been created to protect natural and cultural marine resources. It has exceptional shipwreck preservation due to the cold water; there is good snorkeling and scuba diving too. See 4M.

C CELEBRATIONS

<u>Alpena</u> B*lues Festival:* June
...*Garden Walk:* enjoy other's green thumb, July
...*Maritime Festival:* by the Great Lakes Maritime Heritage Center, see 4M, July

...*Michigan Brown Trout Festival*: fishing tournament, entertainment, food, fun, July

...*Art on the Bay:* juried fine arts, crafts, July
...*Great Lakes Lighthouse Festival:* lifesaving exhibits, nautical entertainment, shipping exhibits, educational, tour the ships in Thunder Bay, Oct.
...*Old US-27 Motor Tour:* see 12C

Premier Video

D DEMOGRAPHICS

Population: 29,600   **Persons per sq. mile:** 52
Largest city: Alpena   **Population:** 10,500
Largest township: Alpena   **Population:** 9,060
Median household income: $36,000
Owner-occupied median house value: $106,000
Persons affiliated with a religious congregation: 78%
Persons below poverty level: 17%
Students receiving school lunch subsidy: 41%

E ENVIRONMENT

Because habitat is the key to wildlife abundance, re-establishing quality uplands and wetlands to benefit all wildlife is the focus and priority of <u>Pheasants Forever</u>. Michigan's 35 chapters and over 5,000 members have, since 1983, completed more than 16,000 habitat improvement projects involving nearly 130,000 acres of public and private land. Creating, restoring and enhancing the quality of open grassland habitat are their primary focus.[Pheasants Forever] See 4F.

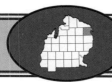
F FLORA & FAUNA

Black Ash

Alice Welch, USDA

White Ash

Alice Welch, USDA

White ash trees are grown commercially for use in making athletic equipment, long tool handles and articles requiring bent wood. Black ash was processed by the American Indians and used to make baskets, thus giving the tree the nickname of hoop or basket ash.

Dave Menke/USFWS

The Ring-necked Pheasant (*MI H&T*) needs an environment of undisturbed low-to-medium high grasses, wetlands, windbreaks and fields of grain and weeds in order to survive. See 4E.

G GOVERNMENT

County: ...created: 1840 **...organized:** 1857
...originally part of: Cheboygan County
Size: 385,000 acres / 574 sq. miles (39 of 83 counties)
The county has 1 city, 8 townships, 8 unincorporated communities and 1 school district.

Michigan State Historic Preservation Office

Alica Bouchard

The Alpena County Courthouse, built in 1935, is an Art Deco monolithic design. It was a Works Pro-

gress Administration project that proved that cement buildings could be built in the winter.
County seat: Alpena
...Homestead property tax: 39 mills
Motto: Alpena: *Water Woods Wildlife; A warm and friendly port*
Alpena Area Convention and Visitors Bureau: *Michigan's Advenshore*

H HISTORICAL MARKERS 4 of 7

Alica Bouchard

Alpena City Hall: 1908, Georgian Revival style; the decision to use Indiana limestone instead of local limestone or cement was very controversial.

Daniel Carter Family: 1856, first settlers, first physician, first teacher, first marriage; donated land for cemetery
Monarch Mill: 1916-1956, Alpena Flour Mill
World's Largest Cement Plant: 1907, home to Portland cement, so named because the stone used to make it resembles the color of the stone from the Isle of Portland in the British Isles
National Register of Historic Places: 5 listings
State Historic Sites: 14 listings

I INFORMATION

Chamber of Commerce: Alpena
Visitor: Alpena Convention and Visitors Bureau, 1-800-4-ALPENA, alpenacvb.com

J JOKES

One foggy night an ore carrier was cruising south in Lake Huron on its way to the St. Lawrence Seaway when a light was spotted in the gloom. The junior radar operator punched in his coordinates and determined that they were on a collision course. He sent out the message "Please change your course 10 degrees NW to avoid immediate collision." The reply came back "You must be joking. I recommend that you change your course." The junior radar operator took the problem straight to his captain, who immediately took charge. "This is the captain," he said, "and I demand that you divert your course. We are an ore

carrier and are simply too big to take quick action." The reply came back, "I don't care how big you are, this is the lighthouse, and you'd better move. Now."

K KINSMAN

Race
American Indian: <1%
Asian: <1%
Black/African American: <1%
Hispanic or Latino: 1%
Other: 1%
White: 97%

Ancestry
German: 25%
Polish: 23%
French: 10%
English: 7%
U.S./American: 6%
Irish: 6%

L LIGHTHOUSE OR LANDMARK

Alisha Bouchard

The 1904 Middle Island Light Station has a renovated foghorn building that allows guests a unique overnight stay. The 77' conical brick tower is one of 7 buildings on the island. There is also a 3-4 hour tour available on Saturday that includes a short boat ride and restoration history.

M MUSEUMS

Alpena *Besser Museum & Planetarium:* art, science, wildlife, American Indians, historic buildings, tug boat

Alisha Bouchard

NPCR

...*Great Lakes Maritime Heritage Center:* 20,000 sq. ft., the full size replica of a wooden Great Lakes schooner will help you explore the Shipwreck Century and many more related displays at the Great Lakes Maritime Heritage Center in Alpena that is part of the National Marine Sanctuary operated by the National Oceanic & Atmospheric Administration (NOAA).; see 4B

N NATURAL RESOURCES

Elevation: 600 – 1,200 feet
Physiography: lake-border plains, hill plains, rolling plains

Forest type: aspen-birch, oak-hickory
Public/private forests: 61% of county

Water in county: 6% of county
  Bay: Thunder Bay
  Lakes: 20 **...largest:** Fletcher Pond
  Rivers: Black, Devils, Thunder Bay
  Rivers & streams: 300 miles

Great Lakes islands: Middle, Sugar, Thunder Bay
Great Lakes shoreline: 61 miles of Lake Huron

NPCR

Avg. sunshine: January: 32%,
                July: 71%
Growing season, avg.: 156 days
  (5-6 temp. zones)
  Last freeze, avg.: May 10 - May 30
  First freeze, avg.: Sept. 15 – Oct. 10
Precipitation, annual avg.:
  rainfall: 28 inches
  snowfall: 67 inches

Temperature (F), avg.: January: high 27°, low 13°
                    July: high 77°, low 58°
  Annual: >90°: 4 days, **<0°:** 11 days
Tornadoes (1930-2010): 14

O ORIGINS

Alpena:[c,co] may be an American Indian word for partridge; 1835

Flanders:[u] local lumber merchant, S.W. Flanders; 1869

Lachine:[u] a railroad man from Lachine, Quebec; 1909

Lakewood:[u] a summer resort subdivision on East Long Lake; 1812

Long Rapids:[t] the long rapids of the Thunder Bay River; 1871

Ossineke:[u] (AH sin eek) from the American Indian name Wawsineke; 1844

P PARKS

National: 1 **State:** 2 **County:** 3 **Local:** 6
Number of campsites: 400

National Underwater Preserve: *Thunder Bay National Marine Sanctuary and Underwater Preserve:* see 4B

State Forest: (44,000 acres) Alpena

...Campground: 2 **...Pathway:** 16 miles

State Park: *Negwegon:* 2,500 acres, rustic, undeveloped, on Lake Huron, no camping

Other: *Partridge Point Wetland:* lagoon and barrier wetland for fresh water coastal marsh, ¼ mile boardwalk; call ahead for tours

...*Island Park & Wildlife Sanctuary:* 17-acre island in the Thunder Bay River

Q QUOTE FROM THE LOCALS

"There are only a few places on this earth where beauty exists alongside industry. Bordered by Lake Huron and state and national forest lands, there's no argument that Mother Nature has a year-round home here. She starts each day by bringing the sun up over Lake Huron and greens or whites the landscape depending on the season. She's dependable; you can plan a multitude of activities around her. The other good news is that Father Time has also visited the area and left established, responsible industries." [MEDC]

R RECREATION & SPORTS

Golf courses: 1
Great Lakes marinas: 2 **Boat slips:** 230
Hiking/skiing/mountain biking trails: 15 miles
Off-road vehicle trails: 10 miles
Public access sites: 9
Public recreational land: 12% of county
Rail-trail: (30 miles) Alpena Bi-Path, Alpena to Cheboygan Trail

Recreational harbor: Alpena Municipal Marina

State-funded snowmobile trails: 30 miles

S STATE OF MICHIGAN

What's the difference between a river, stream, creek, brook, rivulet and rill? There is no general rule that defines what a natural watercourse flowing toward another body of water is called. Sometimes size helped determine the name of the moving water, but mostly the person who first named it determined what it was called. Michigan has over 36,000 miles of rivers and streams.

Big and small rivers and streams feed into the lakes. Michigan has over 11,000 river and stream-fed inland lakes from 3 acres to 22,000 acres in size. Another 13,000 lakes are less than 3 acres each (see 72S).

Ponds, on the other hand, are standing water, either natural or man-made, whose water comes up from the ground or down in the form of precipitation, with no connection to the flowing water of a river. [DNR]

T TRAVEL

Airport: Alpena County Regional
Bus: Indian Trails, Thunder Bay Transportation Authority
Circle Tour: Lake Huron, M-23
Distance to Lansing: 210 miles
Heritage Route: *Recreational:* Sunrise Side Coastal Highway; see 6T
Lights of Northern Lake Huron Tour: Alpena Light, Besser Museum for Northeast Michigan, Middle Island Keeper's Lodge & Boat Tours, Thunder Bay Scuba, Thunder Bay National Marine Sanctuary

Main roads: US-23, M-65, M-32
Memorial Highway: US-23, *United Spanish War Veterans MH:* see 1T

U UNIVERSITIES & COLLEGES

Alpena Community College: est. 1956, 2,000 students. As part of the goal to provide for regional economic development and diverse programming, it has the World Center for Concrete Technology and the Blockmakers Workshop. MCCAA, Lumberjacks

V VARIETY

Alisha Bouchard

Lafarge North America's Alpena Plant is the largest cement plant in North America and is an award-winning technological and market leader in the industry.

W WANDERLUST

Agri-tourism: *AJ's:* strawberries, raspberries, blueberries, cherries, peaches, apples, sweet corn, pumpkins, maple syrup, natural beef
Brewery: Fletcher Street Brewing Company
Cultural: *Alpena Symphony Orchestra:* appreciate, participate and enjoy classical music
Fall colors: late September – early October
Lighthouses, other: *Alpena Light:* 1870, called Sputnik or Little Red, may be one of a kind in U.S.
…Thunder Bay Island: under restoration
…Middle Island: now a lodge, not open to the public
Live theater: *Civic Theatre:* since the 1960s
…Thunder Bay Theatre: resident professional community
Planetarium: Jesse Besser Museum
Shopping mall: Alpena
Walking tour: Alpena: historic homes on Washington, US-23 and M-32 corridors
Wineries: *Stoney Acres:* wine tasting, chocolates, supplies to make your own
Country Cupboard: unique old drug store, antiques

Elowski Grist Mill: 1870s, original milling equipment, nature trails
Fossil dig: at the Lafarge North America Alpena Plant
Sinkholes: 2 of 200 holes are open for public viewing
Sunrise Side Wine & Hops Trail: wineries and breweries in NE Michigan

X X-TRA STUFF

Commercial Port: Alpena
County Fair: *Alpena County Agriculture Society:* Aug./Sept.
Famous people: *…Entertainment*: Michael Bailey Smith
…Sports: Dan Rohn, Kevin Young
Hospital: Alpena Regional Medical Center
Large employers: Alpena General Hospital, Besser Co. (makes concrete products machinery), Wal-Mart, Northeast Michigan Community Service Agency, Welch Aviation (air courier services), Devere Construction, Alpena Public Schools, Lafarge North America (bolder quarrying, hydraulic cement)
The Huron Portland Cement Company is no longer in business (1908-1987). Lafarge North America now owns the Alpena Cement Plant. The plant produces 2.7 million tons of cement annually. See 4V.

Y YESTERYEAR

In 1959, Michigan had the world's largest…
- cement plant in Alpena
- forge in Detroit
- book paper mill in Kalamazoo
- pharmaceutical plant in Kalamazoo
- production of charcoal briquettes in Marquette
- concentration of gray-iron foundries in Muskegon
- factory for making billiard tables and bowling alley equipment in Muskegon
- horsehide tannery in Rockford [Baird]

Z ZOO & ANIMAL PLACES

Zoo: *Dinosaur Gardens Prehistoric Zoo:* 40 acres, life size reproductions of 25 birds and animals

A AGRICULTURE

Land in farms: 20% of county
Number of farms: 410
Size of average farm: 160 acres
Market value of all products: #48 of 83 counties
Crops: ...most acres: forage crops
...highest $ sales: fruits (tart cherries)
Livestock: ...largest number: cattle & calves
...highest $ sales: poultry & eggs
Among the top Michigan counties:
- #1- acres of chestnut trees, aquaculture operations, number of rabbits & their pelts
- #3- acres of tart cherries
- #4- acres of all nuts, pheasants

Dairy, food and meat processing plants: 30
State ranking for harvested trees: #31 of 83 counties
FYI: Michigan has over 1,600 acres of <u>nut</u> trees, including almonds, chestnuts, hazelnuts, pecans and English walnuts, with chestnuts accounting for half the acres. <u>Chestnuts</u> and its sweet chestnut flour is a staple around the world. It has half the calories of other nuts due to a much lower fat content. Growing conditions in Michigan are ideal

for the sweet flavor and rich buttery yellow color of the nut, making Michigan the leading producer of chestnuts in the U.S. And if you can't roast them over an open fire, they can be roasted in the microwave, boiled or steamed. ^{chestnut} growersinc.com See 5F.

Victoria Wessler, www.goinglocal-info.com

B BRIDGE OR BOAT

MDOT Photo and Video Unit

MDOT Historic Bridge: Built in 1932, this bridge on M-88 over the Intermediate River in Bellaire is important because of the significant engineering challenges that had to be overcome since it was immediately below a power dam.

C CELEBRATIONS

<u>Bellaire</u> *Rubber Ducky Festival:* food, parade, rubber-ducky races, Aug.
<u>Central Lake</u> *Collector Car & Truck Show:* around 300 entries in 62 classes, with over 150 awards, June
<u>Elk Rapids</u> *Harbor Days:* a small-town celebration with a big schedule of events, July
...Arts & Crafts Shows: May, July, Aug.

D DEMOGRAPHICS

Population: 23,600   **Persons per sq. mile:** 49
Largest township: Mancelona   **Population:** 3,010
Largest village: Elk Rapids   **Population:** 1,640
Median household income: $40,200
Owner-occupied median house value: $159,000
Persons affiliated with a religious congregation: 27%
Persons below poverty level: 16%
Students receiving school lunch subsidy: 51%

E ENVIRONMENT

"<u>Ice cover on the Great Lakes</u> is highly variable from year-to-year, and is exceedingly important to both water quantity and quality, as well as to shipping and transportation. Widespread ice cover reduces evaporation from the Great Lakes and, therefore, moderates the loss of water from them during the winter. This in turn can contribute to higher water levels the following spring. Huge ice jams can form in Great Lake connecting channels, constricting the flow of water from one lake to another, sometimes creating flooding above the jam and reducing hydro power downstream. When the ice jam finally breaks, the resulting surge of water and ice can damage shoreline properties and structures. Stable ice formation in bays can, however, provide a platform for winter recreational activities such as snowmobiling and ice fishing and, when along shoreline, can protect wetlands and shore zones from erosion." ^{Schaetzl}

F FLORA & FAUNA

Alice Welch, USDA

The chestnut tree is easily identified by its twisted bark. Chestnuts are found inside the spiny burs that open on the tree in autumn and allow the nuts in their shells to fall to the ground. See 5A.

Roger Myers

The Pileated Woodpecker, about the size of a crow, is the largest woodpecker in North America. It makes large, mostly rectangular holes in trees to get to its favorite food, carpenter ants and wood-boring beetle larvae.

G GOVERNMENT

County: ...created: 1840 **...organized:** 1863
...originally part of: Grand Traverse County
Size: 336,000 acres / 477 sq. miles (76 of 83 counties)
The county has 5 villages, 15 townships, 8 unincorporated communities and 7 school districts.

Michigan State Preservation Office

County seat: Bellaire
...Homestead property tax: 38 mills
Motto: <u>Elk Rapids</u>: *A Community With Dedicated Families Working Together for a Better Living*
...<u>Traverse City</u> Convention and Visitors Bureau: *Take Me There*
...<u>Village of Central Lake</u>: *Located in the heart of Antrim County on the Beautiful Chain of Lakes*

H HISTORICAL MARKERS 5 of 8

Antrim County Seat: moving the county seat from Elk Rapids to Bellaire in 1879 started a 25-year controversy that was settled by the state Supreme Court. The courthouse was built in 1905.

Elk Rapids Iron Company: now only ruins; from 1873 to 1915, it made iron with ore from the U.P. It also made charcoal from the hardwoods in the area until the forests were depleted.

Essex: a former lumbering town, now a ghost town

Island House: 1900, Mr. Noble covered a 4-acre sand dune with clay and dark loam, planted trees and built a bridge over the river from his new island

Saint John Nepomucene Catholic Church: 1885, patron saint of Czechoslovakia; Gothic Revival style; fieldstone added in 1926

Monument: The *Hugh J. Gray Cairn* (a cairn is a pile of stones placed as a landmark) is on Cairn Hwy. and contains rocks from all 83 Michigan counties. Mr. Gray was the founder of the West Michigan Tourist Association and considered the Dean of Michigan's Tourist Activity.

Dean Ginther

National Register of Historic Places: 6 listings
State Historic Sites: 13 listings

I   INFORMATION

Chamber of Commerce: Bellaire, Central Lake, Elk Rapids, Mancelona
Visitor: Traverse City Convention and Visitors Bureau, 800-872-8377, traversecity.com

J   JOKES

We're from Michigan. We…
…don't care how cold it is as long as the sun shines.
…don't like the cold, but we've learned to put up with it; and believe it or not, some of us even like it.
…go on vacation to get even closer to one of our 11,000 lakes.
…go through our year from one agricultural season to another.
…think a 55° day in January in Orlando is warm; but a 55° day in July at home is cool.
…know the difference between the Lake Michigan shoreline and the Lake Huron shoreline and have a definite preference.
…love 60° days in March for ourselves, but hate it for the flowers and fruit trees.

K   KINSMAN

Race		Ancestry	
American Indian: 1%		German: 22%	
Asian: <1%		English: 15%	
Black/African American: <1%		Irish: 11%	
Hispanic or Latino: 2%		U.S./American: 10%	
Other: 2%		Polish: 7%	
White: 97%		Dutch: 5%	
		French: 5%	

L   LIGHTHOUSE OR LANDMARK

Dean Ginther

The Chain of Lakes is 14 lakes in Antrim County, running 75 miles north and south and provides water activities for almost any interest. This photo is the north end of Torch Lake (on the left) and Grand Traverse Bay (on the right), at Eastport, looking south.

M   MUSEUMS

Jessie Jakubik

Alden *Depot Park & Museum:* restored 1908 train depot; on Torch Lake, picnic area

Bellaire *Area Historical Museum:* artifacts and graphics from 1865-1965; newspaper collection

Central Lake *Area Historical Society:* community pioneer information in an 1885 restored house; includes children's museum
Elk Rapids *Historical Museum:* in the 1883 Elk Rapids Township Hall that has a mansard roof and other special architectural features
…*Guntzviller's Spirit of the Woods Museum:* American Indian artifacts, Michigan animals, tours

N   NATURAL RESOURCES

Elevation: <600 - 1400 feet
Physiography: hill-lands, plains

Forest type: maple-beech-hemlock, aspen-birch
Public/private forests: 57% of county
Legislatively protected sand dunes: 660 acres

Water in county: 8% of county (land enclosed water)
   Bay: East Arm of Grand Traverse Bay and Grand Traverse Bay of Lake Michigan
   Lakes: 55
      …largest: Torch (#1 depth/MI, #2 size/MI)
            Elk Lake (#2 depth/MI)

Rivers: Cedar, Elk, Grass, Jordan, Intermediate, Manistee (headwaters), Torch
Rivers & streams: 260 miles
Great Lakes shoreline: 27 miles of Lake Michigan
FYI: 21% of this county is water, including part of the East Arm of Grand Traverse Bay, Elk Lake, Torch Lake and The Chain of Lakes.

Growing season, avg.: 113 days (4 temp. zones)
Last freeze, avg.: May 20 – June 5
First freeze, avg.: Sept. 15 – Oct. 5
Precipitation, annual avg.: rainfall: 31 inches
                            snowfall: 96 inches
Temperature (F), avg.: January: high 28°, low 13°
                           July: high 80°, low 55°
Annual: >90°: 7 days, **<0°:** 18 days
Tornadoes (1930-2010): 8

O ORIGINS

Alden:[u] railroad official, state and U.S. senator, William Alden Smith; 1868
Antrim:[co] from County Antrim, Ireland
Bellaire:[v] means pure air; 1879
Central Lake:[v] in the center of the chain of lakes, from Bellaire to Ellsworth; 1869
Elk Rapids:[v] first settler found a pair of elk horns at the mouth of the Meguzee (now Elk) River; 1848
Ellsworth:[v] the first postmaster of the town served under Col. E.E. Ellsworth, the first Union officer to die in the Civil War; 1881
Mancelona:[v] name of the youngest daughter of the first settler; 1869

P PARKS

National: 0   **State:** 3   **County:** 5   **Local:** 16
Number of campsites: 500
State Forest: *Jordan River:*[ww] 44,000 acres, goal is to return the land to a wilderness
...Campground: 2   **...Pathway:** 18 miles
State Game Area: *Petobego:* wetlands shared with Grand Traverse County covering almost 500 acres
Other: *Grass River Natural Area:*[ww] 1,300 acres, part of the Chain of Lakes waterway, includes lakes, meandering rivers, rushing streams, crystal clear creeks in five ecotones; a natural eco-guardian project and adventure in environmental tourism; trails, classes, boardwalks, wheelchair accessible

Q QUOTE FROM THE LOCALS

"Water is the backdrop of life in Bellaire. Swimming, boating, fishing and beach-combing are summer activities that give way in the fall to driving tours along some of Michigan's most scenic back roads. In the winter, snowmobile trails, sledding spots and ...ski slopes provide plenty of fun. Golf swings into action in the spring as the area heats up again."
bellairechamber.org

"Embraced by East Grand Traverse Bay to the west, Elk Lake to the east and Bass Lake to the north, the community of Elk Rapids is one of the most charming of all the harbor towns in Northwest Lower Michigan. ...It is a year-round playground for all types of outdoor activities. Golfing, fishing, boating, hunting, biking, hiking, skiing, exploring – if you are interested in finding your own part of paradise, we invite you to visit us!" elkrapidschamber.org

"When you just want to get away from it all, get a breath of fresh air, and enjoy some quiet time to yourself, the many parks and scenic gems in the Mancelona area provide spectacular views and ideal conditions for that alone time. Some of these secret hideaways are so well hidden, they are unnoticed by many who drive right on by. Whether you are looking for a place to do a little fishing, hiking, have a picnic lunch or take a nap beneath a shade oak tree, Antrim County has the place for you." mancelonachamber.org

Dean Ginther   Dean Ginther

R RECREATION & SPORTS

Blue Ribbon Trout Streams:[1,000] Cedar River, Jordan River
Golf courses: 11
Great Lakes marinas: 2   **Boat slips:** 175
Hiking/skiing/mountain biking trails: 69 miles
Off-road vehicle trails: 39 miles
Public access sites: 32
Public recreational land: 13% of county

Rail-trail: (25 miles) Grass River Natural Area Nature Trail, Jordan River Pathway

Recreational harbor: Grace Memorial Harbor in Elk Rapids

Jessie Jakubik

State/federal wild/scenic/natural river: 2 miles of the Jordan River

State-funded snowmobile trails: 30 miles

Mt. Mancelona: 17 ski runs; deepest natural snow skiing in Lower Michigan

S STATE OF MICHIGAN

<u>Michigan Population Snapshot</u> in selected years

1810: 4,800

1820: 9,000 people in the Michigan Territory, mostly around Detroit

1830: 28,000

1835: 87,000, right before statehood in 1837

1838: 175,000

1840: 212,000

1850: 398,000

1860: 749,000, an increase of 83 times in 40 years

1880: 1,637,000

1900: 2,421,000

1920: 3,668,000

1940: 5,256,000

1960: 7,823,000

1980: 9,262,000

2000: 9,938,000

2010: 9,884,000

NPCR

T TRAVEL

Airport: Antrim County

Bus: Dial-a-Ride

Circle Tour: Lake Michigan, US-31

Distance to Lansing: 180 miles

Main roads: US-31, US-131, M-32, M-66, M-88

Memorial Highways: US-31, *Blue Star MH:* see 3T

…US-31 & US-131, *Green Arrow Route – Mackinac Trail:* don't confuse this Green Arrow Route to Mackinac with the original Green Arrow Route of M-66

Scenic Drive: US-31

Driving tour: take County Road 593 on the east side of Torch Lake for a close-up view of one of the world's most beautiful lakes.

NPCR

U UNIVERSITIES & COLLEGES

None

V VARIETY

Photo courtesy of Shanty Creek Resorts

With four first-class ski resorts, Antrim County is a popular destination for downhill skiing. The Shanty Creek Resorts of Schuss, Summit Mountain and Cedar River offer 53 ski runs, 72 holes of golf, 4 terrain parks and plenty of dining options. See also 5R.

W WANDERLUST

Agri-tourism: *Friske's Farm Market:* U-pick, café, bakery, general store, area fruits and veggies

…*King Orchards:* U-pick, apples, cherries, peaches, apricots, sweet corn, pumpkins

…*Royal Farm:* U-pick, apples, cherries, jams/jellies, bakery, corn maze, greenhouse, flowers

…*Woods Farm:* maple syrup and products

Brewery: Short's Brewing Company

Fall colors: late September – early October

Brownwood Acres: Country Store, Old School House

Deep Woods Press: hand-crafted printed items, bindings and book matter

Traverse Bay Farms: Fruit Advantage "America's Leading Super Fruit Supplement Brand:" juice concentrates, fruit capsules, fruit powders, dried fruits, chocolate covered fruits, fruit butters, fruit salsa; tours available

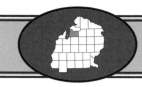
X X-TRA STUFF

County Fair: *Antrim Co. Farm & Family Fair*: Aug.
Famous people: *...Other*: Earl Young
Large employers: Club Corp. International (hotel), Great Lakes Packing (cherries), Go Forward Operating LP (restaurant, motel, amusement), County of Antrim (outpatient clinic, skilled nursing care facility), Elk Rapids Schools, Anchor Lamina (copper foundry), Traverse Bay Manufacturing (clothing)

Jaynne Simpson

Deadman's Hill is the site of several fatal logging accidents that happened over 100 years ago. The mountain was just too steep for the horses pulling rigs carrying the newly cut giant tree logs.

Torch Lake and Elk Lake are considered two of the most beautiful lakes in the world; the water is very clear and a Caribbean blue. The name of Torch Lake is derived from the local American Indians who lit torches for night spear fishing of whitefish and trout. Torch Lake is 19 miles long and is Michigan's second largest inland lake. See 5L, 5O.

Y YESTERYEAR

"In 1871, Hiram H. Bradford located land and prepared a home in the dense wilderness of Mancelona. Mrs. Bradford, walking, carried their youngest son, three months old, in her arms nearly all the way from Spencer Creek, a distance of 12 miles. Their dwelling was the third house built in Mancelona. All their building materials, provisions, etc., had to be procured at Elk Rapids, brought to Spencer Creek by water, and hauled the rest of the way by team. Common lumber was six dollars per thousand, and cost eight dollars per thousand for hauling. They often carried their provisions on their backs, as there were scarcely any teams in the place. Those were days of hardship." Mancelona Historical Society, MIGenWeb

Z ZOO & ANIMAL PLACES

Petting zoo: Brownwood Acres
Watchable Wildlife Viewing Areas:ʷʷ Skegemog Swamp Pathway; see 5P
Drettmann Ranch: the only ranch in the world dedicated to bow hunting trophy whitetail deer
Jordan River Fish Hatchery: under the direction of the U.S. Department of the Interior's Fish and Wildlife Service, it annually propagates up to 2 million yearling lake trout to stock Lake Michigan and Lake Huron

NPCR

Last Chance Kennel: Dogsledding 101, learn all about how to be a dog musher; Nov. -April

A AGRICULTURE

Land in farms: 40% of county
Number of farms: 490
Size of average farm: 190 acres
Market value of all products: #46 of 83 counties
Crops: ...most acres: corn for grain
...highest $ sales: grains: dry edible beans, corn, soybeans, wheat
Livestock: ...largest number: cattle & calves
...highest $ sales: milk & dairy products
Among the top Michigan counties:
• #3- organic production
• #8- acres of dry beans
Dairy, food and meat processing plants: 6
State ranking for harvested trees: #51 of 83 counties
FYI: U.S. Farm Facts: In the U.S. in 1900, there were over 6 million farms averaging less than 200 acres each, for less than 1.2 trillion acres. In 2000, there were just over 2 million farms averaging 500 acres each, for 1 trillion acres. Michigan is ranked 22nd in agricultural cash receipts. California, Texas and Iowa are the first three and New Hampshire, Rhode Island and Alaska are the last three. The top nine states account for 50% of the U.S. agricultural income. [NASS]

B BRIDGE OR BOAT

Charity Island Excursions

The schedule of the Charity Island Excursions ferry to Charity Island changes weekly so that the return trip on the dinner cruise maximizes the beauty of the sunset.

C CELEBRATIONS

AuGres *Car Cruise & Show:* music, arts & crafts, walleye tournament, July
...*Pirates Festival:* at the Harbor of Refuge, games, contests, bands, Aug.
...*Halloween Hallow:* lamppost decorating, Oct.

Omer *Sucker Derby:* "Catch the biggest sucker in the smallest city." April

Standish *Depot Days:* pie baking contest, 5K run/walk, lots of entertainment, Oct.

NPCR

D DEMOGRAPHICS

Population: 15,900   **Persons per sq. mile:** 43
Largest city: Standish   **Population:** 1,510
Largest township: Standish   **Population:** 1,900
Largest village: Sterling   **Population:** 530
Median household income: $35,200
Owner-occupied median house value: $99,900
Persons affiliated with a religious congregation: 36%
Persons below poverty level: 18%
Students receiving school lunch subsidy: 48%
FYI: Omer is the second smallest city in the state with 313 people, according to the 2010 Census. In 2000, they were the smallest with 337 people. Turner is the smallest village in Michigan with a population of 114 in the 2010 census.

E ENVIRONMENT

The Michigan Islands National Wildlife Refuge was started in 1943 and now consists of eight islands in Lake Michigan and Lake Huron. Charity Island and Little Charity Island, in Arenac County, were added in 1999 and Scarecrow and Thunder Bay Islands (part of the Thunder Bay National Marine Sanctuary) are all in Lake Huron. Gull, Hat, Pismire and Shoe Islands (near Beaver Island) are in Lake Michigan. They provide needed sanctuary for migrating and nesting birds, as well as protection for other animals and plants. The U.S. Fish and Wildlife Service is the administrator of this wildlife refuge.

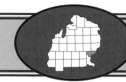
F FLORA & FAUNA

Yellow Birch

Alice Welch, USDA

White Birch

Alice Welch, USDA

The yellow birch tree is used for lumber, flooring and cabinetry. The white birch tree is famous for its paper-like bark that is waterproof and was used by the American Indians to make birch bark canoes. See 6Y.

White sucker 19 inches long

NPCR

The 12"-20" long white sucker is also known as the common sucker, coarse-scaled sucker, brook sucker, gray sucker, mud sucker, sucker mullet, black mullet, slender sucker, June sucker and white horse. Often used as bait, you might find it in the fish market as "freshwater mullet." It is good fried in butter.

G GOVERNMENT

County: ...created: 1883 **...organized:** 1883
...originally part of: Bay & Saginaw Counties
Size: 238,000 acres / 367 sq. miles (81 of 83 counties)
The county has 3 cities, 3 villages, 12 townships, 5 unincorporated communities and 3 school districts.

Andrea Leitch

County seat: Standish
...Homestead property tax: 47 mills
Motto: <u>Standish</u>: *Gateway to the Sunrise Side; The Great Up North Begins Here*

H HISTORICAL MARKERS 1 of 1

Andrea Leitch

Omer Masonic Hall: built in 1890 as the second county courthouse, the Masons bought this church-like building in 1893 when the county seat was moved to Standish.

National Register of Historic Places: 2 listings
State Historic Sites: 5 listings

I INFORMATION

Chamber of Commerce: AuGres, 989-876-6688, augres chamber.com
...Standish Area, 989-846-7867, standishchamber.com

J JOKES

Michiganians don't have accents, so we say, but we do say a few things in our very own way. So if you want to talk like us, say...
..."ant" for aunt.
..."ash-fault" for asphalt.
..."car-ml" for caramel.
..."ciddy" for city.
..."cloze" for clothes.
..."hunnerd" for hundred.

K KINSMAN

Race		Ancestry	
American Indian:	1%	German:	24%
Asian:	<1%	Polish:	14%
Black/African American:	<1%	French:	12%
Hispanic or Latino:	1%	U.S./American:	11%
Other:	2%	English:	8%
White:	97%	Irish:	7%

L LIGHTHOUSE OR LANDMARK

Angela M. Simmons

Charity Island Light is no longer a functioning lighthouse, but is now privately owned and offers tours, dinner and a Bed & Breakfast overnight stay.

M MUSEUMS

Arenac *County Historical Society:* in an 1880s church, recreates vintage homes and businesses

N NATURAL RESOURCES

Elevation: <600 – 1,000 feet
Physiography: lake border plains

Forest type: aspen-birch, elm-ash-cottonwood
Public/private forests: 51% of county
FYI: Of the 15 forest types in Michigan, the aspen-birch hardwood forest has a more open canopy with trees that allow sunlight to penetrate that thus fosters growth of dense underbrush. With over 3 million acres and 40 species of trees, it is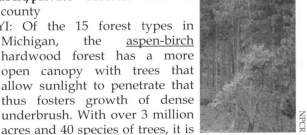

NPCR

the second leading forest type in the state. The most common trees in this forest are quaking aspen, big tooth aspen, red maple, paper birch and balsam fir.
Michigan Forests Forever

Water in county: 1% of county
　Bay: Saginaw Bay of Lake Huron
　Lakes: 10　　**...largest:** Forest Lake
　Rivers: AuGres (aw GRAY), Pine, Rifle
　Rivers & streams: 160 miles

Great Lakes islands: Charity Island
Great Lakes shoreline: 47 miles of Lake Huron

Growing season, avg.: 126 days (2 temp. zones)
　Last freeze, avg.: May 20 - May 25
　First freeze, avg.: Sept. 25 – Sept. 30
Precipitation, annual avg.: rainfall: 28 inches
　　　　　　　　　　　　　snowfall: 45 inches
Temperature (F), avg.: January: high 28°, low 11°
　　　　　　　　　　July: high 82°, low 56°
　Annual: >90°: 8 days, **<0°:** 2 days
Tornadoes (1930-2010): 6

O ORIGINS

Arenac:[co] (AIR a nack) a sandy place
AuGres:[c] (aw GRAY) French for gritty stone; 1862
Charity Island: placed there by the "charity of God," just where the sailors needed it, at the entrance to Saginaw Bay
Omer:[c] the first settler wanted to name it Homer, but there was already a Homer, Michigan, so he dropped the H; 1866
Standish:[c] mill owner, John Standish; 1871
Sterling:[v] lumberman, William Sterling; 1871
Turner:[v] founded by Joseph Turner; 1885
Twining:[v] lumberman, Frederick Twinning; 1894

P PARKS

National: 0　**State:** 3　**County:** 3　**Local:** 9
Number of campsites: 1,700

State Forest: (28,000 acres) Tittabawassee River

State Wildlife Area: *Wigwam Bay:*[ww] 200 acres
Local: *AuGres Boating Access Site & Harbor of Refuge:* dock your boat here and walk to town

NPCR

Q QUOTE FROM THE LOCALS

"Like many small towns in northern mid-Michigan, the height of activity in Omer centers on an influx of people during the spring and summer. The Rifle River that intersects the city attracts thousands per year during the sucker season. Folks from all over the Midwest and Canada line the shores and engage in the sport of sucker fishing in the spring. During the summer, Omer is a popular weekend getaway for those looking to unwind by canoeing or tubing down the scenic river. There are also miles of unspoiled forests surrounding the city that bring in deer hunters from around the country in the fall. Hunting is such a popular sport that the local school in Twining, Michigan, closes for the opening day of deer season rather than face the 50% or more absentee rate that would otherwise occur. Winter also brings snowmobilers and ice fishermen to the surrounding area." wikipedia

NPCR

R RECREATION & SPORTS

Golf courses: 2
Great Lakes marinas: 7   **Boat slips:** 725
Public access sites: 8
Public recreational land: 13% of county
Recreational harbor: AuGres State Dock

State/federal wild/scenic/natural river: 20 miles of the Rifle River

Charter fishing: there are many companies offering charter-fishing adventures on Lake Huron; it's always a great day on the lake

NPCR

Sunrise Side Heritage Bike Ride: 400 miles from Standish to the Mackinac Bridge along the beautiful Lake Huron shoreline; Sept.

S STATE OF MICHIGAN

William M. Ciesla, Forest Health Management International

Since 1998, the Dwarf Lake Iris has been the State Wildflower. This delicate and beautiful endangered and protected flower grows along the northern shorelines of Lake Michigan and Lake Huron.

T TRAVEL

Airport: Standish Industrial
Bus: Indian Trails
Circle Tour: Lake Huron & Sunrise Side via US-23.
Distance to Lansing: 130 miles
Ferry: to Charity Island

Cindy McCarty

Heritage Route: *Recreational:* US-23, Sunrise Side Coastal Highway, 200 miles, from Standish to Mackinaw, offering natural wonders, history and culture

Lights of Northern Lake Huron Tour: Charity Island Lighthouse Bed & Breakfast
Main roads: I-75, US-23, M-13, M-33, M-61
Memorial Highways: US-23, *United Spanish War Veterans MH:* see 1T
…I-75, *American Legion MH:* the American Legion is the largest veterans association in the world
FYI: Over the years, US-23 has been called, in part or as a whole, proposed, promoted or legalized: Artic-Tropic Overland Trail, Blue Water Trail, Dixie Hwy., East Michigan Pike, Huron Shore Hwy., Michigan Pike, Roberts-Linton Hwy., Saginaw Trail, Sweetwater Trail, Theodore Roosevelt International Hwy., Top of Michigan Trail, United Spanish War Veterans Memorial Hwy. and Veterans Memorial Pkwy. Barnett

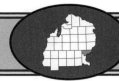
U UNIVERSITIES & COLLEGES

None

V VARIETY

Andrea Leitch

Finished in 1889, the stone for the Standish Depot was hauled in by horse-drawn wagons of the local farmers who donated the materials and their labor to do it. It took stonemasons two years to cut and build the depot. The now renovated building once again serves as the handsome centerpiece in downtown Standish.

W WANDERLUST

Casino: Saganing Eagles Landing
Fall colors: late September to early October
Lighthouses, other: Gravelly Shoal Light, at Point Lookout
State Historic Sites: 5 listings
Singing Bridge: built in 1932 on US-23 over Whitney Drain, it had battle deck plates for its road surface that emitted a high-pitched hum, or "sang" as cars drove across the bridge.

X X-TRA STUFF

County Fair: *Arenac County Agriculture Soc.:* July
Hospital: St. Mary's of Michigan
Large employers: Michigan Department of Corrections, Standish Community Hospital, St. Mary's Medical Center, Sterling Standish Community Schools

Y YESTERYEAR

The major American Indian nations of Michigan in the 1700-1800s belong to a large linguistic group that we now call the Algonquin. The *Chippewa (or Ojibwas)* lived in the U.P. and along the Lake Huron coast north of Saginaw. The *Huron* lived along the shore of Lake Huron in the Thumb and along the shores of Lake St. Clair and Lake Erie. The *Miami* lived in what is now the Berrien and Cass County area. The *Ottawa* lived along Lake Michigan in what we now call the "fruit belt." *The Potawatomi*, by far the largest group, claimed as their homeland about 80% of the lower half of the Lower Peninsula. There were no American Indians in the dense pinewood forests of the interior of the upper half of the Lower Peninsula.

The American Indians all made birch bark canoes in order to navigate the many rivers and lakes of Michigan. The early fur traders and explorers used the birch bark canoe exclusively in their water-based explorations. Consequently, Michigan, because it was the center of fur trading, became famous for the birch bark canoes of the American Indians.

NPCR-2

To make a canoe, first a frame was made of cedar ribs. Large white birch trees were felled and both the outer and inner layer of the strong, lightweight, waterproof and resilient bark was removed in one large piece and then dried. Roots of the white pine tree were used to lash the frame together, to sew large pieces of birch bark together and to attach the bark to the frame. Finally, hot resin of the pine or spruce tree was used to seal and waterproof the seams. Some canoes were large enough to hold up to 10 people and over a thousand pounds of gear and supplies.

Z ZOO & ANIMAL PLACES

Petting zoo: *The Pumpkin Farm:* farm animals, donkeys, buffalo, llamas; wagon ride with story book characters
Watchable Wildlife Viewing Areas:[ww] see 6P

A AGRICULTURE

Land in farms: 46% of county
Number of farms: 1,160
Size of average farm: 140 acres
Market value of all products: #22 of 83 counties
Crops: ...most acres: grain: corn, soybeans
...highest $ sales: grain: corn, soybeans, wheat
Livestock: ...largest number: turkeys
...highest $ sales: milk & dairy products
Among the top Michigan counties:
- #3- rabbits & their pelts, horses sold, turkeys
- #4- goats/meat/other
- #5- beef cows
- #10- milk cows

Dairy, food and meat processing plants: 11
State ranking for harvested trees: #50 of 83 counties
AgBioResearch Centers (MSU): *W.K. Kellogg Biological Station:* 4,000 acres, is a premier inland field research station; includes the Kellogg Bird Sanctuary, Kellogg Farm, Kellogg Biological Laboratories and Lux Arbor Reserve, which is a National Science Foundation's Long-Term Ecological Research site. It is committed to science and ecology education, conservation of natural resources and sustainable agriculture research and demonstration.

FYI: <u>Honeybees</u> provide one service and one product to the agriculture industry. Bees are critically important to the pollination of almost all fruit and vegetable crops. Without them, Michigan's - and the world's - agricultural industry would be devastated. There are beekeepers in every county, even those counties with limited agriculture production.

Most fruit crops need from 1 to 3 beehives per acre for proper pollination, with each hive having 30,000-60,000 bees. In 2007, there were 75,000 colonies of bees on 870 farms in Michigan. The bees produce <u>honey</u> as their winter food source. They collect the nectar from flowers (and in the process pollinate the plants) during warm weather, return to the hive, process the nectar into honey and store it for later use. When more honey is produced than they can use, it is then removed from the hive to become food for human consumption. There was 5 million pounds of honey collected in Michigan

MICHIGAN WILDFLOWER HONEY

NPCR

in 2007. The color of honey is a good indicator of how it will taste. The lighter the honey, the milder the flavor; conversely, the darker the honey, the stronger the flavor. Choose your favorite! See 8F.
michigan.gov, michiganbees.org, USDA

B BRIDGE OR BOAT

Gloria Pennington

MDOT Historic Bridge: Built in 1903, the McKeown Bridge, also called the Sponable Bridge, is a Pratt through truss bridge that is 119 feet long. It spans the Thornapple River off McKeown and Nashville Roads. Now part of the 23-acre McKeown Bridge Park, it is only used by pedestrians and bicycles.

C CELEBRATIONS

<u>Barry County</u> *Thornapple Jazz Festival:* live performances at various locations, April
<u>Delton</u> *Founders Festival:* parade, "art hop," street bowling, rib fest, Taste of Delton, tractor show, Aug.
<u>Hastings</u> *Cerulean Warbler Festival:* celebrating the conservation of North America's fastest declining songbird, June
...*Summerfest:* tennis, basketball and softball tournaments, soccer, roller hockey and weightlifting, parade, car & motorcycle shows, Aug.
<u>Middleville</u> *Heritage Days:* tractor pull, pig roast, pie making contest, crafts, car show, Sept.
<u>Orangeville</u> *Days Festival:* euchre tournament, silent auction, old-fashioned family games, parade, Aug.

D DEMOGRAPHICS

Population: 36,600   **Persons per sq. mile:** 64
Largest city: Hastings   **Population:** 7,350
Largest township: Thornapple   **Population:** 4,570
Largest village: Nashville   **Population:** 1,630
Median household income: $36,000
Owner-occupied median house value: $102,000
Persons affiliated with a religious congregation: 22%
Persons below poverty level: 19%
Students receiving school lunch subsidy: 33%

E ENVIRONMENT

The Pierce Cedar Creek Institute for environmental education has 660 acres that include kettle-hole wetlands, a tall grass prairie, swamp forests and a wetland marsh that has been protected from development and degradation for over 50 years. The institute is a mix between a nature center and biological field station providing educational programs for both the public and higher education institutions. As a top-notch environmental educator, it is a leading force in research that results in awareness, appreciation and preservation of the natural world. There is an education building, visitor center, auditorium and housing, plus the natural features that provide opportunity for many outdoor activities. cedarcreekinstitute.org

F FLORA & FAUNA

Steve Hillebrand/USFWS

Garlic mustard is an invasive noxious weed that is taking over many plant communities. It produces a chemical that ultimately inhibits optimum growth for most plants, including trees in the forest. It should be removed from wherever it is found.

Michigan Farm Bureau

There are about 3,500 different species of bees in North America, but the honeybee is the favorite. More has been written about honeybees than any other species of insect. See 8A.

G GOVERNMENT

County: ...created: 1829 **...organized:** 1839
...originally part of: St. Joseph, Kalamazoo Counties
Size: 369,000 acres / 556 sq. miles (58 of 83 counties)
The county has 1 city, 4 villages, 16 townships with 2 as charter townships, 12 unincorporated communities and 3 school districts.

Michigan State Preservation Office

NPCR

County seat: Hastings
...Homestead property tax: 36 mills
Motto: Barry County Tourism Council: *Explore Barry County*
... Hastings: *We Treasure the Old – Progress with the New; One of the 100 Best Small Towns in America*
... Middleville: *Crossroads to the Future*

H HISTORICAL MARKERS 12 of 22

Carlton Twp. Hall: 1867, in 1981 it was still used and was heated with a wood-burning stove.
Central School: 1931, a truly modern building for the time with many high-end upgrades

Early Hastings: ▪ 1836: village was platted
- 1851: first newspaper
- 1869: first railroad
- 1870s: Dr. William Upjohn practiced here
- 1892: current courthouse was built
- 1919: Ella Eggleston was one of the first women probate judges in the state

Michigan State Preservation Office

George Lowry House: 1894, the asymmetrical composition, stately turret, decorative barge-boards and spindlework typify Queen Anne architecture.

Gov. Kim Sigler: 1894-1953, elected in 1946 after successfully prosecuting legislative graft

Hasting Mutual Insurance Co.: in 1885 it started as the Michigan Mutual Tornado, Cyclone and Windstorm Insurance Company.

Indian Landing – Charlton Park: land donated to the county by Irving Charlton in 1936 was the former home of the Thornapple Band of Ottawa Indians.

John Carveth House: 1886, highly decorative Eastlake designs on an elaborate Queen Anne style

McKeown Road Bridge: 1869-1930s, the last metal truss highway bridge in Barry County; see 8B

Putnam Public Library: the 1884 home in red brick Italianate style was given to Nashville for a library in 1921.

Woodland Town Hall: 1867, handsome two-story Green Revival style with hand-hewn timbers

Yankee Springs Inn: <1853, "Yankee Bill" Lewis of NY, a man known for his hospitality, ran a large inn and stables at this stagecoach stop. See 8O.

National Register of Historic Places: 7 listings
State Historic Sites: 33 listings

I INFORMATION

Chamber of Commerce: Gun Lake, Hastings, Nashville

Visitor: Barry County Tourism Council, 269-945-2454, mibarry.com/tourism

J JOKES

You may live in a Michigan hard water area if…
…your guests ask for a glass of water and you respond "hard or soft?"
…your white clothes don't stay white.
…your two-year-old can actually tell the difference between the kitchen water and the bathroom water.
…you grew up with well water and prefer the taste of iron and minerals in your water.
…everyone you know owns a water softener.
…your water has an odor.
…your clear mugs turn frosted after a year of being washed in the dishwasher.
…your tea kettle has scales.
…your toilet bowl has brown streaks and the inside of the tank has a rusty crust.

K KINSMAN

Race	Ancestry
American Indian: <1%	German: 22%
Asian: <1%	English: 14%
Black/African American: <1%	Dutch: 13%
Hispanic or Latino: 2%	U.S./American: 12%
Other: 2%	Irish: 10%
White: 97%	Polish: 4%

L LIGHTHOUSE OR LANDMARK

Stephen J. Brown

As the nation's "premier automotive history destination," the Gilmore Car Museum has over 200 extraordinary beautiful historic vehicles in 6 restored barns on 90 landscaped acres. There are also collections of pedal cars, hood ornaments, name badges and miniatures, plus the authentic 1941 Blue Moon Diner where you can have lunch. See 8M.

M MUSEUMS

Delton *Bernard Historical Museum:* includes Bernard Hospital, nature trail, school, store, seamstress cottage, blacksmith shop, windmill, gardens

...Bowen Mills Historical Park & Pioneer Farming Village: 19 acres, living history with working water powered grist and cider mill, Civil War era homes and buildings, draft horses; festivals, artisans, weddings, photography

NPCR

Hastings *Historic Charlton Park:* Village, Museum & Recreation Area, 25 historic residences and community buildings were moved here from around the county to help preserve the past so future generations might understand the difficult tasks early inhabitants performed, and to house the extensive collections of Irving Charlton who donated 150,000 artifacts.

James Korringa

Hickory Corners *Gilmore Car Museum:* see 8L

NPCR

N NATURAL RESOURCES

Elevation: 700 - 900 feet
Physiography: rolling plains, hill lands

Forest type: oak-hickory, maple-beech
Public/private forests: 30% of county

Water in county: 3% of county
Lakes: 160 **...largest:** Gun Lake
Rivers: Little Thornapple, Thornapple
Rivers & streams: 270 miles

Growing season, avg.: 139 days (2-3 temp. zones)
Last freeze, avg.: May 5 – May 10
First freeze, avg.: Sept. 30 – Oct. 10
Precipitation, annual avg.: rainfall: 31 inches
snowfall: 52 inches
Temperature (F), avg.: January: high 30°, low 15°
July: high 84°, low 59°
Annual: >90°: 13 days, **<0°:** 11 days
Tornadoes (1930-2010): 19

O ORIGINS

Barry:[co] U.S. Postmaster General under President Andrew Jackson, William Barry
Delton:[u] was supposed to be Dellstown; 1839
Freeport:[v] town founders from Freeport, OH; 1874
Hastings:[c,ct] Eurotas Hastings sold his land with the promise that it would become the county seat; 1836
Hickory Corners:[u] a large hickory tree; 1834
Middleville:[v] close to Indian Middle Village; 1834
Nashville:[v] George Nash drew the village plats; 1837
Rutland:[ct] after Rutland, VT; 1862
Thornapple:[t] abundance of thorn apple trees; 1834
Woodland:[v,t] location in the dense woods; 1837
Yankee Springs: inn owner "Yankee Bill" Lewis and the spring behind his inn; 1836; see 8H

P PARKS

National: 0 **State:** 3 **County:** 2 **Local:** 30
Number of campsites: 2,100
State Game Area: *Barry:*[ww,wba] 15,000 acres, adjacent to Yankee Springs Recreation Area
...Middleville: 3,000 acres, scattered sites

State Recreation Area: *Yankee Springs:*[ww,wba] 5,200 acres, on Gun Lake; 9 lakes, trails, horse trails, camping, swimming, fishing, hunting

Gloria Pennington

County: *Historic Charlton Park:* Village, Museum & Recreation Area, 310 acres of rolling terrain, swim, fish and boat on Thornapple Lake; see 8M
Other: *MAS Otis Bird Sanctuary:* 128 acres, critical habitat for Cerulean Warblers
...The West Michigan Parks and Recreation Inventory: see 3P

Q QUOTE FROM THE LOCALS

"The natural beauty of the Chief Noonday Trail (M-179), coupled with its many recreational and historic sites, makes this an outstanding Heritage Route. This area was once the hunting ground for native woodland [Ottawa] Indians. It continues to be heavily wooded and inhabited by a wide variety of wildlife. A large portion of the road is bordered by state owned land. This is the gateway to the Yankee Springs Recreational area and the Barry State Game Area. The combination of state and local facilities provide the visitor a wide variety of recreational and historic opportunities. Activities available include camping, hiking, swimming, boating, fishing, hunting, biking, horse back riding, water and cross country skiing, berry and mushroom picking, photography and visits to historical sites and museums." michiganhighways.org MDOT See 8W.

Gloria Pennington

R RECREATION & SPORTS

Golf courses: 9
Hiking/skiing/mountain biking trails: 30 miles
Horse racing: harness racing at the county fair, July
North Country National Scenic Trail: yes
Public access sites: 33
Public recreational land: 7% of county
Rail-trail: (30 miles) Paul Henry Thornapple Trail, Yankee Springs Recreation Area
State-funded snowmobile trails: 20 miles

S STATE OF MICHIGAN

Michigan Terrestrial Ecoregions
  Region: Southern Lower Peninsula
  Square miles: 24,000
  Northern Boundary: from the southern part of Saginaw Bay, west to Oceana County
  Landcover: Forest: 23%
  …Agricultural: 50%
  …Wetlands: 8%
  …Urbanization: 9%
  Soils: calcareous and loamy

NPCR

Threats to wildlife and landscape features: industrial, residential and recreational development, invasive species, fragmentation.
Conservation actions are in place.

T TRAVEL

Airport: Hastings City
Bus: Barry County Transit
Distance to Lansing: 40 miles
Heritage Route: *Recreational:* M-179, see 8Q
Main roads: M-37, M-43, M-50, M-66, M-79, M-179
Memorial Highway: M-66, *Green Arrow Route*: named green in honor of Michigan forests and an arrow in honor of Michigan Indians.
Scenic Drive: Bradley to M-37 & 43 via M-179

U UNIVERSITIES & COLLEGES

None

V VARIETY

NPCR

With over 160 lakes and 270 miles of rivers and streams in Barry County, it is easy to find a good place for fishing, swimming, boating, picnicking or just enjoying being by the water and appreciating the beauty.

W WANDERLUST

Agri-tourism: *MOO-ville Creamery:* dairy farm that makes their own milk, ice cream, cheese; retail store and restaurant; see 8Z
Brewery: Waldorf Brewpub & Bistro
Cultural: Thornapple Arts Council
Fall colors: middle October

X X-TRA STUFF

County fair: *Barry County Agricultural Society:* family fun for all ages, 4-H exhibits, July

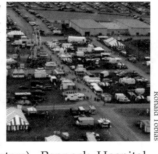

Ronald Tobias

Famous people: *Other:* Irving Charlton, Emil Tyden

Hospitals: Pennock

Large employers: Bradford White (makes water heaters), Pennock Hospital, Hastings Area Schools, Thornapple Kellogg Schools, Flexfab (makes metal, rubber, plastic hose), Hastings Mutual Insurance Co., International Union United (labor organization), Viking (makes fire or burglary resistive products)

Chief Noonday: (1757-1855), was Ottawa Chief Nawehquageezhik (the name on his headstone, but there are several different spellings in historical documents), was born near present day Grand Rapids. He fought with the British against the Americans several times and converted to Christianity around 1830. His American Indian name was translated to English as "noonday." He was well-loved and respected by all who knew him.

Y YESTERYEAR

<u>The Story of Minnie & Ben</u>

In Prairieville Cemetery there is a replica of a dog named Ben, lying on a cement slab guarding the grave of his mistress, Minnie Doster. Minnie was the youngest

Gloria Pennington

child in a family of 12 children; Ben was her dog and they were best friends. She was 16 years old when she died of typhoid fever in 1892. Ben followed the funeral procession six miles to the cemetery and then kept vigil at the gravesite, ignoring all family efforts to bring him home and keep him away from the cemetery. He died, probably of a broken heart that led to starvation, right there next to Minnie's grave. The family couldn't bear to separate them again, so Ben was buried at the foot of Minnie's grave. The family had a replica of Ben made and placed over his burial spot. The inscription reads "My dog Ben." delyon-mi.com

Z ZOO & ANIMAL PLACES

Watchable Wildlife Viewing Areas:ww see 8P
Petting zoo: MOO-ville

NPCR

NPCR

NOTE: (#x/MI) indicates ranking from highest number or percentage (#1) to lowest number or percentage (#83) in Michigan. The significance of either a high or low number depends on the item it describes.

A AGRICULTURE

Land in farms: 64% of county
Number of farms: 850
Size of average farm: 220 acres
Market value of all products: #28 of 83 counties
Crops: ...most acres: corn for grain
...highest $ sales: grains: corn, dry edible beans, soybeans, wheat
Livestock: ...largest number: cattle & calves
...highest $ sales: milk & dairy products
Among the top Michigan counties:
- #1- honey dew melons, watermelons
- #2- cantaloupe, cucumbers and pickles, quail
- #3- potatoes, dry beans
- #5- sugarbeets, other crops and hay, honey

Dairy, food & meat processing plants: 20
State ranking for harvested trees: #83 of 83 counties
FYI: Statewide there are over 1,600 acres of <u>melons</u> grown in Michigan. Bay County is a top producer of cantaloupes and honeydew melons, accounting for 15% of the total crop. A cantaloupe is defined as an orange flesh melon and a honeydew melon has green flesh. A watermelon usually has red flesh, but some varieties are yellow or even pink. All melons are hand picked.

B BRIDGE or BOAT

MDOT Historic Bridge: The Lafayette Ave. Bridge over the Saginaw River in Bay City was voted the most beautiful moveable bridge of the year in 1938.

C CELEBRATIONS

<u>Auburn</u> *Cornfest:* carnival, parade, good times, July
...*Summer Music Fest:* a variety of music styles on 6 evenings throughout the summer
...*Warmbier Farms:* Celebrate Easter, April; Farm Days, Aug.; Harvest Festival, Aug.; Bittersweet, Sept.; Sunflower Festival, Sept.; Festival of the Crow, Sept.; Autumn Festival, Sept.; Pumpkin Festival, Oct.; Festival of the Corn, Oct.; Fall Days, Oct.; Halloween Festival, Oct.

<u>Bay City</u> *State Recreation Area Winter Festival:* free ice fishing contest, snow snake clinic, Feb.
...*Labie Pig Gig:* Midwest Championship Rib Cook-off, pig racing, pig calling, Pigalicious Tasting Trough food demonstration tent, July
...*Rock by the Dock:* dance to the music, July
...*Tall Ship Celebration:* see 9L, July
...*Downtown Wine Walk:* showcasing the eateries and pubs, making friends, Sept.
...*Spring Downtown Divas Weekend:* everything for the lady in your life, May & Oct.

<u>Linwood</u> *National Pickle Festival:* since Bay County is the #2 cucumber-producing county in Michigan, it is only appropriate to have this festival, Aug.

Rachael Walsh

<u>Munger</u> *Potato Festival:* tons of free potatoes, carnival, Las Vegas Casino tent, July
<u>Pinconning</u> *Cheesetown Festival Weekend:* cheese cooking demo, parade, dad pageant, June

D DEMOGRAPHICS

Population: 107,800   **Persons per sq. mile:** 243
Largest city: Bay City   **Population:** 34,900
Largest township: Bangor   **Population:** 14,640
Median household income: $43,700
Owner-occupied median house value: $110,000
Persons affiliated with a religious congregation: 60%
Persons below poverty level: 13%
Students receiving school lunch subsidy: 41%

E ENVIRONMENT

There is a <u>Conservation District</u> in almost every county in the U.S. and in 79 of Michigan's 83 counties. It is a local unit of state government, a link between the local landowner, the government and conservation organizations. It focuses on natural resource problems and solutions. The services include woodland and wildlife improvements, soil information, stream bank stabilization, watershed planning, conserving and restoring wetlands, protecting groundwater, providing tree seedlings, conservation books and workshops. The Bay Conservation District serves this county.

F FLORA & FAUNA

John D. Byrd, Mississippi State University

Heal-all, or self-heal, is an aromatic mint wildflower that historically has been used for sore throats, as a wound dressing and as an herb for cooking.

NPCR

The Eastern American toad, 2"-3.5" is a gardener's friend since they love the cool, loose soils of the garden and they eat insects. They have warts on their skin but they do not cause warts on people.

G GOVERNMENT

County: ...created: 1857 **...organized:** 1857
...originally part of: Saginaw, Midland Counties
Size: 291,000 acres / 444 sq. miles (79 of 83 counties)
The county has 4 cities, 14 townships with 5 as charter townships, 9 unincorporated communities and 4 school districts.

NPCR

NPCR

County seat: Bay City
...Homestead property tax: 46 mills
Motto: <u>Bay City</u>: *A beautiful view...of life*
...<u>Charter Twp. of Monitor</u>: *For Better Living*
...<u>Hampton Charter Twp.</u>: *On the Bay*
...<u>Pinconning</u>: *Cheese Capital of Michigan*

H HISTORICAL MARKERS 12 of 20

Bay City: since its first settlement in the 1830s, the economic basis of the city has been lumbering, coal mining, fishing, ship building and production of beet sugar.

Beet Sugar: since the establishment of the first sugar-beet processing plant opened in 1898 in Bay City, the Saginaw Valley has been the sugar bowl of Michigan.

Center Avenue: between 1870 and 1940, the wealthy built their lavish homes and other monumental public buildings and churches.

First Presbyterian Church: on Center Ave., built of Ionia sandstone in the Richardsonian style in 1893, the bell served as a public timepiece and tolled three times a day.

Allison Short

Michigan State Preservation Office

James Clements Memorial Airport: the Neo-Georgian administration building was built in 1930; James Clements died in WWI and his father made a substantial donation to build the airport.

Midland Street Commercial District: 50 Queen Ann, Romanesque, Georgian Revival, Art Deco and Chicago style buildings built from 1867 to 1929 are on the National Register of Historic Places

Ogaukawning Church: 1847, a Methodist Indian Mission serving Chippewa Indians is now an American Indian social and religious center.

Sage Public Library: 1884, French Chateauesque-style building; merchant and philanthropist Henry Sage built it with a large donation of land and money for materials and books

Saginaw Bay: named after the Sauk Indians, this area has been known for lumbering, schooners hauling logs and lumber and good fishing

St. Stanislaus Kostka Roman Catholic Church: 1890, Polish refugees from Prussia built this Neo-Gothic church

Michigan State Preservation Office

Karen Stoneman

St. Joseph Catholic Church: 1911, designed on the plan of the Church of St. Anne de Beaupre in Quebec City, Canada

"Ten Hours or No Sawdust:" 1885, this was the slogan of sawmill workers who went on strike for a 10-hour day and higher wages. Three months and much contention later, they got the 10-hour day by an act of the state legislature, but did not receive higher wages.

National Register of Historic Places: 14 listings

State Historic Sites: 40 listings

I INFORMATION

Chamber of Commerce: Auburn, Bay City, Pinconning

Visitor: Great Lakes Bay Regional Convention and Visitors Bureau, 800-444-9979, visitgreatlakesbay.org

J JOKES

Michiganians don't have accents, so we say, but we do say a few things in our very own way. So if you want to talk like us, say…

…"loy-er" for lawyer.

…"mack-a-naw," never say mack-a-nack.

…"mow the lawn," not mow the grass.

…"party store" instead of liquor store.

…"pop" for a carbonated beverage, not soda, or soft drink, or cold drink, or cola.

…"win-er" for winter.

K KINSMAN

Race		Ancestry	
American Indian: <1%		German: 27%	
Asian: <1%		Polish: 21% (#2/MI)	
Black/African American: 2%		French: 11%	
Hispanic or Latino: 5%		Irish: 7%	
Other: 3%		English: 6%	
White: 94%		U.S./American: 5%	

L LIGHTHOUSE OR LANDMARK

NPCR

NPCR

Bay City is the home of the Tall Ship Celebration. A Tall Ship is a traditional sailing vessel with multiple masts and riggings that are reminiscent of ships of the past. These sloops, schooners, brigantines, barkentines and consort-barges all sailed the Great Lakes and were the mainstay of Great Lakes commerce and transportation prior to steam engines and railroads. Many of the Tall Ships provide opportunity for visitors to experience the thrill of sailing "the way it used to be." See 9W.

M MUSEUMS

Bay City *Antique Toy & Fire House Museum:* NASCAR room, Tonka room (the largest Tonka Toy collection in the world), Snap-on Tool room, Coca-Cola room, over 80 fire trucks

…*Bay County Historical Museum:* Trails through Time and Seaport to the World exhibits

…*Kantzler Maritime Gallery:* in the Bay County Historical Museum; interactive exhibits of light-houses, ship building and much more

N NATURAL RESOURCES

Elevation: <600 - 800 feet
Physiography: lake-border plains

Forest type: aspen-birch, elm-ash-cottonwood
Public/private forests: 15% of county
National Natural Landmark: *Tobico Marsh:* 1,650 acres, rare example of open fresh water, extensive marshland and a mixed hardwood forest; a major migratory bird flyway; see 9P

NPCR

NPCR

Water in county: 2% of county
  Bay: Saginaw Bay of Lake Huron
  Lakes: 15   **…largest:** Tobico Lagoon
  Rivers: Kawkawlin (caw CAWL in), Pinconning (Pin CON ning), Quanicassee (kwahn icka SEE), Saginaw
  Rivers & streams: 50 miles (#83/MI)

Great Lakes shoreline: 36 miles of Lake Huron

Growing season, avg.: 168 days (#5/MI) (3 temp. zones)
  Last freeze, avg.: May 5 – May 15
  First freeze, avg.: Oct. 5 – Oct. 15
Precipitation, annual avg.: rainfall: 28 inches
                          snowfall: 39 inches
Temperature (F), avg.: January: high 29°, low 15°
                   July: high 82°, low 61°
  Annual: >90°: 10 days, **<0°:** 8 days
Tornadoes (1930-2010): 13

O ORIGINS

Auburn:[c] first settler was from Auburn, Ireland; 1854
Bangor:[ct] first settler was from Bangor, Maine; 1843
Bay City:[c] the Saginaw Bay of Lake Huron; 1835
Essexville:[c] first settler, Ransom Essex; 1850
Hampton:[ct] 1846
Monitor:[ct] means to remind or advise; 1858
Pinconning:[c] from the American Indian word meaning "potato place;" 1872
Portsmouth:[ct] sawmill and village near the mouth of the Saginaw River; 1836
Williams:[ct] possibly for Puritan critic Roger Williams; 1854

P PARKS

National: 0 **State:** 4 **County:** 3 **Local:** 30
Number of campsites: 450
State Game Area: *Crow Island,* in the Saginaw River
…*Tobico Marsh:* 1,800 acres, part of Bay City State Recreation Area, wetland woods, wet meadows, cattail marshlands, oak savannah prairies; staging area for migratory birds; see 9N
State Recreation Area: *Bay City:*[ww] 2,100 acres, 1 mile of Saginaw Bay shoreline, campgrounds, nature trails, interpretive programs; contains one of the largest remaining freshwater, costal wetlands on the Great Lakes; the first wolverine ever verified as living in the wild in Michigan is now on display at the visitor center at Bay City State Recreation Area; see 81F

State Wildlife Area: *Nayan-quing Point:*[ww] 1,400 acres, handicap accessible observation tower

Frank Goeddeke, Sr.

County: *Pinconning Park:*[ww] on Saginaw Bay, large campsites, rental log cabins are ADA accessible; walleye fishing, other water activities
Local: *Wild Haven Park:* cement walkway into shallow waters of Saginaw Bay in Essexville

Q QUOTE FROM THE LOCALS

"Our forefathers knew what they were doing when they decided to settle here along the shore of Michigan's Great Bay. The streams, rivers and bay were a plentiful source of fish and an efficient means of transporting people and goods. Lush forests provided ample lumber for the building of homes and industries. Fertile soil produced bountiful harvests to feed the growing population. Our lives continue to be nourished by the water that surrounds us. We are inspired by our history and enthusiastic about our future." *tourbaycitymi.org*

R RECREATION & SPORTS

Auto racing: *Tri-City Motor Speedway*
Golf courses: 13
Great Lakes marinas: 916   **Boat slips:** 2,000
Hiking/skiing/mountain biking trails: 10 miles
Public access sites: 8
Public recreational land: 2% of county
Rail-trail: (20 miles) Bay City Loop, Anderson Trail
Recreational harbor: Liberty Harbor
Bay City Independents Vintage Base Ball Team: 19th century baseball played in Carroll Park

Riverwalk Linear Parks / Rail Trail: Bay City, 2-mile handicap-accessible fitness course with fishing pier and the "world's most crooked bridge," connects to 7-miles of paved Rail Trail

NPCR

S STATE OF MICHIGAN

Michigan offers at least 24 vehicle <u>license plates</u> that can help raise funds for various causes throughout the state. In 2009, 15 of these were state universities and the others were Agricultural Heritage, Children's Trust Fund, Lighthouse Preservation, Olympic Education, Veteran's Memorial, Water Quality, Wildlife Habitat,

Tom Nugent

Patriotic and Support Our Troops. The initial plate costs $35 above the standard renewal cost and $25 goes to the sponsoring organization. There is a $10 per year renewal fee that goes directly to the sponsoring organization.

Also, and for an additional fee, a Michigan resident may purchase personalized (vanity) plates, historical plates for vintage cars and collector license plates.
Michigan.gov

T TRAVEL

Airport: James Clements Airport & Sea Plane Base
Bus: Bay Metropolitan Transit Authority (BETA); Indian Trails
Circle Tour: Lake Huron via M-13 & M-25
Distance to Lansing: 80 miles
Heritage Route: *Historic:* M-25 in Bay City, is the Center Avenue Historic District with over 80 homes; see 9H
...*Recreation:* M-15, Pathway to Family Fun, 85 miles, Bay City south to Ortonville in Oakland Co. Also called the Miles of Smiles route, it is the scenic alternative to I-75.
Main roads: I-75, US-10, US-23, M-13, M-15, M-25, M-84
Memorial Highways: I-75, *American Legion MH:* see 6T
...I-75 & US-23, *Roberts-Linton Hwy:* around 1910, William Linton and Rolla Roberts were instrumental in the dredging of the Saginaw River in order to deepen the channel
...I-75 & US-23, *Veterans of WWI MH:* in honor of those who served and died in World War I (1914-1918)
Scenic Drive: Port Huron to Tawas City via M-13 & M-25
...Bay City to Ortonville via M-15

U UNIVERSITIES & COLLEGES

Delta College: est. 1961, 16,000 students. As a charter member of the National League for Innovation in the Community College, Delta is devoted to the improvement of learning through experimentation and innovation. MCCAA, Pioneers

V VARIETY

Michigan Farm Bureau

The Michigan Sugar Company, formed in 1906, became a cooperative in 2002, with over 1,000 sugarbeet growers. Their plant in Bay City (along with 3 other Michigan locations) produce nearly 1 billion pounds of sugar annually, making Michigan Sugar the third largest beet sugar producer in the U.S. and the only sugarbeet factory east of the Mississippi River. Look for their Pioneer and Big Chief brand names.

W WANDERLUST

Agri-tourism: *Berry Creek Farm:* U-pick, strawberries, tomatoes, pumpkins, corn maze
…*Downtown Bay City Farmers' Market:* May-Aug.
…*Mike Mulders Farm:* homegrown and picked fresh daily; sweet corn, cherries, apples, tomatoes
…*Warmbier Farms:* home & garden store, U-pick, bedding plants, pumpkins, open all year
…*Witzgall Apple Orchard:* family owned, 40 types of apples, open Labor Day until the apples are gone, or Thanksgiving, whichever comes first
Brewery: Tri-City Brewing Company
Cultural: The Bijou Orchestra (like they used to be in the 19th century)

Fall colors: early October

NPCR

Lighthouses, other: *Saginaw River Rear Range Lighthouse:* on private land, being renovated, not open to the public. "The range light system, which is used by all mariners and maintained by the Coast Guard throughout the United States, was invented by the 15-year-old son of the keeper of this lighthouse." *tourbaycitymi.org*
Live theater: Bay City Players, State Theatre (modeled after an Aztec temple, like Detroit's Fox Theatre), Van Buren Street Dinner Theatre
Planetarium: Delta College
Shopping mall: Bay City Mall
Walking tour: Bay City, The Art & Culture Loop, public buildings, interpretive kiosks, benches, landscaping, public art
Appledore Tall Ships: offers a variety of sailing opportunities for seamanship and freshwater science study, youth travel camps, as well as dinner cruises and autumn color cruises
Bay City Motor Company: vintage cars on display and for sale
Deer Acres: a storybook theme park
Fishing: many opportunities to charter a boat and get on the water for an enjoyable day
Historical boat tours: on the Saginaw Bay
Maritime History Walk: the Riverwalk at Veterans Memorial Park in Bay City

NPCR

Pere Marquette Depot: after sitting vacant for 38 years, the depot was restored and is now the home of the Bay City Convention and Visitors Bureau and others agencies

Pinconning Cheese: it is a Colby-style cheese with 7 different ages from mild to super super sharp. The Pinconning Cheese Co. Deli & Fudge Shoppe has many different kids of cheese and other products, including smoked fish, jerky and sausage.
Watch the Great Lakes freighters in Bay City as they dock at one of the busiest ports in Michigan.

X X-TRA STUFF

County Fair: *Bay County Fair & Youth Exposition:* located in the center of Bay City, it is a true agricultural fair with a large 4-H involvement, Aug.

Famous people: *...Entertainment*: Madonna

...Sports: Art Dore

...Other: Warren Avis, Nate Doan

Hospitals: Bay Regional Medical Center, Bay Special Care Hospital

Large employers: Delta College, Bay Regional Medical Center, General Motors, Saginaw Valley State University, Meijer, Michigan Sugar Co.

NPCR

The Bay City area has been called "the breadbasket of Michigan" due to the rich fertile soil and variety of agricultural production.

The Saginaw River divides Bay City in half.

University Center, home to Delta College and Saginaw Valley State University, lies almost midway between Bay City, Midland and Saginaw.

Y YESTERYEAR

The <u>Michigan Rock and Roll Legends</u> operate a website out of Bay City that is dedicated to "the artists and music that are part of Michigan's rich and diverse rock and roll legacy." To be eligible, the artist must have been born or raised in Michigan, or started their career or lived in Michigan during part of their active career and recorded prior to 1988. Their Top 10 tunes are:

RUNAWAY by Del Shannon [see 13H and 8M]

ROCK AROUND THE CLOCK by Bill Haley and His Comets

NPCR-2

RESPECT by Aretha Franklin

96 TEARS by ? & The Mysterians

DO YOU LOVE ME by The Contours

MY GIRL by The Temptations

I HEARD IT THROUGH THE GRAPEVINE by Marvin Gaye

NIGHT MOVES by Bob Seger & The Silver Bullet Band

MUSTANG SALLY by Wilson Pickett

WHAT'S GOING ON by Marvin Gaye

Z ZOO & ANIMAL PLACES

Watchable Wildlife Viewing Areas:ww see 9P

Petting zoo: *Le Cronier's Baby Acres:* pet, feed and hold the animals; occasional live births; corn maze, tours, wagon rides, pumpkins; April-October

...Warmbier Farms: year-round

"Hey, look, we're in this book." That is what every person who lives or travels in Michigan can say when they look through *Discovering Michigan County by County: Your A-Z Guide to each of the 83 counties in the Great Lakes State.* No matter where they live or where they go, there is something about their personal part of Michigan.

A AGRICULTURE

Land in farms: 9% of county
Number of farms: 205
Size of average farm: 100 acres
Market value of all products: #61 of 83 counties
Crops: ...most acres: forage land
...highest $ sales: fruits (apples, tart cherries)
Livestock: ...largest number: cattle
...highest $ sales: other animals & products
Among the top Michigan counties:
- #2- colonies of bees
- #3- sales of other animal products, including honey
- #7- acres of tart cherries

Dairy, food and meat processing plants: 14
State ranking for harvested trees: #42 of 83 counties
FYI: Since Michigan's varied climate and soils allow farmers to have a wide variety of food and animal production, it can only mean that there must be a wide variety of dairy, food and meat <u>processing plants</u>. Food processing means the process by which fresh food is made ready for the market (like bottled milk) or is preserved for future use. Common methods of preservation include canning, freezing, drying, baking, pickling, making juice, sauces, jams & jellies or wine, making desserts or other prepared dinners, or using another process that is unique to that food (i.e., making sugar from sugar beets or cheese from milk). In 2009, there were 1,620 wholesale food-processing plants, 71 dairy processing plants and 34 meat-processing plants in Michigan employing more than 130,000 residents. ^{MDA, USDA}

Graceland Fruit is the largest single provider of infused dried fruits and vegetables in the world. Their dried apples, wild and cultivated blueberries, cherries, cranberries, raspberries and strawberries are a delicious treat any time of year.

NPCR

B BRIDGE OR BOAT

Sleeping Bear Dune Cruises

The Sleeping Bear Dunes Boat Cruise offers a 2½-3-hour cruise along Sleeping Bear Dunes National Lakeshore on Lake Michigan where you can see bluffs, beaches, dunes and lighthouses on the shore. The building in this picture is the Fog Signal building of the Point Betsie Lighthouse; see 10L.

C CELEBRATIONS

<u>Beulah</u> *Art Fair:* July
...*Fall Fest:* chair lift rides, famous pumpkin carvings, giant pumpkin weigh-in, parade, Oct.
<u>Crystal Lake</u> *Art Show:* July
<u>Frankfort</u> *Shiver by the River:* 2-day Snocross snowmobile race, ice sculpture, winter parade, snowworld, Feb.
...*Art & Craft Fair:* July
...*Concerts in the Park:* Wed., Thurs., & Fri., at different locations in July and August
...*Spring Craft Fair:* June

...*Art Fair:* Aug.

...*Fall Fest:* horse-drawn wagon tours, pumpkin drop on a car, jack-o-lantern auction, parade, Oct.

...*Film Festival:* the best films from prestigious festivals worldwide, Oct.

director@benzie.org

<u>Honor</u> *National Coho Festival:* celebrates the 'salmon run' up the Benzie County rivers; smoked fish contest, lawn tractor races, horseshoes, parade, queen, arts & crafts, flea market, Aug.

Rick Gleason

D DEMOGRAPHICS

Population: 17,500   **Persons per sq. mile:** 55
Largest city: Frankfort   **Population:** 1,290
Largest township: Almira   **Population:** 3,380
Largest village: Benzonia   **Population:** 500
Median household income: $45,600
Owner-occupied median house value: $163,000
Persons affiliated with a religious congregation: 30%
Persons below poverty level: 13%
Students receiving school lunch subsidy: 46%

E ENVIRONMENT

The Michigan Bluebird Society is dedicated to improving the nesting success of the Eastern Bluebird and other cavity-nesting birds through education of members and the general public. They recommend the establishment of a "bluebird trail," a series of nesting boxes in open areas with scattered trees. For complete information on this worthwhile project, see their website at michiganbluebirdsociety.org. Benzie County is also a stopping point for many migrating birds, both in the spring and in the fall. A Benzie birding map is available online at visitbenzie.com. See 10F.

F FLORA & FAUNA

Dr. Thomas G. Barnes/USFWS

The 66 varieties of asters in Michigan are similar, yet each is unique; they come in a variety of colors from white to reddish to blue.

David Menke/USFWS

The eastern bluebird likes open land with scattered trees for perching, nesting and feeding. Nesting boxes are popular in the backyard and help to improve the dwindling nesting habitat for the birds. See 10E.

G GOVERNMENT

County: ...created: 1863 **...organized:** 1869
...originally part of: Grand Traverse, Leelanau Counties
Size: 223,000 acres / 320 sq. miles (83 of 83 counties)
The county has 1 city, 6 villages, 12 townships, 1 unincorporated community and 2 school districts.

Rick Gleason

County seat: Beulah
...Homestead property tax: 31 mills
Motto: Benzie County Visitors Bureau: *Northern Michigan Preserved*
...Beulah: *Your Four Seasons Retreat*
...Elberta: *Come and Play.*
...Frankfort: *on the shores of beautiful Lake Michigan*
...Lake Ann: *Small, But Friendly*

H HISTORICAL MARKERS 8 of 8

Benzonia College: 1858, founded in the remote wilderness by Congregationalists as an "education Christian colony" like Olivet College in Eaton County; it closed in 1918 but did bring coeducational opportunities to northern Michigan.

Benzonia Congregational Church: 1887, Gothic Revival style, now Benzie Area Historic Museum

Bruce Catton: 1899-1978, editor and Pulitzer prize-winning author of Civil War histories; his former home, part of the Benzonia Academy, is now Mills Community House.

Car Ferries on Lake Michigan: 1892, the rail car ferry from Lake Betsie to Kewaunee, WI, was the longest in the world.

Joyfield Cemetery: 1870, the area's first black landowner, William Davis, donated 5 acres for the cemetery; the township's first white settler, Amaziah Joy, is buried here.

Marquette's Death: 1675, Father Jacques Marquette may have died here by the Betsie River, but his bones were reburied in St. Ignace in 1677.

Mills Community House: 1909, called Mills Cottage, it was the girls' dormitory for the Benzonia Academy; now a library & public meeting place.

Pacific Salmon: 1960s, they were introduced into Lake Michigan to control the alewife fish; Coho, Chinook and Kokanee salmon are firmly established in the Great Lakes and have a great impact on the sport fishing industry. See 10Z.

National Register of Historic Places: 9 listings
State Historic Sites: 11 listings

I INFORMATION

Chamber of Commerce: Benzie County
Visitor: Benzie County Visitors Bureau, 800-882-5801, visitbenzie.com

J JOKES

You might be a Michiganian if…
…you call Lake Michigan the West Coast and Lake Huron the East Coast.

…you don't understand why some people think Chicago is such a big deal.
…you find yourself incapable of throwing away cans and bottles even when you are in another state.
…your idea of the seasons is football, basketball, baseball and hockey.
…you know where to get a pony ride for 1¢.
…you had to get a new car because you hit a deer and totaled your old one.

K KINSMAN

Race	Ancestry
American Indian: 1%	German: 24%
Asian: <1%	English: 14%
Black/African American: <1%	Irish: 9%
Hispanic or Latino: 2%	U.S./American: 8%
Other: 2%	Polish: 6%
White: 96%	French: 5%

L LIGHTHOUSE OR LANDMARK

The Point Betsie Lighthouse, built in 1858, is currently operational and can be seen for 15 miles. It is open for tours and events like weddings and memorial services.

M MUSEUMS

<u>Benzonia</u> *Benzie Area Historical Museum:* logging, agriculture, gardens, gift shop

<u>Empire</u> *Northwest Michigan Maritime Museum:* underwater preserve, visitor center, collections

<u>Platte Township</u> *Drake School:* one-room, used 1906-1943, restored; now used to teach kids how school used to be; open for tours

N NATURAL RESOURCES

Elevation: <600 - 1,000 feet
Physiography: hill-lands, lake-border plains, plains

Forest type: maple-beech-hemlock, aspen-birch
Public/private forests: 66% of county
Legislatively protected sand dunes: 6,600 acres

Water in county: 8% of
county
  Lakes: 54
    ...largest: Crystal Lake
    (#9-size/MI)
    (#3-depth/MI)
  Rivers: Betsie, Platte
  Rivers & streams: 100
  miles (#81/MI)

Great Lakes shoreline: 25 miles of Lake Michigan

Growing season, avg.: 159 days (2-4 temp. zones)
  Last freeze, avg.: May 15 – May 20
  First freeze, avg.: Sept. 25 – Oct. 10
Precipitation, annual avg.: rainfall: 32 inches
                    snowfall: 122 inches
Temperature (F), avg.: January: high 29°, **low** 16°
                  July: high 80°, **low** 59°
  Annual: >90°: 6 days, <0°: 5 days
Tornadoes (1930-2010): 4

O ORIGINS

<u>Almira:</u>[t] wife of early settler; 1862
<u>Benzie:</u>[co] originally French for Riviere Aux Bec Scies, or "river of sawbill ducks;" back then the Americans pronounced it Betsie and then refined that to Benzie; 1858
<u>Benzonia:</u>[v] see Benzie above
<u>Beulah:</u>[v] from the Bible, Isaiah 62, when God gave the land of Zion the new name of Beulah; 1880
<u>Elberta:</u>[v] the delicious Elberta peach; 1855
<u>Frankfort:</u>[c] the area reminded an early settler of Frankfort, Germany; 1850
<u>Honor:</u>[v] Honor Gifford, baby daughter of the general manager of the Guelph Patent Cask Co; 1895
<u>Lake Ann:</u>[v] Ann Wheelock, wife of first settler; 1862
<u>Thompsonville:</u>[v] lumber company owner, Sumner Thompson; 1890

P PARKS

National: 1   **State:** 5   **County:** 0   **Local:** 12
Number of campsites: 715
National: south end of the *Sleeping Bear Dunes National Lakeshore:*[wba] 11,000 acres with 10 miles of Lake Michigan coastline; see 45P for a full description of the National Lakeshore

State Forest: (60,000 acres)
  Pere Marquette
...Campground: 5
...Pathway: 19 miles

State Game Area: Betsie River (700 acres)

Q QUOTE FROM THE LOCALS

"No matter what your interests, Benzie County has something for everyone. **See** spectacular scenery, lighthouses, local art and historical sites. **Hear** the leaves rustling from the wind, the waves pounding on the shores, the music of our concerts, the birds and sounds of nature. **Smell** the fresh air of Pure Northern Michigan, the woods in spring or fall and the lake around you. **Taste** the local dishes, desserts and wines all bursting with flavor. **Feel** the sand between your toes, the water as you play in our lakes, the snow crunching under your boots, and the nature that encompasses you as you saunter through our parks." *visitbenzie.com*

R RECREATION & SPORTS

Blue Ribbon Trout Streams:[1,000] Platte River
Golf courses: 5
Great Lakes marinas: 8   **Boat slips:** 470
Hiking/skiing/mountain biking trails: 70 miles
Public access sites: 23
Public recreational land: 32% of county
Rail-trail: (60 miles) Betsie Valley, Michigan Shore to Shore, Platte Plains

Recreational harbor: Frankfort Municipal Marina

State/federal wild/scenic/ natural river: 65 miles of the Betsie River

State-funded snowmobile trails: 52 miles
Park at Water's Edge: 1-acre outdoor water park, pool, climbing wall, sand play area, hot tub

S STATE OF MICHIGAN

Michigan has 1.1 million households served by private wells, more than any other state. It has approximately 25,000 domestic wells drilled per year. Shown here is a typical wellhead and water pressure tank that are needed to bring the water up out of ground. The depth of the well can be from 24' to 400', with the most common depth of 100'-149'.

NPCR   NPCR

The Michigan Department of Environmental Quality, with its Water Well Construction Program, works to protect public health, ground water resources and aquifers by assuring that water wells are constructed, operated and decommissioned in a technically sound manner. They recommend that homeowners have their water wells tested annually for coliform bacteria and nitrates. Michigan.gov/deq

T TRAVEL

Airports: City-County
Bus: Benzie Bus
Circle Tour: Lake Michigan via M-22
Distance to Lansing: 180 miles
Main roads: US-31, M-22, M-115
Memorial Highway: US-31, *Blue Star MH:* see 3T
Northwest Michigan Port of Call Tour: Benzie Area Historical Museum, Point Betsie Lighthouse
Scenic Drive: Frankfort (N) to Suttons Bay via M-22
…Frankfort (S) to Ludington via M-22 & US-31

U UNIVERSITIES & COLLEGES

None

V VARIETY

Brian Confer Photography/Crystal Mountain Resort

Crystal Mountain is a master planned, year-round resort. It features 45 downhill slopes, 36 holes of golf, indoor & outdoor pools, cross-country ski trails and biking trails. With lodging for 1,200, it is a family friendly destination resort.

W WANDERLUST

Cultural: *Benzie Area Symphony Orchestra:* music for every ear by musicians from diverse locals
…*Community Chorus:* Benzie's best voices
Fall colors: late September to early October
Lighthouses, other: *Frankfort North Breakwater:* not open to the public but you can walk on the breakwater to view it
Live theater: Benzie County Players
Gravity Hill: put your car in neutral and it will slowly roll uphill! This optical illusion is due to the lack of a distant horizon for a reference point.
Gwen Frostic Studio: original block prints, nature and verse create art; a "must see" in Benzonia; see 10Y

Rick Gleason

Michigan Legacy Art Park: walk a 1.6-mile nature hiking trail with over 40 impressive pieces of contemporary art that tell the story of Michigan

Owner of M-22 Clothing

M-22 Clothing: Two kite boarding brothers (this is one of them) wanted to express a common passion for Northern Michigan and created M-22 clothing. However, M-22 shares this passion beyond Michigan's borders. It is marked by the simplicity

49

and appreciation for natural wonders such as bays, beaches and bonfires, dunes and vineyards, cottages and friends and family everywhere. M-22 is the feeling you get when you realize there is no other place you would rather be.

X X-TRA STUFF

Commercial port: Frankfort
Famous people: ...*Other*: Bruce Catton
Hospitals: Paul Oliver Memorial
Large employers: Crystal Enterprises (hotel/motel), Smeltzer Orchard (fruit & veggie processor), Continental Industries, Paul Oliver Memorial Hospital, County of Benzie
Benzie County is the smallest county in the state, yet it still sends over 2.4 million cubic feet of trees to the mill every year and is a top ranked producer of honey.

Y YESTERYEAR

Michigan born and educated <u>Gwen Frostic</u> (1906-2001) was an artist inspired by the splendor of nature. She carved the simplified beauty of nature onto linoleum blocks that were used to make her unique (and much emulated) prints. She wrote inspiring verse to accompany those block prints. Her awe-inspiring 1960s home that brings the outside

Rick Gleason

to the indoors is set in a 40-acre wild life sanctuary in Benzonia where visitors from around the world come to see that home, the beauty of nature that was her inspiration and the production facilities for her massive body of work. The home and gift shop are a museum in their own right. As a lifelong friend of Western Michigan University, she is the largest single donor to the school. The Gwen Frostic School of Art is named in her honor.

Z ZOO & ANIMAL PLACES

Watchable Wildlife Viewing Areas:[ww] see 10P
Platte River State Fish Hatchery: It is the largest fish hatchery east of the Mississippi River. Interpretative facilities provide information on the importance of

medium sized rivers to the Great Lakes, the salmon story, how watersheds work and how a hatchery operates; raises Coho and Chinook salmon and is the main egg take station for Coho salmon in the Upper Great Lakes. Tours are available.

NPCR

NPCR

NPCR

A AGRICULTURE

Land in farms: 46% of county
Number of farms: 1,300
Size of average farm: 130 acres
Market value of all products: #15 of 83 counties
Crops: ...most acres: corn for grain
...highest $ sales: fruits, tree nuts, berries
Livestock: ...largest number: hogs & pigs
...highest $ sales: hogs & pigs
Among the top Michigan counties:
- #1- apricots, blackberries & dewberries, cantaloupe, direct to customer sales, English walnuts, grapes, green onions, nectarines, okra, raspberries, strawberries, summer squash
- #2- apples, bell peppers, peaches, plums & prunes, tomatoes, sweet corn, winter squash
- #4- colonies of bees

Lake Michigan Shore American Viticultural Area: 1.3 million acres; U.S. government designated wine grape-growing area
Dairy, food and meat processing plants: 34
State ranking for harvested trees: #59 of 83 counties
AgBioResearch Centers (MSU): *Southwest Michigan Research and Extension Center:* 350 acres, fruit and vegetable breeding and variety evaluations; cherry rootstock testing, peach production and production practices for table and wine grapes are carried out here
FYI: Michigan has almost 15,000 acres of vineyards and Berrien County has more than half of those acres, helping make Michigan fourth in the U.S. for

Michigan Farm Bureau

acres devoted to grapes. Most of Michigan grapes (like Concord) are made into grape juice or jelly, but the state's 60 wineries rank Michigan 13th in wine production with many award-winning products. Most of Michigan's quality wine grapes grow within 25 miles of Lake Michigan. The lake protects the vines with snow in the winter, retards bud opening in the spring, helping to avoid frost damage and extends the growing season in the fall by up to four weeks. Michigan is a leader in the production of fruit wines as well. Wines and winery tourism are a fun and important activity in the state. michiganwines.com, Michigan.gov

B BRIDGE OR BOAT

Hovertechnics

Whether it's on water, land, ice or mud, a hovercraft, made in Eau Clair by Hovertechnics, is a flying experience that will take you places conventional boats can't go. Hovercrafts fly on a cushion of air over the earth's surface. Recreational hovercrafts vary in their seating capacity and horsepower. The rescue hovercraft is specifically designed for professionals engaged in rescue operations. The commercial hovercraft is designed for specific business applications.

C CELEBRATIONS

<u>Baroda</u> *Harvest Feast:* a feast featuring the local bounty (food & wine) and a documentary-style video highlighting the rich agricultural heritage

<u>Benton Harbor</u> *Blossomtime Festival:* Grand Floral

Sabrina LaSota

Parade is the oldest festival in Michigan (1906) and has 25 participating communities; route is from the city of St. Joe across the St. Joseph River to Benton Harbor; blessing of the blossoms; teen, Miss and Mr. pageants; farm tours, Shriners Hospital Tour

<u>Berrien Springs:</u> *Christmas Pickle Parade:* Dec.; see 11X
<u>Coloma</u> *Glad-Peach Festival:* celebrate locally grown gladiolus flowers and tree-ripened peaches; car show, music, fireworks, Aug.

Monica Teichman

<u>Eau Claire</u> *International Cherry Spitting Championship:* July

Niles *Hunter Ice Festival:* ice cream, 150 ice sculptures & competition, kids activities, Jan.

...*Bluegrass Festival:* June

...*Riverfest:* celebrate the St. Joseph River, in, on and by the river; car & truck show, pageant, Aug.

...*Apple Festival:* pie eating & scarecrow contest, kid's parade, fireworks, arts & crafts, Sept.

St. Joseph *Antiques on the Bluff:* premier event, first Sunday of each month, May to October

...*Blossomtime Festival:* see Benton Harbor above

...*Krasl Art Fair:* Art Fair on the Bluffs, one of the top 40 art shows in the nation, July

...*Venetian Festival:* 3 music stages, fireworks, beach events, unique food items, July

D DEMOGRAPHICS

Population: 156,800   **Persons per sq. mile:** 275
Largest city: Benton Harbor   **Population:** 10,000
Largest township: Benton   **Population:** 14,800
Largest village: Berrien Springs   **Population:** 1,800
Median household income: $39,900
Owner-occupied median house value: $135,000
Persons affiliated with a religious congregation: 47%
Persons below poverty level: 17%
Students receiving school lunch subsidy: 49%

E ENVIRONMENT

Of the 95,000 square miles of water in Lake Erie, Lake Huron, Lake Michigan, Lake Ontario and Lake Superior, Great Lakes ownership is divided among the following:

- 40.5%   Michigan
- 35.9%   Ontario, Canada
- 10.6%   Wisconsin
- 4.4%   New York
- 3.6%   Ohio
- 2.3%   Minnesota
- 1.6%   Illinois
- .8%   Pennsylvania
- .2%   Indiana

Having trouble remembering the names of the five Great Lakes? Put your left hand up, palm down, and you can see that Michigan is in the center of the Great Lakes area; we are the *HOME* to (four of the) *five* Great Lakes, just like your five fingers. So count this acronym on your fingers: HOMES= **H**uron, **O**ntario, **M**ichigan, **E**rie and **S**uperior. But also remember the four O's: "**O**h **no**! Michigan's not the home of Lake **O**ntari**o**."

F FLORA & FAUNA

Margret Pooler, USA

These pretty redbud trees, like the ones that line the streets in Buchanan, are native to southern Michigan and are used as ornamental trees. Buchanan is known as the Redbud City.

Joespeh Berger, USA

Black widow spiders are about 1½" long, including their legs. They like to live in undisturbed places outdoors, even in places around the house. Their bite is painful and requires a doctor's visit.

G GOVERNMENT

County: ...**created:** 1829 ...**organized:** 1831
...**originally part of:** Cass County
Size: 371,000 acres / 571 sq. miles (42 of 83 counties)
The county has 8 cities, 9 villages, 22 townships with 9 as charter townships, 21 unincorporated communities and 15 school districts.

NPCR

NPCR

Built in 1838, the Berrien Springs Courthouse is Greek Revival style; it has hand-hewn timbers almost 1 foot square and 40 feet long.
County seat: St. Joseph

...Homestead property tax: 38 mills
Motto: <u>Baroda</u>: *Casual Country Charm*
...<u>Benton Harbor</u>: *Port of Opportunities*
...<u>Berrien County</u>: *Michigan's Great Southwest*
...<u>Berrien Springs</u>: *Christmas Pickle Capital of the World*
...<u>Bridgman</u>: *On the Lake*
...<u>Buchanan</u> Chamber: *Tranquility History Opportunity; Redbud City*
...<u>Coloma</u> Chamber: *Your Gateway to the Paw Paw Lakes*
...<u>Eau Claire</u>: (aw clare) *Cherry Spitting Capital of the World*
...<u>Harbor Country</u> Chamber: *Eight Great Towns, One Great Lake*
...<u>New Buffalo</u>: *On Lake Michigan's Gold Coast*
...<u>Niles</u>: *City of four flags...*
...Southwestern Michigan Tourist Council: *The fun starts here!*
...<u>St. Joseph</u>: *Riviera of the Midwest*

H HISTORICAL MARKERS 17 of 35

Andrews University: 1874 & 1901, oldest Seventh-day Adventist college and the pioneer in a world-wide system of Christian education

The Chapin House: 1884, Queen Anne style, became the Niles City Hall; 1930s Works Progress Administration remodeled outbuildings that became the Fort St. Joseph Museum.

Michigan State Preservation Office

The Dewey Cannon: in 1900, the residents of Three Oaks raised more money, per capita, than any other community in the U.S. to purchase a gun as a memorial to the men on the battleship *Maine*.
Ferry Street School: 1867, school for "colored children" was integrated in 1870
Four Flags Hotel: 1926, named in honor of the nations that had sovereignty over Niles - France, Great Britain, Spain and the United States
The Fruit Belt: 300 miles of Lake Michigan coastal land is uniquely suited to fruit growing.
Gordon Beach Inn: 1924, part of a Jewish resort subdivision; in the 1960s it was purchased by an African-American; restored in 1991.
John and Horace Dodge: (1864 & 1868-1920)

- 1870s: they grew up poor in Niles; spent their free time in their father's machine shop
- 1886: as experienced machinists, they worked in different shops in Detroit
- 1901: started producing auto parts for Olds
- 1903: produced transmissions for Ford; received 50 shares of Ford stock valued at $10,000
- 1913: started the Dodge Brothers Motor Car Company
- 1919: sold their 50 shares of Ford stock back to Ford for $25 million
- 1920: both brothers died in the flu epidemic; their widows sold the company for $146 million

Johnson Cemetery: in this 1800s cemetery with 211 graves, nearly $1/3$ are children age 10 or younger
Israelite House of David: 1903, communal religious community was successful in business

Michigan Central Railroad Niles Depot: 1892

Moccasin Bluff: archeological evidence tells us that people have lived here for 8,000 years
New Buffalo Welcome Center: 1935, on US-12, it was the nation's first Highway Travel Information Center
Old St. Joseph Neighborhood: 1900s, local professionals built magnificent homes; now it is a state historic district
Parc Aux Vaches: or "cow pasture," named by the French for the wild buffalo that grazed here
Ring Lardner: (1885-1933) born in Niles, the sportswriter, humorist and sardonic observer of the American scene wrote for the *Saturday Evening Post*
West Michigan Pike: 1922, paved highway from Chicago to Mackinaw to bring tourists to west Michigan; also known as Red Arrow and Blue Star Memorial Hwy.

National Register of Historic Places: 24 listings
State Historic Sites: 62 listings

I INFORMATION

Chamber of Commerce: Benton Harbor, Berrien Springs-Eau Claire, Buchanan, Niles, Watervliet-Coloma, Harbor Country: Grand Beach, Harbert, Lakeside, Michiana, New Buffalo, Sawyer, Three Oaks, Union Pier; Lakeshore: Baroda, south St. Joseph, Stevensville
Visitor: Southwestern Michigan Tourist Council, 269-925-6301, swmichigan.org

J JOKES

You might be a Michiganian if…

…you look forward to retiring "up north" instead of "down south."

…you know several people who have not hit a deer.

…you've had to use both your car air conditioner and car heater in the same day.

…you know you still have to shovel "lake effect snow."

…you love/hate how the wind chill factor and the humidity index make life more interesting/ hotter/ colder/ unpredictable.

…you know that just because it's 75° today doesn't mean it will be 75° tomorrow. It could be 95° or 55°. And you know what? That's not really funny.

K KINSMAN

Race	Ancestry
American Indian: <1%	U.S./American: 36%
Asian: 2%	Irish: 10%
Black/African American: 15%	English: 9%
Hispanic or Latino: 5%	German: 6%
Other: 4% French: 2%	French: 2%
White: 78%	Scottish-Irish: 1%
	Scottish: 1%

L LIGHTHOUSE OR LANDMARK

Gary Martin Photography

The St. Joseph North Pier Lights, at the entrance to the St. Joseph River Harbor, is a pair of range lights built in 1906-1907 and are a favorite of residents and visitors to the city of St. Joe.

M MUSEUMS

Benton Harbor *Mary's City of David Museum & Tours:* 140 acres, 81 buildings, Historic District

…*Morton House Museum:* 1849, Greek Revival style with touches of Queen Anne

Sarah J. Pion

Berrien Springs *1839 Courthouse Square:* history showcased in the courthouse, sheriff's residence, jail plaza, log house, blacksmith shop

Sarah J. Pion

…*Horn Archaeological Museum at Andrews University:* 8,500 artifacts and objects from Bible lands

…*Natural History Museum at Andrews University:* wooly mammoth, shells, birds, mammals, insects and botanical specimens

Buchanan *Pears 1857 Mill Museum:* restored, rotating exhibits of Buchanan's history, gift shop

Coloma *North Berrien Historical Society:* history of Bainbridge, Coloma, Hagar and Watervliet Twps.

New Buffalo *Railroad Museum:* new replica of the old station highlights the role of the railroad in the development of the area.

Sarah J. Pion

Niles *Fort St. Joseph:* pictographs by Chief Sitting Bull, Victorian decorative arts, Niles contributions

St. Joseph *Curious Kids' Museum:* touch, see, hear, smell and taste the wonders of the world

…*Heritage Museum and Cultural Center:* Fort Miami Heritage Society has exhibits that tell the story of the water, the land and the people.

Three Oaks *Bicycle Museum:* in the 1899 depot, displays of old and unusual bikes, railroad memorabilia and local history

N NATURAL RESOURCES

Elevation: <600 – 1,000 feet
Physiography: hill-lands, lake-border plains

Soil: Gravelly Sand
 Depth: 10"
 Color: dark brown
 Type: loamy sand, lots of gravel
 Details: well-drained gentle slopes to rolling ridges.
 Sub-soil: coarse, incoherent [not in a logical order] gravelly sand
 Agriculture: good for corn, oats, wheat, rye, beans, potatoes, sugar beets and some fruit crops
 NOTE: soil types are not limited to any one county.

Forest type: oak-hickory, maple-beech
Public/private forests: 18% of county
Legislatively protected sand dunes: 4,100 acres
National Natural Landmark: *Grand Mere Lakes:* 1,000 acres, geologically ancient inland lakes; see 11P

...*Warren Woods State Park:* 300 acres, the last climax beech-maple forest in Michigan

Water in county: <1% of county
 Lakes: 60 ...**largest:** Paw Paw
 Rivers: Galien (ga LEAN), Paw Paw, St. Joseph
 Rivers & streams: 500 miles

Great Lakes shoreline: 50 miles of Lake Michigan

Growing season, avg.: 162 days (2 temp. zones)
 Last freeze, avg.: May 5 – May 10
 First freeze, avg.: Oct. 15 – Oct. 20
Precipitation, annual avg.: rainfall: 37 inches (#2/MI)
       snowfall: 70 inches
Temperature (F), avg.: January: high 32°, low 18°
       July: high 82°, low 61°
 Annual: >90°: 11 days, **<0°:** 4 days
Tornadoes (1930-2010): 32

O ORIGINS

Baroda:[v,t] named after a city in India; 1890
Benton Harbor:[c,ct] Thomas Benton, a Missouri senator, helped Michigan attain statehood; a canal was built through the swampland of the Paw Paw River to form a harbor; 1860
Berrien:[co] (BARE e an) John Berrien, Attorney General under President Andrew Jackson
Berrien Springs:[v,t] mineral springs in the area; 1829
Bridgman:[c] lumber company owner George Bridgman; 1856
Buchanan:[c,t] after U.S. Sen. James Buchanan; 1833
Coloma:[c,ct] early settler lived in Coloma, CA; also the name of a western wildflower; 1834
Eau Claire:[v] (aw clare) French for clear water; 1850
Galien:[v,t] (ga LEAN) 1600s French priest map maker, Rene Brehant de Galinee; 1853
Grand Beach:[v] resort on Lake Michigan; 1903
Lake:[ct] area of sand dunes, swamps, woodlands with easy access to Lake Michigan; 1846 [lake-township.org]
Lincoln:[ct] 1827 [berriencounty.org]
Michiana:[v] on the Michigan and Indiana border; 1945
New Buffalo:[c,t] ship captain Whitaker's home port of Buffalo, NY; 1835
Niles:[c,ct] newspaper publisher, Hezekiah Niles; 1690
Oronoko:[ct] Chief Oronoko; (Wikipedia lists 3 other possible originations); 1837
St. Joseph:[c,ct] named after the St. Joseph River which was named by French missionaries; 1780
Shoreham:[v] the length of the village was the Lake Michigan shore line; 1930
Stevensville:[v] Tom Stevens gave land to the railroad; 1872
Three Oaks:[v,t] a cluster of 3 white oak trees; 1850
Watervliet:[c,ct] (water v'LEET) after Watervliet, NY, and means water-ford; 1833

P PARKS

National: 0 **State:** 3 **County:** 5 **Local:** 48
Number of campsites: 1,800

State Park: *Grand Mere:* 1,000 acres, 1 mile of Lake Michigan beach, magnificent sand dunes, blowout dunes, undeveloped natural area; see 11N

Sarah J. Pion

...*Warren Dunes:*[wba,ww] 2,000 acres, 3 miles of Lake Michigan beach, 260' high sand dune, spectacular views, trails, camping, swimming

...*Warren Woods:*[wba] 310 acres on the Galien River; beech-maple climax forest and undisturbed natural area; see 11N

State Underwater Preserve: *Southwest Michigan:* see 3P
State Wildlife Area: Boyle Lake
County: *Galien River:* 86 acres, undeveloped, part of the Great Lakes "New Buffalo Marsh"
...*Silver Beach:* clean wide beach on Lake Michigan with public access to the South Pier
Other: *Fernwood Botanical Gardens:*[ww,wba] 105 acres, woodlands, prairie, cultivated gardens, arboretum, springs, ponds, walking trails, art gallery, nature center, fern conservatory, railway garden

NPCR

...*Sarett Nature Center:*[wv] 350 acres along the Paw Paw River, prime natural habitats, trails

...*Wildflower Blooming Areas:*[wba] Love Creek Nature Center, Niles MDOT Information Center
Mud Lake Bog Nature Preserve: a "textbook" bog because it has all the stages of bog development

Q QUOTE FROM THE LOCALS

"If you've never considered that Michigan's Great Southwest might be the proverbial pot of gold at the end of your rainbow, we'll give you the benefit of the doubt. After all, some might think of our part of the country as a cold, rural, "country cousin" to places like Chicago and Detroit and other Midwestern metropolitan hot-spots, right? Well, we do enjoy beautiful winters here and we do reside close, very close in fact, to some of the most interesting cities in the U.S. Think of Michigan's Great Southwest as a peaceful oasis, nestled next to beautiful Lake Michigan, in a bounteous fruit belt, and full of the amenities that make our region a popular resort community for

people from Chicago and Detroit. Our area offers a rich cultural diversity, wonderful music and art, and all the fun of the great outdoors during every season." michigansgreatsw.com

NPCR

Michigan's Great Southwest is part of an image-building and branding campaign for Berrien County that promotes the area's unique character, products and services on a global basis.

R RECREATION & SPORTS

Golf courses: 14
Great Lakes marinas: 2   **Boat slips:** 2,600
Hiking/skiing/mountain biking trails: 40 miles
Public access sites: 13
Public recreational land: <1% of county
Recreational harbor: New Buffalo Marina, West Basin Marina
State-funded snowmobile trails: 90 miles
Lake Michigan Admirals: play basketball in the American Basketball Association
Lane Automotive: known the world over as a premier supplier of performance parts and accessories for racers, hot rodders, truck and off-road enthusiasts; sponsors the Motor State Challenge amid the lush orchards and vineyards of southwestern Michigan.
Three Oaks Spokes Bicycle Club: hosts annual Apple Cider Century ride through orchard country

S STATE OF MICHIGAN

W.L. French/USFWS

Since 1995, the Painted Turtle has been the State Reptile. It was chosen after some fifth graders from the city of Niles discovered Michigan did not have a state reptile. From 4"-9" long, they are brightly "painted" with red and yellow markings on their soft body and a yellow bottom shell.

T TRAVEL

Airport: Andrews University Airpark, Southwest Michigan Regional, Tyler Memorial, Watervliet Airpark

Amtrak: New Buffalo, Niles, St. Joseph

Bus: Berrien Bus, Indian Trails, Twin Cities Area Transportation Authority

Circle Tour: Lake Michigan via I-94

Distance to Lansing: 125 miles

Historic Harbortowns: Heritage Museum & Cultural Center, Morton House Museum

Heritage Route: *Historic:* <u>US-12 Heritage Trail</u>, 212 miles from Detroit in Wayne County to New Buffalo

in Berrien County, it is among the oldest road corridors east of the Mississippi. US-12, formerly a Sauk Indian Trail from Chicago to Detroit, was called the Chicago Road and the Chicago Turnpike. Now it is known as Michigan Avenue, a consistent name for all the "Main Streets" along the length of the road connecting man, animals, commerce, culture and nature with winding roads and places to explore.

Main roads: I-94, I-196, IS-12, US-31, US-33, M-63, M-140

Memorial Highways: US-31, *Blue Star MH*: see 3T

...US-12, *Iron Brigade*: see 12T

...US-12, *Pulaski MH*: Poland-born Count Casmir Pulaski (1745-1779) fought with the Americans in the American Revolution (1775-1783); he has been given more honors than any other foreigner who fought in the war.

...US-31, *St Joseph Valley Parkway*: originally a by-pass around South Bend, IN and Niles, MI

Michigan Welcome Center: I-94 in New Buffalo

U UNIVERSITIES & COLLEGES

Andrews University: est. 1874, 3,500 students. Seek Knowledge. Affirm Faith. Change the World. ...serious scholarship, quality research and a strong focus on practical Christianity. USCAA, Cardinals

Lake Michigan College: est. 1946, 4,800 students. It is fundamental that a community college assist in meeting the educational, career, cultural, wellness and recreational needs of the community it serves; M-TEC. MCCAA, Indians

V VARIETY

These apple trees in the world's greatest fruit-growing area are bursting with blooms. As pretty as they are, it is just the beginning of the growing process that will eventually provide an apple for your lunch. Driving through the orchards in the spring is a popular activity. See 11A, 80S.

W WANDERLUST

Agri-tourism: *Eckler Farms:* the world's largest single source for ornamental corn products such as gourds and Indian corn

...*Frank Farms:* since 1909, fresh and frozen fruit; vegetables, U-pick

...*Fruit Acres:* apples, peaches, sweet cherries

...*Jollay Orchards:* cherries, raspberries, peaches, apples; market, midway, maze, haunted house

...*Lehman's Orchard:* cherries, apples, pears, dried fruit, trail mixes, fruit wines, hard ciders

...*Nye's Apple Barn:* apples, cherries, peaches, market, gifts, fruit products

...*Springhope Farm:* apples, peaches, U-pick, store

...*Tree-Mendus Fruit Farm:* apricots, apples, cherries, nectarines, plums, "family rent-a-tree"

...*Farm Markets:* Buchanan, Piggot's

Brewery: The Livery

Casino: Four Winds

Cultural: Southwest Michigan Symphony, St. Joseph Municipal Band, Krasl Art Center, Vickers Theatre

Fall colors: middle October

Live theater: Acorn Theater, Buchanan Commons, Howard Performing Arts Center at AU, Mendel Center at LMC, New Buffalo Performing Arts Center, Niles Performing Arts Assoc., Tin Shop Theater, Twin Cities Players, Vickers Theatre

Walking tour: Coloma has historical plaques displayed on each downtown building; St. Joseph Historic District

Wineries: *Contessa Wine Cellars:* tradition and old-world charm with the best of modern amenities

...*Domaine Berrien Cellars:* wines made from grapes grown and hand picked on the family farm

...*Free Run Distillery:* wine made from juice of crushed, not pressed, grapes

...*Hickory Creek:* highest quality estate grown and select local vineyard fruits

...*Karma Vista Vineyards:* a tasting room in the middle of the vineyard on top of the hill

...*Lemon Creek Fruit Farm & Winery:* enjoy the wine, the fruit market, or pick your own fruit

...*Round Barn:* a winery, distillery and brewery that offers wine, brandy and beer tasting

...*St. Julian:* Michigan's oldest, largest and most awarded winery; family-owned since 1921

Sarah J. Pion

...*Tabor Hill:* wine, champagne, restaurant

...*Wyncroft:* artisanal, super-premium wines from estate-grown grapes

Bear Cave: Michigan's only underground cave that is open for tours

Drier's Meat Market: an old-fashioned butcher shop

Harbor Country: Eight Great Towns, One Great Lake: Grand Beach, Harbert, Lakeside, Michiana, New Buffalo, Sawyer, Three Oaks, Union Pier; more art per capita than Second City; sculpture tour, unhurried & quiet, sand dunes with foliage

Southwest Michigan Wine Trail: 12 wineries and tasting rooms along beautiful Lake Michigan

X X-TRA STUFF

American Indian Community: Pokagon Band of Potawatomi Indians

Commercial port: St. Joseph/Benton Harbor

County fair: *Berrien County Youth Fair Assoc.:* Aug.

Famous people: ...*Entertainment*: Ernie Hudson, Arte Johnson, Sinbad

...*Sports*: Muhammad Ali

...*Other*: John & Horace Dodge, Ring Lardner

Hospitals: Community Hospital of Watervliet, Lakeland Regional Health System (5 hospitals)

Large employers: Lakeland Regional Health System, Whirlpool (makes household appliances), Four Winds Casino, Cook Nuclear Plant, Andrews University, Carrier Commercial (makes refrigerated cases), AEP (electric services), Transamerica Distribution (financial services), LECO (makes a variety of equipment)

Benton Harbor and St. Joseph are considered "twin cities" that are divided by the St. Joseph River where

it empties into Lake Michigan; they are connected by the bridge that crosses over the St. Joseph River. Benton Harbor is 92% African-American and St. Joseph is 90% white.

Christmas Pickle: there is no historical evidence of how the tradition got started but there are several interesting tales. Berrien Springs is in the middle of a pickle producing area and the Pickle Packers of America have deemed it the Christmas Pickle Capital of the World. The tradition has morphed from real pickles to a Christmas ornament pickle that has a special place on the Christmas tree.

Y YESTERYEAR

It was recognized by the earliest settlers that the land in southwest Michigan was suitable for fruit production and they began planting various fruit in the 1820s. The Benton Harbor Fruit Market began operations in 1860 and by 1910 it was being promoted as part of southwest Michigan's diversified "fruit belt" of Allegan, Berrien and Van Buren counties; much of the product was shipped to Chicago.

The BHFM was then and still is the World's Largest Fruit Market with hundreds of farmers selling direct to their customers, including a large wholesale business. Over 200 semi-trailers can be loaded at a time. Scientists at Michigan State University consider the area the most productive fruit-growing environment in the *world*. It is the inter-relatedness of the soil, the rolling hills, rainfall and the "lake effect" of Lake Michigan that keeps the weather cooler in the spring and summer and warmer in the fall and winter, that makes perfect growing conditions for fruit. It is no surprise then that Michigan-grown fruit is so wonderful!

michiganfruitbelt.org, offthewater.com

Sarah J. Pion

Z ZOO & ANIMAL PLACES

Petting zoo: *Deer Forest Fun Park:* exotic animals, amusement rides, storybook lane, playland

...*Jollay Orchards:* a family friendly farm

Berrien Springs Fish Ladder[wv] with a series of stair-step pools that allow fish to swim around the hydroelectric power dam on the St. Joseph River near downtown Berrien Springs

Booming Acres Emu Farm: oil, leather, meat

A AGRICULTURE

Land in farms: 75% of county
Number of farms: 1,130
Size of average farm: 220 acres
Market value of all products: #19 of 83 counties
Crops: ...most acres: corn for grain
...highest $ sales: grains: corn, soybeans, wheat
Livestock: ...largest number: hogs & pigs
...highest $ sales: hogs & pigs
Among the top Michigan counties:
- #3- hogs & pigs
- #4- broiler chickens
- #5- corn, sheep & lambs

Dairy, food and meat processing plants: 8
State ranking for harvested trees: #74 of 83 counties
FYI: Most of the 2.4 million acres of <u>corn</u> grown in Michigan is field (dent) corn and that makes it the second largest agricultural commodity in the state, accounting for 15% of agricultural sales. Corn is the primary food source for livestock and is the primary protein in the nation's pet food supply.

The typical grocery store stocks more than 4,000 products containing corn in some form. When the farmer receives $7 a bushel for his corn (an average price), that means there is 13¢ worth of corn in every 16 oz. box of corn flakes. Corn is a natural sweetener for non-diet soft drinks and a natural ingredient in vitamins. Corn is used to make environmentally friendly (biodegradable) printing inks and packaging materials. A "plastic bag" containing just 6% cornstarch and the rest synthetic polymers will decompose in the soil in 3-5 years. Corn is also used in clothing and blankets, carpets, pharmaceuticals and ethanol production. MDA

B BRIDGE or BOAT

MDOT Photo and Video Unit

MDOT Historic Bridge: Built in 1920 for Old US-12 to cross the Coldwater River in Coldwater, it is eligible for the National Register as an excellent representative of a state standard plan riveted Pratt pony truss.

C CELEBRATIONS

<u>Bronson</u> *Polish Festival:* royalty, food, wedding reception, parade, fireworks, talent show, July

<u>Coldwater</u> *Car Show:* up to 1,600 cars, May

The Daily Reporter

NPCR

...*Civil War Days:* living history, encampment, demonstrations, wagon rides, May

...*Old US-27 Motor Tour:* "Back in its day, it was the way." Old US-27 is a designated Michigan and Indiana Historic Road. The goal is to get that same designation in all the US-27 states all the way to Florida. The motor tour is a six-day classic car tour starting in Indiana to Coldwater and then on to Cheboygan with 8 stops in-between plus a stop in Alpena on the "Ride Home," Aug.

...*Strawberry Festival:* fresh, pies, shortcake, June

...*Kites Over Branch County:* fly your own kite or just watch the fun, July

The Daily Reporter

D DEMOGRAPHICS

Population: 45,200   **Persons per sq. mile:** 89
Largest city: Coldwater   **Population:** 10,900
Largest township: Coldwater **Population:** 6,100
Largest village: Quincy   **Population:** 1,650
Median household income: $40,800
Owner-occupied median house value: $113,000
Persons affiliated with a religious congregation: 30%
Persons below poverty level: 18%
Students receiving school lunch subsidy: 41%

E ENVIRONMENT

<u>Ethanol</u> is a high-octane, liquid, domestic, renewable, non-toxic, water-soluble and biodegradable fuel, produced by the fermentation of plant sugars. In the U.S. today, ethanol is typically produced from corn and other grain products. On average, one acre of corn can be processed into 430 gallons of ethanol and 2,600 pounds of distillers' grain that is used as animal feed. However, in the future it may be economical to produce ethanol from biomass resources such as agriculture and forestry wastes or specially grown "energy" crops. <u>E85</u> is the term for motor fuel blends of up to 85% ethanol and 15% gasoline. E85 is considered an alternative fuel under federal and state laws designed to increase our domestic energy security and reduce vehicle emissions. It looks and "fuels" just like regular gasoline; however, ethanol does not contain many of the harmful carcinogens and other toxic chemicals found in gasoline. e85Fuel..com, micron.org

F FLORA & FAUNA

Alice Welch, USDA

Giant hogweed is a public health hazard that is on the Federal Noxious Weed list. It is 15'-20' tall with a 2"-4" diameter stem and 5' wide leaves. If a person comes in contact with the sap from this weed, it can cause severe skin blisters when the skin is later exposed to sunlight.

Dave Dahms

Long-tailed weasels are long (only 10" or less) and slender and use their size advantage to raid the burrows of other animals. They have a black tip on their tail even in the winter when their coat is white. They are nocturnal so they are not often observed in the wild. To "weasel out" of a situation pays tribute to their cunning nature and ability to get into and out of tight situations.

G GOVERNMENT

County: ...created: 1829 **...organized:** 1833
...originally part of: Lenawee, St. Joseph Counties
Size: 332,000 acres / 507 sq. miles (71 of 83 counties)
The county has 2 cities, 3 villages, 16 townships, 11 unincorporated communities and 3 school districts.

Kim W. Kerr

Kim W. Kerr

County seat: Coldwater
...Homestead property tax: 38 mills
Motto: <u>Branch County</u> Tourism Bureau: *Just a Road Trip Away*
...<u>Coldwater</u>: *A Great Place to Live, Work, and Grow*
...<u>Quincy</u>: *Gateway to the Chain of Lakes*

H HISTORICAL MARKERS 13 of 18

Branch County: ▪ 1829: one of 13 counties established by the territorial legislature
- 1842: county seat moved from village of Branch to Coldwater
- 1848: courthouse was built
- 1850s: Chicago Road (now US-12) and the Michigan Southern railroad brought in many settlers
- 1850-1860s: this was a horse training and breeding center; provided 3,000 horses for the Union Army
- 1870-1880s: cigar manufacturing; 13 million cigars were made here in 1882

Kim W. Kerr

Branch County Courthouse Site: in 1972, an arson fire destroyed the 1848 courthouse; the bell and clock were salvaged and citizens contributed money to construct a new Branch County Clock Tower.

Bronson Public Library: 1912, a Carnegie library in the Classic Revival style; see 12Y

The Chicago Road: originally a Sauk Indian trail, then a military road connecting forts in Detroit and Chicago, then a land route that allowed pioneers to get to southern Michigan; it is now US-12 and called Michigan Avenue. See 11T.

City of Coldwater: at the junction of two American Indian trails, they called this area "cold water spring"

First Presbyterian Church: 1869, Romanesque Revival style, 185' steeple

Michigan State Preservation Office

Gov. Cyrus Luce: 1824-1905, active in local and state politics and organizations

Harriet Quimby: 1875-1912, first woman in U.S. to obtain a pilot's license and the first woman to fly over the English Channel; she died in a plane crash.

Michigan Library Association: 1891, Mary Eddy of Coldwater helped to form the state association so other librarians would not have to go to the national meetings to get their information.

Michigan State Preservation Office

Quincy Public Library: Andrew Carnegie and a local man both offered to build the library, but the local man provided the money *and* land as a memorial to his son. See 12Y.

State Public School at Coldwater: 1874, a special state school for neglected, normal and handicapped children

Coldwater Regional Center: for persons of all ages with more serious handicaps; by 1960 there were 2,900 residents

Wing House Museum: 1875, Second Empire style, now the Branch County Historical Museum; see 12M

National Register of Historic Places: 14 listings

State Historic Sites: 32 listings

I INFORMATION

Chamber of Commerce: Branch County, Quincy

Visitor: Branch County Tourism Bureau, 800-968-9333, discover-michigan.com

J JOKES

Welcome to Michigan! You'll need to remember some things in order to navigate the state successfully.

1. We have west Michigan, but no east Michigan, just southeast Michigan and the Thumb. But we have Up North and the U.P.
2. We call our highways by their "given" name: I-69, US-12, M-100, like that.
3. When in Lansing, read the road signs carefully so as not to confuse north and south I-69 with east and west I-69, I-96 and I-496. And if you find yourself going northeast to Flint when you wanted to go south to Coldwater, well, you're not the first.

NPCR

4. Most of our interstate highways are two lanes in one direction. The right hand lane is for those driving the speed limit. The left hand lane is for everyone else who thinks those in the right lane are driving too slow.

K KINSMAN

Race
American Indian: <1%
Asian: <1%
Black/African American: 3%
Hispanic or Latino: 4%
Other: 3%
White: 93%

Ancestry
German: 26%
U.S./American: 14%
English: 12%
Irish: 8%
Polish: 7%
Dutch 3%
French: 3%

L LIGHTHOUSE OR LANDMARK

NPCR

People come to Coldwater from all over Michigan, Indiana and Ohio to experience the thrill of movies at the Capri Drive-In Theater. Built in 1964 with one screen for 1,000 cars, it now features 2 screens serving 850 cars. Gone are the car speakers and their poles, but in their place is stereo sound on FM radio. Good food, friendly people and clean restrooms round out the experience of one the nation's best drive-ins.

M MUSEUMS

Coldwater *Wing House Museum:* Victorian luxury with marble fireplaces in every room, see 12H

Quincy *Historical Society Museum:* in a renovated old church

...*Public Library:* home to display of Grand Army of the Republic (GAR) memorabilia of Union soldiers of the Civil War

NPCR

N NATURAL RESOURCES

Elevation: 900 – 1,000 feet
Physiography: rolling plains, hilly uplands

Soil: Stony, Sandy Loam
  Depth: 18"-24"
  Color: dark brown
  Type: medium textured, gravely and sandy
  Details: many large granite rocks on or below the surface; land is rolling and well drained
  NOTE: soil types are not limited to any one county.

Forest type: oak-hickory, maple beech
Public/private forests: 16% of county

NPCR

Water in county: 2% of county
  Lakes: 110
    ...largest: Coldwater
  Rivers: Coldwater, Fawn, Prairie, St. Joseph, Sauk
  Rivers & streams: 325 miles

Growing season, avg.: 150 days (1-2 temp. zones)
  Last freeze, avg.: May 10
  First freeze, avg.: Sept. 30 – Oct. 5
Precipitation, annual avg.: rainfall: 33 inches
                              snowfall: 48 inches
Temperature (F), avg.: January: high 30°, low 15°
                        July: high 82°, low 59°
  Annual: >90°: 10 days, **<0°:** 10 days
Tornadoes (1930-2010): 17

O ORIGINS

Bronson:[c,t] first settler, Jabez Bronson;, 1828
Branch:[co] John Branch, Secretary of Navy under President Andrew Jackson
Coldwater:[c,t] from the Coldwater River; 1830
Quincy:[v,t] early settler from Quincy, MA; 1830
Sherwood:[v,t] first settler from Sherwood Forest, England; 1832
Union City:[v,t] the Coldwater and St. Joseph Rivers unite here; 1826

P PARKS

National: 0 **State:** 1 **County:** 5 **Local:** 19
Number of campsites: 2,300

State Park: *Coldwater Lake:* 400 acres, undeveloped

County: *Memorial Park:* 30 acres, on Messenger Lake; boat launches, beaches, athletic facilities …*Quincy-Marble Lake:* 60 acres; boating, swimming

Local: *Heritage Park:* swimming pool, softball diamonds, soccer fields, basketball courts, volleyball courts, gym, sledding hill, ice skating rink, roller blade trails, skate board park, tot lot

Q QUOTE FROM THE LOCALS

"The County is a rural farming area located in south central Michigan. Communities popped up along the U.S.-12 Heritage Trail, which was the main thoroughfare from Detroit to Chicago. The rich soils and abundance of lakes brought in more settlers. Also, the Michigan Southern and Indian Northern Railroad opening up the area in 1850 brought even more [settlers]." discover-michigan.com

"Today Branch County is a diverse and thriving rural area with a large agricultural and manufacturing base. Its citizens are committed to family, education and community. The county is also very well-known for its preservation for some of the most beautiful turn-of-the-century architecture." branchareachamber.com

R RECREATION & SPORTS

Auto racing: *Butler Motor Speedway:* $^3/_8$-mile high-banked dirt track
Golf courses: 3
Public access sites: 17
Public recreational land: <1% of county
Coldwater-Marble Lake Chain: 15 miles long

Craig-Morrison Lake Chain: 12 miles long
Log Road Motocross: 1½ miles over hilly terrain
Wolly Bike Rally: 15, 20, 25, 62 and 100-mile rides

S STATE OF MICHIGAN

The State of Michigan <u>Quarter</u> was released in 2004 as part of the 50 State Quarters® Program. It features a topographical outline of Michigan surrounded by the five Great Lakes. 1837 is the year Michigan was admitted to the Union. *E Pluribus Unum* is Latin for "Out of many, one" and is part of the Seal of the United States.

T TRAVEL

Airport: Branch County Memorial
Bus: Branch Area Transit Authority
Distance to Lansing: 70 miles
Heritage Route: *Historic:* US-12 Heritage Trail, see 11T
…*Recreation:* I-69, 80 miles from the state line in Branch County north to Exit 42 in Calhoun County; Connecting Special Places & Extraordinary Landscapes
Main roads: I-69, I-94, US-12, US-27, M-60
Memorial Highways: US-12, *Iron Brigade*: named in honor of the volunteer Civil War troops in the 24th Michigan Infantry who stood like "iron" against the enemy
…I-69, *Purple Heart Trail*: the Purple Heart is given to honor U.S. Armed Forces members who have been wounded or killed in action

Michigan Welcome Center: I-69 in Coldwater

U UNIVERSITIES & COLLEGES

Baker College: see 25U
Grahl Center of Kellogg Community College: in cooperation with Miller College; see 13U

V VARIETY

Great Lakes Glads

Since 1971, Great Lakes Glads have been a premier producer of fresh cut flowers with over 1,200 acres of their beautiful gladiolus, sunflowers and peonies. Branch County is the #1 producer of glads in Michigan; Michigan is the #1 producer of glads in the country; and Great Lakes Glads is the #1 producer of fresh cut gladiolus in the U.S.

W WANDERLUST

Fall colors: middle October
Live theater: 1882 Tibbits Opera House (restored)
Amish Meander: there are 11 shops and stops on this tour; map available
Historic Districts: 6 districts in Coldwater

Little River Railroad: dedicated to the restoration, operation and preservation of historic railroad equipment; 1½ hour ride on the Quincy Flyer

The Daily Reporter

Sauk Trail Trading Post: the largest Minnetonka Moccasin store east of the Mississippi

NPCR

NPCR

X X-TRA STUFF

County fair: *Branch County Agricultural & Industrial Society:* Honeywell Hall Agricultural Museum, Aug.
Hospitals: Community Health Center
Large employers: Michigan Department of Corrections (prisons), Wal-Mart Distribution Center, Community Health Center, GME Construction Products (machine shop), Coldwater Community Schools, Asama Coldwater Manufacturing (makes motor vehicle steering parts), Wal-Mart, Meijer

Y YESTERYEAR

Andrew Carnegie (1835-1919) was a self-educated entrepreneur who used his skills to become "the richest man in the world." He came to America from Scotland as a boy and began working in a factory at age 13. He progressed up the ladder of success as he started a few businesses of his own, culminating in the Carnegie Steel Company that eventually became U.S. Steel. As a multi-millionaire, he believed and said, "The man who dies this rich, dies disgraced." From the 1880s to his death in 1919, he gave away $350 million dollars, or billions of dollars in today's market.

NPCR

His most famous project may be Carnegie Hall in New York or the Carnegie Foundation, but the one that had the most effect on the most people was providing matching funds for free libraries. He provided funding for over 2,500 libraries around the world, including 1,700 libraries in the U.S. and 53 in Michigan. The Bronson Public Library building is one of the few remaining Carnegie Libraries still in its original unaltered configuration. Carnegie.org, wikipedia, Bronson-michigan.com

Z ZOO & ANIMAL PLACES

A.J.'s Bison: buffalos, buffalo meat, gifts, winter robes, horns, socks, soap, more

A AGRICULTURE

Land in farms: 50% of county
Number of farms: 1,180
Size of average farm: 190 acres
Market value of all products: #24 of 83 counties
Crops: ...most acres: corn for grain & silage
...highest $ sales: grains: corn, soybeans, wheat
Livestock: ...largest number: hogs & pigs
...highest $ sales: hogs & pigs
Among the top Michigan counties:
• #1- acres of popcorn, sorghum for syrup, goats
Dairy, food and meat processing plants: 26
State ranking for harvested trees: #60 of 83 counties
FYI: Corn flakes made Battle Creek famous around the world, but breakfast cereals are made from many different <u>grains</u> besides corn, including barley, buckwheat, emmer, spelt, oats, rice, sorghum, rye and wheat too. Historically, grains have been referred to as the "bread or staff of life."

Grains are the world's largest crop and provide more sustenance than any other food. Corn is the world's top crop, but rice and wheat are just behind it. Michigan has 3,000,000 acres in corn and wheat production. See 12A, 13L, 21A, 46A, 71A.

NPCR

B BRIDGE or BOAT

Nathan Holth, HistoricBridges.org

The first of its kind in the U.S., Historic Bridge Park is an outdoor museum featuring historic truss bridges that have been moved to the park and restored.

C CELEBRATIONS

<u>Albion</u> *Winterfest:* Cardboard Classic sled race, Jan.
...*Mother's Day Jubilee:* as the original home of Mother's Day, residents put up "yard cards" to honor mothers, May
...*Festival of the Forks:* celebrates the fork in the Kalamazoo River and local cultures, Sept.

Calhoun County Visitors Bureau

<u>Battle Creek</u> *World's Longest Breakfast Table:* Post, Kellogg and Ralston serve tens of thousands, June

...*Field of Flight:* a major air show and hot air balloon event, July

...*CraneFest:* Sand Hill cranes, Oct.

Prentice Drake

Calhoun County Visitors Bureau

...*International Festival of Lights:* many, many locations throughout the city, Nov. – Dec.

<u>Marshall</u> *Bluesfest:* throughout downtown, July
...*Cruise to the Fountain:* 50's & 60's cars, July
...*Historic Home Tour:* homes and museums, Sept.
...*Scarecrow Days:* displayed on front lawns, Oct.

D DEMOGRAPHICS

Population: 136,000   **Persons per sq. mile:** 192
Largest city: Battle Creek   **Population:** 52,300
Largest township: Emmett   **Population:** 11,770
Largest village: Homer   **Population:** 1,670
Median household income: $39,100
Owner-occupied median house value: $111,000
Persons affiliated with a religious congregation: 33%
Persons below poverty level: 17%
Students receiving school lunch subsidy: 43%

E ENVIRONMENT

The <u>Bernard W. Baker Sanctuary</u> is the Michigan Audubon Society's (MAS) first sanctuary, established in 1941. It is one of 19 Michigan Audubon sanctuaries. With 897 acres, it contains examples of virtually every type of southern Michigan habitat. Although providing residence, nesting habitat and migratory refuge for dozens of bird species, the Sandhill Crane is the star of the show. The sanctuary attracts up to 4,000 of these birds each season. The viewing area is open weekends in October. Bakersanctuary.org See 13F.

F FLORA & FAUNA

Red Oak — Alice Welch, USDA

White Oak — Alice Welch, USDA

Bur Oak — Alice Welch, USDA

The wide variety of uses for the porous, hard, strong and coarse-grained wood from the white oak and red oak trees makes them some of the most valuable timber trees in the state. Of the nine oak species native to Michigan, bur oak trees are relatively fast growing for an oak tree.

Michigan Farm Bureau

Sandhill Cranes are often observed feeding in cornfields and upland grain fields. They are 4'-5' tall with a wingspan up to 7'. They nest in marshes and bogs and are intolerant of human disturbance. If you see or encounter one, leave it alone. See 13E.

G GOVERNMENT

County: ...created: 1829 **...organized:** 1833
...originally part of: St. Joseph, Kalamazoo Counties
Size: 460,000 acres / 709 sq. miles (27 of 83 counties)
The county has 4 cities, 4 villages, 19 townships with 3 as charter townships, 37 unincorporated communities, 1 Census Designated Place and 11 school districts.

Andrea Boughton

Andrea Boughton

County seat: Marshall
...Homestead property tax: 50 mills
Motto: <u>Battle Creek</u>: *Breakfast Capital of the World*
... <u>Calhoun County</u> Visitors Bureau: *It's Battle Creek & So Much More*
...<u>Marshall</u>: *City of Hospitality*
...<u>Springfield</u>: *Picture Yourself in Springfield*

H HISTORICAL MARKERS 11 of 83

Michigan State Historic Preservation Office

Battle Creek Sanitarium: 1866, followed the health principles of the 7th Day Adventist Church; here Dr. John Harvey Kellogg invented flaked cereal. It was later called Percy Jones General Hospital serving 100,000 military patients; the hospital specialized in neurosurgery, plastic surgery and the fitting of artificial limbs from 1942 to 1953; now it is the Hart Dole Inouye Federal Center.
Birthplace of "Old Rugged Cross": a 1912 hymn by Rev. George Bernard, a Methodist minister; see 14H
Birthplace of Famed Song: 1911, two Albion College freshmen wrote "The Sweethearts of Sigma Chi."
C.W. Post: Charles William Post, a patient and sanitarium owner, developed healthy food products and was a pioneer in advertising.
Cereal Bowl of America: the world's leading producers of ready-to-eat cereals are located in Battle Creek; in the early 1900s, there were over 40 cereal manufacturers.

Del Shannon: 1961, Charles Westover (from Coopersville), i.e. Charlie Johnson, i.e. Del Shannon, played "Runaway" here for the first time; the song sold over 6 million records; a granite replica of the Big Top 45 RPM record is on display as part of the historical marker. See 9Y, 70M.

Andrea Boughton

Isaac Crary & John Pierce: 1835, implemented the first statewide plan for public schools and set the example for the rest of the U.S.

Mother's Day in Albion: 1880s, Albion Methodist Church began celebrating Mother's Day as a way to pay tribute to all mothers.

Postum Cereal Company: 1896, C.W. Post created Grape-Nuts & Post Toasties; it is now part of Kraft Foods

NPCR-2

The Starr Commonwealth Schools: 1913, a non-profit home and school for wayward, delinquent and neglected boys; today a nationally recognized childcare organization

W.K. Kellogg Company: 1906, started to sell Toasted Corn Flakes; it became world's largest ready-to-eat cereal manufacturer; by 1917 it produced 9 million boxes of cereal a day

Monument: Civil War Monument in Battle Creek, Underground Railroad: see 39T

NPCR-2

National Historic Landmarks: Marshall Historic Dist.[1,000]

FYI: Marshall has a Michigan State Housing Development Authority designated local historic district, one of 75 such communities in Michigan to have one. Some communities have more than one historic district. A local historic district is a historically significant area that is protected by a historic district ordinance. The local unit of government appoints a historic district commission to review proposed work to the exterior of historic and non-historic resources within the historic district. Exterior work must meet certain guidelines. Designating an area as a local historic district is one of the few ways a community can provide legal protection for its historic resources. Under certain circumstances the historic district may assess the property owners to help raise needed funds. [MSHDA] See 13T

National Register of Historic Places: 41 listings
State Historic Sites: 127 listings

I   INFORMATION

Chamber of Commerce: Albion, Battle Creek, Marshall
Visitor: Calhoun County Visitors Bureau,
   800-397-2240, battlecreekvisitors.org

J   JOKES

Corny cracks about Calhoun County
1. Does a joke about corn automatically make it a corny joke?
2. Did you hear about the cereal killer? He snaps, crackles and pops his victims.
3. How can the Battle Creek be a river?
4. How much confidence can you have in some place called Turkeyville?
5. Battle Creek, hmmm, where the corn flakes and puffs, the sugar pops, the fruit loops, the tart pops, the wheats are mini, the flakes are sugar coated and Tony the Tiger was the singing king!

K   KINSMAN

Race	Ancestry
American Indian: <1%	German: 47% (#1/MI)
Asian: 2%	Irish: 10%
Black/African American: 11%	U.S./American: 9%
Hispanic or Latino: 5%	English: 8%
Other: 5%	Swedish: 5%
White: 82%	Norwegian: 4%

L   LIGHTHOUSE OR LANDMARK

Calhoun County Visitors Bureau

Battle Creek is the global corporate headquarters of the Kellogg Company, the world's leading producer of cereal and a leading producer of many brand name convenience foods. See 13A, 13Y.

M MUSEUMS

Albion *Brueckner Museum & Gladstone Cottage Museum:* on the Starr Commonwealth campus; Victorian era

...Gardner House Museum: history of Albion in the 1875 Second Empire-style Victorian mansion

...Kids 'N' Stuff: exhibits that let the kids play

Battle Creek *Art Center:* changing exhibits, classes, gift shop, features Michigan artists

...Kimball House Museum: elegant 14-room Queen Anne-style, built in 1886

...Kingman Museum of Natural History: one of the first public museums (1871) to be owned and operated by a public school system

...Monument Park: C.W. Post, Sojourner Truth, stone tower (rock of ages)

Marshall *American Museum of Magic:* the only magic museum in the world; artifacts of great magicians

...Capitol Hill School Museum: one-room school

...Grand Army of the Republic Hall Museum: 1902

...Honolulu House Museum: a tribute to the first owner's life in the tropics; built in 1860

...Postal Museum: post office memorabilia; only the Smithsonian postal display is larger

N NATURAL RESOURCES

Elevation: 800 - 1,100 ft.
Physiography: rolling plains, hilly uplands

Forest type: oak-hickory, elm-ash-cottonwood
Public/private forests: 24% of county

Water in county: 1% of county
   Lakes: 80   **...largest:** Duck lake
   Rivers: Kalamazoo, Battle Creek, St. Joseph
   Rivers & streams: 540 miles

Growing season, avg.: 154 days (2 temp. zones)
   Last freeze, avg.: May 5 – May 10
   First freeze, avg.: Oct. 5 – Oct. 10
Precipitation, annual avg.: rainfall: 35 inches
                              snowfall: 45 inches
Temperature (F), avg.: January: high 31°, low 15°
                          July: high 83°, low 60°
   Annual: >90°: 12 days, **<0°:** 9 days
Tornadoes (1930-2010): 16

O ORIGINS

Albion:[c] first settlers were from Albion, NY; 1833
Athens:[v] first settlers were from Athens, NY; 1831
Battle Creek:[c] two American Indians and two surveyors fought it out on the banks of the river; 1824
Burlington:[v] several of the men in the first settlement had served on a Great Lakes gunboat, *Burlington,* in the War of 1812; 1833
Calhoun:[co] John C. Calhoun was Vice President under John Q. Adams and Andrew Jackson, Secretary of War under President James Monroe and Secretary of State under President John Tyler; 1830
Homer:[v] early settlers from Homer, NY; 1832
Marshall:[c] U.S. Chief Justice John Marshall; 1830
Springfield:[c] to honor C.W. Post who was from Springfield, IL; 1904
Tekonsha:[v] (te KON sha) local Pottawattomi chief Tekon-qua-sha; 1832

P PARKS

National: 0   **State:** 1   **County:** 2   **Local:** 10
Number of campsites: 1,800

State Recreation Area: *Fort Custer:* 3,000+ acres, 3 lakes, 1 river, forests, prairie restoration, trails

County: *Kimball Pines:* 100 acres of old urban pines; trails, disc golf
Local: *Leila Arboretum:* 72 acres, 3000+ tree species
...Children's Garden at the Arboretum: 1 acre, guided activities for all
...Ott Biological Preserve: 300 acres, rustic trails
...Willard Beach & Park: on Goguac (GO gwack) Lake
...Whitehouse Nature Center:[ww] 135 acres, Albion College outdoor education center

Q QUOTE FROM THE LOCALS

"Calhoun County is both rich in history and on the cutting edge of tomorrow's technology. [It] offers the serenity of country living and cultural and recreational amenities offered in urban settings …world headquarters for companies." calhouncountymi.org

Prentice Drake

"…abundant natural resources making it the perfect choice for outdoor activities …with a vast variety of entertainment and events you will find something to please the entire family." battlecreekvisitors.org

R RECREATION & SPORTS

Auto racing: *Springport Motor Speedway:* ³/₈-mile high-banked asphalt track
Golf courses: 10
Heritage Water Trail: Kalamazoo River
Hiking/skiing/mountain biking trails: 30 miles
Horse racing: harness racing during fair week

Michigan Heritage Water Trail: Kalamazoo Watershed

North Country National Scenic Trail: yes

Public access sites: 17
Public recreational land: <1% of county
Rail-trail: (20 miles) Battle Creek Linear Park, Main Trail, McClure Riverfront Park
Baseball Parks: Bailey Park, Brown Stadium, Nichols Field, Morrison Field, Convis Softball, Flannery Softball; total seating capacity is almost 10,000
Battle Creek Blaze: football, professionally focused, charity-driven; proceeds given to fight cancer
Battle Creek Bombers: NCAA summer baseball; play at Bailey Park
Battle Creek Knights: International Basketball League; play at Kellogg Arena
Battle Creek Revolution: Mid-Atlantic Hockey League
Victory Park: ice skating rink, Albion

NPCR

S STATE OF MICHIGAN

Michigan was, and still is, a great manufacturing state.
- Manufacturing employs 500,000 people in Michigan.
- About 96% of the manufacturing companies employ fewer than 500 people each and 68% employ fewer than 20 workers.
- Manufacturing accounted for 21% of the state's gross domestic product in 2009.
- Almost 25% of all vehicles produced in the U.S. (and their suppliers) are made in Michigan.
- Over 50% of all office furniture systems made in the U.S. are made in Michigan.
- The state ranks 4th in the U.S. plastics industry.
- Manufacturing accounts for 90% of Michigan exports, the majority of which is shipped to Canada and Mexico. The majority of Michigan exports are the products of small businesses.
- Michigan is second in the nation in manufacturing research and development. More than 85% of North American automotive research and development occurs in Michigan.
- Michigan is a leader in alternative energy and the home to the continents largest lithium-ion battery manufacturer and over 120 wind energy suppliers and manufactures. Michigan Manufacturers Association

T TRAVEL

Airports: Brooks, Claucherty, David's Field, WK Kellogg, Midway
Amtrak: Albion, Battle Creek
Bus: Indian Trails, Greyhound, Battle Creek Transit
Distance to Lansing: 50 miles

Kim Kerr

Heritage Route: *Historic:* BL-94, Marshall,[1,000] the largest National Historic Landmark District in the U.S., with over 850 architecturally significant and diverse buildings. See 13H-FYI.

…*Recreation:* I-69, 80 miles, state line in Branch County north to Exit 42 in Calhoun County; Connecting Special Places & Extraordinary Landscapes
Main roads: I-69, I-94, I-194
Memorial Highways: I-94, *94th Combat Infantry Division MH*: in honor of Michigan troops who trained at Fort Custer and fought with Gen. George Patton in 1945 against the Germans; they suffered a 74% causality rate

…I-94 Bus. Loop, *Dr. Martin Luther King Jr. MH*: Rev. King (1929-1968) spoke at Albion College in 1963
…US-223, *Carlton Road*: see 30X
…M-66, *Sojourner Truth MH*: see 13V
County road names:
…north/south: numbered Mile Roads
…east/west: lettered Drives indicating their position north or south in the county (i.e. L Drive S)
FYI: Over the years, I-194 has been called, in part or as a whole, proposed, promoted or legalized: Martin Luther King Memorial Hwy. [Barnett]

U UNIVERSITIES & COLLEGES

Albion College: est. 1835, 2,000 students. Their guiding principle is 'service-learning' - to enhance the sense of community and common purpose …and to encourage students to reach out beyond the campus. MIAA, Britons

Davenport University: est. 1866, 13,000+ students on 14 Michigan campuses. It is a private school that prepares students for the most in-demand, fastest-growing careers in business, health and technology.

Kellogg Community College: est. 1956, 14,000 students. They provide academic, occupational, general and life-long learning opportunities; exercise leadership, …promote innovation …support economic development activities; M-TEC. MCCAA, Bruins

Miller College: est. 2005, 400 students. They value student learning, critical thinking, oral and written communication skills and an understanding of a globally oriented world; junior and senior level formats with a transfer agreement with Kellogg Community College.

V VARIETY

Andrea Boughton

A nationally known charismatic speaker for abolition, women's rights and human rights for blacks and whites, Sojourner Truth (1797-1883) lived in Battle Creek from 1857 until her death. Her statue can be seen in Monument Park, downtown Battle Creek. See 13H.

W WANDERLUST

Agri-tourism: *Battle Creek Farmers' Market Assoc.*
…*Bosserd Family Farm:* flowers, sweet corn, tomatoes, school tours, beef, pork
…*Harvey's:* asparagus, blueberries, strawberries, chestnuts
Brewery: Arcadia Ales, Dark Horse Brewing Co.
Casino: FireKeepers
Cultural: Art Center of Battle Creek, Bobbit Visual Arts Center at Albion College
Fall colors: middle October
Live theater: Cornwell's Dinner Theater, Franke Center for the Arts
MotorCities National Heritage Area: yes
Planetarium: the Albion College Observatory, built in 1883, is one of the oldest and still active telescopes in the U.S.
Shopping mall: Lakeview Square
Walking tours: Albion, Ghost Tours, Marshall, Historic Purple Gang, Starr Commonwealth
Wineries: *Cherry Creek Cellars:* boutique winery using old world handcrafting
Albion has a lovely brick Main Street.
Alligator Sanctuary: saving lives, making friends
Brooks Memorial Fountain: Marshall, Greek Revival style, evening color light shows, May – Sept.

Andrea Boughton

Cornwell's Turkey Farm: Turkeyville, USA; all turkey restaurant menus, dinner theater, gift shops

Andrea Boughton

Fort Custer National Cemetery: there are 125 National Cemeteries and Michigan has two; Fort Custer is the final resting place for 26,000 people

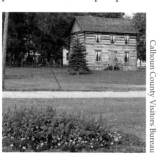

Calhoun County Visitors Bureau

Historic Adventist Village: 19th century living history; health treatments and practices

Southern Exposure Herb Farm: beautiful walking gardens, restored farm buildings, charming gifts

Andrea Boughton

Turtle Lake Resort: the Midwest's Premier Nudist Resort; clothing is optional

A Kalamazoo River canoeing map and guide is available at the visitor's center.

The Fort Custer Industrial Park Mural depicts Battle Creek's manufacturing heritage.

X X-TRA STUFF

American Indian Community: Nottawaseppi Band of Huron Potawatomi Indians

County Fair: *Agricultural & Industrial Soc.,* Aug.

Famous people: ...*Entertainers:* Betty Hutton, Jamie Hynemen, Dick Martin, Jason Newsted
...*Other:* W.K. Kellogg, C.W. Post, Sojourner Truth, John C. Sheehan

Hospitals: Bronson Battle Creek, Oaklawn, Select Specialty, Southwest Regional Rehab., Veterans

Large employers: Denso Manufacturing (makes auto AC), Battle Creek Health System, VA Medical Center, State Farm Insurance, Battle Creek Schools, Kellogg Foods, Kraft Foods, McDonald's of Calhoun, Veterans Health Administration

A coach at Albion College is credited with founding tee-ball, a simplified form of baseball, in 1956.

Y YESTERYEAR

Why did Battle Creek become the <u>Cereal Capital of the World</u>?

In the early 1900s, there were more than 80 cereal companies in Battle Creek and the city would become world famous for the "Big 3" of cereals, Kellogg, Post and Ralston.

The Seventh-day Adventists formed the Western Health Reform Institute in the 1860s and later it became the Battle Creek Sanitarium (the San), an internationally famous hospital and spa. They did not allow caffeine, meat, alcohol, or tobacco, but did promote fresh and healthy food, exercise and fresh air, a rather radical concept at the time. In 1894, W.K. Kellogg was trying to improve the vegetarian diet

of the hospital patients and was experimenting with boiled wheat. He inadvertently left a pot of boiled wheat to stand and the wheat became soft. When he rolled it out and baked it, it was actually very tasty. Later, in 1906, he founded the Battle Creek Toasted Corn Flake Company.

C.W. Post visited the San due to his poor health. He was so impressed with the marketing potential of the products used there that he started his own Postum Cereal Company in 1895. Postum was a cereal beverage. Two year later, he invented Grape Nuts, a unique blend of wheat and barley flours that are baked, dried and ground. While it was baking, it had a grape-like aroma and then a nutty-crunchy texture.

Z ZOO & ANIMAL PLACES

Watchable Wildlife Viewing Areas:[ww] Battle Creek Linear Park, see 13P

Zoo: *Binder Park Zoo:*[ww] 455 acres, has 150 animal species in a natural setting; you can get close to some of the animals

NPCR

Baker Sanctuary: see 13E

Windsong Stable: premier hunter, jumper and equitation facility

Wonder Why Alpaca Farm: all aspects of the alpaca industry and fiber arts

Zukowski's Meadowview Farms: equine activities for all ages and abilities

Bold typeface: this indicates that this heading may be repeated in every chapter, providing that the information about the heading is applicable to the county.

A AGRICULTURE

Land in farms: 58% of county
Number of farms: 810
Size of average farm: 230 acres
Market value of all products: #20 of 83 counties
Crops: ...most acres: corn for grain
...highest $ sales: grains: corn, soybeans
Livestock: ...largest number: hogs & pigs
...highest $ sales: hogs & pigs
Among the top Michigan counties:
- #1- snap beans
- #2- eggplant, hogs & pigs
- #4- organic

Dairy, food and meat processing plants: 12
AgBioResearch Centers (MSU): *Fred Russ Forest:* 530 acres, long-term research on Christmas tree seed production and other projects aimed at preserving the diversity and abundance of Michigan's forests; see 14P

State ranking for harvested trees: #53 of 83 counties
FYI: Hogs and pigs are the 6th largest agricultural commodity group in Michigan with annual sales of over 1.3 million animals producing 460 million pounds of pork. A pig weighs less than 120 lbs. and a hog weighs more than that. These animals are raised on 2,700 farms in the state with 79% of the farms having less than 99 animals each. Pork is now leaner, and therefore healthier, than in previous generations. Cass County has 70 hog farms raising 156,000 animals for your favorite bar-b-que ribs or ham dinner.

Michigan Farm Bureau

Besides providing good food, hogs and pigs are a source of a wide variety of products. For example, pig hair is used in upholstery, bones and skin are used for gloves, garments and glue, hog ovaries are a source of progesterone and estrogen hormones, and fatty acids are used to make lubricants, insecticides, insulation, floor wax and cosmetics. Hogs also produce a number of medical products like insulin to treat diabetes and their skin can be used to help severe burn victims. MDA, USDA

B BRIDGE OR BOAT

NPCR

MDOT Historic Bridge: This abandoned railroad bridge on Thomson Rd. in Howard Twp. was built in 1919. It is eligible for the National Register as an excellent example of an early concrete T-beam bridge with very good historical integrity.

C CELEBRATIONS

<u>Dowagiac</u> *Ice Time:* ice, timber and wood carvers, chili cook-off; Hibernation Sale - show up in your jammies before dawn at the local merchants and get a huge discount, Feb.
...*Beckwick Park Summer Concert Series:* 12 weeks

...*Dogwood Fine Arts Festival:* authors, musicians, storytellers, cooking demos, wine tasting, sculptors, May

Courtesy of SW MI Tourist Council

...*Rod & Roll Classic Auto Show:* Aug.
<u>Pokagon</u> *Kee-Boon-Mein-Kaa Powwow:* dancers, native crafts and food, Sept.

D DEMOGRAPHICS

Population: 52,000   **Persons per sq. mile:** 106
Largest city: Dowagiac   **Population:** 5,890
Largest township: Howard **Population:** 6,200
Largest village: Cassopolis **Population:** 1,700
Median household income: $45,800
Owner-occupied median house value: $132,000
Persons affiliated with a religious congregation: 26%
Persons below poverty level: 16%
Students receiving school lunch subsidy: 43%

E ENVIRONMENT

"The Southwest Michigan Land Conservancy invites you to help protect the local wild and scenic places you care most about: dunes, wetlands, forests, savannahs, prairies, farms and vineyards. It's this diverse beauty that makes the landscape of southwest Michigan a special place to call home. Working together, we can ensure that future generations will continue to enjoy the extraordinary quality of life our natural lands provide. ...We are dedicated to protecting natural areas, historic sites and open spaces, ...encouraging ecologically sound land practices, enabling individuals and organizations to protect land important to wildlife and people...." Currently they have 43 preserves and many are open to the public. swmlc.org

F FLORA & FAUNA

Alice Welch, USDA

Tulip poplar trees, also called yellow poplar, are found only in the eastern United States from southern Michigan to northern Florida. It is the tallest of all the hardwoods, fast growing and a valuable timber tree used from organ making to house siding. The flowers do resemble tulips. The Russ Forest is home to the largest tulip poplar in Michigan, standing 180' tall and it is 300 years old.

Laura Perlick/USFWS

The box turtle is Michigan's only truly terrestrial turtle, living in open woodlands and adjacent meadows near shallow bodies of water. The adult is 4.5"-7.5" long and can live 30 or more years.

G GOVERNMENT

County: ...created: 1829 **...organized:** 1829
...originally part of: Lenawee County
Size: 327,000 acres / 492 sq. miles (74 of 83 counties)
The county has 1 city, 4 villages, 15 townships, 9 unincorporated communities and 4 school districts.

Michigan State Preservation Office

NPCR

The Cass County Courthouse, built in 1899, is a wooden frame building with limestone veneer.
County seat: Cassopolis
...Homestead property tax: 41 mills
Motto: Dowagiac: *Creating Tomorrow*
... Edwardsburg: *Live Bait Capital of the World*
... Greater Dowagiac Chamber: *The Grand Old City*

H HISTORICAL MARKERS 8 of 14

Chain Lake Baptist Church and Cemetery: in the mid-1800s the area's Quaker community provided a haven for fugitive slaves and a stop on the Underground Railroad.

District School House: 1875, a two-room yellow and brick school that could accommodate 110 pupils

Sarah J. Pion

"Old Rugged Cross:" 1913, this popular hymn was sung for the first time by the composer Rev. George Bennard at revival services here. See 13H.

Michigan State Preservation Office

Methodist Episcopal Church: 1862, a barn renovated to be a church, used as a barn again; then in 1998 a church began restoration again; site of the first singing of "The Old Rugged Cross."

Newton House: 1860s, in the Fred Russ Experimental Forest; restored

Poe's Corners: George Poe came from Ohio in 1835; there was eventually a Poe Neighborhood, a Poe's Cemetery, a Poe's Church and a Poe's School.

Sumnerville Mounds: Hopewell Indians lived here in the first century A.D. and six remaining burial mounds are left; the Public Museum of Grand Rapids has artifacts from other mounds in the area

The Underground Railroad: <1860, the Quakers in Vandalia provided shelter for fleeing slaves at this important junction on the Underground Railroad

National Register of Historic Places: 8 listings

State Historic Sites: 26 listings

I INFORMATION

Chamber of Commerce: Cassopolis-Vandalia, Edwardsburg, Dowagiac

Visitor: Southwestern Michigan Tourist Council, 269-925-6301, swmich.org

J JOKES

You might be a Michiganian if…

…you're OK with the Lions losing because you love/hate them anyway.

…you want your son to be a star quarterback so you name him Drew.

…you consider pickled bologna, saltine crackers and Vernor's Ginger Ale a great lunch.

…you've ever said, "It's only 10 below."

…you know how to play euchre.

…your local Dairy Queen is closed November through February.

…you can live with gray skies.

K KINSMAN

Race

American Indian: 1%
Asian: <1%
Black/African American: 5%
Hispanic or Latino: 3%
Other: 4%
White: 89%

Ancestry

German: 27%
U.S./American: 11%
Irish: 10%
English: 10%
Polish: 5%
Dutch: 4%

L LIGHTHOUSE OR LANDMARK

Chris Ryback-Ed Lowe Foundation

Ed Lowe, a native of Cassopolis, founded Kitty Litter in 1947. He used the wealth he gained from that enterprise to create the Edward Lowe Foundation in 1985, a nonprofit organization that supports entrepreneurship research, recognition and educational programs. The foundation focuses on second-stage companies – those that have moved beyond the startup phase and seek significant, steady growth. In addition, the foundation has a secondary mission of land stewardship and is committed to preserving the natural resources and historically significant structures at Big Rock Valley, its 2,600-acre home in southwest Michigan. The campus features renovated farmhouses and converted boxcars for overnight guests, a turn-of-the-century small town as a conference center, the Heritage Center and Information Center Museum.

M MUSEUMS

Cassopolis *Log Cabin Museum:* 1923 building, local artifacts

Decatur *Newton House:* a mid-1800s Quaker home that is now owned by Michigan State University and is part of Russ Forest

Dowagiac *National Heddon Museum:* preserves the history of the Heddon family's many contributions to the fishing tackle industry and to the City of Dowagiac.

NPCR

…*The Museum at Southwestern Michigan College:* interactive adventure in local history and an exploration in science and technology

Edwardsburg *Museum:* in a boarding house

N NATURAL RESOURCES

Elevation: 700 - 900 feet
Physiography: hill-lands, rolling plains

Forest type: oak-hickory, maple-beech
Public/private forests: 24% of county

NPCR

National Natural Landmark: *Newton Woods:* 44 acres, one of the last remaining old-growth, oak-mixed, hardwood stands in the Lower Peninsula

Water in county: 3% of county
    Lakes: 120   **...largest:** Diamond
    Rivers: Dowagiac (do WAW jack)
    Rivers & streams: 230 miles

Growing season, avg.: 144 days (2-3 temp. zones)
    Last freeze, avg.: May 5 – May 10
    First freeze, avg.: Oct. 5 – Oct. 15
Precipitation, annual avg.: rainfall: 37 inches (#2/MI)
                      snowfall: 73 inches
Temperature (F), avg.: January: high 31°, low 15°
                 July: high 84°, low 59°
    Annual: >90°: 16 days (#3/MI), **<0°:** 9 days
Tornadoes (1930-2010): 16

O ORIGINS

<u>Cass:</u>[co] Michigan Territorial Governor, Lewis Cass; see 14Y
<u>Cassopolis:</u>[v] (cass AHPLE us) named after the county; 1829
<u>Dowagiac:</u>[c] (do WAW jack) translated from an American Indian word that meant "foraging ground," where a man could fill all his needs for food, clothing and shelter; 1848
<u>Edwardsburg:</u>[v] county's first merchant, Thomas Edwards; 1828
<u>Howard:</u>[t] Miss Howard from Detroit; 1835
<u>Marcellus:</u>[v] a great Roman general, 1865

Sarah J. Pion

<u>Pokagon:</u>[u,t] (poh KAY gun) Pottawattomi Chief Simon Pokagon, the best-educated full-blooded American Indian in North America and a literary genius; 1838

<u>Vandalia:</u>[v] after Vandalia, NY; 1849

P PARKS

National: 0 **State:** 2 **County:** 6 **Local:** 22
Number of campsites: 1,600
State Game Area: Crane Pond[wba], Three Rivers
County: *Dodd Memorial Park:* 50 acres, fishing, canoe landing, trails, horseshoes, volleyball
...*Fred Russ Forest Park:* see 14V, 14F
...*Lawless:* 720 acres, bike trails, hiking, cross-country trails, disc golf course, soccer field
Local: *Rudolphi Woods:* 325 acres, open space, trails

Sarah J. Pion

Other: *Dowagic Woods Nature Sanctuary:* 384 acres, the largest woodland of virgin soil in Michigan, never plowed, planted or grazed; trails

Courtesy of SW MI Tourist Council

...*Fred Russ Forest Park:* 13 acres, part of the MSU Experimental Station property, home to the largest tulip poplar tree in Michigan; see 14F

...*Newton Woods:* see 14N

Q QUOTE FROM THE LOCALS

"Cass County is both a rich agricultural area as well as a popular tourist spot. It plays a major part in pork production in Michigan as well as other feed crops like soybeans and corn. It also contains over 250 lakes and several nature preserves, which makes for great water sports, hiking and bird-watching." outdoor-michigan.com

NPCR

R RECREATION & SPORTS

Golf courses: 6
Hiking/skiing/mountain biking trails: 10 miles
Public access sites: 24
Public recreational land: 1% of county
State-funded snowmobile trails: 25 miles
Swiss Valley Ski & Snowboard Area: 11 runs, 225' vertical drop, varied terrain for all levels, night skiing, snow making, ski school, Terrain Park with Progression Sessions

S STATE OF MICHIGAN

Michigan, in partnership with local community colleges and through the Michigan Economic Development Corporation, established 18 new technical training centers called Michigan Technical Education Centers, or M-TEC. The college partners with local business communities to ensure that local training needs are met. Opened in 2001 on the Niles Area Campus, the M-TEC at Southwestern Michigan College has a simulated 6,200-square-foot factory, which offers training in die-casting, as well as manufacturing technologies in welding, machining, precision measurement and gauging and metal coating. swmich.edu

T TRAVEL

Airport: Dowagiac Municipal
Amtrak: Dowagiac
Bus: Dowagiac Area Rapid Transit
County road names: ...north/south: Roads
　　　　　　　　　　...east/west: Streets

Distance to Lansing: 100 miles
Heritage Route: *Historic:* US-12 Heritage Trail, see 11T
Main roads: US-12, M-40, M-51, M-60, M-62
Memorial Highways: US-12, *Iron Brigade:* see 12T
...US-12, *Pulaski MH:* see 11T
...M-62, *Veterans MH*
FYI: Over the years, US-12 has been called, in part or as a whole, proposed, promoted or legalized: Chicago Rd, Hoosier Hwy., Iron Bridge Memorial Hwy., Jackson County Roadside Memorial, Michigan Ave., Pulaski Memorial Hwy. and Red Arrow Hwy. Barnett

U UNIVERSITIES & COLLEGES

Southwestern Michigan College: est. 1964, 3,300 students. It is a community college that wants to be the college of first choice for students who have a choice and to meet the needs of students with limited choices. Student Activities Center only.

V VARIETY

NPCR

This modern hog raising facility is a common sight in Cass County, a top producer of hogs.

W WANDERLUST

Agri-tourism: *A-mazing Acres Corn Maze & Pumpkin Patch:* 17-acre corn maze, hayrides, gem mining, pumpkins, gourds, apples, animals
...*Diamond Acre Farm:* ninth generation farm, market, fruits, berries, veggies, flowers
...*Farmer's Markets:* Dowagiac
...*Sprague's Family Fun Farm:* apples, berries, cherries, nectarines, peaches, veggies, corn maze
...*Wicks' Apple House & Cider Mill:* fresh fruits and vegetables, bakers, restaurant, gifts, maze
Fall colors: middle October
Live theater: Beckwith Theatre
Walking tour: Historic Dowagiac

Dowagiac Sculptures: Active Hybrid, Dance of Creation, Resting Dancer, Soldiers & Sailors Monument, Stone Lion

Sarah J. Pion

X X-TRA STUFF

American Indian Community: Pokagon Band of Potawatomi Indians

County fair: *Cass County Agricultural Fair Assoc.:* Aug.

Hospitals: Borgess-Lee Memorial

Large employers: Contech U.S. (makes die-cast products), Southwest Michigan College, Rospatch Jessco (makes wood furniture), Dowagiac Union School District, Lee Memorial Hospital, Borgess Hospital, Edwardsburg Public Schools, K & M Machine Fabricating (machine shop), Smurfit-Stone Container (paperboard mill)

NPCR-2

Dowagiac was the home of Round Oak, makers of potbelly stoves, furnace and kitchen ranges, from the 1860s to 1940s.

Dowagiac is the home of Judd Lumber Company, the oldest lumber company in Michigan, founded in 1859.

Y YESTERYEAR

Lewis Cass: (1782-1866)

- 1782-1812: born in NH, practiced law in OH, served in the War of 1812

- 1813-1831: governor of the Territory of Michigan, which later became the states of Michigan, Wisconsin, Iowa and Minnesota

NPCR-2

- 1829 & 1833: the Michigan Territorial legislature created 12 counties and named 10 of them after President Andrew Jackson and his Cabinet and the Territorial governor. These *Cabinet counties* are Barry, Berrien, Branch, Calhoun, Cass, Eaton, Ingham, Jackson, Livingston and Van Buren.

NPCR-2

- 1831-1836: Secretary of War under President Andrew Jackson
- 1837: Michigan received statehood
- 1845-1848, 1849-1857: U.S. Senator from Michigan
- 1848: Democratic candidate for President (lost to Zachary Taylor)
- 1857-1860: Secretary of State under President James Buchanan

Z ZOO & ANIMAL PLACES

Petting zoo: *A-mazing Acres Corn Maze & Pumpkin Patch:* farm animals, goat walk, bunnyville

Lunkquarium: at Lunkers hunting and outdoor store, Edwardsburg

A AGRICULTURE

Land in farms: 14% of county
Number of farms: 340
Size of average farm: 120 acres
Market value of all products: #62 of 83 counties
Crops: ...most acres: forage land
...highest $ sales: fruits (apples)
Livestock: ...largest number: cattle & calves
...highest $ sales: milk & dairy products
Dairy, food and meat processing plants: 22
State ranking for harvested trees: #34 of 83 counties
FYI: Community Supported Agriculture (CSA) is a new and rapidly expanding opportunity for farmers to provide food for their neighbors, and for those neighbors to be involved in the risks and benefits of being able to receive farm-fresh food on a regular basis. It's the next best thing to having your own backyard garden.

In anticipation of the coming crops and harvest, members purchase shares before the planting season begins. Although each farm may offer different foods and services, the basic CSA concept is the same. All will include a wide variety of vegetables and some may include fruits, eggs, honey, meat or baked goods. Members receive weekly shares of whatever crop is ripe that week. Members may even have the opportunity to be involved on the farm if they so desire.

One of the major benefits to members is that they *know* where and how their food is grown and they become knowledgeable about the natural rhythms and processes involved in growing good food. The farmer, on the other hand, has a predetermined income and a ready market for his products. It is a win-win for everyone. safs.msu.edu

B BRIDGE OR BOAT

Beaver Island Boat Co. & Bill Konway

The Beaver Island Boat Company operates two ferryboats to Beaver Island. The Emerald Isle carries almost 300 passenger and 20 vehicles on the 2-hour, 32-mile trip between Charlevoix and Beaver Island.

C CELEBRATIONS

NPCR

<u>Beaver Island</u> *Celtic Festival:* music, pipes and drums, caber toss (an 18' tree), more games, June

...*Music Festival:* variety and traditions of all music and art in our beautiful world, July
...*Museum Week:* history of the island, July
...*Bite of Beaver Island:* sample the treats, Oct.
<u>Boyne City</u> *National Morel Mushroom Festival:* hunt them in the woods or eat them in restaurants, May
<u>Boyne Falls</u> *Polish Festival:* beer tent, mud run, Aug.
<u>Charlevoix</u> *Summer Solstice Art Show:* high quality art, June
...*Taste of Charlevoix:* food, beer, wine, music, June
...*Trout Tournament:* June
...*Fiber Arts Festival:* July
...*Garden Walk:* public and private gardens, July
...*Street Legends of Charlevoix Classic Car Show:* July
...*Venetian Festival:* boat parade, carnival, sports, live entertainment, fireworks, kids' activities, July
...*Waterfront Art Fair:* a spectacular location for spectacular artists, July
...*Apple Festival:* cider, food, art fair, Oct.
<u>East Jordan</u> *Portside Arts Fair:* juried fine arts on the historic Elm Pointe Estate, Aug.
<u>Walloon Lake</u> *Antique Tractor & Truck Pull:* June
...*Tractor, Engine, & Craft Show:* July

D DEMOGRAPHICS

Population: 35,900   **Persons per sq. mile:** 62
Largest city: Boyne City   **Population:** 3,740
Largest township: Wilson   **Population:** 1,960
Largest village: Boyne Falls **Population:** 300
Median household income: $43,400
Owner-occupied median house value: $166,000
Persons affiliated with a religious congregation: 42%
Persons below poverty level: 13%
Students receiving school lunch subsidy: 39%

E ENVIRONMENT

The Guardian of Lake Charlevoix is the Lake Charlevoix Association. Their mission is to protect the natural quality and beauty of Lake Charlevoix, promote understanding and support for safe and shared lake use, and advocate sensible and sustainable practices for lake use and development. They work with government, non-profit agencies and individuals to meet these goals. Providing hands-on educational experiences for school kids, helping to control invasive species and promoting boating safety are just a few of their programs. lakecharlevoixassociation.org

F FLORA & FAUNA

Alice Welch, USDA

The multiflora rose is a pretty shrub with thorny stems that is a prolific ecological threat to dense woods and prairies and almost any disturbed environment in between. It spreads easily and forms impenetrable thickets that kill any native plants in its way. Although it provides cover for some animals, it is a problem for others. Its out-of-control growth rate is the real issue that makes it a noxious weed.

Steve Hillebrand/USFWS

NPCR-9

Beavers (*MI H&T*), the largest rodent in North America, are still found in Michigan, but not in the large numbers of the 1800s. To spot a beaver dam, look around the edge of a pond or stream for a large group of branches above and below the water.

G GOVERNMENT

County: ...**created:** 1867 ...**organized:** 1869
NOTE: some authorities say it was organized in 1867 and some say 1869
...**originally part of:** Emmet County
Size: 293,000 acres / 417 sq. miles (80 of 83 counties)
The county has 3 cities, 1 village, 15 townships, 2 unincorporated communities and 6 school districts.
County seat: Charlevoix

Bill Luptowski

Jessica Jakubik

...**Homestead property tax:** 34 mills
Motto: Beaver Island Chamber: *America's Emerald Isle –Unspoiled. Unhurried. Unmatched in Natural Beauty*
...Boyne City Chamber: *Home town feel... Small town appeal!*
...Charlevoix: *Charlevoix the Beautiful*
...Charlevoix Area Convention and Visitors Bureau: *Northern Michigan's Freshwater Pearl*
...East Jordan: *Where river, lake and friendly people meet*

H HISTORICAL MARKERS 7 of 10

Big Rock Point Nuclear Power Plant: 1962, the world's first high-power density boiling water reactor; 5th commercial nuclear plant in USA
Greensky Hill Mission: 1850s, was built by American Indians who brought the hand-hewn timbers by canoe from Traverse City, then carried them 2 miles to the site
Horton Bay: 1876, many original buildings remain; young Ernest Hemingway camped at 'the point'

John and Eva Porter Estate: 1920s, an unusual contemporary version of Colonial architecture; now the Portside Art and Historical Soc. Museum

Michigan State Preservation Office

Mormon Kingdom: 1847, Mormon dissenter James Strang established a colony with Strang as authoritarian king. His own followers killed him in 1856. See 15Y

Mormon Print Shop: 1850, published religious works and two newspapers; now home of the Beaver Island Historical Society

Norwood Township Hall: 1884, still operational today

National Register of Historic Places: 21 listings

State Historic Sites: 22 listings

I   INFORMATION

Chamber of Commerce: Beaver Island, Boyne City, Charlevoix, East Jordan

Visitor: Charlevoix Area Convention and Visitors Bureau, 800-367-8557, visitcharlevoix.com

J   JOKES

A short lesson in Michigan weather:

When it is sunny and there is no wind...

- -25°F is when most construction workers go home.
- -15° is just right for ice fishermen.
- -5° is just too cold for everyone else.
- 5° is doable if you're young and strong.
- 15° means you can do all outdoor activities.
- 25° is the perfect winter day.
- 35° means the roads won't ice over.
- 45° is cool but still not warm.
- 55° is pleasant.
- 65° is warm.
- 75° is just right.
- 85° is too hot.
- 95° is unbearable.
- and 105° is the reason we don't live in Austin, Texas.

And when you add clouds, wind and/or humidity to any temperature, *everything changes.* So just forget what you just learned.

K   KINSMAN

Race		Ancestry	
American Indian: 1%		German: 22%	
Asian: <1%		English: 12%	
Black/African American: <1%		U.S./American: 11%	
Hispanic or Latino: 1%		Irish: 11%	
Other: 2%		Polish: 8%	
White: 96%		Dutch: 5%	

L   LIGHTHOUSE or LANDMARK

Bill Lupkiwski

The Beaver Island Light Station was built around 1860 and today is part of an 8-building complex owned by the Charlevoix Public Schools that includes a residential alternative education facility. The tower is open to the public.

M   MUSEUMS

Beaver Island *Marine Museum:* an authentic 1906 net shed, fishing, shipbuilding, shipping disasters displays

...*The Old Mormon Print Shop Museum:* 1850 building; King James Jesse Strang, Irish life, musicians, American Indians, artifacts

...*The Protar Home:* hand hewn logs; Dr. Protar served the people of the island well

Boyne City *Historical Museum:* logging, settlers, railroads, an 1800s "dream cabin"

Charlevoix *Harsha House Historical Museum:* 1891 Victorian style house, player piano, 8' Petoskey Stone tower, local history, period rooms

Courtesy of Charlevoix Historical Society

...*Depot Museum:* 1892, restored, home of the Charlevoix Historical Society

East Jordan *Raven Hill Discovery Center:* science, history and art connect for children and adults through hands-on activities and explorations, both indoors and outdoors

...*Portside Art and Historical Society Museum:* 1940s lodge; smelt, fish stories; student docents in period costumes during the Art Fair

St. James *Old Mormon Print Shop Museum:* now the museum of the Beaver Island Historical Society; it tells the strange story of King James Strang as well as other history of the island. See 15H, 15Y.

N NATURAL RESOURCES

Elevation: <600 – 1,400 feet
Physiography: hill-lands

Forest type: maple-beech-birch-hemlock
Public/private forests: 59% of county
Legislatively protected sand dunes: 2,100 acres

Water in county: 8% of county
  Lakes: 40
    ...largest:
      Lake Charlevoix (#4-size/MI), Thumb Lake (#4-depth/MI)
  Rivers: Boyne, Jordan, Pine
  Rivers & streams: 215 miles

Great Lakes islands: Beaver Islands (4)
Great Lakes shoreline: 100 miles of Lake Michigan

Growing season, avg.: 113 days (4-5 temp. zones)
  Last freeze, avg.: May 20 – June 5
  First freeze, avg.: September 10 - October 5
Precipitation, annual avg.: rainfall: 31 inches
              snowfall: 96 inches
Temperature (F), avg.: January: high 28°, low 13°
         July: high 80°, low 55°
  Annual: >90°: 17 days (#2/MI), **<0°:** 18 days
Tornadoes (1930-2010): 4

O ORIGINS

Bay Shore:[u] located on Little Traverse Bay; 1892
Beaver Island: many beavers lived here; <1849
Boyne City:[c] named after a river in Ireland; 1856
Boyne Falls:[v] falls on the Boyne River; 1874

Charlevoix:[c,co] (SHAR la voy) Jesuit missionary Pierre Charlevoix; 1852
East Jordan:[c] east side of the Jordan River; 1873
Ironton:[u] the Pine Lake Iron Co.; 1879
St. James:[u] James Jesse Strang, founder of the Mormon colony on Beaver Island; 1847
Walloon Lake:[u] earliest settlers were from Wallonia, Belgium; <1872

P PARKS

National: 1 **State:** 3 **County:** 1 **Local:** 19
Number of campsites: 850
National: *Michigan Islands National Wildlife Refuge:* since 1942, Gull, Pismire, Hat and Shoe islands have provided habitat for migratory birds and colonial nesting birds. Closed to the public.

State Forest: *Jordan River:* 44,000 acres

...**Campgrounds:** 2
...**Pathway:** 5 miles

State Park: *Fisherman's Island:* 2,700 acres, not an island, but has 5 miles of unspoiled Lake Michigan shoreline with sand dunes, trails, bogs, trees

...*Young:* 560 acres, on Lake Charlevoix, a "best beach" designation; boat, swim, fish, water ski
State Wildlife Area: *Beaver Island Research:* 10,000 acres

County: *Little Traverse Wheelway:* 26-mile, non-motorized paved trail from Charlevoix to Harbor Springs, with boardwalks over bogs, lake access

...*Beaver Island Recreational Trails:* get a map and go explore this historic island

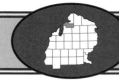
Q QUOTE FROM THE LOCALS

"A setting of natural beauty, a charm that makes people smile – a visit to Charlevoix will convince you that water and land truly couldn't have picked a finer place to meet. Live a memory you'll cherish forever.

"When looking beyond the business of the day, the Charlevoix area provides countless opportunities for fun in the sun, awe amid vibrant fall colors, the thrill of outdoor snow sports and the stillness of woodland wanderings in spring. Each season provides a unique offering of activities that benefit visitors of all ages.

"A love for the water and knowing your neighbor are common denominators for residents and resorters of various backgrounds, interests and stages of life. Despite their differences, these resorters and residents create a fulfilling sense of community. Visitors – whether experiencing Charlevoix for the first or 50th time, easily become part of the social blend."

Charlevoix Area Chamber of Commerce

NPCR

R RECREATION & SPORTS

Blue Ribbon Trout Streams:[1,000] Boyne River
Golf courses: 11
Great Lakes marinas: 29 **Boat slips:** 1,400
Hiking/skiing/mountain biking trails: 110 miles
North Country National Scenic Trail: yes
Off-road vehicle trails: 310 miles
Public access sites: 20
Public recreational land: 20% of county
Rail-trail: (15 miles) Little Traverse Wheelway, Spring Brook Pathway
Recreational harbor: Boyne City Moore Municipal Marina, Beaver Island Municipal Marina, Charlevoix City Marina, East Jordan Municipal Harbor
State/federal wild/scenic/natural river: 70 miles of the Jordan River
State/federal designated wilderness: 12 acres
State-funded snowmobile trails: 10 miles
Beaver Island: Marathon and Half Marathon, Sept.
…The Island Boodle 5K Run: lake and trails, Oct.

Courtesy of Boyne Mountain Resort

Boyne Mountain Resort: all-season vacation resort features 114 downhill ski trails, 8 golf courses and Avalanche Bay, Michigan's largest indoor water park, zip line, much more

Charlevoix Cross Country Ski & Snowshoe Trails: 80 acres, three loops, a lighted trail, rent equipment
Snowmobile Trails (miles): Chandler Hill (34), Charlevoix (19)
Mt. McSauba Ski Hill: city owned, a top ranked small ski area in the USA

S STATE OF MICHIGAN

Lake Michigan Facts
    Size: 6th largest in world
    …3rd largest Great Lake
    Length: 307 miles
    Average depth: 279 feet
    Shoreline (including islands): 1,648 miles
    Special features: world's largest freshwater sand dunes; connected to Lake Huron at the Straits of Mackinaw.
    Borders on: Illinois, Indiana, Michigan, Wisconsin

T TRAVEL

Airports: Boyne City Municipal, Boyne Mountain, Charlevoix Municipal, East Jordan City, Welke, Beaver Island North, Island Airways
Bus: Charlevoix County Transit, Indian Trails
Circle Tour: Lake Michigan via US-31
Distance to Lansing: 190 miles
Ferry: to Beaver Island from Charlevoix
…Ironton Ferry: a four-car cable ferry on Lake Charlevoix connecting Ironton and the direct road to Boyne City; see 15G
Memorial Highways: US-31, *Blue Star MH*: see 3T
…US-131, Green Arrow Route – Mackinac Trail: see 5T
Main roads: US-31, US-131, M-32, M-66, M-75
Scenic Drive: Charlevoix to Harbor Springs via US-31

U UNIVERSITIES & COLLEGES

None

V VARIETY

Mike Barton

The stone houses of Charlevoix are called "Fairy Houses" or "Mushroom Houses" because of their whimsical and irregular shapes. Built of local stones in the early 1900s by a local man, Earl Young, they contribute to the beauty of this area.

W WANDERLUST

Agri-tourism: *Kiteley's Farm Market:* U-pick, strawberries, raspberries, blueberries, veggies, herbs

Fall colors: late September to early October

Lighthouse, other: *Charlevoix Lighthouse:* on the south pier

Walking tours: Charlevoix: Bridge Street, Pine River Channel, Michigan Avenue

Beaver Island is called America's Emerald Isle, unspoiled, unhurried and unmatched in natural beauty. Spend a day or a week absorbing the beauty of land and water, the history, the leisurely pace and the fun shops!

Bullfrog Candle Factory Outlet: top to bottom glow

Castle Farms: a Renaissance castle with magnificent stone towers, beautiful gardens, cobblestone courtyards, maze, garden railroad, open for tours

Bill Luptowski

Dean Ginther

"The Northwest Michigan coastline is known far and wide as the 'Land of the Million Dollar Sunset' and in Charlevoix there are plenty of places to cash in."
Charlevoix Area Chamber of Commerce

X X-TRA STUFF

Commercial port: Charlevoix

Hospital: Charlevoix Area Community

Large employers: East Jordan Iron Works (iron foundry), Boyne USA (hotel/recreation), LexaMar Corp (makes injection molded plastic products), Harbor Industries (makes displays, partitions, fixtures), Grandvue Medical Care Facility, Charlevoix Area Hospital, Honeywell (makes aircraft parts, electricity measuring instruments, etc).

Manhole covers made East Jordan famous.

Y YESTERYEAR

An integral part of the history of this part of the state, including Beaver Island, is "King" James Jesse Strang (1813-1856). A Baptist, a lawyer and a newspaper publisher, among other professions, he converted to the Church of Jesus Christ of Latter Day Saints in 1844, the same year that church founder Joseph Smith was assassinated. Although he wasn't chosen as Smith's direct successor, he did have enough followers and they split from the original church and started their own church, first in Wisconsin and then on Beaver Island. Strang was "king" of his followers and they developed a thriving, although controversial, community on Beaver Island. In 1856, after only six years on the island, some of his former followers assassinated Strang and his 2,600 followers on the island were forcibly evicted. Wikipedia

Beaver Island Historical Society

Z ZOO & ANIMAL PLACES

Petting zoo: *Friske Orchards:* barnyard animals

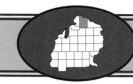
FYI: Whether it is spelled with a "c" like Mackinac County and Mackinac Bridge or with a "w" like Mackinaw City (the only one spelled with a "w"), both words are pronounced exactly the same way. Just remember this simple little rhyme: "I stand in awe of MACK–in-awe."

A AGRICULTURE

Land in farms: 9% of county
Number of farms: 350
Size of average farm: 140 acres
Market value of all products: #57 of 83 counties
Crops: ...most acres: forage crops
...highest $ sales: other crops and hay
Livestock: ...largest number: cattle
...highest $ sales: milk & dairy products
Dairy, food and meat processing plants: 18
State ranking for harvested trees: #19 of 83 counties
FYI: Over 1,000,000 jobs in Michigan are directly related to agriculture (see 1A). These jobs cannot be out-sourced to cheap labor overseas. And during the recent downturn in the economy, the agriculture industry in Michigan did not lose jobs or slow down food production, it increased production.

So if you like/want/must eat, it is mandatory that, as a society, we place a high value on farmland and those who produce our food.

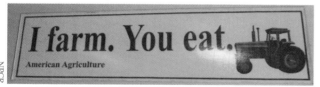

I farm. You eat.
American Agriculture

NPCR

Once farmland is gone, rarely can it be reclaimed for agriculture production again. Once a farmer goes out of business, rarely can he afford to begin farming again (see 29V). Both are limited resources that need to be protected and encouraged. If we, as a state and nation, ever get to the point where most of our food is produced outside of the USA, then we will have very little control over our own lives and destiny, let alone control over the fertilizers, pesticides, sanitation, growing conditions, farm and child labor laws, wages and working and living conditions of those foreigners who are growing and producing the food that we must have.

A strong agriculture production in Michigan and the USA allows our country to be independent and free from foreign control. And that is best for all of us. B VanderMolen

B BRIDGE OR BOAT

The most popular boats in the state are the Mackinac Island ferries, annually carrying 1,000,000 visitors and 600 year-round residents to and from the island.

Arnold Transit Co.

• The Arnold Transit Company's boat is a catamaran.

Sheplers Mackinac Island Ferry

• The Shepler's Ferry will get you to the Island in 16 minutes.

starline@lighthouse.net

• The boats of the Star Line have a 35' Roostertail Spray.
Mackinac Bridge: see 49B

C CELEBRATIONS

FYI: Mackinaw City is in both Emmet County and Cheboygan County. The dividing line is more or less I-75. Emmet County to the west has 80% of the landmass of the city and Fort Michilimackinac. Cheboygan County to the east has most of the downtown area and the docks to Mackinac Island.

Cheboygan *Arts & Crafts Show:* June
...*Summer Concert Series:* June-August
...*Old US-27 Motor Tour:* see 12C
...*Riverfest:* celebrate the Inland Waterway and Cheboygan River; Fish Off cooking competitions, arts & crafts, car show, boat parade of lights, wanigan parade, wanigan & kayak races, Aug.

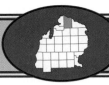
<u>Indian River</u> *Summerfest:* lighted boat parade, car & truck show, beach bash, lobsterfest, pig roast, July

<u>Mackinaw City</u> *Winterfest:* snow carving, sleigh rides, outhouse races, ice fishing, euchre, chili contest, Jan.

...*Mush Dog Sled Race:* Feb.

...*Music in Mackinaw:* summer concerts in the park

...*Arts & Craft Show:* juried, June, Aug.

...*Corvette Crossroads Auto Show:* Aug.

...*Historical Festival:* 1880s baseball, school, Aug.

MDOT Photography Unit

...*International Ironworkers Festival:* friendly competition among the skilled trades, Aug.

...*Labor Day Bridge Walk:* the only day you can walk across the Mackinac Bridge, Sept.; see 49C

...*Big Truck Show & Parade of Lights:* tractor parade across the Mackinac Bridge, Sept.

...*Fort Fright Night at Michilimackinac:* haunted habitat, based on legends of the Fort, Oct.

...*Fort Michilimackinac Pageant:* 400 performers recreate Michigan history of the French, British and American Indians in that area

<u>Wolverine</u> *Lumberjack Festival*: Lumberjack Show, kid's Lumberjack Sport Camp, June

D DEMOGRAPHICS

Population: 26,200   **Persons per sq. mile:** 37
Largest city: Cheboygan   **Population:** 4,870
Largest township: Tuscarora **Population:** 3,040
Largest village: Mackinaw City **Population:** 300
Median household income: $36,900
Owner-occupied median house value: $126,000
Persons affiliated with a religious congregation: 39%
Persons below poverty level: 16%
Students receiving school lunch subsidy: 44%

E ENVIRONMENT

The <u>Michigan Lighthouse Conservancy</u> promotes the preservation of Michigan's lighthouses and life-saving station structures along with the artifacts associated with them. The U.S. Coast Guard has automated all the lights currently in use in Michigan and therefore has no use for many of the unused lighthouses. Without preservation intervention,

these lighthouses will soon vanish due to weather and vandal damage. Many non-profits have been organized to raise money, restore and display this unique part of Michigan and U.S. history. Some lighthouses have been made into museums, some into bed and breakfasts, and some are private homes.

michiganlights.com

F FLORA & FAUNA

Cedar

Alice Welch, USDA

Red Cedar

Alice Welch, USDA

While white cedar trees grow in swamps up north and are used for cabin logs and lumber, the red cedar (really a juniper) grows in the southern Lower Peninsula and is used in the production of cedar chests and pencils.

USFWS

Michigan leads the nation with the most hunters and the largest harvest of the forest game bird, American Woodcock (*MI H&T*). Anyone who walks in the forest also appreciates being able to witness the unique and beautiful courtship flights by the male.

G GOVERNMENT

County: ...created: 1840 **...organized:** 1853
...originally part of: Mackinac County
Size: 510,000 acres / 716 sq. miles (25 of 83 counties)
The county has 1 city, 2 villages, 19 townships, 7 unincorporated communities, 1 Census Designated Place and 3 school districts.

Lynda Tracey

NPCR

County seat: Cheboygan
...Homestead property tax: 38 mills
Motto: Cheboygan County: *Tip of the Mitt*
...Indian River Chamber: *All Trails Lead to Indian River*
...Indian River Visitors Bureau: *Pure Waters. Pure Trails. Pure North.*
...Mackinaw City: *Living History, Making History*
...Topinabee: *The Jewel of Northern Michigan*
...Wolverine: *Home of the Lumberjack Festival*

H HISTORICAL MARKERS 9 of 14

Inland Waterway: the American Indians avoided the treacherous waters of the Straits by using a series of lakes and rivers to get to Little Traverse Bay.

Jessie Jakubik

Jail and Sheriff's Residence: 1880, inmates often did chores for their room and board; the building is now the county historical museum.

Mackinaw City: was home of Ottawa and Ojibwa Indians
• 1715: Fort Michilimackinac built by the French
• 1760: English occupied the Fort
• 1781: English abandoned the Fort and reestablished it on Mackinac Island
• 1847: village was platted
• 1883: incorporated as a village
• 1920s: East and West Michigan Pike brought tourists to the area
Mackinaw City Railroad Dock: prior to 1984, ferry boats shuttled rail cars from Mackinaw City to St. Ignace
Michigan Central Depot at Wolverine: 1906, the railroad promoted Northern Michigan as "curative of hay fever, asthma, bronchial and lung affections" and helped establish Michigan's tourist industry throughout the northern half of the Lower Peninsula.

Michigan State Ferry System: starting in 1923 until the Mackinac Bridge opened in 1957, car ferries were the only way to get from one peninsula to the other; during deer season, 10-hour waits for the ferry were not unusual
Old Mackinac Point Lighthouse: 1889, the light was visible to ships 16 miles away; now it is a maritime museum; see 16L
Old Mill Creek: 1780s, sawmill established to provide lumber for the new fort on Mackinac Island; later included a gristmill, orchard, blacksmith shop and homes. It is now Historic Mill Creek State Park; see 16V
USCG Cutter Mackinaw WAGB 83: 1944-2006, it was able to cut through several feet of lake ice with its six 10-cylinder engines; it is now the Icebreaker Mackinaw Maritime Museum, see 16M
National Register of Historic Places: 10 listings
State Historic Sites: 19 listings

I INFORMATION

Chamber of Commerce: Cheboygan, Indian River, Mackinaw City
Visitor: Indian River Visitors Bureau, 800-EXIT310, irtourism.com
...Mackinaw Area Visitors Bureau, 800-577-3113, mackinaw-city.com

J JOKES

You might be a Michiganian if...

NPCR

...you've never seen a deer crossing the road at one of those deer crossing signs.

...you know Indian River is not the grapefruit capital of Michigan.
...you know that Michigan has more road kill than Texas. They may have armadillos, but we have whitetail deer and opossums.
...you know why Hell and Paradise can be in the same state.
...boats are in your blood.
...you know what paczki's and pasties are, can pronounce them, know when and where to get them, and like them.
...if you know the difference between Cheboygan and Sheboygan.

K KINSMAN

Race
American Indian: 3%
Asian: <1%
Black/African American: <1%
Hispanic or Latino: <1%
Other: 3%
White: 94%

Ancestry
German: 21%
English: 10%
French: 10%
Polish: 9%
U.S./American: 9%
Irish: 9%

L LIGHTHOUSE OR LANDMARK

Prentice Drake

The Old Mackinac Point Lighthouse was built in 1892 and now is part of Mackinac State Historic Parks living history exhibits. It is open for tours and you can climb the tower all the way to the top.

M MUSEUMS

Jessie Jakubik

Cheboygan *County Historical Museum Complex:* log cabin, 1882 Sheriff's Residence and jail, 1912 New Jail, 1997 Spies Hall (for more museum space), tells the story of the rise, fall and rebuilding of Cheboygan

Indian River *Nun Doll Museum:* largest in the world, part of the Cross in the Woods
Mackinaw City *Fort Michilimackinac:* see Emmet County

...Icebreaker Mackinaw Maritime Museum: tour this authentic and retired icebreaker ship

...Old Mackinac Point Lighthouse: see 16 L

Courtesy of Icebreaker Mackinaw Maritime Museum

N NATURAL RESOURCES

Elevation: 600 - 1,000 feet
Physiography: lake-border plains, rolling plains, hill plains

Forest type: aspen-birch, maple-beech-hemlock
Public/private forests: 69% of county

Water in county: 10% of county
    Lakes: 55   **...largest:** Burt Lake
    Rivers: Black, Cedar, Indian, Pigeon, Sturgeon
    Rivers & streams: 420 miles

Great Lakes shoreline: 35 miles Lake Huron

Growing season, avg.: 148 days (7 temp. zones)
    Last freeze, avg.: May 15 – June 15
    First freeze, avg.: August 25 – October 5
Precipitation, annual avg.: rainfall: 28 inches
                           snowfall: 78 inches
Temperature (F), avg.: January: high 27°, low 11°
                    July: high 79°, low 57°
    Annual: >90°: 5 days, **<0°:** 17 days
Tornadoes (1930-2010): 6

O ORIGINS

Afton:[u] a man thought the nearby Pigeon River resembled the Afton River in Scotland; 1887
Aloha:[u] a local man had been to Hawaii; 1903
Burt Lake:[u] Wm. Burt surveyed the area; 1875
Cheboygan:[c,co] (she BOY gun) could be from several Indian words, all with similar pronunciations, meaning "water, sewing needle," or a "place of ore;" 1844
Indian River:[u] the river runs through the city; 1876
Mackinaw City:[v] (MACK in awe) (east of I-75): the English spelling of Mackinac
Mullett Lake:[u] Mr. Mullett surveyed the area; 1849

Topinabee:[u] (TOP in a bee) the Potawatomi chief who gave the land that became Chicago; 1881

Tower:[u] first Michigan woman to be given a military burial, Ellen May Tower; 1899

Wolverine:[v] a mammal and the State of Michigan nickname; 1881; see 9P, 81F

P PARKS

National: 0 **State:** 9 **County:** 0 **Local:** 2
Number of campsites: 2,600
State Forest: Black Lake, Hardwood, Mackinaw

...*Pigeon River Country:* called the Big Wild, 118,000 acres in Cheboygan, Otsego and Montmorency Counties

...**Campground:** 6
...**Pathway:** 90 miles
...*Old Mackinac Point Lighthouse:* see 16L
State Park: *Aloha:* 110 acres, on Mullett Lake, the center of the Inland Lakes Waterways; camping
...*Burt Lake:* 400 acres, part of the Inland Lakes Waterway; 2,000' of beach; trails, camping, fishing
...*Cheboygan:*[ww,wv] 1,250 acres, on Lake Huron; lighthouse ruins, trout fishing in Elliott Creek, camping, trails
State Park, Historic: *Historic Mill Creek Discovery Park:*[ww] see 16V
State Underwater Preserve: *Straits of Mackinac:* 148-square miles in Lake Huron to the east and Lake Michigan to the west; includes 15 shipwrecks and underground geological formations including a 100' rock 'waterfall'
Other: *Inland Waterway:* a 38-mile stretch of rivers and connecting lakes boat route from Lake Huron at Cheboygan to Crooked and Pickerel Lakes in Emmet County. It includes 2 boat locks and places to stop, to eat, to camp or fish along the way. The Indian River, which connects Burt Lake and Mullet Lake, are all part of this wonderful boating opportunity. The river passes under I-75 about a mile north of Exit 310.

Jessie Jakubik

Q QUOTE FROM THE LOCALS

"Lovely surroundings add to the enjoyment of all we do. Mackinaw City offers an abundance of family friendly activities amid an area where nature can be seen at its most magnificent. The Straits of Mackinac itself is spectacular, its deep blue waters dotted with islands. It is a highway between two Great Lakes with green wilderness on both sides, spanned by a great bridge linking two peninsulas. The area boasts twenty-two lighthouses, some historic, some still in the business of protecting sailors from harm. ... There's Mackinac Island, ...there's shopping, ... there's sightseeing. So much to see, so much to do... and so much beauty." mackinawcity.com/visitorguide

"The Cheboygan area...what a delight! Cheboygan is a harbor town for all seasons, with good reasons! Cheboygan hugs the shoreline of Lake Huron and the banks of the Cheboygan River. Boating, fishing, dining, shopping, lodging, hiking, biking, cross country skiing, snowmobiling, hunting,...you'll find it all in Cheboygan." Cheboygan.com

R RECREATION & SPORTS

Blue Ribbon Trout Streams: Black River, Pigeon River, Sturgeon River & West Branch Sturgeon River
Golf courses: 4
Great Lakes marinas: 16 **Boat slips:** 675
Hiking/skiing/mountain biking trails: 160 miles
MI Shore-to-Shore (horse) **Riding & Hiking Trail:** yes
Off-road vehicle trails: 190 miles (#2/MI)
Public access sites: 22
Public recreational land: 36% of county

Rail-trail: (100 miles) (#5/MI) Alpena to Cheboygan Trail, Midland to Mackinac, North Central State Trail

Recreational harbor: Bois Blanc Island Marina, Cheboygan County Marina, Cheboygan Municipal Marina
State/federal wild/scenic/natural river: 50 miles of the Pigeon River
State-funded snowmobile trails: 60 miles
Big Mac Shoreline Scenic Bike Tour: June, Sept.
Mackinaw Bridge Race: run the Bridge, May, October
Zoo-de-Mackinac: 51-mile bike ride followed by huge parties, bands and bar hopping, May

S STATE OF MICHIGAN

According to AAA of Michigan in 2009, the <u>Top 10 driving destinations</u> in the State of Michigan were:

1. Mackinaw City and Mackinac Island (Cheboygan County, Emmet County and Mackinac County)

   FYI: Mackinaw City is also the 7th most popular driving destination in the U.S.

2. Traverse City (Grand Traverse County)
3. Frankenmuth/Birch Run (Saginaw County)
4. Boyne Mountain (Charlevoix County)
5. Dearborn/The Henry Ford Museum and Greenfield Village (Wayne County)
6. Munising (Alger County)
7. Sault Ste. Marie (Chippewa County)
8. Dundee/Cabelas (Monroe County)
9. Saugatuck/Douglas (Allegan County)
10. Lansing (Ingham County)

T TRAVEL

Airport: Cheboygan County
Bus: Indian Trails, Straits Area Regional Ride
Circle Tour: Lake Huron via US-23
Distance to Lansing: 220 miles
Ferry: see 16B
Heritage Route: *Recreational:* Sunrise Side Coastal Highway, see 6T
Lights of Northern Lake Huron Tour: Cheboygan River Front Range Lighthouse, County Historical Museum Complex, Old Mackinac Point Lighthouse, Shepler's Lighthouse Cruises
Main roads: I-75, US-23, M-27, M-33, M-68
Memorial Highways: I-75, *American Legion MH:* see 6T
…I-75, *G. Mennen Williams Hwy.:* "Soapy" Williams (1911-1988) was governor of Michigan from 1949-1961; the Mackinac Bridge was built during his administration.
…I-75, *Prentiss M. Brown MH:* he (1889-1973) was a Michigan U.S. Representative and Senator who is considered the "father of the Mackinac Bridge."
Michigan Welcome Center: Mackinaw City, I-75
Scenic Drive: Cheboygan to St. Ignace via I-75 and US-23

Be sure and stop at the scenic turnout at mile 317 of northbound I-75. It's a great view!

U UNIVERSITIES & COLLEGES

None

V VARIETY

At the Historic Mill Creek Discovery Park, 625 acres, that is part of the Mackinac State Historic Parks, you can hear the rush of water powering a reconstructed sawmill and experience a sawmill demonstration and sawpit method of lumber production. There are also nature trails, a climbing tower, a Water Power Station, a zip line and a naturalist-guided Adventure Tour.

W WANDERLUST

Agri-tourism: *Golden Ripe Orchard:* excellent apples (11 varieties), pumpkins, squash
Fall colors: late September to early October
Lighthouse, other: *Cheboygan Crib, Cheboygan Main, Cheboygan River Front Range, Fourteen Foot Shoal, Poe Reef;* tours available
Live theater: Cheboygan Opera House (1877, restored)
Shopping mall: Mackinaw Crossing

NPCR

NPCR

Walking tour: Mackinaw City Historical Pathway along the waters edge with interpretive signs
Sturgeon River Trips: canoe, kayak, raft or tube

Jessie Jakubik

The National Shrine of the Cross in the Woods: the cross is 55' tall and carved out of one redwood tree and Jesus is a bronze sculpture; staffed by Franciscan Friars.

You can run on the Mackinac Bridge in May, bike it in June and walk it in September.

X X-TRA STUFF

Commercial port: Cheboygan

County Fair: *Cheboygan:* largest fair in northern Lower Michigan, Aug.

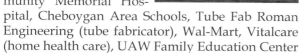

Jessie Jakubik

Hospital: Community Memorial
Large employers: Community Memorial Hospital, Cheboygan Area Schools, Tube Fab Roman Engineering (tube fabricator), Wal-Mart, Vitalcare (home health care), UAW Family Education Center
Cheboygan County has its own Film Industry Support Team.
Great Lakes Boat Building School: to teach quality wooden boat building skills and to preserve craftsmanship
Mackinaw City is not a city, but a village.

Y YESTERYEAR

"From 1841 to 1871 the federal government made land available for $1.25 an acre. Many land grants were made to railroad companies to encourage routes into the forests, thus making new territory accessible for settlements. Some of this land was labeled "swamp," but was, in fact, valuable pine land. Timber cruisers were sent by private investors and speculators to this area to survey and select parcels of the most valuable land for purchasing. These men combed the forest on foot to estimate the yield of timber tracts and assess available river facilities for log drives. Generally, Michigan's white pine was from 15 to 30 inches in diameter and approximately 70 to 160 years old. By 1900 …the stands were depleted and the lumbering industry began its final decline …the results of the philosophy of an 'endless' natural resource." This final decline meant abject poverty for the local residents. cheboygancountymi.org/history

Z ZOO & ANIMAL PLACES

Watchable Wildlife Viewing Areas:ww see16 P
Petting zoo: Cheboygan County Fair
…Indian River Summerfest

Don't forget to check the *BIBLIOGRAPHY & NOTES* at the back of the book for explanations and additional information.

A AGRICULTURE

Land in farms: 18% of county
Number of farms: 450
Size of average farm: 150 acres
Market value of all products: #52 of 83 counties
Crops: ...most acres: forage land
...highest $ sales: grains: corn, wheat
Livestock: ...largest number: cattle
...highest $ sales: milk & dairy products
Among the top Michigan counties:
• #1-short rotation woody crops
Dairy, food and meat processing plants: 5
State ranking for harvested trees: #26 of 83 counties
FYI: Short rotation woody crops are crops that are specifically grown to produce some form of energy. They are considered to be a type of biomass. Biomass is any renewable organic material that can be used to create electricity. Historically, the most common method was the burning of wood. But today, as technology advances, renewable biomass can be converted to liquid fuels and gases that can replace traditional fossil fuels.

Sometimes these crops are grown to produce paper and the waste is used for energy production. Short rotation woody crops include cottonwood, silver maple, black locust, poplar and willow trees. Out of 8,000 acres in the state used for short rotation woody crops, this county has the most acres at around 1,000 acres. See 18F. MDA

B BRIDGE OR BOAT

NPCR

Clare County is famous for its superior lakes. Thousands of tourists are drawn here every year to fish the beautiful waters. Many bring their dinghies with them. These boats are less than 10′ in length and are easy to carry on a car top. They are good for camping trips and for fishing in smaller waters.

C CELEBRATIONS

<u>Clare</u> *Amish Quilt Auction, Antiques, Crafts, & Flea Market:* at Yoder's Amish farm, May & Sept.
...Beat the Winter Blues in Clare!: Feb.
...Irish Festival: Leprechaun contests, bed race, Irish recipe contest, music, dance, March
...Old US-27 Motor Tour: see 12C
<u>Farwell</u> *Lumberjack Festival:* pie eating contest, greased pig contest, skillet toss, chicken chuckin', chainsaw carving, log rolling, lumberjack show, July
<u>Harrison</u> *Frostbite Winter Festival:* snow sculpture, sled judging, parade, soup cook-off, ice fishing, Feb.

D DEMOGRAPHICS

Population: 31,000   **Persons per sq. mile:** 55
Largest city: Clare   **Population:** 3,070
Largest township: Hayes   **Population:** 4,680
Largest village: Farwell   **Population:** 870
Median household income: $32,600
Owner-occupied median house value: $94,000
Persons affiliated with a religious congregation: 22%
Persons below poverty level: 22% (#4/MI)
Students receiving school lunch subsidy: 55%

E ENVIRONMENT

<u>Fuel Saving Tips:</u> help the environment and save money!
1. *Avoid High Speeds:* save about 15% by driving 62 mph instead of 75 mph.
2. *Do Not Accelerate or Brake Hard:* save up to 20% by being slow and steady.
3. *Keep Tires Properly Inflated:* a single tire under-inflated by 2 PSI increases fuel consumption by 1%.
4. *Use A/C Sparingly:* the A/C uses 20% more fuel.
5. *Keep Windows Closed:* open windows on the highway use up to 10% more fuel.
6. *Service Vehicle Regularly:* change that air filter and those spark plugs and keep those fluids up.
7. *Use Cruise Control:* a constant speed saves gas.
8. *Avoid Heavy Loads:* lighten up your life.
9. *Avoid Long Idles:* if you anticipate being stopped for more than 1 minute, shut off the car. Restarting the car uses less fuel than letting it idle for that length of time.
10. *Purchase A Fuel Efficient Vehicle:* a small vehicle with a manual transmission will get the best fuel economy. MichiganGasPrices.com

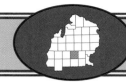

F FLORA & FAUNA

Cottonwood Steve Hillebrand/USFWS

Silver Maple Alice Welch, USDA

Willow Alice Welch, USDA

Short rotation woody crops, such as these cottonwood, silver maple and willow trees, are used for biofuels, bioenergy and bioproducts. They are an economical and sustainable form of alternative energy production; see 18A.

Tom Tetzner/USFWS

Perch can be caught in the many lakes in Clare County and are a favorite dinner entrée at many restaurants. It is the most frequently caught fish in Michigan, both from the inland lakes and the Great Lakes.

G GOVERNMENT

County: ...created: 1840 ...organized: 1871
...originally part of: Isabella, Midland and Mecosta Counties
Size: 369,000 acres / 567 sq. miles (46 of 83 counties)
The county has 2 cities, 1 village, 16 townships, 5 unincorporated communities and 3 school districts.

Sonya Plude

County seat: Harrison
...Homestead property tax: 32 mills
Motto: Clare Chamber: *Up North Begins Here*
…Clare County: *Where the North Begins*
…Farwell Area Chamber: *Remembering the past and looking to the future*

H HISTORICAL MARKERS 4 of 4

Clare Congregational Church: 1909, a Greek cross floor plan that is adapted from fifth and sixth century central plan churches; has a semi-circular roof, European style stencils and stained glass windows from the 1874 church

Michigan State Preservation Office

Harrison: Flint & Pere Marquette Railroad gave a square block to the county for the county seat; named after President William Harrison

NPCR-2

Logging Railroads: after 1870 narrow-gauge railroad lines hauled logs to the sawmills instead of floating them down the river.

Michigan Petroleum Industry: in 1928 Michigan was one of the leading oil producers of the eastern U.S.
National Register of Historic Places: 2 listings
State Historic Sites: 8 listings

I INFORMATION

Chamber of Commerce: Clare, Clare County, Farwell, Harrison
Visitor: Clare County Convention and Visitors Bureau, 989-386-6400, clarecounty.com

J JOKES

You might be a Michiganian if…
…your parents had their honeymoon meal at a Coney Island restaurant.
…you can't understand how people can live in hurricane areas. Blizzards don't destroy your home.

…you've ever worn a snowsuit in the morning and shorts in the afternoon.

…half your friends work at the casino and they're not even American Indians.

…you've picked fresh blueberries the size of acorns and blackberries the size of your thumb.

…it's August and you're sick and tired of hot weather and taking two showers a day.

…you have different hats, coats, outfits and shoes for a 50° day in February, April, July and October.

…you like your swimming and fishing water unsalted.

K KINSMAN

Race
American Indian: <1%
Asian: <1%
Black/African American: <1%
Hispanic or Latino: 2%
Other: 2%
White: 97%

Ancestry
German: 35% (#3/MI)
U.S./American: 14%
English: 13%
Irish: 10%
Polish: 5%
French: 5%

L LIGHTHOUSE OR LANDMARK

NPCR

The MDOT Welcome Center on US-27 in Clare is the unofficial demarcation point between "Up North" and the rest of the Lower Peninsula.

M MUSEUMS

Farwell Area Historical Museum

Farwell *Museum:* 1882 building, formerly the Ladies Library Association, now the Farwell Area Historical Museum Association and Chamber of Commerce

N NATURAL RESOURCES

Elevation: 800 - 1,300 feet
Physiography: hill-lands, upland plains

Forest type: aspen-birch, maple-beech, oak-hickory
Public/private forests: 67% of county

Water in county: 1% of county
 Lakes: 90 **…largest:** Eight Point Lake
 Rivers: Cedar, Clam, Muskegon (muss KEY gun), Tobacco
 Rivers & streams: 330 miles

Growing season, avg.: 126 days (3 temp. zones)
 Last freeze, avg.: May 15 – May 25
 First freeze, avg.: Sept. 20 – Sept. 30
Precipitation, annual avg.: rainfall: 31 inches
                                    snowfall: 52 inches
Temperature (F), avg.: January: high 28°, low 10°
                         July: high 82°, low 56°
 Annual: >90°: 10 days, **<0°:** 17 days
Tornadoes (1930-2010): 9

O ORIGINS

Clare:[c,co] a county in Ireland, 1870
Farwell:[v] Sam Farwell was the son-in-law of the railroad superintendent, 1870
Harrison:[c] U.S. President William H. Harrison, 1877
Lake George: founded by George Lake, 1880

P PARKS

NPCR

National: 0 **State:** 4
 County: 1 **Local:** 10
Number of campsites: 430

State Forest: (51,000 acres) AuSable, Chippewa River

…Campground: 1
 …Pathway: 8 miles

State Park: *Wilson:* 36 wooded acres on Budd Lake, next to the fairgrounds; camping, mini-cabin, tepee

NPCR

Q QUOTE FROM THE LOCALS

"Remember When You...
...drove "Up North" for a long weekend.
...spent a lazy afternoon fishing off the dock.

NPCR

...walked a fragrant wooded trail.
...were greeted on the street with a smile.
...met friends downtown for lunch.
...found a haven of boutique shopping.
Refresh those memories in Clare County!" clarecounty.com

R RECREATION & SPORTS

Blue Ribbon Trout Streams: Cedar River
Golf courses: 5
Hiking/skiing/mountain biking trails: 40 miles
Horse racing: harness racing at the county fair
Off-road vehicle trails: 10 miles
Public access sites: 16
Public recreational land: 14% of county
Rail-trail: (20 miles) Pere Marquette
State-funded snowmobile trails: 30 miles
Snow Snake Mountain Ski & Golf: downhill and cross country skiing, tubing, boarding, terrain park; 18 holes of golf carved out of a hardwood forest

NPCR

S STATE OF MICHIGAN

Go to Michigan.gov/treasury to begin your search for possible unclaimed property. The Michigan Department of Treasury has millions of dollars in lost or forgotten assets from dormant bank accounts, uncashed checks, valuables left in safe deposit boxes and stock certificates. Because the banks or the company entrusted with them consider these properties abandoned and unclaimed, they are turned over to the state, as required by law. The Michigan Department of Treasury is the custodian of these assets and returns them to their owners (or the owner's heirs) when they are rightfully claimed.

T TRAVEL

Airport: Clare County, Clare Municipal
Bus: Clare County Transit, Indian Trails
County road names: ...north/south: Avenues
...east/west: Roads
Distance to Lansing: 90 miles
Main roads: US-27, US-10, M-115, M-51
Memorial Highways: US-127, *Kevin Sherwood MH*: he (1966-2003) was the first Clare County deputy ever killed in the line of duty
...US-10, *Clare County Veterans MH*
Michigan Welcome Center: Clare, on US-27; see 18L

U UNIVERSITIES & COLLEGES

Mid Michigan Community College: est. 1965, 5,000 students. ...to provide educational and community leadership for the development of human ability ...to enable students and the community to achieve success in a global society; M-TEC. Club sports, Lakers

V VARIETY

NPCR

NPCR

Clare County is home to a large community of Amish who enjoy a way of life that is rooted in the land and their community. There are nearly 12,000 Amish residents in Michigan in over 3 dozen communities. Farming is the primary occupation, but construction, farriers, auctioneers and small business owners are well represented. In most communities you can find bakeries, furniture and woodworking shops, general and grocery stores and quilts and handcrafted items for sale. They serve their own people as well as the general public. See 59Q.

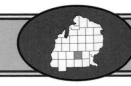
W WANDERLUST

Fall colors: late September to early October
The Clare Police Department owns and operates a bakery called Cops and Doughnuts.

X X-TRA STUFF

County fair: *Clare County Agriculture Society:* Aug.
Hospitals: Mid Michigan Regional Medical
Large employers: Mid Michigan Medical, Renosol (makes vinyl, resins, rubber products), Clare Nursing Home, MidMichigan Community College, Jay's Sporting Goods, Tendercare (skilled nursing), StageRight Corp (makes stage equipment)
The Lincoln-Freeman Storage Field is a depleted gas reservoir converted to storage for natural gas.

Y YESTERYEAR

In May of 1881, Clara Barton, dubbed the "Angel of the Battlefield" during the Civil War, established the <u>American Red Cross</u> in Dansville, NY. Their first disaster relief effort was in September that same year as the Great Michigan Forest Fire burned 70 townships, destroyed over 1,500 homes and left 14,000 people in desperate need of help in the Thumb area of Michigan. Money and supplies came from NY to help the people of Michigan. Working alongside the Port Huron Relief Committee, the Red Cross proved that it could be successful providing relief in times of widespread calamities. The Farwell Museum has displays about the fire and the Red Cross. redcross.org
See 32Y, 58T.

NPCR-2

NPCR-2

Z ZOO & ANIMAL PLACES

NPCR

With 67% of the county as forests that provide habitat for wild animals, there is always the possibility that you will see some anywhere, any time.

From BIBLIOGRAPHY & NOTES…
L LIGHTHOUSE or LANDMARK: When you see "this," you know you're in *this* county!

A AGRICULTURE

Land in farms: 74% of county (3rd of 83 counties)
Number of farms: 1,230
Size of average farm: 220 acres
Market value of all products: #10 of 83 counties
Crops: ...most acres: corn
...highest $ sales: grains: corn, soybeans, wheat
Livestock: ...largest number: cattle
...highest $ sales: milk & dairy products
Among the top Michigan counties:
• #1- chicory, mint, peppermint, spearmint
• #2- milk & dairy products
• #3- cattle, corn for silage, rye for grain
• #7- other crops & hay, sheep, soybeans
Dairy, food and meat processing plants: 13
State ranking for harvested trees: #77 of 83 counties
AgBioResearch Centers (MSU): *Muck Soils Research Center:* 440 acre farm with soil that contains nearly 80% organic matter; carrots, celery, lettuce, onions, potatoes, radishes and sweet corn are the focus of organic soil research in weed, insect and disease control, cultivar evaluations, tillage, crop rotation, subirrigation and nutrient management
FYI: In the 1940s, Michigan was the world's main source of peppermint. But the fungus verticillium wilt nearly wiped out <u>mint</u> production throughout the state. Scientific research has now produced varieties of mint that are resistant to the fungus. Today, St. Johns still calls itself the mint capital of the world with 5,000 acres of peppermint and spearmint crops in the county. Peppermint is named for its pepper-like taste, and spearmint is named for its arrow-shaped flower spires.

Mint leaves are distilled to harvest their oil, a product that is used in many things such as chewing gum, toothpaste, candy and medicine. During harvest in late July and August the fragrant odor of distilling mint is in the air. ^{Michigan.gov}

B BRIDGE OR BOAT

MDOT Historic Bridge: Built in 1901 on Upton Rd. over the Maple River in Duplain Twp., this Parker through truss style that was built by the Detroit Bridge and Iron Works, which built very few metal truss bridges in Michigan. This is the bridge on the seal of the Village of Elsie.

C CELEBRATIONS

<u>Bath</u> *Days Festival:* international bath tub races, parade, fireworks, car show, crafts, Aug.
<u>DeWitt</u> *Ox Roast:* ox burgers, midway, hot air balloon rides, parade, arts & crafts, Aug.

<u>Elsie</u> *Dairy Festival:* in honor of the Dairy industry, July

<u>Fowler</u> *Parade & Festival*
<u>Maple Rapids</u> *Lamplighter Festival:* Sept.
<u>Ovid</u> *Carriage Days:* Sept.

<u>St. Johns</u> *Mint Festival:* mint cooking contest, sports, quilt show, arts & crafts, food, car show, Aug.

...Old US-27 Motor Tour: see 12C

D DEMOGRAPHICS

Population: 75,400   **Persons per sq. mile:** 132
Largest city: St. Johns   **Population:** 7,870
Largest township: DeWitt   **Population:** 14,320
Largest village: Ovid   **Population:** 1,600
Median household income: $58,800 (#2/MI)
Owner-occupied median house value: $169,000

Persons affiliated with a religious congregation: 32%
Persons below poverty level: 8% (#83/MI)
Students receiving school lunch subsidy: 18% (#82/MI)

E ENVIRONMENT

The Michigan Wildlife Conservancy believes that the disappearance of wildlife habitat is a critical problem throughout the state. It does not seek governmental regulation nor does it own or manage land. What it does is provide technical and financial assistance to landowners and managers so they can restore and maintain wildlife habitat on their own land. They are dedicated to the preservation of Michigan's diverse habitats. Their first major wetland restoration project in the early 1980s was the Maple River. With their state office in Bath, they own the Bengel Wildlife Center and provide wildlife education for educators, environmentalists, developer groups, MBA students, local government officials and many more. miwildlife.org

F FLORA & FAUNA

Prentice Drake

One of the first signs of spring is the appearance of the grayish catkins of the pussy willow tree. They are the flower of the species.

Richard Bartlet

The eastern mole is rarely seen, but the evidence of its presence can be very visible. This 6"-8" worm and insect loving insectivore can dig up to 18' per hour in solid earth looking for its food. As they dig, they push the dirt around to create the space for their tunnels. Sometimes these tunnels are visible at the surface. Molehills are the airshaft portion of their underground network of tunnels.

G GOVERNMENT

County: ...created: 1831 **...organized:** 1831
...originally part of: Shiawassee, Kent Counties
Size: 368,000 acres / 572 sq. miles (41 of 83 counties)
The county has 2 cities, 6 villages, 16 townships with 3 as charter townships, 4 unincorporated communities and 6 school districts.

NPCR

NPCR

County seat: St. Johns
...Homestead property tax: 34 mills
Motto: Fowler: *Small Town Big Spirit*
... St Johns: *Mint Festival City*
... Westphalia: *A Family Community*

H HISTORICAL MARKERS 7 of 15

Bath School Disaster: 1927, a school board member uses dynamite to blow up the school, killing 43 people; see 19Y

Gunnisonville: 1853, on land owned by Elihu Gunninson, it was once a proud and thriving community with a community band and historic one-room school that is now a museum.

Joshua Simmons II: 1840, Revolutionary War veteran buried in North Eagle Cemetery

Michigan's Capitol: 1847, when Lansing was chosen as the state capitol, the city did not exist and the first capitol building of 1848 was built in a wilderness [in Ingham County].

Paine-Gillam-Scott House: 1860, restored in 1978, now a museum for the Clinton County Historical Society; see 19M

Philip Orin Parmalee: 1887-1912, early aviation pioneer who took flying lessons at the school run by the Wright brothers; an early innovator of flying techniques, he died in a plane crash.

NPCR

St. John's Church: 1894, neo-gothic style

National Register of Historic Places: 5 listings
State Historic Sites: 28 listings

I INFORMATION

Chamber of Commerce: Clinton County, 989-224-7248, clintoncountychamber.org

J JOKES

You might be from a small town in Michigan if…
…you go to the county fair for your family vacation.
…you know a cow pie isn't made of beef.
…you get up when it's still dark and go to bed when it's still light.
…you know it's a lot more "fun" to watch corn grow than to watch soybeans grow.
…you think a 15 minute drive to somewhere is a long way to go.
…the speed limit doesn't change as the traffic passes through your town.

K KINSMAN

Race
American Indian: <1%
Asian: 1%
Black/African American: 2%
Hispanic or Latino: 4%
Other: 3%
White: 93%

Ancestry
German: 35% (#3/MI)
English: 11%
U.S./American: 10%
Irish: 9%
Polish: 3%
French: 3%
Dutch: 3%

L LIGHTHOUSE OR LANDMARK

NPCR

If this was a scratch 'n sniff book, we could give you the fragrance of mint. But you will just have to settle for this image of a mint distilling operation that produces the mint oil and is the source of the fragrance in the air in mid-to-late summer.

M MUSEUMS

<u>Bath</u> *School Museum*: in the Bath Middle School; history about Bath School disaster

<u>DeWitt</u> *Clinton County Paine-Gillam-Scott Museum:* 3 buildings; property has the largest and oldest magnolia tree in Michigan; see 19H

Laura Hamlin

…*Gunnisonville School*: a one-room schoolhouse that is a living educational museum

NPCR

<u>Elsie</u> *Historical Room:* attached to the library

<u>St. Johns</u> *Clinton Northern Railway:* specializing in 1900s train cars, artifacts; model trains for the public to run

N NATURAL RESOURCES

Elevation: 700 - 900 feet
Physiography: rolling plains

Forest type: maple-beech, oak-hickory, elm-ash-cottonwood
Public/private forests: 15% of county

Water in county: <1% of county
   Lakes: 30   **…largest:** Lake Ovid
   Rivers: Little Maple, Looking Glass, Maple
   Rivers & streams: 320 miles

Growing season, avg.: 148 days (2 temp. zones)
   Last freeze, avg.: May 5 – May 10
   First freeze, avg.: Oct. 5 – Oct. 10
Precipitation, annual avg.: rainfall: 30 inches
                   snowfall: 44 inches
Temperature (F), avg.: January: high 30°, low 14°
          July: high 84°, low 59°
  Annual: >90°: 12 days, **<0°:** 9 days
Tornadoes (1930-2010): 24

O ORIGINS

<u>Bath</u>:[ct,u] for Bath, England, which was named after the mineral baths in that area; 1836

<u>Clinton</u>:[co] NY Gov. DeWitt Clinton; 1837

<u>DeWitt</u>:[c,ct] NY Gov. DeWitt Clinton; 1837

<u>Eagle</u>:[v,t] named for its township;1834

<u>Elsie</u>:[v] name of the first child born in the town; 1857

<u>Eureka</u>:[u] is Greek for 'I have found it' after the town had had four previous names; 1836

<u>Fowler</u>:[v] land owned by Mr. Fowler of Detroit; 1849

<u>Maple Rapids</u>:[v] first settler built his home near the rapids of the Maple River; 1826

<u>Ovid</u>:[v,t] early settlers came from Ovid, NY; 1836

<u>St. Johns</u>:[c] John Swegles named it after himself and a Baptist minister later added the Saint; 1853

<u>Wacousta</u>:[u] (wah COO stah) named after an American Indian maiden who helped thwart an American Indian attack on Fort Detroit in 1763; 1835

<u>Watertown</u>:[ct] named after Watertown, NY; 1841

<u>Westphalia</u>:[v,t] first settlers were farmers from Westphalia, Germany; 1849

P PARKS

National: 0 **State:** 4 **County:** 1 **Local:** 20
Number of campsites: 180

State Game Area: *Maple River:* 4,700 acres, extensive system of wetlands, rugged trails; see 29E

...*Muskrat Lake:* 220 acres, recreational area managed for wildlife habitat and hunting

State Park: *Sleepy Hollow:* 2,600 acres on Lake Ovid and the Little Maple River; summer and winter activities, horse trails, hiking trails, camping

State Wildlife Area: *Rose Lake:*[ww] 4,100 acres, recreation and research area of rolling farmland, oak and lowland woods and marsh; trails, hunting

County: *Motz:* park and facilities were designed for "universal access" for all ages and abilities; lake, picnics, pavilion; a 2010 da Vinci Awards® winner for assistive and adaptive technologies

Local: *Padgett Natural Area:* 70 acres, woods, recreation area, walking and jogging trails

FYI: "Each summer, Michigan's <u>State Park Explorer Programs</u> are offered to campers and day visitors at 41 of Michigan's 97 state parks. Armed with field guides, animal skins, bug boxes and other hands-on materials, state park explorer guides lead informal programs and hikes that feature each location's unique natural, cultural and historic resources. Program topics include forests, insects, night hikes, pond studies and other topics covering the variety of plants, animals and natural features found within each park. These programs are designed for children and adults, often in a family setting." Sleepy Hollow State Park offers this program as a fun summer job for those adults with experience or education in a related field. Michigan.gov

Michigan Department of Natural Resources

Q QUOTE FROM THE LOCALS

"Often referred to as the 'Hub of Michigan,' Clinton County promotes a superb quality of life. Located nearly in the geographic center of Michigan ...it is a great place to live, offering a diversified style of living from rural to in town condos. Housing is ample and affordable. ...It offers its residents stable, established and family-oriented living with access to the cultural and business opportunities of a major metropolitan area. It is a rich and varied agricultural area with about 90 percent of the farmland in the county classified as prime growing soil. The growing of spearmint and peppermint is unique to this area, using the rich black soil that prevails." Clinton County Chamber of Commerce

SLOW DOWN FOR FARMERS
CLINTON COUNTY FARM BUREAU

R RECREATION & SPORTS

Golf courses: 5
Hiking/skiing/mountain biking trails: 30 miles
Public access sites: 6
Public recreational land: 3% of county
The Miracle League of Mid-Michigan: it is committed to providing children and young adults with special needs the opportunity to play baseball in a safe, inclusive, and fun environment, regardless of their abilities.

S STATE OF MICHIGAN

The Michigan State Trunkline Highway System consists of almost 10,000 miles of roads that are maintained by the Michigan Department of Transportation (MDOT).

▪*Interstate Highways:* Designated as I-##, they are always limited access highways. There are 14 in Michigan, with only 3 that actually leave the state. Michigan is a peninsula and most of the highways stop at one of the Great Lakes.

▪*U.S. Highways:* Designated as US-##, can be either limited access 4-lane highways or unlimited access 2-lane or 4-lane roads. Most of these pre-date the interstate system.

▪*State Trunklines:* Designated as M-##, they are not highways or routes or roads, but are called trunklines. They can be concurrent with an Interstate or a US Highway, but most are separate roads. [MDOT]

T TRAVEL

Airport: Capital Region International
Bus: Indian Trails; Clinton Area Transit System (the Blue Bus)
Distance to Lansing: 10 miles
Main roads: I-96, I-69, US-127, M-21
Memorial Highways: I-69, *Purple Heart Hwy.*: see 12T
…I-96, *AmVets MH*: the American Veterans of World War II, Korea and Vietnam, honors all veterans who have served since 1940
…US-127, *Gary Priess MH*: he (1956-2000) was a senior patrol officer with the DeWitt Township Police Department who was killed by a tractor-trailer on US-127
Scenic Drive: see 19V

FYI: Over the years, US-127 has been called, in part or as a whole, proposed, promoted or legalized: Bagley Rd., Center Line Hwy., Fred L. Kircher Freeway., Gary Priess Memorial Hwy., James M. Pelton Firefighters Memorial Hwy., Kevin Sherwood Memorial Hwy., Meridian Road, Townsend National Hwy., Wayne Hwy. and William Howard Taft Memorial Hwy. [Barnett]

U UNIVERSITIES & COLLEGES

Lansing Community College, Clinton County Center

V VARIETY

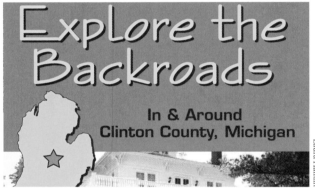

Laura Hamlin

Explore the Backroads In & Around Clinton County Michigan is an excellent online brochure and guide to neat things to see and do in the county. Just go to the Clinton County website to find over 50 unique farms, unusual stores, parks, things to do and places to eat.

W WANDERLUST

Agri-tourism: *Andy T's Farm:* flowers, nursery, corn pumpkins, U-pick, maze, bakers, Christmas trees
…*Peacock Road Tree Farm:* Christmas trees, apples, pumpkins, hayrides, tours, animals, historic cabin
…*Phillips Orchards & Cider Mill:* apples, peaches, pears, melons, potatoes, flowers, market

…*Uncle John's Cider Mill:* apples, cider, bakery, wine, mining sluice, mini-golf, make your own stuffed animal, inflatables, train ride, straw bale maze, apple slingshot, pumpkins, wagon rides, nature trail, car show, arts & craft shows, music

NPCR

...*Wyrick's Orchard:* apples
Cultural: The Depot Center for the Arts
Fall colors: early October
MotorCities National Heritage Area: yes
Shopping Mall: Eastwood Towne Center
Wineries: *Uncle John's Fruit House Winery:* hard cider, grape wines, fruit wines, specialty/honey wines, dessert wines, spirits
Great Lakes Photo Tours: learn to take great images of our beautiful state

Barn art is an American tradition. It's nice to see that this lovely barn and silo, on Grand River Ave. near Portland, still carries on that proud tradition.

Laura Hamlin

X X-TRA STUFF

County fair: *Clinton County 4-H Club Fair:* the fair does not have a midway and is focused solely on the children and their various activities, which gives it its own unique character, Aug.
Famous people: ...*Sports:* Jordyn Weiber
Hospitals: Clinton Memorial, Mem. Healthcare Center
Large employers: Memorial Healthcare Center, St. Johns Public Schools, Mahle Engine Components, Clinton Memorial Hospital, Saylor-Beall Manufacturing (industrial equipment), Wal-Mart, County of Clinton, Keystone Foods (wholesale)

Y YESTERYEAR

Bath School Disaster

"On May 18, 1927, a dynamite blast rocked the Bath Consolidated School, shattering one wing of the building and resulting in the death of thirty-nine children and teachers; dozens more were injured. An inquest concluded that dynamite had been planted in the basement of the school by Andrew Kehoe, an embittered school board member. Resentful of higher taxes imposed for the school construction and the impending foreclosure on his farm, he took revenge on Bath's citizens by targeting their children. Soon after the explosion, as parents and rescue workers searched through the rubble for children, Kehoe took his life and the lives of four bystanders including the superintendent, one student and two townspeople, by detonating dynamite in his pick-up truck as he sat parked in front of the school.

"The destruction of the Bath Consolidated School shared the front page of national newspapers with Charles Lindbergh's transatlantic flight. "Maniac Blows Up School ...Had Protested High Taxes" screamed the headlines of the May 19, 1927, *New York Times.* Michigan Governor Fred Green created the Bath Relief Fund, and people from across the country expressed their sympathies and offered financial support. Michigan U.S. Senator James Couzens gave generously to the fund and donated money to rebuild the school.

"On August 18, 1929, Bath looked to the future and dedicated the James Couzens Agricultural School to its "living youth." A statue entitled, *Girl with a Cat,* sculpted by University of Michigan artist Carleton W. Angell and purchased with pennies donated by the children of Michigan was also dedicated that day."
Michigan Historical Marker

NPCR

During clean up of the school, workers found another 500 pounds of dynamite in the school that had not exploded. In addition, the same morning that he bombed the school, Andrew Kehoe killed his ill wife and set his own home and farm buildings on fire.

Z ZOO & ANIMAL PLACES

Watchable Wildlife Viewing Areas:[ww] see 19P

...*Green Meadows Farms:* it is one of the largest dairy operations in Michigan and the largest herd of registered Holsteins in North America. It is home of the MSU Training Center for Dairy Professionals and has a state-of-the-art manure management system; tours by appointment

NPCR

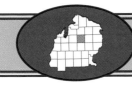
A AGRICULTURE

Land in farms: <1% of county
Number of farms: 40
Size of average farm: 65 acres
Market value of all products: #82 of 83 counties
Crops: ...most acres: forage land
...highest $ sales: other crops and hay
Livestock: ...largest number: laying hens
...highest $ sales: horses, mules, donkeys
Dairy, food and meat processing plants: 3
State ranking for harvested trees: #32 of 83 counties

FYI: The Michigan Farm Market and Agri-tourism Association states, "Agriculture is part of the heritage of Michigan and is the second largest factor in our economy. Michigan farm markets, organic farms, maple syrup producers, wineries and U-pick farms and orchards are all there to welcome visitors for fun on the farm. A tour of Michigan farms could include a creamery, cider mill, petting zoo, pumpkin patch, plant nursery or a tree farm. There is nothing like a day in the Michigan countryside for fresh air, fresh vegetables or maybe a little wine tasting at a Michigan vineyard."

NPCR

Michigan has almost 400 farm markets, ranking it 3rd in the nation. For a statewide, region, county, or product directory, go to michiganfarmfun.com for complete information. Or you can pick up a printed directory at all Michigan Welcome Centers or your local Farm Bureau Office. See *W WANDERLUST* for each county in this book to get a partial listing of farms, orchards and wineries that you can visit.

Jessie Jakubik

Jessie Jakubik

B BRIDGE OR BOAT

Adolph M. Greenert

Jessie Jakubik

The AuSable River Boat dates back to the mid-1800s when this style of boat was used to transport tools and supplies to logging camps. Now these boats are used only on the AuSable and Manistee Rivers for fly-fishing. With flat bottoms and a wide beam, the boat is poled from the rear to move it downstream.

C CELEBRATIONS

Grayling *Woodshaving Days:* historic steam-powered sawmill cutting logs, wood carving, wood burning, woodcrafters, 1800s vintage baseball, July

...*Black Iron Days:* blacksmith skills, weavers & wool spinners, wood carvers & woodcrafters, Aug.

Grayling Visitors Bureau

...*Harvest Fest:* antique tractor parade, fiber arts demonstration, arts & crafts, Oct.

...*Old US-27 Motor Tour:* see 12C

...*Wellington Farms USA Festivals:* Farm by Lantern Light (Dec.), Music concerts (May-Aug.), Dairy Days (June), Punkin' Chunkin' (Oct.)

D DEMOGRAPHICS

Population: 14,100   **Persons per sq. mile:** 25
Largest city: Grayling   **Population:** 1,880
Largest township: Grayling   **Population:** 5,830
Median household income: $36,900
Owner-occupied median house value: $110,000
Persons affiliated with a religious congregation: 24%
Persons below poverty level: 19%
Students receiving school lunch subsidy: 51%

E ENVIRONMENT

Michigan Trout Unlimited is a conservation organization whose mission is to conserve, protect and restore Michigan's coldwater fisheries and their watersheds that support wild trout and salmon. Michigan TU serves as a coordination and communication link between the 21 individual Trout Unlimited chapters in Michigan and the national TU organization. It works to ensure that the importance of wild trout and salmon and their habitats are not forgotten in the many land use and resource issues that threaten our precious wild salmonid resources. It has over 7,000 members that advocate for the prudent management of these resources including on-the-ground stream improvements, angler and steward education, research, partnerships and collaboration with other conservation groups and governmental agencies, and policy development. Trout Unlimited also sponsors a Fly-fishing School and a Youth Trout Camp.

The AuSable River and Manistee River are known world-wide for their trout. Michigan tu.org

F FLORA & FAUNA

NPCR

The white and red pines of the Old Growth stand in the Hartwick Pines State Park, estimated to be around 375 years old, shows us what northern Michigan looked like before the logging era of the late 1800s. See 20M, 20P, 20T.

Jessie Jakubik

Grayling trout, once abundant in northern Michigan streams, is now extinct in Michigan. This was due to deforestation in the late 1800s and the resulting logs that clogged the rivers as well as to the introduction of non-native fish species. See 20H.

G GOVERNMENT

County: ...created: 1840 **...organized:** 1879
...originally part of: Cheboygan, Antrim, Kalkaska Counties
Size: 361,000 acres / 558 sq. miles (56 of 83 counties)
The county has 1 city, 6 townships and 1 school district.

Jessie Jakubik

County seat: Grayling
...Homestead property tax: 40 mills
Motto: Crawford County: *Heart of Northern Michigan*
...Grayling: *The heart of the north; Canoe Capital of the World*
...Grayling Visitors Bureau: *Make Grayling Your Place to Stay*

H HISTORICAL MARKERS 6 of 7

Beginning of State Reforestation: 1903 marked the beginning of replanting and fire protection for the cut-over and burned-over lands of the 1800s; the first state forest was organized in Crawford and Roscommon counties.

Michigan Grayling: these were 12'-15' long fish that had a thyme-like odor, a long wavy dorsal fin, with a gamy but delicious taste; see 20F

Chief Shoppenagon: Chippewa Chief David Shoppenagon came to this area in the 1870s and was a guide for sportsmen; he made canoes and paddles by hand and lived to be over 100 yrs. old.

Jessie Jakubik

Thomas E. Douglas: he owned a sawmill, a general store and blacksmith shop, and in 1916 he built and operated the Douglas House, a sportsmen's club that drew auto pioneers Ford, Dodge and Nash. Today the house is a B & B, the North Branch Outing Club.

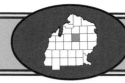

Officer's Club: 1917, is a southern style building built on 14,000 acres donated by Rasmus Hanson; it became part of the Michigan National Guard Officer Corps. See 20L.

32ⁿᵈ Red Arrow Division: in 1917 all of Michigan's National Guard troops were sent to Camp Grayling. While fighting in France in 1918, they earned the name "Red Arrow" for their swift assaults through German lines.

National Register of Historic Places: 3 listings

State Historic Sites: 11 listings

I INFORMATION

Chamber of Commerce: Grayling

Visitor: Grayling Visitors Bureau, 800-937-8837, grayling-mi.com

J JOKES

The Five Rules of Fishing
1. The least experienced fisherman always catches the biggest fish.
2. The worse your line is tangled the better the fishing is around you.
3. Fishing will do a lot for a man but it won't make him truthful.
4. Cook a man a fish and you feed him for a day. Teach a man how to fish and he's gone the whole weekend.
5. Don't use your thumb as a hook holder.

NPCR

K KINSMAN

Race

American Indian: <1%

Asian: <1%

Black/African American: <1%

Hispanic or Latino: 1%

Other: 1%

White: 97%

Ancestry

German: 25%

English: 13%

U.S./American: 10%

Irish: 9%

Polish: 7%

French: 6%

L LIGHTHOUSE or LANDMARK

Michigan State Historic Preservation Office

NPCR

Camp Grayling is a National Guard training facility with 147,000 acres in 3 counties. Much of that land, the Hanson Military Reservation, is accessible to the public for hunting, fishing, snowmobiling and other recreational uses. See 20H, 20S.

M MUSEUMS

<u>Grayling</u> *Bottle Cap Museum:* 10,000 pieces of Coca Cola memorabilia in the Dawson and Stevens Classic 50's Diner

Dawson & Stevens

Cathy Oleniczak

...*Crawford County Historical Museum:* in a restored 1882 train depot, extensive displays of riverboats, home life, Bear Archery, saloon, logging and a 1929 railroad caboose

...*Hartwick Pines Logging Museum:* built by the Civilian Conservation Corps in 1935, it has extensive displays of logging life and work in the 1800s steam-powered sawmill. It is part of the Michigan Historical Museum System. See 20F, 20P.

Michigan State Historic Preservation Office

...*W.J. Beal Tree Planting:* 1888, forest restoration and experimentation of 40 tree species to study how to rebuild the forests after clear-cut logging of the 1800s

...*Wellington Farms, USA:* "Where It's Always 1932;" 60 acres, open-air interpretive museum, features displays, exhibits, natural beauty, authentic in every historical detail; see 20C

Wellington Farms

Jessie Jakubik

Lovells *Historical Society:* Lone Pine School House Museum; Museum of Trout Fishing History: early fishing cabins

N NATURAL RESOURCES

Elevation: 1,110 – 1,300 feet
Physiography: upland-hills, plains, hill-lands

Forest type: pine-aspen, oak-hickory, birch
Public/private forests: 85% of county

Water in county: <1% of county
   Lakes: 40
     ...**largest:** Lake Margrethe
   Rivers: Au Sable (aw SAHBle), Manistee
   Rivers & streams: 200 miles

NPCR

Growing season, avg.: 110 days (1 - 2 temp. zones)
   Last freeze, avg.: May 30
   First freeze, avg.: Sept. 15 – Sept. 20
Precipitation, annual avg.: rainfall: 32 inches
                  snowfall: 93 inches
Temperature (F), avg.: January: high 26°, low 9°
                 July: high 81°, low 54°
   Annual: >90°: 8 days, **<0°:** 8 days
Tornadoes (1930-2010): 9

O ORIGINS

Crawford:[co] Revolutionary War soldier Col. William Crawford was killed in 1782; 1876
Frederick:[u] pioneer settler, Frederick Barker; 1874
Grayling:[c] the abundant grayling trout; 1874
Lovells:[v] 1889

P PARKS

National: 1   **State:** 11   **County:** 1   **Local:** 2
Number of campsites: 1,200
National: *Huron-National Forest:* 38,000 acres, part of 300,000 acres in 5 counties; est. in 1909 on former "logged out" lands that are once again lush forests
State Forest: (167,000 acres) Au Sable
...**Campgrounds:** 14   ...**Pathway:** 11 miles

State Park: *Hartwick Pines:*[ww] 10,000 acres, on the AuSable River featuring Old Growth Pines; logging museum, Michigan Forest Visitor Center; camping, fishing, hunting, trails; see 20F, 20M

Michigan State Preservation Office

Other: *Hanson Hills Recreation Area and Winter Sports Park:* Grayling Recreation Authority has downhill ski areas, year-round sports for all and operates the Grayling Fish Hatchery

Q QUOTE FROM THE LOCALS

"The Grayling area is a sanctuary for those who seek the great outdoors. When you're here, you enter "River Time Zone" – where time has no meaning.

NPCR

Year-round, Grayling offers casual adventures for outdoor enthusiasts. Seventy percent of the land in Crawford County is owned by either the State or Federal government, allowing public access to literally thousands of acres." Grayling Visitors Bureau

R RECREATION & SPORTS

Blue Ribbon Trout Streams:[1,000] AuSable River-Main, South, & East Branches; Big Creek-West & East Branches; Manistee River

Golf courses: 2

Hiking/skiing/mountain biking trails: 175 miles

MI Shore-to-Shore (horse) **Riding & Hiking Trail:** yes

Off-road vehicle trails: 80 miles

Public access sites: 30

Public recreational land: 60% of county

Rail-trail: (60 miles) Aspen, Grayling Bicycle Turnpike, Hartwick Pines, Mertz Grade, Midland to Mackinac

State/federal wild/scenic/natural river: 140 miles (#2/MI) of the AuSable and Upper Manistee Rivers

State-funded snowmobile trails: 85 miles

AuSable River Canoe Marathon: 120 miles, "longest, richest, and toughest canoe race in North America"

The Grayling Visitors Bureau lists the following outdoor activities available in this county:

- *biking:* 8 trails, natural beauty, easy to hilly
- *bird watching:* get out your identification book
- *canoe & kayak:* 3-5 MPH current, beautiful scenery
- *cross country skiing:* 6 groomed areas
- *downhill skiing:* at Hanson Hills; headlight nights
- *fall color tours:* evergreen and hardwood forests
- *fishing:* 100+ miles of cool, clear trout streams
- *geocaching:* over 300 caches within 25 miles
- *golf:* over 30 courses within a 1 hour drive
- *hunting:* deer, hares, squirrel, turkey, grouse, more
- *ice fishing:* lake, bass, bluegill, walleye, pike
- *morel mushrooms:* black, white, yellow, tan
- *motorcycles:* dozens of scenic rides
- *ORV:* 29 miles of the Frederic Loop ORV Trail
- *skijoring:* your dog pulls you on your x-country skis
- *ski walking:* not too much snow, use poles
- *snowmobiling:* thousands of acres, miles of trails
- *snowshoeing:* when there is lots of snow

Forbush Corner Cross Country Skiing: is a unique system of rolling and wooded trails designed for different ability levels

S STATE OF MICHIGAN

The Michigan Army National Guard's mission is to assist the federal government and to protect Michigan. It maintains 60 armories throughout the state. Camp

Grayling, with 147,000 acres in 3 counties, is the largest National Guard training facility in the U.S. where over 10,000 troops from around the Midwest come annually for their military training. It has 600 home-based soldiers and employs 200 local civilians. Michigan.gov See 20L, 20H

T TRAVEL

Airport: Crawford County Air Terminal

Bus: Indian Trails

Distance to Lansing: 140 miles

Main roads: I-75, US-27, M-18, M-72, M-93

Memorial Highway: I-75, *American Legion MH*: see 6T

Scenic Drive: *Virgin Pines Scenic Drive*: an 8-mile loop through Hartwick Pines State Park

…*Old Growth Forest Trail:* 1¼ mile walking loop through the old trees at Hartwick Pines State Park, see 20F

U UNIVERSITIES & COLLEGES

None

V VARIETY

Log buildings, whether large or small or simple or elegant, are used as cabins and homes and for commercial businesses. They are popular throughout

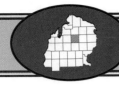

Michigan, but especially "up north," here in Crawford County and the Upper Peninsula. The logs may be of pine or cedar. Each log may be one solid tree trunk or may be laminated for increased benefits. They are milled flat on two sides for ease of stacking and weatherproofing. Interior walls may be the log themselves or drywall. Buildings come in a large variety of kits for the do-it-yourselfer or they may be custom designed for a one-of-a-kind, distinctively unique home.

W WANDERLUST

Agri-tourism: *Grayling Farmers' Market:* fruits, veggies, meat, flowers from the local farmers; see 20A
…*Wellington Farm Park:* maze, pumpkins, corn; see 20M
Fall colors: late September – early October
See also 20R.

X X-TRA STUFF

Hospitals: Mercy
Large employers: Camp Grayling, Mercy Hospital, Crawford AuSable Schools, Springs Window Fashions (makes kiln dried lumber, hardware, millwork), Weyerhaeuser (lumber sawing & planning, wood products), County of Crawford, Centennial Healthcare (skilled nursing)

Y YESTERYEAR

Verse 1 (of 22 verses) of *THE SETTLER'S STORY*, by Will Carlton (1845-1912). See 32X.

"It ain't the funniest thing a man can do –
Existing in a country when it's new;
Nature – who moved in first – a good long while –
Has things already somewhat her own style,
And she don't want her woodland splendors battered,
Her rustic furniture broke up and scattered,
Her paintings, which long years ago were done
By that old splendid artist-king, the Sun,
Torn down and dragged in Civilization's gutter,
Or sold to purchase settlers' bread-and-butter.
She don't want things exposed, from porch to closet-
And so she o'nags the man who does it.
She carries in her pockets bags of seeds,
As general agent of the thriftiest weeds;
She sends her blackbirds, in the early morn,
To superintend his fields of planted corn;
She gives him rain past any duck's desire –

Then may be several weeks of quiet fire;
She sails mosquitoes – leeches perched on wings –
To poison him with blood-devouring stings;
She loves her ague-muscle to display,
And shake him up – say every other day;
With careful, conscientious care, she makes
Those travellin' poison-bottles, rattlesnakes;
She finds time, 'mongst her other family cares,
To keep in stock good wild-cats, wolves, and bears;
She spurns his offered hand, with silent gibes,
And compromised with the Indian tribes
(For they who've wrestled with his bloody art
Say Nature always takes an Indian's part).
In short, her toil is every day increased,
To scare him out, and hustle him back East;
Till fin'lly, it appears to her some day,
That he has made arrangements to stay;
Then she turns 'round, as sweet as anything,
And takes her new-made friend into the ring,
And changes from a snarl into a purr:
From mother-in-law to mother, as it were."

Z ZOO & ANIMAL PLACES

Petting zoo: Wellington Farm Park
Watchable Wildlife Viewing Areas:ww Deward Tract (headwaters of the Manistee River), Fletcher Plains; see 20 P

Grayling Fish Hatchery: raises brook, brown and rainbow trout for stocking the local rivers; you may also fish at the fish hatchery.

A AGRICULTURE

Land in farms: 59% of county
Number of farms: 1,200
Size of average farm: 180 acres
Market value of all products: #32 of 83 counties
Crops: ...most acres: corn for grain
...highest $ sales: grains: corn, soybeans, wheat
Livestock: ...largest number: cattle & calves
...highest $ sales: milk & dairy products
Among the top Michigan counties:
• #2- onions, protected nursery stock, radishes
• #3- maple syrup
Dairy, food and meat processing plants: 35
State ranking for harvested trees: #66 of 83 counties
FYI: Michigan Farm Bureau (MFB) is the premier grassroots farmers' organization in the state with farmer, farm related and non-farm members. There are 67 county Farm Bureaus in the state with members in every county. "Farm Bureau is an independent, non-governmental, voluntary organization governed by and representing farm and ranch families united for the purpose of analyzing their problems and formulating action to achieve educational improvement, economic opportunity and social advancement and, thereby, to promote the national well-being."

MFB is part of the American Farm Bureau Federation (AFBF) that is the nation's largest farm organization. The stated mission of the AFBF is to work through grassroots organizations to enhance and strengthen the lives of rural Americans and to build strong, prosperous agricultural communities.

Farm Bureau Insurance, Michigan's Insurance Company©, is one of the services offered to the members. Michigan Farm Bureau and Farm Bureau Insurance both have their state office in Eaton County. michfb.com

The staff and volunteers of Michigan Farm Bureau worked very hard on obtaining many of the pictures for this book. MFB has generously donated their share of the profits to the Michigan Foundation for Agriculture. (See Acknowledgements at the front of the book.)

B BRIDGE OR BOAT

The Grand Princess Riverboat is available for river tours along the Grand River in Grand Ledge during Island Days. This boat is available for travel to any location for many events around the state as long as there is sufficient water in which to operate.

C CELEBRATIONS

Bellevue *Car, Truck, & Motorcycle Show:* July
...*Antique Tractor Show:* August
Charlotte *Bluegrass Festival:* June

...*Celebrate Charlotte:* a Great Place, music, craft show, hot air balloons, June

...*Frontier Days:* rodeo, parade, saloon, crafts, Sept.

...*Michigan Apple Festival:* at the Country Mill, Sept.

Delta *Rocks:* kids' activities, June
Eaton Rapids *Dam Festival:* on the island, June
Grand Ledge *Winter Thaw:* snow and ice activities, Feb.

...*Yankee Doodle Days:* follies, river activities, June

...*Island Art Fair:* juried arts & crafts, Aug.

...*Color Cruise & Island Festival:* pioneers, Oct.

<u>Olivet</u> *Fire Fighters Fest:* to raise money, July

<u>Potterville</u> *Gizzard Fest:* the one and only, June

<u>Vermontville</u> *Maple Syrup Festival:* locally made sweet treats, April

Prentice Drake

D DEMOGRAPHICS

Population: 107,800   **Persons per sq. mile:** 187

Largest city: Charlotte   **Population:** 9,100

Largest township: Delta   **Population:** 32,400

Largest village: Bellevue   **Population:** 1,280

Median household income: $52,300 (#5/MI)

Owner-occupied median house value: $155,000

Persons affiliated with a religious congregation: 30%

Persons below poverty level: 10%

Students receiving school lunch subsidy: 27%

E ENVIRONMENT

The United States is the #1 trash-producing country in the world. In fact, the average American family of four produces over *three tons*, that's 6,000+ pounds, of garbage annually. CARA, the <u>Charlotte Area Recycling Authority</u>, provides opportunity to recycle some of those wasted resources. They take aluminum (cans, foil, siding, windows, etc.), appliances, athletic shoes, batteries (automotive & household), boxboard, cartridges (ink & toner), cell phones, cooking oil & grease, corrugated cardboard, eye glasses, glass (bottles, cookware, dinnerware, jars, mirrors, etc.), junk mail, light bulbs, magazines, metals (brass, copper, iron, lead, steel, tin, zinc), newspapers, office paper, phone books, plastics (detergent containers, milk jugs, water bottles, etc.), shopping bags, Styrofoam, vinyl siding and more. ^{CARA}

Do what you can, wherever you live, to make your home and our world a better place.

F FLORA & FAUNA

Jan Samenek, State Phytosanitary Administration

Norway Maple

Sugar Maple

Alice Welch, USDA

The Norway maple tree is the most common maple tree in urban areas due to its rapid growth, pleasing shape and ability to withstand city smoke and dust. The sugar maple provides the sap for making maple syrup and the hard maple wood for floors and bowling alleys.

John Collins/USFWS

When they feel their life is in danger, skunks (*MI H&T*) will spray their offensive odorous fluid that causes nausea and burning of the eyes and nose of the attacker. Their only natural enemies are automobiles and large birds since other mammals with a keen sense of smell (except some really dumb dogs) tend to avoid them.

G GOVERNMENT

County: ...created: 1829 ...organized: 1837

...originally part of: St. Joseph, Kalamazoo and Calhoun Counties

Size: 371,000 acres / 576 sq. miles (37 of 83 counties)

The county has 5 cities, 5 villages, 16 townships with 3 as charter townships, 16 unincorporated communities, 1 Census Designated Place and 11 school districts.

County seat: Charlotte

...Homestead property tax: 41 mills

Motto: <u>Bellevue</u>: *Believe in Bellevue*

...<u>Charlotte</u>: *Celebrate Charlotte. It's a Great Place*

...<u>Delta Township</u>: *a great place to live, work and play!*

...<u>Eaton Rapids</u>: *The Only Eaton Rapids on Earth*

...<u>Grand Ledge</u> Chamber of Commerce: *Small Town. Natural Wonders. Endless Opportunity.*

...<u>Potterville</u>: *Home of the World Famous Gizzard Fest*

...<u>Vermontville</u>: *Home of the Maple Syrup Festival*

H HISTORICAL MARKERS 11 of 37

Austin Blair: 1861, Governor of Michigan during Civil War, lived in Eaton Rapids for a few years; see 23Y, 38H

Eaton County: the only county in Michigan with three existing county courthouses: 1845, 1885, 1979

Eaton County Courthouse Square: 1885 courthouse and sheriff's residence; museum, restored

G.A.R.: 1866, Grand Army of the Republic veterans

Fitzgerald Park: "Big rocks," Spiritualist Camp, summer theater

Lauren Dickinson & The Country Capitol: after becoming governor in 1939 at age 80, he conducted much of the state's business out of his farm home in Eaton Township.

Miller Dairy Farm No. 1: 1896, home of the Miller Ice Cream chain of ice cream shops; now owned by the Eaton Rapids Area Historical Society

Olivet College: 1844, Rev. Shipherd and 39 followers arrived by ox-cart to this oak grove wilderness for the purpose of starting a Christian college for all people and races. See 23U.

Red Ribbon Hall: 1878, temperance, no alcohol

Saratoga of the West: 1869, Eaton Rapids had mineral water health resorts.

VFW National Home: 1924, for families of veterans; it is still serving families today.

National Register of Historic Places: 16 listings

State Historic Sites: 59 listings

I INFORMATION

Chamber of Commerce: Bellevue, Charlotte, Eaton Rapids, Grand Ledge, Potterville (Chamber of Business)

Visitor: Greater Lansing Convention and Visitors Bureau, 888-252-6746, lansing.org

J JOKES

You might be an Eatontonian if...

...you know the difference in pronunciation of Charlotte, NC and Charlotte, MI.

...you can locate the only Eaton Rapids on earth.

...you always take a sweatshirt to the beach.

...you prefer pure maple syrup on your pancakes.

...you know how to get to Podunk.

...you know why the head of the chicken was missing.

...you like to eat your way through Eaton County.

K KINSMAN

Race		Ancestry	
American Indian: <1%		German: 24%	
Asian: 2%		English: 13%	
Black/African American: 6%		U.S./American: 11%	
Hispanic or Latino: 5%		Irish: 9%	
Other: 4%		Dutch: 4%	
White: 88%		Polish: 4%	

L LIGHTHOUSE OR LANDMARK

General Motors, LLC 2011

NPCR

The General Motors Lansing Delta Township Assembly plant was built in 2006 with over 3 million square feet of space. It is the only automotive manufacturing facility in the world to receive LEED (Leadership in Energy and Environmental Design) certification for green building design, construction, operations and maintenance solutions. This car on display is the Acadia, assembled at this plant.

M MUSEUMS

<u>Bellevue</u>: artifacts from first county settlement

<u>Charlotte</u> *Courthouse Square:* restored 1885 courthouse, one-room schoolroom, period displays; see 23H

NPCR

<u>Eaton Rapids</u> *Historical Society*: the historical village includes the Miller Ice Cream Factory and Parlor, Miller Dairy Farm with the longest barn in Michigan, the Miller house, Plains Road Church and Wright School.

Grand Ledge Chamber of Commerce

<u>Grand Ledge</u> *Historical Society:* includes a Gothic Revival home that houses the museum, the Opera House, the Grand Ledge Chair Company and the Ledges Playhouse

<u>Sunfield</u> *Historical Society Museum*: to tell our story
<u>Vermontville</u>: tours of local historic sites

N NATURAL RESOURCES

Elevation: 800 - 1,000 feet
Physiography: rolling plains

Forest type: maple-beech, elm-ash-cottonwood
Public/private forests: 22% of county

Water in county: <1% of county
 Lakes: 34 **...largest**: Pine Lake
 Rivers: Battle Creek, Grand, Thornapple
 Rivers & streams: 207 miles

Growing season, avg.: 133 days (2 temp. zones)
 Last freeze, avg.: May 5 – May 10
 First freeze, avg.: Sept. 30 – Oct. 5

Precipitation, annual avg.:
 rainfall: 33 inches
 snowfall: 48 inches

Some summers, like 1988, it just doesn't rain at all.

NPCR

Temperature (F), avg.: January: high 30°, low 13°
 July: high 84°, low 57°
 Annual: >90°: 15 days, **<0°:** 15 days
Tornadoes (1930-2010): 28

O ORIGINS

<u>Bellevue</u>:[v] French for beautiful view; 1835
<u>Charlotte</u>:[c](shar-LOT) wife of Ed Bostwick, one of four men who developed the town; 1835
<u>Delta</u>:[ct] bend in Grand River looked like the Greek letter "delta;" 1842
<u>Dimondale</u>:[v] dam and mill owner Isaac Dimond; 1840
<u>Eaton</u>:[co] John Eaton, U.S. Sec. of War under President Andrew Jackson
<u>Eaton Rapids</u>:[c] Eaton Co. and Grand River rapids; 1838
<u>Grand Ledge</u>:[c] the Grand River with 1 mile of sandstone outcroppings along the shore; 1848
<u>Mulliken</u>:[v] railroad contractor Mr. Mulliken; 1888
<u>Olivet</u>:[c] Biblical Mt. Olives, founded to build a Congregationalist community and college; 1844
<u>Potterville</u>:[c] sawmill owner Linus Potter; 1844

Sunfield:[v] early settler Abram Chatfield filed the paperwork to have the township named after him. By the time it reached Lansing, the ink had smeared. The state clerk couldn't read it, so he called it "Some field," which eventually became Sumfield and then Sunfield; 1836 [Sunfield]

Vermontville:[v] Congregationalists from VT; 1836

P PARKS

National: 0   **State:** 0   **County:** 4   **Local:** 21
Number of campsites: 20

County: *Fitzgerald Park:* 78 acres, 60 ft. sandstone ledge rock formations on the Grand River; walking paths along the river and through the woods and meadows; picnic facilities, ball fields

Prentice Drake

…*Fox Park:* 100 acres, Public Observatory, lake
…*Keehne Environ. Park:*[ww] boardwalk through swamp

…*Lincoln Brick Park:* 90 acres, active beehive

Other: *Woldumur Nature Center:*[ww] 188 acres, fields & forests along the Grand River, interpretive center

NPCR

Q QUOTE FROM THE LOCALS

"Eaton County enjoys a small-town lifestyle in close proximity to the local urban centers of Lansing, Battle Creek, and Grand Rapids. The rolling landscape, picturesque towns, high quality education institutions, a rural way of life, and competent and thoughtful leadership, make it a wonderful place to live and do business." eatoncounty.org

NPCR

R RECREATION & SPORTS

Golf courses: 8
Heritage Water Trail: Battle Creek River
Hiking/skiing/mountain biking trails: 12 miles
Horse racing: harness racing during fair week
Public access sites: 5
Public recreational land: <1% of county
Rail-trail: (5 miles) Paul Henry Thornapple
Alliance Lake Softball Park: 4 fields, lighted
Rock climbing: Grand Ledge has the only public rock-climbing venue in the state.
The Capital Center: a 176,000+ sq. ft. multi-use sports facility; two ice rinks, Aim High Sports basketball center, gymnastics area, multi-use area for a variety of sports

S STATE OF MICHIGAN

<u>What Makes a Great Place</u>? When people roll up their sleeves and get to work to make their community a "place," great things happen.

10 Benefits of Creating a Great Place:
1. There are jobs people want.
2. People are healthy.
3. The community is involved.
4. The environment is sustainable.
5. There is culture and diversity.
6. There are lots of opportunities for entertainment and recreation.
7. People can make good use of their time.
8. People can walk and kids can bike to where they want to go.
9. People feel safe.
10. There's a sense of belonging.

How can this happen?
1. Agriculture plays an important role: celebrate and preserve Michigan's agriculture diversity.
2. Growing Michigan's economy: nurture innovation, learn new skills and create good jobs.
3. Feeling connected: be a part of your community - volunteer, help your neighbor, be generous.
4. Something for everyone: markets, festivals, concerts, recreation. Enjoy each other!
5. Keep it green: trees, flowers, streams & lakes, clean air.
6. Within easy reach: walk, bike, drive, bus; spend less time commuting and more time living
7. Be safe and healthy: walk, talk, exercise, see and be seen, go to the parks, eat well.
8. Celebrating differences: something old, something new, someone old, someone new [MSU Land Policy Institute]

T TRAVEL

Airports: Abrams, Fitch-Beach

Bus: Indian Trails; EATRAN (*EA*ton County *TRAN*sportation Authority)

Distance to Lansing: 20 miles

Main roads: I-496: Ransom E. Olds Freeway, (founder of Oldsmobile Co. in early 1900s); I-69, I-96, M-50, M-66, M-78, M-79

Memorial Highways: M-43, *Frank D. Fitzgerald MH*: from Grand Ledge, (1885-1939) was Michigan's Secretary of State and then Governor who was the only governor to die while in office.

…M-188, *Elgie G. Hanna MH*: the only alumnus of the Veterans of Foreign Wars National Home for Children in Eaton Rapids to be killed in action during the Vietnam War

County road names: …north/south: Roads
                          …east/west: Highways

FYI: Over the years, I-69 has been called, in part or as a whole, proposed, promoted or legalized: Central Michigan International Hwy., Central Michigan Pike, Chevrolet-Buick Hwy., Pearl Harbor Memorial Hwy., Purple Heart Hwy. and Veterans Memorial Hwy. ^{Barnett}

U UNIVERSITIES & COLLEGES

Olivet College: est. 1844; 1,200 students. It is the second oldest college in the nation to admit women and people of all races. The Olivet Plan is a nationally recognized and distinctive approach to liberal arts with an intentional focus on individual and social responsibility. MIAA, Fighting Comets

Great Lakes Christian College: est. 1949; 200+ students. Affiliated with Christian Church/Churches of Christ, it seeks to glorify God by preparing students to be servant–leaders in the church and the world. Intellectual, Spiritual & Personal Growth. NCCAA, Crusaders

From BIBLIOGRAPHY & NOTES…

H HISTORICAL MARKERS: At the discretion of the author, not all historical markers have been included.

V VARIETY

Courtesy of The English Inn

This 10,000 square foot Tudor Revival house on the Grand River was built in 1928 by the president of the Oldsmobile Corporation. From 1940-1962, it was the residence of the Catholic Bishop of Lansing. Since 1989 when it was renovated, it has been the home of the English Inn, where the gracious spirit of the past survives in fine dining, including other opportunities such as overnight accommodations, weddings, banquets and conference facilities.

W WANDERLUST

Agri-tourism: *Country Mill:* apples, cider, bakery, gifts, tours, family fun on the farm

…*Pray Farms:* best sweet corn in town, melons

Cultural: Charlotte Performing Arts Center

Fall colors: middle October

Live theater: Community theater troupes in Bellevue, Grand Ledge, Olivet, Vermontville

MotorCities National Heritage Area: yes

Planetarium: Olivet College

Shopping mall: Lansing Mall

Michigan Back Roads: This website out of Bellevue, michiganbackroads.com, has as its focus the back roads of Michigan where you can find small historic towns, historic destinations, unusual destinations, unique lodging and local shops. The information categories are: Attractions, Books, Festivals, Good Food, Great Shops, Historic Destinations, Lodging, Made in Michigan, Quiet Places, Terrific Towns, Up North, Web Magazine, live Road Trip Shows for groups and organizations and Scenic Drives & Trails. Three books are also available.

Walking tours: Grand Ledge, Charlotte

Whenever you are downtown in any of the many wonderful small cities and villages throughout the state, be sure to LOOK UP and appreciate the architectural details of the buildings that line any Main Street. Notice the many details, the shape of the windows and possibly the eyebrows over the windows. See how many other features you can find that are no longer a part of modern building construction.

Wineries: *Mighty Mac Winery:* apple wine, apple wine with blueberries, cherries or maple syrup
Old Road Dinner Train: Charlotte, murder mystery
The Amish in the area: bakery, oak furniture shop, grocery store, general store

X X-TRA STUFF

County Fair: *4-H Agricultural Society:* the oldest county fair in Michigan, started in 1855, July
Famous people: *...Entertainment:* A. Whitney Brown
...Politics: Elly Peterson
...Sports: Wayne Terwilliger
...Other: Emerson Boyles
Hospitals: Eaton Rapids Medical Center, Hayes Green Beach Memorial Hospital
Large employers: General Motors (car assembly); Meijer Distribution Center, Auto-Owners Insurance, Spartan Motors (makes motor home & fire truck chassis), Hayes Green Beach Memorial Hospital, Magnesium Products of America (makes die-cast auto parts)
Johnson's Workbench: a top leader in providing quality domestic and exotic kiln-dried lumber from around the world, woodworking machinery, tools
Olivet is a college town without a fast food burger restaurant.

The AL!VE Health and Wellness Center in Charlotte, an exciting new venue for wellness, is a destination that refreshes, reassures and reawakens us to a world of creative

well-being. It is the first of its kind in the nation.
The State Secondary Complex is home to a variety of State of Michigan offices, including the Michigan State Police Training Academy. It is secondary to

the primary state offices located in downtown Lansing. Around 3,000 people work there.

The Strange School, on Strange Hwy., is a tuition-free public one-room school for grades K – 5.

Y YESTERYEAR

Austin Blair, 1818-1894, was born in New York and moved to Michigan in 1841 where he lived for a few years in Eaton Rapids. He was elected Eaton County clerk during that time. An attorney, he held various county and state positions and was chairman of the committee that formed the Republican Party in Jackson in 1854, where he was living at the time. He was governor of Michigan from 1861-1865, during the years of the Civil War. While governor, he worked tirelessly raising money to support the 90,000 troops that Michigan sent to support Lincoln and the Union war effort. To show their gratitude for his leadership during those difficult years, the Michigan legislature, in 1895, commissioned a statue in his memory. That statue still stands on the east side of the State Capitol building in Lansing. See also 23H, 33H.

Z ZOO & ANIMAL PLACES

Watchable Wildlife Viewing Areas:ww see 23 P
Petting zoo: *Country Mill:* fishpond too
Sundance Riding Stables: lessons, hayrides

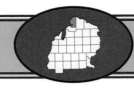

FYI: Whether it is spelled with a "c" like Mackinac County and Mackinac Bridge or with a "w" like Mackinaw City (the only one spelled with a "w"), *both words are pronounced exactly the same way.* Just remember this simple little rhyme: "I stand in awe of MACK–in-awe."

A AGRICULTURE

Land in farms: 13% of county
Number of farms: 290
Size of average farm: 140 acres
Market value of all products: #63 of 83 counties
Crops: …most acres: forage land
…highest $ sales: other crops & hay
Livestock: …largest number: cattle
…highest $ sales: milk & dairy products
Dairy, food and meat processing plants: 14
State ranking for harvested trees: #29 of 83 counties
FYI: How big is an acre? Historically, an acre is about what one man and his ox could plow in one day. Mathematically, it is 43,560 square feet, in any shape whatsoever; a square acre is 209'x209'. Practically, an acre is approximately 91 yards of a football field, or seven city home lots or mobile home lots that are 50'x125' each. There are 640 acres in a square mile.

B BRIDGE OR BOAT

NavSource.org

There have been three ships with the name *USS Michigan.* Launched in 1843 and retired in 1912, this ship was the U.S. Navy's first iron-hulled warship and the only one to cruise the Great Lakes. If you had been on shore in Emmet County in the 1800s, no doubt you would have seen her sailing on Lake Michigan. (The second *USS Michigan* was an ocean-going battleship that operated 1908-1922 and then was scrapped. The third ship, launched in 1980, is a nuclear-powered submarine and is still on active duty.)

C CELEBRATIONS

FYI: Mackinaw City is in both Emmet and Cheboygan County. The dividing line is more or less I-75. Emmet County to the west has 80% of the landmass of the city and Fort Michilimackinac (MISH ill a mack in awe). Cheboygan County to the east has most of the downtown area and the docks to Mackinac Island.

Alanson *Riverfest:* "An Inland Water Route Celebration," storytelling camp, pie eating contest, river stories, boat races, light boat parade, August

Harbor Springs *Taste of Harbor Springs:* Sept.

…*Waterfront Wine Festival:* local music, June
Mackinaw City: *Fort Fright Night at Michilimackinac:* haunted habitat, based on legends of the Fort, Oct.
…*Fort Michilimackinac* (MISH ill a mack in awe) *Pageant:* 400 performers re-create Michigan history of the French, British and American Indians in that area, May
…see also Cheboygan County, Mackinaw City
Pellston *Celebration:* food, beer, parade, June
Petoskey *Art in the Park:* juried, fine art, July
…*Festival on the Bay:* music, sandcastles, cruises, arts & crafts, water events, sunsets, Aug.
…*Winter Blues Festival:* blue night parade, hot-dish cook off, snowman building contest, music, Feb.

D DEMOGRAPHICS

Population: 32,700	**Persons per sq. mile:** 70
Largest city: Petoskey	**Population:** 5,670
Largest township: Bear Creek	**Population:** 6,200
Largest village: Alanson	**Population:** 740

Median household income: $49,000
Owner-occupied median house value: $181,000
Persons affiliated with a religious congregation: 44%
Persons below poverty level: 12%
Students receiving school lunch subsidy: 34%

E ENVIRONMENT

The <u>Little Traverse Conservancy</u> works to protect the scenic and natural character of Northern Michigan. They have volunteers and projects in Charlevoix, Cheboygan, Chippewa, Emmet and Mackinac counties. Since 1972 they have protected over 25,000 acres and more than 70 miles of streams. Projects have included forests, sand dunes, many nature and island preserves, water projects and conservation and farm easements. ltconservancy.org

F FLORA & FAUNA

Choke Cherry

Alice Welch, USDA

Pin Cherry

Alice Welch, USDA

Both the choke cherry and the pin cherry are members of the rose family and are common in burn-over lands and fencerows. The choke cherry fruit is extremely bitter for humans but delicious for the birds. The pin cherry is tart and makes good jelly.

Frank Laubach

Carp can be found in the Great Lakes, inland lakes, ponds and rivers. The several species found in Michigan can grow to be 6-30 pounds. This fish is fun to catch just using canned kernel corn, but they are caught and released because, as bottom feeders, they are not safe to eat.

G GOVERNMENT

County: ...created: 1840 **...organized:** 1853
...originally part of: Mackinac County
Size: 310,000 acres / 468 sq. miles (77 of 83 counties)
The county has 2 cities, 3 villages, 16 townships, 2 unincorporated communities and 5 school districts.

Erika Fettig

NPCR

County seat: Petoskey
...Homestead property tax: 35 mills
Motto: <u>Alanson</u>: *A Place to enjoy... A Place to Remember*
...<u>Emmet County</u>: *Quality of life is everything.*
...<u>Mackinaw City</u>: *Living History. Making History.*
...<u>Pellston</u>: *The Icebox of the North*

H HISTORICAL MARKERS 10 of 18

Andrew J. Blackbird House: 1815-1908, an Odawa Indian educated in Euro-American schools, an author, councilor and a postmaster who helped establish a reservation for his people; see 24M, 7Y

Bay View / Bayview Association:[1,000] >1875, built as a Methodist camp to encourage scientific and intellectual development within a religious community, it now has one of Michigan's most spectacular collections of Victorian era architecture.

Michigan State Preservation Office

Erika Fettig

Ephraim Shay: 1839-1916, invented the popular Shay locomotive that had a patented gear-drive mechanism that revolutionized the logging industry by allowing timber to be cut [and hauled to the sawmill] year-round and not just in the winter; see also 83H, 83Y

Fort Michilimackinac (MISH ill a mack in awe)*:*
- 1715: built by the French
- 1761: British troops took over
- 1763: Chippewa Indians took over
- 1764: British troops got it back
- 1781: British moved to Mackinac Island and the old fort soon reverted to the wilderness; 24L

Grand Rapids & Indiana Railroad Depot: 1889, the railroad opened the Little Traverse Bay area to resort and commercial development.

Harbour Inn: 1900, the deep harbor, pollen-free air, scenic woods and ski resorts of the area attracted visitors who needed a good place to stay.

Holy Childhood of Jesus School: 1829, a school for the American Indians

The Legs Inn: 1930s, named for stove legs that trim the roofline; an eclectic stone and timber building filled with driftwood and tree roots made into fantastical creatures and furniture

Michigan State Preservation Office

Michigan's First Jewish Settler: 1761, Ezekiel Solomon came from Germany, served with the British army, was an active fur trader and owned a general store with several other men.

Passenger Pigeons: this area was a major nesting place for these birds. Millions of these 12"-16" birds were killed, packed in barrels and shipped from Petoskey. Once the most numerous birds in North America, they were extinct by 1914. See 32F.

National Historic Landmarks: Bay View Association; Ernest Hemingway Cottage (Windemere); Fort Michilimackinac (MISH ill a mack in awe); see 24L

National Register of Historic Places: 51 listings

State Historic Sites: 66 listings

I INFORMATION

Chamber of Commerce: Harbor Springs, Mackinaw City, Petoskey Regional

Visitor: Mackinaw Area Visitors Bureau, 800-577-3113, mackinawcity.com

J JOKES

You know it's cold and blowing in Michigan when…
…there's frost on the *inside* of your window.
…the snow makes that crunching sound under your feet and tires.
…teenagers wear hats and gloves.
…the county snow plow drivers take their snow plow trucks home for the night just to keep them warm.
…the de-icing fluid keeps freezing on your car windshield.
…the kids are praying for the snow days to end and to go back to school.
…the snow drifts caused by the wind are more troublesome than the snow itself.

K KINSMAN

Race		Ancestry	
American Indian:	4%	German:	24%
Asian:	<1%	English:	11%
Black/African American:	<1%	Irish:	11%
Hispanic or Latino:	1%	Polish:	9%
Other:	2%	U.S./American:	8%
White:	93%	French:	4%
		Dutch:	4%

L LIGHTHOUSE OR LANDMARK

Kelly Turner

Colonial Historic Michilimackinac (MISH ill a mack in awe) is a 1770s'-era, authentically reconstructed fort with 1 million artifacts and live historical reenactments. It is a Michigan State Park and a U.S. National Historic Landmark that is on the National Register of Historic Places. See 24M.

M MUSEUMS

<u>Alanson</u> *Inland Water Route Historical Society Museum:* preserving the history of the water route, displays and artifacts from all communities on the Route, logging, railroad use, gift shop

<u>Harbor Springs</u> *Andrew Blackbird House:* American Indian artifacts in his home; see 24H

Michigan State Historic Preservation Office

...History Museum: in the former city hall, Odawa Indians, missionaries, homesteaders, loggers, merchants, resorter displays

<u>Mackinaw City</u> *Fort Michilimackinac* (MISH ill a mack in awe)*:* a Michigan Historic State Park with costumed guides and living history demonstrations; see 24L

Prentice Drake

...Mc Gulpin Point Lighthouse Museum: built in 1868, restored in 2009; climb the winding stairs to the top

<u>Oden</u> *Michigan Fisheries Visitor Center:* scale model of Great Lakes watershed, interpretive displays, interactive exhibits, Stream Viewing Chamber; see 24Z

<u>Petoskey</u> *Little Traverse History Museum:* in a large railroad depot, Ernest Hemingway exhibit, extensive photo collection, Victorian parlor

Erika Fettig

N NATURAL RESOURCES

Elevation: 600 - 1,200 feet
Physiography: hill-lands

Forest type: maple-beech-birch-hemlock
Public/private forests: 67% of county
Legislatively protected sand dunes: 3,800 acres

Water in county: 3% of county
  Bay: Little Traverse Bay of Lake Michigan
  Lakes: 20   **...largest:** Crooked Lake
  Rivers: Bear, Carp Lake, Crooked, Maple
  Rivers & streams: 100 miles (#81/MI)

Great Lakes islands: Temperance, Waugoshance
Great Lakes shoreline: 75 miles of Lake Michigan

Growing season, avg.: 158 days (5 temp. zones)
  Last freeze, avg.: May 20 – June 10
  First freeze, avg.: September 15 – October 5
Precipitation, annual avg.: rainfall: 30 inches
                snowfall: 100 inches
Temperature (F), avg.: January: high 27°, low 15°
            July: high 78°, low 58°
  Annual: >90°: 5 days, **<0°:** 1 day (#83/MI)
FYI: Pellston holds the record for Michigan's lowest recorded temperature of 53°F below zero. It has over 40 days per year with temperatures below 0°F while the rest of the county averages 1 day. Beginning in November it averages the coldest temperatures in the state and is one of the coldest places in the nation.pellstonmi.com

Erika Fettig

Tornadoes (1930-2010): 5

O ORIGINS

<u>Alanson</u>:ᵛ railroad official Alanson Cook; 1875
<u>Bay View</u>:ᵘ a grand view of Little Traverse Bay; 1875
<u>Carp Lake</u>: a great quantity of fish in the lake; 1880
<u>Conway</u>:ᵘ the family of Conway Dodge gave a school and church to the community; 1878
<u>Cross Village</u>:ᵘ the Jesuit missionaries erected a large cross on the bluff; <1799
<u>Emmet</u>:ᶜᵒ Irish patriot Robert Emmet
<u>Harbor Springs</u>:ᶜ the harbor on Little Traverse Bay and the many springs in the area; 1742
<u>Mackinaw City</u>:ᵛ (MACK in awe), west of I-75: the English spelling of Mackinac; 1634
<u>Pellston</u>:ᵛ Mr. Pell platted the village; 1882

<u>Petoskey</u>:ᶜ (pe TAH ski) from the name of Odawa Chief Ignatius Petosega who owned the land on which the city was built; 1852

Erika Fettig

P PARKS

National: 0   **State:** 3   **County:** 3   **Local:** 16

NPCR

Number of campsites: 1,000
State Forest: (67,000 acres) Hardwood

State Park: *Petoskey:* 300 acres, sandy beach on Little Traverse Bay, camping, 2 trails, fishing and beautiful sunsets

...*Wilderness:*[ww,wv] 11,000 acres, on Lake Michigan, rustic cabins and bunkhouses, 12 trails, forests; this is one of the unique places in the state where you can watch the sunrise and sunset over the water from the same location.

Sunrise — Prentice Drake

Sunset — Prentice Drake

Same Location — NPCR

State Park, Historic: *Colonial Historic Michilimackinac* (MISH ill a mack in awe): see 24L
County: *Camp Pet-O-Se-Ga:* 300 acres, a 1930s boys' camp, now a historic/modern park
...*Cecil Bay:* 800 acres, 1-mile shoreline on Lake Michigan; fishing, swimming, boardwalk
...*Headlands:* 550 pristine acres with 2 miles of undeveloped Lake Michigan shoreline on the Straits of Mackinac; group facilities, trails

Other: *Inland Waterway:* a 38-mile river and connecting lakes boat route from Lake Huron at Cheboygan to Crooked and Pickeral Lakes; also includes Burt and Mullett Lakes and the Crooked, Indian and Cheboygan Rivers

NPCR

...*Wildflower Blooming Area:* Sturgeon Bay Natural Area

Q QUOTE FROM THE LOCALS

"Many find that the benefits of living in northern Michigan far outweigh the more suburban or even urban settings such as Detroit, Grand Rapids and Chicago. Relocation is common in our area, especially for those wishing to retire or raise a family. Those seeking a more small-town America type of environment where there is greater freedom and safety will find what they are looking for here in Emmet County. Emmet County is proud to be one of the sought-after destination communities located within the Snow Belt. For those who wish to spend their free time sailing the blue waters of Lake Michigan, golfing world class courses, schussing down the slopes, and enjoying all the great north has to offer, Emmet County is their destination."
harborspringschamber of commerce.com

R RECREATION & SPORTS

Blue Ribbon Trout Streams: Maple River
Golf courses: 11; (Bay Harbor, Links, Quarry, Preserve [1,000])
Great Lakes marinas: 6   **Boat slips:** 420
Hiking/skiing/mountain biking trails: 95 miles
North Country National Scenic Trail: yes
Off-road vehicle trails: 40 miles
Public access sites: 7
Public recreational land: 25% of county
Rail-trail: (50 miles) Mackinac Bridge, Petoskey to Mackinaw, Little Traverse Wheelway

Recreational harbor: Harbor Springs Municipal Marina, Petoskey Marina, Mackinaw City Municipal Marina

State-funded snowmobile trails: 115 miles

Dean Ginther

For the best fishing of the day, charter boat fishing trips are usually scheduled to leave around sunrise for the morning trip and return around sunset from the evening trip.

NPCR

Ski Resorts: *Boyne Highlands:* 1,000 with a vertical drop of over 550 ft. for skiing, also offers zipline adventures, Nordic skiing, tubing, snowshoeing, horse-drawn wagon rides, dog sledding and a host of other wonderful four-season activities

Boyne Highlands Resort

Nub's Nob

...*Nub's Nob:* with 53 ski slopes and trails on 3 separate peaks, also offers NASTAR Racing, league and speed series racing and was voted #1 in the Midwest for terrain parks; many more awards

S STATE OF MICHIGAN

NPCR

Since 1965, the Petoskey stone has been the State Stone. It is formed from fossilized coral and is characterized by the six-walled coral structure. It can be found on the beaches of Lake Michigan in the Petoskey and Charlevoix areas and has even been found along the Lake Huron shore as well.

T TRAVEL

Airports: Harbor Springs, Pellston Regional
Bus: Indian Trails, Straits Area Regional Ride
Circle Tour: Lake Michigan via US-31
Distance to Lansing: 200 miles
Heritage Route: *Scenic:* M-119, Tunnel of Trees, 28 miles, Harbor Springs to Cross Village
Main roads: I-75, US-31, US-131, M-68, M-108, M-119

Memorial Highways: US-31, *Blue Star MH:* see 3T
...US-131, *Green Arrow Route– Mackinac Trail:* see 5T
Northwest Michigan Port of Call Tour: Colonial Michilimackinac, Crooked Tree Arts Center, Little Traverse History Museum
Scenic Drive: *Wilderness Park Drive:* from Mackinaw City west to the end of the peninsula

...*Petoskey and Bay View Scenic Drive:* US-31 from Charlevoix to Harbor Springs

Dean Ginther

NPCR

...*Tunnel of Trees:* M-119 between Cross Village and Harbor Springs, a beautiful canopy of mature broadleaf and pine trees surround the road

U UNIVERSITIES & COLLEGES

North Central Michigan [Community] College: est. 1958, 3,000 students. Your growth. Our mission. Offers an exceptional education close to home ... enjoy a small-town setting and unmatched natural beauty while you take the next step ...on your path to success. Gym and fitness center only.

V VARIETY

Erika Fettig

Shopping in downtown Petoskey's Historic Gaslight District is a resort town delight and something everyone looks forward to when they visit this area.

W WANDERLUST

Agri-tourism: *Pond Hill Farm:* your local farm for organic food, flowers and family fun; market, café

Casinos: Odawa Casino Resort

Cultural: *Great Lakes Chamber Orchestra:* performs in the Tip of the Mitt area

…Blissfest Music Organization: to preserve and promote cultural heritage and diversity with a focus on folk and roots music, dance, oral history and crafts from America and all cultures

Fall colors: late September to early October

Lighthouses, other: *Little Traverse Lighthouse:* built in 1884 at the entrance to Little Traverse Bay, it is unique with its rare square pyramidal tower; private property

…Petoskey Pierhead: at the end of the breakwater

… Waugoshance & White Shoal: both can be seen from tour boats

Live theater: *Crooked Tree Arts Center:* in an historic church; art gallery, performances, classes

…Little Traverse Civic Theatre: to enrich, educate and entertain

Walking tours: East Mitchell Street Historic District

Wineries: *Mackinaw Trail:* enhancing life with exceptional wine; in Petoskey and Mackinaw City

…PleasantView Vineyards & Winery: specializes in unusual, eclectic blends from American Varietal grapes; tasting room, B & B

Learn Great Foods: culinary farm tours linking sustainable farming, great cooking & environment

Petoskey Pedicab: rent yourself environmentally friendly transportation

There is a replica of the late 1600s' cross that is planted on the bluff overlooking Cross Village.

X X-TRA STUFF

American Indian Community: Little Traverse Bay Band of Odawa Indians

County Fair: *Emmet-Charlevoix County Fair:* Aug.

Hospital: Northern Michigan

Large employers: Northern Michigan Hospital, Burns Clinic Medical Clinic, Ltbb Gaming (hotel/motel), Bay Harbor Co. (developer), Wal-Mart, Home Depot, Manthei (makes hardwood veneer, plywood), Petoskey Plastics (injection molded plastics)

Bay Harbor was the site of the largest reclamation project in North America. After nearly 100 years of quarrying limestone and cement production, the industrial debris covered 2 square miles that included 5 miles of Lake Michigan shoreline.

Ernest Hemingway spent the summers of his childhood at Walloon Lake.

Petoskey has received the honor of being selected as one of the best small towns in America and one of the best places to retire by the authors of the books *The 100 Best Small Towns in America* and *America's 100 Best Places to Retire.*

Y YESTERYEAR

"In 1851, the Bear River Indians had petitioned the Presbyterian Board for a school for their children. They asked in the petition that the children be taught in English, not in the Indian language, and this was done at Mr. Porter's school. The reports sent back to headquarters during the years indicated that the children were making good progress in writing, spelling, reading and ciphering. The attendance record was not too good. Except for periodic lapses at maplesugaring time, etc. the situation was improved by providing each child with bread and molasses at noon. The Porter women were stuck with the bread-making and as a rule it was a daily chore, twelve loaves a day."

Emmet.migenweb.net The History of the Petoskey Area by Harriet Kilborn

Z ZOO & ANIMAL PLACES

Watchable Wildlife Viewing Areas:[ww] see 24P

Petting zoo: *Pond Hill Farm*

Oden State Fish Hatchery: one of the most advanced fish culture facilities of its kind; Michigan Fisheries Visitor Center; rears brown trout, rainbow trout

A AGRICULTURE

Land in farms: 31% of county
Number of farms: 990
Size of average farm: 130 acres
Market value of all products: #35 of 83 counties
Crops: ...most acres: soybeans
...highest $ sales: grains: corn, soybeans, wheat
Livestock: ...largest number: cattle
...highest $ sales: milk & dairy products
Among the top Michigan counties:
• #1- alpacas
• #2- English walnuts
• #3- organic production and organic acres
Dairy, food and meat processing plants: 34
State ranking for harvested trees: #65 of 83 counties
FYI: The USDA, United States Department of Agriculture, has an annual budget of around $150 billion dollars, or 6% of the entire U.S. Federal Budget. Seventy percent of the USDA budget is for nutrition assistance programs like food stamps and school lunch programs. The balance is for the following programs that help *promote, protect and preserve America's food supply and natural resources*: Forest Service, Natural Resources Conservation Service, Farm Service Agency, Foreign Agricultural Service, Risk Management Agency, Rural Utilities Service, Rural Housing Service, Rural Business Cooperative Service, Food Safety and Inspection Service, Agricultural Research Service, National Institute of Food and Agriculture, Economic Research Service, National Agricultural Library, National Agricultural Statistics Service, Agricultural Marketing Service, Animal and Plant Health Inspection Service, Grain Inspection and Packers and Stockyards Administration. USDA

B BRIDGE OR BOAT

Genesee County Park and Recreation Commission

The Genesee Belle Paddlewheel Riverboat offers sightseeing cruises on Mott Lake of the Flint River.

C CELEBRATIONS

Flint *Back to the Bricks Cruise and Car Show:* 12-mile route, 30+ stops, automotive displays, Aug.
...*Festival of Quilts:* multiple sites throughout the county, demonstrations, sales, raffle, Sept.
Flushing *Cruise Nights:* at the A & W Drive-In Restaurant, monthly, April-Oct.
...*Walleye Festival:* fish the Flint River, outdoor expo, fish dinner, March
Montrose *Blueberry Festival:* 2 parades, mud bog, blueberry baked goodies, music, dog show, Aug.
Otisville *Fun Days Celebration:* a fun event for the entire family, car & truck show, Sept.
Swartz Creek *Hometown Days:* carnival, fine craft show, car show, expo tent, mobile zoo, weekend after Memorial Day

D DEMOGRAPHICS

Population: 425,800   **Persons per sq. mile:** 665
Largest city: Flint   **Population:** 102,400
Largest township: Flint   **Population:** 31,900
Largest village: Goodrich   **Population:** 1,860
Median household income: $41,600
Owner-occupied median house value: $123,000
Persons affiliated with a religious congregation: 37%
Persons below poverty level: 19%
Students receiving school lunch subsidy: 43%

E ENVIRONMENT

Protecting Michigan's Vanishing Native Lakeshore
"Shoreline development along lakes often results in the 'cleaning up' of the lot and alteration of the native vegetation. Trees are cut and pruned while dead trees and fallen limbs are chain sawed and burned. The forest undergrowth is often removed and replaced with a lawn. Herbicides are sometime used to eliminate the shoreline plants. The wild native shoreline is replaced with a highly ordered 'suburban lawn' setting. As a result, many lakes today have little or none of their original native shoreline remaining. The shoreline is a transition zone where aquatic species such as frogs, turtles and fish merge with land species such as minks, raccoons and blue herons. The wild lakeshore is one of the most biologically diverse, plant and animal rich environments on earth and needs to be protected and preserved." MSU Extension

F FLORA & FAUNA

Alice Welch

The American linden tree, also called American basswood, has heart-shaped flowers and the bark of older trees have neat vertical ridges. It is a soft wood that is used for model building, hand carving, and string and wind instruments.

David Menke/USFWS

Bobwhite Quail (*MI H&T*) can be hunted in 27 of Michigan's counties, including Genesee. They thrive in grasslands, brush and young trees, and need cropland as a food source. Although they like to stay under cover, you know they are around when you hear their distinctive "bob-WHITE" whistle.

G GOVERNMENT

County: ...created: 1835 **...organized:** 1835
...originally part of: Lapeer County
Size: 416,000 acres / 640 sq. miles (33 of 83 counties)

The county has 11 cities, 5 villages, 17 townships with 10 as charter townships, 4 unincorporated communities, 3 Census Designated Place and 19 school districts.

Laura Hamlin

County seat: Flint
...Homestead property tax: 48 mills
Motto: Davison: *City of Flags*
... Linden: *Where Yesterday Meets Today*
... Montrose: *Home of the Blueberry Festival*
... Otisville: *Where Life is Worth Living*

H HISTORICAL MARKERS 13 of 57

Buick Motor Company: 1908, was the nation's largest auto factory and made 8,800 cars that year
Buick Open: 1957, the first corporate sponsored PGA Tour event; was won by Billy Casper
Charles Nash: in 1890 he started as a cushion stuffer in Durant's carriage shop; he went on to run General Motors.
Fenton House: 1856, one of the oldest hotels in continuous operation in Michigan
Flint Road Cart Factory/Durant-Dort Carriage Company: 1906, largest producer of horse-drawn vehicles in the U.S., with 56,000 units

The Flint Sit-Down: 1937, for 7 weeks, striking auto workers shut down auto production, resulting in war-like conflicts; General Motors finally accepted the United Auto Workers (UAW) as the workers' bargaining agent; see 25T.

Flint-Genesee County Convention & Visitor's Bureau

Glenwood Cemetery: 1857, features rolling landscape and winding roadways, which were unusual at the time
Henry Crapo: 1804-1869, successful lumberman and railroad developer who became mayor of Flint, a state senator and Governor of Michigan
Resisting Slavery: 1840s, the Genesee County Anti-Slavery Society stood against the evils of slavery.

Sarah Emma Edmonds: 1841-1898, a Canadian woman who joined the Union Army as a man, Franklin Thompson; for 2 years was a successful soldier; 20 years later received an Army pension

Michigan School for the Deaf: 1854, originally the Michigan Asylum for Educating the Deaf and Dumb; "to educate deaf children so they may earn a living …may have culture enough to enjoy that living …(and) may be fitted for citizenship"

Vehicle City: first in the production of wagons and carriages; then became second only to Detroit in the production of automobiles; see 25L

Voiture 1116 40 et 8: WWI veterans formed this chapter of the American Legion; the name means 40 men and 8 horses, which was the capacity of boxcars that they rode in during the war.

Flint-Genesee County Convention & Visitor's Bureau

Monument: 1937 Sit-down Strike; see above and 25T

National Historic Landmark: Durant-Dort Carriage Company Office
National Register of Historic Places: 66 listings
State Historic Sites: 125 listings

I INFORMATION

Chamber of Commerce: Clio, Davison, Fenton, Flint, Flushing, Grand Blanc, Linden-Argentine, Montrose, Swartz Creek
Visitor: Flint Area Convention and Visitors Bureau, 810-232-8900, geneseefun.com

J JOKES

You may be a retiree of the automobile industry if…

…no one wants to hire you because your only skill is putting a bumper on a car.

…you no longer have a union steward to "protect your behind" when you screw up.

…your automotive stock lost 100% of its value.

…you had to say good-bye to that first-class pension and health benefits after the restructuring. But that's OK, Social Security and Medicare will make up the difference.

…you know you will survive because your spouse is employed, and not in the automotive industry.

…you always knew GM really stood for Generous Motors.

…now you realize you should have worn those earplugs the company required you to wear. Huh! Wha'd ya' say?

K KINSMAN

Race		Ancestry	
American Indian:	<1%	German:	15%
Asian:	<1%	English:	9%
Black/African American:	21%	U.S./American:	9%
Hispanic or Latino:	3%	Irish:	9%
Other:	3%	Polish:	5%
White:	75%	French:	4%

L LIGHTHOUSE OR LANDMARK

Laura Hamlin

For over 100 years, Flint has been the Vehicle City. Originally (1899-1940s), there were 7 arches on Saginaw St. that provided lighting and celebrated Flint as the world's largest volume manufacturer of horse drawn carriages. Currently there are 2 replicas of the original arches in downtown Flint, a city that became known for General Motors and Buick vehicles.

M MUSEUMS

Davison *Historical Society & Museum:* to preserve history; wooly mammoth bone, military artifacts

Flint *Children's Museum:* where the power of hands-on play inspires lifelong learning

Flint Childrens Museum. Explore.Play.Learn Kimberly S. Roddy

Flint-Genesee County Convention & Visitor's Bureau

...Institute of Arts: 70,000 works of art from around the world; classes, concerts, lectures, events

...Labor Museum and Learning Center: history of the working class and the labor movement

...Sloan Museum: history of the birthplace of General Motors, world's largest collection of antique Buicks, American Indian and pioneer life, Science Discovery Center, hands-on history experiences

Laura Hamlin

...Stockton Center at Spring Grove: local history, Civil War memorabilia; the first St. Joseph Hospital

...Whaley Historical House Museum: 1885 restored Queen Anne home, history of the family and Flint

Flushing *Area Historical Museum:* in an 1888 restored train depot; museum and cultural center

Grand Blanc *Heritage Museum:* in an 1885 church building; to discover, document, collect, preserve, research and exhibit the history of the area

Montrose *Historical and Telephone Pioneer Museum:* making connections with the past; antique phone equipment, farm implements, household items

Otter Lake *Historical Museum:* in an old fire station

N NATURAL RESOURCES

Elevation: 600 - 900 feet
Physiography: rolling plains, lake border plains

Forest type: oak-hickory, elm-ash-cottonwood
Public/private forests: 2% of county (#82/MI)

Water in county: 1% of county
   Lakes: 80   **...largest:** CS Mott
   Rivers: Flint, Thread
   Rivers & streams: 355 miles
   Waterfall: manmade at Stepping
    Stone Falls

NPCR

Growing season, avg.: 152 days (3
   temp. zones)
   Last freeze, avg.: May 5 – May 15
   First freeze, avg.: Sept. 20 – Sept. 30
Precipitation, annual avg.: rainfall: 29 inches
                  snowfall: 49 inches
Temperature (F), avg.: January: high 29°, low 14°
              July: high 81°, low 59°
Annual: >90°: 8 days, **<0°:** 11 days
Tornadoes (1930-2010): 42 (#1/MI)

O ORIGINS

Burton:[c] local farmer, John Burton; 1831 [wikipedia]
Clayton:[ct] in honor of Rev. Clayton of NY; 1836
Clio:[c] (KLEE oh) Greek goddess of history and poetry; 1837[Clio]
Davison:[c,t] Judge Norman Davison; 1842
Fenton:[c] village platter, lawyer Wm. Fenton; 1834
Flint:[c] from the American Indian word for the rocky bed of the river; 1819
Flushing:[c,ct] early settlers from Flushing, NY; 1835
Gaines:[v] Gen. EP Gaines, a friend of the first settler; 1836
Genesee:[co,t] (gen a SEE) many early settlers from Genesee County, NY; 1833
Goodrich:[v] three Goodrich brothers; 1835
Grand Blanc:[c,t] name given by the American Indians to a husky trader and means 'Big White;' 1823
Lennon:[v] village founder, Peter Lennon; <1880
Linden:[c] the linden tree; 1835
Montrose:[c,ct] man who wanted to impress his Scottish friends by naming the town after a town in Scotland; 1835
Mt. Morris:[c,ct] many settlers from Mt. Morris, NY; 1833
Mundy:[ct] Lt. Gov. Edward Mundy; 1833
Otisville:[v] land owner, Francis Otis; 1851
Otter Lake:[v] many otters in the lake; 1838
Swartz Creek:[c] 'swartz' is German for black; 1836

P PARKS

National: 0 **State:** 1 **County:** 21 **Local:** 45
Number of campsites: 1,300

Laura Hamlin

State Park: *Seven Lakes:* 1,400 acres, farmland, rolling hills, forests and water make an endless variety of topography and ecosystems; camping, fishing, boating, hunting, mountain biking

County: *Crossroads Village & Huckleberry Railroad:* authentic mid-1800's town with 34 buildings offering many activities and rides for all ages including the authentic Baldwin steam locomotive

Laura Hamlin

...*Elba Equestrian Complex:* 4,500 acres, camp with your horse and ride, ride, ride
...*For-Mar Nature Preserve and Arboretum:*[wv] 380 acres, rare trees, 7 miles of hiking trails, Foote Bird Museum, gardens, visitor center, ed. programs

NPCR

...*Holloway Reservoir Regional Park:* 5,500 acres, including Elba Equestrian Complex; beaches, canoe and boat launches, fishing sites, a snowmobile area and toboggan hill and 2,000 acre Holloway Reservoir with its dam on the Flint River

...*The Mounds:* premier off-road vehicle park

FYI: Genesee County has Michigan's largest county park system. It has 21 parks for its citizens and visitors with more than 11,000 acres of woods, rivers, lakes, trails, beaches and campgrounds.

NPCR

Q QUOTE FROM THE LOCALS

"Flint is in transition from an industrial powerhouse to a diverse community with strong colleges and universities, first-class medical facilities and a thriving downtown. Flint was named the "Vehicle City" for its carriage works at the turn of the 20th Century and then became famous as the birthplace of General Motors and United Auto Workers. After decades of decline, Flint now is driving forward again with the entrepreneurial spirit that has always typified America. From the innovative Chevy Volt engine to the unique Swedish Biogas technology, from the fast-growing University of Michigan-Flint to the acclaimed Flint Farmers' Market, Flint has a bright future as the hub of Mid-Michigan." Dayne Walling, Mayor of Flint

R RECREATION & SPORTS

Auto racing: *Auto City Speedway:* ¼-mile and ½-mile paved oval track
Golf courses: 22
Hiking/skiing/mountain biking trails: 15 miles
Public access sites: 5
Public recreational land: <1% of county
Rail-trail: (1 mile) Southern Links
Crim Festival of Races: cultivate fitness as a community and family value, Aug.
Flint Fire: play basketball in the American Basketball Association
Flint Fury: play football in the Mid Continental Football League at Atwood Stadium
Flint Rampage: play football in the United States Football Alliance at Atwood Stadium
Flint Rogues: play rugby in the Michigan Rugby Football Union at Longway Park
Michigan Warriors: play hockey in the North American Hockey League at Perani Arena
The Buick Open, a PGA Tour golf tournament, was held at the Warwick Hills Golf and Country Club from 1957 through 2009.

S STATE OF MICHIGAN

Although Michigan is 11th in size and 8th in population of all U.S. states, it is 2nd in the number of billboards with over 16,000. Many people feel the proliferation of billboards pollutes the visual beauty of the state. In 2007, new legislation was passed that would limit the growth and regulate the environmental impact

of billboards. With the expansion of the Specific Service Signing (logo signs for gas, lodging and food) on the state interstate highways and the blue Tourist-Oriented Directional Signs on the state trunklines, the need for billboards can be

reduced. Some states ban all billboards. In Michigan, certain communities with smaller populations have the right to ban billboards in their jurisdiction. *Scenic Michigan*

On the other hand, many people consider billboards an economic and informational necessity, and enjoy the variety.

T TRAVEL

Airport: Athelone Williams, Bishop International
Amtrak: Flint
Bus: Indian Trails
Distance to Lansing: 50 miles
Heritage Route: *Recreation:* M-15, Pathway to Family Fun, see 9T
Main roads: I-69, I-75, I-475, US-23, M-13, M-15, M-21, M-54, M-121
Memorial Highways: I-69, *Chevrolet-Buick Freeway*: early Flint car manufacturers Louis Chevrolet (see below) and David Buick (see I-475)
…I-69, *Louis Chevrolet Freeway*: he (1878-1941) started the Chevrolet Motor Company in 1911 in Flint, where he designed automobiles and engines; in 1915 he joined William Durant when General Motors was formed
…I-69, *Veterans MH*
…I-75, *American Legion MH*: see 6T
…I-75 & M-57 intersection, *Bernie Bordon Memorial Overpass*: he was born in 1929 in Clio and later received the gratitude of his follow residents when they petitioned to have an overpass named after him.
…I-475, *David Dunbar Buick Freeway*: he (1854-1929) started the Buick (car) Manufacturing Company; in 1908, when William Durant was the manager of the company, it was the #1 car manufacturer in the U.S.
…I-475, *UAW Freeway*: founded in Detroit in 1935, the United Automobile Workers signed their first contract with General Motors in 1937.
…US-23, *United Spanish War Veterans MH*: see 1T
…M-54, *Marine Corps League MH*

…M-54, *UAW Sitdown Strike MH*: in 1937 the autoworkers sat down at their jobs at Chevrolet in Flint and refused to work or leave the plant, resulting in the recognition of the United Automobile Workers as their bargaining agent. See 25H.
…M-121, *Disabled American Veterans Hwy.*: the organization provides help to those who have been injured while on active duty in the U.S. Armed Forces.

Scenic Drive: Bay City to Ortonville via M-15

U UNIVERSITIES & COLLEGES

Baker College of Flint: est. 1911, 35,000 students statewide. It is the largest independent college in Michigan with emphasis on job specific career training; 14 locations plus online degrees.
Davenport University: see 13U
ITT Technical Institute: Of the 125 ITT schools offered in 38 states and serving 80,000 students, there are six campuses and learning centers located in Michigan. It provides accredited, technology-oriented undergraduate and graduate degree programs.
Kettering University: est. 1919, formerly General Motors Institute, 2,600 students. It is ranked #1 in the U.S. for Industrial & Manufacturing Engineering; offers degrees in management, manufacturing operations, engineering and information technology. Intramural sports, Bulldogs
Mott Community College: est. 1923, 12,000 students. With over 100 programs, MCC provides high quality, accessible and affordable educational opportunities and services …that promote student success; M-TEC. MCCAA, NJCAA, Bears
University of Michigan-Flint: est. 1956, 8,000 students. Action-oriented academics are at the heart of the UM-Flint experience with commitment to the development of the next generation of "Leaders and Best." Intramural sports
University of Phoenix: It is the nation's largest private university, specializing in the education of working adults … with degrees that are highly relevant, accessible and efficient… on campus, online, or a combination of both; 11 locations in Michigan.

V VARIETY

Laura Hamlin

The Stepping Stone Falls is part of the C.S. Mott Dam on the Flint River that creates Mott Lake. There are walking trails in the park and the falls are illuminated after dark.

W WANDERLUST

Agri-tourism: *Almar Orchards:* since 1885, some organic, fruits, veggies, market, hayrides, tours
…*Flint Farmers' Market:* open Tuesday, Thursday and Saturday all year
…*Koan's Orchards:* peaches, apples, cider, bakery, country store, maple syrup, festivals
…*Montrose Orchards:* since 1913; apples, asparagus, blueberries, cherries, pears, pumpkins; market and bakery with pies, donuts and bread
…*Trim Pines Farm:* nursery, Christmas trees, hayride and bonfires, organic gardens
Turtlebee & Honeytree Farms: educational classes, field trips, beekeeping, beef, pork, lamb

Flint-Genesee County Convention & Visitor's Bureau

Cultural: *Flint Cultural Center:* includes the Public Library, Sloan Museum, Youth Theatre, Institute of Arts, Institute of Music, Longway Planetarium, Whiting Auditorium
…*Flint Symphony Orchestra:* classical and family concerts
Fall colors: early October
Live theater: Buckham Alley Theatre, Central Academy Theatre, City Theatre, Vertigo Productions, Theatre for Original Productions
MotorCities National Heritage Area: yes
Planetarium: Longway at Sloan Museum

Shopping mall: East Towne, Valley
Walking tour: Flint River Walk, Flushing River Walk
Wineries: *Burton Winery:* Vintner's Cellar make-your-own

Applewood: the 1916 self-sustaining farm estate of the C. S. Mott family, 34 acres, with heritage apples and over 100 different perennials and spectacular gardens; home of the Ruth Mott Foundation; a horticultural laboratory

Flint-Genesee County Convention & Visitor's Bureau

NPCR

Flint weather ball: on top of the Citizens Bank building in Flint; red means higher temps, blue means lower temps, yellow means no change and blinking means precipitation.

General Motors Truck Assembly Tour: 810 232-8902
Krupp's Novelty Shop: the Lawn Ornament Capital of America
US-23 Drive-in Theater: movies begin at dusk.

X X-TRA STUFF

County fair: *Genesee Co. Agricultural Society:* Aug.
Famous people: …*Entertainment*: Sandra Bernhard
Hospitals: Genesys, Healthplus, Hurley, McLaren
Large employers: General Motors, Delphi (warehouse & loading), Hurley Medical Center, Genesys Regional Medical Center, McLaren Regional Medical Center
The 235-acre former automobile manufacturing complex known at Buick City is the USA's largest brownfield.
Great Getaways TV is a television series on PBS featuring travel destinations and outdoor adventures in Michigan, Canada and the northern Midwest. In their travels, host Tom O'Boyle talks to local residents about vacation and recreation opportunities in their area. It is produced in this county.

Y YESTERYEAR

In 1904, successful carriage manufacturer <u>William "Billy" Durant</u> (1861-1947) of Flint invested in the Buick Motor Company and made it very successful. He was the driving force behind the initial success of [Louis] Chevrolet as well and the formation of General Motors in 1913 by merging 13 auto manufacturers

NPCR-2

that included Oldsmobile and Cadillac and 10 parts suppliers such as Fisher Body. His genius was this new concept of an umbrella auto company that allowed many brands of cars with different lines to flourish under its leadership. A rival of Henry Ford, and unlike Ford, he strove to make cars for various income levels and tastes by diversifying styles. After leaving GM, he went on to start his own company, Durant Motors, but it was not successful. He lost his wealth in the 1930s depression and never regained wealth or prominence again.

<u>Charles Stewart Mott</u>, (1875-1973), was a wheel and axel maker in New Jersey when Billy Durant recruited him to come to Flint as an original partner in the creation of General Motors in 1913. He was on the GM Board of Directors for 60 years. Although he was a good businessman, he will be forever remembered for his generous philanthropy through the C.S. Mott Foundation that he started in 1926. The primary grant making program areas for the foundation are Civil

NPCR

Society, Environment, Flint Area and Pathways Out of Poverty. In 2000, the Mott Foundation had estimated assets of almost $3 billion and made over 600 grants totaling $154 million. His legacy continues to live around the world.

Z ZOO & ANIMAL PLACES

Petting zoo: Almar Orchards & Farm, Little Pumpkin Patch, Porter's Orchard Farm Market & Cider Mill, Trim Pines Farm

Watchable Wildlife Viewing Areas:[ww] Grand Blanc Commons

American Association of Riding Schools: all levels, ages, styles

Discovering Michigan County by County is the only book where all counties are treated equal. Every county has a story to tell. There's no other book or online site like it!

A AGRICULTURE

Land in farms: 21% of county
Number of farms: 560
Size of average farm: 120 acres
Market value of all products: #55 of 83 counties
Crops: ...most acres: forage land
...highest $ sales: grains: corn, soybeans, wheat
Livestock: ...largest number: cattle
...highest $ sales: milk & dairy products
Among the top Michigan counties:
• #2- deer
Dairy, food and meat processing plants: 5
State ranking for harvested trees: #33 of 83 counties
FYI: Start2Farm is an online resource for beginning farmers and ranchers sponsored by the USDA's National Agricultural Library and the American Farm Bureau Federation. Education, training, mentoring and outreach materials are available to help those who have decided to pursue a career in agriculture. There is a special focus on beginning farmers and ranchers with limited resources: those who may be socially disadvantaged, immigrant farm workers and other farm workers who want to begin their own operations. This online library also helps support rural development. Start2farm.gov

Jorie Porter/Start2Farm.gov

B BRIDGE OR BOAT

NPCR

The tour boat *Riversong*, docked on Smallwood Lake, used for the Northern Tittabawassee (tit a ba WAH see) River Cruise, was originally built for tours on the historic Erie Canal and Mississippi River.

C CELEBRATIONS

Beaverton *Good Ole' Days:* Aug.
Gladwin *Arts & Crafts Festival:* July
...*Classic Car Show:* July
...*Carriage Festival:* parade of more carriages in one place than you've ever seen before; French and Indian Encampment, Gen. Custer Encampment, carriage rides, horse events, Aug.: see 26V

D DEMOGRAPHICS

Population: 25,700   **Persons per sq. mile:** 51
Largest city: Gladwin   **Population:** 2,930
Largest township: Tobacco   **Population:** 2,570
Median household income: $36,900
Owner-occupied median house value: $119,000
Persons affiliated with a religious congregation: 25%
Persons below poverty level: 19%
Students receiving school lunch subsidy: 47%

E ENVIRONMENT

The Michigan Agriculture Environmental Assurance Program (MAEAP) is an innovative, proactive program that helps farms of all sizes and all commodities voluntarily prevent or minimize agricultural pollution risks. MAEAP teaches farmers how to identify and prevent environmental risks and comply with state and federal environmental regulations. There are three phases of a MAEAP system:
1. education
2. on-farm risk assessment
3. third-party verification

Farmers who successfully complete the program are rewarded by becoming verified in either livestock, farmstead, or cropping. MAEAP was developed by a coalition of agricultural producers, commodity groups, state and federal agencies, and conservation and environmental groups. Look for their signs here and around the state on farms that have completed the program and earned their certification. MAEAP.com

Paul Jackson

F FLORA & FAUNA

Alice Welch, USDA

The beech tree is known for the steel-gray or ash-gray color of its bark, its firm and leathery leaves, its beechnuts as a favorite animal food and its hard wood that is used for furniture, charcoal, chemical distillation and fuel.

Colin Macdonald

The male Ruffed Grouse (*MI H&T*), often called a partridge, makes a distinct drumming sound with its wings that is part of the mating ritual. Listen for it as you walk through the woods in late spring.

G GOVERNMENT

County: ...**created:** 1831 ...**organized:** 1875
...**originally part of:** Saginaw and Midland Counties
Size: 330,000 acres / 507 sq. miles (70 of 83 counties)
The county has 2 cities, 15 townships, 9 unincorporated communities and 3 school districts.

Courtesy of Gladwin County Historical Society

Courtesy of Gladwin County Historical Society

County seat: Gladwin
...**Homestead property tax:** 38 mills
Motto: <u>Gladwin County</u> Chamber: *Near North*

H HISTORICAL MARKERS o

State Historic Sites: 1 listing

I INFORMATION

Chamber of Commerce: Gladwin County, 800-789-4812, gladwincountychamber.org

J JOKES

You may be a Michiganian when all your relatives describe their in-state honeymoon destinations in the following terms. Can you guess where they went?
1. horses, fudge and grand old homes
2. tulips, windmills and wooden shoes
3. cherries, wine tours and sand dunes
4. dogs, grouse and carriages
5. sand dunes, wine and the art coast of Michigan
6. tall ships, blue water and an international bridge
See the end of this chapter for the answers.

K KINSMAN

Race		Ancestry	
American Indian: <1%		German: 28%	
Asian: <1%		U.S./American: 11%	
Black/African American: <1%		English: 11%	
Hispanic or Latino: 1%		Irish: 9%	
Other: 1%		Polish: 7%	
White: 98%		French: 6%	

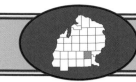
L LIGHTHOUSE OR LANDMARK

NPCR

Unique in the woods and water of Gladwin County is Riverwalk Place on the Cedar River. It offers luxury overnight suites, condominiums, boutiques and shopping, offices, dining and a salon and spa.

M MUSEUMS

Courtesy of Gladwin County Historical Society

Gladwin: *Gladwin County Historical Society:* many log cabins, town tours, scheduled events

N NATURAL RESOURCES

Elevation: 700 - 900 feet
Physiography: lake-border plains, hill lands

Forest type: aspen-birch, elm-ash-cottonwood, maple-beech
Public/private forests: 57% of county

Water in county: 2% of county
  Lakes: 40   **...largest:** Wixom
  Rivers: Cedar, Molasses, Sugar, Tittabawassee (tit a ba WAH see), Tobacco
  Rivers & streams: 470 miles

NPCR

Growing season, avg.: 126 days (4 temp. zones)
  Last freeze, avg.: May 10 – May 25
  First freeze, avg.: September 20 – October 5
  Precipitation, annual avg.: rainfall: 31 inches
                              snowfall: 52 inches
  Temperature (F), avg.: January: high 28°, low 10°
                          July: high 82°, low 56°
    Annual: >90°: 10 days, **<0°:** 17 days
Tornadoes (1930-2010): 10

O ORIGINS

<u>Beaverton:</u>[c] town founders were lumbermen from Beaverton, Ontario, Canada; 1863
<u>Gladwin:</u>[c,co] British Maj. Henry Gladwin, who in 1763, protected Fort Detroit from Indian assaults; 1875
<u>Winegars:</u>[u] local landowner W.S. Winegar; 1888

P PARKS

National: 0   **State:** 3   **County:** 1   **Local:** 4
Number of campsites: 660
State Forest: *Tittabawassee River:* 86,000 acres
...Campground: 3   **...Pathway:** 3 miles
State Game Area: *Gladwin Game Refuge:* 35,000 acres
Local: *Gladwin City Park and Campground:* on the Cedar River, swimming, tennis & basketball courts

Other: *Gladwin Field Trial Area:* dogs hunting for wild grouse in sanctioned events; nationally acclaimed; part of the Gladwin Game Refuge

Sonya Plude

Q QUOTE FROM THE LOCALS

"Not on the way to anywhere and not a quick stop off an expressway, Gladwin County is a special destination awaiting those who would like to visit, live or do business in a great rural community in the 'Near North.'

"Visitors and residents find hunting, hiking, color tours, photography, riding ORVs and snowmobiles, and just plain exploring favorite pastimes in the woods, while others find enjoyment in fishing, boating, canoeing, kayaking, tubing and swimming on nearly 50 lakes and over 400 miles of streams. Manufacturing, agriculture, retail and service industries are strong mainstays in a community filled with good, hard-working people." Tom Tucholski, Gladwin County Chamber of Commerce President

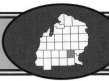
R RECREATION & SPORTS

Blue Ribbon Trout Streams: Cedar River
Golf courses: 3
Hiking/skiing/mountain biking trails: 40 miles
Horse racing: harness racing at the county fair
Off-road vehicle trails: 90 miles
Public access sites: 12
Public recreational land: 26% of county
Rail-trail: (40 miles) Midland to Mackinac

NPCR

Lost Arrow Resort: "The Closet Place to Far Away;" guided deer and pheasant hunts, shooting range, fishing, hayrides, river cruise, pool, restaurant

Gladwin Community Arena: ice-skating for all ages and events; roller skating, basketball, fitness center

Sugar Springs: "Mid Michigan's Finest Recreational Community;" 4,000 acres, 2 all-sport lakes, championship golf course, 1,200 home sites

Larry M. Fees

S STATE OF MICHIGAN

In 2005, the top Michigan manufacturing sectors were (in descending order of number of employees):
1. transportation equipment (198,000 employees)
2. fabricated metal products
3. machinery
4. plastic and rubber products
5. food
6. chemicals
7. primary metals
8. furniture and related products
9. printing and related support activities
10. computer and electronic products
11. nonmetallic mineral products
12. paper
13. wood products
14. electrical equipment, appliance and components (11,500 employees)

In 2007, the top 5 counties with the highest employment in the manufacturing sector (Wayne, Macomb, Kent, Oakland, Ottawa) accounted for 52% of all the manufacturing jobs in Michigan. [Schaetzl] Gladwin County is an important part of the machinery manufacturing sector; see 26X.

T TRAVEL

Airport: Gladwin Zettel Memorial
Bus: Gladwin City/County Transportation
Distance to Lansing: 110 miles
Main roads: M-18, M-30, M-61

U UNIVERSITIES & COLLEGES

None

V VARIETY

Bob Frei

The parade at the Carriage Festival Parade is the old-fashioned equivalent of the modern day car show. This is the way it used to be when everyone had a horse and buggy for transportation.

W WANDERLUST

Agri-tourism: *Fruitful Orchard & Cider Mill:* 30 kinds of apples, bakery, country store, tours
…The Wild Pumpkin: pumpkins, giant pumpkins, corn & straw maze, spend the day on the farm
Cultural: Gladwin Council of the Arts
Fall colors: late September to early October
Live theater: Gladwin Area Friends of the Theatre

Walking tours: Riverwalk in Gladwin

Nancy Buzzell

Stone Cottage Garden: specializes in hybrid daylilies and all varieties of perennials; tranquil and display gardens surrounding the old stone cottage

X X-TRA STUFF

County fair: *Gladwin County Fair Assoc.:* July
Famous people: *...Politics:* Debbie Stabenow
Hospitals: Mid Michigan Medical Center-Gladwin
Large employers: Gladwin Community Schools, Brown Machine (makes printing and plastic working machinery), Mid Michigan Medical Center-Gladwin, Lyle Industries (makes plastic working machinery and metal forming machine tools), Mid Michigan Gladwin Pines (nursing home), Gladwin County
FYI: Oil was discovered in Gladwin County in the 1930s. One of the by-products of petroleum is plastic. Dow Chemical Company, a major developer and manufacturer of plastics, is in Bay County adjacent to Gladwin County on its southeastern border. The process of making plastic items is called thermoforming. To make a plastic item is to (1) heat a sheet of plastic, (2) use heat and pressure to form that plastic into a shape on a mold and (3) trim off the excess plastic. In the 1940s Gaylord Brown and others turned Gladwin County and Beaverton into the Thermoforming Capital of the World by making the machines that made the plastic items. Today this is still an important industry in this area; see 26S. Sigsby

Y YESTERYEAR

During the past 100 years or so, invasive pests have played havoc with the trees in Michigan as well as the U.S. and Canada.

- From 1900 to 1940, 4 billion American chestnut trees were wiped out nationwide due to fungus blight. Chestnut was a superior building lumber; many old split rail fences were chestnut.
- Starting in 1928 and peaking in the 1950s, a fungus spread by beetles wiped out 90% of the elm trees. Cities had planted this type of tree by the thousands (Detroit planted 400,000) because they were fast growing and provided stately, cathedral-like shade canopies.
- Introduced into the U.S. in the 1990s, the emerald ash borer has the potential to wipe out 700 million ash trees in Michigan alone before it runs its course. It takes only 5 years for a tree to die. If you see a dead tree that still has most of its branches, it's probably an ash tree. In many urban areas, 10-25% of the trees are ash.

Dead trees become a hazard as they fall on houses and power lines. Removal is expensive for both homeowners and municipalities. But for those who cut their own and burn wood to heat their home, there will be good supply of free wood for years to come. When you travel, please remember: Don't Move Firewood. See emeraldashborer.info/Michiganinfo.cfm for complete information on this on-going environmental hazard.

Many research universities are actively involved in developing disease resistant varieties of these popular and beautiful trees.

Z ZOO & ANIMAL PLACES

Petting Zoo: *Aunt Tudes Petting Farm:* farm animals, wool, crafts, mazes & crafts
...The Wild Pumpkin Farm: fall fun on the farm

(J JOKES)

Answers: 1. Mackinac Island, Mackinac County
2. Holland, Ottawa County
3. Traverse City, Grand Traverse County
4. Gladwin, Gladwin County
5. Saugatuck, Allegan County
6. Port Huron, St. Clair County

A AGRICULTURE

Land in farms: 20% of county
Number of farms: 520
Size of average farm: 120 acres
Market value of all products: #50 of 83 counties
Crops: ...most acres: forage crops
...highest $ sales: fruits: sweet and tart cherries
Livestock: ...largest number: colonies of bees
...highest $ sales: cattle
Among the top Michigan counties:
- #2- sweet cherries, pears
- #3- pounds of honey
- #4- colonies of bees, tart cherries

Old Mission Peninsula American Viticulture Area: 19,000 acres, U.S. government designated wine grape-growing area
Dairy, food and meat processing plants: 56
State ranking for harvested trees: #43 of 83 counties
AgBioResearch Centers (MSU): *Northwest Michigan Horticultural Research Center:* studies apricots, cherries, peaches, plums and wine grapes
FYI: Cherry trees grow well in the hills and sandy soil of the Grand Traverse area. Lake Michigan tempers the Arctic cold in the winter and cools the hot air of summer. There are 3,800,000 cherry trees in this area of Michigan and Grand Traverse County is the #2 producer of <u>sweet cherries</u>. Sweet, or Bing cherries, are handpicked and are eaten fresh, dried, or made into maraschino cherries. The third week of July is usually when the sweet cherries are at their peak. usacherries.com

Grand Traverse County and the surrounding counties are the Cherry Capital of the World. The Traverse City area consists of Antrim, Benzie, Grand Traverse, Kalkaska and Leelanau counties.

B BRIDGE OR BOAT

This 1986, 224' former Navy submarine surveillance ship, now the *T/S State of Michigan*, is one of the training vessels for the Great Lakes Maritime Academy. T/S means training ship. This training vessel, along with sailboats, a utility boat, a research vessel and a tugboat, provide hands-on learning experience for the cadets at the Academy. See 28U.

C CELEBRATIONS

<u>Interlochen</u> *Wine, Food, and Fine Arts Festival:* May
...Arts Festival: world-renowned artists
<u>Traverse City</u> *National Cherry Festival:* 175 events, all things cherry; tour the orchards, July

<u>Old Mission Peninsula</u> *Blossom Days:* hosted by the wineries, May

D DEMOGRAPHICS

Population: 87,000   **Persons per sq. mile:** 187
Largest city: Traverse City   **Population:** 14,500
Largest township: Garfield   **Population:** 16,300
Largest village: Kingsley   **Population:** 1,480
Median household income: $49,100
Owner-occupied median house value: $175,000
Persons affiliated with a religious congregation: 47%
Persons below poverty level: 11%
Students receiving school lunch subsidy: 31%

E ENVIRONMENT

The Grand Traverse Regional Land Conservancy consists of five counties in beautiful northwest Michigan. Its goal is to protect significant natural, scenic and farm lands - now and for all future generations. Their efforts are focused on unique farmlands, critical watersheds, wildlife habitats and one-of-a-kind sand dunes in the area. Lands are either purchased by or donated to the Conservancy. The funds to purchase these lands come from donations and special property taxes approved by local residents. The preservation success of Old Mission Peninsula has set a national standard for excellence. gtrlc.org

F FLORA & FAUNA

Alice Welch, USDA

Witch hazel is a shrub whose leaves and bark are used in the production of a product called Witch Hazel that is used as an herbal remedy to dry and cleanse skin. It may have been named because its branches were used as dowsing rods to locate water, or to "witch" a well.

Discovering Michigan County by County is just like having your own personal tour guide as you travel throughout the great state of Michigan.

NPCR

The opossum is the only marsupial that is native to someplace other than Australia. They pretend to be dead to avoid being eaten by predators. That kind of "playing dead" behavior in humans is called "playing possum."

G GOVERNMENT

County: ...**created:** 1851 ...**organized:** 1851
...**originally part of:** Mackinac County
Size: 316,000 acres / 465 sq. miles (78 of 83 counties)
County seat: Traverse City
...**Homestead property tax:** 37 mills
The county has 1 city, 2 villages, 13 townships with 2 as charter townships and 2 school districts.

Michigan State Preservation Office

NPCR

The Grand Traverse County Courthouse, built in 1900 for $36,000, was remodeled in 1980 for $1.7 million.
Motto: Interlochen Chamber: *20 Lakes within 20 Minutes*
...Kingsley: *a little bit of paradise*
...Traverse City Convention and Visitors Bureau: *Take Me There*

H HISTORICAL MARKERS 7 of 10

City Opera House: 1891, Victorian, with excellent acoustics

Congregation Beth El: 1885, Michigan's oldest synagogue

Grand Traverse Bay: home of Chippewa and Ottawa Indians

Hesler Log House: 1854, on Old Mission Peninsula, was moved to this site and restored

Interlochen: • <1800s: Ottawa Indians lived in the pine forest *between the lakes.*
- late 1800s: all the pine trees were cut except the ones in the area between the lakes.
- 1917: the virgin pine area between the lakes was purchased to become one of the first state parks.
- 1918: Camp Interlochen opened as a girls' recreational camp.
- 1922: Camp Penn opened as a boys' recreational camp.
- 1928: National High School Orchestra Camp opened on the former girls' and boys' camps.
- 1931: NHSOC became the National Music Camp.
- 1942: NMC affiliated with University of Michigan.
- 1960: Interlochen Music Academy was charted and provides year-round training in the creative arts; see 28W.

Novotny's Saloon: 1886, semi-pro baseball team

Traverse City Regional Psychiatric Hosp.: 1885-1985, served 50,000 clients

National Register of Historic Places: 11 listings

State Historic Sites: 27 listings

I INFORMATION

Chamber of Commerce: Fife Lake, Interlochen, Traverse City

Visitor: Traverse City Convention and Visitors Bureau, 800-872-8377, traversecity.com

J JOKES

You might be a Michiganian if...

...you know where to visit the cherry capital of world.

...you ever participated in a cherry pit spitting contest.

...you know why there are cherry pits along the side of the road, and you helped put them there.

...Acme reminds you of the Road Runner because he always gets his supplies from Acme. Michigan, no doubt.

...you wish there was an Interstate Highway connecting I-75 and Traverse City.

...you hope to get a glimpse of The Bear or The Wolverine.

...when someone mentions Ford, you don't know if they're talking about cars, tractors, trucks, museums, expressways, the Detroit Lions or Presidents.

K KINSMAN

Race	Ancestry
American Indian: 1%	German: 25%
Asian: <1%	English: 11%
Black/African American: 1%	Irish: 11%
Hispanic or Latino: 2%	U.S./American: 8%
Other: <1%	Polish: 7%
White: 99%	French: 4%

L LIGHTHOUSE OR LANDMARK

The Old Mission Lighthouse is located at the end of Old Mission Peninsula. Built it 1870, it is almost halfway between the North Pole and the equator.

M MUSEUMS

<u>Traverse City</u> *Dennos Museum Center* at Northwestern Michigan College: visual and performing arts

...*Art Center & Gallery:* northwestern Michigan artists & craftsmen

137

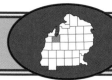

...*History/Heritage Center:* 1903 Carnegie library building; contains 10,000 Midwest Indian artifacts in the Con Foster Museum; Victorian parlor, railroad history, logging, changing displays

Rick Gleason

Rick Gleason

...*Great Lakes Children's Museum:* hands-on, interactive

...*Music House Museum:* automatic musical instruments

N NATURAL RESOURCES

Elevation: <600 - 1,100 feet
Physiography: hill-plains, plains

Soil: Sandy loam
  Depth: 8-12"
  Color: dark gray or brown
  Type: sandy loam with a high % of organic matter
  Details: surface is level to gently rolling with good drainage; easy to till
  Agriculture: very good for orchard fruits and other general farm crops
  NOTE: soil types are not limited to any one county.

Forest type: maple-beech-hemlock, aspen-birch, oak-hickory
Public/private forests: 56% of county

Water in county: 6% of county
  Bay: East Arm and West Arm of Grand Traverse Bay of Lake Michigan
  Lakes: 80   ...**largest:** Long Lake
  Rivers: Betsie, Boardman
  Rivers & streams: 170 miles

Great Lakes peninsula: Old Mission
Great Lakes shoreline: 56 miles of Lake Michigan

Growing season, avg.: 132 days (4 temp. zones)
  Last freeze, avg.: May 20 – June 5
  First freeze, avg.: Sept. 10 – Sept. 30

Precipitation, annual avg.: rainfall: 30 inches
                    snowfall: 87 inches
Temperature (F), avg.: January: high 26°, low 13°
              July: high 81°, low 57°
  Annual: >90°: 9 days, **<0°:** 13 days
Tornadoes (1930-2010): 3

O ORIGINS

Acme:[u] Greek for the 'highest point'; 1864
Bates:[u] Traverse City Railroad secretary, Thomas Bates; 1891
East Bay:[u] east arm of Grand Traverse Bay; 1867
Fife Lake:[v] state highwayman, William Fife; 1872
Garfield:[ct,t] U.S. President James A. Garfield; 1882
Grand Traverse:[co] the larger of the 2 bays on the west coast of Michigan
Interlochen:[u] (IN-ter-lock-in) "between two lakes," Green and Duck Lakes; 1890; see 28H
Kingsley:[v] platted by Judson W. Kingsley; 1874
Old Mission: a Presbyterian mission church; 1839
Traverse City:[c] (TRA vers) French voyagers found a zigzag course around Lake Michigan shoreline is a "long distance;" 1847.

P PARKS

National: 0   **State:** 9   **County:** 5   **Local:** 34
Number of campsites: 1,900
State Forest: *Pere Marquette*
...**Campground:** 6   ...**Pathway:** 45 miles
State Game Area: *Petobego:* wetlands shared with Antrim County covering almost 500 acres

State Park: *Traverse City:* 45 acres, 700 ft. sandy beach on Lake Michigan, beautiful and on the bay

Rick Gleason

...*Interlochen:* 190 acres, Michigan's first state park in 1917; cabins, tepees, swimming, fishing, events

Courtesy of www.chrisdoyal.com

State Underwater Preserve: *Grand Traverse Bay Great Lakes State Bottomland Preserve:* 295 square miles, 19± shipwrecks, wharf & dock remains, coastal wetlands

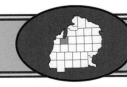
County: *Beitner:* 5 acres in Nature Education Reserve; access for Boardman River activities

…Medalie: 15 acres, fishing, canoe launch

…*Bill Carls Nature Preserve:* 160 acres, one of the most botanically diverse and beautiful properties in Grand Traverse County, it is now protected from development by the Grand Traverse Regional land Conservancy (see 28E) and was their first project.

Rick Gleason

…*Power Island:* 202 acres, on west arm of Grand Traverse Bay

…*Twin Lakes:* 175 acres, lodge, dormitory to rent

Rick Gleason

…*Maple Bay Park and Natural Area:* 400 acres, agricultural, wetlands, woodlands, sand dunes, beaches, all being developed

Local: *Clinch Park:* marina, train; an urban beach

Q   QUOTE FROM THE LOCALS

"Traverse City area is flourishing with a robust and varied economic base. Tourism is a major factor, with 80% of tourists coming from Michigan. The majority come to enjoy the water related activities, including sightseeing. Vineyards and wine making are gaining importance every year. Adding to the community's health is retail and medical facilities, oil and gas companies, as well as family activities and culture."

mytraversecity.com

R   RECREATION & SPORTS

Auto racing: *Cherry Speedway:* 3/8-mile oval dirt track
Blue Ribbon Trout Streams:[1,000] Boardman River & North and South Branch
Golf courses: 8; Traverse City area is ranked 12th in the world by *Golf Digest*; The Bear was designed by Jack Nicklaus[1,000] and The Wolverine was designed by Gary Player.[1,000]
Groomed cross-country ski trails: 10
Hiking/skiing/mountain biking trails: 140 miles

MI Shore-to-Shore (horse) **Riding & Hiking Trail:** yes
North Country National Scenic Trail: yes
Off-road vehicle trails: 75 miles

Public access sites: 26

NPCR

Public recreational land: 21% of county
Rail-trail: (60 miles) Leelanau, Michigan Shore to Shore, Traverse Area Recreation Trail (TART), VASA Pathway
Recreational harbor: Traverse City Clinch Marina
State or Federal wild/scenic/natural river: 65 miles of the Boardman River
State-funded snowmobile trails: 60 miles
TART jogging/bike trail: Tom's West Bay to Acme
Traverse City Beach Bums: play baseball in the Frontier Independent Professional Baseball League at Wuerfel Park
Try steelhead salmon fishing in the Boardman River.

S   STATE OF MICHIGAN

The <u>Most Visited Counties in Michigan</u>, annually and by the season, are:
- Allegan: spring, summer
- Berrien: annual, summer, winter
- Cheboygan: summer
- Emmet: summer, winter
- Grand Traverse: annual, summer, fall, winter, spring
- Ingham: annual, fall, winter, spring
- Isabella: annual, fall, winter, spring
- Kalamazoo: fall, winter
- Kent: annual, summer, fall, winter, spring
- Mackinac: annual, summer, fall
- Oakland: annual, fall, winter, spring
- Ottawa: summer
- Saginaw: annual, summer, fall, winter, spring
- Washtenaw: annual, fall, spring
- Wayne: annual, summer, fall, winter, spring [Schaetzl]

T   TRAVEL

Airports: Cherry Capitol, Lake Ann, Green Lake, Sea Plane Base, Sugar Loaf
Bus: Indian Trails; Traverse Area Recreation Trail (TART)
Circle Tour: Lake Michigan via US-31, M-37, M-22
Distance to Lansing: 180 miles
Heritage Route: *Scenic:* M-22, Leelanau Scenic Heritage Route, 64 miles, Traverse City to Empire

...*Scenic:* M-37, Old Mission Peninsula, [1,000]
18 miles, Traverse City to Old Mission
Main roads: US-31, M-37, M-72, M-113
Memorial Highways: US-31, *Blue Star MH:* see 3T
Northwest Michigan Ports of Call Tour: Grand Traverse Heritage Center, The Tall Ship Manitou

U   UNIVERSITIES & COLLEGES

Davenport University: see 13U
Northwestern Michigan College: est. 1951, 4,500 students. A community college, a community of learners... providing academic degrees/programs, personal enrichment, cultural activities, and corporate and customized training; M-TEC. Intramural sports
Great Lakes Maritime Academy: est. 1969, 100 students. A division of Northern Michigan College and Ferris State University; the nation's only freshwater academy... to train men and women to serve as business professionals and Merchant Marine officers on Great Lakes and ocean ships. See 28B.

V   VARIETY

Cindy A. Ratowski

Whether in the marina or on the lake, whether large or small, the sailboats on Grand Traverse Bay are a beautiful sight that everyone enjoys. Shown here is

the tall ship Manitou that is available for daily 2-hour sails, a 4-day sailing trip, a bed & breakfast overnight stay and a variety of specialty cruises.

W   WANDERLUST

Agri-tourism: *Gallagher's Centennial Farm:* beef, dairy, pork, cherries, veggies, cheese, bakery
...*Hoxsie's Farm Market:* cherries, apples, pumpkins
...*Jacob's Corn Maze:* 4+ miles of trails, U-pick, apples, pumpkins, raspberries
...*Stoney Beach Farm:* strawberries, cherries, tomatoes
Brewery: North Peak Brewing Co., Right Brain Brewery, Traverse Brewing Co.
Casino: Turtle Creek
Cultural: Traverse Symphony Orchestra
Fall colors: late September to early October
Live theater: City Opera House, Old Town Playhouse, State, Theatre North
Shopping malls: Cherry Land, downtown Traverse City, Grand Traverse
Walking tours: Boardman River and River Walk
Wineries:

Paul Jackson

...*Bowers Harbor:* dynamically expressive varietal
...*Brys Estate Vineyards:* European vinifera grapes
...*Chateau Chantel:*[1,000] bed & breakfast , tours, tasting, seminars
...*Chateau Grand Traverse:* 100's of awards

...*Grey Hare:* bed & breakfast, boutique vineyards

Rick Gleason

...*Peninsula Cellars:* in a one-room schoolhouse
Barns of Old Mission: 10 stops along this quilt trail

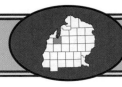
Grand Traverse Pie Company:[1,000] Would you like some pie for dessert?

Grand Traverse Resort & Spa:[1,000] 900 acres, golf, dining, water activities, Dog Dreams Inn

Interlochen Center for the Arts:[1,000] is among the top 10 nonprofit corporations in the U.S.

Courtesy of Interlochen Center for the Arts

…*Arts Camp:* intensive training during the summer

…*Arts Academy:* residential fine arts high school

…*Arts Festival:* 700+ yearly concerts & exhibitions

…*Public Radio:* classical music, news, serving NW lower Michigan

Old Mission Peninsula General Store: everything you knew an original, old time general store should be

Rick Gleason

Rogers Observatory: NMC, astronomy education

Sleeping Bear Dunes: see 45L, 45P

Traverse City Film Festival: 100 screenings of foreign, American independents, documentaries

X X-TRA STUFF

Commercial port: Traverse City

County Fair: *Northwestern Michigan Fair:* Aug.

Hospital: Munson Medical Center

Large employers: Munson Medical Center, Traverse City Area Public Schools, Grand Traverse Resort & Spa, Sara Lee Bakery (frozen pies & desserts), Lear Corp (electromechanical devices), Tower Automotive (automotive stampings)

Grand Traverse County is the…

…#2 MI area for dollars spent for pleasure activities.

…#2 MI county for number of licensed charter boats.

…#2 MI county for sweet cherries.

…#3 MI county & #3 U.S. county for tart cherry production.

Site Selection Magazine has twice named Traverse City the top small town in America when it comes to business growth.

Travel America Magazine named the Traverse City area one of the best vacation destinations in the world.

Y YESTERYEAR

In his <u>1883 historical account</u> of life in the Grand Traverse region, Dr. M.L. Leach tells about the <u>Ottawa Indians</u>. "The fish in the lakes, during the proper season, furnished an abundant supply of food. They were caught in gill nets made of twine manufactured from the inner bark of the slippery elm (Ulmus fulva). The manufacture of the twine was part of the work of the women. The bark was macerated in the lye of wood ashes to remove the mucilage, beaten to separate the fibers and spun by hand. It was the work of the women also, to dress the game, cure the skins, cultivate their limited corn-fields, pound the corn in wooden mortars and prepare the hominy, gather the fuel and perform the general drudgery of the household. The men, when not engaged in fishing or the chase, or in forays into the homes of distant tribes (for all distant tribes were considered lawful plunder), reclined in listless idleness in the shelter of their bark wigwams, or engaged in the athletic sports common among the Algonquin people."

Z ZOO & ANIMAL PLACES

Watchable Wildlife Viewing Areas:[ww] Sand Lakes Quiet Area

Zoos: *Clinch Park Zoo & Museum:* MI animals and fish

Gateway Ranch: Alpaca breeding and fiber ranch

Don't forget to check the *BIBLIOGRAPHY & NOTES* at the back of the book for explanations and additional information.

A AGRICULTURE

Land in farms: 78% of county
Number of farms: 1,040
Size of average farm: 275 acres
Market value of all products: #7 of 83 counties
Crops: ...most acres: corn
...highest $ sales: grains: corn, soybeans, wheat
Livestock: ...largest number: hogs
...highest $ sales: milk & dairy products
Among the top Michigan counties:
• #3- sales of cattle
• #4- hogs, soybeans
• #5- organic production
• #6- sugarbeets
Dairy, food and meat processing plants: 9
State ranking for harvested trees: #64 of 83 counties
FYI: Barns and their silos are the quintessential symbol of farm life in America. Silos, whether tall and thin or short and fat, are used for storing bulk materials. Some are used to hold grain like corn or wheat. Others hold silage that is fed to cattle or sheep. Silage is made from the entire plant, not just the grain, like in corn silage. Many other grass

Michigan Farm Bureau

crops can be harvested into high nutrition silage and stored for later use for the animals. As the silage in the silos ferments, it converts sugars to acids and uses all the oxygen present in the crop material, thus allowing the silage not to spoil. *wordiq.com*

B BRIDGE OR BOAT

NPCR

A jon boat is a good fishing boat for the Maple Rapids River. Its flat bottom allows it to get into the shallow water of the wetlands.

C CELEBRATIONS

<u>Alma</u> *Highland Festival:* Celtic entertainment, highland dancing, open pipe band championship, traditional ceilidh (social gathering with Gaelic folk music and dancing), Scottish pageantry, parade, border collie sheep-herding, harp classes, May

Courtesy of Alma Highland Festival and Games

<u>Ashley</u> *Trading Days:* car show, race, music, June
<u>Ithaca</u> *Hometown Fun Fest:* Aug.
...*Old US-27 Motor Tour:* see 12C

D DEMOGRAPHICS

Population: 42,500   **Persons per sq. mile:** 75
Largest city: Alma   **Population:** 9,400
Largest township: Pine River   **Population:** 2,280
Largest village: Breckenridge   **Population:** 1,330
Median household income: $36,800
Owner-occupied median house value: $96,000
Persons affiliated with a religious congregation: 33%
Persons below poverty level: 20%
Students receiving school lunch subsidy: 40%

E ENVIRONMENT

At Mile Marker #106, US-127 passes over the Maple River, which at that point is part of the <u>Maple River State Game Area</u>. The state's game areas are set aside to protect and improve the habitats for wildlife species and to improve hunting opportunities. This SGA is the largest (9,000 acres) contiguous wetland complex in mid-Michigan and includes floodplains, lowlands, marshes, upland grasslands, agriculture lands and forests that provides habitat for many types of birds and waterfowl plus numerous other land animals. There are trails for

NPCR

walking, blinds for hunting and bird watching, including a barrier-free blind, boardwalks in the cattails and trails on top of the dikes. These dikes hold the water that creates the ponds that are the home for many waterfowl. Get off the highway and experience it yourself! DNRE

F FLORA & FAUNA

Jan Miller/USFWS

Look out for poison ivy! The middle leaf is symmetrical and has a longer stalk than the other two asymmetrical leaves. The plant has hairy tendrils but does not have a prickly stem. It grows along the edge of fields and forests and anywhere else it wants. Look for 3 green leaves, with young leaves that are red; the fall has red and orange leaves, while the winter has white, waxy berries on a leafless plant.

Dan Sudia/USFWS

The Tufted Titmouse can be found year-round in Michigan where they like moist woodlands and wooded residential areas and city parks. They store their food in trees or under objects on the ground, mate for life and have 10 different calls.

G GOVERNMENT

County: ...**created:** 1831 ...**organized:** 1855
...**originally part of:** Saginaw, Clinton Counties
Size: 366,000 acres / 570 sq. miles (43 of 83 counties)
The county has 3 cities, 3 villages, 16 townships, 18 unincorporated communities and 6 school districts.

Deb Schmuker

County of Gratiot

County seat: Ithaca
...**Homestead property tax:** 39 mills
Motto: <u>Alma</u>: *Scotland, USA*
...<u>Breckenridge</u>: *A Country Village Along the Way*
...<u>Gratiot Area</u> Chamber: *A Great Place to Work, Play and Do Business*
...<u>Gratiot County</u>: *Great Things. In the Palm of Your Hand*
...<u>Ithaca</u>: *Cherishing Our Past...Living for the Future*
...<u>St. Louis</u>: *Middle of the Mitten*

H HISTORICAL MARKERS 6 of 7

Alma College: 1886, the Presbyterian Synod of Michigan established and endowed a college of learning to the glory of God and to the dignity of men.
Gratiot County: named after Gen. Charles Gratiot; settlers began arriving in 1846 and a Lutheran Indian mission was started.
Lumberjack Park: 1926, former shanty boys, lumberjacks and riverdrivers purchased the last 40-acre tract of white pine in the county.

Karen Stoneman

Michigan Masonic Home: 1929, diverse residential and nursing care facility operated by the Grand Lodge of Free and Accepted Masons of Michigan

Saginaw & Gratiot County State Road: 1869, 32-mile plank road from Saginaw to St. Louis, now M-46
Saginaw Valley and St. Louis Railroad: 1873, built alongside the plank road and allowed for export of agricultural and lumbering products
National Register of Historic Places: 7 listings
State Historic Sites: 22 listings

I INFORMATION

Chamber of Commerce: Gratiot Area, 989-463-5525, gratiot.org

J JOKES

You'll never be a good dairy farmer if...
...you don't like to get up early so you can be in the barn at 4:00 A.M. for the *first* milking of the day.
...tons of manure turns your stomach.

…you insist on taking off work for illness, vacations, weekends, holidays, mental health days and personal days.

…you insist on time and a half overtime pay for any work week over 40 hours, which, of course, is every week of the year.

…you insist double time for holidays. Isn't this what unions are for?

…you can't handle debt and uncertain market prices.

…you don't like white mustaches.

NEXT 2 MILES

NPCR

K KINSMAN

Race
American Indian: <1%
Asian: <1%
Black/African American: 6%
Hispanic or Latino: 5%
Other: 3%
White: 91%

Ancestry
German: 24%
U.S./American: 17%
English: 13%
Irish: 7%
Polish: 4%
French: 3%
Scottish: 3%

L LIGHTHOUSE OR LANDMARK

Deb Schmuker

The largest wind farm in Michigan sits on 30,000 acres among corn and soybean fields in the "sweet spot" for catching winds in northeast Gratiot County. Once completed, this DTE Energy site will have 133 wind turbines that will produce enough electricity for 50,000 homes for 20 years. The tower is 330' tall and each blade is 130' long. There is another wind farm under construction in the county too. It would take 3,300 wind turbines to produce 25% of Michigan's energy needs.

M MUSEUMS

<u>Breckenridge-Wheeler</u> *Area Historical Society:*
…*Plank Road Museum:* local artifacts
…*Drake Memorial House:* 1900s country doctor's home; research library

<u>Ithaca</u> *Gratiot County Historical Museum:* in an 1881 red brick Victorian house, 1850s-1950s artifacts

Deb Schmucker

<u>St. Louis</u> *Depot Museum:* 1917 Republic truck, transportation items

N NATURAL RESOURCES

Elevation: 600 - 800 feet
Physiography: rolling plains, lake border plains

Soil: Clay
Depth: 6"-9"
Color: brown or black
Type: silty, clay loam
Details: darker and loamier where percentage of organic matter is higher
Sub-soil: bluish-gray clay
Agriculture: good for sugar beets and other general crops
NOTE: soil types are not limited to any one county.

Forest type: maple-beech, aspen-birch, oak-hickory
Public/private forests: 13% of county
FYI: Of the 15 forest types in Michigan, the <u>northern hardwood</u> forest was the most common forest type in the NE United States when Michigan was settled and lumbered in the 1800s. It is still the most common forest type in the state with 40% of the forest landscape and it makes up half of the state's hardwood forests. It is home to 70 tree species; the most common trees in this forest are sugar maple, red maple, basswood, hemlock and beech. Michigan Forests Forever

NPCR

Water in county: <1% of county
   Lakes: 15   **...largest:** Rainbow Lake
   Rivers: Bad, Maple, Pine
   Rivers & streams: 240 miles

Growing season, avg.: 152 days (2 temp. zones)
   Last freeze, avg.: May 15 – May 20
   First freeze, avg.: Oct. 5 – Oct. 10
Precipitation, annual avg.: rainfall: 30 inches
                   snowfall: 42 inches
Temperature (F), avg.: January: high 29°, low 14°
              July: high 84°, low 59°
   Annual: >90°: 13 days, <0°: 11 days
Tornadoes (1930-2010): 27

O   ORIGINS

<u>Alma</u>:[c] probably the daughter of Mr. Gargett; 1853
<u>Ashley</u>:[v] railroad promoter and builder, John Ashley;
   1883
<u>Breckenridge</u>:[v] mill owners Dan and Justin
   Breckenridge; 1860
<u>Gratiot</u>:[co] (GRA shut) Gen. Charles Gratiot (1786-
   1855) was involved in the Battle of Mackinac Island
   and the building of Fort Gratiot to protect the St.
   Clair River and Lake Huron at Port Huron.
<u>Ithaca</u>:[c] second settler was from Ithaca, NY; 1850
<u>Perrinton</u>:[v] the firm of attorney Mr. Perrin had large
   land interests in this area; 1886
<u>St. Louis</u>:[c] Gen. Charles Gratiot was from St. Louis,
   MO; 1853

P   PARKS

National: 0 **State:** 2 **County:** 2 **Local:** 12
Number of campsites: 550
State Game Area: Maple River[ww] and Gratiot-
   Saginaw, covering 15,000 acres; see 29E
County: *Paul Hubscher*: 60 acres, man-made lake,
   swim, fish, hike
...*Reed:* 100 acres, 6 pavilions, man-made lake, sand
   volleyball, disc golf,
   maple-beech forest

Other: *Forest Hill Nature
   Area:* 90 acres, gently rolling hills, willow thickets,
   woodlots, trails

Karen Stoneman

Q   QUOTE FROM THE LOCALS

"Between the hustle and bustle of major metropolitan areas and the peaceful tranquility of some of the world's largest lakes, tucked safe and secure in the palm of Michigan's Lower Peninsula, lies Gratiot County. It's a community that prides itself on maintaining rural values where people still care about their neighbors, yet its proximity to Saginaw, Lansing, Grand Rapids and Detroit allows residents to enjoy a combination of outstanding local activities and a wide variety of cultural and entertainment events.

"...agriculture accounts for about 70 percent of all land use. The rich, fertile soil, which is among the finest in the state, is ideal for growing dry beans, corn, sugar beets, soybeans and wheat. Beef cattle and dairy farms comprise the largest portion of the area's livestock operations. But possibly the biggest contribution agriculture has made is instilling a work ethic that has been carried on from generation to generation, making Gratiot County a fertile ground for employers looking to fill new industrial or commercial jobs." Gratiot.org/CommunityGuide

R   RECREATION & SPORTS

Golf courses: 6
Hiking/skiing/mountain biking trails: 3 miles
Horse racing: harness racing at Ithaca Ag Expo
Public access sites: 3
Public recreational land: 4% of county
Rail-trail: (10 miles) Fred Meijer Heartland

S   STATE OF MICHIGAN

Lee Karney/USFWS

Since 1931, the American Robin, affectionately called Robin Redbreast, has been the <u>State Bird</u>. Voted on by the Michigan Audubon Society, it is described as the best known and best loved of all the birds in the state. Most of the robins in the state migrate to Mexico in the winter, but there are always a few hardy ones that hang around southern Michigan. The first sighting of this songbird is considered a sign of spring.

T TRAVEL

Airport: Gratiot Community
Bus: Alma & St. Louis Dial-a-Ride, Indian Trails
Distance to Lansing: 50 miles
Main roads: US-127, M-46, M-57
Memorial Highways: US-27, *Veterans MH*

U UNIVERSITIES & COLLEGES

Alma College: est. 1886, 1,400 students. It is a private liberal arts college that highlights personalized education, social responsibility and extraordinary achievements; includes Scottish heritage studies. MIAA, Scots. See 29H.

V VARIETY

Farming is land, labor and machinery intensive.

The tractor is the engine that pulls the train of crop production.

Michigan Farm Bureau

Michigan Farm Bureau

First, the ground is plowed to break it up and to plow under any remaining vegetation from last year's crop.

Then a disc is used to break up the plowed clumps and prepare the ground for the seed.

Michigan Farm Bureau

Michigan Farm Bureau

The seed is put into the ground with the planter.

Depending on the crop, sometimes plowing, planting and even fertilizing can all be done in a one-step operation.

Even with all that input of time and money to get the crop planted, there is no guarantee of a good and/ or profitable harvest. The farmer has little control over the market conditions that set the selling price of his agricultural product. There is little that can be done to control the effects of weather (too hot, too cold, too much rain, not enough rain, hail, wind storms, etc.) and ever present and extensive crop damage by fungi, insects and wild animals.

When the grain crop is ready for harvest (in this picture it is field corn) the combine (COM bine) is used. The combine *combines* the harvesting steps of cutting the corn stalk, picking the corn, removing the corn husk and shelling the corn from the cob, which prior to 1850, were all separate steps done by hand. The corn is loaded into the waiting wagon, which can either be emptied into a larger vehicle like a live bottom semi-truck, or driven straight to the local elevator to be emptied.

Michigan Farm Bureau

W WANDERLUST

Deb Schmuker

Fall colors: early October
Live theater: GEM Theater

Planetarium: Alma College

Wineries: *Hometown Cellars:* full service, make your own

X X-TRA STUFF

County fair: *Gratiot Agricultural Society:* June
...Gratiot County Fair for Youth: July
Hospitals: Gratiot Medical Center
Large employers: Gratiot Medical Center, Michigan Correctional Facilities, Michigan Masonic Home (skilled nursing facility), Wal-Mart, Department of Corrections, Alma College, International Automotive (motor vehicle parts), GTE

Y YESTERYEAR

In 1869, some travelers were enjoying the water flowing from a well alongside the Pine River that had been dug in search of salt brine. One of the men had a hand that was crippled by rheumatism. After only 4 minutes of soaking his hand in the water, he regained movement and flexibility that had been long lost. Local people started bathing in and drinking this water and claimed improved health or complete cures of their ailments.

"The unexpected discovery of miraculous water in a flowing well in the small, backwoods settlement in St. Louis, Michigan, was to push the town into the national lime-light within months. It was a discovery that would have a significant influence on the town for a century."

By the next year, hundreds of people were coming from around the country to bathe in the miraculous mineral water. A bathhouse was built that could provide 500 baths a day. It was just the beginning of luxurious improvements, including heating the water for the comfort of winter guests. Stagecoaches, boarding houses and restaurants were all flourishing and a building boom was in full progress.

Many famous people came to the St. Louis Magnetic Springs and their claim of cures helped spread the word of the magical water. Testing showed the water contained sulfate of lime, bicarbonate of soda and magnesia, and had a magnetic element to it too.

Mineral baths became popular around the state including the discovery of wells in Alpena, Eaton Rapids, Fruitport, Grand Ledge, Hubbardston, Midland and Spring Lake. All claimed medicinal qualities for their water, but only St. Louis and Alpena claimed magnetic qualities. rootsweb.ancestry.com

NPCR

NPCR

Z ZOO & ANIMAL PLACES

Watchable Wildlife Viewing Areas:[ww] see 29P
Double Eagle Dairy: 3,500 cows, educational, observation deck, tours available

From BIBLIOGRAPHY & NOTES...

O ORIGINS:
[c] = current city
[co] = current county
[ct] = current charter township
[t] = current township
[u] = current unincorporated place
[v] = current village

A AGRICULTURE

Land in farms: 70% of county
Number of farms: 1,670
Size of average farm: 160 acres
Market value of all products: #18 of 83 counties
Crops: ...most acres: corn
...highest $ sales: grains: corn, soybeans, wheat
Livestock: ...largest number: hogs & pigs
...highest $ sales: milk & dairy products
Among the top Michigan counties:
• #2- number of farms, number of dairy farms
• #4- goats for milk, sheep & lambs
Dairy, food and meat processing plants: 16
State ranking for harvested trees: #70 of 83 counties
FYI: Milk is the largest agricultural commodity produced in Michigan (25% of the total agriculture sales) with 2,600 farms raising over 344,000 milking cows. Michigan is 7th in the nation for dairy production. Sixty-eight percent of Michigan farms have fewer than 99 cows each while the remaining farms have 84% of the entire state herd.

One cow, which can eat up to 90 pounds of food and drink 35 gallons of water every day, produces about 8.5 gallons (136 cups) of milk per day. (Cows only produce milk for about 10 months out of a 12-14 month milking/gestational year.) It takes

Michigan Farm Bureau

about 19 cups of milk to make 1 pound of American cheese and 39 cups of milk to get enough cream to make a pound of butter.

Milk and dairy products are the best way to get the calcium your body needs. In addition to bottling the milk, Michigan's 70 dairy processing plants make milk into a large variety of cheeses, ice creams, yogurts, butter and sour cream. MDA, National Dairy Council, USDA

NPCR

B BRIDGE OR BOAT

NPCR

This is just one of 17 bridges crafted in the 1930s by two Mexican artisans for local businessman, W.H.L. McCourtie on his estate, *Aiden Lair*. Using metal rods as the skeleton, it is a complex process of shaping, molding, staining and texturizing wet cement so that the finished product looks like real trees, although fanciful ones. McCourtie Park and the bridges are open to the public. See 30H.

C CELEBRATIONS

Camdem *Farmers Day Festival:* tractor and truck pulls, chicken bar-b-que, parade and much more, to support the local fire department, Aug.

Jonesville *Riverfest:* clean up the St. Joe River, boat and foot races, crafts, May

Hillsdale *Civil War Reenactment:* at the Poor House, June; see 30X

...County *Car Show & Summerfest:* classic cars, ribfest, bands, at the fairgrounds, June

...*Fiddlers Convention:* workshops, music, fun, June

...*Old Time Farm Festival:* vintage tractor games, traditional old foods, old style crafts, at the Poorhouse, Aug.

Litchfield *Sweet Corn Days:* good food, music, fun, Aug.

Montgomery *Frog Eye Festival:* soap box derby, duck drop, bikini contest, frog jumping, July

North Adams *Heritage Days:* parade, tractor/pedal pulls, classic cars, outhouse races, Aug.

Reading *Festival Days:* Soapbox derby, truck and tractor pull, Aug.

Waldron *Labor Day Festival:* raising money for local non-profits; 24-hour softball tournament, Sept.

D DEMOGRAPHICS

Population: 46,700   **Persons per sq. mile:** 78
Largest city: Hillsdale   **Population:** 8,300
Largest township: Somerset   **Population:** 4,620
Largest village: Jonesville   **Population:** 2,260
Median household income: $38,100
Owner-occupied median house value: $119,000
Persons affiliated with a religious congregation: 24%
Persons below poverty level: 17%
Students receiving school lunch subsidy: 45%

E ENVIRONMENT

The Friends of the St. Joseph River was established to bring together the communities of the St. Joseph River Watershed in both Michigan and Indiana in order to work as one unit to clean and restore the river and all the lakes, rivers and streams within the watershed. Critical wetland identification and prioritization is important. It is also important that government bodies and individual landowners have the necessary education and knowledge about wetland functions so proper decisions can be made to protect and manage these vital areas. The all-volunteer organization is working hard to accomplish these goals.FOTSJR.org

F FLORA & FAUNA

Alice Welch, USDA

By definition, a thistle is a weed that has prickles that are long, sharp and dense. Some species are native, but most are exotic, invasive species. The giant bull thistle is common in mown lawns where they can be stepped on with bare feet; along roadsides they can grow to 6' tall.

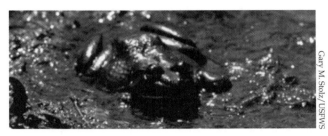

Gary M. Stolz/USFWS

The North American bullfrog (3"-6" long) likes warm, shallow water. They will sit and wait for their next carnivorous meal to come by and use their long tongue to catch it. They are known for their enormous legs that are used for jumping and racing, and providing frog legs for dinner.

G GOVERNMENT

County: ...**created:** 1829 ...**organized:** 1835
...**originally part of:** Lenawee County
Size: 388,000 acres / 599 sq. miles (36 of 83 counties)
The county has 3 cities, 6 villages, 18 townships, 21 unincorporated communities and 8 school districts.

Michigan State Preservation Office

County seat: Hillsdale
...**Homestead property tax:** 37 mills
Motto: Allen: *Antique Capital of Michigan*
...Hillsdale: *It's the People*
...Litchfield: *Curfew Shall Not Ring Tonight*
...Reading: *Traditional Values Progressive Spirits*

H HISTORICAL MARKERS 8 of 13

Moses Allen: a veteran of the War of 1812, he claimed his land on the prairie here in 1827, two years before the U.S. was ready to sell it.

NPCR

College Baptist Church: 1868, Romanesque style designed after European cathedrals

Congregational Church of Litchfield: 1870, Gothic style; first meeting of the Christian Endeavor Society

Grosvenor House: 1874, Elijah Myers was the architect of this house; he then went on to design the State Capitol building, of which Mr. Grosvenor was chairman of the building committee; see 30M.

Hillsdale: • <1839: inhabited by Potawatomi Indians
- 1839: first settler
- 1843: Hillsdale became county seat; Michigan Southern Railroad came through town
- 1851: first Hillsdale County Fair
- 1855: Hillsdale College opened
- 1869: city received its charter

Hillsdale College: • 1844: organized by Freewill Baptists as Michigan Central College in Spring Arbor, was the first college in Michigan to grant degrees to women
- 1853: moved to Hillsdale
- 1855: chartered by the legislature, renamed Hillsdale College with an independent board of trustees

Michigan and Ohio Railroad Depot: 1883, in Moscow, this simple Stick Style building was a big deal when it opened.

W.H.L. McCourtie: 1872-1933, a cement tycoon who sought to make a model town and gave free white paint to any homeowner that needed it; he sponsored many community events.

Monument: *Sultana:* a steamboat overloaded with over 2,000 Union soldiers returning home in 1865, many from Hillsdale County, exploded on the Mississippi River and killed 1,800 passengers in what is known as America's greatest maritime disaster.

...*Squaw-Field Monument:* a beautiful large red pudding stone rock has an arrow head shaped plaque that states, "SQUAW-FIELD SITE OF THE LAST CAMP OF THE POTTAWATOMIE INDIANS UNDER CHIEF BAW BESSE MOVED TO IOWA 1840."

...*Tri-state:* at the point where Michigan, Indiana and Ohio meet

National Register of Historic Places: 8 listings

State Historic Sites: 27 listings

I   INFORMATION

Chamber of Commerce: Hillsdale County, 517-439-4341, hillsdalecountychamber.com

...Litchfield, 517-542-2921

J   JOKES

It's a good spring in Michigan when…

- …you can sleep with your window open at night even if your electric blanket is still on 'low.'
- …you can get through the whole spring without having to cover your new tomato plants.
- …someone invites you to go smelt fishing with them.
- …the ladies don't have to wear their winter coats over their Easter dresses.
- …you can open your backyard pool Memorial Day weekend.
- …the mosquitoes are tolerable.
- …there's no snow on April Fool's Day.
- …only half the blossoms on the fruit trees are killed by frost.
- …the local radio stations are *not* having a contest to see who can guess when the last of the giant piles of snow in the Meijer parking lot will melt.
- …you make time to walk in the woods while the wildflowers are still in bloom and before the poison ivy encroaches on the path.

K   KINSMAN

Race	Ancestry
American Indian: <1%	German: 28%
Asian: <1%	U.S./American: 15%
Black/African American: <1%	English: 13%
Hispanic or Latino: 2%	Irish: 9%
Other: 2%	Polish: 4%
White: 97%	French: 4%

L LIGHTHOUSE or LANDMARK

This is Hillsdale College's historic Central Hall and clock tower. In 2011, *U.S. News & World Report* ranked the college as the #1 Michigan liberal arts school. In a stroll down Liberty Walk you will find 7 statues including Thomas Jefferson, Margaret Thatcher and Ronald Reagan. See 30U.

M MUSEUMS

<u>Jonesville</u> *Grosvenor House Museum:* High Victorian Italianate design, 32 rooms, 8 Italian marble fireplaces, each of a different color

<u>Hillsdale</u> *Historical Society Museum:* called the Poor House, is in the original (1854) County Poor House that inspired the famous poem "Over the Hill to the Poor House" by Will Carlton; see 30X

N NATURAL RESOURCES

Elevation: 900 – 1,200 feet
Physiography: hilly uplands, rolling plains

Forest type: oak-hickory, maple-beech
Public/private forests: 19% of county

Water in county: <1% of county
   Lakes: 80 ...**largest:** Second Lake
   Rivers: St. Joseph
   Rivers & streams: 300 miles

Growing season, avg.: 136 days (3 temp. zones)
   Last freeze, avg.: April 30 – May 10
   First freeze, avg.: Oct. 5 – Oct. 15
Precipitation, annual avg.: rainfall: 38 inches (#1/MI)
                 snowfall: 57 inches
Temperature (F), avg.: January: high 30°, low 15°
            July: high 82°, low 58°
  Annual: >90°: 8 days, **<0°:** 11 days
Tornadoes (1930-2010): 24

O ORIGINS

<u>Allen</u>:[v,t] Capt. Moses Allen; 1827
<u>Camden</u>:[v,t] settler from Camden, NY; 1837
<u>Hillsdale</u>:[c,co,t] topography of hills and dales; 1834
<u>Jonesville</u>:[v] the Jones brothers from Ohio; 1829
<u>Litchfield</u>:[c,t] early settlers from Litchfield, CT; 1834
<u>Montgomery</u>:[v] county clerk allowed the settlers to register the village for free if they would name it after him; 1870
<u>North Adams</u>:[v] in Adams Township; 1835
<u>Osseo</u>:[u] named for an American Indian chief; 1840
<u>Pittsford</u>:[u] named after Pittsford, NY; 1833
<u>Reading</u>:[c,t] named after Reading, PA; 1840
<u>Somerset</u>:[t] named after Somerset, NY; 1832
<u>Waldron</u>:[v] local congressman, Henry Waldron; 1835

P PARKS

National: 0 **State:** 2 **County:** 2 **Local:** 23
Number of campsites: 1,200

NPCR

State Game Area: 2,400+ acres, Adams Twp., Lost Nations[ww], Somerset[ww]

Local: *McCourtie Park:* 42 acres, with 17 Mexican folk art cement bridges that are sculpted to look like trees; see 30B

Other: *Fireman's Park:* pavilion, bicycle/nature trail
…*Lewis Emery Park:* five man-made fishing ponds with handicap accessible piers
…*Mrs. Stock's Park:* information kiosk; community concerts and art shows
…*Owen Memorial Park:* 25 acres, playground area, Frisbee golf course
…*Slayton Arboretum:* at Hillsdale College

NPCR

Q QUOTE FROM THE LOCALS

"Get off the beaten path…visit yesteryear in one of the beautiful outposts in the tri-state region. Lose yourself in historical locations, stay in a cozy bed and breakfast, visit antique shops, explore quaint villages and enjoy the many recreational opportunities. Discover the byways through the hills and dales of our county. Hillsdale County is a rural oasis in Michigan located at the bottom of the mitten where the Ohio and Indiana borders meet. Our county has a proud heritage and is actively building for the future. The area is perfect for scenic drives past rolling farmlands, through charming downtowns and around the many lakes and ponds, where nature and tranquility connect." Hillsdale County Chamber of Commerce

R RECREATION & SPORTS

Golf courses: 5
Hiking/skiing/mountain biking trails: 10 miles
Horse racing: harness racing during fair week

North Country National Scenic Trail: yes
Public access sites: 9
Public recreational land: <1% of county
Rail-trail: (8 miles) Baw Beese, Firemans Park
Camden Mud Bogs: every August

S STATE OF MICHIGAN

The Department of Community Health keeps statistics on <u>Baby Names</u>. The 10 Most Popular *names for girls* in Michigan in selected years are noted here.
1950: Linda, Mary, Susan, Patricia, Barbara, Nancy, Kathleen, Sandra, Deborah, Carol
1960: Mary, Susan, Karen, Linda, Patricia, Debra, Kimberly, Cynthia, Deborah, Pamela
1970: Jennifer, Lisa, Michelle, Kimberly, Amy, Angela, Dawn, Kelly, Melissa, Julie
1980: Jennifer, Sarah, Amanda, Melissa, Jessica, Nicole, Angela, Heather, Amy, Elizabeth
1990: Ashley, Jessica, Amanda, Brittany, Samantha, Sarah, Stephanie, Megan, Nicole, Emily
2000: Emily, Hannah, Madison, Alexis, Olivia, Lauren, Samantha, Sarah, Taylor, Kayla
2010: Sophia, Isabella, Olivia, Ava, Emma, Madison, Addison, Abigail, Ella, Chloe
See 46S for *boys'* names.

T TRAVEL

Airport: Hillsdale Municipal
Distance to Lansing: 70 miles
Heritage Route: *Historic:* US-12, *Heritage Trail:*, see 11T
Main roads: US-12, US-127, M-34, M-49, M-50
Memorial Highways: US-12, *Iron Brigade:* see 12T
…US-12, *Pulaski MH:* see 14T
…US-223, *Carlton Road:* see 13T
FYI: Over the years, US-27 (now US-127) has been called, in part or as a whole, proposed, promoted or legalized: Artic-Tropic Overland Trail, Center Line Hwy., Luce Rd., Townsend National Hwy., Veteran's Memorial Hwy. and William Taft Memorial Hwy. Barnett

U UNIVERSITIES & COLLEGES

Jackson Community College, Clyde LeTarte Center
Hillsdale College: est. 1844, 1,300 students. This liberal arts college has two main principles - academic excellence and institutional independence in that it does not accept federal or state taxpayer subsidies for any of its operations. Chargers, GLIAC

V VARIETY

Deb Schmuker

The hills and dales of Hillsdale County go up and down. (Does this sound familiar? A line from the U.S. Army Song says, "Over hill, over dale, we will hit the dusty trail…")

W WANDERLUST

Agri-tourism: *Glei's:* veggies, apples, pumpkins, Christmas trees, bedding and vegetable plants
…*Meckley's Flavor Fruit Farm:* U-pick apples, cider, bakery, maze, pumpkins, pig roasts, hayrides
…*Farm Markets:* Hillsdale County
Culture: Hillsdale College Sage Center for the Arts
Fall colors: middle October
Live theater: Sauk
Shopping mall: Allen Antique Barn

Kelli Williams

Green Top Country Village: antique shops in a variety of old buildings

X X-TRA STUFF

County fair: *Hillsdale County Agricultural Society:* "The Most Popular Fair on Earth." Classic, century old fair buildings bring historic charm to the fairgrounds as visitors enjoy modern entertainment, livestock, skills exhibits and delicious fair time food. Sept.
Famous people: …*Entertainment:* Jason Robards
Hospitals: Hillsdale Community Health Center
Large employers: Tenneco (makes vehicle mufflers), Hillsdale College, Eagle-Picher Automotive (makes OEM parts), Walker Manufacturing Division of Tenneco (makes OEM exhaust parts), Hi-Lex Controls (makes vehicle parts), Hutchinson FTS (makes motor vehicle AC parts), Nyloncraft of Michigan (makes processed plastics)

"The first 'Free School' in Michigan was in Jonesville as well as the first school district with a defined curriculum. The longest continuously operated primary school building in Michigan is currently being used as Jonesville Middle School." Jonesville.org

Hillsdale County has two famous poets:

NPCR

…*Will Carlton:* (1845-1912) a graduate of Hillsdale College in 1869, he published the poem "Over the Hill to the Poorhouse" in 1872 about an older woman, willing to work but unable to support herself. Her beloved children didn't want to take care of her so they sent her to the county home for the poor. The poem gained national fame and Carlton became a well-respected poet for the rest of his life. See 20Y.

Kelli Williams

…*Rose Hartwick Thorpe:* (1850-1939) wrote the poem "Curfew Must Not Ring Tonight" in 1867 when she was 16 years old and a student at Litchfield High School. The poem was set in Oliver Cromwell's England (1650) where the heroine's lover was unjustly accused of being a spy and was to be executed when the curfew bells rang that night. She prevented the bell from ringing and was ultimately considered a hero. Hartwick wrote, edited and published many other poems, stories, books and magazines throughout her life.

Gospel Barn: an inspired and unique gospel music theater with an atmosphere of fun and fellowship centered on Christ
Ray's Tavern: in Reading, noted in *USA Today* for their famous burgers

Y YESTERYEAR

Michigan-Ohio War, also known as the Toledo War

In the early 1800s as the U.S. was expanding westward, a dispute arose between the Michigan Territory and the State of Ohio. Due to conflicting and differing interpretations of state and federal laws, both governments claimed the 468 square mile

"Toledo Strip" that ran from Lake Erie westward just south of the Michigan counties of Monroe, Lenawee and Hillsdale. Ohio was able to stop Michigan's admission into the Union as a result of the dispute. In 1835, both sides raised militias and faced one another across the Maumee River in Toledo. No war was ever fought. Facing pressure from Congress, Michigan capitulated and let Ohio have the land.

As the loser of this dispute, Michigan received the Upper Peninsula. In 1837, Michigan entered the Union as a free (i.e. not supporting slavery) state. But Michigan became the eventual winner of the war when copper and iron were discovered in the U.P. and timber became a valuable resource. World Book Encyclopedia

If you have comments, suggestions, corrections or updates, please email these to: info@discovermichigancountybycounty.com And thanks for reading this book and taking time to share your thoughts!

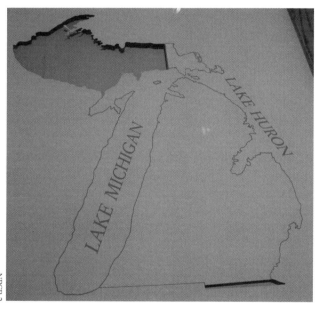

On display in the Michigan Historical Museum in Lansing is a travel trunk with the address of Toledo, Michigan, thought to have been used by Michigan Militia during the 1835-1836 "war."

Z ZOO & ANIMAL PLACES

Watchable Wildlife Viewing Areas: see 30P
Petting zoo: *Meckley's Flavor Fruit Farm*

A AGRICULTURE

Land in farms: 81% of county
Number of farms: 1,390
Size of average farm: 315 acres
Market value of all products: #3 of 83 counties
Crops: ...most acres: corn
...highest $ sales: grains: corn, soybeans, wheat
Livestock: ...largest number: cattle
...highest $ sales: milk & dairy products
Among the top Michigan counties:

- #1- corn for silage, dairy farms, dry edible beans, haylage & grass silage & greenchop, milk cows, sugarbeets, wheat
- #3- corn for grain, colonies of bees
- #4- honey

Dairy, food and meat processing plants: 19
State ranking for harvested trees: #81 of 83 counties
FYI: Nationally, Michigan is the 4th largest beet sugar producer with 3-4 million tons of sugarbeets. That represents 90% of the sugarbeet production east of the Mississippi River. This county has about one-third of the state's 150,000 acres of sugarbeets. Michigan produces 1 billion pounds of sugar a year. Look for the Pioneer and Big Chief brands processed by Michigan Sugar Company, the only beet sugar processor in Michigan. Beet sugar and cane sugar are chemically identical. There are many by-products of sugarbeet processing, including animal feed, production of yeast, vinegar, citric acid and antibiotics. MDA, MFB

The sugarbeet is a root crop that grows underground. Each beet is about 10"-12" long and weighs 3-5 pounds, which, after processing, produces 1 tablespoon of natural sugar. The leftover beet pulp is then used as cattle feed. See 32V.

Don't forget to take this copy of *Discovering Michigan County by County* with you on your next road trip. As you drive throughout the state it will help you to understand what is significant in each and every county.

B BRIDGE OR BOAT

NPCR

Charter boat fishing is a popular activity on any of the Great Lakes. Usually the trip is a half a day and sometimes you come home with your limit and sometimes you don't. The charter service cleans the fish for you and prepares it for your freezer.

C CELEBRATIONS

Huron Daily Tribune

<u>Bad Axe</u> *Hatchet Festival:* hatchet throwing contest, mobile animal exhibit, music, Pure Pro Wrestling, June

<u>Bay Port</u> *Fish Sandwich Festival:* original sandwiches that "take two hands to hold one," Aug.

<u>Caseville</u> *Shanty Days:* polar dip, chili cook-off, Feb.
...*Country Ribstock:* ribs, sand castles, walleye tournament, music, car show, poker, dancing, June
...*Cheeseburger in Caseville:* a week of many events with cheeseburger and Jimmy Buffet themes, Aug.

<u>Harbor Beach</u> *Maritime Festival:* one of the world's largest personal watercraft events in the world's greatest man-made harbor, July

<u>Kinde</u> *Polka Fest:* Sept.
<u>Port Austin</u> *May Fest:* car show, pig roast, poker run, music, poetry reading, May
...*Festivale Italiano:* June
...*Pirates on the Great Lakes Fishing Festival:* Aug.

Port Hope *ABC Day:* (Antiques, Bean Soup, Crafts & Collectibles) take a stroll back in time, Aug.

Sebewaing *Michigan Sugar Festival:* parade, candy drop, Sweet Adelines, historic tours, queen, June

Huron Daily Tribune

D DEMOGRAPHICS

Population: 33,100   **Persons per sq. mile:** 40
Largest city: Bad Axe   **Population:** 3,130
Largest township: Colfax   **Population:** 1,880
Largest village: Sebewaing **Population:** 1,960
Median household income: $38,500
Owner-occupied median house value: $105,000
Persons affiliated with a religious congregation: 75% (#3/MI)
Persons below poverty level: 15%
Students receiving school lunch subsidy: 45%

E ENVIRONMENT

Built in 2007, the 3,200-acre Harvest Wind Farm was Michigan's first commercial-scale wind project. There are 32 wind turbines, each 397 feet tall, with blade lengths of 131 feet. A minimum wind speed of 8 mph is needed to operate the turbines. The $94 million investment can provide enough electric power to run 15,000 homes. WolverinePower Cooperative.com

F FLORA & FAUNA

Gary M. Stolz/USFWS

Bladderwort is a freshwater, underwater, carnivorous aquatic plant that ingests prey from protozoa to young tadpoles. The "hollow pod" structure is the sophisticated bladder that catches and digests the prey.

Wikipedia: Alexander Wilson

The Pigeon River and Village of Pigeon were named for the huge flocks of Passenger Pigeons that fed from the marshy swamps along the banks of the river. Observers said the flocks were so thick that, when in flight, they darkened the sky. By 1914, the pigeons were extinct. See 24H.

G GOVERNMENT

County: ...created: 1840 ...organized: 1859
...originally part of: Saginaw, St. Clair, Sanilac Counties
Size: 545,000 acres / 837 sq. miles (18 of 83 counties)
The county has 2 cities, 9 villages, 28 townships, 13 unincorporated communities and 15 school districts.

NPCR

NPCR

County seat: Bad Axe
...Homestead property tax: 42 mills
Motto: <u>Bad Axe</u> Chamber: *the hub of the Thumb*

...<u>Bay Port</u> Chamber: *Where the Fish Caught the Man*

...<u>Caseville</u>: *Perch Capital of Michigan*
...<u>Harbor Beach</u>: *World's Greatest Man-made Harbor*
...<u>Huron County</u>: *Your Welcoming Neighbor*
...<u>Huron County</u> Visitor's Bureau: *Where the Countryside Meets the Lakeshore*
...<u>Pigeon</u>: *Good Life in a Small Town*
...<u>Port Austin</u> Chamber: *Visit the 'Thumb'!*
...<u>Port Hope</u>: *The little town with the Big WELCOME!*
...<u>Sebewaing</u>: *Sugar Beet Capital*

H HISTORICAL MARKERS 15 of 17

Bay Port Fishing District: 1920-1930s, one of the largest freshwater commercial fishing ports in the world

Charles G. Learned House: <1839, prosperous farmer Learned updated this house in the French Second Empire Style.

Frank Murphy: 1890-1949, held state, U.S. and international government positions; as a U.S Supreme Court judge he clarified labor's right to strike; he was born and is buried here.

Great Fire of 1881: a 3-day fire that burned a million acres in Huron and Sanilac counties with at least 125 deaths; this was the first disaster relief of the newly established American Red Cross; see 32Y.

Huron City: destroyed by the fire of 1871, then rebuilt, and destroyed again by the fire of 1881, then rebuilt again; a few homes remain from this period.

Indian Mission: the original 1849 log mission house of the Lutheran missionaries who wanted to convert the American Indians; by 1854 it was sold because the American Indians had left the area.

John C. Liken: a successful businessman who owned several sawmills, factories and stores

John C. Martini House: John Liken built five Stick Style houses for his children; only this one remains.

Owendale: 1896, after the sawmill burned, the area turned from lumbering to agriculture.

Pigeon Depot: 1883, now the Pigeon Historical Society Museum

Pointe aux Barques Lighthouse: 1857, was run by Michigan's first female light keeper

Port Hope Chimney: 1858, all that remains of a lumber mill destroyed by the fires of 1871 & 1881

St. Mary of Czestochowa Roman Catholic Church: 1933, the "Queen of Poland," built to maintain Polish identity

Stagecoaches: 1800s, slow and rough travel; improved when better roads were built

White Rock School: 1909, had 25 students, teacher was paid $40 per month; now the Huron County Historical Society Museum

Monument: *Caseville Civil War Monument*
National Register of Historic Places: 26 listings
State Historic Sites: 43 listings

I INFORMATION

Chamber of Commerce: Bad Axe, Caseville, Harbor Beach, Pigeon, Port Austin, Sebewaing
Visitor: Huron County Visitors Bureau, 800-35-THUMB, huroncounty.com

J JOKES

You might be from a small town in Michigan if...
...without thinking, you wave to all oncoming traffic.
...you don't buy all your fruits and vegetables at the grocery store.
...your "main drag" in town is two blocks long.
...your town doesn't have a McDonald's.

…you put pennies in the parking meter just for the excitement of seeing the dial move.

…the downtown stores close at 5:00 PM.

…you know it's better to mow in December than to shovel in October.

K KINSMAN

Race
American Indian: <1%
Asian: <1%
Black/African American: <1%
Hispanic or Latino: 2%
Other: <1%
White: 97%

Ancestry
German: 39% (#1/MI)
Polish: 19%
U.S./American: 8%
English: 7%
Irish: 6%
French: 4%

L LIGHTHOUSE OR LANDMARK

Michigan State Historic Preservation Office

Built in 1857, Pointe aux Barques (point oh barks) means "point of little boats" because the water is shallow and therefore dangerous to larger vessels. This active Lighthouse is now part of Lighthouse County Park and adjacent to Thumb Area Great Lakes State Bottomland Preserve. The keeper's house is a museum.

M MUSEUMS

<u>Bad Axe</u> *Allen House Museum:* 1902 Dutch Colonial style home that is nearly unchanged

…*Museum of Local History:* mid-to-late 19th century artifacts, fire hose drying tower

Courtesy of D.A. McDonald, Huron County Historical Society

…*Pioneer Log Village:* largest collection (6 individual museums) of authentically restored pioneer log buildings in Michigan; home of the Log Cabin Society of Michigan that celebrates and sponsors over 100 log cabins and events in Michigan each June

<u>Elkton</u> *Log Cabin Museum:* 1865

<u>Harbor Beach</u> *Grice House Museum:* life in the past

…*Murphy Museum:* Frank Murphy, former Michigan governor and U.S. Supreme Court Justice

<u>Parisville</u> *St. Mary's Historical Museum:* in an authentic Polish settlement log cabin that is the oldest in U.S.

<u>Pigeon</u> *Depot Museum:* railroad artifacts, household items, farm tools, clothing, pianola, military items

<u>Port Austin</u> *Huron City Historic District:* restored 1880s lumbering village, 7 buildings including the 1876 Pointe aux Barques Life Saving Station

<u>Port Hope</u> *Pointe aux Barques Lighthouse Museum:* antiques, shipwreck information; see 32H, 32L

<u>Sebewaing</u> *Historical Society:* Charles Liken Home, Old Sebewaing Township Hall

…*Luckhard Museum:* 1845 mission, pioneer and American Indian relics

N NATURAL RESOURCES

Elevation: 600 – 800 feet
Physiography: lake-border plains, rolling plains

Forest type: maple-beech-hemlock, aspen-beech
Public/private forests: 12% of county

NPCR

Water in county: 3% of county
  Bay: Wild Fowl Bay of Saginaw Bay of Lake Huron
  Lakes: 8   **…largest:** Rush
  Rivers: Black, Cass, Pigeon, Pinnebog
  Rivers & streams: 940 miles

Great Lakes islands: 4
Great Lakes peninsula: Thumb
Great Lakes shoreline: 93 miles of Lake Huron

Growing season, avg.: 144 days (3-4 temp. zones)
Last freeze, avg.: May 10 – May 20
First freeze, avg.: Oct. 5 – Oct. 20
Precipitation, annual avg.: rainfall: 29 inches
snowfall: 54 inches
Temperature (F), avg.: January: high 28°, **low** 13°
July: high 81°, **low** 57°
Annual: >90°: 8 days, **<0°:** 11 days
Tornadoes (1930-2010): 13

O ORIGINS

Bad Axe:[c] an early surveyor found a broken axe in an old hunter's cabin and noted the place as Bad Axe Camp on his map; 1861

Caseville:[v] large landowner, Leonard Case; 1836

Elkton:[v] first settler killed a huge elk that got tangled in his wife's clothesline; 1886

Grandstone City:[u] grind-stones were quarried, shaped and shipped around the world; 1834

Harbor Beach:[c] a more descriptive name of the town than Sand Beach, its former name; 1837

Huron:[co] from the French word meaning "wild boar" because they thought the Mohawk haircuts of the Wyandot warriors looked like the bristles on a wild boar's neck bigorrin.org

Kinde:[v] storekeeper, John Kinde; 1884

Owendale:[v] sawmill owners and cousins, both named John Owen; 1877

Parisville:[u] early pioneer settler was born near Paris, France; 1854

Pigeon:[v] wild pigeons in the area; 1888; see 32F

Port Austin:[v] lumber firm owner P.C. Austin built a dock and put a light on it; it was Austin's Dock, then Austin Port, now Port Austin; 1839

Port Hope:[v] the place where two men drifting in a skiff made land; 1855

Sebewaing:[v] (SEE ba wing) American Indian word for crooked creek; 1845

Ubly:[v] misspelling of Ubley, England, hometown of an early settler; 1865

P PARKS

National: 0 **State:** 4 **County:** 4 **Local:** 11
Number of campsites: 2,400
State Game Area: Gagetown, Rush Lake[wv], Verona
State Park: *Port Crescent:*[ww] 600 acres on Saginaw Bay, 3 miles of sandy beach, boardwalk, hunting, fishing, swimming, trails, camping

…*Albert Sleeper:* 720 acres on Saginaw Bay, sandy beach, forest, wetlands, dunes, trails; Michigan Gov. Sleeper (1917-1920), from Huron County, sign-ed the law that created the state park system .

State Wildlife Area: *Wild Fowl Bay:*[ww] 12,000 acres
State Underwater Preserve: *Thumb Area:* 276 square miles of Lake Huron that contains 19 major shipwrecks, sea caves and grindstones
County: *Huron County Nature Center-Wilderness Arboretum:*[ww] 280 acres
…*Lighthouse:* 120 acres, Lighthouse Museum

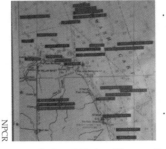

…*Thumb Area Great Lakes State Bottomland Preserve:* the only preserve in the state that is part of a county park system; see above

…*Wagener:* 132 acres, camping, Harbor Beach Nature Trails

Local: *Sand Point Nature Preserve:* 140 acres

Q QUOTE FROM THE LOCALS

"Michigan has a green Thumb! And not just in the usual sense. Huron County's lush, fertile farmland has a border of deeper green – shady willow green, spicy pine green, immense oak green. At the Lake Huron Shoreline, cropland is separated from sandy beaches by deep, cool forests. We have the loveliest countryside and lakeshore imaginable – all for your enjoyment." huroncounty.com

R RECREATION & SPORTS

Auto racing: *Owendale Speedway:* ¼-mile oval clay track …*Ubly Dragway:* ⅛ mile dragstrip
Golf courses: 6
Great Lakes marinas: 20   **Boat slips:** 1,000
Hiking/skiing/mountain biking trails: 20 miles
Horse racing: harness racing during fair week
Michigan Heritage Water Trail: Tip of the Thumb
Public access sites: 13
Public recreational land: 2% of county
Rail-trail: (1 mile) Harbor Beach Bike-Pedestrian Path

Recreational harbor: Bay-port Harbor of Refuge, Caseville Marina, Harbor Beach Marina, Port Austin State Harbor, Sebewaing Marina

Huron County EDC

Kayak Rendezvous: June
Thumb Area OffShore Challenge Fishing Tournament: June

S STATE OF MICHIGAN

Lake Huron Facts
  Size: 5th largest in world
    2nd largest Great Lake
  Length: 206 miles
  Average depth: 195 feet
  Shoreline (including 30,000 islands): 3,827 miles
  Special features: islands, Georgian Bay, Saginaw Bay, scenic beauty
  Borders on: Michigan and Ontario, Canada

T TRAVEL

Airport: Huron County Memorial
Bus: Huron Transit
Circle Tour: Lake Huron via M-25
Distance to Lansing: 130 miles
Main roads: M-19, M-25, M-53, M-142
Memorial Highway: M-53, *Earle MH:* see 44T
Scenic Drive: M-25 follows Lake Huron for 75 miles

U UNIVERSITIES & COLLEGES

None

V VARIETY

Huron County EDC

The homely, humble sugarbeet has the appearance of a large rock. These piles of sugarbeets are just waiting to be made into sugar, a process which takes only 4-5 hours. Harvested in October, it takes until March to process the entire crop of Michigan sugarbeets. See 32A.

W WANDERLUST

Agri-tourism: *Leipprandt Orchards:* apples, cider, peaches, bakery, gifts, Christmas room
…*Willow Ridge Farm Market:* flowers, fruits, berries, veggies, pickles, jams, brown eggs
Fall colors: late September
Lighthouse, other: Harbor Beach Breakwater Light, Port Austin Reef Light
Live theater: Harbor Beach Community Theatre, Port Austin Community Players
Wineries: *Dizzy Daisy Winery & Vineyard:* 35 varieties of grapes, 30 different wines, sampling
Bay Port Fish Company: free guided tours of a real fish market; on the shores of Lake Huron
Farm Tours: Maplewood Farm, Sandy Acres Llama Farm, Shadow Hollow Suri Alpacas

X X-TRA STUFF

Commercial port: Harbor Beach
County fair: *Huron Community Fair Assoc.:* Aug.
Famous people: …*Entertainment*: Bob Murawski, Tami Ginden
…*Politics*: Frank Murphy
…*Sports*: Tom Bers
…*Other*: Terry Camp, Lillian Jackson Braun
Hospitals: Harbor Beach Community Hospital, Huron Medical Center, Scheurer Hospital

Large employers: Thumb Plastics (makes injection molded products), Axly Tool & Bushing (makes cast steel, copper foundry), Huron Casting (makes alloy steel, foundry), Tower Automotive (makes stamped products), Scheurer Hospital, Huron Medical Center, Thumb Tool & Engineering (makes dies and tools)

Parisville was one of the first Polish-American settlements in the U.S. in 1848.

In this county in 2010, there were still 5, one-teacher schools with 10-20 students each and 2, two-teacher schools with 24-27 students each.

Y YESTERYEAR

The summer and fall of 1881 were extremely hot and dry with the rivers at record lows and some swamps had even dried up. The fire of 1871 had ended the timber era but left downed timber everywhere. The underbrush began to grow uninhibited. The Thumb area was called "as dry as a man after eating salt mackerel." Residents were still engaged in clearing the land from the logging and previous fire remnants and they cleared the land by burning. On Sept. 5, 1881, hurricane intense winds blew in from the southwest and the whole land exploded into fire. Approximately 300 people died, 15,000 were made homeless and 3,400 buildings were destroyed. The <u>Great Fire of 1881</u> was the worst three days in the history of the Thumb. However, this tragedy launched Clara Barton's three-week-old American Red Cross into national prominence as the premier disaster relief organization. [Schultz] See also 32H, 18Y, 58T.

Z ZOO & ANIMAL PLACES

Watchable Wildlife Viewing Areas:[ww] see 32P

From the INDEX...

[1,000] This notation indicates that the noted item is on the *1,000 Places To See Before You Die* list (and book of the same name) by Patricia Schultz.

A AGRICULTURE

Land in farms: 66% of county
Number of farms: 950
Size of average farm: 200 acres
Market value of all products: #26 of 83 counties
Crops: ...most acres: corn
...highest $ sales: grains: corn, soybeans, wheat
Livestock: ...largest number of: cattle
...highest $ sales: milk & dairy products
Among the top Michigan counties:
- #1- quail
- #2- sod
- #3- mules, burros and donkeys
- #4- maple syrup, sheep and goat operations

Dairy, food and meat processing plants: 42
State ranking for harvested trees: #75 of 83 counties
AgBioResearch Centers (MSU): *South Campus Field Research Facilities:* on the Michigan State University campus, 18 research units/centers specializing in animal science, botany and plant pathology, crop and soil sciences, forestry and horticulture; focus is on developing more nutritious food, producing crops with fewer or no pesticides, clean water, wetland preservation, land use and techniques to detect the organisms that cause food-born illness
FYI: The mission of the Michigan Department of Agriculture and Rural Development (MDARD), formerly the MDA, is "To protect, promote and preserve the food, agricultural, environmental and economic interests of the people of Michigan." Under their jurisdiction are not only all aspects of agriculture, including food safety and animal health, but environmental stewardship, fairs, exhibitions, horse racing, food law and restaurant licensing, weights and measures, and retail motor fuel outlet licensing as well. Michigan.gov See 68A.

B BRIDGE OR BOAT

Laura Hamlin

The *Michigan Princess* Riverboat, a triple deck river big wheel paddle boat on the Grand River, has a capacity of 500 guests, and offers lunch and dinner cruises, mystery cruises and parties of all kinds.

C CELEBRATIONS

Lizzie Williams

East Lansing *Art Festival:* premier juried, May

...*Great Lakes Folk Fest.:* celebrating heritages, Aug.
...*Fountain Square Concert Series:* Ann Street Plaza, Concert Series: mid-Michigan musicians, June-Aug.

MessageMakers

...*Moonlight Film Festival:* outdoors, July-Aug.

...*Summer Solstice Jazz Festival:* Michigan musicians, June

...*Winter Glow:* music & food, Dec.

Mason *Down Home Days:* family activities, Sept.
...*Sun Dried Music Fest:* variety of music styles, Aug.

Lansing *Fiesta:* Hispanic arts and traditions, May
...*Woldumar Nature Center:* American Heritage Festival, Sept.; Wildflower Weekend, May
...*Juneteenth Celebration:* commemorate the ending of slavery in the U.S. by celebrating the joys of liberty, educating the community about African-American heritage and promoting positive cultural interaction
...*Riverbank Traditional Pow Wow:* bringing American Indian culture to the community, June

Greater Lansing CVB

...*Common Ground Music Festival:* 7 days, 80,000 attendees, top tier entertainment, July

...*Car Capital Celebration:* a salute to the contribution made by the auto industry, Aug.
...*Old US-27 Motor Tour:* see 12C
...*Michigan Mosaic Music Festival:* celebrate diversity and unity; bands, dance, dragon boat races, ethnic foods, labor displays, car & motorcycle show, Aug.

Raymond Holt

...Old Town: Festival of the Sun, Festival of the Moon, June; Jazzfest, Aug.; Bluesfest, Sept., Oktoberfest, Oct., Dickens Village, Dec.

...Silver Bells in the City: light parade, arts, Dec.

...Wonderland of Lights: Potter Park Zoo, Nov.-Dec.

Stockbridge *A Day in the Village:* June
Williamston *Red Cedar Jubilee:* June

Greater Lansing CVB

D DEMOGRAPHICS

Population: 281,000
Largest city: Lansing
Largest township: Meridian
Largest village: Webberville
Median household income: $43,000
Owner-occupied median house value: $140,000
Persons affiliated with a religious congregation: 40%
Persons below poverty level: 19%
Students receiving school lunch subsidy: 40%

Persons per sq. mile: 503
Population: 114,300
Population: 39,700
Population: 1,270

E ENVIRONMENT

The College of Agriculture and Natural Resources (CANR) at Michigan State University offers the following undergraduate majors: Agribusiness Management, Agriscience, ANR Communications, Animal Science, Biosystems Engineering, Construction Management, Crop and Soil Sciences, Dietetics, Entomology, Environmental Economics and Policy, Environmental Soil Sciences, Environmental Studies and Applications, Fisheries and Wildlife, Food Industry Management, Food Science, Forestry, Horticulture, Interior Design, Landscape Architecture, Packaging, Park-Recreation and Tourism Resources, and Technology Systems Management. Other specializations include Agronomy, International Agriculture, Marine Ecosystem Management, Natural Resources Recreation, and Science-Technology-Environment and Public Policy. The graduates of these programs become the leaders in agricultural, natural resources and environmental fields.

F FLORA & FAUNA

Red Clover

Maddie List/USFWS

White Clover

USFWS

Red clover is used as a cover crop and forage or pasture for animals; it also grows wild. White clover likes a mowed environment so it is found in lawns, parks and roadsides. It is the white clover where one four-leaf clover will be found for every 10,000 three-leaf clovers.

Gary M. Stolz/USFWS

The five-lined skink, 5"-8" long, is a member of the lizard family; it has small legs yet it is sometimes mistaken for a snake. It likes wooded or partially wooded areas and needs to bask in the sun.

G GOVERNMENT

County: ...**created:** 1829 ...**organized:** 1838
...**originally part of:** Washtenaw, Jackson, Eaton Counties
Size: 359,000 acres / 559 sq. miles (55 of 83 counties)
The county has 5 cities, 3 villages, 16 townships with 3 as charter townships, 5 unincorporated communities, 4 Census Designated Place and 12 school districts.

Michigan State Preservation Office

NPCR

County seat: Mason

...Homestead property tax: 45 mills

FYI: The City of Lansing, in Ingham County, is the capital of Michigan and Mason is the Ingham County seat. Michigan is the only state in the nation where the state capital and the local county seat are not the same city.

Motto: <u>East Lansing</u>: *The Home of Michigan State University*

...<u>Lansing</u>: *Where Michigan Works*

...<u>Leslie</u>: *The place to be!*

...<u>Williamston</u>: *Discover the Charm*

H HISTORICAL MARKERS 30 of 88

Box 23 Club: provides support for Lansing Fire Dept.

Chief Okemos: 1775?-1885, leader of local Saginaw Chippewa Indians; means Little Chief

RE Olds Museum

Collegeville: 1887, platted subdivision next to MSU

Curved Dash Oldsmobile: 1901, the first moving assembly line was invented by R.E. Olds; the song *My Merry Oldsmobile* was written about this car.

The Grand River: Michigan's longest river, 270 miles from Hillsdale County to Grand Haven on Lake Michigan

Grand River Trail: American Indian trail, now US-16 and M-43

Harry J. Eustace Hall: MSU, 1888, first separate horticultural lab in U.S.

Horatio Earle: 1905, "the father of good roads," helped open Michigan to commerce and tourism; see 44T

Ingham County Courthouse: 1904, Gov. Bliss said, "a meeting place for farmers, mechanics, business and professional men."

Kern Hotel Fire: 1934, 34 people died

Lansing Becomes State Capitol: 1847, free land, equidistant from Detroit, Mt. Clemens, Monroe; at the mouth of Grand and Kalamazoo Rivers [sic]

Malcolm X Home site: 1925-1965, lived locally in 1930s; spokesman for the oppressed everywhere

Michigan Automobile Assoc.: est. 1920, to promote and protect the interests of franchised dealers

Michigan Dental Assoc.: est. 1856, first state dental society in the U.S.

Michigan Manufacturer's Assoc.: est. 1902, first to promote worker's compensation and group insurance

Michigan Millers Mutual Insurance Co.: est. 1881, by four mill owners, to provide fire insurance

Michigan Pharmacists Assoc.: est. 1883, to regulate drug distribution and pharmacist licensing

Michigan Sheriffs' Assoc.: est. 1877, to help each other detain, arrest and convict criminals

Michigan State Medical Society: est. 1866, created state public health department in 1873

Michigan State Police: est. 1917 during WWI for protection from German agents and radical labor groups

Michigan State University: est. 1855; College Hall, where Beaumont Tower now stands, the first building in the U.S. for the teaching of scientific agriculture; a model for all land-grant colleges

Old Newsboys: as a truant officer, George E. Palmer began raising money to buy shoes for needy kids because he determined that was the main reason some kids were not attending school.

Ransom Eli Olds: 1897, started Olds Motor Vehicle Co. which later became the Oldsmobile Division of General Motors

State Bar of Michigan: est. 1935, to improve the justice and delivery of legal services

State Capitol: 1879, 267' spired dome; Michigan white pine, copper and slate used extensively

State Highway Dept.: est. 1905; roads were quagmires of sand, mud and clay; bicyclists led the way for road reform.

Town of Michigan: 1847, name of Michigan's capital before it was named Lansing in 1847; see 33Y

Michigan State Preservation Office

Union Depot: 1902-1972; Chateauesque conical towers and cut stone arches; now Clara's Restaurant

Turner-Dodge House: 1858, classic revival style; 33M

Michigan State Preservation Office

Wolverine Boys / Girls State: 1937 /1941, by American Legion to promote good citizenship

Monument: statue of Michigan's Governor during the Civil War, Austin Blair; see 23H, 23Y, 38H

National Historic Landmarks: Michigan State Capitol; see 33L

National Register of Historic Places*: 41 listings

State Historic Sites: 125 listings

I INFORMATION

Chamber of Commerce: Lansing, Leslie, Mason, Michigan, Williamston

Visitor: Greater Lansing Convention and Visitors Bureau, 888-252-6746, lansing.org

J JOKES

<u>Driving in Michigan</u>

1. A right lane construction closure is just a game to see how many people can cut in line by passing you on the right as you sit in the left land waiting for the same jerks to squeeze their way back in before hitting the construction barrels.
2. Under no circumstances should you leave a safe distance between you and the car in front of you, no matter how fast you're driving. If you do, somebody else will fill in the space, putting you in an even more dangerous situation.
3. Never get in the way of a car that needs extensive bodywork. Michigan is a no-fault insurance state and the other driver may feel there is nothing to lose. Or he may be just looking for free repairs.
4. They teach you in kindergarten that red means stop, green means go and yellow means caution. They forget to mention that orange means keep your cool while sitting through mind-numbing stop-and-go construction traffic.
5. In July you can ignore the "Ice forms on bridges before roads" signs. It's not gonna' happen. Not even in the U.P.

K KINSMAN

<u>Race</u>
American Indian: <1%
Asian: 5%
Black/African American: 12%
Hispanic or Latino: 7%
Other: 6%
White: 76%

<u>Ancestry</u>
German: 19%
English: 10%
Irish: 8%
U.S./American: 6%
Polish: 5%
Italian: 4%

FYI: Of U.S. cities with over 100,000 people, Lansing has the highest percentage (4.1%) of people who identify themselves as multiple-race black. Lansing State Journal

L LIGHTHOUSE OR LANDMARK

Paul Jackson

Built in 1888, the State of Michigan Capitol Building is restored and *very* beautiful. It is open for free guided tours, Monday through Friday. You simply must take the tour when you're in town.

M MUSEUMS

<u>Lansing</u>: *All Around the African World Museum:* contributions of those from African descent

…*Impression 5 Science Museum:* hands-on learning

…*Michigan State Capitol Building:* you need to see it!

…*Michigan Historical Museum:* 26 galleries include 1957 Auto Show, copper mine, WWII, one-room school, American Indians, threestory relief map and much more; descriptions of all the galleries are available online; part of the Michigan Historical Museum System (see FYI below)

Laura Hamlin

…*Michigan Supreme Court Learning Center:* hands-on gallery to help us understand the judiciary processes

...*Michigan Women's Historical Center & Hall of Fame:* contributions of Michigan women

...*R.E. Olds Transportation Museum:* history of area transportation since 1883; vintage cars

...*Telephone Pioneer Museum:* telephone memorabilia

...*Turner-Dodge House:* Classical Revival architecture, gardens, costumed guides; see 33H

REO Olds Museum

Laura Hamlin

<u>Meridian Township</u>: *Meridian Historical Village:* includes authentic plank road tollhouse, one room schoolhouse and general store

...*Nokomis Learning Center:* learn about Native Americans of the Great Lakes region

<u>Michigan State University</u>: *Athletics Hall of Fame:* the best from 24 sports

...*Eli and Edythe Broad Art Museum:* a world-class facility; committed to exploring international contemporary culture and ideas through art

...*Museum:* discover the wonders of the natural world and different cultures

NPCR

FYI: The <u>Michigan Historical Museum System</u> consists of 11 museums and historic sites throughout the state that are your pathway to fun and discovery. Be sure to visit them when you are in the following counties: Crawford, Delta, Ingham, Iosco, Jackson, Lenawee, Keweenaw, Mackinac, Marquette and Sanilac.

N NATURAL RESOURCES

Elevation: 800 – 1,000 ft.

Physiography: rolling plains
Forest type: maple-beech, oak-hickory
Public/private forests: 17% of county

NPCR

National Natural Landmark: *Toumey Woods Natural Area:* on the MSU campus, an extremely rare example of a virgin stand of beech-maple forest

Laura Hamlin

Water in county: <1% of county
Lakes: 30   **...largest:** Lake Lansing
Rivers: Grand, Red Cedar
Rivers & streams: 230 miles

Avg. sunshine: January: 35%   July: 74%
Growing season, avg.: 144 days (2 temp. zones)
  Last freeze, avg.: May 5 – May 10
  First freeze, avg.: Oct. 5 – Oct. 10
Precipitation, annual avg.: rainfall: 29 inches
                snowfall: 39 inches
Temperature (F), avg.: January: high 29°, low 14°
            July: high 83°, low 59°
 Annual: >90°: 10 days, **<0°:** 12 days
Tornadoes (1930-2010): 26

O ORIGINS

<u>Dansville</u>:[v] Daniel Crossman platted the village; Dr. Daniel Weston was first postmaster; 1844
<u>Delhi</u>:[ct] many settlers from Delhi, NY; 1837
<u>East Lansing</u>:[c] east of Lansing; 1849
<u>Haslett</u>:[u] James Haslett, founder of a summer camp for Spiritualists at Pine Lake; 1879
<u>Holt</u>:[u] postmaster general, John Holt; 1837
<u>Ingham</u>:[co] (ING um) Samuel Ingham, Secretary of Treasury under President Andrew Jackson; 1839
<u>Lansing</u>:[c,ct] after Lansing Twp. and Lansing, NY; John Lansing was a NY Revolutionary War hero; 1837
<u>Leslie</u>:[c] the Leslie family living in NY; 1836
<u>Mason</u>:[c] Michigan's first and youngest (age 24) governor, Stevens T. Mason; 1836; see 53O
<u>Meridian</u>:[ct] the eastern boundary of the township was the principal meridian; 1841; see 33P, 63Y
<u>Okemos</u>:[u] (OAK em us) a Chippewa Chief, means "little chief;" 1839
<u>Stockbridge</u>:[v] after Stockbridge Twp.; 1835
<u>Webberville</u>:[v] postmaster Herbert P. Webber; 1867
<u>Williamston</u>:[c] Williams brothers built a dam, sawmill and gristmill on the Red Cedar River; 1834

P PARKS

National: 0 **State:** 1 **County:** 13 **Local:** 61
Number of campsites: 750
State Game Area: ʷʷ (5,000 acres) Dansville
State Park: *Meridian-Baseline:* 88 acres, not open to the public; it preserves the spot where all township, range and section survey lines begin for the state. By 1819, the American Indians had ceded their lands to the settlers in the Treaty of Detroit and the Treaty of Saginaw. The western boundary for the Treaty of Detroit later became the principal meridian, or north-south line, for land surveys. Meridian Road, which divides Ingham County in half, is named for this line. See 60Y, 63Y.

County: *Burchfield /River-bend Nature Area:* 500 acres, mountain biking trails, swimming, to-bogganing

NPCR

...*Capital Connector Trail System:* 23 miles of trails along the Grand River, through Potter Park Zoo, connecting major recreation centers in the county with downtown Lansing; walk, run, bike, or skate

...*Lake Lansing Parks:* 400+ acres, on Lake Lansing, the largest lake within 30 miles; 5 miles of hiking/cross-county ski trails, swimming, boating, ball fields

Laura Hamlin

Local: *Adado Riverfront Park:* on the Grand River, designed for Lansing festivals
...*Frances Park:* formal rose garden with over 150 varieties; overlooks the Grand River; picnic shelter
...*Harris Nature Center:* guided tours available
...*Washington Park:* softball field, ice rink

Other: *Baker Woodlot:* MSU, 170 acres, the forest of Michigan's past; level paths, ponds, swamps

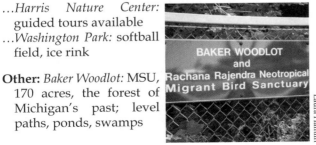

BAKER WOODLOT and Rachana Rajendra Neotropical Migrant Bird Sanctuary

Laura Hamlin

...*Fenner Nature Center:*ʷʷ self-guided nature trails through woods, interpretive center, herb garden
...*Wildlife Viewing Sites:* River Bend Natural Area, Rayner Park

Q QUOTE FROM THE LOCALS

"Ingham County is the heartland of Michigan, a hub of government, culture, and commerce. The county stands as the demographic center of the state – 90 minutes to 90 percent of Michigan's population. It is the crossroads of Michigan via freeways, railroads, and air transportation systems. The imposing State Capitol, the sculptured beauty of Michigan State University, and an energetic and prosperous General Motors industrial base working hand in hand with a bountiful agricultural society to form the most stable economy in the state." Michigan.org.

R RECREATION & SPORTS

Auto racing: *Spartan Speedway:* the track the stars call home; ¼-mile paved track
Golf courses: 20
Hiking/skiing/mountain biking trails: 50 miles
Public access sites: 4
Public recreational land: 1% of county
Rail-trail: (10 miles) Lakeland, Lansing River Trail
Baseball Academy of Mid-Michigan: plays indoors
Hope Soccer Complex: 6 state-of-the-art fields, World Cup ratings
John Smoltz Baseball Academy: instructional

Lansing Lugnuts: minor league baseball plays at Cooley Law School Stadium (previously Olds-mobile Park) on the Jackson (National Life) Field

NPCR

Lansing Capitals: International Basketball League; only play away games
Michigan State University offers 12 men's and 13 women's varsity sports.

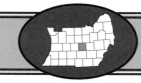
FYI: <u>Michigan Trails and Greenway Alliance</u> seeks to promote a statewide system of trails and greenways for environmental and cultural preservation. Trails are important because they help connect people to nature; they provide opportunity for exercise and family activities; they help children get to school safely; and they are good for Michigan's economy. The organization sponsors many activities throughout the state. michigantrails.org

S STATE OF MICHIGAN

In Michigan, a resident either lives in a non-incorporated township, or an incorporated city or village. <u>Where a person lives</u> determines some of the laws that govern them, to whom taxes are paid and what services are provided. There are 1,860 local units of government in Michigan.

• *Census Designated Place (CDP):* These are communities that do not have their own incorporation status and are still governed by a township or county. They have a high population density, have their own identity, may have their own zip code and schools, and are recognized in the U.S. Census.

• *Charter Township:* These were created by the state legislature in the 1940s, in part, to protect the townships from annexation by larger cities.

• *City:* Cities are incorporated, have local governmental powers and are not part of a township; size is not a determining factor.

• *County:* Michigan is one of 20 states that has a county form of government. Michigan's 83 counties vary widely in their organization and function.

• *Township:* It is a unit of local government created in the 1800s when transportation and communication were very limited. They provide some of the services needed by the residents.

• *Unincorporated community:* It can be a Census Designated Place (see above), but most often is an area that at one time may have been the site of the local one-room schoolhouse or post office. They might have few or no businesses, and someone may have converted the old one-room schoolhouse to a home or business. Some

may be very populous communities. It is governed by the township and county.

• *Village:* Some villages are incorporated and some are not. They all have some self-governing authority but have less governing powers than a city; they still remain part of the township. They can be larger or smaller than cities. Michigan.gov

T TRAVEL

Airports: Capital Region International is in Clinton County; Mason Jewett

Amtrak: East Lansing

Bus: Capital Area Transportation Authority (CATA), Indian Trails

Distance to Lansing: You're already here!

Main roads: I-69, I-96, I-127, I-496

Memorial Highways: I-96, *AmVets MH*: see 19T

…I-496, *Olds Freeway*: Ransom Eli Olds (1864-1950) was the founder of the Olds Motor Vehicle Company in Lansing that eventually became part of General Motors.

…US-127, *James M. Pelton Firefighters Memorial*: he (1943-2001) was a volunteer fireman for 39 years and the first full-time fire chief in Mason when he was killed by someone who ran a stop sign.

…M-43, *Frank D. Fitzgerald MH*: see 23T

U UNIVERSITIES & COLLEGES

Thomas M. Cooley Law School: est. 1972; 3,200 students. It is the largest law school in the country with 4 campuses in Michigan and 1 in Florida. Cooley stands firm in its belief that the study of law should not be an esoteric pursuit, or the practice of law an elitist profession.

Davenport University: see 13U

Lansing Community College: est. 1957; 40,000 students. LCC exists so that all people have educational and enrichment opportunities in career and workforce development, general education, developmental education and personal enrichment; M-TEC. MCCAA, Stars

Michigan State University: est. 1858; 47,000 students. As a pioneer land-grant institution, MSU strives to discover practical uses for theoretical knowledge and to speed the diffusion of information to the residents of the state, the nation and the world. Big 10, Spartans

V VARIETY

Laura Hamlin

The first Spartan statue at Michigan State University was a 9'7" terra cotta sculpture (largest in the world) that stood outdoors from 1945 to 2005. It has been relocated indoors at Spartan Stadium. In 2005, an exact replica of the original Spartan was cast in bronze and now stands at the north end of Demonstration Hall Field in the same spot as the original statue.

W WANDERLUST

Agri-tourism: *Farmers' Markets:* Allen Street, City of East Lansing, Meridian Township, Williamston
…Shawhaven Farm: maze, pumpkins, lambs, tours
Brewery: Harper's Restaurant & Brewpub
Cultural: *Greater Lansing Ballet Company:* semi-professional
…Lansing Symphony Orchestra: music, outreach

Live theater: All-of-us Express Children's Theatre, Lansing Civic Players, Mid-Michigan Family Theatre, Peppermint Creek Theatre Company, Riverwalk, Starlight Dinner Theatre, Stormfield, Wharton, Williamston
MotorCities National Heritage Area: yes
Planetarium: Abrams at Michigan State University; Lansing Community College
Shopping malls: Antique District of Williamson, Frandor, Mason Antiques District, Meridian Mall
Walking tours: *Michigan Walk of Fame:* honors Michigan residents with a bronze plaque in the sidewalk in downtown Lansing who have made significant contributions to the state or nation
…Old Town: brochure available or download to MP3; kid-friendly scavenger hunt
Wineries: *Burgdorf's:* family-owned, wines, tours
Gardens: *Cooley Gardens:* 100 years old, hidden and serene
…Horticulture Gardens: MSU, 14-acre living laboratory that supports and integrates teaching, research and service for the Department of Horticulture; Michigan 4-H Children's Garden, perennial and annual gardens, vegetable demonstration garden

Laura Hamlin

jbastion@lansing.org

…Shigematsu Memorial Garden: a traditional Japanese garden to experience Japanese culture

…W.J. Beal Botanical Gardens: MSU, 5,000 species; oldest continuously operated garden of its type in U.S.

Dairy Store: MSU-made ice cream and cheese for sale; production viewing area for visitors plus informational videos on dairy products

NPCR

Planet Walk: Part of the River Trail, the planets are displayed in scale for size and distance for a two-mile walk.
Urban Options: energy and environmental demonstration house for resource efficiency

X X-TRA STUFF

County Fair: *Ingham:* 4-H & FFA recognition, Aug.

Fall colors: early October

Famous people: ...*Entertainment*: Jim Cash, Wally Pleasant, Steven Segal

...*Sports*: Earvin "Magic" Johnson, Todd Martin, John Smoltz

...*Other*: Larry Page

Hospitals: McLaren-Greater Lansing, Sparrow Health, Sparrow Specialty

Large employers: State of Michigan, General Motors (car assembly), Sparrow Health System, Lansing School District, McLaren-Greater Lansing Medical Center, Leona Group (management of charter schools), Jackson National Life Ins. Co., Michigan State University, Lansing Community College

FYI: There are only 51 capit*o*ls in the U.S. and the Michigan State Capit*o*l is one of them. This capitol, spelled with an 'o,' means the building in which a state legislature meets. All the other capitals, such as capital letters, capital city, and capital, meaning money, are spelled with an 'a.'

Laura Hamlin

The Shrimp Farm Market: Michigan's first shrimp farm is in an industrial park in Okemos.

Y YESTERYEAR

In 1847, the Michigan legislature, with 13 sites to choose from and after voting 51 times, finally chose Lansing Township in Ingham County to be the site of the new state capital and capitol. It had free land that was available, it was centrally located in the southern half of the Lower Peninsula and it was more in the

NPCR-2

center of the population. The problem was there was no town and no roads to get there, and only eight people lived there. Consequently, Lansing was a forest *designed* to be a capital, not just a city *designated* as a capital.

Z ZOO & ANIMAL PLACES

Watchable Wildlife Viewing Areas:[ww] see 33P

Petting Zoo: Rowe's Farm Market, Shawhaven Farm

NPCR

Zoo: *Potter Park:* 100 acres along the Red Cedar River, 450 animals, picnics, rides, year-round

Michigan State University:

...*Butterfly House:* free-flying butterflies

...*MSU Farms:* self-guided tours of the dairy, sheep, horse and swine farms

NPCR

NPCR

...*The Bug House:* crawling with a collection of creepy critters

A AGRICULTURE

Land in farms: 64% of county
Number of farms: 1,200
Size of average farm: 200 acres
Market value of all products: #5 of 83 counties
Crops: ...most acres: corn
...highest $ sales: grains: corn, soybeans, wheat
Livestock: ...largest number: hogs & pigs
...highest $ sales: milk & dairy products
Among the top Michigan counties:
- #1- ostriches
- #2- beef cows
- #4- total livestock sales
- #5- dairy cows

Dairy, food and meat processing plants: 21
State ranking for harvested trees: #56 of 83 counties
AgBioResearch Centers (MSU): *Clarksville Research Center:* this 440-acre station focuses on small fruits and tree fruits with the aim of making agricultural production more profitable and efficient for growers, while offering environmentally responsible methods to control pests; also includes organic research plots.
FYI: The biggest issues in <u>organic farming</u> are soil nutrients, weed and pest control, seed origins and quality of the end product. "Organic farming is a non-synthetic input farming system that strives for the most environmentally sustainable farming practices available today. This system is defined more by the processes and practices organic farmers follow than by the inputs they do or do not use. Many consumers are often willing to pay a premium for organically grown food that they consider healthier and grown more environmentally friendly." new-ag.msu

As defined by the Michigan Department of Agriculture (MDA), an organic farm is one that grows an agriculture product for commercial sales and is certified by a federal, state or private program approved by the MDA. Organic production is a system that is managed according to certain standards. It strives for site-specific conditions that integrate cultural, biological and mechanical practices that foster cycling of resources, promote ecological balance and conserve biodiversity. The MDA keeps a Certified Organic Farm Registry. In 2007, Michigan had over 600 farms with more than 50,000 acres in organic production and that number continues to grow each year. Eighty percent of Michigan's organic acres are in beans and grains.
MDA, USDA

B BRIDGE OR BOAT

MDOT Photo and Video Unit

MDOT Historic Bridge: Built in 1867 on White's Bridge Rd. over the Flat River in Keene Twp., this covered bridge has hand-hewed dimensional lumber that is secured with wooden pegs and hand-cut nails. It is known as White's Covered Bridge.

C CELEBRATIONS

<u>Belding</u> *Applefest:* Sept.
...Homecoming: twilight parade, car show, plant walk (like a cake walk), Sept.
...Music in the Park: June - Aug.
<u>Ionia</u> *Farm Power Show:* tractor pulls, shingle mill demonstration, thrashing competition, more, June
...Music & Art on the Green: June-Aug.

...Autumn Celebration: Chili Dawg Challenge, carnival, costume contest, live shows, Oct.

NPCR

<u>Lake Odessa</u> *Art in the Park:* juried, July
...Fair: livestock shows, petting zoo, truck & tractor pulls, midway, quilt parade, June
<u>Lyons</u> *Island Fest:* on DeVore Island, June
<u>Portland</u> *Riverfest:* Aug.
<u>Saranac</u> *Bridge Festival:* Aug.

D DEMOGRAPHICS

Population: 63,900   **Persons per sq. mile:** 112
Largest city: Ionia   **Population:** 11,400
Largest township: Boston   **Population:** 4,380
Largest village: Saranac   **Population:** 1,330
Median household income: $46,900
Owner-occupied median house value: $124,000

Persons affiliated with a religious congregation: 36%
Persons below poverty level: 16%
Students receiving school lunch subsidy: 38%

E ENVIRONMENT

"Our quality of life is protected when open space is preserved. Air, water, and wildlife benefit from natural habitats, and open space landscapes are attractive and enhance community values. Preservation of farmland ensures continuation of farming in mid-Michigan. Therefore, the purpose of the Mid-Michigan Land Conservancy is:

1. to conserve natural, scenic, recreational, and agricultural lands and their natural diversity in mid-Michigan so rural landscapes are preserved and

2. to encourage and promote the preservation of these lands and their natural diversity through education and other assistance." The MMLC operates in Clinton, Eaton, Hillsdale, Ingham, Ionia, Jackson and Shiawassee counties. midmilandcons.org

F FLORA & FAUNA

Alice Welch, USDA

Chicory may be the most common roadside weed in Michigan, standing 3'-4' tall with its bright blue flowers waving as you pass by in your car. The taproot has been used to make tea or to flavor coffee.

From BIBLIOGRAPHY & NOTES...

F FAUNA: (MI H&T) indicates that Michigan allows Hunting and Trapping of this animal with the proper training, permits, licensing and within the season.

Bill Buchanan/USFWS

The name raccoon *(MI H&T)* comes from the Latin word that means "the washer," and this animal requires easy access to water in order to wash its food. They are active at night and use their very dexterous front paws to get into mischief with their human neighbors.

G GOVERNMENT

County: ...created: 1831 ...organized: 1837
...originally part of: Kent County
Size: 371,000 acres / 573 sq. miles (40 of 83 counties)
The county has 3 cities, 7 villages, 16 townships and 11 school districts.

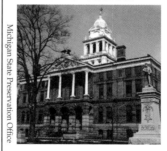

Michigan State Preservation Office

NPCR

The Ionia County Courthouse, built in 1885, is the largest structure ever built of Ionia sandstone; this Classic Revival structure has marble floors and 14 marble fireplaces.
County seat: Ionia
...Homestead property tax: 35 mills
Motto: Belding: *live. grow. naturally.*
...Ionia: *A Great Place To Visit, A Better Place To Live; Your Home in the Heartland*
...Ionia Area Chamber: *More Than You Imagine*
...Lake Odessa: *Welcome to Our Friendly Port*
...Portland: *City of Two Rivers*

H HISTORICAL MARKERS 9 of 18

Alvah N. Belding Library: 1918, Classical Revival architecture built by a son to honor his parents

Belrockton Dormitory: 1906, the Belding Brothers Co. was a major silk manufacturer and Belding was known as the 'Silk City of the World.' This was one of 3 dormitories for single women who worked in the silk factory; it is now the Belding Museum.

Fred W. Green Home: 1872-1936, while governor of Michigan he expanded the fish planting program and added seven state parks; his home is mission-style.

Michigan State Preservation Office

Frederick Hall House: 1870, Italian Villa style, now a library

John and Harriet Blanchard House: 1881, substantial Italianate House with variegated sandstone from the local quarry; now the Ionia County Museum

John C. Blanchard: 1822-1905, the epitome of a self-made man, he left NY when he was 14, worked as laborer in Detroit, bought 40 acres of land for $50 when he was 15; co-owned the Ionia Sandstone Quarry and became a lawyer and philanthropist.

Pere Marquette Railway Depot: 1923, typical of Michigan railroad stations; now renovated for offices

Ionia Area Chamber of Commerce

The Roadside Table: 1929, the first picnic table along a highway right-of-way; idea caught on and became an emblem of Michigan's hospitality

White's Bridge: 1867, in constant use since it was built, proof that it was well made; see 34B

National Register of Historic Places: 15 listings

State Historic Sites: 39 listings

I INFORMATION

Chamber of Commerce: Belding, 616-794-9890, beldingchamber.org

…Ionia Area, 616-527-2560, ioniachamber.org

…Lake Odessa, 616-374-0766, lakewoodareacoc.org

J JOKES

You might be from a small town in Michigan if…

…driving 20 minutes to a larger town is not worth the gas or the effort.

…WalMart is your favorite destination.

…your local Farm & Fleet has pretty much everything you need anyway.

…those retirees who eat out every meal eat in the same restaurant every day.

…what's left of the high school class of 1940 still gets together once a month for lunch.

…you can get almost anything you need as long as you don't require a large selection or like to do comparison shopping.

…you cannot tolerate traffic congestion of any kind.

K KINSMAN

Race		Ancestry	
American Indian:	<1%	German:	29%
Asian:	<1%	U.S./American:	15%
Black/African American:	5%	English:	12%
Hispanic or Latino:	4%	Irish:	9%
Other:	3%	Dutch:	5%
White:	92%	French:	3%
		Polish:	3%

L LIGHTHOUSE OR LANDMARK

Ionia Free Fair

The Ionia Free Fair, "World's Largest Free Fair," has no admission. The fair was started in 1915 by Ionia mayor Fred Green (who would eventually become Governor of Michigan), partly because as a boy he couldn't get into fairs because he had no money for admission. The central theme has always been to highlight agriculture and farm life while showcasing talents of the surrounding communities.

M MUSEUMS

Belding *Museum:* in the former Belrockton Dormitory; silk thread history, refrigerators, more

Ionia *County Museum:* in the 1880s Blanchard mansion that is unchanged, preserved, beautiful

Lake Odessa *Area Historical Museum:* in the restored 1888 onion-dome depot; period displays, genealogy

Saranac *Historical Depot Museum:* Grand Trunk Railroad and Saranac area history

NPCR

N NATURAL RESOURCES

Elevation: 700 - 900 feet
Physiography: rolling plains

Forest type: maple-beech, oak-hickory
Public/private forests: 20% of county

Water in county: <1% of county
   Lakes: 30   **...largest:** Long
   Rivers: Flat, Grand, Looking Glass, Maple
   Rivers & streams: 460 miles

Growing season, avg.: 137 days (2 temp. zones)
   Last freeze, avg.: May 5 – May 10
   First freeze, avg.: Oct. 5 – Oct. 10
Precipitation, annual avg.: rainfall: 32 inches
                     snowfall: 44 inches
Temperature (F), avg.: January: high 30°, low 14°
                  July: high 84°, low 58°
   Annual: >90°: 15 days, **<0°:** 12 days
Tornadoes (1930-2010): 19

O ORIGINS

Belding:[c] silk maker, Hiram Belding; 1839
Clarksville:[v] store owner, Clark Howard; 1840
Hubbardston:[v] mill owner, Thomas Hubbard; 1836
Ionia:[c, co,t] (i OWN ya) an ancient Greek province; 1833
Lake Odessa:[v,t] 3 lakes in Odessa Twp.; 1880
Lyons:[v] Lucius Lyon said it would become one of the most important towns in Michigan; 1833
Muir:[v] railroad superintendent, H.K. Muir; 1854
Palo:[v] Palo Alto was the site of the first battle and the first victory in the Mexican War; 1857
Pewamo:[v] (pa WA mo) American Indian chief from this area; 1857
Portland:[c,t] a port on the Looking Glass River; 1833
Saranac:[v] (SAR a nac) after a NY resort town, in hopes of attracting settlers from that state; 1836

P PARKS

National: 0   **State:** 6
County: 2   **Local:** 31
Number of campsites: 1,000

Prentice Drake

State Game Area: Flat River, Grand River, Maple River, Portland, Saranac-Lowell, 15,000 acres

State Recreation Area: *Ionia:* 4,500 acres, rolling hills, babbling brooks, open meadows, forested ridges; a lake nestled in the hills and the Grand River winding its way through woods and fields; camping, equestrian trails, swimming, boating

County: *Bertha Brock Park:* 186 acres, rolling hills, deep woods, 3 picturesque stone bridges, rustic charm of Palmer Lodge; camping, hiking, fishing
Local: *Fred Thwaites Grand River Trail:* boardwalk
...*Riverfront Linear Park:* 8 miles in Portland
...*Silk City Nature Trail:* paved, along the Flat River, bask in nature's beauty
Other: *The West Michigan Parks and Recreation Inventory,* see 3P

Q QUOTE FROM THE LOCALS

"Ionia invites you to savor the simple pleasures of life throughout our county and discover the many benefits our communities have to offer. Ionia is nestled in the heart of the Grand River Valley, 'In the Middle of it All.' Our communities feature beautifully renovated downtown business districts and modernized industrial centers with picturesque countryside along the scenic Grand, Flat, Looking Glass and Maple Rivers. We have rich farmlands, beautiful homes and a location that provides easy access to metropolitan areas of Mid and West Michigan.

"Ionia County is home to numerous recreational and cultural opportunities where our history is combined with a vibrant future. Our area offers excellent educational opportunities and a broad spectrum of medical services. The strength of the

labor force in Ionia is rooted in a past that cherished hard work and innovation. Its bright future is ensured by our merchants and business owners' dedication to providing 'Hometown Service Beyond Expectations.'" Ionia Area Chamber of Commerce

R RECREATION & SPORTS

Randy Ellen Photography

Auto racing: *I-96 Speedway:* ½-mile track; ¼-mile track for hobby stock, mini stock; ⅛–mile track for motorcycles, quads, go-karts; off-road park

…Mid Michigan Raceway Park: ⅓-mile semi banked clay oval track

Golf courses: 6
Hiking/skiing/mountain biking trails: 25 miles
Horse racing: harness racing at the Lake Odessa Fair
Public access sites: 15
Public recreational land: 3% of county
Rail-trail: (30 miles) Ionia Recreation Area, Portland Riverwalk, Rivertrail Park
State/federal wild/scenic/ natural river: 15 miles of the Flat River
State-funded snowmobile trails: 3 miles

NPCR

Double R Ranch Resort & Golf: water activities, horseback riding, hay rides, hiking, golfing

S STATE OF MICHIGAN

"The <u>Department of Corrections</u> administers Michigan's adult prison, probation, and parole systems. The department has jurisdiction over all adults convicted of felonies who are sentenced to prison. Convicted felons who are not sentenced to prison terms are either sentenced to a county jail term or are supervised in the community through a system called probation. Probation services for felons are provided by the Department for various felony courts in Michigan's counties."

State prisons in Ionia include Bellamy Creek Fac-

PRISON AREA
DO NOT PICK UP
HITCHHIKERS

NPCR

ility, Ionia Maximum Facility, Michigan Reformatory and Michigan Training Unit. In 2004 these facilities employed around 2,000 people. Michigan.gov See 38S.

T TRAVEL

Airport: Ionia County
Bus: G & M Coach
Distance to Lansing: 40 miles
Main roads: I-96, M-21, M-44, M-50, M-66, M-91
Memorial Highways: I-96, *AmVets MH:* see 19T
…M-66, *Green Arrow Route:* see 8T

Scenic drive: Riverside Drive from Lyons to Saranac

Prentice Drake

U UNIVERSITIES & COLLEGES

None

V VARIETY

Benz Aviation

Benz Aviation is mid-America's largest glider base and soaring center. This flight experience is the closest thing available to flying free like a bird.

W WANDERLUST

Agri-tourism: *Paulson's Pumpkin Patch:* apples, peaches, tomatoes, sweet corn, broccoli
Fall colors: early October
Live theatre: *Ionia Theatre:* live shows and first-run movies
Walking tour: Downtown Ionia Historic District; Ionia Sandstone Quarry
Ionia County Historic Home Tour: May

X X-TRA STUFF

County fair: *Ionia County Fair Association:* to highlight agriculture and farm life while showcasing the talents of surrounding communities, July; see 34L
...*Lake Odessa Civic & Agricultural Assoc.:* June
Famous people: ...*Politics*: Brian Calley, Fred Green
...*Other*: Harlan Bretz
Hospitals: Sparrow Ionia
Large employers: Department of Corrections, Ventra (stamped parts), TRW Automotive (steering parts), Meijer, Ionia County Intermediate School District, Matcor (stamped automotive parts)
On the southwest corner of I-96 and M-66 is Herbruck Poultry Ranch, home to 2.5 million chickens that supply eggs for all the McDonald's Restaurants east of the Mississippi River. At another location, Herbruck's is also the largest producer of organic eggs in the U.S.

Y YESTERYEAR

"Of all the states in the Union, <u>Michigan</u> is perhaps the <u>least typical</u>. It is unique geographically because it consists of two large peninsulas, because it lies in the midst of the upper Great Lakes, and because of the striking difference between the soils, climate, and vegetation of those parts of the state lying north of the 43rd parallel and those lying south of this line. [The 43rd parallel runs through Ionia County.] Its highly industrialized southeastern region is in sharp contrast to the sparsely settled Upper Peninsula and northern half of the Lower Peninsula. Michigan is heavily dependent on a singe industry: automotive manufacturing. Portions of the state, however, rely on the tourist and vacation industry as the backbone of their economy. It is a state that has experienced boom periods in the fur trade, land speculation, mining, lumbering, and automobile manufacturing, each of which has been followed by severe depressions." [Dunbar]

NPCR

Z ZOO & ANIMAL PLACES

Homestead Acres: a rare breed and fiber farm with alpacas, llamas, sheep; tours

NOTE: (#x/MI) indicates ranking from highest number or percentage (#1) to lowest number or percentage (#83) in Michigan. The significance of either a high or low number depends on the item it describes.

A AGRICULTURE

Land in farms: 13% of county
Number of farms: 315
Size of average farm: 150 acres
Market value of all products: #53 of 83 counties
Crops: ...**most acres:** forage land
...**highest $ sales:** grains: corn, soybeans, wheat
Livestock: ...**largest number:** cattle
...**highest $ sales:** milk & dairy products
Dairy, food and meat processing plants: 4
State ranking for harvested trees: #47 of 83 counties
FYI: The <u>Michigan Agricultural Surplus System</u> (MASS) is the driving force behind the fresh fruits and vegetables that are donated to Michigan food banks, soup kitchens and shelters throughout the state to help feed needy families. Farmers and food processors donate their excess product that is transported, packaged and distributed at no cost to the recipients. Around 6 million pounds of fresh food is donated each year to help feed over 1 million people. MASS is funded through a grant from the Michigan Department of Agriculture. ^{MASS}

B BRIDGE OR BOAT

Sonya Plude

The *AuSable River Queen* paddlewheel boat offers a 2-hour trip on the AuSable River. You will see beautiful scenery and may even see the bald eagles that nest along the river or perhaps some Trumpeter Swans.

C CELEBRATIONS

<u>East Tawas</u> *Tawas Point Celebration Days:* celebration of American Heritage, blacksmithing, muzzle loader shows, spinning, weaving, wood carving, fishing derby, much more, June

Leisa Sutton

<u>Oscoda</u> *Sunrise Side Wood-carvers Show:* carvers from all over the U.S., May

...*Art on the Beach:* 150 artisans, July
...*Gagaguwon Traditional Pow Wow:* July
...*Paul Bunyan Festival:* chainsaw carving, lumberjack show, car show, beer, bands, Sept.
...*Super Boat Tournament:* fish Lake Huron, Aug.
<u>Tawas City</u> *Tawas Point Birding Festival:* seminars and field trips, May

D DEMOGRAPHICS

Population: 25,900   **Persons per sq. mile:** 47
Largest city: East Tawas   **Population:** 2,810
Largest township: Oscoda   **Population:** 7,000
Median household income: $34,000
Owner-occupied median house value: $102,000
Persons affiliated with a religious congregation: 45%
Persons below poverty level: 19%
Students receiving school lunch subsidy: 58% (#3/MI)

E ENVIRONMENT

The <u>Wildflower Association of Michigan</u> encourages the preservation and restoration of Michigan's native plants and native plant communities. One of their first accomplishments was to address the lack of commercial growers who could provide Michigan native wildflower seeds. As a result, the Michigan Native Plant Producers Association was formed with the results that now there is a consistent supply of good seed. Native plants can be incorporated into home landscapes where they are easy to grow and maintain. The use of wildflowers lowers water use and improves water quality, provides food and shelter for wildlife and helps reduce global warming.
wildflowersmich.org

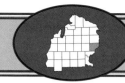
F FLORA & FAUNA

Alice Welch, USDA

The Jack pine tree and its resulting forests are the home of the Kirtland's Warbler, which must have the younger, smaller trees for survival. At maturity, these trees can grow up to 100' tall. It is the most northerly pine in the U.S.

George Lou/USFWS

Northern Lower Michigan is the only place in the world where the endangered Kirtland's Warbler nests. The DNR and the U.S. Forest Service have set aside certain lands with an on-going management plan to ensure that these birds have the nesting grounds they need.

G GOVERNMENT

County: ...**created:** 1840 ...**organized:** 1857
...**originally part of:** Saginaw, Cheboygan Counties
Size: 362,000 acres / 550 sq. miles (60 of 83 counties)
The county has 3 cities, 11 townships with 2 as charter townships, 5 unincorporated communities, 2 Census Designated Place and 4 school districts.

Sonya Plude

NPCR

County seat: Tawas City
...**Homestead property tax:** 33 mills
Motto: <u>AuSable</u>: *Where The Mighty AuSable River Meets The Great Lake Huron!*
...<u>East Tawas</u>: *On Michigan's Sunrise Side*
...<u>Hale</u>: *Gateway to Northern Michigan*
...<u>Oscoda</u> Chamber: *naturally.*
...<u>Tawas City</u>: *Proud of Our Past, Confident of Our Future*

H HISTORICAL MARKERS 8 of 10

Alabaster: this area is named after a type of gypsum that was found here and was used as fertilizer and in plaster; now gypsum is used in wallboard.
Cooke Hydroelectric Plant: 1910, one of six on the AuSable River; has a transmission line 125 miles long to Flint to provide that city with electricity
Hydroelectric Power: with advances in electricity in the 1880s, Michigan's extensive water resources were used to produce electricity and helped fuel Michigan's growth as a premier industrial state.
Dock Reserve: refugees from the 1911 fire that destroyed Oscoda and AuSable spent their first night here on the dock where they waited for rescue.
Five Channels Dam Workers Camp: 1911, for construction workers and their families; included water and sewage system, icehouse, school, washroom, store, boardinghouse
Lumbering on the Huron Shore: between 1866 and 1896, 12 billion board feet of lumber were removed from the forest from Iosco to Alpena.

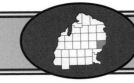
Monument: *Lumberman's Monument:* see 35V
National Register of Historic Places: 4 listings
State Historic Sites: 12 listings

I INFORMATION

Chamber of Commerce: Oscoda-AuSable, Tawas Area
Visitor: Oscoda Area Convention and Visitors
Bureau, 877-8-OSCODA, oscoda.com

J JOKES

You might be a Michiganian if…

…your school classes were cancelled because it was too cold.

…your school classes were cancelled because it was too hot.

…someone complains about the weather and you tell them to wait 2 hours because it will change.

…your idea of a traffic jam is 15 cars waiting to pass an orange barrel.

…you like going to the festivals named after fruits, vegetables, dairy products or any food items in general.

…your car rusts out before you need new brakes.

NPCR

…you support the preservation of forests, farmland and wetlands because they have a direct impact on your wallet.

…you never forget that 10% unemployment still means 90% employment.

K KINSMAN

Race
American Indian: <1%
Asian: <1%
Black/African American: <1%
Hispanic or Latino: 2%
Other: 2%
White: 96%

Ancestry
German: 23%
English: 12%
Irish: 11%
U.S./American: 10%
Polish: 8%
French: 7%

L LIGHTHOUSE or LANDMARK

Michigan State Historic Preservation Office

The Tawas Point Light, built in 1875, is the only true Victorian-era style station on the Great Lakes. It is restored, has a museum and tours; overnight stays are possible. It is part of the Michigan Historical Museum System.

M MUSEUMS

<u>East Tawas</u> *Iosco County Historical Museum:* lumbering, railroads, American Indians, fishing, military, much more

<u>Hale</u> *Michigan Museum of Military Transport Foundation:* preserves and displays current and historic military vehicles, uniforms equipment and paraphernalia

<u>Oscoda</u> *AuSable-Oscoda Historical Museum:* American Indian artifacts, commercial fishing, shipwrecks, logging, Paul Bunyan legend, railroads, the 1911 fire

…*Lumberman's Monument:* see 35V

…*Melvin Motorcycle Museum:* antique and rare motorcycles from around the world

…*Wurtsmith Aviation Museum of the Yankee Air Force:* 3 hangers, Huey helicopter, T-33 Jet trainer, other planes being restored, displays

Deb Schmucker

N NATURAL RESOURCES

Elevation: <600 – 1,000 feet
Physiography: hill-lands, lake border plains, plains

Forest type: aspen-birch, oak-hickory, pine, elm-ash-cottonwood
Public/private forests: 70% of county

Water in county: 3% of county
  Bays: Tawas
  Lakes: 50
    ...largest: Foote Dam Pond
      Loon Lake (#8-depth/MI)
  Rivers: AuGres (aw GRAY), AuSable (aw SAHBle), Pine
  Rivers & streams: 260 miles

NPCR

Great Lakes shoreline: 36 miles of Lake Huron

Growing season, avg.: 131 days (2-3 temp. zones)
  Last freeze, avg.: May 25 – May 30
  First freeze, avg.: Sept. 25 – Sept. 30
Precipitation, annual avg.: rainfall: 29 inches
                          snowfall: 50 inches
Temperature (F), avg.: January: high 29°, low 11°
                      July: high 80°, low 56°
Annual: >90°: 6 days, **<0°:** 23 days
Tornadoes (1930-2010): 12

O ORIGINS

AuSable:[ct] (aw SAHBle) French for "on the sandy river;" 1848
East Tawas:[c] (TAH wahss) east of Tawas City; 1862
Hale:[u] lumberman from NY, CD Hale; 1880
Iosco:[co] (eye AH skoe) American Indian word that means "water of light;" 1849
Long Lake:[u] a long L-shaped lake; 1894
National City:[u] the National Gypsum Co. opened a quarry in 1925; 1884
Oscoda:[u] (ahs CODE a) from Indian words meaning "pebble stones" and "prairie;" 1867
Tawas City:[c] (TAH wahss) either from the Ottawa Indian tribe, or Chippewa chief Otawas; 1854
Whittemore:[c] named by friends of well known local man, Frank Whittemore; 1879

P PARKS

National: 7 **State:** 2 **County:** 1 **Local:** 15
Number of campsites: 1,800

NPCR

National: *Huron National Forest:* 112,000 acres, established in 1909 on former "logged out" lands that are once again beautiful forests

...Tuttle Marsh Wildlife Area:[ww] 5,000 acre wetland complex, permanent and temporary home to many bird species, bears, bobcats, deer, muskrats, beaver, mink, weasel, otter, fox, coyote, insects and reptiles

Deb Schmucker

State Forest: (25,000 acres) Ogemaw, Oscoda
...Campground: 1
State Park: *Tawas Point:*[ww] 180 acres, called the "Cape Cod of the Midwest;" on Tawas Bay with shallow water for warm swimming; camping, trails, fishing; home of the Tawas Point Lighthouse
County: *Old Orchard Park:* 140 acres on Lake Huron, camping, boat launch
Other: *Veteran's Memorial Park:* 6 acres under continuing development, circle of flags

Q QUOTE FROM THE LOCALS

"Iosco County is overflowing with space to play in the great outdoors. As the months pass, the natural landscape takes on a new outlook, from springtime flowers to the fully blossomed trees of summer to the colorful landscape of fall and the white blanket of winter. Regardless of the season, Iosco County's pristine water and natural landscape welcome you.

"One of our hidden treasures is the number of arts and crafts studios in the area. Here you will find just about anything handmade, including pottery, jewelry, paintings, ceramics, furniture, wood workings and much more. The county is also home to a vibrant cultural scene of music, dance and theater." developiosco.org

R RECREATION & SPORTS

Auto racing: *Whittemore Speedway:* Michigan's oldest speedway; asphalt oval
Blue Ribbon Trout Streams: AuGres River-East Branch
Golf courses: 5
Great Lakes marinas: 15
Groomed cross-country trails: *Corsair Ski Trails:* 60 km of interconnecting trails that cross forests, meadows, hills and valleys
...Highbanks: backcountry ski touring overlooks AuSable River Valley

Hiking/skiing/mountain biking trails: 80 miles
MI Shore-to-Shore (horse) **Riding & Hiking Trail:** yes
Off-road vehicle trails: 75 miles
Public access sites: 11
Public recreational land: 38% of county
Recreational harbor: East Tawas State Dock, Oscoda Harbor of Refuge
State/federal wild/scenic/natural river: 10 miles of the AuSable River
State-funded snowmobile trails: 90 miles
Fishing: located midway between the cool waters of Lake Huron and the warm waters of Saginaw Bay means that you may catch both cold water and warm water fish in the same Tawas Bay fishing trip

Kiteboarding: combines wakeboarding, surfing, snowboarding and paragliding and can be done on water, land or snow

John Davidson

Canoeing and Kayaking: on the world famous Au-Sable River
Canoe Races: Klondike in March; Curley Memorial in July; Weyerhaeuser AuSable River International Canoe Marathon in July

S   STATE OF MICHIGAN

The names of Michigan's 83 counties are a variety that reflects our natural resources and the heritage of our American Indian, French, British and American ancestors:

- 21 are named for natural features and local geography.
- 18 are named for American Indian tribes, chiefs, or use an American Indian word that is descriptive of something unique about that local place.
- 14 are named after politicians.
- 9 are words "made-up" by Henry Schoolcraft, author and Indian Agent, by combining American Indian, Arabian and Latin words to make American Indian-sounding words; see 75Y.
- 5 are named for counties in Ireland.
- 4 are named after military men.
- 4 are named after missionaries or explorers.
- 4 are named after non-Americans.
- 2 are named after state employees.
- 2 have names with unclear origins.

T   TRAVEL

Airports: Oscoda-Wurtsmith, Iosco County
Bus: Indian Trails
Circle Tour: Lake Huron via US-23
Distance to Lansing: 150 miles
Heritage Route: *Recreational:* Sunrise Side Coastal Highway; see 6T
Lights of Northern Lake Huron Tour: Tawas Point Lighthouse
Memorial Highways: US-23, *United Spanish War Veterans MH:* see 1T
Main roads: US-23, M-55, M-65

Scenic Drive: *National Scenic Byway:* Lumberman's Monument Auto Tour Scenic Drive via the River Road Scenic Drive; follows the south side of the Au Sable River 23 miles between M-65 and Oscoda

NPCR

…Tawas City to Cheboygan via US-23

U   UNIVERSITIES & COLLEGES

Alpena Community College, *Huron Shores Campus:* est. 1969, 200 students. It is housed in the renovated Headquarters Building of the former Wurtsmith Air Force Base and is a full service extension center.

V   VARIETY

Sonya Plude

The Lumberman's Monument consists of a 14' bronze statue featuring the timber cruiser, the sawyer and river men who felled the mighty pine trees to build the cities and supply lumber for the treeless prairies. There is an interpretive center with excellent

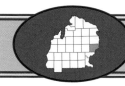

information on the lumbering era in Michigan, outdoor and hands-on displays and activities, and spectacular and diverse lookouts across the AuSable River Valley. This could include a view into an eagle's nest if you bring your binoculars.

W WANDERLUST

Brewery: Wiltse's Brew Pub
Cultural: Corsair Concert Series, Tawas Area Community Band, et al., Tuesday Night Live
Fall colors: late September to early October

Sonya Plude

Live theater: Tawas Bay Players Community Theater, Shoreline Players

Iargo Springs: on the River Road Scenic Byway, a American Indian holy place; CCC trail 300' down to the spring

X X-TRA STUFF

Commercial port: Alabaster, Port Gypsum
County fair: *Iosco County Agricultural Society*, July
Hospitals: St. Joseph Health System
Large employers: Tawas St. Joseph Health Services, Oscoda Area Schools, Plastic Trim (makes extruded plastic products), Tawas Area Schools, Kmart, Phoenix Composite Solutions (makes aircraft parts), Tendercare (skilled nursing home), Wal-Mart

In 2006, the State of Michigan declared Oscoda the official home of the legendary Paul Bunyan because the first published stories about the oversized lumberjack were published here in 1906. It should be noted, though that cities throughout the U.S. and even Europe claim to be the "official" home of the "real" Paul Bunyan.

Deb Schmucker

Wurtsmith Air Force Base: now decommissioned and redeveloped as a renaissance zone, it was the home of U.S. Air Force Air Defense Command and the Strategic Air Command.

Y YESTERYEAR

In the 1800s the <u>natural resources of the area provided the main source of food and occupation</u>. The rivers provided a variety of fresh fish and the forests provided trees that were made into lumber. In the 1870s salt brine wells were discovered. Wood residues from lumber sawmills provided fuel for the fires that evaporated the water from the salt brine to make salt. The salt was then used as a preservative for the fish industry. The lumbering industry ended in 1911 when much of northeast Michigan was destroyed by fire. The wells are still there, the fish are still there and the trees have grown back, but their need for one another is no longer there. ^Iosco County

Gypsum, the mineral with a thousand uses, is also found in Iosco County. Its suitability for economical mass production and insulating qualities has made it indispensable to the building industry. Since 1902, the U.S. Gypsum Co. has operated the Alabaster quarry. developiosco.org

NPCR-2

Z ZOO & ANIMAL PLACES

NPCR

Watchable Wildlife Viewing Areas:^ww see 35P

Bald Eagle sightings: along the AuSable River
Sunrise Side Nature Trail and Exotic [rare animals] *Park*
Tawas Point: an important stop for migrating birds and waterfowl and monarch butterflies
Tuttle Marsh Wildlife Area: any Michigan wild animal is a possibility

A AGRICULTURE

Land in farms: 53% of county
Number of farms: 1,020
Size of average farm: 190 acres
Market value of all products: #31 of 83 counties
Crops: ...most acres: soybeans
...highest $ sales: grains: corn, soybeans, wheat
Livestock: ...largest number: cattle
...highest $ sales: milk & dairy products
Among the top Michigan counties:
- #4- alfalfa
- #5- hay
- #6- pheasants

Dairy, food and meat processing plants: 10
State ranking for harvested trees: #57 of 83 counties
FYI: The Michigan Barn Preservation Network (MBPN) promotes appreciation, preservation and rehabilitation of Michigan barns, farmsteads and rural communities. Barns are economic resources and symbols of our agriculture heritage. They are attractive images on the landscape. The MBPN is committed to rehabilitation of barns for agricultural, commercial, residential and public uses. With their

home office in Mt. Pleasant, they offer barn and stable tours throughout the state, help sponsor quilt barn trails and the Barn Mural Project, and provide resources for barn owners interested in saving their beautiful old barn. *mibarn.net*

NPCR

B BRIDGE OR BOAT

NPCR

The Fisher Covered Bridge in Deerfield Nature Park crosses the Chippewa River. The park also has another pedestrian bridge and two swinging bridges.

C CELEBRATIONS

<u>Blanchard</u> *Days:* fire truck parade, ball tournaments, tractor pulls, kids' events, June

Stanley Delo Photography

...Steam and Gas Show: tractors and equipment, threshing demos, tractor parade, softball, Aug.

<u>Mt. Pleasant</u> *Festival of Banners:* public art displays, May-Nov.
...Max & Emily's Summer Concert Series: local and national musical talent, June-Aug.

Lynette Henson

...Special Olympics State Summer Games: 3,000 athletes participate in 10 sports, June

...Summer Festival: in Island Park, timber show, softball, pedal pullers, duck race, June

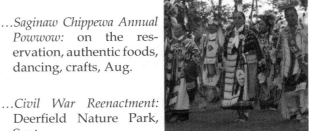

Frank Cloutier

...Saginaw Chippewa Annual Powwow: on the reservation, authentic foods, dancing, crafts, Aug.

...Civil War Reenactment: Deerfield Nature Park, Sept.
...Outdoor Summer Concert Series: at Soaring Eagle Casino, May-Sept.
...Indigenous Peoples Art Market: American Indian Juried Art show, music, dance, Oct.
...Mardi Gras: parade, New Orleans bayou food, Oct.
<u>Shepherd</u> *Maple Syrup Festival:* pancakes, parade, classic cars, tractor and horse pulls, bingo, April
...Salt River Bluegrass Festival: July
...Blues & Barbeque: Rally in the Alley, beer tent, live music, Aug.
<u>Weidman</u> *Daze:* pancake breakfast, car show, horseshoe tournament, light & siren parade, July

D DEMOGRAPHICS

Population: 70,300   **Persons per sq. mile:** 122
Largest city: Mt. Pleasant   **Population:** 26,000
Largest township: Union   **Population:** 12,900
Largest village: Lake Isabella   **Population:** 1,680
Median household income: $36,000
Owner-occupied median house value: $131,000
Persons affiliated with a religious congregation: 28%
Persons below poverty level: 27% (#1/MI)
Students receiving school lunch subsidy: 33%

E ENVIRONMENT

The mission of the <u>Michigan Loon Preservation Association</u> is to conserve and enhance the Common Loon population through research, habitat protection and restoration, species protection and public awareness and involvement. The Common Loon is currently a threatened species in Michigan and is protected by state and federal laws. Their estimated population in Michigan is less than 500 breeding pairs; they return to the same territory to nest year after year. The average life expectancy of a loon is 15-30 years. ^{michiganloon.org} See 37F.

F FLORA & FAUNA

Art Cameron

The sweet Joe-Pye weed is a tall (4'-10') plant that is an herb, a wildflower, a butterfly plant and an ornamental plant. It is named after an American Indian herbalist.

From BIBLIOGRAPHY & NOTES...

F FLORA & FAUNA: All Flora and Fauna can be found in the county where they are listed but are not limited to that county unless otherwise stated.

NFW/USFWS

The Common Loon can be up to 3' long. Their almost violent mating dance and eerie wails make them symbolic of our wild northern lakes and marshes. They are very sensitive to human disturbance so their habitat needs to be protected. See 37E.

G GOVERNMENT

County: ...**created:** 1831 ...**organized:** 1859
...**originally part of:** Saginaw, Midland Counties
Size: 370,000 acres / 574 sq. miles (38 of 83 counties)
The county has 1 city, 3 villages, 16 townships with 1 as a charter township, 8 unincorporated communities, 2 Census Designated Place and 5 school districts.

Deb Schmucker

Deb Schmucker

County seat: Mt. Pleasant
...**Homestead property tax:** 43 mills
Motto: <u>Mt. Pleasant</u> Area Convention and Visitors Bureau: *Wow!*

H HISTORICAL MARKERS 6 of 10

Central Michigan University: privately organized in 1892, became Michigan's second state-supported normal (teacher education) school in 1895
Doughty House: the oldest house in Mt. Pleasant, balloon frame pioneer architecture; Mr. Doughty helped found CMU.

Indian Cemetery: 1850s-1860s, only a few grave markers are visible.

Isabella County Seat / The Founding of Mt. Pleasant: 1860, to encourage settlement on land that he owned, lumberman David Ward deeded five acres to Isabella County and platted the village of Mt. Pleasant.

Power House: 1908, Shepherd's first electric plant, now home of the Shepherd Area Historical Society

Schoolhouse: 1893-1934, it was the Mt. Pleasant Indian Industrial School; in 1934 it was the Mt. Pleasant branch of the Michigan Home and Training School.

Deb Schmucker

Joyne Neyer

Monument: The *Michigan Vietnam Memorial and Bridge* includes a series of brick monuments honoring those who lost their lives in the war. Mt. Pleasant has WWI, WWII and Korean Memorials also.

National Register of Historic Places: 4 listings
State Historic Sites: 14 listings

I INFORMATION

Chamber of Commerce: Mt. Pleasant, Shepherd
Visitor: Mt. Pleasant Area Convention and Visitors Bureau, 888-772-2022, mountpleasantwow.com

J JOKES

You might be a graduate student at Central Michigan University if…

…there is a desk in the library you consider "yours."

…you can tell the time of day by the traffic flow in the library.

…you know you're a better teacher than the professor of the undergraduate class you are teaching in his place.

…the students in that class wholeheartedly disagree with you.

…the students in that class can't understand your English because of your heavy foreign accent even though you're considered 'proficient' in English.

K KINSMAN

Race	
American Indian:	3%
Asian:	<1%
Black/African American:	2%
Hispanic or Latino:	3%
Other:	3%
White:	89%

Ancestry	
German:	28%
English:	10%
Irish:	10%
U.S./American:	7%
Polish:	6%
French:	4%

L LIGHTHOUSE OR LANDMARK

Soaring Eagle Casino

The Soaring Eagle Casino, with its hotel and entertainment programs, is the most publicized and visible landmark in Isabella County.

M MUSEUMS

<u>Mt. Pleasant</u>: at Central Michigan University:

…*Michigan High School Coaches Association Hall of Fame:* for those outstanding coaches who have coached high school sports for at least 25 years

Deb Schmucker

…*Museum of Cultural and Natural History:* Michigan history with a worldwide perspective

…*University Art Gallery:* faculty and student art as well as guest artists

…*Ziibiwing Center of Anishinabe Culture and Lifeways:* museum and cultural center built to share the history of the Saginaw Chippewa Indian Tribe of Michigan with the rest of the world

Courtesy of the Ziibiwing Center of Anishinabe Culture and Lifeways-Jennifer Jones, photographer

Shepherd *Area Historical Society:* historical one room schoolhouse, Power House Museum

...*Rail Museum:* in the 1890s Ann Arbor Railroad Depot

N NATURAL RESOURCES

Elevation: 700 - 1,000 feet

Physiography: hill-lands, rolling plains, lake-border plains

Forest type: maple-beech, aspen-birch, oak-hickory, elm-ash-cottonwood

Public/private forests: 28% of county

NPCR

Water in county: <1% of county
  Lakes: 50 ...**largest:** Lake Isabella
  Rivers: Chippewa (CHIP a wah), Coldwater, Pine, Salt
  Rivers & streams: 330 miles

Growing season, avg.: 144 days (2 temp. zones)
  Last freeze, avg.: May 10 – May 15
  First freeze, avg.: Sept. 30 – Oct. 5
Precipitation, annual avg.: rainfall: 30 inches
                                snowfall: 36 inches
Temperature (F), avg.: January: high 29°, low 13°
                           July: high 83°, low 58°
Annual: >90°: 11 days, **<0°:** 10 days
Tornadoes (1930-2010): 18

O ORIGINS

Beal City:[u] grocery store owner, Mr. Beal; 1880

Blanchard:[u] village founder and lumberman, Peter, and first postmaster, Herbert, Blanchard; 1878

Brinton:[u] charcoal manufacturer, Oscar Brinton; 1862

Isabella:[co] Queen Isabella of Spain

Lake Isabella:[v] named after the county

Leaton:[u] settler and attorney, John Leaton; 1871

Mt. Pleasant:[c] a better location than the first site chosen for the county seat; 1863

Rosebush:[v] James and Rose Bush gave the railroad land for a depot; 1844

Shepherd:[v] lumberman, Isaac Shepherd; 1857

Union:[u] the township officials were on the side of the Union in the Civil War; 1861 [Wikipedia]

Vernon City:[u] Mt. Vernon, home of George Washington; 1870

Weidman:[u] lumber mill owner, John Weidman; 1884

Winn:[u] a Mr. Winn; 1867

P PARKS

National: 0 **State:** 1 **County:** 8 **Local:** 25
Number of campsites: 300
State Forest: *Chippewa River:* 1,800 acres
State Game Area: *Edmore:* 160 acres, scattered sites
County: *Deerfield Nature Park:* 600 acres, on the Chippewa River, artesian well, sledding, beach
...*L.A. McDonald Wildlife Sanctuary:* 11-acre wetland adjacent to the Pere Marquette Rail Trail
The parks in the county are all connected by more than 8 miles of paths or sidewalks.

Q QUOTE FROM THE LOCALS

"Q. How has gaming affected the [Saginaw Chippewa] tribe? A. Through the resiliency of our ancestors we have endured and overcome many obstacles that were placed before us. The recent success of our gaming and entertainment operation has enabled us to better provide for the needs of our community. Housing, health care and educational opportunities have greatly improved in the past twenty years. Our economic success has also given us the means to begin to reclaim the history of our people and share it with the rest of the world." [sagchip.org]

R RECREATION & SPORTS

Auto racing: *Mt. Pleasant Speedway:* $3/8$-mile clay track; home of the Xtreme100

Golf courses: 9

Hiking/skiing/mountain biking trails: 8 miles

Joe Nevills

Horse racing: *Mt. Pleasant Meadows:* only track east of the Mississippi River that offers mixed breed harness racing

Public access sites: 9
Public recreational land: <1% of county
Rail-trail: (8 miles), Pere Marquette
Le Tour De Mont Pleasant: professional cyclists, family fun ride, promoting health & wellness, June
Michigan's Central Swing: a play and stay program with 12 top-rated golf courses in Central Michigan
Morey Courts: court sports, ice arena, tournaments
Skate War: one of the largest amateur skateboard/inline competitions in the nation, July

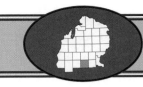
Tom Bowl: each year since 1989, the #1 and #2 college football teams have been invited to play this bowl game in Beal City. Every year each team has declined the offer.

S STATE OF MICHIGAN

The Michigan Department of Transportation (MDOT) has some very useful driver information on their website. There is a map showing

construction projects throughout the state (Quick Links: Mi Drive) and whether it is a total or partial closure of the road, plus more details. There is also information on bridges and bridge clearances, current traffic speed on the Interstate Highways, current accident information and weather information.

The Quick Links: Lane Closures offers detailed information on a regional or county level with information on specific roads on specified dates, currently or in the future.

The Quick Links: State Map site offers 40 city maps similar to what would be found in the printed State Transportation map if there was room for them all.

The MDOT Online Services include:

1. Construction Projects and Travel Delays including reporting potholes, projects under study and those explained above
2. Maps and Getting Around including ferries, a city-to-city distance and time calculator, and detailed information for truckers
3. Doing Business with MDOT including Adopt a Highway, contractor and construction information and filing a damage claim
4. Alternatives to Driving including aeronautics, bicycling (see 50S), carpools and rideshares, and a cost to commute calculator

There is so much more information that it is impossible to mention it all in this small space. Go online and become familiar with all that the State of Michigan has to offer its citizens and visitors.

T TRAVEL

Airport: Lake Isabella Airpark, Mt. Pleasant Municipal
Bus: Indian Trails, Isabella County Transportation Commission
Distance to Lansing: 64 miles
Main roads: US-10, US-127, M-20

U UNIVERSITIES & COLLEGES

Central Michigan University: est. 1892, 21,000 students. They prepare students for varied roles as responsible citizens and leaders in a democratic and diverse society…using excellent teaching and student-focused learning. MAC, Chippewas

Davenport University: see 13U

Saginaw Chippewa Tribal College: est. 1998, 150 students. It is a two-year tribally controlled college developed to increase access to higher education for the tribal community …in an educational empowerment process that is aimed at preserving and maintaining Saginaw Chippewa tribal culture.

V VARIETY

Central Michigan University has the fourth largest enrollment among Michigan's 15 public universities, including 21,000 students on campus, 7,000 enrolled online and at more than 60 locations throughout Michigan and North America.

W WANDERLUST

Agri-tourism: *Papa's Pump-kin Patch & Country Farm Market:* Michigan's largest farm toy store, a recreational and educational farm for kids of all ages; U-pick, asparagus, strawberries, sweet corn, wagon rides, corn maze

Deb Schmuker

Brewery: Mountain Town Station

Casino: *Soaring Eagle:* big name entertainment all year 'round; see 37L

Cultural: Central Michigan University events

Fall colors: early October

Live theater: Broadway, Bush Theatre

Central Michigan University Annual Pow-Wow: part of the American Indian Program at CMU, March

X X-TRA STUFF

American Indian Community: *Saginaw Chippewa Tribe:* the 138,000 acres of the Isabella Indian Reservation was set aside by the treaties of 1855 and 1864; the tribe is now the largest employer in Isabella County. sagchip.org

NPCR

County fair: *Isabella County Youth & Farm Science Fair:* Aug.

Hospitals: Central Michigan Community

Large employers: Central Michigan University, Meijer, Delfield (cooking equipment), Mt. Pleasant Public Schools, STT (security, detective), Morbark (makes manufacturing machines), Michigan Dept. of Community Health (psychiatric hospital), Central Michigan Community Hospital, Saginaw Chippewa Indian Tribal Government

Y YESTERYEAR

Prior to the coming of the Europeans, the estimated 15,000 American Indians in Michigan had no concept of land ownership. They felt the land provided them with their life and therefore belonged to all peoples. The issue of land use and ownership provided most of the conflicts between the natives and the newcomers. Michigan had no "Indian wars," although there were occasional skirmishes.

Beginning in 1783 with the Treaty of Paris, Great Britain ceded all its land to the U.S., including the land that would become the State of Michigan. However, by law, the *land* remained the property of the local American Indian tribes (who didn't even know they *owned* it) until the U.S. took it from them by treaty. Over the years, the American Indians were given cash, goods, and promises for their land, but sometimes the government didn't always pay fair value or keep the treaties.

In all, there were 11 treaty cessions between the American Indians of Michigan and the U.S. government between 1795 and 1842. After 1825, all U.S. treaties with the American Indians implemented the government policy of relocating the American Indians west of the Mississippi River.

From 1838-1840, a majority (but not all) of the Potawatomi tribe was rounded up and moved to Missouri, then to Iowa, then to Kansas, then finally to the Indian Territory around 1875.

It is estimated that less than half of all of the American Indians of Michigan were actually removed from Michigan to the western states. Dunbar

Z ZOO & ANIMAL PLACES

Florence J. Maxwell Audubon Woods Preserve: owned by the Chippewa Watershed Conservancy, 40-acre Audubon bird sanctuary, 110 species of birds

From BIBLIOGRAPHY & NOTES...

F FAUNA: (MI H&T) indicates that Michigan allows Hunting and Trapping of this animal with the proper training, permits, licensing and within the season.

A AGRICULTURE

Land in farms: 39% of county
Number of farms: 1,200
Size of average farm: 150 acres
Market value of all products: #36 of 83 counties
Crops: ...most acres: corn
...highest $ sales: grain: corn, soybeans, wheat
Livestock: ...largest number: cattle & calves
...highest $ sales: milk & daily products
Among the top Michigan counties:
• #3- beef cows, all goats, sheep & lambs
• #5- horses
Dairy, food and meat processing plants: 21
State ranking for harvested trees: #58 of 83 counties
FYI: Michigan is second only to California in the diversity of agricultural products produced in the state. The ability to produce a wide variety of different kinds of crops is due to the many microclimates around the state that are a result of the effect of the Great Lakes on the weather and the varied soil types that are a result of glacial activity. Michigan produces an average of 30% of the food its residents consume. At over $7 billion per year in gross farm sales, agriculture is the second largest industry in the state with over $71 billion in economic impact (see 1A). Manufacturing is the leading industry and tourism is third.

The United States Department of Agriculture (USDA) tracks the following 200 agriculture crops and livestock produced in Michigan:

• alfalfa (hay, seed), alpacas, apples, apricots, aquaculture (catfish, trout, other food fish, baitfish, ornamental fish, sport or game fish, other), aquatic plants, asparagus
• barley, beans (lima, snap), bedding & garden plants, beets, berries (blackberries & dewberries, tame blueberries, wild blueberries, cranberries, currents, raspberries, strawberries, other), birdsfoot trefoil seed, bison, buckwheat, broccoli, Brussels sprouts, bulbs & tubers (& corms & rhizomes), burros
• cabbage (Chinese, head), canola, carrots, cattle & calves (beef, milk, other), cauliflower, celery, cherries (sweet, tart), chicory, Christmas trees (cut), clover seed (crimson, red), collards, colonies of bees, corn (for grain, for silage), cucumbers & pickles, cut flowers & florist greens, cuttings & seedlings (& liners & plugs)
• daikon, dairy products, deer, dill, donkeys, dry edible beans (azuki, black, cranberry, great northern, kidney, navy, pinto, small red, yellow eye), dry edible peas, ducks
• eggs, eggplant, elk, emmer & spelt, emus, escarole & endive
• flower seeds, foliage plants (indoor), forage land
• garlic, geese, ginseng, goats (mohair produced, milk goats, meat produced), grapes, greenhouse food crops (fruits & berries, vegetable & herbs, tomatoes)
• hay (small grain, other tame, wild), haylage & grass silage & green chop (all, alfalfa, other), herbs (fresh cut), hogs & pigs, honey collected, horses & ponies, horseradish
• kale
• lettuce (head, leaf, romaine), llamas
• maple syrup, melons (cantaloupe, honeydew, watermelon), mink, mint (peppermint, spearmint), mules, mushrooms, mustard greens
• nectarines, nursery stock, nuts (almonds, chestnuts, hazelnuts, pecans, English walnuts, other nuts)

Michigan Farm Bureau

• oats, okra, onions (dry, green), ostriches, other field and grass seed crops, other floriculture crops, other nursery crops
• parsley, peaches, pears, peas (Chinese, sugar, snow, green), peppers (bell, others), persimmons, pheasants, pigeons or squab, plums & prunes, popcorn, potatoes, potted flowering plants, poultry (broilers, layers, pullets, other), proso millet, pumpkins
• quail
• rabbits, radishes, rhubarb, rye, ryegrass seed
• sheep & lambs & wool production, short-rotation woody crops, sod, sorghum (grain, silage), soybeans, spinach, squash (summer, winter), sugarbeets (seeds, sugar), sunflowers (oil, seed), sweet corn (fresh, seed), sweet potatoes
• timothy seed, tomatoes, triticale, turkeys, turnips, turnip greens
• vegetables/other, vegetable seeds, vegetable transplants, vetch seed
• watercress, wheat (spring, winter), wild rice

B BRIDGE OR BOAT

Stacey Choate

MDOT Historic Bridge: The stone veneer of this 1925 handsome bridge over the S. Branch River Raisin in Brooklyn is on a mill site that was purchased by Henry Ford in 1921. Using power generated from a giant water wheel near this site, Ford made auto parts at this location from 1934 until 1967.

C CELEBRATIONS

Brooklyn *Race Fest Classic Car Cruise:* get ready for the Michigan International Speedway season, June

Jackson *Blues Festival:* a blues festival for blues fans, by blues musicians, June

NPCR

…*Cascades Civil War Muster:* the longest running, biggest Civil War Muster and reenactment in the Midwest, Aug.

NPCR

…*Hot Air Jubilee:* hot air balloons, crafts, auto show, plus the features of Ella Sharp Park, July

…*Michigan Shakespeare Festival:* plays and activities that inspire, attract and educate a broad-based audience about the Bard, July & Aug.

…*Rose Festival:* to further civic pride; queens pageant, parade, party in the park, crafts, June

…*Storyfest:* professional storytellers weave their magic with words, May

Hanover *Rust and Dust Days:* many activities using antique farm equipment, antique sawmill, tractor pulls, demonstrations of 1900s life skills, Aug.

Michigan Center *Carp Carnival:* the fishing tournament is only part of the fun, June

D DEMOGRAPHICS

Population: 160,200   Persons per sq. mile: 227
Largest city: Jackson   Population: 33,500
Largest township: Blackman   Population: 24,000
Largest village: Brooklyn   Population: 1,200
Median household income: $46,500
Owner-occupied median house value: $135,000
Persons affiliated with a religious congregation: 35%
Persons below poverty level: 14%
Students receiving school lunch subsidy: 42%

E ENVIRONMENT

Helping the Grand River live up to its name, the Grand River Environmental Action Team (GREAT) seeks to promote the protection and preservation of the Grand River Watershed in Jackson County through activities and educational programs. With headwaters in Jackson County at the Liberty Dam in Liberty Twp., the Grand River is the longest river (260 miles) in Michigan. As the second largest watershed in the state, it empties into Lake Michigan.

Jackson County sits on one of the largest aquifers in North America. In addition, some of the largest remaining wetlands in Lower Michigan are located in this watershed, which has over 200 miles of navigational waterways and hundreds of small lakes. The GREAT sponsors 22 different canoe trails in and around Jackson alone. great-mi.org

F FLORA & FAUNA

Charles Peirce

The Michigan lily is a wildflower common to prairie areas and can be found throughout both peninsulas and many other states, too.

In many states as well as Michigan, crows *(MI H&T)* are considered small game and can be hunted. They are considered scavengers of road kill and human garbage. They are a loud, messy and destructive presence in orchards and cornfields as well as urban areas.

USFWS

G GOVERNMENT

County: ...**created:** 1829 ...**organized:** 1832
...**originally part of:** Washtenaw County
Size: 463,000 acres / 707 sq. miles (29 of 83 counties)
The county has 1 city, 6 villages, 19 townships with 3 as charter townships, 13 unincorporated communities, 4 Census Designated Place and 13 school districts.

Kim W. Kerr

County seat: Jackson
...**Homestead property tax:** 41 mills
Motto: <u>Brooklyn</u>: *A Place for All Seasons*
...<u>Jackson County</u>: *Integrity Leadership Collaboration Responsiveness Accountability*
...<u>Jackson County</u> CVB: *Down to Earth People Reaching New Heights*

H HISTORICAL MARKERS 19 of 30

Austin Blair: governor of Michigan from 1860-1864, raised money to send the Michigan Volunteer Infantry Regiment, the first soldiers from the western states, to fight for the Union; see 23H, 23Y

Camp Blair: 1863-1866, rendezvous and hospital for Union troops in Michigan
Ed Cross Farm: 1863-1938, after farming his land for 50 years, lost it in the Great Depression
Ella Sharp Museum: Ella died in 1912 and left the 600-acre farm to Jackson for a park; her 1855 house is now the museum.

Michigan State Preservation Office

First Congregational Church: 1859, Romanesque Revival style; raised up 8' in 1871 to add lower-level classrooms

First State Prison: 1838, a temporary wooden structure enclosed by a fence of tamarack poles
First United Methodist Church: the 1922 Neo-Gothic style building was built around the 1868 church.

Michigan State Preservation Office

First Universalist Church: 1866, Gothic Revival style reflects New England origins of the original 13 families who started the Universalist Society.

Hanover High School: 1911-1962, now the local history museum with many displays; historical agricultural park under development
Hanover-Horton Schools: 1945, consolidated as the Hanover-Horton Rural Agricultural School District
Huron Potawatomi Indian Village: Wabkezhik opposed federal government resettlement plans.
Spring Arbor: 1831, founded on a Potawatomi Indian settlement
Jackson Area: was known as a stopping place for westbound travelers on the Territorial Road, for the Grand River, for the birth of the Republican Party and for state prisons
Jacksonburg Public Square: 1830s, residents convinced Jackson would be the state capital
Paddock-Hubbard House: 1845, Greek Revival style, now part of the Concord Historic District; museum
St. John's Church: 1857, first congregants were Irish immigrants who fled Ireland during the potato famine of 1845, coming to American mining towns like Jackson.

Spring Arbor College: 1963, roots go back to 1873; Albion College and Hillsdale College got their start here too.

Under the Oaks: 1854, when the anti-slavery meeting was held the crowd was large and the day was hot, so they moved outside to an oak grove; a state-wide slate of candidates were selected and the Republican Party was born; see 38Y.

Michigan State Preservation Office

Wellman General Store: 1886, triple-brick Victorian-style structure exemplifies small town midwestern general stores of the 1880s

National Register of Historic Places: 22 listings
State Historic Sites: 58 listings

I INFORMATION

Chamber of Commerce: Brooklyn-Irish Hills, Napoleon
Visitor: Experience Jackson, 800-245-5282, experiencejackson.com

J JOKES

You may be a good Michiganian if…
…you enjoy, oops, at least tolerate, bone-chilling cold and stifling hot weather.
…you look forward to the change of seasons for the change in the weather, the change in the scenery, the change of your wardrobe, the change of activities, the change in your mood and the change in your utility bill.
…given the chance, you'd be the last one to turn off the lights.
…you take your summer vacation in-state.
…you appreciate your kids moving to a city that has a direct flight from your favorite airport.
…you always have a state map and county map book in your car, even if you have a GPS. (And now, you always carry *Discovering Michigan County by County* with you in your car, too. Don't leave home without it!)

K KINSMAN

Race
American Indian: <1%
Asian: <1%
Black/African American: 8%
Hispanic or Latino: 3%
Other: 4%
White: 88%

Ancestry
German: 22%
English: 13%
U.S./American: 12%
Irish: 10%
Polish: 8%
French: 3%
Italian: 3%

L LIGHTHOUSE OR LANDMARK

Kenny Price of K Price Photos

Cascade Falls, in the 460-acre Cascade Park, is a 500' wide, 1930s art deco lighted fountain with 16 waterfalls. There are nightly light and water shows in the summer. The park also has paddleboats, a golf course and three fireworks displays a year.

M MUSEUMS

Teresa Choate

Concord *Mann House:* furnished late Victorian home; part of the Michigan Historical Museum System

NPCR

Grass Lake *Michigan Whitetail Hall of Fame Museum:* trophy bucks, live deer

NPCR

NPCR

...*Waterloo Farm and Dewey School Museum:* includes farm house, log house, bake house, windmill, milk cellar, granary, workshop, ice house, one-room school; local history

...*Whistle Stop Park Depot:* displays of local interest

Hanover Lee Conklin Antique Reed Organ Museum: 95 fully restored & working organs, restoration workshops; in the Hanover-Horton Museum

Stacey Choate

Jackson *Cascades-Sparks Museum:* an eclectic collection of local memorabilia

NPCR

...*Ella Sharp Museum of Art and History:* 5 galleries of art and history; farmhouse and interpretive center, historic village; restaurant, educational and entertaining programs; all in the Ella Sharp Park

Spring Arbor *Ye Olde Carriage Shop:* 40 old cars including 15 that were made in Jackson

N NATURAL RESOURCES

Elevation: 900 – 1,100 feet
Physiography: hilly uplands, rolling plains

Soil: Sand
 Depth: 12"
 Color: black
 Type: fine, loamy sand
 Details: low and flat, often swampy areas
 Agriculture: corn, wheat, grains, oats, celery
 NOTE: soil types are not limited to any one county.

Forest type: oak-hickory
Public/private forests: 18% of county
National Natural Landmark: *Black Spruce Bog Natural Area:* 120 acres, a boreal bog forest illustrating the climax stage of succession in a sphagnum bog ecosystem

Water in county: 3% of county
 Lakes: 130 **...largest:** Lake Columbia
 Rivers: Grand, Kalamazoo, Portage, River Raisin
 Rivers & streams: 320 miles

Growing season, avg.: 152 days (2-3 temp. zones)
 Last freeze, avg.: May 1 – May 10
 First freeze, avg.: Oct. 5 – Oct. 15
Precipitation, annual avg.: rainfall: 29 inches
 snowfall: 39 inches
Temperature (F), avg.: January: high 29°, low 15°
 July: high 83°, low 61°
 Annual: >90°: 13 days, **<0°:** 10 days
Tornadoes (1930-2010): 16

O ORIGINS

Blackman:[ct] first settler, Horace Blackman; 1830
Brooklyn:[v] after Brooklyn, NY; 1832
Concord:[v,t] since all the settlers were living in harmony; 1832
Grass Lake:[v,ct] a grass-filled lake; 1829
Hanover:[v,t] settler from Hanover, Germany; 1836
Jackson:[c,co] first Jacksonburgh, then Jacksonopolis; named after Pres. Andrew Jackson; 1827
Michigan Center:[u] the east-west center of the state; 1834
Munith:[u] after Munich, Germany; <1880
Napoleon:[u] in honor of Napoleon Bonaparte; 1830
Parma:[v,t] pioneers from Parma, NY; 1833
Pleasant Lake:[u] first called Spring Lake; 1836
Rives Junction:[u,t] in Rives Township at the junction of two railroads; 1834
Sandstone:[ct] large deposit of sandstone; 1832
Spring Arbor:[u,t] large spring in the area; 1838
Springport:[v,t] many springs in the area; 1836
Vandercook Lake:[u] pioneer settler, Henry Vandercook

P PARKS

National: 0 **State:** 2 **County:** 16 **Local:** 11
Number of campsites: 3,000
State Game Area: Grass Lake, Sharonville, Waterloo

State Recreation Area: *Waterloo:*[wba, ww] 20,000 acres of scattered parcels, 11 lakes, 47 miles of trails, visitor center, cabins, lodges, school, horse trails, 7 campgrounds, hunting, boating, swimming, fishing, mountain biking

NPCR

Local: *Ella Sharp Park:* 560 acres, major golf course and golfing opportunities, flower gardens, hiking trails, pool, sports facilities; includes the Ella Sharp Museum and farms

KIM W. Kerr

Other: *The Dahlem Conservancy:*[ww] 300 acres, ecology farm, gardens, forests, prairies, rolling meadows, marshes, ponds, special needs trail; to bridge the gap from the human to the natural environment

Q QUOTE FROM THE LOCALS

"Jackson is one of Michigan's best-kept secrets. Jackson strikes just the right balance between downtown excitement, rich history, natural beauty, culture and outdoor fun. It is a place to celebrate all of the good things life has to offer – music, sports, culture, festivals, and fabulous food. The county is blessed with rolling hills, beautiful lakes, and the headwaters of several major rivers. The terrain is perfect for four seasons of recreation including hiking, golfing, water recreation, hunting and fishing, bird watching, camping, snowmobiling and more. Jackson County is a bird lover's paradise, with dozens of native and migratory bird species flocking to our forests, fields, marshes and lakes. The county has consistently been rated one of the 10 most affordable housing markets in the U.S." [jccvb.org]

R RECREATION & SPORTS

Auto racing: *Michigan International Speedway:* see 46R
Golf courses: 21
FYI: Jackson County was ranked #4 in value in the nation by *Golf Digest* and has a national reputation for the number, quality and affordability of good golf courses.

Hiking/skiing/mountain biking trails: 40 miles
Public access sites: 8
Public recreational land: 3% of county
Rail-trail: (10 miles) Falling Waters

S STATE OF MICHIGAN

The Michigan Department of Corrections (MDOC) maintains an Internet site that contains information about 300,000 Michigan prisoners, parolees and probationers. If a person has been under the jurisdiction of the MDOC within the last three years, then the Offender Tracking Information System (OTIS), which includes the Sex Offender Registry, will have information about that person. OTIS does not contain information about prisoners in county jails or city lockups, only those in the state prison system. See 34S.

T TRAVEL

Airport: Jackson County Reynolds Field

Amtrak: Jackson

Bus: Greyhound, Jackson Transportation Authority
Distance to Lansing: 38 miles
Main roads: I-94, US-127, M-50, M-60, M-99, M-106

Kim W. Kerr

Memorial Highways: US-127, *Haskell L. Nichols MH:* (1896-1991) served a total of 34 years in the Michigan House and Senate
FYI: Over the years, I-94 has been called, in part or as a whole, proposed, promoted or legalized: Austin Blair Memorial Hwy., Blossom Hwy., Blue Water Trail, Detroit Industrial Hwy., Detroit-Lincoln-Denver Hwy., Edsel Ford Expy., James G. O'Hara Frwy., Liberty Hwy., 94th Combat Infantry Division Memorial Hwy., Underground Railroad Memorial Hwy., Victory Hwy. and Willow Run Expy. [Barnett]

U UNIVERSITIES & COLLEGES

Baker College of Jackson: see 25U
Jackson Community College: est. 1928, 10,000 students. Their mission is to assist the learner in identifying and achieving their educational goals; they value integrity, caring, collaboration, quality, inclusion, service and leadership. MCCAA, Jets

New Tribes Bible Institute: est. 1955, 400 students on 2 campuses (MI and WI). It provides students with a solid Biblical foundation with a clear missions emphasis and challenges them to consider how they can impact their world for Christ.

Spring Arbor University: est. 1873/1928/1963, 4,000 students. They encourage lifelong involvement in the study and application of the liberal arts, total commitment to Jesus Christ as the perspective for learning, and critical participation in the contemporary world. MCC, Cougars

V VARIETY

Jackson County Chamber of Commerce

Jackson County Chamber of Commerce

Built in 1926, the State Prison of Southern Michigan was the largest walled prison in the world (57 acres enclosed by 34' high walls) with almost 6,000 inmates who lived in 10'l x 6'w x 7.5'h individual cells. This site was closed in 2007 and prisoners are now housed in other facilities. See 38W.

W WANDERLUST

Agri-tourism: *Farm Markets:* Adams, Grand River, Hearthstone, Page Avenue, Pregitzer, Sodt's Berry Farm

Cultural: Jackson Symphony Orchestra, Jackson Youth Symphony Orchestra

Fall colors: middle October

Live theater: Center Stage Jackson, Michigan Theatre, Potter Center,

MotorCities National Heritage Area: yes

Planetarium: Hurst at Ella Sharp Park

Shopping mall: Westwood

Walking tour: *Jackson Historical Home & Buildings Tour:* 300 notable homes in the 15-block district

Wineries: ...*Chateau Aeronautique Winery:* fine wines in an airpark lifestyle

...*Lone Oak Vineyard Estate:* SE Michigan's oldest and largest commercial vineyard

...*Sandhill Crane Vineyards:* estate-bottled wines, tasting room is surrounded by vineyards

...*Sleeping Bear Winery & Taste of Michigan store:* a fun approach to wines and Michigan products

...*Southeast Michigan Pioneer Wine Trail:* brochure is available at local wineries

Old State Prison / Armory Arts Tour: tour the old prison, underground tunnels and cellblocks; plus shop at the arts village that was once the State Prison of Southern Michigan; see 38V.

Michigan State Preservation Office

X X-TRA STUFF

County fair: *Jackson County Fair:* Aug.

Hospitals: Allegiance Health

Large employers: Allegiance Health, Department of Corrections, Consumers Energy, Michigan Automotive Compressor, Jackson Public Schools, Great Midwest News (wholesale books, newspapers), Jackson Community College

There are more than 50 lakes within a 10-mile radius of Brooklyn and some call it the "Heart of the Lakes."

Y YESTERYEAR

Birth of the Republican Party

Slavery and anti-slavery sentiments were running high all around the country.

▪*Feb. 1854:* An anti-slavery faction of the Whig Party in Wisconsin vowed to start a new political party if the Kansas-Nebraska Bill was made into law.

▪*May 1854:* Congress passed the Kansas-Nebraska Bill that permitted slavery in the new territories of Kansas and Nebraska if the people voted for it.

▪*July 1854:* As a result of the meeting in Wisconsin, the delegates met in Jackson, MI, and formally adopted the name *Republican*.

▪*1856:* The Republican anti-slavery presidential candidate lost the 1856 election and the party knew they could not win the presidency on the slavery issue alone. Therefore, the party broadened its appeal by endorsing the transcontinental railroad and Western development, Federal aid to improve harbors and rivers, and agreed to permit slavery in states where it already existed.

▪*1860*: The Republican Party nominated moderate anti-slavery candidate Abraham Lincoln, who won the presidential election.

▪*April 1861*: The southern states considered Lincoln too radical and 11 of them voted to leave the Union and thus the Civil War began. ^{Worldbook Encyclopedia}

See 38H.

NPCR-3

NPCR-3

Z ZOO & ANIMAL PLACES

Watchable Wildlife Viewing Areas:^{ww} Haehnle Audubon Sanctuary; see 38P

Bellairs Fiber Farm & Sheep Shed: tours

The Buffalo Ranch: wagon rides to see and feed the buffalo; burgers, general store

Indian Brook Aquaculture Farm: rainbow trout hatchery and fishing for them in the lake

Michigan Whitetail Hall of Fame Museum: feed the deer

Sandhill Llamas: pet and learn about llamas

Many Sandhill Cranes come to Jackson County to roost during October.

Bold typeface: this indicates that this heading may be repeated in every chapter, providing that the information about the heading is applicable to the county.

A AGRICULTURE

Land in farms: 39% of county
Number of farms: 850
Size of average farm: 170 acres
Market value of all products: #8 of 83 counties
Crops: ...most acres: corn for grain
...highest $ sales: nursery, greenhouse, floriculture
Livestock: ...largest number: hogs & pigs
...highest $ sales: milk & dairy products
Among the top Michigan counties:

- #1-bedding plants, colonies of bees, cuttings & seedlings & liners & plugs, flower seeds, greenhouse square footage, rabbits, sales of floriculture & greenhouse products
- #2- greenhouse tomatoes, greenhouse vegetables and herbs, potted flowering plants, sheep & lambs, pounds of honey
- #3- indoor foliage plants, sheep
- #5- hogs

Dairy, food and meat processing plants: 43
State ranking for harvested trees: #62 of 83 counties
AgBioResearch Centers (MSU): *Kellogg Experimental Forest:* tree breeding and genetics
FYI: In 2008, Michigan was 3rd in the nation and Kalamazoo County 1st in the state for floriculture production. This category includes bedding & garden plants, cut flowers and cut florist greens, foliage plants and potted flowering plants. There are 1,300+ commercial floriculture growers in the state.

Kalamazoo County is the #1 bedding plant producer in the U.S. Bedding plants, most often flowers, are grown (usually in a greenhouse) from seed to near-blooming or blooming size before being shipped to the consumer to plant for seasonal flowers or foliage. These plants add beauty and enjoyment to any garden or landscape.

Kalamazoo County is the #1 U.S. producer of geraniums, hanging flower baskets and Easter lilies. kalcounty.com, Michigan.gov/mda See 39L.

Michigan Farm Bureau

B BRIDGE OR BOAT

Sarah J. Pion

The Augusta Creek Covered Bridge, privately built in 1973, was moved near the WK Kellogg Forest and is now open to the public.

C CELEBRATIONS

Kalamazoo *Kalama-Do-Dah Day and Parade:* silly, zany, fun, June
...Great Winter Adventure: ice sculptures, chili cook off, Jan.
...Living History Show: largest show in U.S. devoted to pre-1890 supplies and crafts, March
...Maple Sugar Festival: at the Kalamazoo Nature Center, March

...Art Fair: Bronson Park, June

...Greekfest: heritage & culture, June

John A. Lacko

...Art on the Mall
- *Black Arts Festival:* minority artists, July
- *Blues Fest:* local & national musicians, July
- *Taste of Kalamazoo:* eat, drink and be merry, July
- *Ribfest:* ribs and beer, Aug.
- *Scottish Festival:* everyone welcome, Aug.
- *Street Rod Nationals:* 2,000+ cars that are 30 years and older, Sept.
- *Irish Festival:* Sept.

John A. Lacko

...*Michigan Festival Of Sacred Music*: International artists at various churches and unique venues, Nov.

...*New Year's Eve Fest*: dozens of venues around town, Dec.

<u>Portage</u> *Summer Entertainment Series:* family events, June-July

<u>Vicksburg</u> *Showboat:* musical revue, Feb.

...*Old Car Festival:* evolution of the auto, June

D DEMOGRAPHICS

Population: 250,300   **Persons per sq. mile:** 445
Largest city: Kalamazoo   **Population:** 74,300
Largest township: Kalamazoo   **Population:** 21,900
Largest village: Vicksburg   **Population:** 2,300
Median household income: $42,300
Owner-occupied median house value: $146,000
Persons affiliated with a religious congregation: 35%
Persons below poverty level: 20%
Students receiving school lunch subsidy: 41%

E ENVIRONMENT

"The <u>Michigan Groundwater Stewardship Program</u> (MGSP) provides information and assessment tools for residents and farms to help them identify risks to groundwater. The MGSP coordinates local, state, and federal resources to help reduce those risks. Technical assistance and education resources, as well as cost-share funds, address agricultural, turf grass and household audiences." Specialists are available at the MSU Extension office and the Kellogg Biological Station. *kalcounty;.com*

F FLORA & FAUNA

Dr. Thomas G. Barnes/USFWS

Dutchman's breeches (4"-8" tall) can be found in the woodlands in the spring. [Breeches are a full, knee-length pant fitted at the bottom.]

NPCR

Eastern cottontail rabbits *(MI H&T)* are most common in southern Michigan. They require an edge-dependent habitat where two different habitats meet, such as brushy thickets, dry and grassy wetland edges, hayfields, grassy cornfields, bushy fencerows, orchards and gardens.

G GOVERNMENT

County: ...**created:** 1829 ...**organized:** 1830
...**originally part of:** St. Joseph County
Size: 371,000 acres / 562 sq. miles (53 of 83 counties)
The county has 4 cities, 5 villages, 15 townships with 5 as charter townships, 5 unincorporated communities, 5 Census Designated Place and 9 school districts.

Sarah J. Pion

County seat: Kalamazoo
...**Homestead property tax:** 52 mills
Motto: <u>Kalamazoo County</u>: *to govern...to protect...to serve*
...<u>Kalamazoo County</u> Convention and Visitors Bureau: *You'll be back We promise*
...<u>Parchment</u>: *The Paper City*
...<u>Vicksburg</u>: *The Village with a Vision*

H HISTORICAL MARKERS 11 of 45

Edward Israel Artic Pioneer: 1881, born and buried in Kalamazoo, part of Greeley's expedition to the Artic Ocean, the nation's first polar expedition

First Women's Club in Michigan: 1879, first club in the nation to have its own building

West Main Hill Historic District: 1888, an innovative plat of curving, tree-lined streets

Indian Fields: an 1800 Potawatomi village; now part of the Kalamazoo airport

Kalamazoo Celery: 1872, Dutch farmers made Kalamazoo famous for the celery grown in the muck fields.

Kalamazoo School Case: 1858, the right of school districts to levy taxes and therefore provide free schools (vs. private schools requiring tuition) for all children

Kalamazoo State Hospital: 1848, Michigan's first state institution for the treatment of mental patients

Sarah J. Pion

Lincoln at Kalamazoo: 1856, his only speech in Michigan

Michigan State Grange: 1873, an agricultural organization to "educate and elevate the American farmer;" very influential and innovative at the time

South Street Historical District: 1841-1915, reflects the spectrum of fashionable domestic architecture with the Italian Revival style most prevalent

NPCR-2

The Upjohn Company: 1886, the four Upjohn brothers started their pill-making factory with "friable" (easily crumbled, i.e. digestible) pills.

National Register of Historic Places: 49 listings

State Historic Sites: 100 listings

I INFORMATION

Chamber of Commerce: Kalamazoo Regional
Visitor: Kalamazoo County Convention and Visitors Bureau, 800-888-0509, discoverkalamazoo.com

J JOKES

You might be from Michigan if…

…you know there is no zoo in Kalamazoo. But there is the Air Zoo.

…half the people you know say they are from Detroit, but you don't personally know anyone who lives there now.

…you know that Kalamazoo actually exists and it isn't that far from Hell (Michigan).

…you know that Kazoo is a town and not just a toy.

…you know how to get to Village of Climax. From Kalamazoo, go south on Lover's Lane… turn toward I-69…

…you install security lights on your house and garage but leave the buildings unlocked.

…you spend your retirement winters in Florida living in a park model trailer.

K KINSMAN

Race
American Indian: 1%
Asian: 2%
Black/African American: 11%
Hispanic or Latino: 4%
Other: 5%
White: 82%

Ancestry
German: 18%
Dutch: 12%
English: 10%
Irish: 8%
U.S./American: 7%
Polish: 5%

L LIGHTHOUSE OR LANDMARK

Sarah J. Pion

These greenhouses remind you why Kalamazoo County is the #1 county in Michigan for floriculture production and the #1 county in the U.S. for bedding plant production. Michigan has over 1,200 acres (over 1.9 square miles) of greenhouses and Kalamazoo County has about 23% of them. See 39A.

M MUSEUMS

<u>Kalamazoo</u> *Air Zoo:* 50 historic aircraft, full motion flight stimulators, hands-on activities, world's largest indoor mural

Courtesy of the Kalamazoo Air Zoo

...*Institute of Arts:* exhibits, auditorium, classes

...*Public Library:* 2002 National Library of the Year

Sarah J. Pion

...*Kalamazoo Valley Museum:* hands-on and interactive history, science and technology; mummy, planetarium

<u>Galesburg</u> *Historical Museum*

<u>Portage</u> *Celery Flats Historical Area:* understand the era when Kalamazoo was the Celery City

...*National Miniatures Trust Museum:* dolls, dollhouses, accessories

...*WK Kellogg Manor House:* restored estate, tours

<u>Vicksburg</u> *Museum:* 1904 railroad station, revolving exhibits, wildlife observation

N NATURAL RESOURCES

Elevation: 700 - 900 feet
Physiography: rolling plains, hill plains

Forest type: oak-hickory, elm-ash-cottonwood, maple-beech
Public/private forests: 22% of county

Water in county: 3% of county
   Lakes: 100   ...**largest:** Gull Lake
   Rivers: Kalamazoo, Portage
   Rivers & streams: 365 miles

Growing season, avg.: 164 days (2 temp. zones)
   Last freeze, avg.: May 5 – May 10
   First freeze, avg.: Oct. 5 – Oct. 10
Precipitation, annual avg.: rainfall: 35 inches
                 snowfall: 73 inches
Temperature (F), avg.: January: high 31°, low 16°
          July: high 85°, low 61°

NPCR

Annual: >90°: 18 days (#1/MI), **<0°:** 6 days
Tornadoes (1930-2010): 27

O ORIGINS

<u>Augusta</u>:[v] the first postmaster was from Augusta, Maine; 1832

<u>Climax</u>:[v] the climax of the search for a place to settle; 1835

<u>Comstock</u>:[ct,v] Gen. Horace Comstock had the area surveyed and established the village; 1830

<u>Cooper</u>:[ct] Mrs. Horace Comstock was the niece of James Fennimore Cooper, who wrote his novel about Michigan frontier life, *Oak Openings*, in this locality; 1834

<u>Galesburg</u>:[c] village founder George L. Gale; 1835

<u>Kalamazoo</u>:[c,ct,co] from the American Indian name meaning "reflecting river," or perhaps "boiling water;" 1829

<u>Oshtemo</u>:[ct] American Indian word meaning "head waters;" <1857

<u>Parchment</u>:[c] the Kalamazoo Vegetable Parchment Co. paper mill was built here in 1909

<u>Portage</u>:[c] from Portage Creek; 1830. (Portage means the act of carrying goods or boats over land from one body of water to another.)

<u>Richland</u>:[v] from Richland Township, possibly from rich farmland in the area; 1832

<u>Schoolcraft</u>:[v] Michigan's Indian Agent, Henry Schoolcraft, 1831; see 75Y

<u>Texas</u>:[ct] after the state of Texas, when Texas revolted against Mexico's rule; 1829

<u>Vicksburg</u>:[v] John Vickers platted the village; 1830

P PARKS

National: 0   **State:** 2   **County:** 6   **Local:** 34
Number of campsites: 750
State Game Area: Fulton, Gourdneck
State Linear Park: *Kal-Haven Trail:*[ww] a 34-mile rail trail between Kalamazoo and South Haven

State Recreation Area: *Fort Custer:* 3,000 acres, includes 25 miles of trails for hiking, bridle, mountain biking, dog sledding, cross-county skiing; swimming, boating, fishing and more; also includes Fort Custer National Cemetery

Sarah J. Pion

State Wildlife Area: *Augusta Creek State Fish & Wildlife Area:* 400 acres, holistic management
County: *Cold Brook:* 276 acres, access to 3 lakes
...*Markin Glen:* 190 acres, handicap accessible
...*Prairie View:* 208 acres, 2 lakes
...*River Oaks:* 270 acres, 20 AYSO soccer fields

...*Scotts Mill Historic Park:* 110 acres, 1860s working water-powered gristmill; great wedding spot

Sarah J. Pion

Local: *Bronson Park:* downtown Kazoo, named after the first white settler in the area, Titus Bronson

Sarah J. Pion

...*Kalamazoo Nature Center:*[ww,wba] 1,000 acres, voted by other nature centers as the #1 nature center in the U.S.

...*West Lake Nature Center:*[ww] 80 acres, over 2 miles of barrier free trails

Other: *Kellogg Experimental Forest:* Michigan State University owned, premier research forest; trails open to the public

Q QUOTE FROM THE LOCALS

"This place with the memorable name is also brimming with out-of-the-ordinary things to see and do. World-class museums, colorful ethnic festivals, top-notch arts and entertainment, unique culinary flavors, charming wineries and microbreweries and vibrant downtown scenes minutes from expansive nature trails and sandy shores...in short, excitement year-round!

"And we can't forget to mention the warm, welcoming people who live and work here. At every corner, you'll find a kind word, impeccable service and a can-do attitude. It exists in everyone from the Discover Kalamazoo team to the hospitality experts at our various attractions, to the folks who call this place home. They're the real reason we can confidently say that whether you stay with us for a day or a week, you'll be back. We promise." discoverkalamazoo.com

R RECREATION & SPORTS

Auto racing: *Galesburg Speedway:* ¼-mile flat oval track a with figure eight
...*Kalamazoo Speedway:* ³/₈-mile banked oval track with 14° average banking; NASCAR sanctioned
Golf courses: 21
Hiking/skiing/mountain biking trails: 90 miles
Horse racing: harness racing during fair week
Michigan Heritage Water Trail: Kalamazoo Watershed
North Country National Scenic Trail: yes
Public access sites: 19
Public recreational land: 2% of county
Rail-trail: (80 miles) Fort Custer Recreation Area, Kal-Haven, Kalamazoo River Valley, Portage Creek Celery Flats
State-funded snowmobile trails: 6 miles
USTA Boys' 18 & 16 National Tennis Championships: at Kalamazoo College, Aug.
Gull Lake Yacht Club: maintains several fleets and races every weekend in the summer

David Roush

Kalamazoo River Valley Trail: 12 ft. wide, paved, for non-motorized traffic, part of a 130 mile connected trail from Battle Creek to South Haven

Kalamazoo Wings: play ice hockey in the Eastern Conference Hockey League at Wings Stadium; the team celebrates some of the holidays with green ice on St. Patrick's Day, pink ice on Valentine's Day, orange ice on Halloween and a golden ice game sponsored by McDonald's.

S STATE OF MICHIGAN

In 2011, ten Michiganians were listed on the *Forbes list of The 400 Richest People in America.* Three of these are from Kalamazoo County.
The following information on each person includes their:
- Michigan ranking 1-10.
- *Name:*
- age at the time of the 2011 Forbes publication;
- Forbes list ranking: # American billionaires ranking / # world's billionaires ranking;
- source of their wealth;
- current miscellaneous information;

- current residence;
- estimated net worth ^{Forbes.com}

1. *Frederik Meijer:* age 91; #57 / #223; he and his father started Meijer Thrifty Acres in 1962; philanthropist, donated land and sculpture for Frederik Meijer Gardens and Sculpture Park; Grand Rapids, MI; $4.7 billion.

2. *Richard Devos:* age 85; #62 / #254; co-founder of Amway; owns the Orlando Magic; Ada, MI; $4.2 billion

3. *Ronda Stryker:* age 57; #170 / #440, granddaughter of Homer Stryker (1894-1980) who invented mobile hospital beds and other medical equipment; Stryker Corp. Board member; interests include special education, empowerment of women, non-traditional college students; Portage, MI; $2.1 billion

4. *Alfred Taubman:* age 87; #182 / #512; real estate and pioneer of mall development; philanthropist, donated extensively to U of M and others; Bloomfield Hills; $2.3 billion

5. *Mike Ilitch:* age 81; #238 / #736; founded Little Caesars Pizza in 1959; owns the Detroit Tigers and the Detroit Red Wings, involved in many philanthropic endeavors; Detroit, MI; $1.7 billion

6. *Manuel "Matty" Moroun:* age 83; #252 / #701; multiple transportation interests, owner of the Ambassador Bridge; Grosse Pointe Shores, MI; $1 billion

7. *Roger Penske:* age 74; #290 / #879; race car driver and racing team owner, Penske Auto Group is the world's second largest automotive group; he is still active in many transportation-related industries; Birmingham, MI; $1.4 billion

8. *John Stryker:* age 53; #332 / #782; grandson of Homer Stryker (1894-1980) who invented mobile hospital beds and other medical equipment; active in gay rights and protecting apes and chimpanzees; Kalamazoo, MI; $1.6 billion

9. *William Ford, Sr.:* age 86; #385 / #993; grandson of Henry Ford, retired from active involvement of the Ford Motor Company; owns the Detroit Lions; Grosse Pointe Shore, MI; $1.2 billion

10. *John Brown:* age 76; #385 / #938; retired president and chief executive of Stryker Corp.; his management took the company global; runs four miles a day; Kalamazoo, MI; $1.3 billion

T TRAVEL

Airports: Kalamazoo/Battle Creek Intl.
Amtrak: Kalamazoo
Bus: Indian Trails, Metro Transit
County road names: ...north/south: number Streets
...east/west: letter Avenues
Distance to Lansing: 70 miles
Main roads: I-94, US-131
Memorial Highways: US-131, *Underground Railroad MH*: operating from 1830 to 1860, local people provided escape routes for slaves; they used the language of the railroad to describe their activities.
...I-94 Bus. Loop, *AmVets MH*: see 19T
...M-96, *Fort Custer MH*: established in 1917 as Camp Custer to train soldiers for WWI, named after Michiganian Gen. George Armstrong Custer; see 58V

U UNIVERSITIES & COLLEGES

Kalamazoo College: est. 1833, 1,300 students. The mission of K College is to prepare its graduates to better understand, live successfully within, and provide enlightened leadership to a richly diverse and increasingly complex world. MIAA, Hornets

Kalamazoo Valley Community College: est. 1966, 11,400 students. They are bound neither to traditional forms of education nor to traditional methods of communication, but strive to meet the needs of students, community and nation; M-TEC. MCCAA, Cougars

University of Phoenix: see 25U

Western Michigan University: est. 1904, 25,000 students. Dynamic and student-centered, it is focused on delivering high quality undergraduate instruction, advancing its graduate division and fostering research activities. MAC, Broncos

Don't forget to check the *BIBLIOGRAPHY & NOTES* at the back of the book for explanations and additional information.

V VARIETY

Art Cameron

Michigan leads the nation with over 2,000,000 flats of impatiens sold annually. Impatiens were so named because they are impatient, shooting their seeds out of their pods. They add a lot of intense color to any landscape or hanging basket.

W WANDERLUST

Agri-tourism: *Avalon Farms Homegrown:* hydroponic greenhouses, tomatoes, herbs, broccoli, tours
…*Centre Street Market:* the best of local farms
…*Gull Meadow Farms:* fruit, bakery, U-pick
Brewery: Bell's Brewery, Olde Peninsula Brewpub & Restaurant
Cultural: Kalamazoo Institute of Arts
Fall colors: middle October

Live theater: *Barn Theater:* a converted 1940s dairy barn is the home of Michigan's oldest resident summer stock theatre.

Michigan State Preservation Office

…Civic; Farmers Alley; Miller Auditorium (WMU); Knockabout; New Vic; State
MotorCities National Heritage Area: yes
Planetarium: Universe at Kalamazoo Valley Museum
Shopping malls: Crossroads, Kalamazoo
Walking tours: Kalamazoo
Wineries: *Lawton Ridge:* cool climate viticulture
…*Peterson & Sons:* chemical-free wines
…*Tempo Vino Winery:* custom wine and labels
The Train Barn: features O, S, HO and N gauge items; 23,000 sq. feet of train layout

X X-TRA STUFF

County Fair: *Kalamazoo Co. Agricultural Soc.*, Aug.
Famous people: …*Sports:* Greg Jennings, Derek Jeter, Duane Young
…*Other:* Edna Ferber, Bill Hybels
Hospitals: Borgess, Bronson (2)
Large employers: Pharmacia (pharmaceuticals; formerly Upjohn Co)., Schafer Bakeries, Bronson Hospital, Borgess Hospital, Borgess Health Alliance, Kalamazoo Public Schools
From Kalamazoo, it is 140 miles to Detroit and 150 miles to Chicago.
In 2007, the City of Portage received 12 state and national awards for excellence in various areas.
The American Foundation for the Blind rates Kalamazoo as one of the three top cities in the U.S. for the Sight Impaired. WMU has a Department of Blindness and Low Vision Studies, offering 4 master's degree programs.
The Greater Kalamazoo United Way has the highest per capita giving for cities its size in the U.S.
The Kalamazoo Promise is a program that provides free college tuition for any student who graduates from the Kalamazoo Public Schools. Financed by anonymous donors, the goal is to make the greater Kalamazoo area even greater.
The nation's first permanent pedestrian mall was opened in downtown Kalamazoo in 1959; it has since been returned to street traffic.
Throughout its history, Kalamazoo has been known as Bronson, the Burr Oak City, the Celery City, the Debt-Free City, the Mall City, the Paper City and the Windmill City.
Yes, there really is a Kalamazoo.

Y YESTERYEAR

The most popular of the many songs that mention Kalamazoo by name is the 1942 Glenn Miller song, *I've Got a Gal in Kalamazoo.* "I'm going to Michigan to see the sweetest gal in Kalamazoo zoo-zoo-zoo-zoo-zoo."

In 1962, Lucky Starr included Kalamazoo in the song *I've Been Everywhere.* "…Nebraska, Alaska, Opelika, Baraboo, Waterloo, Kalamazoo, Kansas City, Sioux City…"

Down on the Corner by Credence Clearwater Revival (1969) made reference to the Gibson guitars that were made in Kalamazoo from 1902-1980s, and some models were named Kalamazoo. "Poorboy twangs

the rhythm out on his Kalamazoo..."

Kalamazoo is an unusual word and has a good rhyming quality in its last syllable; it has been used in that capacity without any meaningful relationship to the city or county. Since 1990 there have been several songs with the name *Kalamazoo*. Ben Folds sang, "… ran up a tab and all the way from Kalamazoo; …we had been driftin' all the way from Kalamazoo…" In his song, Mike Carver says, "There's one thing I never want to do And that's be a predator down in Kalamazoo." In the Primus song, Kalamazoo is mentioned in every verse. In a song by Luna, Kalamazoo is never even mentioned at all.

Z   ZOO & ANIMAL PLACES

Watchable Wildlife Viewing Areas:ww see 39P
Battle Creek Riding Club: fine equine facilities
Hillcrest Equestrian Center: lessons, tours, camps
Kellogg Bird Sanctuary: MSU, near Gull Lake, 180 acres, interpretive trails, open 365 days a year

Larry Burdick

Larry Burdick

Sarah J. Pion

Kellogg Dairy Center: MSU, exhibits, research, teaching, demonstrations, self-guided trail

Reindeer Ranch: the first 4-H reindeer program in the lower 48 states; research projects; meat and jerky products

From BIBLIOGRAPHY & NOTES:

U UNIVERSITIES & COLLEGES

• Information is from the website of each school.
  Est.: year school was established
 # students: current enrollment; number is rounded

Athletic Conferences abbreviations:
  Big 10: Big 10, Div. I
  CCHA: Central Collegiate Hockey Association, Div. I
  GLIAC: Great Lakes Intercollegiate Athletic Conference, Div. II
  HL: Horizon League, Div. l
  MAC: Michigan Athletic Conference, Div. I
  MCC: Mid-Central College Conference
  MCCAA: Michigan Community College Athletic Association
  MCHA: Midwest Collegiate Hockey Association, Div. III
  MIAA: Michigan Intercollegiate Athletic Association (the nations oldest athletic conference), Div. III
  NAIA: National Association of Intercollegiate Athletics
  NCCAA: National Christian College Athletic Association
  NCHA: Northern Collegiate Hockey Association, Div. III
  NJCAA: National Junior College Athletic Association
  Summit League: Div. I
  USCAA: United States Collegiate Athletic Association, Div. II
  WHAC: Wolverine-Hoosier Athletic Conference, Div. II
  WIAC: Wisconsin Intercollegiate Athletic Conference, Div. III

A AGRICULTURE

Land in farms: 6% of county
Number of farms: 220
Size of average farm: 105 acres
Market value of all products: #65 of 83 counties
Crops: ...most acres: forage land
...highest $ sales: vegetables: potatoes
Livestock: ...largest number: laying hens
...highest $ sales: horses, ponies, mules, burros, donkeys
Among the top Michigan counties:
- #6- rye for grain
- #7- potatoes
- #9- Christmas trees

Dairy, food and meat processing plants: 9
State ranking for harvested trees: #25 of 83 counties
FYI: With offices in all 83 Michigan counties, Michigan State University Extension brings the research and knowledge of the academic world and applies it at the local level to meet local needs. Extension educators, specialists and program associates are trained to translate the university's research of 30 academic departments and 8 Michigan State University colleges into educational programs that help families, entrepreneurs and community leaders apply that knowledge. They provide excellent information in the areas of agriculture, community development, environment, health and wellness, home and garden, and youth and family. Included in these are a wealth of printed materials and online information on hundreds of related subjects, the 4-H and Master Gardener programs and land issues of any kind. They are a major resource that is available to all Michigan citizens. Just stop by, call or go online. MSUE

B BRIDGE OR BOAT

D & R Sports

With over 1 million registered boats, more than any other state in the U.S., fishing on Michigan's lakes and streams is easy with a boat designed especially for fishing, like this all-purpose bass fishing boat. They sit higher in the water so they can handle rougher waters. This is a good family fishing boat.

C CELEBRATIONS

NPCR

Kalkaska *National Trout Festival:* to celebrate the Heritage of our Natural Resources, Trout Fishing and Sportsmanship, April

...Winterfest-Mid-West International Dog Sled Races: since 1965, the longest continuous running race in Michigan; largest sprint race purse, $6,000; only race in the state with an unlimited/open class; Ice Bowl Disc Golf tournament raises funds for Meals on Wheels, Jan.

D DEMOGRAPHICS

Population: 17,200   **Persons per sq. mile:** 31
Largest township: Kalkaska   **Population:** 2,700
Largest village: Kalkaska   **Population:** 2,020
Median household income: $40,000
Owner-occupied median house value: $108,000
Persons affiliated with a religious congregation: 19% (#83/MI)
Persons below poverty level: 17%
Students receiving school lunch subsidy: 52%

E ENVIRONMENT

Serving 40 counties in Michigan, including Kalkaska County, the Michigan Water Stewardship Program provides information and assessment tools for those farmers, turf grass managers and private households that use pesticides and nitrogen fertilizers. It is a volunteer and locally driven program that works to reduce the risks to groundwater from these applications. MDARD

F FLORA & FAUNA

Alice Welch, USDA

The tamarack tree is a conifer that loses its needles in the fall. It is a hard, strong and durable softwood that is used for poles and posts.

Robert H. Pos/USFWS

Rainbow trout can live in Michigan's coldwater streams. They are known as steelheads when they live in the Great Lakes.

G GOVERNMENT

County: ...created: 1840 **...organized:** 1871
...originally part of: Grand Traverse, Antrim Counties
Size: 365,000 acres / 560 sq. miles (54 of 83 counties)

The county has 1 village, 12 townships and 1 school district.

NPCR

County seat: Kalkaska
...Homestead property tax: 37 mills

H HISTORICAL MARKERS 2 of 2

Excelsior Town Hall: 1901, built for $1,192; from 1907-1926, housed the first rural high school in Michigan established under the law of 1901

Rugg Pond Dam: the dam was erected in 1904 by a private company; it was sold to Consumer Power Co. in 1950 and then to Kalkaska County in 1953. The Army Corp of Engineers condemned the dam in 1980; in 1982 the local citizens formed the Rugg Pond Natural Area to save the dam and preserve the area.

NPCR

State Historic Sites: 4 listings

I INFORMATION

Chamber of Commerce: Kalkaska, 231-258-9103, kalkaskami.com
Other: visitkalkaska.com

J JOKES

You may be a cheapskate in Michigan if...
...you look forward to the snow melting so you can scour the sides of the road for those cans and bottles worth 10¢ each.
...fishing, hunting, trapping and wild berry picking is more than just seasonal entertainment.
...you know which leaves make the best toilet paper.

…you don't recycle for the benefit of the environment; you recycle for the benefit of your own wallet.

…you never give to local charities; you only take what you can get from them.

…you never give of your time, money or labor to help anyone.

…you're proud to be known as a tight-fisted, penny-pinching, stingy cheapskate.

K KINSMAN

Race	Ancestry
American Indian: <1%	German: 25%
Asian: <1%	English: 12%
Black/African American: <1%	Irish: 10%
Hispanic or Latino: 1%	U.S./American: 10%
Other: 2%	Polish: 6%
White: 97%	French: 5%

L LIGHTHOUSE OR LANDMARK

Harold Sheffer

Kalkaska's Rainbow Trout Fountain is a fitting symbol for the area's top ranked trout streams and the National Trout Festival.

M MUSEUMS

Harold Sheffer

Kalkaska *Historical Society & Museum:* in the old train depot; see the smokehouse made from a single tree trunk; much of Kalkaska today looks like it did 100 years ago.

N NATURAL RESOURCES

Land: Elevation: 1,000 – 1,300 feet
Physiography: hill-lands, plains, upland plains

Forest type: aspen-birch, pine-oak, elm-ash-cottonwood
Public/private forests: 74% of county

Water in county: 1% of county
   Lakes: 80   **…largest:** Lake Skegemog
   Rivers: Boardman, Manistee, Rapid River
   Rivers & streams: 280 miles

Growing season, avg.: 110 days (2-3 temp. zones)
   Last freeze, avg.: May 30 – June 5
   First freeze, avg.: Sept. 10 – Sept. 20
Precipitation, annual avg.:
   rainfall: 31 inches
   snowfall: 126 inches
Temperature (F), avg.:
   January: high 26°, low 9°
   July: high 81°, low 54°

   Annual: >90°: 8 days, **<0°:** 26 days

Tornadoes (1930-2010): 8

NPCR

O ORIGINS

<u>Kalkaska:</u>[v,co] an American Indian word of unknown meaning; some say it means "flat table land;" some say it means "burned over territory"
<u>Rapid City:</u>[u] located on the Rapid River, 1891
<u>South Boardman:</u>[t,u] where the railroad crossed the south branch of the Boardman River, 1874

P PARKS

National: 0   **State:** 5   **County:** 2   **Local:** 2
Number of campsites: 220
State Forest: Kalkaska (155,000 acres)

…**Campgrounds:** 3
  …**Pathway:** 10 miles

NPCR

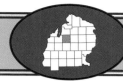
Other: *Skegemog Lake Wildlife Area:* 3,300 acres, one of finest, most ecologically significant areas in the Lower Peninsula; home to beavers, egrets, minks, otters and many other wildlife; miles of trails and a large bridge through the swamp that allows you to get close to the action; bring your insect repellent

Dean Ginther

Q QUOTE FROM THE LOCALS

These miscellaneous remarks from Robert Barnard are part of his unofficial guide to the things to see and do in Kalkaska County and can be found at visitkalkaska.com. On a bus ride from Arizona to Kalkaska when he was 15 years old, he said, "I watched as the forests (in Missouri, Indiana and Southern Michigan) with their heavy undergrowth changed to the type we have here; forests without the vines, saplings and undergrowth. These forests draw people to wander them. Places where you can see considerable distance under a hardwood canopy."

Additional information from visitkalkaska.com states: "Maximize the enjoyment in your vacation by benefiting from an informed, experienced and well-connected adventure guide. If you're new to an area, why spend your time finding the ideal location, etc. when you can gain the advantage of the know-how of an experienced guide?

"Of course any mention of Kalkaska should also include a reference to our National Trout Festival. It's big, really BIG." visitkalkaska.com

NPCR-2

R RECREATION & SPORTS

Blue Ribbon Trout Streams:[1,000] Boardman River-North & South Branches, Manistee River & North Branch
Golf courses: 3
Hiking/skiing/mountain biking trails: 40 miles
MI Shore-to-Shore (horse) **Riding & Hiking Trail:** yes
North Country National Scenic Trail: yes
Public access sites: 26

Public recreational land: 42% of county
Off-road vehicle trails: 140 miles (#4/MI)
Rail-trail: (1 mile) Skegemog Lake
State-funded snowmobile trails: 55 miles
State/federal wild/scenic/natural river: 20 miles of the Upper Manistee River
The headwaters for the Boardman River are in this county; the river is considered one of the 10 top trout streams in the state.

SEASONAL ROAD NOT SNOWPLOWED BY THE KALKASKA COUNTY ROAD COMMISSION

ROAD IMPROVEMENTS WILL NOT BE AT COUNTY EXPENSE

NPCR

Iceman Cometh Challenge: 27-mile mountain bike race from Kalkaska to Traverse City; 3,700 riders, $35,000 in prizes, November
Kaliseum Recreation Complex: fitness center, pool, ice rink, athletic and community activities

S STATE OF MICHIGAN

Since 1990, the Kalkaska Soil Series has been the State Soil. It is one of 500 different kinds of soils in Michigan and is unique to the State. It occurs in 29 counties in both peninsulas, covering over 1 million acres. It is a well-drained soil with 24" to 48" of multicolored

NPCR

sand. This soil supports sugar maple and yellow birch hardwood timber, and some Christmas trees, potatoes and strawberries. In addition, its filtering abilities add to the quality of the lakes and streams wherever it is found. Michigan.gov

T TRAVEL

Bus: Indian Trails
Distance to Lansing: 160 miles
Main roads: US-131, M-66, M-72
Memorial Highways: US-131, *Green Arrow Route – Mackinac Trail:* see 5T
…M-66, *Green Arrow Route:* see 5T

U UNIVERSITIES & COLLEGES

None

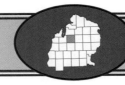
V VARIETY

Alice Welch, USDA

Excellent fly-fishing brings fishermen from around the world to Kalkaska County. This type of fishing is different from standard fishing in that a specialized, hand-tied artificial fly is used on a fly rod using a fly line. No weights or lure or bobber is used, so the casting method has a whole different technique to it. It is a skill that has to be learned.

W WANDERLUST

Fall colors: late September to early October

Kalkaska Shoe Tree: on the west side of US-131 just north of Kalkaska; nobody knows for sure how it started, but over the years, people have hung hundreds of pairs of shoes on this tree.

Skegemog Swamp Pathway:[wba] uses an old rail way through areas of unusual beauty; crosses a running water swamp with wooden walkways and bridges

NPCR

Woodland Creek Furniture Company: the ambience of nature in a refined-rustic display of furnishings and accessories

X X-TRA STUFF

County fair: *Kalkaska County Agricultural Fair*: Aug.
Hospitals: Kalkaska County
Large employers: Kalkaska County Hospital, Kalkaska Public Schools, Kalkaska Memorial Health Center, Wayne Wire Cloth Products (makes wire products, blowers & fans, screw machine parts, more), WellTech (oil field services), Shell Western E & P (oil/gas exploration services)
Michigan Heritage & Research Foundation: owns 80 acres of pristine land overlooking Lake Skegemog; plans are to build a center as a memorial to men and women from Michigan who have devoted their lives (michiganfallenheroes.org) so that the state, country and world are a better place.

NPCR

This county is an interesting mix of Camp Grayling and the Kirkland Warbler protected area, along with high forest hills and lots of swamps.

Y YESTERYEAR

Between 1860 and 1900, 15 major rail lines built 10,000 miles of train track in Michigan, much of it with government grant money aimed at providing the lumber industry with easier access to their markets. The early growth of Kalkaska County can be attributed to lumber and railroads too. [In this book, the *O ORIGINS* section for each county uses a double underline to indicate communities that were founded as a direct result of railroad activity.] The railroads figured that the settlers would begin farming. But in many places, the land was sandy and poor and much of this area did not lend itself to wide-scale and profitable farming.

So, in an effort to increase their business, the railroads began promoting northern Michigan as a resort area, including hunting and fishing opportunities. (Even the Grand Hotel on Mackinaw Island was financed by 3 different railroads.) There were many health and recreation activities, camps and colonies established for summer visitors, all of which were serviced by the railroads. But you know the rest of the story. Once the automobile became the premier mode of transportation, all railroads began to decline.

Kalkaska County has recovered from the lumbering years, the trees have been replanted and it is now considered one of the great "untouched" counties in the Lower Peninsula. [Dunbar]

NPCR

Z ZOO & ANIMAL PLACES

Skegemog Lake Wildlife Area: see 40P
Blue Ribbon Trout Streams[1,000]

A AGRICULTURE

Land in farms: 30% of county
Number of farms: 1,190
Size of average farm: 140 acres
Market value of all products: #6 of 83 counties
Crops: ...most acres: corn for grain
...highest $ sales: nursery, greenhouse, floriculture
Livestock: ...largest number: turkeys
...highest $ sales: milk & dairy products
Among the top Michigan counties:
- #1- apples, nursery stock, potted flowering plants
- #2- alpacas, bedding & garden plants
- #3- floriculture crops, non-citrus fruit, sweet corn
- #4- number of horses
- #5- market value of all crops

Dairy, food and meat processing plants: 105
State ranking for harvested trees: #41 of 83 counties
FYI: <u>Apples</u> are the largest and most valuable fruit crop in the state and Kent County is Michigan's largest apple-producing county. Statewide there are 37,000 acres of apple trees containing 7.5 million apple trees on less than 1,000 family-run farms. All

apples are hand picked. These trees produce 800 million pounds of apples with a $700 million impact on the economy. About 60% of Michigan apples are made into pies, fresh-cut slices [like McDonalds], or made into apple cider.

michiganapples.com

Wherever there are apples, it is only natural to have <u>cider mills</u> producing apple cider. Usually several different apple varieties are pressed together to maximize the flavor. Each cider mill has its own blend of apples for what they consider the best flavor. Fresh cider is made in the fall and sold locally at the cider mill and farm markets. Many apples are

commercially processed into apple juice, which unlike cider, is strained and pasteurized for a long shelf life. Hard cider is an alcoholic drink made from fermented apple cider and was common in colonial times. It is now a specialty at some cider mills and wineries. MDA

B BRIDGE OR BOAT

The Fallasburg Covered Bridge, built in 1871, is a single span at 14'x100' and is still open to vehicle traffic. It crosses the Flat River in the Fallasburg Pioneer Village on the Fallasburg Park Road. See 41M.

C CELEBRATIONS

<u>Byron Center</u> *Byron Days:* parade, activities, July

<u>Cedar Springs</u> *Red Flannel Fest:* (Cedar Springs is the former home of a red flannel clothing manufacturer.) bands, queen contest; everyone wears red, Oct.

<u>Grand Rapids</u> *Blues on the Mall:* Wednesday nights in July and July
...*Festival of the Arts:* the nation's largest all-volunteer arts festival, June
...*Grand Rouge Living History Encampment:* a time line of military and civilian living from colonial times to present day, Sept.
...*Polish Harvest Festival:* celebrate Polish heritage with food, beer tent, music, activities, Aug.
...*Celebration on the Grand:* a community festival celebrating life in Grand Rapids, Sept.
...*Hispanic Festival:* largest Hispanic festival in West Michigan; music, dance, food, fun, Sept.
... *ArtPrize®:* an international art competition and social experiment where anyone can be an artist, any space can be a venue and everyone has a voice; awarding the world's largest prize for art; Sept. and Oct.
...*Pulaski Days Annual Celebration:* to remember Revolutionary War hero, Gen. Casimir Pulaski, Oct.; see 11T

Renee McCauley

<u>Lowell</u> *Showboat Sizzlin'* *Summer Concerts:* for 10 weeks on Thursdays in the summer, local talent

...*Fallasburg Fall Festival:* celebrate the bridge, Oct.
...*Riverwalk Festival:* water activity, duck race, July

D DEMOGRAPHICS

Population: 603,000   **Persons per sq. mile:** 704
Largest city: Grand Rapids   **Population:** 188,000
   2nd largest city: Wyoming   Population: 72,100
   3rd largest city: Kentwood   Population: 48,700
Largest township: Plainfield   **Population:** 31,000
   2nd largest twp.: Byron   Population: 20,300
Largest village: Sparta   **Population:** 4,140
Median household income: $47,700 (county)
   Grand Rapids: $37,200
   Wyoming: $43,200
   Kentwood: $45,800
Owner-occupied median house value: $148,000
Persons affiliated with a religious congregation: 53%
Persons below poverty level: 15%
Students receiving school lunch subsidy: 42%

E ENVIRONMENT

"<u>Preserve America</u> is a 2003 Bush White House initiative that encourages and supports community efforts to preserve and enjoy our priceless cultural and natural heritage. The goals of the initiative include a greater shared knowledge about the nation's past, strengthened regional identities and local pride, increased local participation in preserving the country's cultural and natural heritage assets, and support for the economic vitality of our communities." Grand Rapids is a Preserve America Community with 6 local historic districts that have 2,000 structures and 70 local landmarks. The city encourages restoration and revitalization programs, specialized zoning, tax credits, and has received Preserve America grants.

preserveamerica.gov

F FLORA & FAUNA

NPCR

The black locust tree is a member of the pea or legume family and grows to 40'-60' tall. Since it has an extensive root system, it is used in erosion control, reclaiming wasteland by spreading roots that have sprouts that hold the soil in place on steep hillsides and gullies.

Steve Thompson/USFWS

Coyotes (*MI H&T*) can live in a wide range of habitats including forests, grasslands, deserts and swamps. They also have a high tolerance for human activities and can live in suburban, agricultural and urban areas. Be alert! You might see one.

G GOVERNMENT

County: ...created: 1831   **...organized:** 1836
...originally part of: Kalamazoo County
Size: 559,000 acres / 856 sq. miles (16 of 83 counties)
The county has 9 cities, 5 villages, 21 townships with 6 as charter townships, 12 unincorporated communities, 4 Census Designated Place and 19 school districts.

Renee McCauley

Renee McCauley

Renee McCauley

County seat: Grand Rapids

...Homestead property tax: 30 mills

Motto: <u>Cascade</u>: *Serene vistas... Plentiful trees... Two rivers... One community*

...<u>Cedar Springs</u>: *A great place to Live, Work & Play*

...<u>East Grand Rapids</u>: *A Better Place to Live*

...<u>Grand Rapids</u>: *Michigan's West Coast; The Furniture City*

...<u>Grand Rapids / Kent County</u> Convention and Visitors Bureau: *Experience Grand Rapids*

...<u>Grandville</u>: *Charting New Courses ...*

...<u>Lowell</u> Area Chamber: *The Next Place to Be!*

...<u>Kent City</u>: *Our Town is Your Town*

...<u>Kentwood</u>: *A Community Effort*

...<u>Plainfield</u>: *Rolling Plains and Beautiful Fields*

...<u>Walker</u>: *From Solid Roots...Strong Branches*

H HISTORICAL MARKERS 13 of 48

Ada Covered Bridge: built in 1867, restored in 1941; now closed to traffic

Renee McCauley

Arthur Hendrick Vandenberg: 1884-1951, a U.S. Senator from 1929-1951, involved in creating the Marshall Plan, FDIC, NATO and Military Assistance

Baw-wa-ting: American Indian for "the rapids." Over 2,000 years ago, Hopewellian Indians built burial mounds here that were destroyed in the 1800s as "GR" grew. A park at Grand Valley State University recognizes the former American Indian village.

The Castle: 1884, a spectacular home in the Heritage Hill area; Chateauesque Style architecture with Scottish granite, parquet floors

Fallasburg Pioneer Village: 1839, John Fallas built a sawmill and established a chair factory that was a forerunner of the Kent County furniture industry; see 41B, 41M.

Furniture Industry: by the end of the 1800s, Grand Rapids was the furniture capital of America, with buyers coming here from around the world.

May House: 1908, this Frank Lloyd Wright Prairie-style house was his first house in Michigan; see 41M.

Courtesy Gerald R. Ford Library

President Gerald R. Ford: 1913-2006, the 38th president of the U.S., a Grand Rapids native, a U.S. Representative from Grand Rapids and the only president from Michigan; see 41L, 41M

Michigan State Preservation Office

Sixth Street Bridge: 1886, its rust-resistant wrought iron Pratt trusses make it the longest and oldest remaining metal bridge in Michigan.

Toledo, Saginaw & Muskegon Railway Depot: 1888, typifies country combination-type depot; restored by Michigan Railroad Historical Society in 1973

Veteran's Cemetery: 1886, designed in the form of a Maltese cross

Veterans' Facility: 1885, serving the physical, emotional and spiritual needs of many disabled and needy veterans

Voigt House: 1895, an elegant and perfectly preserved Victorian mansion; now a museum

Monument: *Kent County Civil War Monument*

National Historic Land-marks: *Norton Mounds Group*: 13 important and well-preserved Hopewell Indian burial mounds dating from 400 B.C. to 400 A.D.; owned by the Grand Rapids Public Museum; found in Millennium Park

Photo from the collection of Grand Rapids Public Museum

National Register of Historic Places: 43 listings
State Historic Sites: 103 listings

I INFORMATION

Chamber of Commerce: Cedar Springs, Grand Rapids, Grandville, Lowell, Rockford, Sparta, Wyoming-Kentwood
Visitor: Grand Rapids / Kent County Convention and Visitors Bureau, 800-678-9859, experiencegr.com

J JOKES

You might be from a "big city" in Michigan if…

…you really don't care about the accessibility of museums, symphonies, ballet and art classes.
…you like having lots of choices for live concert events, though the louder the better.
…the closest you've been to a farm is the grocery store, and that really doesn't count.
…you think that any county with less than 25,000 people couldn't possibly have anything worthwhile to do and be of any interest to you.
…you think that only your immediate metropolitan area really counts for anything.
…you think it's "creepy" to be any place where there are no people or buildings.
…you think that every other community is just like yours.
…outdoor things really don't interest you.

K KINSMAN

Race
American Indian: <1%
Asian: 2%
Black/African American: 10%
Hispanic or Latino: 10%
Other: <1%
White: 80%

Ancestry
Dutch: 20%
German: 15%
English: 8%
Irish: 7%
Polish: 7%
U.S./American: 6%

L LIGHTHOUSE OR LANDMARK

Renee McCauley

The Gerald R. Ford Presidential Library (in Ann Arbor) and Museum (in Grand Rapids) are part of Presidential Libraries system of the National Archives and Records Administration. The museum provokes emotions that stimulate learning, reflection and a sense of democratic citizenship. See 41H, 41M, 41T.

M MUSEUMS

<u>Ada</u> *Averill Historic Museum:* home, barn, artifacts
<u>Byron</u> *Area Historic Museum:* artifacts, documents
<u>Grand Rapids</u> *Art Museum:* a new building in 2007 that is LEED certified (see 23L), with educational facilities to help teach children about the visual arts; 5,000 works of art in the collection
…*Children's Museum:* celebrates childhood and the joy of learning
…*Gerald R. Ford Museum:* America's most entertaining presidential museum; see 41H, 41L, 41T
…*Public Museum:* world-class history, nature, cultural heritage, furniture, 1928 carousel

…*Frederik Meijer Gardens & Sculpture Park:*[1,000] 100+ sculptures, gardens, trails, Michigan's largest tropical conservatory

Frederik Meijer Garden and Sculpture Park-William J. Herbert

Courtesy of Steelcase Inc.

…*Meyer-May House*: a Frank Lloyd Wright original Prairie-style house that has been meticulously restored by the Steelcase Corp.

...*Urban Institute for Contemporary Arts:* Michigan's largest multi-disciplinary arts center; visual, performance, literature, film, music, dance

Lowell *Area Historical Museum:* enrich, delight and inspire through preservation and presentation

Plainfield *Hyser Rivers Museum:* in a restored 1852 Greek Revival house

...*Voigt House Victorian Museum:* 1895 mansion with original furnishings

Rockford *Historical Museum:* 150 years of history

Renee McCauley

N   NATURAL RESOURCES

Elevation: 600 – 900 feet
Physiography: rolling plains, hill lands

Forest type: maple-beech, oak-hickory
Public/private forests: 28% of county

Water in county: 2% of county
  Lakes: 180   **...largest:** Wabasis Lake
  Rivers: Coldwater, Flat, Grand, Rogue, Thornapple
  Rivers & streams: 770 miles

Avg. sunshine: January: 30%   July: 72%
Growing season, avg.: 154 days (3 temp. zones)
  Last freeze, avg.: May 5 – May 15
  First freeze, avg.: Sept. 30 – Oct 10
Precipitation, annual avg.: rainfall: 38 inches (#1/MI)
                    snowfall: 71 inches
Temperature (F), avg.: January: high 29°, low 15°
                    July: high 83°, low 60°
Annual: >90°: 12 days, **<0°:** 9 days
Tornadoes (1930-2010): 37 (#3/MI)

O   ORIGINS

Ada:[u] Ada Smith, daughter of first postmaster; 1821
Byron Center:[u] in Byron Township; 1836
Caledonia:[v,ct] named after Caledonia, NY; 1838
Cascade:[u,ct] the fine fall of the water; 1845
Casnovia:[v] means new home; 1850
Cedar Springs:[c] cedar trees and many springs; 1855
Comstock Park:[u] after Rep. Charles Comstock; 1838
East Grand Rapids:[c] east of Grand Rapids; 1832
Fallasburg:[u] first settler, J. Wesley Fallas; 1939

Forest Hills:[u] lush, rolling, woodland terrain
Grand Rapids:[c,ct] 1 mile rapids on Grand River; 1820
Grandville:[c] a village on the Grand River; 1834
Kent:[co] NY state chancellor, James Kent
Kent City:[v] from Kent County; 1870
Kentwood:[c] the woods in SE Kent County; 1967
Lowell:[c,ct] in Lowell Township, which was named after Lowell, NY; 1847
Northview:[u] north of Grand Rapids
Plainfield:[ct] rolling plains and beautiful fields; 1837
Rockford:[c] from Rockford, IL; 1844
Sand Lake:[v] located by a sandy, shallow lake; 1869
Sparta:[v] from Sparta (a Greek military city-state) Township; 1848
Walker:[c] from Walker Township; 1836
Wyoming:[c] American Indian word meaning "at the big flat river;" 1859

P   PARKS

Federal: 0   **State:** 5   **County:** 34   **Local:** 71
Number of campsites: 971
State Game Areas: 5 areas covering 8,000 acres
State Linear Park: *White Pine Trail State Park:* Kent County is the southern end of the longest rail-trail in the state that runs 93 miles north to Cadillac.
County: *Blandford Nature Center:*[ww] 140 acres, wildlife hospital, trails and boardwalks, Community Supported Agriculture farm (see 15A), guided walks, educational programs

...*Millennium Park:* 1,500 acres are being returned to urban green space; beach, splash pad, 20 miles of trails; NYC Central Park is the model and Millennium Park will be twice as big as Central Park.

Renee McCauley

Other: *Ah-Nab-Awen Park:* 6.5 acres, on the site of an American Indian Village; means "resting place." It is the site of many city festivals in downtown Grand Rapids. Prior to the building of Grand Rapids, there were around 40 burial mounds in the area; they no longer exist.
...*Frederik Meijer Gardens & Sculpture Park:* see 41M
...*The West Michigan Parks and Recreation Inventory:* see 3P
Wildflower Viewing Sites:[wba] Aman Park, on M-45, six miles west of Grand Rapids; Christiansen Nature Center

Q QUOTE FROM THE LOCALS

"With a healthy economy, low taxes, affordable housing, and Midwestern hospitality, Kent County offers the best in both business and family locations. The area has begun to experience significant employment increases in the educational and health service industry." This is due, in part, "to a strong but highly diversified base of industries, an excellent work force, educational opportunities, excellent employer/employee relations, good location and transportation facilities, utilities and possibly the most important, quality of life." accesskent.com

R RECREATION & SPORTS

Auto racing: *Grattan Raceway:* Feel the Rush, Experience the Thrill; winding and hilly
Golf courses: 31
Hiking/skiing/mountain biking trails: 90 miles
North Country National Scenic Trail: yes.

FYI: The North Country National Scenic Trail is a premier footpath that runs 4,600 miles through NY, PA, OH, MI, WI, MN and SD. With their national headquarters in Lowell, it works with the National Park Service to build, maintain and promote hiking paths that link communities, forests and prairies. northcountrytrails.org

Renee McCauley

Public access sites: 24
Public recreational land: 1% of county
Rail-trail: (80 miles) East West, Fred Meijer Millennium, Grand River Edges, Kent Trails, Paul Henry Thornapple, White Pine
State/federal wild/scenic/natural river: 140 miles (#1/MI) of the Flat and Rogue Rivers
State-funded snowmobile trails: 35 miles
Grand Rapids Griffins: the primary affiliate of the National Hockey Leagues' Detroit Redwings; play at Van Andel Arena
Kent Trails: 15 miles, paved, non-motorized, handicap accessible
Rhoades McKee Triathlon: swim, bike, run, Sept.
The 25K Fifth Third [Bank] Riverbank Run has 10,000 runners from around the world.

West Michigan Whitecaps: a Class A, professional minor league baseball team affiliated with the Detroit Tigers; play at Fifth Third Ballpark

NPCR

S STATE OF MICHIGAN

In 1999, Michigan created the Life Sciences Corridor that will make four of Michigan's research institutions - Wayne State University (Detroit), the University of Michigan (Ann Arbor), Michigan State University (East Lansing) and the Van Andel Institute (Grand Rapids) – among the nation's most important in the development of biotechnology applications. The development of important life-saving technology will make Michigan a major focus in the biotechnology industry…from cancer research to treatment of cardiovascular disease; the potential of biotechnology applications is staggering. Michigan will invest $1 billion over 20 year; other public and private investment is expected also. state.mi.us/migov/gov/pressrelease

T TRAVEL

Airports: Gerald R. Ford International, Lowell City, Sparta
Amtrak: Grand Rapids
Bus: Greyhound, Indian Trails, The Rapid
County road names: …north/south: named Avenues
…east/west: numbered Roads are in the north part of the county; numbered Streets are in the south part of the county; however, there are a few other named Avenues, Roads and Streets.
Distance to Lansing: 60 miles
Main roads: I-196, I-96, US 131
Memorial Highways: I-96, *AmVets MH*: see 19T
…I-196 Business Route, *Cesar E. Chavez Way*: he (1927-1993) formed the National Farm Workers Association in 1962 to help migrant and seasonal field workers.
…I-196, *Gerald R. Ford Freeway*: he (1913-2006) was a U.S. Representative from Michigan and was the House Minority Leader who became Vice President when Spiro Agnew resigned, and then became President when Richard Nixon resigned in 1974; see 41H, 41L, 41M.
…M-6, *Paul B. Henry Freeway*: see 70T

FYI: The City of Grand Rapids is divided into quadrants, NW, NE, SW, SE. Every building in the city has one of those designations as part their street address.

FYI: Over the years, I-196 has been called, in part or as a whole, proposed, promoted or legalized: Central Michigan Pike and Gerald R. Ford Frwy. [Barnett]

U UNIVERSITIES & COLLEGES

Aquinas College: est. 1886, 2,300 students. An inclusive education rooted in the Catholic Dominican tradition; named after St. Thomas Aquinas, a 13th century Dominican scholar. WHAC, Saints

Calvin College: est. 1876, 4,200 students. It is a distinctively Christian, academically excellent liberal arts college that shapes minds for intentional participation in the renewal of all things. Named after John Calvin, 16th century reformer; part of the Christian Reformed Church. MIAA, Knights

Calvin Theological Seminary: est. 1876, 300 students. Students are committed to grow in the understanding of the Word, to be formed by it and to proclaim it to others…for contemporary ministry around the world…to serve everywhere.

Thomas M. Cooley Law School: see 33U

Cornerstone College: est. 1941, 1,900 students. It is an inter-denominational, Christ-centered school… to enable individuals to apply unchanging biblical principles in a rapidly changing world. WHAC, Golden Eagles

Davenport University: see 13U

Grace Bible College: est. 1939, 200 students. To develop passionate servants of Jesus Christ… emphasizing the integration of biblical truth, ministry experience and character transformation. WHAC, Tigers

Grand Rapids Community College: est. 1914, 14,000 students. …Priority is to be student-centered, collaborative and flexible; school has maintained a solid reputation as a premier transfer institution and is nationally recognized for both its liberal arts and occupational programs; M-TEC. MCCAA, Raiders

Grand Rapids Theological Seminary: est. 1948, 340 students. It prepares biblically and culturally informed ministry leaders for service through Christ's church.

ITT Technical Institute: see 25U

Kendall College of Art and Design: est. 1928, 1,000 students. Students are prepared to become working artists and leaders in art and design; school partnered with Ferris State Univ. in early 2000s.

Kuyper College: est. 1939 as Reformed Bible Institute, 300 students. The school seeks to place ministry-focused people in ministry and professional areas of leadership around the world to meet spiritual and social challenges. NCCAA, Cougars

University of Phoenix: see 25U

V VARIETY

Renee McCauley

This 54'l x 43'h x 30'w steel sculpture has sat in Calder Plaza in front of the Grand Rapids City Hall since 1969. Custom designed for the city and for the space by world-renowned sculpture Alexander Calder (1898-1976), it is called *La Grande Vitesse* and refers to the great swiftness of the Grand River. Local residents simply refer to it as The Calder. At the time, it helped revitalize the downtown area and has since become a symbol of success for the city.

W WANDERLUST

Agri-tourism: <u>Farms</u> *Bos Greenhouse & Farms:* since 1913, apples, asparagus, berries, broccoli, cauliflower & more veggies all the way to zucchini
…*Country Basket:* U-pick, apples, pumpkins, cider, blueberries, honey, flowers
…*Dairy Discovery:* tours of SwissLane Dairy
…*Ed Dunneback:* strawberries, apples, cherries
…*Farm Markets:* Byron Center, Plainfield Township
…*Fryear's Little Red Market:* family owned for 100 years
…*Heidi's Farm Stand:* a cornucopia of local products
…*H & W:* local Michigan products and gifts
…*Krupp:* asparagus, raspberries, strawberries
…*Sandy Bottom Berries:* blueberries, flowers
<u>Orchards</u> *Blok:* apples, peaches, nectarines, veggies
…*Steffens Orchard Market:* 250 acres of apples, tours, many other items
…*Wells:* apples, cherries, pears, squash, maze

Brewery: B.O.B.'s (Big Old Building) Brewery, Founders Brewing Company, Grand Rapids Brewing Co., Schmohz Brewing Company, The Hideout Brewing Company

Cultural: *Grand Rapids Ballet:* Michigan's only professional ballet company

The George Balanchine Trust

...Grand Rapids Symphony: regular season plus summer outdoor concerts

...Opera Grand Rapids: 3 productions a year at DeVos Hall

Fall colors: early October

Live theater: Actors' at Spectrum, Broadway at Grand Rapids, Community Circle, DeVos Performance Hall, Civic Theater, Jewish, Master Arts, Peter Martin Wege, St. Cecilia Music Center

Planetarium: Chaffee at Public Museum of Grand Rapids; Veen in Lowell

Shopping malls: Rivertown Crossing, Woodland

Walking tours*: Heritage Hills:* a national, state and local Historic District, has 1,300+ homes in over 60 architectural styles dating from the 1840s

Michigan State Preservation Office

Renee McCauley

Wineries: *Robinette's:* hard cider, fruit wines, tasting
ARTisans Market: on Fulton Street, a summer, traditional, open market that is affordable and inclusive
Grand River Folk Arts Society: folk dance or concerts every Saturday

Grand Rapids Outdoor Sculpture & Historic Buildings: includes 6 Alexander Calder sculptures, Riverwalk path, unique architecture

NPCR

X X-TRA STUFF

County Fair: Kent Co. 4-H Agricultural Assoc., Aug.

Famous people: *...Entertainment:* Steven Ford, Anthony Kiedis, Kevin Max, The Good Luck Joes
...Politics: President Gerald Ford, Peter Secchia
...Sports: Gary Hogeboom, Chris Kaman, Tom Lehman
...Other: Chris Van Allsburg, Roger Chaffee, Jack Lousma

Hospitals: Helen DeVos Children's, Forest View, Mary Free Bed Rehab, Metro Health, Pine Rest Christian Mental Health, Saint Mary's, Spectrum Butterworth, Spectrum Blodgett, Spectrum Kent Community

Large employers: Spectrum Health, Meijer (groceries, general merchandise), Steelcase (office furniture), Spartan Stores (grocery wholesaler), Grand Rapids Public Schools, Alticor (parent company of Amway), Foremost Insurance, Wolverine Worldwide (shoes)

East Grand Rapids is known for its affluence and lake front mansions on Reeds Lake. The high school has over 100 state championships in almost all sports and activities.

The movie *American Pie* was based on the East Grand Rapids High School days of Adam Herz.

GR has a very large philanthropic community.

GR has been named an All-American city 3 times, a Top 10 for Business by *Forbes*, #6 Fishing City by *Field & Stream* and #5 healthiest towns by *Men's Health.*

GR was the first city in the U.S. to add fluoride to its drinking water.

Gypsum plaster mines can be found in this county. Gypsum is used in building materials, agriculture, airplanes and automobiles.

Kent County is home for the *world headquarters* of: Alticor and Amway (cleaning, health and beauty, wellness products), American Seating (office furniture), Bissell Homecare (cleaning products), Gordon Food Service, Meijer (groceries & general merchandise), Old Orchard (juices), Spartan Stores (groceries), Steelcase (office furniture), Universal Forest Products (wood & alternative wood products), Wolverine Worldwide (shoes), X-Rite (measures special effect paints) and Zondervan (Christian publishers).

Once the "furniture capital" of the U.S., GR is now the "office furniture capital."

NPCR-4

The Grand Rapids Home for Veterans is in this county. County has the most with over 2,000. See 68S.

Y YESTERYEAR

Why did Grand Rapids become the <u>Furniture Capital of America</u>?

Grand Rapids happened to be situated more or less on the dividing line between the soft wood forests (pine, spruce, cedar) to the north and hard wood forests (ash, maple, walnut) to the south. From the beginning, it was a lumbering and sawmill town.

The Flat, Rouge and Grand Rivers provided sufficient opportunity to transport cut lumber via barges, or to float those huge cut tree logs to Grand Haven, where they could be shipped to Illinois or Wisconsin. In 1855, Michigan produced more lumber than the next three states combined.

Because of these natural resources, men with skills in all areas of the lumber industry were drawn to Grand Rapids and set up their own sawmills, cabinetry and furniture-making shops, building supplies and support supplies (varnish, hinges, saws, etc). Many were creative and innovative and made advancements that affected furniture-making throughout the U.S. They brought in European skilled wood workers to improve their offerings. In the late 1800s, Grand Rapids furniture makers cooperatively established the "furniture fairs" and people came from all over the country and the world to purchase the high quality furniture that was made in Grand Rapids. Elliott

NPCR-4

Z ZOO & ANIMAL PLACES

Petting Zoo: Country Basket, Dairy Discovery, Fruit Ridge Hayrides, Krupp Farms, Orchard Hill Farms

Watchable Wildlife Areas:[ww] Grand Rapids Fish Ladder, Pickerel Lake; see 41P

Zoo: *John Ball Zoological Garden:* 110 acres, 1,000 animals, aquarium and children's zoo

Blandford Nature Center: native wild animals

Alpacas: Circle R Ranch

Dairy Discovery: tours of Swiss Lane Dairy, Saturdays, April-Oct.

From BIBLIOGRAPHY & NOTES...

L LIGHTHOUSE or LANDMARK: When you see "this," you know you're in *this* county!

A AGRICULTURE

Land in farms: 6% of county
Number of farms: 190
Size of average farm: 115 acres
Market value of all products: #75 of 83 counties
Crops: ...most acres: forage land
...highest $ sales: hay
Livestock: ...largest number: cattle
...highest $ sales: milk & dairy products
Dairy, food and meat processing plants: 3
State ranking for harvested trees: #38 of 83 counties
FYI: Agriculture in the State of Michigan 2007

Michigan is among the top states in the U.S. for dollar sales of these USDA designated commodity groups (see 1A):

- #3- cut Christmas trees & short rotation woody crops
- #5- fruits & berries
- #6- nursery & greenhouse
- #9- vegetables
- #7- milk & dairy products
- #10- other animals

Michigan farm operator characteristics:
- 47% say farming is their primary occupation
- 15% of farmers are women
- 90% of farmers are white
- 56 years, age of the average farmer [USDA]

B BRIDGE OR BOAT

D & R Sports Center

Bass boats can be seen on any lake in Lake County and throughout Michigan, too. They are low and sleek and are built to fish with two or three anglers on board. The boat has a livewell to keep the catch alive and an electric trolling motor on the front of the boat.

C CELEBRATIONS

<u>Baldwin</u> *Turkey Hunters Rendezvous and State Calling Championships:* March
...*Blessing of the Bikes:* Michigan's "original," thousands of motorcycle enthusiasts, May
...*Troutarama:* celebrate fishing, July
...*Shrine of the Pines Craft Show:* Sept.
<u>M-37</u> *West Michigan's Longest Yard Sale:* in Lake and Newaygo Counties along M-37, June
<u>Idlewild</u> *Music Fest:* all that jazz, July
<u>Irons</u> *Bluegrass Jamboree:* Sept.

NPCR

<u>Luther</u> *Logging Days:* lumber & logging heritage, July

D DEMOGRAPHICS

Population: 11,500 **Persons per sq. mile:** 20
Largest township: Chase **Population:** 1,140
Largest village: Baldwin **Population:** 1,210
Median household income: $29,400 (#83/MI)
Owner-occupied median house value: $94,000
Persons affiliated with a religious congregation: 30%
Persons below poverty level: 23% (#3/MI)
Students receiving school lunch subsidy: 87% (#1/MI)

E ENVIRONMENT

"Michigan's <u>physical landscape</u> mainly reflects the actions of the major glacial lobes that retreated from the state between about 18,000 and 11,000 years ago, acting upon a complex assortment of bedrock lithologies. This situation produced an intricate and tangled pattern of glacial landforms and sediments that surpass all other Midwest states in their complexity, and form the basis for the state's important agricultural, timber, recreational and aggregate [sand and gravel] economies.

"...Our economic success has come, however, at a high environmental price. Highly permeable drift and extensive lakes and wetlands make the state very susceptible to surface and groundwater contamination.

"...Michigan's environmental challenge is to continue to protect and enhance its glacial resources at a time of diminishing state appropriations." Schaetzl

F FLORA & FAUNA

Alice Welch, USDA

Cattails are found worldwide and were here before the European settlers. They grow in or near water. The plant provides both food and habitat for wild animals. Humans can eat the entire plant. Whether boiled or pickled, it tastes like cucumbers or cabbage. It can even be ground into flour, made into thatch roofing, woven into hats, or used as stuffing for pillows.

Largemouth Bass Robert H. Pos/USFWS

Smallmouth Bass Robert H. Pos/USFWS

The smallmouth bass likes the cool, clear water of the Great Lakes where the lake bottom is rock or gravel. The largemouth bass likes warm shallow water and lives among the vegetation close to shore. The length of the upper jaw of the species determines their name.

G GOVERNMENT

County: ...created: 1840 **...organized:** 1871
...originally part of: Oceana, Mason, Newaygo Counties
Size: 367,000 acres / 568 sq. miles (44 of 83 counties)
The county has 2 villages, 15 townships, 4 unincorporated communities and 2 school districts.

Ryan Fox

County seat: Baldwin
...Homestead property tax: 43 mills
Motto: Idlewild: *Yesterday's Jewel...Tomorrow's Treasure*
...Lake County: *Endless Nature, Timeless Rhythms, Boundless Adventure*

H HISTORICAL MARKERS

Brown Trout: the first recorded planting of brown trout in the U.S. was planted in the Pere Marquette River in 1884.
Lake County: 1849, lumbering, farming and tourism are chief activities in this county.
National Register of Historic Places: 3 listings
State Historic Sites: 6 listings

I INFORMATION

Chamber of Commerce: Idlewild African American, 231-745-4742, iaacc.com
...Lake County, 231-745-4331, lakecountymichigan.com

J JOKES

UNDERNEATH ALL IS THE LAND.
Here's a few diverse perspectives on *undeveloped* land:

• *The ATV-er:* Give me a big, loud, noisy machine that tears up the land and anything else that gets in my way. Love that smell of spent fuel and used rubber.
• *The Birder:* Shhhhh, look up and listen carefully. Let's see how many more species we can spot and add to our yearly total.
• *The Conservationist:* All the plants, animals and the water *must* be managed properly for now and in the future so there will always be wild animals to hunt.
• *The Criminal:* This might be a good place to (fill in the blank) _____ because there's no one around here to watch me.
• *The Developer:* Oooh, what could I build here?
• *The Environmentalist:* Maybe we can find an endangered species or critical wetlands. Then no one can do anything with this land.
• *The EPA:* Ignorance of the law is no excuse. Do it our way or pay the fines and we will make an example out of you.
• *The Farmer:* Let's call the Conservation District Office and find out what will grow best on this land.
• *The Fisherman:* If it doesn't have a lake or a river, it's not worth much.

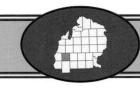

- *The Forrester:* Do any of these trees need to be harvested?
- *The Geologist:* Gas? Oil? Water reservoir? Iron ore? Copper? Gypsum? Salt? Salt brine? Limestone? Gold?
- *The Hunter:* Wonder if I can get permission to hunt deer on this land? Who needs permission anyway?
- *The Land Owner:* It's my land; I should be able to do what I want with it!
- *The Naturalist:* All land, anywhere, is worth observing the flora and fauna that resides within. Where's my camera?
- *The Recreationalist:* Ah, the great outdoors where the sky in blue and the air is fresh. Looks like a good place to hike, bike or ski. Glad I didn't forget my GPS and bug repellant.
- *The Shopper:* I can't believe people can live around here. There's absolutely nothing to do and no place to go.
- *The Tax Assessor:* The township can't take in enough money to even pay for the snow plowing of these roads.
- *The Tourist:* Are we there yet? How many more miles to the next gas station and restroom?

K KINSMAN

Race
American Indian: <1%
Asian: <1%
Black/African American: 9%
Hispanic or Latino: 2%
Other: 3%
White: 87%

Ancestry
German: 20%
U.S./American: 13%
Irish: 8%
English: 8%
Dutch: 6%
Polish: 4%
French: 4%

L LIGHTHOUSE or LANDMARK

Frank P. Zwemmer

Sixty-two percent (8,300) of the housing units in this county are vacation, seasonal, or occasional homes, the highest percentage of any Michigan county. US Census

M MUSEUMS

Michigan State Historic Preservation Office

<u>Baldwin</u> *Shrine of the Pines Museum:* world's largest display of rustic pine furniture; in a Northwoods hunting lodge with an observation deck; trails by the river

<u>Idlewild</u> *Historic Cultural Center:* tells the Idlewild story of the founders and the famous African-Americans who were part of this famous retreat

<u>Luther</u> *Logging Museum*

N NATURAL RESOURCES

Elevation: 800 – 1,200 feet
Physiography: rolling plains, plains, hilly uplands

Soil: Silt Loam
  Depth: up to 10"
  Color: light to medium brown
  Type: little or no organic matter, homogenous [uniform size] texture with no gravel
  Details: surface is easily tilled, but there are often large boulders and rocks; land is rolling with good drainage.
  Agriculture: grain, hay and other general farm crops
  NOTE: soil types are not limited to any one county.

Forest type: pine-oak-aspen, hickory
Public/private forests: 86% of county (#4/MI)

Water in county: 1% of county

NPCR

  Lakes: 156[Lake County]
    ...largest: Big Star Lake

  Rivers: Baldwin, Little Manistee, Pere Marquette (mar KET), Pine
  Rivers & streams: 250 miles

Growing season, avg.: 111 days (2 temp. zones)
  Last freeze, avg.: May 25 – May 30
  First freeze, avg.: Sept. 20 – Sept. 25
Precipitation, annual avg.: rainfall: 34 inches
                  snowfall: 83 inches

Temperature (F), avg.: January: high 29°, low 11°
July: high 83°, low 55°
Annual: ...>90°: 12 days, **...<0°:** 19 days
Tornadoes (1930-2010): 3

O ORIGINS

Baldwin:[v] Michigan Gov. Henry Baldwin; 1870
Branch:[u] north branch of the Pere Marquette R.; 1873
Chase:[u] Gov. Chase of Ohio; 1887
Idlewild:[u] named after Lake Idlewild; 1912 [The locals like to say the men are idle and the women are wild.]
Irons:[u] the Irons family, early settlers; 1894
Lake:[co] many lakes in the county _{lakecountymichigan.com}
Luther:[v] sawmill owner, BT Luther; 1880
Nirvana:[u] Buddhist form of the highest heaven; 1874

P PARKS

National: 7   **State:** 6
County: 0   **Local:** 0
Number of campsites: 1,050

Ryan Fox

National: *Manistee National Forest:* 112,000 acres, part of the 600,000 acres in 8 counties; prime salmon fishing in the forest rivers

State Forest: *Pere Marquette:* 60,000 acres
...Campground: 5   **...Pathway:** 18 miles

Q QUOTE FROM THE LOCALS

"Lake County is truly a county for all seasons. It offers year-round enjoyment to all its residents and guests. State and Federal lands make up over 48% of our county and provide outstanding opportunities for hiking, bird watching, swimming, camping, cross-country skiing and wildlife viewing. We have several hundred miles of trails for snowmobile and ORV riding, many lakes and rivers for year-round fishing and thousands of acres of forest land for a full slate of hunting activities. The Pere Marquette River is known worldwide for its excellent trout and salmon fishing and for some of West Michigan's most scenic canoe trips."

NPCR

lakeclontymichigan.com

R RECREATION & SPORTS

Blue Ribbon Trout Streams: Baldwin Creek, Little Manistee River, Pere Marquette River & Little South Branch, Pine, Sable-Big
Golf courses: 1
Hiking/skiing/mountain biking trails: 60 miles
North Country National Scenic Trail: yes
Off-road vehicle trails: 160 miles (#3/MI)
Public access sites: 36 (#2/MI)
Public recreational land: 47% of county
Rail-trail: (50 miles) Irons Area, North Country National Scenic Trail, Pere Marquette, Wellston Area
State/federal wild/scenic/natural river: 105 miles of the Pere Marquette and Pine Rivers
State-funded snowmobile trails: 135 miles
The county has over 300 miles of ATV/ORV trails.

S STATE OF MICHIGAN

Michigan Terrestrial Ecoregions
  Region: Northern Lower Peninsula
  Square miles: 17,000
  Southern Boundary: from the southern part of Saginaw Bay west to Oceana County.
  Landcover: Forest: 67%
  ...Agricultural: 4%
  ...Wetlands: 20%
  ...Urbanization: 2%
  Soils: forest soils and loamy sands and sandy loams.
  Threats to wildlife and landscape features: industrial, residential and recreational development, invasive species, fragmentation, altered fire regime.
Conservation actions are in place. _{Michigan.gov}

NPCR

T TRAVEL

Airport: Baldwin Municipal
County road names: ...**north/south**: named Roads
　　　　　　　　　　...**east/west**: numbered Roads
Distance to Lansing: 140 miles
Main roads: US-10, M-37
Memorial Highways: M-37, *WWII Veterans MH*
FYI: Over the years, US-10 has been called, in part or as a whole, proposed, promoted or legalized, Artic-Tropic Overland Trail, Dort Hwy., Top of Michigan Trail and Veterans Memorial Hwy. ^{Barnett}

U UNIVERSITIES & COLLEGES

None

V VARIETY

Ryan Fox

Summer, fall, winter or spring, the beauty of nature is everywhere you look in Lake County. Enjoy it, appreciate it and please come back and visit again.

W WANDERLUST

Fall colors: late September to early October

X X-TRA STUFF

Large employers: Baldwin Family Health Care, County of Lake, Baldwin Community School District, Lake County Care Center (skilled nursing), GEO Group (management services), Star Foods & Family Center (variety stores)

Y YESTERYEAR

From the 1920s to the 1960s, Idlewild was a thriving community known as the Black Eden. It was one of few places in the Midwest where African-Americans could own vacation property and experience the pleasures of outdoors and Up North living. As both a seasonal resort and year-round community, it attracted middle and upper class African-Americans and became a center for intellectuals as well as famous black entertainers from throughout the country. At its peak, it was the most popular resort in the Midwest with 25,000 seasonal visitors. After the passage of the 1964 Civil Rights Acts, racial discrimination became illegal and African-Americans were allowed to vacation and purchase property anywhere. Idlewild declined as a community during the next few decades, but in the 1990s began the slow process of remaking itself into a vibrant community again. ^{iaacc.com}

NPCR

Z ZOO & ANIMAL PLACES

NPCR

With 86% of this county covered in forests, forest dwelling animals are everywhere. And yes, there are rivers in the forest.

A AGRICULTURE

Land in farms: 42% of county
Number of farms: 1,300
Size of average farm: 130 acres
Market value of all products: #34 of 83 counties
Crops: ...most acres: soybeans
...highest $ sales: corn, soybeans, wheat
Livestock: ...largest number: pheasants
...highest $ sales: milk & dairy products
Among the top Michigan counties:
- #1- beets, bison, elk, parsley, pheasants
- #2- horses, poultry farms
- #4- organic farms, sheep & goat farms
- #5- animal farms

Dairy, food and meat processing plants: 18
State ranking for harvested trees: #68 of 83 counties
FYI: There are over 500 privately owned <u>bison, deer and elk</u> farms in Michigan. Many of these are private hunt clubs that provide prime hunting opportunities for their members; others are farms that raise the animals to provide specialty meats for consumers. Clothing, footwear and purses are made from the hide of these animals and antler velvet is used as a natural health dietary supplement. Michigan.gov

Bison — Michigan Farm Bureau
Deer — Michigan Farm Bureau
Elk — Gary Zahm, USFWS

B BRIDGE or BOAT

Elizabeth Motz

MDOT Historic Bridge: The Silverwood Road Bridge over the North Branch of the Flint River is "the last noteworthy historic bridge in Lapeer and a spectacular example of a skewed mid-size concrete camelback bridge."

C CELEBRATIONS

<u>Almont</u> *Country Heritage Tours:* Michigan's most anticipated self-guided fall event, featuring art, agriculture and antiques, Oct.
<u>Columbiaville</u> *Days:* Small Town USA, July
<u>Imlay City</u> *Blueberry Festival:* pie eating contest, parade, fireworks, entertainment stages, Aug.
...Summer Concert Series
<u>Lapeer</u> *Days Festival:* parade, carnival, Aug.
<u>Metamora</u> *Country Days and Balloon Festival:* Celebration of the Horse, Blessing of the Hounds, parade, music, food, fireworks, Aug.

D DEMOGRAPHICS

Population: 83,300   **Persons per sq. mile:** 135
Largest city: Lapeer   **Population:** 8,840
Largest township: Mayfield   **Population:** 7,960
Largest village: Almont   **Population:** 2,670
Median household income: $51,300
Owner-occupied median house value: $172,000
Persons affiliated with a religious congregation: 33%
Persons below poverty level: 9% (#82/MI)
Students receiving school lunch subsidy: 28%

E ENVIRONMENT

Since 1985, the <u>Conservation Reserve Program</u> has encouraged farmers to voluntarily plant permanent areas of grass and trees on land that needs protection from erosion. This vegetative cover may include grass filter strips or riparian buffer trees that filter runoff or wastewater that will flow into steams, lakes, wetlands or sinkholes. Living snow fences protect both the existing landscape and livestock from wind and snow damage. Grass waterways help protect soil from erosion during storms. Shallow water areas provide cover and water for wildlife. Vegetation planted in the area surrounding the wellhead of a municipal water supply helps protect that water supply from contamination. USDA

F FLORA & FAUNA

Alice Welch, USDA

Wild columbine is native to Michigan and the Midwest and is one of only a few flowers pollinated by hummingbirds. It is 2'-3' feet tall and likes full sun to partial shaded open woods.

Lamar Gore/USFWS

Foxes *(MI H&T)* are found in all Michigan counties. They especially thrive in areas with fallow and cultivated fields, meadows, bushy fence lines, woody stream borders, and low shrub cover along woods and beaches. The fox will eat almost anything from fruits and berries to small animals and the contents of garbage cans.

G GOVERNMENT

County: ...created: 1822 **...organized:** 1835
...originally part of: Oakland County
Size: 424,000 acres / 654 sq. miles (32 of 83 counties)
The county has 2 cities, 7 villages, 18 townships, 14 unincorporated communities, 1 Census Designated Place and 6 school districts.

Elizabeth Motz

Elizabeth Motz

County seat: Lapeer
...Homestead property tax: 28 mills
Motto: Lapeer Chamber: *Work ·Shop ·Play*

H HISTORICAL MARKERS 12 of 15

Columbiaville Depot: 1893, Romanesque inspired style, built by a millionaire lumber baron to spur development of the village; he gave the depot to the railroad.

Elizabeth Motz

Michigan State Historic Preservation Office

Currier House: 1854, octagonal rooms promised a healthy living environment.

Dryden Depot: 1883, the board-and-batten building was built partly with private money to induce the railroad to come to town; now the Dryden Museum
General Squier Park: George Squier (1865-1934) was a world-renowned scientist and inventor who opened his estate to the public when he was alive, then left it to Lapeer County after he died. See 44P.
Imlay City Grand Trunk Depot: 1927, a Grant Trunk design, now the Imlay City Historical Museum
Grettenberger Field: built as a 1930s WPA project
Henry Stephens Memorial Library: 1917, Georgian Revival Style, in the local National Historic District
Ladies Library Hall: 1885, the Ladies Library Association built this building for books and live entertainment; they also did charitable work.

Lapeer County Courthouse: built in 1845, the oldest courthouse in Michigan that serves its original purpose; an impressive Greek Revival style with Doric columns and a three-tiered tower; see 44G, seal

NPCR

Elizabeth Motz

Lapeer Public Library: 1923 Georgian Revival style, now named after Lapeer-born Newberry Award winning children's author, Marguerite De Angeli

Tuttle House: 1890, Queen Anne style built by planning mill owner Columbus Tuttle; house featured in his grand-daughter's, Marguerite deAngeli's, 1936 book *Ted and Nina Have a Happy Rainy Day*

William Peter Mansion: penniless immigrant becomes a wealthy businessman and builds this fine Italianate home

National Register of Historic Places: 24 listings

State Historic Sites: 43 listings

I INFORMATION

Chamber of Commerce: Imlay City, 810-724-1361, imlaycitymich.com

…Lapeer Area; lapeerareachamber.org

…Metamora, 810-678-6222, metamorachamber.org

J JOKES

You may be a rich man in Michigan if…

…your cars are never more than 6 months old.

…nobody knows for sure what you do for a living.

…you're in debt up to your eyeballs but you sure do look good.

…you never worked for the auto industry.

…you can't understand why the guy working for you making $10 an hour can't pay his bills on time.

…you're not as rich as you used to be.

…your maxed out Social Security income is just pocket change.

K KINSMAN

Race
American Indian: <1%
Asian: <1%
Black/African American: 1%
Hispanic or Latino: 4%
Other: 3%
White: 96%

Ancestry
German: 24%
English: 12%
U.S./American: 10%
Irish: 10%
Polish: 9%
French: 4%
Italian: 4%

L LIGHTHOUSE OR LANDMARK

Peter Gilles

The Metamora Hunt is "real foxhunting country with nearly 100 magnificent square miles of hilltops, trees, stone walls, lush meadows, coops, babbling brooks, bridges, woods, ditches and big, green, grassy wide-open fields (and horse farms) that will take your breath away." metamorahunt.com See 44Q.

M MUSEUMS

<u>Attica</u> *Museum:* quaint building and displays

<u>Columbiaville</u> *Historical Society Museum:* in the Village Library; arrowheads, furniture, preserved birds

<u>Dryden</u> *Historical Society:* museum inside the Dryden railroad depot, local artifacts

<u>Hadley</u> *Flour and Feed Mill:* see 44V

<u>Imlay City</u> *Historical Museum:* 7,000 items

<u>Lapeer</u> *County Historical Museum:* pioneer household items, Michigan Gov. John T. Rich display

…*Davis Brothers Farm Shop Museum:* 1800s agricultural implements, hand tools

<u>Metamora</u> *Historical Society:* in the 1888 Old Town Hall and Opera House; artifacts, lovely stage

North Branch *Village Orr Museum:* horse drawn vehicles, antique cars (a rare 1907 Model S Ford)
Otter Lake *Area Historical Museum:* local interest

N NATURAL RESOURCES

Elevation: 700 – 1,000 feet
Physiography: hilly uplands, rolling plains

Forest type: oak-hickory, maple-beech, elm-ash-cottonwood
Public/private forests: 26% of county

NPCR

Water in county: <1% of county
  Lakes: 85
    ...largest: Halloway Reservoir
  Rivers: Flint (headwaters)
  Rivers & streams: 590 miles

Growing season, avg.: 130 days (3 temp. zones)
  Last freeze, avg.: May 10 – May 20
  First freeze, avg.: Sept. 30 – Oct. 10
Precipitation, annual avg.: rainfall: 34 inches
               snowfall: 48 inches
Temperature (F), avg.: January: high 29°, low 13°
              July: high 83°, low 58°
  Annual: >90°: 12 days, <0°: 12 days
Tornadoes (1930-2010): 20

O ORIGINS

Attica:[t,u] first it was Mill Station, then Elk Lake, then finally named after its township; 1851
Almont:[v] in honor of Mexican Gen. Juan Almont; 1828
Clifford:[v] Clifford Lyman, son of village founder; 1862
Columbiaville:[v] early settlers from Columbia County, NY; 1847
Dryden:[v] in honor of English poet, John Dryden; 1840
Hadley:[t,u] from 1907 to 1957, a member of the Hadley family was the postmaster; 1834
Imlay City:[c] first landowner, William Imlay; 1870
Lapeer:[c,co] (la PEER) American version of the French word that means "stones" in the Flint River; 1831
Metamora:[v] American Indian word meaning "among the hills" or an American Indian character in an 1840s play; 1843
North Branch:[v] north branch of the Flint River; 1856
Otter Lake:[v] lake with many otters; 1838

P PARKS

National: 0   **State:** 2   **County:** 7   **Local:** 16
Number of campsites: 275
State Game Area: Lapeer

State Recreation Area: *Metamora-Hadley:* 720 acres, on Lake Minnewanna, camping, fishing, hunting, boating, trails, fishing pier

Elizabeth Motz

County: *General Squier Park:* 80 acres, General's "Country Club for Country People" was donated to the county in 1934; renovated historical buildings, trails, sledding, picnics, site of Mill Race Water Park; see 44H

Elizabeth Motz

...*Torzewski:* 69 acres on Pero Lake, amphitheater, trails, fishing, pontoon boat rental

Other: *Seven Ponds Nature Center:*[ww] 7 glacial lakes, cedar swamp, marshes, fields, woodlands, grass prairie, trails, boardwalks, viewing towers, butterfly garden, wildflower garden, wildfowl feeding

Elizabeth Motz

Q QUOTE FROM THE LOCALS

"The Metamora Hunt is still as exciting and challenging as it was when founded in 1928. Membership includes local landowners, as well as those who travel some distance to 'follow the hounds.' Hounds and riders go out twice weekly, Wednesdays and Saturdays, from August through March. The Hunt provides the area with special color and Tradition. There are few sights as fine as the hunt meeting just as dawn breaks over the Metamora Hills, with riders in their traditional hunting clothes and carefully groomed horses following the huntsman and hounds. The sounds of the Hunt horn and the cry of the pack are special treats that go with living in Metamora. Foxhounds hunt red or gray fox, and lately coyotes. The hunt is a non-blood sport." designworksjewelry.com See 44L.

R RECREATION & SPORTS

Auto racing: *Lapeer International Dragway:* no speed limit; the fun place to race
Golf courses: 8
Hiking/skiing/mountain biking trails: 10 miles
Public access sites: 8
Public recreational land: 3% of county
Rail-trail: (30 miles) Polly Ann, Southern Links
Polar Place Arena Complex: ice arena with 2 NHL-sized rinks, multi-level dance floor and stage suitable for many different events

S STATE OF MICHIGAN

The State of Michigan's Department of Treasury, has a Property Tax Estimator website at https://treas-secure.state.mi.us/ptestimator/ptestimator.asp.

You can enter a State Equalized Value (SEV) or a Taxable Value (TV) for any property. Then you must enter the county, the city, village, or township, and the school district. That will give you the estimated property tax.

In Michigan, property taxes are based on 50% of the buyer's purchase price of the property (if it was purchased for fair market value), and for that first year the SEV and TV are the same. Each year after that, the SEV and TV may change, but probably at different rates. Taxes are levied on the TV and the TV cannot go up more that 5% per year. That means that property taxes cannot go up more than 5% per year.

In years when the real estate market is rising, the SEV, or the estimated market value of the property, may go up by any amount, with no effect on property taxes. In years when the real estate market is falling, the SEV may go down, and the TV may go up or down until it reaches the level of the SEV. The TV can never be higher than the SEV. Michigan.gov

T TRAVEL

Airport: Dupont-Lapeer
Amtrak: Lapeer
Bus: Greater Lapeer Transportation Authority
County road names: Mile roads in Metro Detroit start at 0 Mile Rd. (Ford Rd.) in Wayne County and proceed north through Oakland County to 50 Mile Rd. (Bowers Rd.) in Lapeer and St. Clair County; many have dropped their Mile road designation and now just use named roads.

Distance to Lansing: 70 miles
Main roads: I-69, M-24, M-53, M-90
Memorial Highways: I-69, *DeWayne T. Williams MH*: see 77T
…I-69, *Veterans MH*
…M-53, *Earle MH*: Horatio Earle (1855-1935) was the "Father of Good Roads" who advocated for paving the mud and dirt roads of Michigan and promoting tourism.

NPCR-2

Scenic Drive: *Metamora Horse Country Drive:* five sections southeast of Metamora within the boundaries of Dryden Rd., Barber Rd., Rock Valley Rd., Brocker Rd. and Blood Rd.

U UNIVERSITIES & COLLEGES

Mott Community College, Lapeer Extension: est. 1989, 5,000 students. Students can complete many basic educational requirements close to home.

V VARIETY

Lamar Gore/USFWS

The Hadley Flour and Feed Mill was built in the 1870s. Mill Creek supplied the water flow for the water turbine that powered the wooden and metal gears that turned the grindstone that ground the grain. The mill is now a 3-story museum in the Hartwig Community Park that helps to remind visitors of their heritage.

W WANDERLUST

Agri-tourism: *Brookwood Fruit Farm:* U-pick tart cherries with free pitting, apples, peaches, tours

Cultural: Lapeer Center for the Arts

Fall colors: early October
Live theater: Pix
Walking tour: *Piety Hill Historic District:* Lapeer, 29 homes and churches from the mid-1800s

Elizabeth Motz

Elizabeth Motz

Roadside Attractions: crashed airplane is part of the sign of this unique shop that is like a museum, but everything is for sale

Past Tense Country Store: arts & antiques, cider mill, floral & gardens, tearoom, celebrations, gifts

X X-TRA STUFF

County fair: *Lapeer Agricultural Soc.,* Aug.
…Eastern Michigan Fair: Aug.
Hospitals: Lapeer Regional Medical Center
Large employers: Ultra Air Products (makes HVAC parts), Lapeer Regional Medical Center, County of Lapeer, MI Department of Mental Health, Meijer, MI Department of Corrections, Albar Industries (paints), Pinnacle Foods Group (frozen specialties), Dott Industries (makes plastic, glass & metal products), Lapeer Stamping (makes auto parts), Champion Bus (makes bus bodies)

Y YESTERYEAR

A variety of "<u>plagues</u>" caused havoc in the pioneer wilderness. In the mid-1800s, deer mice, each 5"-8" long, destroyed the crops and ate the settlers' homes and their belongings. One fall one farmer caught 2,000 mice in his house alone! Wolves, squirrels and blackbirds also plagued pioneer families. State and county bounties were paid on wolves and blackbirds.

There were massive squirrel hunts. One such hunt during the Fourth of July celebration resulted in 5,700 squirrel tails. Out of necessity, the settlers had to be self-sufficient with every seed planted and every meager possession vital to their survival. ^{Schultz}

Z ZOO & ANIMAL PLACES

Petting zoo: *Ruby Farms of Michigan:* includes cider mill, pumpkins, cut your own Christmas trees
Watchable Wildlife Viewing Areas: see 44P
Shamrock Farms B & B: on a working Thoroughbred Racehorse Farm, petting zoo

The author would like to note that she couldn't possibly include everything about each county. She intentionally has not included restaurants and lodging because so many other fine destination guides already do that. She has not included phone numbers and addresses because the Internet is so easily available to most people. But she has included things that you will not find in any other general travel book or website. Enjoy your trip through the state as you read *Discovering Michigan County by County!*

A AGRICULTURE

Land in farms: 24% of county
Number of farms: 450
Size of average farm: 125 acres
Market value of all products: #41 of 83 counties
Crops: ...most acres: tart cherries
...highest $ sales: fruits
Livestock: ...largest number: cattle
...highest $ sales: cattle & calves
Among the top Michigan counties:
- #1- acres & sales of sweet cherries, sales of tart cherries, plums & prunes, ryegrass seed
- #2- acres of fruit, acres of tart cherries, chestnuts
- #6- organic production

Leelanau Peninsula American Viticulture Area: over 1,000 acres of wine grapes; U.S. government designated wine grape-growing area
Dairy, food and meat processing plants: 41
State ranking for harvested trees: #67 of 83 counties

FYI: Although tart cherry production is spread out along 8 Lake Michigan counties of the Lower Peninsula, Leelanau County is #1 for tart cherry sales and the #2 tart cherry-producing county with more than 9,500 acres of tart cherry  trees. Michigan produces up to 75% of the U.S. crop of these bright red cherries. There are more tart cherries produced in Michigan than in any other place in the world.

Tart cherries are used for pies, jams, jellies, juice and dried fruit, but are rarely eaten fresh. It takes 8 pounds of fresh cherries to make one pound of dried cherries. It is tart cherry juice that research has shown to have a wide variety of health benefits, from pain relief to antioxidants to improving sleep.

If you want to eat your cherries fresh, though, ask for sweet cherries (see 28A). February is National Cherry Month, so celebrate with a cherry pie for Valentine's Day and Presidents' Day. Michigan.gov

B BRIDGE OR BOAT

Manitou Island Transit offers ferry rides to both North and South Manitou Islands and Good Harbor Bay cruises as well.

C CELEBRATIONS

Empire Winterfest: ice skating, curling, polar bear dip, pool tournament, Feb.

...Asparagus Festival: a unique celebration of spring; listed in MSN Travel as one of the world's weirdest festivals, May
...Anchor Day: themes, races, parade, July
...Dunegrass: blues festival, Aug.
...Heritage Days: Oct.

Leland *Wine & Food Festival:* local wines, food, music, beautiful view, June

Port Oneida Fair: experience life of the late 1800s and early 1900s sponsored by many historic preservation groups in the area, Aug.

Suttons Bay *Blues Festival:* Leelanau's finest foods, wines, brews & ciders, July

D DEMOGRAPHICS

Population: 21,700   **Persons per sq. mile:** 62
Largest city: Traverse City (partial)   **Population:** 190
Largest township: Elmwood   **Population:** 4,500
Largest village: Suttons Bay   **Population:** 620
Median household income: $54,900 (#3/MI)
Owner-occupied median house value: $239,000 (#1/MI)

Persons affiliated with a religious congregation: 40%
Persons below poverty level: 10% (#81/MI)
Students receiving school lunch subsidy: 28%

E ENVIRONMENT

Since 1988, the Leelanau Conservancy has worked to conserve the land, water and scenic character of Leelanau County. As one of the premier land trusts in the U.S., they have preserved over 7,000 acres of land and 27 miles of shoreline/stream and river frontage and farmland; they monitor water quality and have created over 20 Natural Areas and Preserves. With 2,800 members, they also develop and maintain trails through mixed forests, along fragile sandy shores, into blowout dunes and wetlands; they lead hikes, rescue wildflowers and tirelessly work to benefit the beautiful Leelanau Peninsula. the converancy.com

F FLORA & FAUNA

Alice Welch, USDA

The wild fox grape is the source of many cultivated grape varieties. An important food in the wildlife chain, it can also be made into jams and jellies. The vine, also called skunk grape, can climb over 30' tall.

James Harding

Green frogs are 2"-5" and can be green, greenish brown, brownish, yellowish green, olive or blue. They can be found in any inland water area helping to control the local insect population.

G GOVERNMENT

County: ...created: 1840 **...organized:** 1863
...originally part of: Grand Traverse County
Size: 234,000 acres / 348 sq. miles (82 of 83 counties)
The county 3 villages, 11 townships with 1 as a charter township, 10 unincorporated communities, 1 Census Designated Place and 4 school districts.

Rick Gleason

NPCR

County seat: Leland
...Homestead property tax: (Leland Twp.) 18 mills

231

H HISTORICAL MARKERS 9 of 10

Michigan State Preservation Office

Bingham's District No. 5 Schoolhouse: built in 1877, used as school, church, township hall; now restored

Early State Parks: the Michigan state parks system began in 1919, with most properties on beautiful lakes; D. H. Day State Park (honoring the first chairman of the State Park Commission, see 45T) was the first state park; it is now part of Sleeping Bear Dunes National Lakeshore. See 45L, 45P.

Empire Lumber Co.: well equipped hardwood mill; destroyed by fire twice, 1906 and 1917

Great Lakes Sport Fishery: 1920s, Great Lakes sport trolling for trout began in Grand Traverse Bay.

Michigan State Preservation Office

Grelickville: 1883, the steam powered sawmill cut 8.5 million feet of hardwood lumber.

Leland Historical District (Fishtown): 1880s, commercial fishing then and now

Old Settlers Park: 1893, a picnic to honor early and elderly pioneers

Omena Presbyterian Church: 1858, an American Indian and white church, it is relatively unchanged; now used in the summer only

St. Wenceslaus Church and Cemetery: 1914, Late Gothic Revival style church reflects Bohemian [Czechoslovakia] heritage of 1860s settlers; ornate metal grave markers

Monument: *Manning Memorial Light:* see 45W

National Register of Historic Places: 21 listings

State Historic Sites: 34 listings

I INFORMATION

Chamber of Commerce: Glen Lake, 231-334-3238, visitglenarbor.com

…Leelanau Peninsula, 231-994-2202, leelanauchamber.org

…Suttons Bay, 231-271-5077, suttonsbayarea.com

J JOKES

You may be a tourist in Michigan if…

…you think the only things to see in Michigan are Greenfield Village, Mackinac Bridge and Mackinac Island, the Soo Locks, Traverse City and any beach town on Lake Michigan.

…you only go where the interstates go.

…the destination is more important than the journey.

…you never take a two-lane road even when it has enhanced scenic beauty and quaint towns.

…you'd rather walk a mile in the mall than walk a mile in the forest.

…you marvel at the green grass, the green trees and all that blue water. Michigan's just not like Arizona.

…if water, water, everywhere is your idea of a good time.

…the Caribbean is too long of a drive.

…you're not a wine snob.

…you'd rather sit on the beach than go into the water.

…you're amazed how enjoyable it is to swim in "unsalted water."

K KINSMAN

Race		Ancestry	
American Indian:	4%	German:	23%
Asian:	<1%	English:	11%
Black/African American:	<1%	Polish:	10%
Hispanic or Latino:	4%	Irish:	9%
Other:	2%	French:	6%
White:	93%	U.S./American:	5%

L LIGHTHOUSE OR LANDMARK

National Park Service

Sleeping Bear Dunes National Lakeshore offers spectacular scenery, scenic drives, museums and sand dunes on Lake Michigan. See 45P, 45Y.

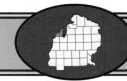
M MUSEUMS

<u>Empire</u> *Area Museum:* 4 buildings, unique displays

<u>Glen Haven</u> *Cannery Boathouse Museum:* largest public exhibit of Great Lakes small craft

National Park Service

National Park Service

...Sleeping Bear Point Coast Guard Station Maritime Museum: 1930s era U.S. Coast Guard life-saving station.

FYI: From 1871 to 1915, the U.S. Life-Saving Service, nationwide, saved over 178,000 people, with a success rate of 99%.

<u>Leelanau</u> *Grand Traverse Lighthouse Museum:* a working lighthouse built in 1858; see 45W

...Historical Museum: exploring the past, understanding the present and imagining the future; Anishinaabe arts, past and present; New Manitou Passage

N NATURAL RESOURCES

Elevation: 600 - 1,000 feet
Physiography: hill-lands

Soil: Fine Sand
  Depth: 4"-20"
  Color: dark gray to black
  Type: fine sand
  Details: level surface with natural drainage
  Sub-Soil: same texture, but with less organic matter
  Agriculture: crop value depends on the amount of organic matter; found along the Lake Michigan coastline; very good for small fruits
NOTE: soil types are not limited to any one county.

Forest type: maple-beech-birch-hemlock, spruce-fir
Public/private forests: 54% of county
Legislatively protected sand dunes: 11,000 acres

Water in county: 7% of county
  Bay: West Arm of Grand Traverse Bay; Grand Traverse Bay of Lake Michigan; Good Harbor
  Lakes: 40 **...largest:** Lake Leelanau Glen (#7/depth/MI)
  Rivers: Crystal
  Rivers & streams: 60 miles (#82/MI)

Great Lakes islands: North Manitou, South Manitou
Great Lakes peninsula: Leelanau
Great Lakes shoreline: 150 miles of Lake Michigan

Growing season, avg.: 130 days (2 temp. zones)
  Last freeze, avg.: May 20 – May 25
  First freeze, avg.: September 5 – September 10
Precipitation, annual avg.: rainfall: 35 inches
  snowfall: 145 inches (#6/MI; #1/Lower Peninsula)
Temperature (F), avg.: January: high 27°, low 14°
                           July: high 81°, low 56°
  Annual: >90°: 6 days, **<0°:** 11 days
Tornadoes (1930-2010): 3

NPCR

O ORIGINS

<u>Empire</u>:[v] schooner *Empire* became icebound in the harbor; 1851
<u>Glen Arbor</u>:[u] dense mass of wild grapes grew entwined in the treetops; 1848
<u>Greilickville</u>:[u] sawmill operator Godfrey Grelick; 1875
<u>Leelanau</u>:[co] (LEE la naw) American Indian word meaning "delight of life;" 1905
<u>Leland</u>:[u] (LEE lund) lee land side is exposed to the wind; 1853
<u>Maple City</u>:[u] the abundance of maple trees; 1865
<u>Northport</u>:[v] on Northport Bay; 1852
<u>Omena</u>:[u] American Indian for "is it so?;" 1852
<u>Suttons Bay</u>:[v] land owned by Harry Sutton; 1854

P PARKS

National: 1 **State:** 3 **County:** 2 **Local:** 24
Number of campsites: 830
National: *Sleeping Bear Dunes National Lakeshore:*[ww,wba,1,000] 71,000 acres with 35 miles of Lake Michigan coastline; Visitors Center has information on the park, natural and human history of area; 1920s Glen Haven General Store, Cannery Boat House Museum and the Blacksmith Shop with a working blacksmith; South Manitou Island Visitor Center was once a

general store; Dune Climb and Duneside Interpretive Trail; camping by and swimming in Lake Michigan; South Manitou Island Lighthouse is open for tours; North Manitou Island is managed as a wilderness; Coast Guard Station Maritime Museum; 21 lakes; Port Oneida Rural Historic District is a 1900s era farm that is being restored; 11 other historic farms and buildings; Pierce Stocking Scenic Drive

National Park Service

FYI: In 2011, Sleeping Bear Dunes National Lakeshore was named by <u>Good Morning America</u> as the Most Beautiful Place in America. Viewers of the TV show nominated places and then voted on the top 10.

Courtesy of www.chrisdoyal.com

State Forest: Pere Marquette (5,000 acres)

State Game Area: 1,200 acres, South Fox Island of the Beaver Island Wildlife Research Area; North Manitou Island

State Park: *Leelanau:*^{wba} 1,300 acres, on the tip of the little finger, home of Grand Traverse Lighthouse

LEELANAU STATE PARK

Rick Gleason

Courtesy of www.chrisdoyal.com

State Underwater Preserve: *Manitou Passage:* 16 shipwrecks in and around the Manitou Islands and the mainland; clear water, excellent diving

Q QUOTE FROM THE LOCALS

"The Lower Peninsula of Michigan is often described as a 'mitten.' The Leelanau Peninsula can be described as the 'little finger' of that mitten. Others call the Leelanau Peninsula the Third Coast or North

Coast. With dunes that rise high over Lake Michigan offering sweeping views, acres of farmland filled with cherry trees and grapevines and a vast variety of recreation opportunities, describing Leelanau County with words alone is difficult.

"The peninsula is home to many wineries that produce award-winning varieties. Farmers markets celebrate the agricultural heritage of the area offering a wide selection of locally grown produce.

"Don't let Leelanau's rural character and small towns fool you. We love arts and culture here, too. Leelanau is home to many very talented artists who are inspired by the beauty of our peninsula. The area offers an impressive variety of musical events, art exhibitions and cultural events in addition to our collection of galleries and shops.

"Leelanua is one of those places that you really have to see to believe. A great place to live, work or play." lee.timberlakepublishing.com

R RECREATION & SPORTS

Golf courses: 4
Great Lakes marinas: 15   **Boat slips:** 600
Hiking/skiing/mountain biking trails: 140 miles
MI Shore-to-Shore (horse) **Riding & Hiking Trail:** begins here in Empire on Lake Michigan and goes east to Oscoda on Lake Huron
Public access sites: 17
Public recreational land: 23% of county
Rail-trail: (10 miles) Leelanau Trail
Recreational harbor: Grelick-Elmwood Twp. Marina, Leland Twp. Marina, Northport Marsten Dam Marina, South Manitou Island, Suttons Bay Marina

NPCR

S STATE OF MICHIGAN

Since 1998, *The Legend of Sleeping Bear* by Kathy-jo Wargin has been the <u>State Children's Book</u>. It is a beautifully illustrated book that retells an Ojibwe Indian tale of the origination of the Sleeping Bear Dunes. See 45Y for a brief summary of the tale.

T TRAVEL

Airport: Sugar Loaf Resort
Circle Tour: Lake Michigan via M-22
Distance to Lansing: 200 miles
Ferry: to North and South Manitou Islands

Heritage Route: *Scenic:* M-22, Leelanau Scenic Heritage Route, 64 miles, Traverse City to Empire

Main roads: M-22, M-72, M-109, M-201, M-204, M-209

Memorial Highways: on M-22, *Carl Oleson Jr. Bridge:* a tackle & bait shop owner who loved the waters and the fish in this part of Northern Michigan

...M-109, *D.H. Day Hwy.:* David Henry Day (1858-1928) was a positive influence in the development of this area and a model for timber conservation, a pioneer cherry grower and the first State Park Commissioner. See 45H.

Northwest Michigan Port of Call Tour: Grand Traverse Lighthouse Museum, Leelanau Historical Museum, Sleeping Bear Dunes National Lakeshore, Sleeping Bear Point Maritime Museum

Scenic Drive: *Suttons Bay to Frankfort* via M-22

...*Pierce Stocking Scenic Drive:* 7.4 miles in the National Lakeshore, includes covered bridges, 4 overlooks; features ecology, dunes, forests; get an interpretive guide at the Visitor Center.

U UNIVERSITIES & COLLEGES

None

V VARIETY

Paul Jackson

The harvesting of tart cherries is done mechanically with a machine that shakes the trees, causing the ripe cherries to fall from the tree. They are then loaded into vats of cold water that cools them down before they are transported to the processor to be made into your favorite cherry product.

W WANDERLUST

Agri-tourism: *Black Star Farms:*[1,000] B & B, winery, creamery, farm market, café, local specialty processed foods

...*Gallagher Farm Market:* fresh fruits and vegetables in season, local wines, jam & jellies

...*Farm 651:* eco-agricultural vineyard, hops farm, apple orchard, cherries; education, research

Casino: Leelanau Sands

Cultural: *Leelanau Community Cultural Center:* the Old Art building; classes, performances, exhibits

Fall colors: late September – early October

Michigan State Preservation Office

Lighthouses, other: *Grand Traverse:* 1858 lighthouse and museum; see 45M

...*Manning Memorial Light:* 1990, built by his friends as a memorial for fisherman Robert Manning

...*South Manitou Island:* 1871, climb up the 117 steps of the circular staircase; see 45P

Walking tours: *Fishtown:* 145-year-old fishing village, a living legacy of maritime culture; shopping, good restaurants

Wineries:[1,000] *Bel Lago Vineyards & Winery:* family-owned vineyards produce cool climate classic wines

...*Black Star Farms:*[1,000] world-class wines, cheese, B&B inn, equestrian facility, recreational trails

...*Chateau De Leelanau Vineyard & Winery:* fine wines from this new and progressive wine country

...*Chateau Fontaine:* 17 acres of pinot gris, chardonnay, gewürztraminer, pinot noir & merlot

...*Cherry Republic Winery:* 9 cherry wines from the people who know cherries!

...*Ciccone Vineyard & Winery:* award-winning wines and food products

...*Circa Estate Winery:* invokes Old World European regions in a cellar ambience and a soothing palette

...*Forty-Five North Vineyard and Winery:* Leelanau Co. shares the 45th parallel with Bourdeaux, France

Rick Gleason

NPCR

...*Gill's Pier Vineyard & Winery:* award-winning wines in an exquisite atmosphere

...*Good Harbor Vineyards:* whatever beneficial actions are taken with the grape vines make better tasting wines

...*Good Neighbor Organic Winery:* certified organic wines, farm, hard ciders; micro brewery

...*L. Mawby Vineyards:*[1,000], wines are living things, raised with care, giving voice to our joie de vivre

...*Leelanau Wine Cellars:* established in 1977 to produce quality, affordable, consumer-friendly wines

...*Longview Winery:* the possibilities of life – grapes, wines, ourselves

...*Raftshol Vineyards:* produces over 1,000 cases of Bordeaux varietal red wines

...*Shady Land Cellars:* every wine is a product of a thousand details...an expression of place

...*Silver Leaf Vineyard & Winery:* an artisan's approach that reflects unique character

...*Tandem Ciders:* artisanal hard ciders that connect the land, the farmer, the apples, the cider

...*Willow Vineyard:* tasting room has panoramic view of W. Traverse Bay; European influenced vineyards

Cherry Republic: ALL things very cherry delicious

Jayme Simpson

Cove Restaurant: eat by the river and watch the salmon as they swim upstream.

X   X-TRA STUFF

American Indian Community: Grand Traverse Bay Ottawa and Chippewa Indians

Large employers: Grand Traverse Band of Ottawa Indians (gaming commission, hotel/motel, real estate), Leelanau Memorial Health Center, Suttons Bay Public Schools, Easling Construction, National Park Service

The Homestead Resort AMERICA'S FRESHWATER RESORT: adjacent to the Sleeping Bear Dunes National Lakeshore; on the Manitou Passage; Lake Michigan beaches, homes, condos, golf, luxury living where the great Northwoods and the Great Lakes meet.

Y   YESTERYEAR

NPCR

<u>The Legend of Sleeping Bear</u>   Long ago, along the Wisconsin shoreline, a mother bear and her two cubs were forced into Lake Michigan to escape a raging forest fire. The bears swam for many hours, but eventually the cubs tired and lagged behind. Mother bear reached the shore of Michigan and climbed to the top of a high bluff to watch and wait for her cubs. Too tired to continue, the cubs drowned within sight of the shore and their mother. The Great Spirit Manitou, impressed by the mother bear's faith and determination, created two islands (North and South Manitou Island) to mark the spot where the cubs disappeared, and then created a solitary dune where the faithful mother bear still watches and waits for her cubs. NOTE: Once a towering and impressive dune, over the years the winds have reduced it to a fraction of its original size. See 45S.

Z   ZOO & ANIMAL PLACES

Watchable Wildlife Viewing Areas:[ww] see 45P
Petting zoo: Black Star Farms

> *From BIBLIOGRAPHY & NOTES...*
>
> **H HISTORICAL MARKERS:** At the discretion of the author, not all historical markers have been included.

A AGRICULTURE

Land in farms: 72% of county
Number of farms: 1,690 (#1/MI)
Size of average farm: 205 acres
Market value of all products: #11 of 83 counties
Crops: ...most acres: soybeans
...highest $ sales: grains: corn, soybeans, wheat
Livestock: ...largest number: cattle
...highest $ sales: milk & dairy products
Among the top Michigan counties:
- #1- other peppers, revenue from grains
- #2- corn for grain, head cabbage, llamas, soybeans
- #4- wheat
- #5- goats

Dairy, food and meat processing plants: 17
State ranking for harvested trees: #63 of 83 counties
FYI: Michigan's <u>wheat</u> crop is grown on approximately 523,000 acres and the sale of wheat represents 3% of the state's annual agriculture sales. It is generally "winter wheat" that is planted in the fall, grows a few inches, winters over under the snow and is a lush green during early spring when everything else is still brown. It is then harvested in the summer when it is 3'-4' tall and the grains are ripe.

When the farmer receives $10 a bushel for his wheat (an average price), that means there is 17¢ worth of wheat in every 16 oz. loaf of bread. Most Michigan-grown wheat is milled right here in the state and the high quality flour is used in breads and baked goods, as soup thickeners and other products, including Michigan's huge cereal industry.

After the edible wheat grains are removed from the plant, the leftover stalk is now called straw and it is primarily used for animal bedding. MSU Extnsion, USDA

Michigan Farm Bureau

Michigan Farm Bureau

B BRIDGE OR BOAT

Kim W. Kerr

MDOT Historic Bridge: Called the "rainbow" arch bridge, this 1926 bridge at Merrick St. over the S. Branch River Raisin in Adrian was designed by an engineer from Adrian. This style of bridge was common in other midwestern states but not so common in Michigan.

C CELEBRATIONS

<u>Adrian</u> *Art-A-Licious:* art, music, food, free family fun, Sept.
...Open Air Paint Out Event: artists set up outdoors and do their creative work while you watch, Aug.
<u>Blissfield</u> *River Raisin Festival:* river racin', July
<u>Clinton</u> *Fall Festival:* car show, parade, raffle, Sept.
<u>Lenawee</u> *County Heritage Festival:* living history, lost arts, saw milling, antique tractors & engines, Sept.
<u>Morenci</u> *Town & Country Festival:* queen's contest, man pageant, arm wrestling, dog show, old guys vs. young guys softball game, bingo, beer, June
<u>Onsted</u> *Old Time Country Harvest Day Festival:* Sept.
<u>Tecumseh</u> *Appleumpkin Festival & Westfest:* make a scarecrow, kids' activities, waterball tournament, activities all over town, Sept.
...Ice Sculpture Festival: snowmen too, Jan.

<u>Tipton</u> *Oh! These Irish Hills Festival:* celebrate the beauty of the place, the spirit of its people, the progression of its history, Sept.

Norm Emmons

D DEMOGRAPHICS

Population: 100,000   **Persons per sq. mile:** 133
Largest city: Adrian   **Population:** 21,100
Largest township: Madison **Population:** 8,600
Largest village: Blissfield **Population:** 3,340
Median household income: $46,700
Owner-occupied median house value: $146,000
Persons affiliated with a religious congregation: 40%
Persons below poverty level: 13%
Students receiving school lunch subsidy: 46%

E ENVIRONMENT

The <u>Raisin Valley Land Trust</u> was established to use all reasonable means to preserve, enhance and maintain the natural, historical and cultural qualities that define the Raisin Valley. This includes preserving rural landscapes, preservation of historical structures and active farmland, supporting creation of parks, having input into development throughout the county, promoting public awareness and preservation of the natural and historical features around the upper River Raisin Watershed, and working with other organizations and governments to accomplish these goals. rvlt.org

F FLORA & FAUNA

Robert E. Schutzki, Dept of Horticulture, Michigan State University

Michigan may not be considered a "southern" state, but magnolia trees are alive and well and thrive in southern Michigan.

Kevin D. Arvin

The woodchuck (*MI H&T*), also known as the groundhog, likes to live where there is rolling farmland, grassy pastures, small woodlots and brushy fence lines. They have underground tunnel systems that can be 5' deep and 70' in length. This can cause extensive damage to buildings, farmland and machinery. They can be hunted year-round.

G GOVERNMENT

County: ...**created:** 1822 ...**organized:** 1826
...**originally part of:** Wayne County
Size: 487,000 acres / 751 sq. miles (23 of 83 counties)
The county has 4 cities, 8 villages, 22 townships with 3 as charter townships, 11 unincorporated communities, 1 Census Designated Place and 12 school districts.

Michigan State Historic Preservation Office

NPCR

County seat: Adrian
...**Homestead property tax:** 39 mills
Motto: <u>Adrian</u>: *respect for the individual voice, service for the common good…*
...<u>Clinton</u>: *A Little Town with a Big Heart*
...<u>Deerfield</u>: *We care about all of our neighbors and friends.*
...<u>Hudson</u> Chamber: *Small Town Big Heart*
...<u>Morenci</u>: *A Comfortable Blend of Tradition and Progression*
...<u>Tecumseh</u>: *Innovative Timeless Inviting*

H HISTORICAL MARKERS 17 of 47

Adrian College: began in 1859 with Wesleyan Methodist origins, it had strong anti-slavery sentiments; now affiliated with the [United] Methodist Church

Kelly Drlicka

Adrian Monthly Meetinghouse & Raisin Valley Friends Church: 1835, Michigan's oldest surviving Friends organization and one of the oldest houses of worship in Michigan

Adrian Union Hall: 1863, now called the Croswell Opera House and Fine Arts Association

Al Meyers Airport: is a privately owned airport for public use; Mr. Myers (1908-1976) made airplanes here during WWII to 1966; also site of airplane restoration services, especially the Meyers planes

Camp Williams: 1861, was the site for training soldiers in the Fourth Michigan Volunteer Infantry for the Civil War

Site of the Clinton Inn: built in 1830, Henry Ford moved it to Greenfield Village in 1927.

Erie & Kalamazoo Railroad: 1833, the first railroad west of the Allegheny Mountains was 33 miles long between Adrian and Toledo, OH; at first the train was pulled by horses.

NPCR

Payne-Smith-Kimball House: 1840, Greek Revival style house with a portico of twin fluted Ionic columns flanked by square Doric piers was "one of the most monumental in Michigan;" now a community center in Clinton

Lake Shore and Michigan Southern Railway: 1869, between Buffalo, NY, and Chicago, IL, it was vital to transporting settlers and the goods they needed.

Oakwood Cemetery: 1848, Victorian era, park-like setting, wooded pathways, variety of monuments

Sacred Heart Hall: 1922, Neo-Classical and Romanesque Revival building was built by the Adrian Dominican Sisters as a teacher's college for women; now part of Sienna Heights College. See 46U.

Michigan State Historic Preservation Office

St. John's Episcopal Church: 1835, oldest remaining Episcopal Church building in Michigan; original hand-hewn beams, wainscoting, stained glass windows

Kim W. Kerr

St. Joseph's Church and Shrine: the stone church with the red tile roof was built in 1863; in 1932 the fourteen outdoor Stations of the Cross were started.

Taft Memorial Hwy.: 1930, to promote automobile tourism, from Sault Ste. Marie, MI, to Fort Myers, FL; the Taft Memorial Highway Association lobbied for modern roads and bridges along their routes.

Walker Tavern: 1832, famed stagecoach and pioneer wagon stop; restored as museum in 1921, it is now part of the Michigan Historical Museum System. See 46M.

Wooden Stone School: Rev. Wooden built the fieldstone school in 1850; it is now restored.

Woodstock Manual Labor Institute: 1844, started by an African American for "colored people and others," it was one of the nations first integrated schools.

Monument: *An Gorta Mor* ("The Great Hunger") *Memorial*: to remember the victims of the Irish Potato Famine of 1845-1850

NPCR

...Civil War Memorial: Adrian
National Register of Historic Places: 24 listings
State Historic Sites: 86 listings

I INFORMATION

Chamber of Commerce: Adrian, Blissfield, Clinton, Hudson, Lenawee County, Onsted, Tecumseh

Visitor: Lenawee County Conference and Visitors Bureau, 800-536-2933, visitlenawee.com

J JOKES

You may like a Michigan winter if you appreciate…

…the wildlife drama at your bird feeder.

…the brilliance of new fallen snow on a sunny day.

…sitting *in* your house and looking *out* the window at the bird drama and the new fallen snow.

…having someone else shovel your sidewalk and driveway.

…when and where snow can melt on a 24° day.

…when 35° is just a cool day and not a cold one.

…when the weatherman predicted 20 inches of snow and you're disappointed you *only* got 10 inches.

…gray and brown as your favorite colors.

K KINSMAN

Race
American Indian: <1%
Asian: <1%
Black/African American: 3%
Hispanic or Latino: 8%
Other: 4%
White: 92%

Ancestry
German: 21%
English: 12%
U.S./American: 10%
Irish: 10%
French: 4%
Polish: 2%

L LIGHTHOUSE OR LANDMARK

The Michigan International Speedway, with over 1,400 acres, seats 137,000 people in the grandstand and bleachers with another 150,000 people in the infield and outfield areas. See 46R.

M MUSEUMS

<u>Adrian</u> *Lenawee County Historical Museum:* a former Carnegie library that is Romanesque styling; extensive collections

<u>Blissfield</u> *Depot Museum:* home of the Old Road Dinner Train

<u>Clinton</u> *Southern Michigan Railroad Museum:* a 14-mile historic train ride through the countryside

<u>Hudson</u> *History Museum:* Civil War, WWI & WWII items, doctor, dentist, pharmacy items, railroad

…*Thompson House Museum & Gardens:* 1890 Queen Anne style, Oriental and English art

<u>Onsted</u> *Cambridge Junction Historic State Park:* 80 acres, also known as the Walker Tavern Historic Site, was a major stopping place for stagecoaches traveling between Detroit and Chicago; visitor center and restored tavern tells the story of stagecoach travel in Michigan; discover Michigan's agricultural and travel heritage at this 1840s stagecoach stop; part of the Michigan Historical Museum System

<u>Tecumseh</u> *Area Historical Museum:* in the 1913 Old Stone Church building; illuminating the relevance of history in our lives today

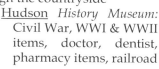

N NATURAL RESOURCES

Elevation: 700 – 1,000 feet
Physiography: lake-border plains, rolling plains, hilly uplands

Forest type: elm-ash-cottonwood, oak-hickory, maple-beech
Public/private forests: 11% of county

Water in county: 7% of county
   Lakes: 60 **…largest:** Devils Lake
   Rivers: River Raisin
   Rivers & streams: 620 miles

NPCR

Growing season, avg.: 156 days (3 temp. zones)
   Last freeze, avg.: April 30 – May 10
   First freeze, avg.: Sept. 30 – Oct. 10
Precipitation, annual avg.: rainfall: 33 inches
                snowfall: 32 inches
Temperature (F), avg.: January: high 31°, low 15°
              July: high 84°, low 60°
   Annual: >90°: 15 days, **<0°:** 9 days
Tornadoes (1930-2010): 34

O ORIGINS

Addison:[v,ct] land owner, Addison Comstock; 1835
Adrian:[c,ct] Roman emperor, Hadrian; 1826
Blissfield:[v,t] first settler, Hervey Bliss; 1824
Britton:[v] local storekeeper, John Britton, paid $500 to the railroad to have the town named after him; 1881
Cement City:[v] having three previous names, the name of the village was changed again after a cement company started there in 1900; 1838
Clayton:[v] Presbyterian minister, Rev. Clayton; 1836
Clinton:[v,t] NY Gov. DeWitt Clinton; 1830
Deerfield:[v,t] numerous deer in the area; 1826
Hudson:[c] early land owner, Dr. Daniel Hudson; 1833
Lenawee:[co] (LEN a way) Shawnee word meaning "Indian" [lenaweehistory.com]
Morenci:[c] named by two settlers; 1834
Onsted:[v] settler John Onsted; 1884
Raisin:[ct] wild grapes growing on the banks of the river reminded early travelers of raisins; 1835
Tecumseh:[c,t] (te COME SUH) Shawnee chief Tecumseh; 1824

P PARKS

National: 0 **State:** 4 **County:** 4 **Local:** 45
Number of campsites: 9,370 (Michigan International Speedway has 9,000 campsites, making it the largest registered campground in Michigan)
State Game Area: Onsted
State Park: *Walter J. Hayes:* 650 acres on Wamplers Lake and Round Lake, in the heart of the Irish Hills; camping, swimming, fishing, close to MIS racetrack
State Park, Historic: *Cambridge Junction Historic State Park:* see 46M
State Recreation Area: *Lake Hudson:* 2,800 acres, muskie fishing, game hunting, camping, geo-caching, swimming, boating; a designated dark sky preserve for observing the night sky

County: *Bicentennial:* 80 acres, hiking trails through virgin timbers and prairie grass fields

Norm Emmons

…*Ramsdell:* 180 acres, rolling hills, fishing ponds, wildlife, native tallgrass prairie
Other: *Hidden Lake Gardens:* 775 acres, developed by Harry Fee in 1920s–1940s to create a series of pictures in landscape gardens; now owned by Michigan State University; open to the public, walk or drive through the grounds; there is every shade of green in the world. Beautiful!

Norm Emmons

Prentice Drake

Q QUOTE FROM THE LOCALS

"Irish settlers who came to the U.S. seeking a new beginning must have been green with envy when they discovered a place in southeast Michigan that was so reminiscent of their native land. What these immigrants discovered was a green, pristine

NPCR

assemblage of rolling hills, grassy meadows, large stands of oak and other indigenous trees and beautiful lakes. They quickly colonized the area and hence came its name: <u>The Irish Hills</u>. It developed into a tourist destination in the 1920s. The Hills wants to continue to be a tourist destination. Its allure is unique because it doesn't offer the high-end restaurants, fancy motels and transportation infrastructure… That's not necessary, the basic beauty and amenities are still as wholesome as ever. What's going on is a stepped up endorsement of the built-in charm that gives the Irish Hills its special magnetism."

Dave Woolford, *Splendor in Tact…the Irish Hills*, irishhills.com See 46V.

R RECREATION & SPORTS

Auto racing: *Michigan International Speedway:* 2-mile oval track, 73' turns, 18° banking; NASCAR Nationwide Series, Sprint Cup Series and Camping World Truck Series; one of the country's premier racing facilities; see 46L, 46P

Golf courses: 9

Hiking/skiing/mountain biking trails: 10 miles

Horse racing: harness racing during fair week

Public access sites: 8

Public recreational land: <1% of county

Rail-trail: (21 miles) Kiwanis, Heritage Park

Lenawee Christian Family Center: cafe, bowling, fitness center, gym, racquetball, auditorium, track, soccer, baseball, volleyball, walking path

Michigan Cup Snowmobile Grass Drags: longest running grass drag event in the state, Oct.

Courtesy of "Michigan Cup Grass Drags" Onsted, MI

S STATE OF MICHIGAN

The Department of Community Health keeps statistics on <u>Baby Names</u>. The 10 Most Popular *names for boys* in Michigan in selected years are noted here.

1950: Robert, Michael, James, David, John, Thomas, William, Richard, Gary, Charles

1960: Michael, David, James, Robert, Mark, John, Thomas, William, Timothy, Steven

1970: Michael, David, James, Robert, John, Jeffrey, Scott, Christopher, Brian, Mark

1980: Michael, Jason, Christopher, Matthew, David, James, Robert, Ryan, Joshua, Joseph

1990: Michael, Joshua, Matthew, Christopher, Andres, Ryan, Kyle, Nicholas, David, Justin

2000: Jacob, Joshua, Michael, Nicholas, Andrew, Tyler, Matthew, Zachary, Joseph, Ryan

2010: Jacob, Ethan, Noah, Michael, Logan, Aiden, Alexander, Mason, Andrew, William

See 30S for *girls'* names.

T TRAVEL

Airport: Lenawee County, Al Meyers

Bus: Dial-A-Ride

Distance to Lansing: 70 miles

Heritage Route: *Historic: US-12 Heritage Trail*, see 11T

Main roads: US-12, US-127, M-34, M-50, M-52, M-156

Memorial Highways: US-12, *Iron Brigade:* see 12T
…US-12, *Pulaski MH:* see 14T
…US-223, *Carlton Road:* see 30X

Scenic Drive: any roads in the Irish Hills

FYI: Over the years, US-223 has been called, in part or as a whole, proposed, promoted or legalized: Carleton Rd., Erie & Kalamazoo Trail, Kalamazoo-Deering Trail and Michigan-Erie Hwy. Barnett

U UNIVERSITIES & COLLEGES

Adrian College: est. 1859, 1,600 students. A liberal arts college in the United Methodist tradition, it is committed to the pursuit of truth and to the dignity of all people…to achieve a more socially just society. MIAA, Bulldogs

Siena Heights University: est. 1919, 2,300 students on campus and in 8 degree completion centers in Michigan; a Catholic school founded and sponsored by the Adrian Dominican Sisters to help people become more competent, purposeful and ethical. WHAC, Saints

V VARIETY

NPCR

The Irish Hills are one the prettiest areas of Michigan. It's always worth the drive to see the scenery and experience the ambience of this place that looks so much like Ireland. See 46Q.

W WANDERLUST

Agri-tourism: *Applewood Orchards:* fancy varieties
...*Kapnick Orchards:* apples, peaches, U-pick, bakery, cider mill, tours, wagon rides, pumpkins
...*Farm Markets:* Adrian, Blissfield, Madison, Hathaway House, Hudson, Tecumseh Area, Walker Tavern
Cultural: Adrian Symphony Orchestra
Fall colors: middle October

Norm Emmons

Live theater: Croswell Opera House (oldest, continuously operated community theater in Michigan); dinner theater
...Tecumseh Center for the Arts
MotorCities National Heritage Area: yes
Planetarium: Robinson at Adrian College
Shopping mall: Adrian
Walking tour: Adrian architecture and walking tour, Tecumseh Art Walk
Wineries: *Cherry Creek Vineyard & Winery:* in an 1870s one-room school; making wines for 100 yrs.
...*J Trees Cellars:* Blissfield
...*Pentamere Winery:* the "five seas" of the Great Lakes; old-fashioned winemaking craftsmanship meets innovative design
...*Southeast Michigan Pioneer Wine Trail:* brochure is available at local wineries
Antique Alley: there are at least 22 antique stores and malls in the county

Blissfield Model Railroad: HO scale of the Chesapeake & Ohio and Clinchfield railroads; 1,300 sq. feet display area with 1,500' of mainline track
Mystery Hill: gravity defying vortex; wax museum, horror show, oddity collections

Old Road Dinner Train: the Murder Mystery Dinner Train on the historic Adrian-Blissfield Railroad

Norm Emmons

X X-TRA STUFF

County fair: *Lenawee County Agricultural Society:* Aug.
Famous people: ...*Entertainment:* Danny Thomas
...*Politics:* Gov. Charles Croswell
Hospitals: Bixby, Herrick Memorial, Thorn Health Center
Large employers: Pro-Medica Health system, Inteva Products (makes injection-molded plastic products), Michigan Department of Corrections (prison), L & W (makes auto parts), Wacker Chemical (makes silicones), Adrian Mall

Y YESTERYEAR

Almost every town in Michigan, no matter how small, had a train station. For everything you ever wanted to know about trains and railroads in Michigan, including Michigan's Internet Railroad History Museum, go to *michiganrailroads.com* and explore the wealth and depth of information they have on trains, depots, train-watching spots, model

NPCR

train club, train museums, tourist trains, a timeline of the rise and fall of trains and much, much more.

Lenawee County is home to the Old Road Dinner Train and Southern Michigan Railroad, both offering train excursions. See 46M, 46W.

Z ZOO & ANIMAL PLACES

3 Bar B Ranch: indoor rodeo, bull riding, team roping, barrel racing, mutton bustin' (children riding goats)

A AGRICULTURE

Land in farms: 26% of county
Number of farms: 800
Size of average farm: 120 acres
Market value of all products: #40 of 83 counties
Crops: ...most acres: corn
...highest $ sales: grain: corn, soybeans, wheat
Livestock: ...largest number: cattle
...highest $ sales: milk & dairy products
Among the top Michigan counties:
• #1- angora goats; mules, burros, & donkeys
Dairy, food and meat processing plants: 18
State ranking for harvested trees: #49 of 83 counties
FYI: Over 1,600 farms in Michigan have 4,400 <u>mules, donkeys and burros</u> and this county has the most farms (66) with the most animals (200+).

Mules are the offspring of a male donkey and a female horse and cannot reproduce. Although the size of an average horse, the mule is stronger, has more endurance and eats less food than a horse. Locally they are popular for pulling wagons and plows and are much beloved by their owners for their intelligence and common sense.

Historically donkeys are from Europe and the smaller burro is from Central America. Donkeys are often kept as guard animals to protect sheep and cattle herds from coyotes and dogs because they have the ability to recognize danger. Both donkeys and burros are kept as pets for their owners and as companions for horses and other animals. luckythreeranch.com, Daryl Schultz

Mules
Alice Welch, USDA

Donkeys
Michigan Farm Bureau

Burro
Alice Welch, USDA

Bold typeface: this indicates that this heading may be repeated in every chapter, providing that the information about the heading is applicable to the county.

B BRIDGE OR BOAT

NPCR

Pontoon boats are versatile and offer many opportunities for water and sun activities. Whether you call the Chain of Lakes in Livingston and Washtenaw Counties the Portage Chain of Lakes or the Pinckney Chain of Lakes or the Huron River Chain of Lakes, many residents think of it as 'Pontoon Heaven.'

C CELEBRATIONS

<u>Hamburg</u> *Festival and Railroad Days:* ride the train, Taste of Hamburg, tours, night creatures, Sept.

<u>Howell</u> *Melon Festival:* the famous Howell melon, melon ice cream, Made in Michigan arts & crafts, farm tours, melon carving, melon wine, Aug.
The honey sweet Howell melon is a hybrid cantaloupe that thrives in the soil and climate of Livingston County and is the only one sold at the Howell Melon Festival.

Downtown Howell annual events thanks the community for their continued support

Sheryl Smith

...Michigan Challenge Balloon Festival: state championship of hot air ballooning, June

D DEMOGRAPHICS

Population: 181,000   **Persons per sq. mile:** 319
Largest city: Howell   **Population:** 9,500
Largest township: Hamburg   **Population:** 21,200
Largest village: Fowlerville   **Population:** 2,900

Median household income: $46,700
Owner-occupied median house value: $77,000
Persons affiliated with a religious congregation: 37%
Persons below poverty level: 15%
Students receiving school lunch subsidy: 12% (#83/MI)

E ENVIRONMENT

Livingston County is blessed with a rich diversity of natural features like lakes, wetlands and a variety of forests, farmlands and abundant wildlife. The Livingston Land Conservancy works with landowners and communities to protect the open space in the county. The fastest growing means of protecting land is the conservation easement, a legal agreement between the landowner and a land trust that permanently limits the scope and type of development while leaving the land in private ownership. Each conservation easement is unique, specifically tailored to the particular land being protected as well as to the particular situation of the landowner. livingstonlandconservancy.org

F FLORA & FAUNA

Field bindweed, also called wild morning glory, is a pesky plant that winds around or binds other plants and can smother and kill them.

Unlike honeybees (see 8A) that use hives, bumblebees make their nests in a protected niche like underground holes, holes in walls or trees, or under rocks. If threatened, they can sting more than once. There are 200 different bee species in Michigan and all are important to the pollination process.

G GOVERNMENT

County: ...created: 1833 ...organized: 1836
...originally part of: Shiawassee, Washtenaw Counties
Size: 375,000 acres / 568 sq. miles (45 of 83 counties)
The county has 2 cities, 2 villages, 16 townships with 3 as charter townships, 4 unincorporated communities and 6 school districts.

County seat: Howell
...Homestead property tax: 37 mills
Motto: Brighton: *Where quality is a way of life...*
...Hamburg Twp.: *a great place to grow*
...Hell: *The Hysterical Town*

H HISTORICAL MARKERS 12 of 28

Ann Arbor Railroad: 1885, Howell raised $20,000 to induce the Toledo, Ann Arbor & Northern Michigan Railroad to the town; later the railroad was renamed the Ann Arbor Railroad, 1895; see 47M

Brighton District No. 8 School: 1885-1956, now the Brighton Area Historical Museum.

Brighton Village Cemetery: 1837, 17% of burials are for children under 10 years old, a reminder of the hardships faced by early Michiganians

Florence B. Deering Museum: 1891, in a former general mercantile store and now a museum; named after the local librarian who collected and assembled Hartland memorabilia

Frank Hecox House: 1887, Second Empire style; with mansard roof, it is the 'house of seven gables'

245

Howell Carnegie Library: 1906, Neoclassical style; steel entrepreneur Andrew Carnegie funded over 2,500 free public libraries throughout the English-speaking world. See 12Y.

Michigan State Historic Preservation Office

Michigan State Historic Preservation Office

Kinsley Bingham: 1818-1861, house is Greek Revival style; in 1843 at age 25 he left NY and said "Give me $500 and let me go to Michigan and I'll be governor in two years." He was elected the nation's first Republican governor in 1854.

Old Town Hall: 1878, now home of City of Brighton Arts, Culture and History Center

George O. Winegar

St. Augustine Church: 1895, High Victorian Gothic style; this church in Howell was elaborate for a rural community.

St. Stephen's: 1844, funds for the building were solicited from back East and Hamburg, Germany

Spanish American War Regiments: 1898, ten men volunteered for every one who could be accepted into the military.

Tom Walker's Grist Mill: from 1869 to 1969, grain was ground for no more than 7 cents a bag; (now the Parshallville Grist Mill that makes apple cider)

National Register of Historic Places: 12 listings
State Historic Sites: 34 listings

I INFORMATION

Chamber of Commerce: Brighton, Hartland, Howell; *PLHH:* Pinckney, Lakeland, Hamburg, Hell

Visitor: Livingston County Convention and Visitors Bureau, 800-686-8474, lccvb.org

J JOKES

You might be a certified MSU Master Gardener if…

…you and your spouse, both master gardeners, have his and her flower beds.

…everyone at work is your new best friend during tomato season.

…the highlight of your Disney Vacation was the Behind the Seeds Tour of Living with the Land.

…you're out of space in your yard so you start planting flowers in your neighbor's yard.

…you can't leave town in July or August because there's another vegetable ripe every week.

…earthworms, frogs, bluebirds and bats are your friends.

…you love the smell of newly turned soil and the feel of the dirt between your fingers.

…you never cease to be amazed at a sprouting seed.

K KINSMAN

Race	Ancestry
American Indian: <1%	German: 21%
Asian: <1%	Irish: 12%
Black/African American: <1%	English: 11%
Hispanic or Latino: 2%	Polish: 10%
Other: 2%	U.S./American: 85
White: 97%	Italian: 4%

L LIGHTHOUSE OR LANDMARK

NPCR

The 4,000 acres of forests, meadows and lakes, and the Huron River of the Island Lake State Recreation Area are part of 50,000 acres of parks and recreation areas in this county. And yes, there are islands in Island Lake. Get the 'up north' experience in southeast Michigan. This park has the largest state park shooting range and a hot air balloon port.

ℳ MUSEUMS

Brighton *Area Historical Society:* operates the 1885 Lyon School and gives historical tours of area

Fowlerville *Livingston Centre Historical Village:* 1900s buildings from around the county

Hamburg *Historical Museum:* in a historic building

Hartland *Deering Museum:* in the Old Town Hall

Howell *Depot Museum:* collection of artifacts

Livingston *County Courthouse:* 1889, restored; see 47G

N NATURAL RESOURCES

Elevation: 800 – 1,000 feet
Physiography: hilly uplands, rolling plains

Forest type: oak-hickory, maple-beech
Public/private forests: 27% of county

Water in county: 2% of county
   Lakes: 160   **...largest:** Whitmore
   Rivers: Red Cedar (& Middle and West Branch), Portage, Shiawassee (shy a WAH see)
   Rivers & streams: 470 miles

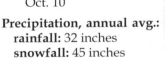

Growing season, avg.: 158 days (1-2 temp. zones)
Last freeze, avg.: May 10

First freeze, avg.: Oct. 5 – Oct. 10

Precipitation, annual avg.:
   rainfall: 32 inches
   snowfall: 45 inches
Temperature (F), avg.: January: high 28°, low 14°
                   July: high 81°, low 60°
  Annual: >90°: 7 days, **<0°:** 11 days
Tornadoes (1930-2010): 24

O ORIGINS

Brighton:[c,ct] many settlers from Brighton, NY; 1832

Fowlerville:[v] first settler, Ralph Fowler; 1836

Green Oak:[ct] many openings in the oak forests; 1830

Gregory:[u] farmer, Halstead Gregory; <1884

Hamburg:[t] early settlers from Hamburg, Germany; 1835

Hartland:[u,t] named after its township; 1831

Hell:[u] after a distillery was built, there were numerous drunken fights and many a wife would say that her husband had "gone to Hell;" 1841

Howell:[c,t] named after its township; 1834

Livingston:[co] Edward Livingston, U.S. Secretary of State under President Andrew Jackson

Oak Grove:[u] a better name than Chemungville; 1839

Pinckney:[v] middle name of the town founder's brother; 1836

P PARKS

National: 0 **State:** 6 **County:** 1 **Local:** 9
Number of campsites: 1,500
State Game Area: Gregory, Oak Grove
State Linear Trail Park: (13 miles) Lakeland

State Recreation Area:
Brighton: 5,000 acres, high irregular hill ranges, oak forest, thick hedgerow, open space, grassy & shrub marshes, dense swamp, timber, several lakes; horse camp and trails, camping, boating, hunting, fishing

...*Island Lake:*[ww,wba] see 47L

...*Pinckney:* 11,000 acres, 40 miles of multi-use trails & horse trails offer backcountry experience; boating, swimming, chain of excellent fishing lakes

State Wildlife Area: Unadillia

Other: *Howell Conference & Nature Center:* 270 acres, owned by the Presbytery of Detroit, its mission is to provide opportunities for mental, physical and spiritual growth designed to enhance our relationships with God, nature, and our brothers and sister throughout the world; educational programs, wildlife rehabilitation; see 47Z

...*Huron-Clinton Metropolitan Authority:* regional special park district of Livingston, Macomb, Oakland, Washtenaw and Wayne Counties; 13 Metroparks, 24,000 acres along the Huron and Clinton Rivers; picnic, swimming, fishing, boating, hiking, golfing, nature study and winter sports are offered; included in this county:

* *Huron Meadows Metropark:* 1,500 acres, get that 'up north' feeling; golf, water ski, cc ski, hike
* *Kensington Metropark:* 4,500 acres of wooded, hilly terrain; 1,200 acre Kent Lake; splash park, Island Queen tour boat, golf & disc course, nature center, farm center, bike, hike, fish, swim, boating

...*Wildflower Viewing Site:*[wba] MDOT rest area, eastbound I-96

Q QUOTE FROM THE LOCALS

"Livingston County is made up of an eclectic blend of unique communities… Enjoy the area's hamlet-like, picturesque villages by taking a scenic drive through the country. Winding curves, gentle rolling hills, serene lakes, lush farmlands and vast canopies of tall graceful trees are just a few of the pleasing landscapes a visitor can expect to see. Outstanding seasonal recreational opportunities include Michigan's tallest outdoor climbing wall, hiking, biking, boating, fishing, canoeing, horseback riding, in-line skating, zip line and a high ropes adventure course." LCCVB visitors guide

R RECREATION & SPORTS

Golf courses: 14
Hiking/skiing/mountain biking trails: 60 miles
Horse racing: harness racing at the fairgrounds
Public access sites: 11
Public recreational land: 5% of county
Rail-trail: (50 miles) Brighton Recreation Area, Island Lake State Park, Lakeland
State/federal wild/scenic/natural river: 20 miles of the Huron River
Hell Survivors: world-renowned paintball players
Mt. Brighton Ski: 130 acres, 26 trails, 250' vertical drop; terrain park

S STATE OF MICHIGAN

The Year in the Life of a Michigan Home Gardener
- *January:* sitting by the fireplace browsing through the seed catalogues and longing for more sunshine and warm weather
- *February:* strolling through the greenhouse just to smell the soil and feel the warmth of the sun
- *March:* the days are above freezing, the sap is running and it's maple syrup time
- *April:* time to get out the rototiller and prepare the ground for planting
- *May:* asparagus and rhubarb are the first to push their way up from the newly warming ground; now it's finally time to plant the annual crops
- *June:* picking strawberries and making strawberry pies, strawberry freezer jam and strawberry shortcake

- *July:* picking sweet cherries and blueberries and praying for enough rain and heat units for the rest of the summer; hoeing, weeding, hoeing, weeding, hoeing, weeding

- *August:* feasting on melons, peaches, sweet corn, tomatoes, green beans and new potatoes; canning and freezing the summer bounty to enjoy all winter long; the flowers are beautiful, too
NPCR

- *September:* picking apples, making cider and pies
- *October:* carving pumpkins, savoring baked butternut squash and decorating with gourds
- *November:* now is the time to prepare the garden for its long winter's sleep
- *December:* cut your own Christmas tree; enjoying all your canned and frozen fruits and vegetables

NPCR

T TRAVEL

Airport: Brighton Field, Livingston County
Distance to Lansing: 45 miles
Main roads: I-96, US-23, M-36, M-59, M-106
Memorial Highways: I-96, *AmVets MH:* see 19T
…US-23, *United Spanish War Veterans MH:* see 1T
…M-59, *Vietnam Veterans MH:* in honor of those who served and died (58,000 Americans) in the Vietnam War (1957-1975)

U UNIVERSITIES & COLLEGES

Cleary University: see 81U
Damnation University: spoof website where you can get your diploma from DAM-U; get over sixty spoof diplomas like the one from the School of Agriculture with a Bachelor's Degree in Green Thumbology.
Mott Community College, Livingston Center: M-TEC

V VARIETY

Wallace Berrie & Co, Inc.

Gardening is America's # 1 hobby. And in any garden, or lawn, at least a *few* weeds will grow. Good luck!

W WANDERLUST

Agri-tourism: *DeGroot's Strawberries:* U-pick, wagon rides, apples

...*Farm Markets:* Brighton, Fowlerville, Hartland, Sundays in Howell, Winter Marketplace

...*Roeske Farms:* Hartland Farms; turkeys, beef, pigs, eggs, veggies

...*Runkel Orchards:* only have the Runkel apple variety

...*Spicer Orchards Farm Market, Cider Mill & Winery:* apples, strawberries, blueberries, peaches, tomatoes, sweet corn, wagon rides, U-pick

...*Turk Farms:* farming the old fashioned way; pork, lamb, chicken, rabbit, goat, eggs, fruit, veggies

Cultural: Brighton Art Guild, Brighton Center for the Performing Arts, Howell Opera House, Hartland Music Hall

Fall colors: middle October

Live theater: Hartland Players, Livingston Players, Community Theatre of Howell, Phoenix Players, Pinckney Players

MotorCities National Heritage Area: yes

Shopping mall: Green Oak Village Mall, Tanger Outlet Center

Walking tour: 7 tours of Historic Howell

Deb Schmucker

Wineries: *Howell's MainStreet Winery:* taste the wines and take the ghost tour, too

...*Spicer's Carriage House Cellars:* orchard grown fruit wines, grape wines, hard cider blends

Heavenly Scent Herb Farm: flowers, herbs, workshops, festivals, gift shop, delightful & beautiful

Hell: stop by this small unincorporated community and shop at Screams Ice Cream and Hell in a Hand Basket (gifts), or just enjoy the splendid out doors of this family friendly destination.

NPCR

Livingston Antique Outlet: Michigan's largest indoor antique mall

X X-TRA STUFF

County fair: *Fowlerville Agricultural Society:* July

Famous people: ...*Politics*: Kinsley Bingham (see 47H)

...*Sports*: Charlie Gehringer

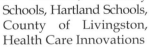

National Baseball Hall of Fame Library, Cooperstown, New York

Hospitals: St. Joseph Mercy, Woodland Health Center

Large employers: Citizen Insurance Co. of America, St. Joseph Mercy Hospital, Ogihara America (stamped auto parts), Intier Automotive Interiors, Pinckney Schools, Hartland Schools, County of Livingston, Health Care Innovations

NPCR

Castaway Café: Michigan's largest indoor play structure for children and adults

Y YESTERYEAR

"Following the War of 1812, the Federal Government provided any veteran of that war with <u>160 acres of free land in Michigan</u>. However, surveyors indicated that the land in and around Livingston County was extremely wet and poorly suited for farming. Since this caused many of the soldiers to accept free land in Missouri rather than in Michigan, the Governor requested a new survey. This second survey found much of the rolling hills and sparsely wooded land well suited for agricultural uses. Rather than give this exceptional land away, the State began to sell the originally free section parcels for $2.00 to $3.00 per acre.

"Indian trail ways through Livingston County formed some of the major transportation corridors of today, including Grand River Ave. and White Lake Road. The development of the Grand River Road from Detroit to Lansing proved to be an impetus to growth with a stagecoach stop in Howell." co.Livingston.mi.us

NPCR-2

Z ZOO & ANIMAL PLACES

Petting zoo: DeGroot's Strawberry Farm
Watchable Wildlife Viewing Areas:ᵂᵂ see 47P
Zoo: *Wild Wonders Wildlife Park:* woodland, meadows and wetland habitats with their animals; part of the Howell Conference & Nature Center; see 47P
Highwater Corral at Hill Creek Ranch: trail rides through 1,000 acres

NPCR

NPCR

Discovering Michigan County by County is the only book where all counties are treated equal. Every county has a story to tell. There's no other book or online site like it!

A AGRICULTURE

Land in farms: 20% of county
Number of farms: 475
Size of average farm: 130 acres
Market value of all products: #37 of 83 counties
Crops: ...most acres: soybeans
...highest $ sales: nursery, greenhouse, floriculture
Livestock: ...largest number: cattle & calves
...highest $ sales: cattle & calves
Among the top Michigan counties:
- #1- Brussels sprouts, collard greens, dill, herbs, kale, lettuce, sweet corn, watermelon
- #2- beets, cut flowers & florist greens, nursery stock, pumpkins

Dairy, food and meat processing plants: 66
State ranking for harvested trees: #73 of 83 counties
FYI: There are almost 10,000 acres of sweet corn grown in Michigan on over 1,000 farms producing over 100 million pounds. This county grows the most with about 10% of the crop. Sweet corn is best eaten the day it is picked, so find your nearest local farm market and visit often! There are many delicious varieties grown throughout the state and everyone has their favorite. A summer meal of sweet corn, fresh tomatoes, fresh green beans and new potatoes from your own garden or the local farm market, is one of the things that make summer in Michigan so wonderful!

Sweet corn grown for human consumption and field corn grown for animal feed or ethanol are not the same thing. MDA

Michigan Farm Bureau

B BRIDGE or BOAT

NPCR

Macomb County is the fresh water boating capital of the world with more registered pleasure boats (40,000) than any other county in the U.S. It has 75 marinas and 8,500 boat slips. See 50L.

C CELEBRATIONS

<u>Mount Clemens</u> *Stars & Stripes Festival:* fireworks, music, July

Robert Eichelberger

<u>Richmond</u> *Area Good Old Days Festival:* voted Michigan's Best Small Town Festival, Sept.

<u>Romeo</u> *The Michigan Peach Festival of Romeo:* homemade peach pies, fly-in, peachy queen contest, car show, sports tournaments, night parade, children's parade, floral parade, Sept.

<u>Sterling Heights</u> *Sterling Fest:* bands, music, concerts, food, arts & crafts, midway, June

D DEMOGRAPHICS

Population: 841,000   **Persons per sq. mile:** 1,752
Largest city: Warren   **Population:** 134,000
   2nd largest city: Sterling Heights   Population: 130,000
   3rd largest city: St. Clair Shores   Population: 54,700
Largest township: Clinton   **Population:** 96,800
   2nd largest twp.: Macomb   Population: 79,600
   3rd largest twp.: Shelby   Population: 73,800
Largest village: New Haven   **Population:** 4,600
Median household income: $50,700 (county)
   Warren: $44,600
   Sterling Heights: $61,000
   St. Clair Shores: $49,000
Owner-occupied median house value: $164,000
Persons affiliated with a religious congregation: 44%
Persons below poverty level: 11%
Students receiving school lunch subsidy: 28%

E ENVIRONMENT

<u>Michigan Green Schools</u> is a non-profit agency dedicated to assisting all Michigan schools, public and private, in achieving environmental goals. These goals include protecting the air, land, water and animals of our state, along with world outreach through good ecological practices and teaching of educational stewardship. It began as an idea from students and teachers of Hartland Consolidated School District (Livingston County) in 2005 and was signed into state legislation in 2006. There are 20 Points of Energy and Environmental Savings Activities that schools can

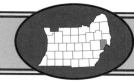
do. If they participate in 10 activities, they are a Green School; if they do 15, they are an Emerald School; and if they do all 20 points, they are an Evergreen School. School enrollment in the program is voluntary and annual, and in 2010 there were over 500 participating schools statewide and 70 of them were in Macomb County. michigangreenschool.us

F FLORA & FAUNA

Dr. Thomas G. Barnes, USFWS

Bloodroot is a spring woodland flower that is 8"-15" tall. The roots contain a reddish sap that historically has been used as a red dye and as a treatment for warts.

Craig Koopie, USFWS

The Peregrine Falcon is pictured on the Macomb County website logo. As it dives for its prey of other birds or animals, it can reach speeds of 200 mph, making it the fastest animal on earth.

G GOVERNMENT

County: ...created: 1818 **...organized:** 1818
...originally part of: Wayne County
Size: 310,000 acres / 480 sq. miles (75 of 83 counties)
The county has 12 cities, 3 villages, 11 townships with 5 as charter townships, 1 unincorporated community and 23 school districts.

Kelly Turner

NPCR

County seat: Mount Clemens
...Homestead property tax: 44 mills
Motto: <u>Armada</u>: *A rich past and a bright future*
...<u>Center Line</u>: *Out of the past   Into the future...*
...<u>Chesterfield</u>: *the gateway to Anchor Bay*
...<u>Eastpointe</u>: *Gateway to Macomb County*
...<u>Ray</u>: *the jewel of Macomb County*
...<u>Richmond</u>: *With Time for You*

H HISTORICAL MARKERS 29 of 58

Alexander Macomb: War of 1812 hero, Chief Army Engineer who built military roads in the Great Lakes area, Commander in Chief of U.S. Army from 1828-1841

Crocker House: 1869, moved in 1908, moved again in 1976 to this location; now the Crocker House Museum; see 50M

Detroit Arsenal Tank Plant: 1941, built over 22,000 tanks (one-quarter of U.S. tank production) during WWII; closed in 1997

Edsel & Eleanor Ford House: 1927, the design and many of the materials came from England; on an 87-acre estate; house is now available for public use

Robert Eichelberger

Erin-Warren Fractional District No. 2 School: 1872-1921, called the Halfway School in the village of Halfway (now Eastpointe), midway between Mt. Clemens and Detroit; now owned by the East Point Historical Society

General Motors Technical Center: between 1949-1985, 31 International Style buildings were built; is a model corporate research and development park

Gov. Alex Groesbeck: 1872-1953, 3-term Michigan

Gov. Alex Groesbeck: 1872-1953, 3-term Michigan governor in the 1920s; M-97 in named after him.

Baltimore's mineral bath & summer resort era; now owned by the New Baltimore Historical Society

Holcombe Beach: 9,000 BC; in 1961, archeologists found evidence of an early Paleo-Indian settlement living here in tundra-like terrain

Kolping Chapel: 1932, Neo-Gothic structure is reminiscent of European wayside shrines; made from stones and shells from around the world

Lake St. Clair: 1679, French explorers entered the lake on Aug. 12, the feast day of Sainte Claire of Assisi, who started the Franciscan nuns

Michigan State Historic Preservation Office

Loren Andrus House: 1860, Michigan's most elaborate remaining Octagon house, said to be a spacious design that offered healthier air circulation and an abundance of light

Methodist Episcopal Church: 1926, local paper called it a "Monument to Unity of Action"

Milk River Settlement: was called L'Anse Creuse, meaning "deep bay"

Mount Clemens Mineral Bath Industry: was a world-renowned spa center from 1843 to 1940

Packard Proving Grounds: 1929 complex of buildings, laboratories, test tracks; Packard Motor Car Company set the standard for luxury and design

Richmond Center for the Performing Arts: 1887, once a Gothic Revival-style church

Robert Eichelberger

Sacred Heart Church: 1861, German, Belgian, Irish & French families built a log structure seating 300

Saint Joseph Sanitarium and Bath House: 1899, Mt. Clemens was called "The Great Health & Pleasure Resort of Michigan"

Sanford/Weller House: 1878, Victorian era Eastlake Style remodeled in 1920s to reflect the 'more modern' Colonial Revival style

Selfridge Field: 1917, Lt. Thomas Selfridge, the nation's

Selfridge Field: 1917, Lt. Thomas Selfridge, the nation's first military pilot, was killed in 1908 while flying with Orville Wright.

solid log construction covered with clapboards; now the Selinsky-Green Farm House Museum; see 43 M

Shoreline Interurban Railway: 1898-1927, 26-miles from Mt. Clemens to Detroit; it was a major factor in the growth of Detroit's suburbs.

Spring Hill Farm: 1830s, a shelter in the side of a hill was part of the Underground Railroad; the farm was owned by Joe Louis in the early 1940s.

"The Thing:" 1884, the first recorded self-propelled vehicle in Michigan, with a single cylinder steam engine with a tubular boiler, seated 4 people.

Thomas Edison: 1862, saved the life of the railroad agent's daughter from being hit by a train; in gratitude the agent taught him railroad telegraphy, which provided employment for him for many years; some of his first inventions were based on the telegraph. See 77H, 77M.

Utica Nike Base: 1955-1974, one of 15 missile bases to protect the Detroit area from nuclear attack by the Soviet Union

Village of Warren: retains its individual identity in its historic churches, homes and businesses

William Austin Burt: 1792-1858, legislator, surveyor, millwright; invented the first patented typewriter, solar compass and Equatorial sextant

National Register of Historic Places: 13 listings

State Historic Sites: 65 listings

I   INFORMATION

Chamber of Commerce: *Anchor Bay*: Chesterfield Twp., Ira Twp., Lenox Twp., New Baltimore, New Haven; Eastpointe, Metro East, Richmond, Romeo-Washington, St. Clair Shores, Sterling Heights, Utica, Warren

…Macomb County Chamber of Commerce, 586-493-7600, central-macomb.com

Visitor: Detroit Metro Convention and Visitors Bureau, 800-DETROIT, visitdetroit.com

J   JOKES

You may be an automotive industry retiree if…

…you retired after 30 years of work, at age 48, with a full pension and full medical benefits, just so you could get away from "the shop."

…you expect to collect those benefits until you die at

…you expect to collect those benefits until you die at age 90, and then your 60-year-old third wife can collect them until she dies at age 100.

up to be. After all, how much golfing and fishing can a fella' do?

...you spent seven years in the Jobs Bank program for "laid-off" workers watching TV at the UAW hall and collecting 100% of your salary.

...you LOVE the union.

...working at the "the shop" is now considered the good ol' days and you really do miss it.

K KINSMAN

Race
American Indian: <1%
Asian: 3%
Black/African American: 9%
Hispanic or Latino: 2%
Other: 3%
White: 85%

Ancestry
German: 18%
Polish: 17%
Italian: 14%
Irish: 8%
English: 6%
U.S./American: 4%
French: 4%

L LIGHTHOUSE OR LANDMARK

NPCR

The Nautical Mile, in St. Clair Shores on Lake St. Clair, has the largest concentration of marinas and watercraft in the Midwest. A place for all seasons, it offers attractions, entertainment, dining, shopping, sports, recreation and special events throughout the year. See 50B.

M MUSEUMS

Chesterfield *Twp. Historical Park:* one-room school, log cabin, cobblers shop, working blacksmith shop

Clinton *Twp. Historical Village:* 1880s Moravian Hall;

Clinton *Twp. Historical Village:* 1880s Moravian Hall; locks from Clinton-Kalamazoo Canal, log cabin living history museum

the 1920s Albert Kahn house resembles Cotswold village cottages; see 50H

Mount Clemens *Crocker House Museum:* home & garden walks, authentically decorated rooms

...*Michigan Transit Museum:* in a train depot, to display and operate mass transportation systems, trains, streetcars, elevated trains, caboose; rides

U.S. Government photo by Mr. John Swanson courtesy of the Selfridge Military Air Museum

...*Selfridge Military Air Museum & Air Park:* to preserve the heritage and tradition of the Air National Guard in Michigan; over 30 planes, restoration facilities, gift shop, Adopt-A-Plane

Ray *Wolcott Mill Metropark Historic Center:* old mills, history of American barns, antiques

Michigan State Historic Preservation Office

St. Clair Shores *Selinsky-Green Farmhouse Museum:* learn about early rural 1900s life in this area; see 50H

Sterling Heights *Upton House:* 1887 Victorian Italianate style, quilts, military memorabilia

Warren *Bunert One-Room School Museum:* the way it used to be

N NATURAL RESOURCES

Elevation: 600 - 800 feet
Physiography: lake-border plains, rolling plains

Forest type: oak-hickory, elm-ash-cottonwood, maple-beech
Public/private forests: 20% of county

Water in county: <1% of county
  Bay: Anchor, L'Anse Creuse
  Lakes: 40   ...**largest:** Lake St. Clair
  Rivers: Au Vase, Clinton, Milk
  Rivers & streams: 300 miles

NPCR

Growing season, avg.: 174 days (#2/MI) (3-4 temp. zones)

Last freeze, avg.: April 25 – May 10

First freeze, avg.: Oct. 10 – Oct. 20

Precipitation, annual avg.:
rainfall: 28 inches
snowfall: 34 inches

NPCR

Temperature (F), avg.: **January:** high 30°, low 17°
July: high 82°, low 62°

Annual: >90°: 8 days, **<0°:** 5 days
Tornadoes (1930-2010): 19

O ORIGINS

Armada:ᵛ,ᵗ (ar MAY da) unknown meaning; 1834

Center Line:ᶜ the middle of three American Indian trails from the fort at Detroit to the trading posts of the north; 1863

Chesterfield:ᶜᵗ English Lord Chesterfield; 1830
_{chesterfieldtwp.org}

Clinton:ᶜᵗ NY Gov. DeWitt Clinton

Eastpointe:ᶜ formerly East Detroit; 1831

Fraser:ᶜ village founder, Alex Fraser; 1857

Harrison:ᶜᵗ 1859

Macomb:ᶜᵒ Gen. Alexander Macomb, see 50H

Memphis:ᶜ named after Memphis, Egypt, and means "a place of good abode;" 1834

Mount Clemens:ᶜ Christian Clemens bought a distillery here and was the first postmaster; 1795

New Baltimore:ᶜ 1796

New Haven:ᵛ 1835

Richmond:ᶜ named after Richmond, NY; 1837

Romeo:ᵛ lady who suggested it thought it was short, musical, classical and uncommon; 1821 _{villageofromeo.org}

Roseville:ᶜ tavern-keeper, William Rose; 1836

Shelby:ᶜᵗ Gen. Isaac Shelby (1759-1826) was the first governor of Kentucky; 1824

St. Clair Shores:ᶜ on Lake St. Clair; 1779

Sterling Heights:ᶜ first settler, Azariah Sterling; 1835

Utica:ᶜ (u DUH ca) many settlers from Utica, NY; 1817

Warren:ᶜ Gen. Joseph Warren (1741-1775)was a doctor and Major General who served as a private soldier; he was killed in the 1775 Battle of Bunker Hill in Boston, MA; 1837

Washington:ᶜᵗ President George Washington; 1821

P PARKS

National: 0 **State:** 2 **County:** 4 **Local:** 125
Number of campsites: 160
State Park: *Wetzel:* 900 acres, undeveloped, hiking, hunting, snowmobiling, cross-country skiing

Robert Eichelberger

State Game Area: Chesterfield Twp., St. Clair Twp.

State Recreation Area: *Shadbush Tract Nature Study Area:* 70 acres, on the Clinton River, tamarack swamp, unusual plants

State Wildlife Area: Salt River Marsh

County: *Freedom Hill:* 100 acres, pavilions, picnic areas, nature trail, outdoor amphitheatre

• **Other:** *Huron-Clinton Metropolitan Authority:* see 47P; included in this county (all have golf courses):

• *Metro Beach Metro-park:*ʷʷ 770 acres, nature center, 1-mile shoreline trail on Lake St. Clair Metropark, boardwalk, 3 marinas, swimming pool

NPCR

• *Stony Creek Metropark:* 4,500 acres, "up north" feeling, lush woodlands, lake, wetlands, tall grass prairies, nature center

• *Wolcott Mill Metropark:* 2,600 acres, 4 parks in one: a current working farm, 1840s Wolcott Mill, Historic Center, and woods and trails

Q QUOTE FROM THE LOCALS

"From upscale cosmopolitan centers to quintessential small towns and villages, Macomb County offers lifestyle choices for every taste and preference. And, whatever the neighborhood, Macomb County offers the most affordable housing in the region – partly due to the consistently low tax base, affordable homeowner and car insurance rates, and utility rates. People who live (and work) in Macomb County have access to all of the "extras" that constitute quality of life issues: top rated public schools, recreation and green space, places to go and things to do including 2,100 restaurants, shopping including 4 malls, and 40 farm markets, and 6 hospitals." _{macombcounty.mi.gov}

R RECREATION & SPORTS

Golf courses: 47
Great Lakes marinas: 75   **Boat slips:** 8,500 (#1/MI)
Hiking/skiing/mountain biking trails: 10 miles
Public access sites: 6
Public recreational land: 3% of county
Rail-trail: (50 miles) Clinton River Spillway, Macomb County Hike & Bike, Macomb Orchard Trail, Stoney Creek Metropark

NPCR

Recreational harbor: Metro Beach Metropark Marina, Mt. Clemens Harbor of Refuge

S STATE OF MICHIGAN

Bicyclists have all the same rights and responsibilities as the driver of any other vehicle and can be ticketed for violating Michigan traffic laws. One or more of the following behaviors cause more than half of all urban car-bike crashes:
Cyclists:
1. Cycling against the direction of traffic
2. Failure to yield when required
3. Running a stop sign or red light
4. Cycling at night without required lighting
5. Riding into a street at mid-block
Motorists:
1. Failure to yield to a cyclist when required
2. Unsafely passing a cyclist
3. Right or left turn immediately in front of a cyclist
4. Driving too fast for conditions
5. Opening driver-side door into a cyclist's path[Michigan.gov]

T TRAVEL

Airport: Berz-Macomb, Macomb, Romeo
Bus: Greyhound, SMART
Circle Tour: Great Lakes via I-94
County road names: ...east/west: Mile roads from 8 Mile to 38 Mile Rd.; see 44T
Distance to Lansing: 90 miles
Main roads: I-75, I-96, I-696, M-3, M-28, M-53, M-59, M-97, M-102
Memorial Highways: I-94, *James O'Hara Freeway:* he (1925-1989) was a U.S. Representative from Michigan from 1958 to 1977 and was one of the architects of the Great Society

...I-696, *Walter P. Reuther Hwy.:* see 63T
...M-3, *Ronald W. Reagan MH:* he (1911-2004) was President of the U.S. from 1981-1989
...M-53, *Christopher Columbus Freeway:* an Italian (1451-1506) who is given credit for discovering America for Spain, this road honors all Italians in Michigan
...M-53, *Earle MH:* see 44T
...M-53, *POW/MIA Freeway:* in honor of those Prisoners of War and Missing in Action in all wars
...M-59, *Veterans MH*
...M-59, *Vietnam Veterans MH:* see 47T
...M-102, *Columbus MH:* an Italian (1451-1506) who is given credit for discovering America for Spain, this road honors all his many achievements

U UNIVERSITIES & COLLEGES

Baker College of Mt. Clemens: see 25U
Davenport University: see 13U
Macomb Community College: est. 1954, 59,000 students. It is the largest grantor of Associate's Degrees in Michigan, ranking it in the top 2% nationally; 3 campuses; M-TEC. MCCAA, Monarchs
University of Phoenix: see 25U

V VARIETY

Kelly Turner

Selfridge Air National Guard Base is home to the 127th Wing that flies KC-135 and A-10 planes. In addition, every branch of the military has a presence on this base.

W WANDERLUST

Agri-tourism: *Backyard Boutique:* fresh cut flowers, designer pumpkins
...*Blake's Big Apple:* U-pick, apples, strawberries, cherries, bakery, tours, wagon rides

…*Blake's Orchard:* apples, peaches, veggies, pumpkins, Christmas trees, bakery, wagon rides

…*DeMeulenaere Farms:* asparagus, green beans, broccoli, cherries, blueberries, flowers, Christmas trees

…*Kutchey's Farm Market:* family farm, fruits, veggies, bedding plants

…*Stoney Creek Orchard & Cider Mill:* U-pick, apples, raspberries, tours, maple syrup, market, wagon ride

…*Westview Orchards & Cider Mill of Romeo:* family farm, apples, peaches, bakery, tours, maze, honey

…*Wolcott Mill Metropark Farm Center:* working farm, educational programs and guided tours, animals

…*Farm Markets:* Boyka's, Bruce Twp., Mt. Clemens, Shelby Twp., Vantage Point, Warren

Brewery: Dragonmead Microbrewery, Great Baraboo Brewing Co., Kuhnhenn Brewing Co., Sherwood Brewing Company

Cultural: Anton Art Center, Warren Fine Arts Center, Community Chorus, Concert Band, Symphony Orchestra

Fall colors: middle October

Prentice Drake

Live theater: Richmond Community Theatre, Warren Civic Theatre

MotorCities National Heritage Area: yes

Shopping Mall: Lakeside, Macomb, The Mall at Partridge Creek, Universal

Tour Lake St. Clair: includes 25 destinations on and around Lake St. Clair

X X-TRA STUFF

County fair: *Armada Agricultural Society:* A True Country Fair, Aug.

Famous people: …*Entertainment:* Eminem, Kid Rock, Uncle Kracker

…*Sports:* Dick Engberg

Hospitals: Mount Clemens Regional Medical Center, St. John Macomb, St. John North Shores, Henry Ford Macomb-Clinton Twp., Henry Ford-Warren, Henry Ford-Mt. Clemens

Large employers: General Motors, St. John Health, MI Air National Guard, Chrysler, Ford, Administrative Employer Services (management consulting), General Dynamics Land Systems (makes military amphibian tanks), Mt. Clemens Regional Medical Hospital, U.S. Department of Defense

In 2007, the Michigan Economic Development Corporation listed 16 different Chrysler, Ford and General Motors locations within the county with a total employment of 55,000.

As of 2006, for the 25th consecutive year, Macomb County won more awards from the National Association of Counties than any other county in Michigan.

Y YESTERYEAR

"Michigan Fever" was in full swing beginning in the 1830s. The American Indians had been removed to west of the Mississippi River and that allowed land surveyors to come in and prepare the land to be sold. The Erie Canal had been completed and settlers could get to Detroit via Lake Ontario and Lake Erie. Land was $1.25 per acre in 80-acre plots, cash only. Land speculators bought much of the land at that time and then sold it to the settlers as they came from Europe, back east, Indiana and Ohio. geo/msu.edu See also 5S.

NPCR-2

NPCR-2

Z ZOO & ANIMAL PLACES

Watchable Wildlife Viewing Areas: ww see 50P

Petting zoo: Blake's, Millers Big Red, Westview Orchards, Wolcott Mill Metropark Farm Center

From BIBLIOGRAPHY & NOTES…

W WANDERLUST: We always recommend you call ahead to check on the operating status of any venue!!! Check the Internet for contact information or call the Visitor Information listed in *I INFORMATION* in the chapter.

A AGRICULTURE

Land in farms: 13% of county
Number of farms: 360
Size of average farm: 130 acres
Market value of all products: #59 of 83 counties
Crops: ...most acres: forage land
...highest $ sales: fruits (tart cherries, apples)
Livestock: ...largest number: laying chickens
...highest $ sales: cattle & calves
Among the top Michigan counties:
• #2- (tied)-strawberries
• #5- acres of Christmas trees
• #9- sale of Christmas trees, acres of tart cherry trees
Dairy, food and meat processing plants: 16
State ranking for harvested trees: #39 of 83 counties
FYI: Strawberries are grown in almost every county in Michigan, so there is probably a U-pick farm or farm market not far from you. June is strawberry season in the Lower Peninsula and July is their season in the U.P. Most of the Michigan crop is purchased from local farm markets and eaten fresh. A hand-picked, vine-ripened Michigan strawberry is much more flavorful and juicier than berries purchased at the grocery store other times during the year. Berrien County, the top strawberry county in the state, grows around 110 acres of strawberries, and Manistee and Van Buren counties have about 80 acres each. All strawberries are hand-picked. The value of the Michigan strawberry crop is around 6 million dollars. MDA, USDA

Michigan Farm Bureau

Fresh Michigan strawberries purchased from the local farm market or a roadside stand virtually shout "school is out and summer is here."
NOTE: Who picks Michigan crops? See 51X.

From BIBLIOGRAPHY & NOTES...

C CELEBRATIONS: Most Independence Day and Christmas activities have not been included since most communities have these events.

B BRIDGE OR BOAT

Travel Dynamics International

Manistee is just one of eleven stops for the Great Lakes Cruise Ship *MV Yorktown*. International travelers especially enjoy cruising the upper Great Lakes because of their outstanding natural beauty, the lure of the undeveloped forests, the quaint villages and the ocean-like expanse of the Great Lakes themselves. Travel Dynamics International of New York began providing these tours in 2011.

C CELEBRATIONS

Rick Gleason

Arcadia *Daze:* July
Bear Lake *Days:* July

...Scarecrow Festival: Oct.

Copemish *Heritage Days:* Aug.
Kaleva *Heritage Days:* Aug.
...Log Cabin Outdoor Theater: live entertainment on Fridays in August
Manistee *Manistee National Forest Festival:* boat parade, fish boil, fireworks on Lake Michigan, July; see 51F
...A Chickadee Christmas: at Lake Bluff Bird Sanctuary, Dec.
Marilla *Sugar Bush Fest:* maple-sugaring tours, April
...Strawberry Social: local and homemade, June
Onekama *Concert in the Park:* Mondays, July, Aug.
...Days: Aug.

D DEMOGRAPHICS

Population: 24,800   **Persons per sq. mile:** 46
Largest city: Manistee   **Population:** 6,230
Largest township: Manistee   **Population:** 3,570
Largest village: Eastlake   **Population:** 510
Median household income: $41,000
Owner-occupied median house value: $126,000
Persons affiliated with a religious congregation: 52%
Persons below poverty level: 14%
Students receiving school lunch subsidy: 47%

E ENVIRONMENT

As part of the Michigan Audubon Society, the Lake Bluff Bird Sanctuary was once landscaped as an arboretum and has California Redwood and Giant Sequoia trees among its 70 types of trees and shrubs. But as a major migratory flyway, the sanctuary offers sanctuary to over 170 bird species. The site boasts 76 acres with 1,500 feet of Lake Michigan frontage, maintained trails, overnight accommodations and an onsite manager. There is a Migration Week every September that offers guided bird watching tours and environmental education for young birders and families. michiganaudubon.org

F FLORA & FAUNA

The family of hickory trees can grow to 100' and are known for wood that combines strength, toughness, hardness and flexibility. The wood is used to make bows and cabinetry, its wood chips are used to cure and barbecue meats and its edible nuts are loved by squirrels and people alike.

Donna Dewhurst, USFWS

The Black-capped Chickadee received its name from its most familiar call of *chick-a-dee-dee-dee*. The more *dees*, the greater the alarm the bird is communicating to other chickadees and other species of birds. They are year-round residents in Michigan and a frequent visitor to winter bird feeders.

G GOVERNMENT

County: ...created: 1840 ...organized: 1855
...originally part of: Mackinac, Ottawa, Oceana, Grand Traverse Counties
Size: 358,000 acres / 544 sq. miles (62 of 83 counties)
The county has 1 city, 5 villages, 14 townships with 1 as a charter township, 8 unincorporated communities and 2 school districts.

Rick Gleason

County seat: Manistee
...Homestead property tax: 41 mills
Motto: Manistee: *Victorian Port City*
...Manistee County: *Fishing Capital of the Midwest*
...Kaleva: *It Feels Good*
...Manistee County Convention and Visitors Bureau: *Naturally more*
...Onekama: *The Two Lake Town* [Lake Michigan & Portage Lake]

H HISTORICAL MARKERS 9 of 14

Harriet Quimby: (1875-1912), was the first American woman to receive an aviation license and to fly solo over the English Channel; she died in a plane crash.

The Bottle House: 1941, built of 60,000 glass pop bottles; now the Kaleva Historical Museum; see 51M

Rick Gleason

First Congregational Church: 1892, an architect known as the "father of the skyscraper," designed the beautiful Romanesque church with stained glass widows, soaring rafters, hand-carved pews.

Great Fire of 1871: a hot dry summer and strong winds burned towns up and down the Lake Michigan coast and all the way to Lake Huron. See 74Y.

Michigan State Historic Preservation Office

Kaleva: 1900, founded by Finnish immigrants who took pride in their home, family and country

Manistee City Library: 1905, Beaux Arts Classicism design

Manistee's Fire Hall: 1889, Romanesque Revival style architecture with brick, cut-stone, French plate glass, trimmed with galvanized iron and with a copper covered dome; the first "fire truck" was a horse-drawn steam engine.

Our Savior's Lutheran Church: 1875 Danish architectural features; weathervane-topped spire

Ramsdell Theater: 1903, Thomas Jefferson Ramsdell built this theatre and his son painted the dome and lobby murals.

National Historic Land-marks: *SS City of Milwaukee* is the last remaining traditional Great Lakes passenger and railroad car ferry and is permanently moored in Manistee. It ran from 1930 to 1981 and now is open for tours and overnight stays.

NPCR

National Register of Historic Places: 12 listings
State Historic Sites: 28 listings

I INFORMATION

Chamber of Commerce: Manistee
Visitor: Manistee County Convention and Visitors Bureau, 877-626-4783, visitmanisteecounty.com

J JOKES

You'll *never* hear a Michiganian say that he …
…loves the nine-month orange barrel season.
…gets sick and tired of green trees and green grass.
…wishes that the weather would always be the same.
…sure would like Michigan to have toll roads.
…doesn't like to go to the lake.
…wished we lived in a hurricane area.
…thinks fall foliage colors are boring.

NPCR

K KINSMAN

Race		Ancestry	
American Indian: <1%		German: 24%	
Asian: 3%		Polish: 17%	
Black/African American: 9%		U.S./American: 9%	
Hispanic or Latino: 2%		English: 9%	
Other: 3%		Irish: 7%	
White: 85%		Swedish: 4%	
		French: 4%	

L LIGHTHOUSE OR LANDMARK

Brian Blatz

Walk out to the end of the pier in Lake Michigan to the Manistee North Pierhead Lighthouse and enjoy the beautiful view. Built in 1872 after the Great Fire of 1871 destroyed the previous structure, it is 39' tall and is a symbolic icon of the Victorian Port City of Manistee.

M MUSEUMS

<u>Arcadia</u> *Area Historical Museum:* furniture, railroad, shipping, shipwrecks, the schooner Minnehaha, much more; award-winning website

<u>Brethren</u> *Heritage Museum*

Lyle Matteson, Arcadia Area Historical Society

Rick Gleason

<u>Kaleva</u> *Bottle House Museum:* home made of 60,000 glass bottles; other exhibits; see 51H

...*Railroad Depot:* railroad history, switch engine

<u>Manistee</u> *County Historical Museum:* old time drug store exhibit, period rooms, a very large Victorian antique and photograph display

...*Manistee Art Institute:* a permanent home for Manistee's artistic legacy; visual arts

...*Our Savior's Historical Museum*

<u>Marilla</u> *Historical Museum & Pioneer Place:* period buildings, artifacts, enjoy an old-fashioned tea

N NATURAL RESOURCES

Elevation: <600 - 900 feet
Physiography: lake-border plains, plains, hill-lands

Forest type: oak-hickory, birch-aspen, pine
Public/private forests: 70% of county
FYI: Of the 15 forest types in Michigan, the nut-bearing trees of the oak-hickory hardwood forest were the most widely distributed forest in the eastern half of the U.S. With over 2 million acres it is the third leading forest type in the state. The most common trees in this forest are northern red oak, white oak, black oak, red maple, and big tooth aspen are among the 63 species of trees that make up this forest. _{Michigan Forests Forever}
Legislatively protected sand dunes: 600 acres

Water in county: 3% of county
  Lakes: 40   ...**largest:** Portage Lake
  Rivers: Betsie, Little Manistee, Manistee (MAN is TEE), Pine

Rivers & streams: 275 miles
Great Lakes shoreline: 25 miles of Lake Michigan

Growing season, avg.: 108 days (3-5 temp. zones)
  Last freeze, avg.: May 15 – May 25
  First freeze, avg.: Sept. 25 – Oct. 15
Precipitation, annual avg.: rainfall: 29 inches
                      snowfall: 78 inches
Temperature (F), avg.: January: high 29°, low 9°
               July: high 81°, low 54°
  Annual: >90°: 6 days, **<0°:** 25 days
Tornadoes (1930-2010): 2

O ORIGINS

<u>Arcadia</u>:[u] a mountainous region of Greece; 1866
<u>Bear Lake</u>:[v] lake is shaped like a bear; 1863
<u>Brethren</u>:[u] a colony of settlers from the Church of the Brethren (German Baptist); 1900
<u>Copemish</u>:[v] (COPE mish) American Indian for "big beech tree;" 1883
<u>Eastlake</u>:[v] on the east shore of Manistee Lake; 1870
<u>Kaleva</u>:[v] (KAL a va) from the national Finnish epic poem, *Kalevala;* 1894
<u>Manistee</u>:[c,co] (MAN is TEE) from an American Indian word meaning "the sound the wind makes when it blows through the trees in the forests," or it may mean "a river with islands at the mouth of the river;" 1840
<u>Marilla</u>:[u] sister of original Twp. Board member; 1866
<u>Onekama</u>:[v] (oh NECK a ma) from the American Indian word for Lake Oneka-ma-engk, meaning "portage;" 1845
<u>Wellston</u>:[u] first postmaster, Adelmer Wells; 1885

P PARKS

National: 7   **State:** 3   **County:** 2   **Local:** 34
Number of campsites: 1,600

NPCR

National: *Manistee National Forest:* 87,000 acres, est. in 1938 on logged-out abandoned lands and partly replanted by the CCC

State Forest: (20,000 acres) Pere Marquette
...**Campground:** 1

State Game Area: Manistee River

Rick Gleason

State Park: *Orchard Beach:* 200 acres, on a bluff overlooking Lake Michigan with stairway to beach

Rick Gleason

State Recreation Area: *Tippy Dam:* 78 acres, the only state recreation area in the state with boating access and overnight camping

Other: Manistee River Trail with suspension bridge and waterfall

Hiking/skiing/mountain biking trails: 80 miles
North Country National Scenic Trail: yes
Public access sites: 23
Public recreational land: 31% of county
Rail-trail: (60 miles) Big "M," Irons Area, North County National Scenic Trail, Wellston Area
Recreational harbor: Arcadia Veterans Memorial Marina, Manistee Marina, Portage Lake Harbor of Refuge
State/federal wild/scenic/natural river: 45 miles of the Betsie and Pine Rivers
State-funded snowmobile trails: 110 miles
State recreational public access sites: 23

Rick Gleason

Manistee National Golf & Resort: two par 71 courses

Onekama "Shake Down" Fishing Tournament: May

Q QUOTE FROM THE LOCALS

"'Authentically Manistee has the finest collection of historical buildings in the State of Michigan' states the Michigan Historic Preservation Office. A visit to beautiful Manistee County will take you back in time. You will be swept away to an era when logging, agriculture and the railroad were key elements in developing this great land. Our museums are full of intriguing information and artifacts about the people,

Rick Gleason

places and industries that helped carve out this fascinating and unique area of northwest Michigan. The struggles and triumphs of these early settlers can be felt throughout the area as you explore our museums and view the landscape where they first set foot."

visitmanisteecounty.com

R RECREATION & SPORTS

Auto racing: *Northern Michigan Dragway:* ⅛-mile-asphalt strip track
…*Manistee County Fairgrounds:* ½ mile slightly banked dirt oval track
Blue Ribbon Trout Streams:[1,000] Bear Creek, Pine River
Golf courses: 6
Great Lakes marinas: 20   **Boat slips:** 890

S STATE OF MICHIGAN

There are oil and gas wells in 63 of Michigan's 83 counties with over 11,000 active wells statewide, all in the Lower Peninsula. Fourteen thousand private mineral owners earn more than $80,000,000 in royalties annually. Manistee County is the #2 producer of crude oil with over 100 million barrels and the #2 producer of natural gas with 600 billion cubic feet annually. Michigan-produced barrels of oil provide 4% of the state's annual demand. Michigan's natural resources are a great source of pride to its

Rick Gleason

residents. To preserve and protect these resources, the oil and gas industry works hard to minimize its impact on the environment. State-of-the-art technology has made current operations quieter, cleaner and more efficient than ever before.

wmich.edu/geology

T TRAVEL

Airports: Manistee County Blacker Airport
Circle Tour: Lake Michigan via US-31 & M-22
Distance to Lansing: 130 miles
Historic Heritage Route: M-22 from Manistee to Traverse City

Main roads: US-31, M-42, M-55, M-66

Memorial Highways: US-31, *Blue Star MH*: see 3T
…M-55, *Gold Star MH*: during WWI families who had a relative who died in the war displayed a flag with a gold star; this memorial highway was planted with black walnut trees in 1924.

Northwest Michigan Port of Call Tour: Manistee County Historical Museum, Orchard Beach Aviation (fly along Lake Michigan Shoreline), *SS City of Milwaukee*, Water Bug Tours (lighthouse and sunset tour on Lake Michigan)

Scenic Drive: Frankfort to Ludington via US-31

U UNIVERSITIES & COLLEGES

West Shore Community College, *Manistee County Center;* see 53U

V VARIETY

The City of Manistee reflects its 1880's lumber town millionaire heritage with elegant mansions and ornate Victorian architecture. During that time, Manistee had more millionaires per capita than anywhere else in the United States. See 51Q.

W WANDERLUST

Agri-tourism: *Urka Farms:* strawberries, U-pick

Brewery: Tahquamenon Falls Brewery & Pub

Casinos: Little River Casino Resort

Cultural: Manistee Art Institute is in the historic Ramsdell Theatre; Manistee Symphony Orchestra

Fall colors: late September to middle October

Live theater: Manistee Civic Players

Walking tours: Manistee Riverwalk, Historic Arcadia, Kaleva Centennial Walkway

Gravity Hill: Arcadia; optical illusion of going uphill when you should be going downhill

Kaleva Grasshopper: 4 ft. tall welded metal statue honoring St. Urho who drove the grasshoppers out of Finland and saved the grapes

Rockin' R Ranch: horseback, carriage, stagecoach and hayrides, campfire meals, much more

Victorian Manistee Tours: homes and history

If you arrive early in the morning, you can see this machine cleaning and grooming the Lake Michigan beach in Manistee.

X X-TRA STUFF

American Indian Community: Little River Band of Ottawa Indians

Commercial port: Manistee

County fair: *Manistee County Agricultural Society:* Aug.

Hospital: West Shore Medical Center

Large employers: Little River Band of Ottawa Indians (casino, resort, government), Michigan Department of Corrections, Oaks Correctional Facility, Packaging Corp. of America (makes corrugated containers), West Shore Medical Center

FYI: <u>Migrant labor</u> is an integral part of Michigan agriculture. Harvesting the crops is near the end of the long crop production process. The Michigan Department of Labor lists 38 fruits and vegetables

plus bedding plants, bulbs, hay harvest, nursery plants, sod and Christmas trees on their Migrant and Seasonal Farm Worker Program list. In addition to harvesting, this type of work includes bagging, bailing, cleaning, grading, hoeing, loading, packing, planting, potting, processing, pruning, shearing, shipping, sorting, thinning, training, transplanting and weeding. michiganlabor.org

In an article in the Grand Traverse Insider reviewing a study by the Leelanau County League of Women Voters regarding migrant visa issues, it states " 'Care for and harvesting of crops is a critical, labor-intensive aspect of our agriculture. Without adequate labor, asparagus, apples, or grapes might go unharvested; corn isn't detasseled, and crops are left to rot in the field. The work is difficult and uncomfortable, the hours are long, the weather is a factor, and the jobs are seasonal. Michigan workers don't step up to take agricultural jobs, even with the state's high rate of unemployment. Without workers, our area farmers and processors are at risk of closure or bankruptcy.' "

Half of all Michigan crops need to be harvested by hand. This " 'requires a large labor pool for a very short time-span… Young workers [local] are largely unskilled in agricultural work, and prefer tourism-related summer jobs to short-term harvest work. The same is true of older workers who seek summer employment.' "

Michigan suffers from a chronic shortage of skilled migrant workers, primarily due to the Federal H-2A (seasonal agricultural worker permits) that severely limits the number of legal migrants who are allowed into the entire United States, only 30,000. In addition, the rules and regulations that govern this legislation are overly cumbersome and inflexible to both the grower and the migrant as well. Most state legislators are " 'clueless about the problems facing the agricultural community' and 'a streamlined agricultural migrant visa program that would enhance the potential for agricultural employers to hire legal, skilled workers when needed,' is urgently required.' " morningstarpublications.com 2-20-12

Above all, the Mexican migrants who come to work in Michigan want respect and a good relationship with the growers, good pay and good housing, and plan to return home to Mexico. Overall, the growers consider them decent, hard-working people who will do whatever it takes to get the crops harvested. There is an extensive network of job openings lists and recruitment services to place the right person with a certain skill set in the right job. Good housing for migrant workers is essential to retain good workers who return year after year. Michigan has 870 licensed housing sites including 4,000 living units with a capacity for 23,000 persons. In addition, Michigan has health services, day care and education services for migrant workers and their families. michigan.gov/mdard

The ability of Michigan farmers to increase fruit and vegetable production is limited by the amount of good, reliable and legal migrant farm workers who are allowed into the United States.

Y YESTERYEAR

"Although far from exhausted, Michigan's forest resources are only a fraction of what they once were. They have been wastefully exploited and plundered. Conservation and replanting are only a recent development, but considerable strides have

Never Again.

NPCR-6

been made… In retrospect, it appears regrettable that the exploitation of Michigan's timber resources did not proceed in a slower manner, and that some degree of regulation and control of timber harvesting was not instituted before it was too late. In the twentieth century the people of Michigan have become much more aware of the value of their natural resources and have taken steps to preserve and renew them so far as it is possible to do so." Dunbar We've come a long way in 100 years. See 48A, 53A, and 60A.

Z ZOO & ANIMAL PLACES

Watchable Wildlife Viewing Areas: ww Hamlin Lake Marsh, 100 acres; Lake Bluff Audubon Center, 100 acres; Manistee River; North Country Trail

A AGRICULTURE

Land in farms: 23% of county
Number of farms: 450
Size of average farm: 170 acres
Market value of all products: #42 of 83 counties
Crops: ...most acres: forage land
...highest $ sales: vegetables
Livestock: ...largest number of: cattle & calves
...highest $ sales: milk & dairy products
Among the top Michigan counties:
...#2- asparagus, elk
...#10- acres of fruit & nut trees
Dairy, food and meat processing plants: 20
State ranking for harvested trees: #48 of 83 counties
FYI: Michigan's <u>Fruit Belt</u> consists of parts of 16 counties along the Lake Michigan shoreline from Charlevoix to Berrien County, and even includes 2 counties that are not on Lake Michigan (Kent and Newaygo). The soil (sandy loam), the climate (modifying the extremes of hot and cold), and topography (rolling hills that provide protection from frost) all come together to make excellent fruit growing conditions. Each of the counties has from 1,000 to 25,000 acres of orchards.

Michigan-developed "Red Haven" peaches are famous throughout the country and have become the most widely planted variety of peach in the world. In addition to peaches, other tree fruits include apples, apricots, cherries, nect-  arines, pears, persimmons, and plums and prunes. Most tree fruits are hand picked. Then, of course, there are the berry fruits (see 80A) and grapes (see 11A) too. Michigan is a great place to live and eat!
geo.msu, Michigan.gov/mda

B BRIDGE OR BOAT

Michigan State Historic Preservation Office

The 60-mile trip to Manitowoc, WI, on the *SS Badger* takes four hours. You can rent a stateroom, eat, sleep, watch movies, play games, or sit on the deck and enjoy the sun, the wind and the water while you cross Lake Michigan.

C CELEBRATIONS

<u>Ludington</u> *Fine Arts Fair:* July
...*Sweet Summer Celebration:* of arts, culture: July
...*Gold Coast Artisan Fair:* Aug.
<u>Scottville</u> *West Michigan Old Engine Club:* spring, summer & fall
...*Harvest Festival:* Sept.

D DEMOGRAPHICS

Population: 17,500　**Persons per sq. mile:** 73
Largest city: Ludington　**Population:** 8,100
Largest township: Hamlin　**Population:** 3,400
Largest village: Custer　**Population:** 280
Median household income: $38,000
Owner-occupied median house value: $94,000
Persons affiliated with a religious congregation: 39%
Persons below poverty level: 19%
Students receiving school lunch subsidy: 48%

E ENVIRONMENT

<u>Ludington Pumped Storage Plant</u> is an 840-acre reservoir and is one of the world's largest electric "batteries." To produce electricity, water is pumped in from Lake Michigan during the night. During the day it is pumped back out so that it flows over and turns large

265

turbines on its way back to the lake. Built in the early 1970s, this Consumers Power plant generates enough electricity to serve 1.4 million residential customers. Great care is taken to protect the environment by preventing fish from getting caught in the intake valves. From the observation deck one can observe the beautiful landscaped grounds of the plant as well as Lake Michigan, Stearns Beach and North Pierhead Light. Ludingstonarea.com

F FLORA & FAUNA

Tom Comish, USFWS

The fireweed herb is one of the first plants to grow in burned or logged areas and along roadsides. As other plants are established, it dies out, but its seeds remain in the ground for many years. When another fire or other conditions clear out the area, the seeds germinate and the plants begin to grow again.

Gary M. Stolz, USFWS

The badger likes upland grasslands such as meadows and hayfields. Although an important living component of many Michigan ecosystems and fairly common, they are secretive and rarely seen.

G GOVERNMENT

County: ...created: 1840 **...organized:** 1855
...originally part of: Ottawa, Oceana Counties
Size: 327,000 acres / 495 sq. miles (73 of 83 counties)
The county has 2 cities, 3 villages, 15 townships with 1 as a charter township and 3 school districts.

Rick Gleason

The Mason County Courthouse was built in 1893. It is Richardsonian Romanesque-style structure using Jacobsville sandstone from the U.P.
County seat: Ludington
...Homestead property tax: 38 mills
Motto: Ludington Area Convention and Visitors Bureau: *Up North, Close By*
...Scottville: *Crossroads of Mason County; Home of the world famous Scottville Clown Band*

H HISTORICAL MARKERS 9 of 11

A Bygone Lumbering Town: 1888, Hamlin was wiped out when the milldam broke.
Armistice Day Storm: Nov. 11, 1940, one of Lake Michigan's greatest storms sank and damaged ships
Big Sable Point Lighthouse: 1867, lumber carriers, steamers and tourist still rely on this lighthouse
Marquette's Death: 1675, Father Pere Marquette died somewhere near here along the Lake Michigan shore.
Notipekaago: the place of the skulls, site of a 1700s American Indian battle
SS Pere Marquette 18: 1910, the car ferry mysteriously sank with the crew and many passengers.
Scottville: 1882, two men tossed a coin - the winner, Hiram Scott, named the town and the loser, Charles Bain, named the streets.
SS Badger: built in 1952, renovated in 1992, provides truck, car and passenger service to Wisconsin
Ludington Car Ferries: began in 1875; first railroad car ferry in 1892; first steel railroad car ferry on the Great Lakes in 1897
National Register of Historic Places: 5 listings
State Historic Sites: 18 listings

I INFORMATION

Chamber of Commerce: Ludington & Scottsville

Visitor: Ludington Area Convention and Visitors Bureau, 800-542-4600, pureludington.com

J JOKES

You may be a second-generation southern-born Michiganian if…

…you were in fourth grade before you knew "worsh" was actually spelled and pronounced "wash."

…you cook with bacon drippings.

…you plan to retire to your parents' home town down south.

…using an outhouse is not offensive.

…your parents came to Michigan because that's where the best jobs in America were. You're thinking about leaving Michigan because those good jobs went south, literally and figuratively.

…you wished you lived in the south because all the good country music is about southern living.

K KINSMAN

Race		Ancestry	
American Indian: 1%		German:	24%
Asian: <1%		Polish:	10%
Black/African American: <1%		English:	9%
Hispanic or Latino: 4%		Irish:	8%
Other: 3%		U.S./American:	8%
White: 95%		Swedish:	5%

For many years the author was a step-on-guide, giving tours of the Lansing area to busloads of tourists. She knew from her research in preparing for that job that there was no central location for the information she needed for her tourist clients. So she wrote *Discovering Michigan County by County: Your A-Z Guide to each of the 83 counties in the Great Lakes State* with the casual tourist in mind. She knew that they wanted to know a little bit about a lot of things and enjoyed laughing at some jokes, too. So as you read this book, it is just like having your own personal tour guide.

L LIGHTHOUSE OR LANDMARK

Michigan State Historic Preservation Office

The 112' tall Big Sable Point Lighthouse was built in 1867; you can climb the tower.

M MUSEUMS

<u>Ludington</u> *Rose Hawley Museum:* in White Pine Village; see below

From the Collection of the Mason County Historical Society

…*Historic White Pine Village:* 29 buildings, self-guided tours with signs, artifacts, archives

…*Sandcastles Children's Museum:* hands-on

N NATURAL RESOURCES

Elevation: <600 – 1,000 feet
Physiography: rolling plains, lake border plains, plains

Forest type: maple-beech-hemlock, oak-hickory, pine-oak, aspen-birch
Public/private forests: 53% of county
Legislatively protected sand dunes: 6,400 acres

Water in county: 3% of county
  Lakes: 60   **...largest:** Hamlin Lake
  Rivers: Big Sable River, Lincoln, Pere Marquette
  Rivers & streams: 240 miles
  Great Lakes shoreline: 28 miles of Lake Michigan

Growing season, avg.: 139 days (3-5 temp. zones)
  Last freeze, avg.: May 15 – May 25
  First freeze, avg.: Sept. 20 – Oct. 15
Precipitation, annual avg.:
  rainfall: 32 inches
  snowfall: 83 inches
Temperature (F), avg.:
  January: high 29°, low 16°
  July: high 80°, low 58°
    Annual: >90°: 4 days, <0°: 6 days
Tornadoes (1930-2010): 6

NPCR

O ORIGINS

Custer:[v] Gen. George Custer; 1876
Epworth Heights:[u] the Epworth League (adult education) of the Methodist Episcopal Church; 1894
Fountain:[v] after a local spring; 1882
Free Soil:[v] an anti-slavery party; 1855
Ludington:[c] lumberman, James Ludington; 1847
Mason:[co] Michigan's first and youngest (age 24) governor, Stevens T. Mason; 1855
FYI: Stevens T. Mason (1811-1843) is the youngest state governor in American history. His father was a political appointee, but Stevens was more astute than his father. Lewis Cass (14Y) appointed him Secretary of the Michigan Territory when he was 19 years old and he helped steer Michigan toward statehood. He became Michigan's first governor in 1835 and served until 1840.
Pere Marquette:[ct] at the mouth of the Pere Marquette River; 1847
Scottville:[c] sawmill owner, Mr. Scott; 1874

P PARKS

National: 2 **State:** 2 **County:** 2 **Local:** 18
Number of campsites: 2,270
National: *Manistee National Forest:* 60,000 acres, part of 600,000 acres in 8 counties; prime salmon fishing in forest rivers
State Game Area: Pere Marquette

State Park: *Ludington:*[ww] 5,300 acres, on Lake Michigan, "the queen of the State Parks," sand dunes, ponds, marshlands, forests, sugary white beach sand, Hamlin Lake, interpretive programs

Rick Gleason

State Recreation Area: *Lake Michigan:* 4,500 acres

State Wilderness Area: *Nordhouse Dunes:* 3,500 acres, part of Manistee National Forest, lakeshore dunes ecosystem of 3,500-year-old dunes that are 140' tall

Local: *Cartier Park:* 68 acres, natural area, on Lincoln River
...*Hamlin Lake Beach:* warm, shallow water

...*Stearns Park:* on Lake Michigan, lighthouse, rated #1 public beach in Michigan

Rick Gleason

Q QUOTE FROM THE LOCALS

"Whether you're seeking an exhilarating encounter with nature, a tranquil escape, or a stimulating cultural scene, you've come to the right place. ...From east to west and north to south, Mason County's friendly communities abound with delights. A productive fruit belt, its orchards and fields provide a bounty of goodness found at farmers markets, stands and U-pick operations. Hidden treasures await the keen eye on the antique trail, while the area's colorful maritime legacy is revealed by shipwrecks, an iconic car ferry, lighthouses

and museum displays. We invite you to settle in, stay a while and bask in the many pleasures earning the Ludington area its reputation as one of Michigan's most popular destinations." ludingtonarea.com/destinationguide

R RECREATION & SPORTS

Blue Ribbon Trout Streams: Little Manistee River, Pere Marquette River, Sable, Big Sable

Golf courses: 2

Rick Gleason

Great Lakes marinas: 10
  Boat slips: 500

Hiking/skiing/mountain biking trails: 40 miles
Horse racing: harness racing during fair week
North Country National Scenic Trail: yes
Off-road vehicle trails: 20 miles
Public access sites: 26
Public recreational land: 20% of county

NPCR

Rail-trail: (30 miles) Nordhouse Dunes Trail System, North Country National Scenic Trail

Recreational harbors: Ludington Harbor View, Ludington Municipal Marina

State/federal wild/scenic/natural river: 130 miles (#3/MI) of the Pere Marquette River and streams
State-funded snowmobile trails: 15 miles

Annual Lake Jump: March, to raise money for local non-profits

Ludington Offshore Classic Fishing Tournament: largest freshwater salmon tournament in U.S., July

Ludington Daily News

Snowshoe making classes: Ludington State Park, Jan.
West Shore Community College: ice arena, recreation center

S STATE OF MICHIGAN

Building vibrant, energetic cities that attract jobs, people and opportunity to the state is the key component of the 2003 Michigan economic vision, Cool Cities. It is part of an urban strategy to revitalize communities, build community spirit and retain our "knowledge workers" who are leaving the state in large numbers. The guiding principles for growth revitalization and momentum for the communities are:

- Support innovation
- Grow our talent
- Embrace diversity
- Invest in and build on quality of place
- Think regionally and act locally
- Make new connections

With an emphasis on concepts like the 'Creative Class' and urban pioneers, it is about creating hot jobs in cool neighborhoods and encouraging people to live, work and shop right here in Michigan. Scottville participates in this program. coolcities.com

NPCR

T TRAVEL

Airport: Mason County
Bus: Ludington Mass Transit Authority
Circle Tour: Lake Michigan via US-31
Distance to Lansing: 160 miles
Ferry: *SS Badger* to Manitowoc, WI
Historic Harbortowns: *Ludington:* Big Sable Point Lighthouse, *SS Badger* Car Ferry, White Pine Village
Main roads: US-31, US-10, M-116
Memorial Highways: US-10, *Veterans MH*
…US-31, *Blue Star MH:* see 3T
…US-31, *Pere Marquette HM:* in honor of Pere (French for Father) Jacques Marquette (1637-1675), pioneer missionary and explorer
Scenic Drive: Ludington to Frankfort via US-31 & M-22

U UNIVERSITIES & COLLEGES

West Shore Community College: est. 1966, 1,600 students. WSCC strives to make the community a better place in which to learn, live, work and prosper… with the core values of learning, integrity, excellence, inclusiveness and creativity.

V VARIETY

NPCR

The well-known Scottville Clown Band, with over 300 members, performs annually at over 60 events throughout the state.

W WANDERLUST

Agri-tourism: *Orchard Market:* asparagus, cherries, strawberries, melons, veggies, restaurant
Brewery: Jamesport Brewing Co.
Fall colors: late September to early October

Lighthouse, other: *North Breakwater:* 1936, on the pier at Stearns Park

Live theater: WSCC Center Stage Theater
Driving tour: see the blossoms in the orchards in the spring.

Rick Gleason

Ludington Area Center for the Arts: arts community

Ludington's Historic Murals: on downtown buildings

West Michigan Old Engine Club: 22-acre park, machinery

Rick Gleason

Waterfront Sculpture Park & Playground: on the harbor

X X-TRA STUFF

Commercial port: Ludington
County fair: *West Michigan Fair:* emphasis on local agricultural and domestic pride with youth, adult, commercial and non-profit participation; barn brawl wrestling, rodeo, chuck wagon races, July
Hospitals: Memorial Medical Center of West Mich.
Large employers: Memorial Medical Center, Wal-Mart, Indian Summer Cooperative (makes applesauce, pickles, salad dressings, etc)., Jackson Pandrol (makes RR equipment), Mason County Central School District, Metalworks (makes furniture parts), Ludington Area Schools, Meijer

Rick Gleason

Ludington is the top fishing port on Lake Michigan with over 65 licensed charter boats.

Y YESTERYEAR

A Very Brief History of Michigan
1600s
Pre-1618: Michigan had an estimated 15,000 American Indians throughout the state. See 37Y.
1618: first white man (French) passed through Michigan at what is now Port Huron.
1622: first white men (French) landed at what is now Sault St. Marie.
1668: Father Jacques Marquette (French) started the first permanent settlement in Michigan at Sault St. Marie. See 52L.
1671: the first military outpost was built by the French, on the north side of the Straits of Mackinac (now St. Ignace).
1700s
1701: Fort Pontchartrain was built at what is now Detroit, by Frenchman Antoine de la Mothe Cadillac, to provide security for the fur trading industry.
1715: the military fort in St. Ignace was rebuilt on the south side of the Straits of Mackinac and was called Fort Michilimackinac.
1762: the British took over Fort Detroit.
1783: The Revolutionary War ended and with the Treaty of Paris the territory that is now Michigan was given to the U.S.

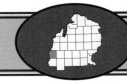
1787: Congress formed the Northwest Territory (NW of the Ohio River) to include the land that would later become Michigan, Ohio, Indiana, Illinois, Wisconsin and part of Minnesota.

1796: the British finally withdrew from Detroit.

1800s

1803: Ohio became a state and Michigan became part of the Territory of Indiana.

1805: the Territory of Michigan was created with Detroit as the capital. See 5S.

1813: Lewis Cass was the military governor at Detroit of the Territory of Michigan. See 14Y.

1818: the great migration from the Eastern states began when the land was opened to public sales. See 5S.

1821: with the signing of the Treaty of Chicago, the Ottawa, Ojibwa and Potawatomi Indians ceded their lands south of the Grand River to the U.S. government. See 37Y.

1825: the Erie Canal (NY) opened and allowed people and goods to move both east and west. See 53Y.

1831: Stevens T. Mason, age 19, became acting governor for the Michigan Territory. See 53O.

1835: Mason was elected as Michigan's first and youngest ever governor. See 53O.

1836: Michigan "lost" the Toledo War and received the Upper Peninsula as a consolation. See 30Y.

1837: Michigan was admitted to the Union as a free state to balance out Arkansas as a slave state.

1847: Lansing became the new state capital. See 33Y.

1861: Michigan soldiers were the first from the west to arrive in Washington DC for the Civil War. See 23Y.

1879: The new (and current) capital building in Lansing was completed. See 33L.

1896: Ransom E. Olds of Lansing and Henry Ford of Dearborn both test gasoline-powered autos. See 82Y.

1900s

1904: Buick Motor Company began in Flint. See 25Y.

1914: Ford Motor Company adopted $5 a day wage for 8 hours of work.

1918: there were over 135,000 Michigan men in WWI.

1941: auto plants were converted to the production of war materials for WWII and Michigan becomes known as the "Arsenal of Democracy." See 58Y.

1957: the Mackinac Bridge was completed. See 49B, 49Y.

1960s: the Motown record industry was born. See 9Y.

1974: Gerald R. Ford became the 38th President of the United States. See 41H.

1992: the fully restored Michigan Capitol was rededicated.

1990s: it was a decade of economic growth when statewide tax cuts were established.

2000s

2000s: the national economic downturn hits Michigan manufacturing very hard; 857,000 jobs were lost. See 13S, 26S.

2010: Michigan is determined to reposition itself as a first-class state in which to live, work and play [Michigan.gov] See Michigan.gov and *Discovering Michigan County by County*, chapters 1 to 83.

Z   ZOO & ANIMAL PLACES

Watchable Wildlife Viewing Areas:[ww] see 53P
Amber Elk Ranch: 103 acres, tours, education, hunt
Llamas Etc: a llama adventure!

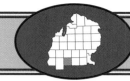
A AGRICULTURE

Land in farms: 32% of county
Number of farms: 850
Size of average farm: 135 acres
Market value of all products: #30 of 83 counties
Crops: ...most acres: forage land
...highest $ sales: grains: corn, soybeans, wheat
Livestock: ...largest number: hogs & pigs
...highest $ sales: hogs & pigs
Among the top Michigan counties:
- #1- alfalfa seed, number of hog farms
- #2- maple syrup, rye for grain, wild hay
- #3- alfalfa, hay, potatoes
- #4- dairy farms, forage land
- #7- number of animal farms

Dairy, food and meat processing plants: 12
State ranking for harvested trees: #40 of 83 counties

FYI: <u>4-H Youth Develop-ment</u> is the youth education program of Michigan State University Extension. Working cooperatively in all 83 Michigan counties with the state and county government, 4-H pro-vides over 275,000 kids

Michigan Farm Bureau

18 USC 707

non-formal educational opportunities to help them thrive in a complex and changing world. Known for its roots in plant and animal education, now the program opportunities are as diverse as the Extension Service and MSU itself. Half of the youth membership lives in rural towns and half of the youths live in towns of more than 10,000 people, including suburbs and large central cities. "I pledge...my HEAD to clearer thinking, my HEART to greater loyalty, my HANDS to larger service, my HEALTH to better living, for my club, my community, my country and my world." Michigan State University Extension

NPCR

NPCR

B BRIDGE OR BOAT

Deb Schmucker

This 250' wooden bridge across the Muskegon River on the Riverwalk in Big Rapids provides handicap accessibility, fishing platforms and benches if you just want to sit and enjoy the scenery.

C CELEBRATIONS

<u>Big Rapids</u> *Riverdays Festival:* music, dawgs, arts & crafts, antique tractors, walk the Riverwalk, Sept.
<u>Morley</u> *Celebration on the Pond:* boat cruise, parade, car & tractor show, baking contest, horseshoes, Aug.

<u>Remus</u> *Wheatland Music Festival:* all ages and abil-ities welcome, 3 stages, all performing arts, all year 'round

Jennifer Marfio

D DEMOGRAPHICS

Population: 42,800 **Persons per sq. mile:** 77
Largest city: Big Rapids **Population:** 10,600
Largest township: Morton **Population:** 3,850
Largest village: Mecosta **Population:** 460
Median household income: $37,800
Owner-occupied median house value: $122,000
Persons affiliated with a religious congregation: 27%
Persons below poverty level: 21%
Students receiving school lunch subsidy: 49%

E ENVIRONMENT

Michigan has about 5.5 million acres of <u>wetlands</u>, half of the original acreage in the state. Landowners can actually restore their land to a wetland if they so desire. Wetlands are vital for surface water filtration and flood control, wildlife habitat, erosion control and are a vital part of the food cycle. Almost every animal is dependent upon wetlands sometime during

its life cycle. Various governing authorities have different definitions of what constitutes a wetland, therefore giving rise to some controversy. Depending on the definition that is applied will determine what soils, plants and water conditions constitute a wetland. Wetlands are commonly referred to as a bog, swamp, or marsh, but they can also be grassy meadows, shrubby fields, or mature forests with high water tables. DNRE; Chuck Nelson

F FLORA & FAUNA

Steve Hillebrand, USFWS

Although it is attractive, purple loosestrife is a persistent invasive species that can be observed along many roadsides. It spreads vigorously in moist soil and crowds out more desirable native wetland species.

George Gentry, USFWS

The Great Blue Heron, the largest heron in North America, is a common sight in shallow water in marshes, ponds and along lakeshore and stream edges; they are somewhat tolerant of human habitat. Its length is around 4' with a wingspan of 6'.

G GOVERNMENT

County: ...created: 1840 **...organized:** 1858
...originally part of: Newaygo County
Size: 365,000 acres / 556 sq. miles (57 of 83 counties)
The county has 1 city, 4 villages, 16 townships with 2 as charter townships, 7 unincorporated communities, 1 Census Designated Place and 5 school districts.

Jennifer Marfio

Jennifer Marfio

County seat: Big Rapids
...Homestead property tax: 38 mills
Motto: Big Rapids: *Small Town Charm With Some Big City Fun*
...Mecosta County: *Visions for the future, Values of the past; Tubing Capital of Michigan*
...Remus: *Farms Friends Families*

H HISTORICAL MARKERS 10 of 12

Anna Howard Shaw: 1847-1919, partly due to extreme hardship as she helped her mother farm their land, she believed women were equal to men; she was a suffragist, ordained minister, medical doctor, orator and temperance leader.

Frank Barry: 1853-1902, owned a sawmill, a planning mill, a livery, 2 general stores, 2 hotels, 2 restaurants, a pharmacy and hardware store in the village that he named after himself, Barryton.

Ferris State College: founded by Woodbridge N. Ferris in 1884 as the Big Rapids Industrial School, to provide practical training for all who have a desire to study and learn. See 54L.

First United Methodist Church: 1907, domed Beaux Arts-style building reflects a trend in using Early Christian architectural forms from the fourth and fifth centuries

Jennifer Marfio

Mineral Well: 1890, mineral baths and the Natural Medicinal Water firm were found in this area.

Negro Settlers: 1860s, they were farmers and woodsmen; the schools and churches of the area were integrated.

Nisbett Block: 1906, large building with a massive decorative exterior of rough-cut granite, elaborate parapets and heavy Romanesque columns.

Jennifer Marfio

Jennifer Marfio

Old Mecosta Jail House: 1893-1965, jail and sheriff's residence; Queen Anne style architecture of red brick with gable and hip roofs and turret

Parish Fish Hatchery: 1881-1964, raised salmon and brown trout fingerlings; now part of a county park

Wheatland Church of Christ: 1893, oldest Disciples of Christ church in western Michigan built mainly by and for blacks

National Register of Historic Places: 2 listings

State Historic Sites: 15 listings

I INFORMATION

Chamber of Commerce: Mecosta County

Visitor: Mecosta County Area Convention and Visitors Bureau, 231-796-7640, bigrapids.org

J JOKES

You might be a Michigan farmer's daughter if…

…4-H has taught you things they don't teach in school anymore, like cooking, canning, sewing, leadership and personal responsibility.

…you actually know people who cook, can and sew, and who take leadership and personal responsibility seriously. You're still deciding if you're going to do that or not.

…you ever wished there was an aftershave that smelled like fresh cut hay.

…unlike the chores of your city friends, your chores actually add to the economic viability of your family. Sometimes you like that and sometimes you don't.

…you know the difference between red, green, blue, yellow and orange tractors and have a definite opinion about the merits and demerits of each one.

…you think that all the other jokes about farmer's daughters aren't very funny.

K KINSMAN

Race	Ancestry
American Indian: <1%	German: 26%
Asian: <1%	English: 11%
Black/African American: 3%	U.S./American: 10%
Hispanic or Latino: 2%	Irish: 9%
Other: 2%	Polish: 5%
White: 94%	Dutch: 4%
	French 4%

L LIGHTHOUSE or LANDMARK

Bob Frei

As the Tubing Capital of Michigan, the Muskegon River in Mecosta County is a popular summer activity for residents and visitors, kids and adults, and even babies and dogs. Bring your own tube or rent one and get pick-up service at the end of your river trip.

M MUSEUMS

<u>Barryton</u> *Area Museum:* a one-room schoolhouse with an attached museum for historical items

<u>Big Rapids</u> at Ferris State University

• *Antique Pharmacy*
• *Card Wildlife Education Center:* a natural history museum, 180 wildlife specimens
• *Jim Crow Museum of Racist Memorabilia:* to promote racial tolerance

...*Mecosta County Historical Museum:* Wooten Desk, historical displays, traveling museum

<u>Remus</u> *Area Historical Society Museum:* Our Past, Your Future; a century of development

Carl Jefts

N NATURAL RESOURCES

Elevation: 800 – 1,000 feet
Physiography: hilly uplands, rolling plains, hill-lands

Forest type: aspen-birch, maple-beech-birch-hemlock, oak-hickory
Public/private forests: 47% of county

Water in county: 2% of county
  Lakes: 85   **...largest:** Chippewa
  Rivers: Chippewa (CHIP a wah), Little Muskegon, Muskegon (muss KEY gun)
  Rivers & streams: 290 miles

Growing season, avg.: 128 days (2 temp. zones)
  Last freeze, avg.: May 15 – May 20
  First freeze, avg.: Sept. 25 – Sept. 30
Precipitation, annual avg.: rainfall: 32 inches
                      snowfall: 71 inches
Temperature (F), avg.: January: high 28°, low 11°
                    July: high 82°, low 56°
  Annual: >90°: 8 days, **<0°:** 16 days
Tornadoes (1930-2010): 11

O ORIGINS

<u>Barryton</u>:[v] local entrepreneur, Frank Barry; 1894; see 54H
<u>Big Rapids</u>:[c,ct] the largest of many rapids on the Muskegon River; 1853
<u>Canadian Lakes</u>:[u] a resort community
<u>Chippewa Lake</u>:[u] the Chippewa Indians; 1870
<u>Green</u>:[ct] Green family erected first frame building; 1854
<u>Mecosta</u>:[v,co] (ma COST a) a Potawatomi chief whose name meant "big bear;" 1851
<u>Morley</u>:[v] 1869
<u>Paris</u>:[u] fisherman and hunter, John Parish; 1851
<u>Remus</u>:[u] surveyor, landowner, William Remus; 1869
<u>Rodney</u>:[u] lumber firm partner, Rodney Hood; 1879
<u>Stanwood</u>:[v] a splendid stand of timber; 1870
<u>Sylvester</u>:[u] early lumberman, Sylvester Dresser; 1868

P PARKS

National: 0 **State:** 4 **County:** 7 **Local:** 16
Number of campsites: 1,800
National Forest: Manistee
State Forest: Pere Marquette   **...Campground:** 1
State Game Area: 13,000 acres, Haymarsh Lake[ww], Martiny Lake
State Linear Trail Park: *White Pine State Park:* 92 miles from Cadillac to Comstock Park
State Recreation Area: *Hungerford Lake:* 13 mile multi-use trail system
State Wildlife Area: *Featherbed Marsh:* 430 acres, within the Haymarsh Lake State Game Area
County: *Brower Park:* 280 acres, boat access to Muskegon river; camping, fishing

...*School Section Lake Park:* 86 acres, camping, beach, rustic log cabin lodge for large groups

Jennifer Marfio

Q QUOTE FROM THE LOCALS

"Mecosta County truly is the 'County for Every Season.' There is no better place to work, raise a family or vacation. The county's prospering rural economy allows our residents to enjoy a family-friendly atmosphere and a high quality of life. The diversified economy of Mecosta County is centered on agriculture, higher education, retail and a broad range of manufacturing provides a high level of economic stability.

"A beautiful place to visit, you will find Mecosta County to be a relaxing and fun experience for the whole family… Mecosta is located in western Michigan, and its central location makes it appealing for those seeking to explore our wealth of natural resources. Mecosta County is a serene vacation spot and a welcoming, safe place to call home for both families and businesses." mecostacounty.org

R RECREATION & SPORTS

Auto racing: *Mid Michigan Motorplex:* drag racing
Golf courses: 3, including award-winning Tullymore and St. Ives
Hiking/skiing/mountain biking trails: 25 miles

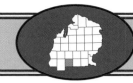
Horse racing: harness racing during fair week
Public access sites: 25
Public recreational land: 4% of county
Rail-trail: (25 miles) White Pine
Hunt clubs: *Sanctuary:* because there's more to the hunt than the kill
…*Super G Ranch:* 445 acres, guided hunts for deer, elk, buffalo, pheasant; lodge with home cooking

S STATE OF MICHIGAN

Human activity accounts for 95% of all <u>wildfires</u> in Michigan, the out of control burning of grass, weeds, crops, brush or forests. Careless debris burning (trash, grass, leaves, brush) is the source of most of these wildfires. A free "burn permit," to burn brush legally, is required everywhere in the state when there is no snow on the ground. Although permits are not needed for campfires, care must always be taken to prevent the fire from spreading to nearby vegetation.

Wildfire Prevention Week is in April to bring attention to the fact that the greatest threat of wildfires is in April and May before the green grass comes up and the trees sprout their new foliage. There are 10,000 to 12,000 wildfires each year in Michigan; they then become the responsibility of local and state firefighters to extinguish.

This shameful waste **WEAKENS AMERICA !**
Remember – Only you can **PREVENT FOREST FIRES** NPCR

The most visible symbol of wildfire prevention is Smokey Bear of the "Only You Can Prevent Wildfires" fame. Smokey, a mascot for the U.S. Forest Service, was created in 1944 to educate the public about the dangers of forest fires.

Not all fires in the wild are bad since certain ecosystems need periodic low-intensity fires to remain healthy. Controlled burns have become an important wildfire prevention tool to remove highly flammable dry undergrowth that could intensify a real forest fire. Michigan.gov

T TRAVEL

Airport: Roben-Hood
Bus: Indian Trails
County road names:
 …**north/south:** numbered Avenues
 …**east/west:** named and numbered Roads
Distance to Lansing: 110 miles
Main roads: US-131, M-21, M-66
Memorial Highway: M-66, *Green Arrow Route*: see 8T

U UNIVERSITIES & COLLEGES

Ferris State University: est. 1853, 10,000 students. It offers an integrative education where theory meets practice with partnerships and career-oriented, broad-based education for careers, responsible citizenship and lifelong learning. GLIAC, Bulldogs

V VARIETY

Bob Frei

The 8½ feet bronze statue on a 5-foot pink granite die stone base honors Woodbridge N. Ferris (1853-1928), founder of Ferris State University; he was also a Michigan governor from 1913-1918 and a U.S. Senator from 1922-1928. See 54H.

W WANDERLUST

Agri-tourism: *Farm Markets:* downtown Big Rapids, The Villages at Tullymore
…*Four Green Fields Farm:* pumpkins, 8-acre haunted corn maze
Cultural: Artworks, Rankin Gallery at FSU
Fall colors: early October; get a color tour map from the Mecosta County Area CVB
Live theater: STAGE-M
Walking tour: *Big Rapids Riverwalk:* 2.64 miles, multi-functional trail along the Muskegon River
Amish Tour: includes 21 homes and stores where you can purchase fresh meat, live animals, fruits and vegetables, home furnishings and furniture, and much more. See 18V.

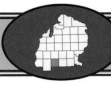

Mecosta County Historical Attractions Tour: the brochure lists 21 stops on this tour.

Sculptures: on the FSU campus and throughout the county; these 20'+ tall steel sculptures convey the power and strength that comes from education. Words and brief messages that define Ferris State University are engraved into the steel.

Ferris State University Photographic Services

X X-TRA STUFF

County Fair: *County Agricultural Fair Association:* Mecosta County 4-H fair is a great chance for the youth in the county to show all the work they've put into their projects; July.

NPCR

Hospitals: Mecosta County General

Large employers: Wolverine World Wide (makes footwear), Wal-Mart, Big Rapids Components (makes furniture parts), Mark IV (makes auto parts), Fluid Routing Solutions (makes steel & iron pipes, more), Haworth (makes office furniture), Mecosta County General Hospital, Mecosta-Osceola Intermediate School Dist., Meijer, Ice Mountain Spring Water (bottled water)

Canadian Lakes is a private resort development of five combined lakes with building lots for homes and cottages.

Cran-Hill Ranch: is devoted to being a ministry through which God is transforming lives into the image of Christ through youth camps, family camping, retreats and Christian Adventures; 360 acres, horses, lakes, high ropes course, archery, crafts, petting farm, much more

Jennifer Marfio

Eiffel Tower: in Paris, Michigan, is 20' tall and was built in 1980 by high school students using left over WPA metal bed frames from the 1930s

Y YESTERYEAR

Making <u>maple syrup</u> was an important American Indian activity. The sap was put into large wooden troughs made from tree trunks that were either hollowed out by an ax or burned out by fire. The American Indians boiled the sap in the same manner as they cooked their food: they heated stones in the fire and then dropped the red-hot stones into the sap in the trough. As soon as the stones were cool, they took them out and replaced them with more hot stones, continuing this way until the sap was boiled down to syrup. Remember, it takes 40 gallons of sap to make one gallon of syrup! They continued to boil it down even more to make granulated maple sugar. See 54A.

Z ZOO & ANIMAL PLACES

Watchable Wildlife Viewing Areas:ww see 54P

...Card Wildlife Education Center: at FSU, see 54M

Outback Lodge and Stables Bed and Breakfast: 700 acres, working horse ranch, ride horses, sleigh or wagon rides; and hike, ski or snowmobile

A AGRICULTURE

Land in farms: 27% of county
Number of farms: 570
Size of average farm: 160 acres
Market value of all products: #39 of 83 counties
Crops: ...most acres: corn
...highest $ sales: grains: corn, soybeans, wheat
Livestock: ...largest number: cattle & calves
...highest $ sales: milk & dairy products
Among the top Michigan counties:
• #1- greenhouse fruits and berries, vegetable seeds
Dairy, food and meat processing plants: 13
State ranking for harvested trees: #69 of 83 counties
FYI: The <u>Michigan FFA Association</u>, formerly Future Farmers of America, is a leadership, personal growth and career development organization for students enrolled in agriscience education programs in high school and college. With over 5,000 members in rural, urban and suburban schools, FFA provides leadership and learning opportunities in agricultural-related science, business, technology and production farming. Wearing their distinctive blue corduroy jackets, they can be identified as the future leaders of the agriculture industry in Michigan and the U.S.
michiganffa.com

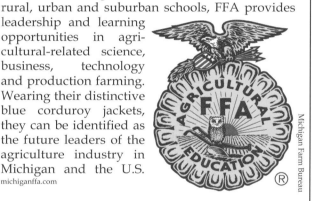

Michigan Farm Bureau

B BRIDGE OR BOAT

Karen Stoneman

The Tridge, in the Chippewassee Park in downtown Midland, is a three-way pedestrian bridge over The Forks, the point where the Tittabawssee (tit a ba WAH see) and Chippewa Rivers meet.

C CELEBRATIONS

<u>Midland</u> *Folk Music Festival:* stage shows, Aug.
...Michigan Antique & Collectible Festivals: 1,000 vendors, swap meet, car show, June, July, Sept.
<u>Oil City</u> *Rock & Reggae Music Festival:* at Salt River Acres, Aug.
<u>Sanford</u> *Freedom Festival: Parkapalooza:* bands, bands, bands, Sept.
...Founders' Day Festival: demonstrations of wood-carving, American Indian basket & beadwork, spinning, blacksmithing; pig roast, parade, music, Sept.

D DEMOGRAPHICS

Population: 83,600   **Persons per sq. mile:** 161
Largest city: Midland   **Population:** 41,700
Largest township: Larkin   **Population:** 5,140
Largest village: Sanford   **Population:** 860
Median household income: $51,000
Owner-occupied median house value: $132,000
Persons affiliated with a religious congregation: 46%
Persons below poverty level: 12%
Students receiving school lunch subsidy: 28%

E ENVIRONMENT

The <u>Little Forks Conservancy</u> partners with private landowners in or near the Tittabawassee (tit a ba WAH see) River Watershed to permanently protect and preserve the unique natural features and cultural resources that add quality of life in the community. Currently they are working on purchasing 419 acres along an undeveloped two-mile stretch of the river that includes wildlife habitat, forests, wetlands and farmland. By preserving this diverse ecosystem as the natural floodplain that it is, it will be treasured for generations to come. littleforks.org

To order additional copies of this book, go to discovermichigancountybycounty.com. Books are shipped the following business day.

F FLORA & FAUNA

Alice Welch, USDA

Spotted knapweed is an aggressive invasive species that reduces wildlife forage and increases water runoff, soil erosion and stream sedimentation.

Alice Welch, USDA

The Blanding's turtle, 6"-10" in length, is common in the Lower Peninsula but is also protected by Michigan law as a special concern species. They are threatened by wetland degradation and road mortality. Look for their yellow marking on the shell and neck to identify them.

G GOVERNMENT

County: ...created: 1831 **...organized:** 1850
...originally part of: Saginaw County
Size: 338,000 acres / 521 sq. miles (66 of 83 counties)
The county has 2 cities, 1 village, 16 townships with 2 as charter townships, 8 unincorporated communities and 4 school districts.

Deb Schmucker

NPCR

Among Michigan county courthouses, the 1926 Midland County Courthouse is singularly unique in its styling (Tudor), materials used (developed by Dow) and funding for the construction (partly by private donations). See 56H.
County seat: Midland
...Homestead property tax: 37 mills
Motto: <u>Midland</u>: *City of Modern Explorers; A Million Brilliant Possibilities*

H HISTORICAL MARKERS 4 of 5

Midland County Courthouse: 1926, rustic Tudor Revival style architecture, using material developed by the Dow Chemical Company; mosaics and murals depict county history; see 56G

Origins of the Salt Industry: early settlers used salt for preserving fish and other foods, curing meats and tanning hides as well as for cooking. The 1935 state convention provided for state control of salt springs and salt lands in Michigan.

State Salt Well No. 1: 1838, site of first (failed) attempt to drill a salt well on the salt springs of the Tittabawassee River; Michigan went on to become a leading salt producer in the U.S. See 82N.

Michigan State Historic Preservation Office

The Upper Bridge: 1908, the Currie Parkway Bridge, a 140-foot steel Pratt through-truss; in 1988 an arch was added for support.

National Historic Landmark: Herbert H. Dow (chemist) House, see 56Y; Alden B. Dow (architect) Home and Studio (he was Herbert's youngest son), see 56L
National Register of Historic Places: 26 listings
State Historic Sites: 23 listings

I INFORMATION

Chamber of Commerce: Midland, Sanford
Visitor: Great Lakes Bay Regional Convention and Visitors Bureau, 800-444-9979, visitgreatlakesbay.org

J JOKES

You may be a rich man in Michigan if…
…your second home is on Mackinac Island.
…your third home is in West Palm Beach.
…you've got condos in Traverse City when you're golfing and in Marquette when you're downhill skiing.
…your yacht is moored at Lake Macatawa and your sailing vessel at the Detroit Yacht Club.
…you never drive to your weekend destination, but always fly your private plane.
…you've got all the latest electronic gadgets at each of these locations.
…you're too busy to go to any of your properties or to play with any of your toys. Life is just so busy and work is so demanding.
…you have several full time "asset managers" to take care of all this personal property.

K KINSMAN

Race		Ancestry	
American Indian: <1%		German: 29%	
Asian: 2%		English: 11%	
Black/African American: 1%		U.S./American: 10%	
Hispanic or Latino: 2%		Irish: 9%	
Other: 2%		Polish: 6%	
White: 95%		French: 5%	

L LIGHTHOUSE OR LANDMARK

Michigan State Historic Preservation Office

Midland is the home of Dow Chemical Company. The legacy of the Dow family is evident throughout the City of Midland, including the Alden B. Dow Home and Studio that is a National Historic Landmark. This

20,000 sq. ft. structure is more than a museum and it is open for tours. See 56M, 56Y.

M MUSEUMS

Deb Schmucker

<u>Midland</u> *Alden B. Dow Home and Studio:* see 56L

Midland Center for the Arts: it includes:
- *Dow Museum of Science & Art:* visual art and science exhibitions to educate, inspire, stimulate

In Heritage Park:
- *Bradley Home Museum and Carriage House:* authentic Victorian Gothic architecture
- *Doan Midland County History Center:* hands-on interactive exhibits
- *Dow Historical Museum:* the evolution of the chemical and pharmaceutical industries
- Heritage Park

<u>Sanford</u> *Centennial Museum:* 1870-1910 buildings: school, log cabin, depot, general store, one-room school, chapel, township hall; lumber camp, antique farm implements

N NATURAL RESOURCES

Elevation: 600 - 800 feet
Physiography: lake-border plains

Forest type: aspen-birch, elm-ash-cottonwood, maple-beech
Public/private forests: 52% of county

NPCR

Water in county: <1% of county
   Lakes: 20   **…largest:** Sanford
   Rivers: Chippewa (CHIP a wah), Pine, Salt, Tittabawassee (tit a ba WAH see), Tobacco
   Rivers & streams: 310 miles

Growing season, avg.: 152 days (3-4 temp. zones)
   Last freeze, avg.: May 5 – May 15
   First freeze, avg.: Sept. 30 – Oct. 10
Precipitation, annual avg.: rainfall: 29 inches
                      snowfall: 38 inches
Temperature (F), avg.: January: high 29°, low 15°
               July: high 83°, low 60°
  Annual: >90°: 11 days, **<0°:** 8 days
Tornadoes (1930-2010): 9

O ORIGINS

Averill:[u] first postmaster, Averill Harrison; 1868
Coleman:[c] Seymour Coleman gave 160 acres to the railroad in return for a depot here; 1870
Edenville:[u] the natural beauty of the area; 1854
Hope:[u] named after the township; 1856
Larkin:[ct] landowner, lumberman, John Larkin; 1876
Midland:[c,co,ct] in the middle of the state; 1836
Oil City:[u] oil discovered here in 1928
Sanford:[v] land owner and village platter, Charles Sanford; 1864

P PARKS

National: 0 **State:** 2 **County:** 6 **Local:** 41
Number of campsites: 930
State Forest: (942,000 acres) Chippewa (CHIP a wah) River, Tittabawassee (tit a ba WAH see) River
...Campground: 2 **...Pathway:** 8 miles
County: *Pine Haven Recreation Area:* 325 acres, diverse terrain for skiing, biking, hiking
...*Sanford Lake Park:* ½ mile of soft, sandy beach, spray park, boating, fishing, swimming
Local: *Chippewassee Park:* home of the Tridge, a skateboard park, Rail Trail, summer concerts, Farmers' Market, festivals
...*Emerson Park:* 50 acres, home of Currie Stadium, softball tournaments, inline hockey rink
Nature Center: *Chippewa:*[ww] 1,150 acres, meandering trails, 1870 homestead farm

Other: *Chippewa Nature Center:* 1,200 acres, woodland, wetlands, rivers, upland fields, trails, Visitor Center with hands-on exhibits, naturalist

...*Dow Gardens:* 100 acres, arboretum, original gardens of the Dow homestead, open for tours

Q QUOTE FROM THE LOCALS

"In Midland, every day is a work of art. From exquisite galleries to colorful create-your-own masterpiece studio spaces, it's easy to see the beauty of this rare community. When you're not soaking up the arts and culture that surround you, you'll enjoy our downtown shopping district, exceptional sports venues and more. A million brilliant possibilities await you in Midland..." visitgreatlakesbay.org

R RECREATION & SPORTS

Golf courses: 4

Hiking/skiing/mountain biking trails: 30 miles
Horse racing: harness racing during fair week
Off-road vehicle trails: 40 miles
Public access sites: 2
Public recreational land: 12% of county
Rail-trail: (110 miles, #4/MI) Midland to Mackinac, Pere Marquette

Great Lakes Loons: Single-A (Low A) partner of the Los Angeles Dodgers; play baseball at Dow Diamond; mascot Lou E. Loon

Michigan Amateur Softball Association Hall of Fame: in Midland
Midland Civic Arena: 1,000-seat, figure and speed skating, hockey
Midland Community Center: 200,000 sq. ft, for recreations, sports, arts
Midland Curling Club: at the Curling Center
Midland Soccer Club: with 16 irrigated fields
Mid Michigan Ice: professional women's fastpitch softball
Mud Creek Crawl: off-road 5K and 10K race

S STATE OF MICHIGAN

As you drive through rural Michigan, you may see those fancy green and yellow signs in the yard of farm homes. The homeowners are the proud recipients of a Centennial Farm designation. A Centennial farm is a working farm of 10 or more acres that has been continuously owned by the same family for at least 100 years. The sign highlights the family farm's contribution to Michigan's development. There are over 6,000 certified Centennial Farms in Michigan.

There is also a Sesquicentennial Farm Program for those Centennial farms that have reached 150 years of same family ownership.

Michigan's electrical utility companies are the official sponsors of these signs that commemorate the dramatic changes electricity brought to farm operation and family life. The Centennial Farm Program is part of the Historical Society of Michigan, the state's official historical society. Michigan.gov

Paul Jackson

T TRAVEL

Airport: Jack Barstow
Bus: Greyhound
Distance to Lansing: 90 miles
Main roads: US-10, M-18, M-20, M-30, M-47

U UNIVERSITIES & COLLEGES

Davenport University: see 13U
Northwood University: est. 1959, 3,000 students. The Northwood Idea incorporates the lessons of the American free-enterprise society into the college classroom with technical, manufacturing, marketing, retail and ethics-driven management; other schools in Florida, Texas, & overseas. GLIAC, Timberwolves

V VARIETY

NPCR

NPCR

Dahlia Hill is unlike any other dahlia garden. There are eight terraces planted with 3,000 dahlias in over 250 varieties. In downtown Midland, it is maintained by volunteers and is open to the public free of charge.

W WANDERLUST

Agri-tourism: *Downtown Midland Area Farmers' Market:* Wed. & Sat., great selection
Cultural: *Midland Center for the Arts*: Concerts, Festivals & Film, Museum, Theater & Musicals, Heritage Park, Science Museum
Fall colors: early October
Live theater: Midland Center for the Arts
Shopping mall: Midland
Walking tour: *Chippewa Trail:* 3 miles, interpretive stops, unique landscape

Dow Gardens: 110 acres, all season botanical garden & conservatory, children's garden, Whiting Forest, Visitor Center, streams, ponds, covered bridge

Deb Schmucker

Santa House: designed in the style of the Midland Courthouse

X X-TRA STUFF

County fair: *Midland County Agricultural and Horticultural Society:* July
Hospitals: Midland
Large employers: Dow Chemical (makes plastics, alkalis, chlorine, fungicides, herbicides), Dow Corning Silicon Energy, Midland Hospital Assoc., MidMichigan Medical Center, Midland Public Schools, Dow Corning, Midland Community Center
"In 1994, a meteorite known as the 'Coleman meteorite' fell near the city [of Coleman], which is coincidental because the community schools' mascot are the Coleman Comets." wikipedia
Midland is nicknamed the City of Beautiful Churches because of the wide variety of denominations and architectural styles.
"On a per capita basis, Midland County has more resident engineers, chemists and metallurgists than any other area in the nation." Michigan.org/medc

Y YESTERYEAR

Why did Midland become the home of Dow Chemical Company?

Eons ago, Michigan was covered by a salt sea and the remains of that sea are still deep in the earth's crust. Herbert Dow (1866-1930) was born in Canada and lived and went to school in the U.S. As a chemistry student in college, he did research on salt brines. He found that the salt brines in Midland had high levels of bromine. At the time, bromine was a major ingredient in pharmaceuticals and photography. He developed a less expensive process of extracting the bromine from the salt brine. In 1896, after some business ups and downs, he moved to Midland and started the Dow Chemical Company. He continued to do research and expand the role of chemistry in our society and today the Dow Chemical Companies have plants in 120 countries around the world. midlandcounty.org, wilipedia

Z ZOO & ANIMAL PLACES

Watchable Wildlife Viewing Areas:ww see 56P

If you have comments, suggestions, corrections or updates, please email these to: info@discovermichigancountybycounty.com
And thanks for reading this book and taking time to share your thoughts!

A AGRICULTURE

Land in farms: 24% of county
Number of farms: 390
Size of average farm: 225 acres
Market value of all products: #33 of 83 counties
Crops: ...most acres: forage land
...highest $ sales: grains: corn, soybeans, wheat
Livestock: ...largest number of: cattle & calves
...highest $ sales: milk & dairy products
Among the top Michigan counties:
- #1- acres of Christmas trees
- #6- forage land
- #7- corn for silage, sales of dairy products
- #9- cattle
- #10- market value of all livestock

Dairy, food and meat processing plants: 5
AgBioResearch Centers (MSU): *Lake City Research Center*: studies beef cattle breeding, optimum grazing grass and legume combinations, potatoes
FYI: The mission of the AgBioResearch Centers (formerly the Michigan Agricultural Experiment Station) is to engage in innovative, leading-edge research that combines scientific expertise with practical experience to generate economic prosperity, sustain natural resources and enhance the quality of life in Michigan, the nation and the world. A network of 18 on-campus laboratories in East Lansing and 14 off-campus centers around the state provide nearly 400 AgBioResearch scientists the opportunity to focus their research and outreach activities on the agricultural and natural resource needs of particular parts of the state. agbioresearch.msu.edu

State ranking for harvested trees: #22 of 83 counties
FYI: Missaukee County, with its sandy soil, has almost 9,000 acres of Christmas trees and is the #1 producer in the state, accounting for nearly 30% of all cut Christmas trees. In 2007 Michigan had over 40,000 acres planted for Christmas tree production, with tree farms in all counties but Wayne County. The climate, soils and topography of Michigan permits the production of many popular species of Christmas trees including Austrian Red, Scotch and White Pine, Balsam, Concolor, Douglas and Fraser Fir, and Black Hills, Colorado Blue and White Spruce. The total Michigan annual harvest is over 1.5 million trees that help to make a merry Christmas for many families throughout the country. Michigan.gov, MDA

Michigan Farm Bureau

B BRIDGE OR BOAT

Hobie Cat Company

Whether it is sailing on Lake Missaukee or one of the Great Lakes, sailing a double-hulled catamaran offers a safe and stable opportunity to enjoy the best of Michigan's Water Wonderland.

C CELEBRATIONS

Lake City *Greatest 4th in the North:* parade, fireworks, carnival, battle of the bands, arts & crafts, July
...Festival of the Pines: lumberjack contests, history in the Park, prince & princess contest, parade, lots of food, music, Sept.
McBain *Hughston's Cow Camp:* rodeo, barrel racing, Sept.

D DEMOGRAPHICS

Population: 14,800   **Persons per sq. mile:** 26
Largest city: Lake City   **Population:** 840
Largest township: Lake   **Population:** 2,800
Median household income: $38,700
Owner-occupied median house value: $113,000
Persons affiliated with a religious congregation: 33%
Persons below poverty level: 15%
Students receiving school lunch subsidy: 48%

E ENVIRONMENT

Included in the Department of Natural Resources list of Endangered & Threatened Species are 2 amphibians, 22 birds, 24 fish, 19 insects, 6 mammals, 14 mollusks, 4 reptiles and over 330 plants. The DNR works with many units of government and private organizations in an effort to protect both the animal

or plant and its habitat from further declines. The Michigan Wildlife Action Plan provides a common strategic framework and information resource to aid in conservation of Michigan's aquatic and terrestrial wildlife, for both public and private efforts, whether large or small. [Michigan.gov] See 48E.

F FLORA & FAUNA

The snow trillium, so named because it blooms in March and April when there may still be snow on the ground, is on the State of Michigan Endangered and Threatened Species list.

The Barn Owl is also on the State of Michigan Endangered and Threatened Species list. They tend to nest in abandoned buildings and they help control rodents and other pests. Many people put up nesting boxes to help restore the species.

G GOVERNMENT

County: ...**created:** 1840 ...**organized:** 1871
...**originally part of:** Antrim, Grand Traverse Counties
Size: 366,000 acres / 567 sq. miles (47 of 83 counties)
The county has 2 cities, 15 townships, 6 unincorporated communities and 2 school districts.

County seat: Lake City
...**Homestead property tax:** 34 mills
Motto: Lake City: *Christmas Tree Capital of Michigan*

H HISTORICAL MARKERS o

National Register of Historic Places: 3 listings
State Historic Sites: 2 listings

I INFORMATION

Chamber of Commerce: Lake City Area, 231-839-4969, lakecitymich.com

J JOKES

We're from Michigan. We...
...think 85° is hot, no matter what, when, where or how.
...don't like H[3]: heat, humidity and hazy days.
...know our cars and trees.
...never take locally grown fruits and vegetables for granted.
...always take locally grown fruits and vegetables for granted.
...assumed everyone had green grass in their yard, until our first trip to the Southwest.
...always take our vacations where there is water.
...know that when we're in a drought, the grass will die and the weeds will thrive.

K KINSMAN

Race
American Indian: <1%
Asian: <1%
Black/African American: <1%
Hispanic or Latino: 2%
Other: 2%
White: 97%

Ancestry
Dutch: 25% (#3/MI)
German: 18%
U.S./American: 11%
English: 10%
Irish: 7%
French: 4%
Polish: 4%

L LIGHTHOUSE OR LANDMARK

NPCR

It is a joy to drive through this area and see the rows and rows of trimmed evergreens just waiting to get big enough to be "real" Christmas trees.

M MUSEUMS

NPCR

Lake City *Missaukee Park Historical Museum*

N NATURAL RESOURCES

Elevation: 1,000 – 1,300 feet
Physiography: hilly uplands, upland plains

Forest type: aspen-birch, maple-beech-hemlock, pine-oak
Public/private forests: 65% of county

Ellen Vanderwaal

National Natural Landmark: *Dead Stream Swamp:* 12,000 acres, northern white cedar swamp, the climax in bog forest development

Water in county: 1% of county
  Lakes: 30 **largest:** Lake Missaukee (miss SOCK key)
  Rivers: Clam, Manistee, Muskegon (muss KEY gun)
  Rivers & streams: 210 miles

Growing season, avg.: 108 days (2 temp. zones)
  Last freeze, avg.: May 25 – May 30
  First freeze, avg.: Sept. 15 – Sept. 20
Precipitation, annual avg.: rainfall: 29 inches
                                snowfall: 78 inches
Temperature (F), avg.: January: high 26°, low 9°
                          July: high 81°, low 54°
  Annual: >90°: 6 days, **<0°:** 25 days
Tornadoes (1930-2010): 9

O ORIGINS

Lake City:[c] adjacent to Lake Missaukee; 1868
McBain:[c] settler, sawmill owner, Gillis McBain; 1887
Merritt:[u] village founder, Charles Merritt; 1908
Missaukee:[co] (miss SOCK key) the local American
  Indian chief was named Nesuakee; 1901

P PARKS

National: 0   **State:** 3   **County:** 3   **Local:** 7
Number of campsites: 500

State Forest: (94,000 acres) Missaukee SF includes the Missaukee Dead Stream Swamp; Pere Marquette

...Campground: 4
  ...Pathway: 11 miles
State Wildlife Area: 6,500 acres, Houghton Lake Wildlife Research Area is also in Roscommon County

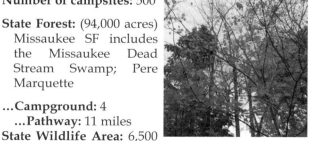

NPCR

County: *Missaukee County Park:* 33 acres on Lake Missaukee, white sand beach, excellent swimming, camping, boat docking, picnic area

Q QUOTE FROM THE LOCALS

"In Missaukee County we are surrounded by lakes, streams, woods, parks, campgrounds and an abundance of wildlife. The majority of us have a lake or stream suitable for fishing, swimming or boating within ten miles of our homes. Our streams have brook, brown and rainbow trout. The lakes have bass, walleye, northern pike, crappie, pan fish and perch. For those who enjoy hunting, Missaukee County has over 100,000 acres of wild public land in which grouse, woodcock, turkeys, ducks and white tail deer reside. For cross-country skiers, snowmobilers, off-road vehicles and hikers, there are over a hundred miles of marked and groomed wilderness trails in our forestlands. In the spring, you will find many people with their heads down looking for morel mushrooms. They will also find beefsteak and other kinds of spring fungus."

NPCR

lakecitymich.com

R RECREATION & SPORTS

Auto racing: *Merritt Raceway:* 3/8-mile banked dirt oval track
Blue Ribbon Trout Streams:[1,000] Clam River
Golf courses: 5
Hiking/skiing/mountain biking trails: 5 miles
Off-road vehicle trails: 70 miles
Public access sites: 7
Public recreational land: 28% of county
Rail-trail: (10 miles) Michigan Shore to Shore
State-funded snowmobile trails: 50 miles
Jack Pine Enduro Race: also known as the Cowbell Classic; since 1923, it is the oldest running motorcycle endurance race in the U.S.
Missaukee Ski Mountain: city owned, 3 towropes

S STATE OF MICHIGAN

Michigan has about 2 million White-tailed deer and every year at least 65,000 of them are involved in reported car-deer crashes, an average of one every 8 minutes. About 80% of these crashes are on 2-lane roads between dusk and dawn. Each year car-deer crashes cause $130,000,000 in vehicle damages.

If you see a deer on the road in front of you, please follow these guidelines.
1. When you see one deer, chances are there will be more than one. SLOW DOWN.
2. If you know you're going to hit a deer, DON'T SWERVE. Brake firmly, hold onto the steering wheel and bring your vehicle to a controlled stop. It is better to hit the deer than lose control of your car where you might hit a tree or roll over the car.
3. Notify the police and your insurance company. Michigan.gov See 62S, 68S.

USFWS

T TRAVEL

Distance to Lansing: 130 miles
Main roads: M-55, M-66
Memorial Highway: M-66, *Green Arrow Route:* see 8T

U UNIVERSITIES & COLLEGES

None

V VARIETY

Ellen Vanderwaal

Michigan has over 6,000 miles of designated snowmobile trails throughout the state. The DNR is responsible for maintaining the system of trails. They work closely with private organizations like the Missaukee Trail Blazers whose members are responsible for grooming over 50 miles of trails.

W WANDERLUST

Fall colors: late September to early October

NPCR

X X-TRA STUFF

County fair: *Missaukee Agriculture Youth Show*: has supreme support from the agricultural community, Aug.

Famous people: ...*Entertainment*: Burt Reynolds

Large employers: Lake City Forge (makes ferrous auto forgings), McBain Rural Agricultural School District, Autumwood Nursing Home, John A Biewer of Toledo (sawing & planing mill)

Stoney Corner Wind Farm: 28 windmills in 2011

Y YESTERYEAR

"With the crash of the local lumber industry in the early 20th century, Missaukee County settled into an agricultural economy. Where the land was good, farmers thrived, but many just eked out a living. Much of Missaukee County's soil is sandy and poor, not well suited to pasturing livestock.

NPCR

"But the growth of the auto industry downstate had an unexpected side effect on <u>Missaukee's economy</u>. Assembly line workers and their families began to head northward for vacation and recreation time in Missaukee's still wild lands, lakes and rivers. Tourism eventually became a strong element of the local economy, especially in the decades after WWII. Many vacationers bought summer cottages here and later winterized them into retirement homes.

"Forestry, dairy farming, tourism and...Christmas trees. In the 1960s and 1970s, Missaukee County's sandy soil was to be a perfect medium for growing many varieties of Christmas trees, and another leg of the local economy was born. Missaukee is now in the heart of Michigan's Christmas tree-growing district."

lakecitymi.com

Z ZOO & ANIMAL PLACES

The whole county is a wildlife wilderness wonderland.

From the INDEX...

1,000 This notation indicates that the noted item is on the *1,000 Places To See Before You Die* list (and book of the same name) by Patricia Schultz.

A AGRICULTURE

Land in farms: 58% of county
Number of farms: 1,120
Size of average farm: 185 acres
Market value of all products: #17 of 83 counties
Crops: ...most acres: corn
...highest $ sales: grains: corn, soybeans, wheat
Livestock: ...largest number: laying hens
...highest $ sales: cattle & calves
Among the top Michigan counties:
- #1- catfish, cabbage, tomatoes
- #2- cauliflower, other peppers
- #3- cantaloupes
- #4- pumpkins, sweet corn
- #5- floriculture, soybeans

Dairy, food and meat processing plants: 11
State ranking for harvested trees: #80 of 83 counties
FYI: Aquaculture is the production of fish and seafood in a safe and environmentally sensitive manner. Michigan has nearly 70 licensed aquaculture facilities that produce trout (rainbow, brook, brown), bass, bluegill, catfish, shrimp and sunfish. This county is the state leader for catfish production.

The U.S. currently imports 84% of its seafood consumption. With its ample water supply, Michigan is looking to the future to expand its production of seafood aquaculture to provide jobs and to make locally grown food even more available to state residents and for international markets also.
Michigan.gov, michiganaquaculture.org

B BRIDGE OR BOAT

D & R Sports Center

Bay boats are generally smaller, fiberglass boats that are intended for use in shallow, wide-open waters that are not exposed to rough waters. Although sometimes thought of as a saltwater boat, they are still the perfect boat for fresh water fishing in Lake Erie.

C CELEBRATIONS

Monroe County Historical Museum

<u>Dundee</u> *Lantern Tours:* costumed volunteers tell stories at night about people and events of 200 years ago.

...Mayfly Music Festival: variety of music, June

<u>Estral Beach</u> *Pointe Mouillee Waterfowl Festival:* decoy carving, wildlife art show, duck and goose calling, retriever training seminar, hip-boot race, Sept.

<u>Monroe</u> *River Raisin International Fife and Drum Muster:* one of the most important musters in the U.S. with all the most important units in attendance, parade, June

...River Raisin Jazz Festival: fastest growing music festival in Michigan, Aug.

Monroe County Convention & Tourism Bureau

From BIBLIOGRAPHY & NOTES...

C CELEBRATIONS: Just a few of the activities for each celebration have been listed; there are many more activities at each event.

D DEMOGRAPHICS

Population: 152,000   **Persons per sq. mile:** 276
Largest city: Monroe   **Population:** 20,700
Largest township: Bedford   **Population:** 31,100
Largest village: Dundee   **Population:** 3,960
Median household income: $53,200 (#4/MI)
Owner-occupied median house value: $165,000
Persons affiliated with a religious congregation: 54%
Persons below poverty level: 11%
Students receiving school lunch subsidy: 27%

E ENVIRONMENT

MyEcoVille is an affordable, value-packed environmental website *template* that is used to educate residents and increase local waste diversion and sustainability in the community. The Monroe County Environmental Health Division hosts this website. It is the place to go for information on residential and business recycling, buying recycled products, reuse programs, garbage collection, sustainability initiatives, recycling bins, events, news, environmental education and MyEcoVideos. Monroe. co.mi.myecoville.com

F FLORA & FAUNA

Photo by R.G. Micka Lotus Garden Club of Monroe County

The American lotus is the world's largest aquatic flower and can be found along the shore of the Lake Erie marshes. The flower is 7"-11" across with leaves that are up to 2' in diameter. The Michigan Legislature named it the Official Symbol of Water Quality in Michigan.

R. Town–USFWS

The muskrat *(MI H&T)* is found in the marshy areas of Lake Erie and was used for both food and clothing by the pioneers. The 12" long rodent is still abundant today. Muskrat dinners are a popular treat in this county during Lent since the mammal is a Catholic approved fish substitute (from a 1700s tradition) for meat.

G GOVERNMENT

County: ...created: 1817 **...organized:** 1817
...originally part of: Wayne County
Size: 361,000 acres / 551 sq. miles (59 of 83 counties)
The county has 4 cities, 5 villages, 1 Census Designated Place, 15 townships with 3 as charter townships, 17 unincorporated communities and 10 school districts.

Monroe County Historical Museum

Monroe County Historical Museum

County seat: Monroe
...Homestead property tax: 38 mills
Motto: <u>Monroe County</u>: *Walleye Capital of the World; Golf Capital of Michigan*

H HISTORICAL MARKERS 5 of 10

Gen. George Armstrong Custer: see 58V
Sighting the Enemy: 1910, a statue of Gen. Custer in downtown Monroe; see 58V
Michigan: Historic Crossroads: in the heart of the upper Great Lakes, many American Indian waterways and trails, French and British exploration and control

Michigan: Twenty-sixth State: 1837, became the lumbering, copper and iron ore capital of the U.S. in the 1880-1890s, and a manufacturing giant in the 1900s

Peter Seitz Tavern & Stagecoach Inn: 1856, on the North Custer plank toll road that was built of wooden boards to aid travel during the "muddy season;" a single-family home since 1899

FYI: In addition, the Monroe County Historical Society has placed over 60 Historical Markers throughout the county that help tell the interesting story of the area.

Monroe County Historical Museum

Monument: *George Armstrong Custer Equestrian Monument:* see 58V

National Register of Historic Places: 14 listings
State Historic Sites: 32 listings

I INFORMATION

Visitor: Monroe County Convention and Tourism Bureau, 734-457-1030, monroeinfo.com

J JOKES

Welcome to Michigan! You will need to remember some things in order to navigate the state successfully.
1. The Michigan Left means you have to turn right in order to go left. Actually it's one right turn and two left turns.
2. We have two Peninsulas, an Upper and a Lower. People from the **U**pper **P**eninsula are called Yoopers (as in U-pers), but people from the Lower Peninsula are not called Loopers. Actually, they aren't called anything, except by Yoopers who call them Trolls because they live under The Bridge.
3. "The Bridge" is the Mackinaw Bridge, and only the Mackinaw Bridge, unless you live in Wayne County or St. Clair County or Chippewa County, where theirs is just "the bridge."
4. When asked, "How far is it to The Bridge?" Michiganians answer in time, not miles. "Why, it's only 3½ hours to The Bridge."
5. We have a Northern Michigan area, but no real Southern Michigan area. We go Up North, but we don't go down south, we go down state. Anything north of Clare is Up North. We can go to the Thumb, the little finger, the palm of the mitten or the top of the mitten.

K KINSMAN

Race
American Indian: <1%
Asian: <1%
Black/African American: 2%
Hispanic or Latino: 3%
Other: 3%
White: 94%

Ancestry
German: 29%
U.S./American: 9%
Polish: 8%
French: 8%
Irish: 8%
English: 7%

L LIGHTHOUSE OR LANDMARK

Tom Nugent

According to Monroe County Convention and Tourism Bureau, Cabela's World's Foremost Outfitters is the state's #1 tourist destination with 6,000,000 visitors annually. Not only do they have hunting, fishing, camping and outdoor gear, they have educational and entertainment services as well. See 16S.

M MUSEUMS

<u>Dundee</u> *Old Mill Museum:* fashion, furniture, farm life, American Indians, Henry Ford

<u>Monroe</u> *County Historical Museum:* early maps, American Indians, the French, George Custer, Bronco McKart

…Labor History Museum: labor history in Monroe Co.

…Martha Baker Country Store Museum: 1860s one-room school is now a 1918 country store

...*Navarre Anderson Trading Post Complex:* 1789, French-Canadian home, the oldest wooden residence still standing in the state, includes cookhouse and barn

Michigan State Historic Preservation Office

Monroe County Historical Museum

...*Vietnam Veterans Historical Museum:* 1,500 original era artifacts; staffed by Vietnam veterans

Temperance Banner Oak School: 1870s, one-room

N NATURAL RESOURCES

Elevation: 600 - 700 feet
Physiography: lake-border plains

Forest type: elm-ash-cottonwood, oak-hickory
Public/private forests: 19% of county
FYI: Of the 15 forest types in Michigan, the swamp hardwoods (commonly called elm-ash-cottonwood) are characterized by wet soils and fluctuating water levels. They cover over 2 million acres with 57 species of trees. The most common trees in this forest are red maple, silver maple, black ash, green ash and cedar. Michigan Forests Forever

NPCR

Water in county: 2% of county
  Bay: North Maumee
  Lakes: 40
    ...**largest:** fly ash dilution pond
  Rivers: Huron, River Raisin
  Rivers & streams: 460 miles

Great Lakes islands: Gard, American Indian (part of the international Wildlife Refuge)
Great Lakes peninsula: Lost, Woodtick
Great Lakes shoreline: 57 miles of Lake Erie

Growing season, avg.: 180 days (#1/MI) (4 temp. zones)
  Last freeze, avg.: April 25 – May 10
  First freeze, avg.: Oct. 5 – Oct. 20
Precipitation, annual avg.: rainfall: 31 inches
        snowfall: 33 inches

Temperature (F), avg.: January: high 32°, low 17°
        July: high 84°, low 63°
  Annual: >90°: 16 days (#3/MI), **<0°:** 6 days
Tornadoes (1930-2010): 30

O ORIGINS

Azalia:[u] the daughter of a railroad executive; 1869
Carleton:[v] Michigan poet, Will Carleton (see 30W, 20Y); 1872
Dundee:[v,t] a village in Scotland; 1823
Estral Beach:[v] *estral* is Spanish for star; 1925
Frenchtown:[ct] a hundred French families from Canada came here in just four years; 1780-1784
Luna Pier:[c] means "moon overlooking the pier;" 1900s
Maybee:[v] mill owner, William Maybee; 1873
Milan:[c] formerly called Tolanville, Farmersville and Woodward's Mill; 1836
Monroe:[c,co,ct] U.S. President James Monroe (1758-1831); 1780
Petersburg:[c] farmer, Richard Peters; 1824
South Rockwood:[v] settler from Rockwood, Ontario; 1863
Temperance:[u] original owners of the land deeded all the lots they sold so that no liquor could be used, made, or sold on the property; 1884

P PARKS

National: 1 **State:** 5 **County:** 4 **Local:** 28
Number of campsites: 1,500

National: *River Raisin National Battlefield Park:* Visitor Center, Heritage Trail, driving tour; in 1813, during the War of 1812, hundreds of local citizens and 901 American soldiers were killed here, more than any other single battle of the war.

Monroe County Historical Museum

State Game Area: (6,500 acres) Erie, Petersburg, Pointe Aux Peaux, Pointe Mouillee
State Park: *Sterling:* on Lake Erie, 1,300 acres, 1 mile of beach; shore fishing, fishing lagoons, trails, camping, boating, swimming
State Wildlife Area: *Plum Creek Bay:* 400 acres

Other: *Detroit River International Wildlife Refuge:* a joint effort of the U.S. and Canada, with 48 miles along the Detroit River and Lake Erie to provide safe refuge for millions of migratory birds; eagle tours, byways to flyways bird driving tour, hawk watch

Monroe County Convention & Tourism Bereau

Q QUOTE FROM THE LOCALS

"The River Raisin has provided valuable resources and quality of life to citizens of and visitors to Historic Monroe County since our founding in the 1700s. The Indians referred to the river as "Numasepp," or River of Sturgeon, reflecting the river's value as a source of food and course water. Our founders, the early French settlers of this area, named it "Riviere Aux Raisins" or River of Grapes. Early records tell of vast amounts of wild grapes that grew along the fertile banks. This beautiful river was used as a means of transportation and an awesome venue for numerous types of recreation and get-togethers." Do You Know Monroe? with Johnnie Tourism monroeinfo.com

R RECREATION & SPORTS

Golf courses: 21
Great Lakes marinas: 43
…**Boat slips:** 4,800 (#3/MI)
Hiking/skiing/mountain biking trails: 8 miles
Public access sites: 10
Public recreational land: 2% of county
Recreational harbor: Bolles Harbor of Refuge, Monroe Harbor of Refuge
Southern Michigan Timberwolves: minor league football

S STATE OF MICHIGAN

Lake Erie Facts
Size: 11th largest in world;
4th largest Great Lake
Length: 241 miles
Average depth: 62 feet
Shoreline (including islands): 871 miles
Special features: warmest, most biologically productive
Borders on: Michigan, New York, Ohio, Pennsylvania, and Ontario, Canada

T TRAVEL

Airport: Monroe Custer
Bus: Lake Erie Transit
Circle Tour: Lake Erie via I-75
Distance to Lansing: 100 miles
Historic Heritage Route: 2 miles of Monroe St. in Monroe
Main roads: I-75, I-275, US-23, US-24, US-223, M-50
Memorial Highways: I-75, *American Legion MH:* see 6T
…I-275, *Philip A. Hart MH:* he (1912-1976) was a U.S. Senator from Michigan who was instrumental in creating the Pictured Rocks and Sleeping Bear Dunes National Parks.
…US-23, *United Spanish War Veterans MH:* see 1T
…US-24, *Fallen Soldiers of Iraqi Freedom MH*

…M-125, *Clara Barton MH:* she (1821-1912) is best known as the founder of the American Red Cross in 1881; she also was a Civil War nurse and worked tirelessly after the war finding missing soldiers and marking graves. See 18Y, 32Y.

NPCR

…M-125, *Veterans Memorial Road*
Michigan Welcome Center: US-23 in Dundee; I-75 near Monroe
FYI: Dixie Hwy. was once an American Indian trail between Detroit and Toledo; it became Michigan's first highway in 1829.
FYI: Over the years, I-75 has been called, in part or as a whole, proposed, promoted or legalized: Algonquin Trail, American Legion Memorial Hwy., Arctic-Tropic Overland Trail, Bicentennial Freedom Way, Blue Water Trail, Center Line Hwy., Charles J. Rogers Interchange, Chrysler Freeway., Dixie Hwy., East Michigan Pike, Fisher Freeway, G. Mennen Williams Hwy., Prentiss M. Brown Memorial Hwy., Seaway Freeway and Veterans of World War I Memorial Hwy. Barnett

U UNIVERSITIES & COLLEGES

Monroe Community College: est. 1964, 4,700 students. It provides a variety of higher education opportunities to enrich the lives of the residents of Monroe County. Intramural sports.

V VARIETY

George Armstrong Custer (1839-1877) was raised in Monroe and graduated from West Point. He led the Michigan Calvary Brigade in the Great Sioux War of 1876 in what would become known as Custer's Last Stand. He died with 266 others at the Battle of Little Big Horn in Montana, a battle that has been studied by historians ever since. Some consider him a hero and others think he was a fool.

W WANDERLUST

Agri-tourism: *Bennett's Orchard & Country Store:* U-pick, apples, peaches, cider, pumpkins, flowers
…*Calder Dairy and Farms:* since 1946, milk in glass bottles, home delivery, ice cream, farm tours
…*Whittaker's Berry Farm:* strawberries, raspberries
Farmers Market: Monroe, Parran's
Brewery: Original Gravity Brewing Co.
Fall colors: middle October
Lighthouse, other: Toledo
Live theater: River Raisin Centre for the Arts, La-Z-Boy Center at MCC, Monroe Community Players
MotorCities National Heritage Area: yes
Shopping mall: Mall of Monroe, Monroe Factory Shops

Monroe Muskrat Project: look for Francois, the mascot of the Monroe County Convention and Tourism Bureau, and his decorated muskrat statues around Monroe.

X X-TRA STUFF

County fair: *Monroe County Fair Association:* Michigan's finest fair; the steam locomotive Little Smokey is ready for you to ride; the 1883 Little Brown Bear House is open for storytelling; the 1857 Eby log cabin is open for tours; during fair week in August.

Hospitals: Memorial, Mercy Memorial

Large employers: Automotive Components Holdings (makes auto parts), Memorial Hospital, International Trans Co. (auto parts), National Galvanizing (hot-rolled steel), Detroit Edison (electric steam services), Cabela's (retail sporting goods), La-Z-Boy (makes chairs), Guardian Industries (makes glass), Monroe Shock Absorbers

Detroit Edison Monroe Power Plant: twin 800' towers are the world's largest

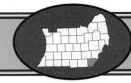

Enrico Fermi Nuclear Generating Station: these two units (only one is operational now) on Lake Erie are owned by DTE Energy and provide low-cost, carbon-free electricity for southeastern Michigan.

NPCR

Lake Erie produces more walleye fish than all the other Great Lakes combined.

Monroe County: has the largest 4-H club program in Michigan with 2,000 youth members, 123 clubs, 1,200 adult volunteers; in addition, another 9,000 youth are touched by 4-H programs. See 54A.

…is the #1 county in the state for licensed Charter Boat Captains

…is the #1 county in the state and the #7 county in the nation for golf holes per capita

The oldest Centennial Farm in Michigan was established in Frenchtown Township in 1809.

FYI: **Lake Ontario Facts**

Size: 14th largest in world;
  5th largest Great Lake
Length: 193 miles
Average depth: 283 feet
Shoreline (including islands): 712 miles
Special features: baymouth bars create lagoons, sheltered harbors and wetlands
Borders on: New York and Ontario, Canada

Y YESTERYEAR

"As World War II broke out in Europe, Detroit [and the surrounding area] started producing airplanes, tanks, and other war materials. After the attack on Pearl Harbor, the auto industry dedicated all of its efforts and resources to winning the war and played a significant role in the Allied victory. Michigan's success earned it the title of "Arsenal of Democracy" throughout the world. Since over 600,000 Michigan men and women served in the Armed Forces, women did

NPCR-2

much of the labor at the plants. 'Rosie the Riveter' was a nickname given to these hardworking women who contributed so much to the war effort." *Portraits of Michigan*

NPCR-2

NPCR-2

Z ZOO & ANIMAL PLACES

Detroit River International Wildlife Refuge: see 58P

Don't forget to check the *BIBLIOGRAPHY & NOTES* at the back of the book for explanations and additional information.

A AGRICULTURE

Land in farms: 54% of county
Number of farms: 1,200
Size of average farm: 200 acres
Market value of all products: #14 of 83 counties
Crops: ...most acres: corn
...highest $ sales: potatoes, vegetables
Livestock: ...largest number: cattle & calves
...highest $ sales: milk & dairy products
Among the top Michigan counties:
- #1- acres & revenue of all vegetables [includes carrots, cucumbers, peas, snap beans], honey, potatoes
- #2- colonies of bees
- #3- Christmas tree sales, oats, snap beans
- #5- alfalfa, cattle farms, dairy farms

Dairy, food and meat processing plants: 15
State ranking for harvested trees: #52 of 83 counties
AgBioResearch Centers (MSU): *Montcalm Research Center:* with emphasis on potatoes and dry beans, scientist are studying all factors of production to make the least possible environmental impact.

FYI: Potatoes are Michigan's #1 produce crop with over 50,000 acres in production; Michigan is the #1 state for producing "new" potatoes and potatoes for potato chips. Of the 1.5 billion pounds of potatoes produced annually, 70% are made

Michigan Farm Bureau

into potato chips, 20% are sold fresh, 5% are processed and 5% are used for next year's seed. The estimated value of the Michigan potato crop is 100 million dollars. The average person consumes 50 pounds of fresh potatoes each year and 82 pounds in chips, frozen, and other potato products. This county has about 16,000 acres of potatoes, making it the "potato capital of Michigan." Michigan.gov, mipotato.com

Michigan Farm Bureau

Round white potatoes are the most popular Michigan grown potato. It is good for any type of cooking and is made into potato chips. The potato chip processors are in Detroit, making Detroit "the potato chip capital of the world." See 82X.

B BRIDGE OR BOAT

NPCR

A personal watercraft (PWC), both the sit-down and stand-up variety, is very popular on lakes and rivers anywhere in Michigan.

C CELEBRATIONS

<u>Carson City</u> *Frontier Days:* hot air balloon shoot-out, pie baking contest, 3 parades, June
<u>Edmore</u> *Potato Festival:* air dogs, parade, car & bike show, ice cream social, fireworks, Aug.

Courtesy of the Daily News Greenville

<u>Greenville</u> *Danish Festival:* Hans Christian Andersen play, Lego contest, Danish food, Tivoli Gardens, Grand Dansk Parade, queen, music, food, Aug.

<u>Howard City</u> *Burley Park Antique & Collectible Market & Car Show:* 5 days, May-Oct.
...Harvest Festival: quilts, bow shooting, motorcycles, parade, tractor pull, pizza eating contest, farmer's market, pumpkin painting, Sept.
<u>Lakeview</u> *Summerfest:* fireman's parade, strawberry shortcake, horseshoes, ice cream, June
<u>Sheridan</u> *Springfest:* queen, parade, carnival, horseshoes, car show, garden tractor pull, May
<u>Sidney</u> *Heritage Festival:* at the Montcalm Heritage Village; one-room schoolhouse demonstration, quits, music, vintage baseball, gospel sing, Aug.
<u>Stanton</u> *Old Fashioned Days:* talent show, fireman's parade, volleyball, softball, mud ball, car show, Aug.
<u>Trufant</u> *Jubilee:* kiddie parade, fireman's parade, car show, BBQ, Sept.

D DEMOGRAPHICS

Population: 63,000   **Persons per sq. mile:** 90
Largest city: Greenville   **Population:** 8,500
Largest township: Eureka   **Population:** 3,960
Largest village: Howard City   **Population:** 1,810
Median household income: $38,100
Owner-occupied median house value: $115,000
Persons affiliated with a religious congregation: 32%
Persons below poverty level: 20%
Students receiving school lunch subsidy: 45%

E ENVIRONMENT

The <u>Organization for Bat Conservation</u> is dedicated to protecting bats, other wildlife and the ecosystems they need to survive. They provide more live shows and media events than any other bat organization in the U.S. They also do bat rescue from all over the world and these animals are on display at the Bat Zone (in Oakland County). They have ideas for bat house projects and information on using bats for insect control and relocation of bats to suitable habitats. Since much prime bat habitat has been destroyed, they suggest providing bat houses as an alternative for the bats so they do not have to live in human dwellings. It should be noted that in the last 50 years, less than 40 people have gotten rabies from a wild bat bite. See 59F.

F FLORA & FAUNA

Ohio State Weed Lab Archive, The Ohio State University

Lambs quarter is a nutritious, edible weed similar in taste to spinach or chard with an earthy, mineral rich taste. It is very common in gardens and landscaped areas and is generally removed as a nuisance weed.

Organization for Bat Conservation

Big brown bats have a wingspan of 13"-16" and are the most common bat in cities and rural areas. They are highly adaptable to their environment. As an insectivore whose favorite meal is beetles, each bat can eat 2,000 – 6,000 insects a night. This flying mammal is a night predator and returns to its roost during the day where it hangs upside down to digest its food. See 59E.

G GOVERNMENT

County: ...**created:** 1831 ...**organized:** 1850
...**originally part of:** Ionia County
Size: 461,000 acres / 708 sq. miles (28 of 83 counties)
The county has 3 cities, 6 villages, 20 townships with 1 as a charter township, 3 unincorporated communities and 7 school districts.

Ryan Fox

County seat: Stanton
...**Homestead property tax:** 40 mills

From BIBLIOGRAPHY & NOTES...

D DEMOGRAPHICS: Owner-occupied median house value: The value of Michigan real estate declined an average of 26% from 2006 to 2011.

H HISTORICAL MARKERS 2 of 3

Greenville: 1844, John Green was founder, dam and sawmill owner, and financier of early business, so Green's Village was changed to Greenville in 1871.

Michigan State Historic Preservation Office

St. Paul's Episcopal Church: 1856, was built by Congregationalists and moved to this site in Greenville in the 1880s.

National Register of Historic Places: 2 listings
State Historic Sites: 10 listings

I INFORMATION

Chamber of Commerce: Carson City, Edmore, Greenville, Lakeview, Panhandle Area, Trufant
Visitor: Montcalm County Community Information, Center, montcalm.org

J JOKES

You might be a long distance truck driver from Michigan if…

…you used to haul Michigan-made auto parts but now you haul imported auto parts.

…the only reason you live in the country is to have a lot big enough to park your rig.

…you can't wait to get home and you can't wait to get on the road again.

…sometimes you hate your job/boss/truck/wife, and sometimes you love your job/boss/truck/wife, and sometimes that is all in one day.

…you know how hard it is to discipline your kids over the phone.

…you know the rest of the world doesn't understand about your way of life.

…your Detroit Lions ball cap used to get laughed at everywhere you went, but lately you're getting a little R E S P E C T.

K KINSMAN

Race
American Indian: <1%
Asian: <1%
Black/African American: 2%
Hispanic or Latino: 3%
Other: 2%
White: 94%

Ancestry
German: 23%
English: 13%
U.S./American: 12%
Irish: 10%
Dutch 6%
Danish: 6%

L LIGHTHOUSE OR LANDMARK

This statue of the Little Mermaid helps commemorate Greenville's Danish (Denmark) heritage. Written in 1837 by Hans Christian Anderson, the story is about a mermaid and her love for a handsome prince. The statue was created by a local artist.

Greenville Chamber of Commerce

M MUSEUMS

Edmore *Old Fence Rider Historical Center:* western heritage
…*Pine Forest Historical Forest Museum:* rare collectibles, in an old church

Greenville *The Fighting Falcon Military Museum:* Greenville is the home to the most famous combat glider of WWII, the CG-4A.

Deb Schmucker

...*Flat River Historical Museum:* 2 buildings, gardens; American Indian, Danish, logging and local history

...*Oakfield Pioneer Heritage:* on Podunk Rd., kids puzzle sheet for historical exhibits

Lakeview *Area Museum:* in an old well house

Sidney *Montcalm Heritage Village:* 26 historical building with 100s of artifacts, at MCC campus

N NATURAL RESOURCES

Elevation: 700 - 900 feet
Physiography: rolling plains

Forest type: maple-beech, oak-hickory, birch-hemlock, elm-ash-cottonwood
Public/private forests: 29% of county

Water in county: 1% of county
   Lakes: 130   ...**largest:** Big Whitefish
   Rivers: Flat, Pine
   Rivers & streams: 480 miles

Growing season, avg.: 140 days (3-4 temp. zones)
   Last freeze, avg.: May 5 – May 20
   First freeze, avg.: Sept. 25 – Oct. 4
Precipitation, annual avg.: rainfall: 33 inches
                      snowfall: 55 inches
Temperature (F), avg.: January: high 29°, low 14°
                July: high 84°, low 58°°
Annual: >90°: 14 days, **<0°:** 10 days
Tornadoes (1930-2010): 14

O ORIGINS

Carson City:[c] boomtown Carson City, Nevada; 1850
Crystal:[u] on Crystal Lake; 1853
Edmore:[v] town founder, Edwin Moore; 1878
Entrican:[u] George Entrican, early Union soldier; 1879
Greenville:[c] first settler, John Green; 1844
Howard City:[v] railroad attorney, Wm. Howard; 1868
Lakeview:[v] west bank of Tamarack Lake; 1858
McBride:[v] sawmill owner, Alexander McBride; 1874
Montcalm:[co] French military commander in the French and Indian War, Marquis Louis de Montcalm; 1844
Pierson:[v] first settler, David Pierson; 1856
Sheridan:[v] Civil War Gen. Philip Sheridan; 1851
Six Lakes: six lakes now connected by channels; 1876
Stanton:[c] Edwin Stanton, Sec. of War under President Lincoln; 1862
Trufant: early settler, Emery Trufant; 1871

P PARKS

National: 0 **State:** 5 **County:** 6 **Local:** 14
Number of campsites: 2,300
National Forest: *Manistee:* 1,800 acres

State Game Areas: (24,000 acres), Edmore, Flat River, Langston, Stanton, Vestaburg

State Linear Trail Park: White Pine State Park, 92 miles from Cadillac to Comstock Park

County: *Flat River Nature Park:* 69 acres, over 4,000 feet of frontage on the beautiful Flat River
...*Ford Lincoln Park:* on Townline Lake, group facilities include bunkhouse, heated cabins, kitchen & dining hall; boating, fishing, swimming
Other: *Comden-Towle Model Forest:* 40 acres, by the Montcalm Conservation District to demonstrate techniques for timber improvement, forestry and sustainable nature areas; trails, picnic shelter, visitors' center
...*The West Michigan Parks and Recreation Inventory:* see 3P

Q QUOTE FROM THE LOCALS

"Based on the faith and customs of their forefathers, the Amish place a premium on stability. In the midst of modern agricultural farms, integrated manufacturing, and state-of-the-art healthcare facilities, the Amish eliminate fads, social status, and worldly stresses and allurements. They provide their daily basic requirements for themselves and their families. Part of their lifestyle is creating hand-crafted items, baked goods or fresh produce to sell in order to supplement their needs." *greenvillemi.org*

The Greenville Chamber of Commerce has a map of local Amish farms and shops where you can "step back in time." You can find fresh produce and baked goods, handmade quilts or furniture and enjoy talking to the local Amish proprietors. See 18V.

R RECREATION & SPORTS

Auto racing: *Crystal Motor Speedway:* The Dirt Racer's Destination!
…*Mid-Michigan Motorplex:* ¼-mile drag strip
Golf courses: 7
Hiking/skiing/mountain biking trails: 10 miles
Public access sites: 29
Public recreational land: 5% of county
Rail-trail: (45 miles) Fred Meijer Heartland, White Pine
State/federal wild/scenic/natural river: 80 miles of the Flat River
Moreland's USA Sports Park: 2.5 miles of Supercross track, 3 miles of Hare Scramble Trails

S STATE OF MICHIGAN

<u>Tree City USA</u> is a program sponsored by the Michigan Department of Natural Resources, Urban and Community Forestry Program and the National Arbor Day Foundation. It recognizes communities and utilities for their commitment to quality tree care. A community must commit to four standards:

1. a tree board or department
2. tree ordinance for planting, maintenance and removal

3. a community forestry program with a designated budget of at least $2 per capita; (the average expenditure is $8 per capita)
4. Arbor Day observances and proclamation

There are around 125 Tree Cities, Tree Line and Tree Campus USA in Michigan, including Howard City. *Michigan.gov.dnr*

T TRAVEL

Airport: Lakeview-Griffith Field, Greenville Mun.
Distance to Lansing: 70 miles
Main roads: US-131, M-46, M-57, M-66, M-82, M-91
Memorial Highways: M-66, *Green Arrow Route*: see 8T
…M-82, *Korean War Veterans MH*: in honor of those who served and died in this military conflict from 1950-1953

U UNIVERSITIES & COLLEGES

Montcalm Community College: est. 1965, 3,000 students. It is a leader in creating a learning community, contributing to shared economic, cultural and social prosperity for all our citizens. M-TEC. Intramural & club sports

V VARIETY

In 1934, Dutch immigrant, Hendrik Meijer (MY er), was a barber who opened a small grocery store in Greenville to help his customers during the Depression. An innovator in the grocery store business, he was among the first to use advertising, grocery carts and conveyor belts, as well as keeping costs down and quality up. <u>Meijer</u> opened his first food and general merchandise store in 1962 as Meijer Thrifty Acres and created a new retail model that has

NPCR

been copied worldwide. Fred Meijer, son of Hendrik and head of the company, left a legacy of philanthropy around the Grand Rapids area, including the Frederik Meijer Gardens & Sculpture Park. (See 39S). Today, Meijer has almost 200 stores in five states and employees 60,000 people.

W WANDERLUST

Agri-tourism: *Anderson & Girls Orchards/Gifts:* apples, peaches, bakery, hayrides, pumpkins

...*Klackle Orchards:* the Family Fun Farm (the Disney of family farms), U-pick, cider, maze, bakery

Cheryl Strautz

Fall colors: early October

Live theater: Hans Christian Andersen Theatre, Flat River Community Players, the Barn Theatre at MCC

X X-TRA STUFF

County fair: *Montcalm County Fair Asso.:* July
Famous people: ...*Sports*: Greg Cadaret, Ty Hallock
Hospitals: Carson City, Kelsey Memorial, Sheridan Community, Spectrum Health United Memorial
Large employers: Michigan Department of Corrections, Meijer, Spectrum Health United Memorial Hospital, Carson City Hospital, Federal Mogul (makes bearings, power transmission equipment), Clarion Technologies (molded plastic), Greenville Tool & Die, Vertis (offset printing)

Y YESTERYEAR

"Early settlement of the Montcalm County area by Native Americans is documented as far back as 8000 B.C. along the Flat River near Greenville. By 1800 A.D., more Europeans were arriving in the Great Lakes area, crowding out the existing native populations. When the settlers arrived in this area in the late 1830s, there were only remnants of the Ottawa,

Chippewa and Potawatomi Indian tribes who had ceded their lands under the Treaty of Washington in 1836." Montcalm org See 37Y.

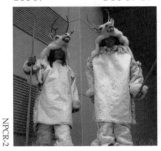

NPCR-2

NPCR-5

Z ZOO & ANIMAL PLACES

Cheryl Strautz

Petting zoo: Anderson & Girls Orchards, Klackle Orchards

NOTE: (#x/MI) indicates ranking from highest number or percentage (#1) to lowest number or percentage (#83) in Michigan. The significance of either a high or low number depends on the item it describes.

A AGRICULTURE

Land in farms: 6% of county
Number of farms: 140
Size of average farm: 160 acres
Market value of all products: #70 of 83 counties
Crops: ...most acres: forage land
...highest $ sales: corn, soybeans, wheat
Livestock: ...largest number: cattle
...highest $ sales: dairy products
Dairy, food and meat processing plants: 4
State ranking for harvested trees: #14 of 83 counties
FYI: Michigan Forest Facts

- About 50% of Michigan is covered in forests.
- All the wood in Michigan forests, if piled into a stack 8' wide and 4' tall, would stretch around the world 10 times!
- Each year Michigan adds 8,000 miles to that pile of timber (#2 above), more than any other state.
- The most common trees in Michigan are the sugar maple, red maple, quaking aspen, northern white cedar and northern red oak.
- The maple-beech-basswood upland hardwood forest makes up over half of the Michigan forest and is on the increase.
- Most of Michigan's forest lies in the northern two-thirds of the state. But even in the lower third where there are more farms, cities and roads, a person is never more than a 30-minute drive from a forest. uptreeid.com

B BRIDGE or BOAT

NPCR

Boats have to be prepared for the winter season. Many boats are covered with shrink-wrap to protect them from the elements. The blue color absorbs the sun's heat, allowing the snow and ice to melt and slide off easily. A wood frame on the inside of the boat, industrial strapping, heavy plastic blue shrink-wrap and a heat gun with a 5" flame is what it takes to get the job done. Think of the boat as being in hibernation, just waiting for the warm weather so it can emerge from its long winter sleep and once again be out on the water doing its thing.

C CELEBRATIONS

Atlanta *Elk Festival:* parade, chicken throwing contest, pie eating, bubble gum blowing, Sept.
Hillman *Mill River Days:* celebrate rich heritage on the Thunder Bay River, July
...*VJ Day Festival:* fish fry, car show, quilt raffle, pig roast, elk viewing, fireworks, Aug.
Lewiston *Morel Mushroom Festival:* May
...*Auto Show:* June
...*Annual Timberfest & Arts & Crafts in the Park:* food, music, fun, Aug.

D DEMOGRAPHICS

Population: 9,800   **Persons per sq. mile:** 18
Largest township: Albert   **Population:** 2,530
Largest village: Hillman (partial)   **Population:** 700
Median household income: $32,800
Owner-occupied median house value: $104,000
Persons affiliated with a religious congregation: 41%
Persons below poverty level: 19%
Students receiving school lunch subsidy: 57%
FYI: Forty-eight percent (4,400) of all housing units in this county are vacation, seasonal, or occasional homes. US Census

E ENVIRONMENT

"The Thunder Bay River Watershed is a vast river system well known for its high water quality and aesthetically pleasing scenery. Year-round outdoor recreational opportunities within the watershed are seemingly endless and include canoeing, camping, hiking, hunting, fishing, golfing, wildlife viewing, skiing, swimming and snowmobiling. The area is also unique in the fact that the western half of the watershed is host to the only elk herd population in Michigan. The 1,200 square miles of the watershed is in 5 counties...and exhibits a mix of forests, wetlands, open spaces, agriculture and developed areas." Thunder Bay River Watershed Initiative

F FLORA & FAUNA

Alice Welch, USDA

The white pine trees of Michigan were once the greatest stands in the world. Although most of the original stands are gone, they are being replanted and managed for use in the construction industry. See 60S.

Gary Zahm, USFWS

Elk can weigh up to 1,000 pounds and range over 3 counties in this area. Fall is the best time to see them as the males round up their harems and fend off rivals with their loud bugling. See 60L, 60P.

From BIBLIOGRAPHY & NOTES...

H HISTORICAL MARKERS: At the discretion of the author, not all historical markers have been included.

G GOVERNMENT

County: ...created: 1840 **...organized:** 1881
...originally part of: Cheboygan, Alpena Counties
Size: 360,000 acres / 548 sq. miles (61 of 83 counties)
The county has 1 village, 8 townships, 3 unincorporated communities and 3 school districts.

Jessie Jakubik

Jessie Jakubik

County seat: Atlanta
...Homestead property tax: (Briley Twp). 23 mills
Motto: <u>Atlanta</u> Chamber: *Elk Capital of Michigan Since 1986*
...<u>Lewiston</u> Area Chamber: *All Seasons are Picture Perfect in Lewiston*

H HISTORICAL MARKERS 3 of 5

Angusdale Stock Farm: 1901, Cephas Buttles bought 25,000 acres of cutover timber land and sold small farms to immigrants; the soil was too poor for farming and by the 1920s his dream had died. See 48Y.
Big Rock: 1882, the rock marks the spot of a former settlement.

Camp Lunden: 1933, former site of a CCC camp; what remains today is a landscaped earthen scale model of the state of Michigan with an artesian well feeding the lakes.

State Historic Sites: 4 listings

I INFORMATION

Chamber of Commerce: Atlanta, 989-785-3400, atlantamichiganchamber.com
...Hillman, 989-742-3739, hillmanmichigan.org
...Lewiston Area, 989-786-2293, lewistownchamber.com

J JOKES

You might be a rural Michiganian if…

…your water is all-natural, untreated, not chlorinated, and comes directly to you from under the ground and right into your home.

…you have an on-site sewer treatment facility, commonly know as a septic system.

…you don't have to pay a quarterly water and sewer bill to "the city."

…your property taxes are a lot less than those of your city friends.

…your municipal services are also a lot less than those of your city friends.

…what some people call the "middle of nowhere," you call "home sweet home."

NPCR

K KINSMAN

Race
American Indian: <1%
Asian: <1%
Black/African American: <1%
Hispanic or Latino: <1%
Other: 2%
White: 98%

Ancestry
German: 28%
English: 13%
U.S./American: 10%
Irish: 9%
Polish: 8%
French: 7%

L LIGHTHOUSE OR LANDMARK

Jessie Jakubik

The largest herd of wild elk (see 60F) east of the Mississippi River can be found in Pigeon River County State Forest, and that makes Atlanta the Elk Capital of Michigan. The elk range is roughly from Gaylord to Indian River to Onaway to Hillman.

M MUSEUMS

<u>Hillman</u> *Brush Creek Mill:* 22′ stainless steel water wheel, classes, group tours

N NATURAL RESOURCES

Elevation: 700 - 1,300 feet
Physiography: hill-lands, rolling plains

Forest type: aspen-birch, maple-beech-hemlock, oak-hickory, pine
Public/private forests: 82% of county

NPCR

Water in county: 2% of county
 Lakes: 100
  …largest: West Twin Lake
 Rivers: Black, Thunder Bay
 Rivers & streams: 310 miles

Growing season, avg.: 106 days (3 temp. zones)
 Last freeze, avg.: May 30 – June 10
 First freeze, avg.: Aug. 30 – September 15
Precipitation, annual avg.: rainfall: 28 inches
                snowfall: 66 inches
Temperature (F), avg.: January: high 28°, low 9°
                July: high 81°, low 54°
 Annual: >90°: 8 days, **<0°:** 23 days
Tornadoes (1930-2010): 6

O ORIGINS

<u>Atlanta</u>:[u] the area reminded a Civil War veteran of Atlanta, Georgia; 1881
<u>Canada Creek Ranch</u>:[u] local Canada Creek; 1939
<u>Hillman</u>:[v] founded by John Hillman; 1880
<u>Lewiston</u>:[u] after Lewiston, NY, which was named after Morgan Lewis, Governor of NY; 1892
<u>Montmorency</u>:[co] Count Morenci was a Revolutionary War patriot; and/or possibly means "mountain moor" since the county has some boggy land; 1840

P PARKS

National: 0 **State:** 8 **County:** 0 **Local:** 3
Number of campsites: 740
National Wildlife Refuge: 40 acres
State Forest: *Thunder Bay River:* over 120,000 acres, headwaters of Thunder Bay River

...*Pigeon River Country:* called the Big Wild, 118,000 acres in Cheboygan, Otsego and Montmorency Counties

NPCR

...**Campgrounds:** 7

...**Pathway:** 94 miles

State Game Area: 5 areas covering 20,000 acres

State Park: *Clear Lake:* 290 acres, quiet, secluded, abundant wildlife; swimming, boating, fishing

Local: *Emerick Park:* on Thunder Bay River; camping, picnics, good fishing

Q QUOTE FROM THE LOCALS

NPCR

"Summer: Summer days can be spent on sandy beaches, picnicking, soaking up rays of sunshine and then cooling off in the clear blue waters.

"Fall: Red and orange fall days offer miles of breathtaking scenes of Mother Nature at her best.

"Winter: Crystal white winter days can be spent downhill skiing, on snowmobiles, or cross-country skiing on beautiful groomed trails enjoying wildlife in their natural surroundings.

"Spring: Wake up to sparkling mornings of clean, cool air that will fill you with energy to...spend a day hunting the elusive morel mushroom or just enjoying the wildflowers." Lewiston Chamber of Commerce

R RECREATION & SPORTS

Auto racing: Sno*Drift rally racing events are run on snow-covered gravel surface roads in January.

Blue Ribbon Trout Streams: Black River & East Branch, Canada Creek, Gilchrist Creek, Hunt Creek

Golf courses: 2

Hiking/skiing/mountain biking trails: 70 miles

MI Shore-to-Shore (horse) **Riding & Hiking Trail:** yes

Off-road vehicle trails: 140 miles (#5/MI)

Public access sites: 20

Public recreational land: 37% of county

State/federal wild/scenic/natural river: 1 mile of the Thunder Bay River

State-funded snowmobile trails: 60 miles

Canada Creek Ranch is a private hunting, fishing and recreation club on 13,500 acres.

Elk County Snowmobile Trails link up with other trails going north and south.

This county allows ATV's on county roads.

The Voyer Lake Shooting Range has a covered shooting area with 100, 50 and 25 yard shooting ranges.

S STATE OF MICHIGAN

Alice Welch, USDA

Since 1955, the White Pine has been the State Tree. It was the great white pine forest of northern Michigan that provided building timber for much of the Midwest in the late 1800s. The lumber boom lead the way in establishing communities and transportation networks that helped lay the groundwork for much of Michigan's early wealth. See 60F.

T TRAVEL

Airports: Atlanta Municipal, Garland, Hillman
Distance to Lansing: 150 miles
Main roads: M-32, M-33

U UNIVERSITIES & COLLEGES

None

V VARIETY

Thunder Bay Golf

Thunder Bay Golf

Thunder Bay Resort offers year-round Elk Viewing Carriage Rides with Percheron draft horses pulling the wagon or sleigh. A 5-course gourmet dinner is then cooked over the antique wood stove in the elk antler cabin. *USA Today* named the winter sleigh ride one of the "10 Best Sleigh Rides" in North America. The Resort also offers a variety of accommodations, golfing, quilt retreats, fishing and hunting, and many more fun opportunities.

W WANDERLUST

Fall colors: late September to early October

X X-TRA STUFF

County Fair: *Montmorency County 4-H Fair Association:* Aug.
Large employers: Wayne Wire & Cloth Products (makes filters, blowers, valves, wire), Hillman Community School District, Medilodge Group (skilled nursing), Thunder Bay Community Health Services, H-B Carbide (makes machine tool cutting accessories)
Almost 50% of the housing units in this county are seasonal units, reflecting the large growth in hunt clubs and vacation homes.
Montmorency County is one of the more remote and untouched areas of the state.

Y YESTERYEAR

Prior to statehood in 1837, Michigan was surveyed and divided into one-mile square blocks called sections. Thirty-six sections were then added together to form a township. Most townships are therefore six miles by six miles, or 36 square miles. (There are, of course, exceptions throughout the state). Townships were then added together to form counties. The system of surveying land in advance of settlement assured an orderly pattern of land distribution. The public-lands policies of the United States determined not merely the pattern of land sales, but also the kind of society that would emerge in Michigan - a society of small, independent farmers. See 33P, 63Y.

NPCR-2

NPCR-6

Z ZOO & ANIMAL PLACES

Watchable Wildlife Viewing Areas:ww Fletcher Floodwaters, Tomahawk Creek Flood Area

"Hey, look, we're in this book." That is what every person who lives or travels in Michigan can say when they look through *Discovering Michigan County by County: Your A-Z Guide to each of the 83 counties in the Great Lakes State.* No matter where they live or where they go, there is something about their personal part of Michigan.

A AGRICULTURE

Land in farms: 25% of county
Number of farms: 525
Size of average farm: 150 acres
Market value of all products: #23 of 83 counties
Crops: ...most acres: corn
...highest $ sales: fruits, tree nuts, berries
Livestock: ...largest number: turkeys
...highest $ sales: milk & dairy products
Among the top Michigan counties:
• #2- turkeys
• #8- fruit, tree nuts, berries
Dairy, food and meat processing plants: 22
State ranking for harvested trees: #45 of 83 counties

FYI: Look around you. No matter where you are, chances are you will see some green grass, called <u>turfgrass</u> in the industry. Michigan has almost 2 million acres in grass, 83% of which is residential lawns and, in descending order,  the rest is in golf courses, parks, MDOT highway roadsides, schools, cemeteries and sod farms. Turfgrass is a $1.9 billion dollar industry in this state.

Michigan State University, in partnership with Muskegon Community College, offers a certificate in the Landscape and Lawn Management Program. There is much research being done at MSU to improve the varied grass needs of Michigan with its many different climates and soils. michiganturfgrass.org

B BRIDGE OR BOAT

The *Lake Express Ferry* offers daily 2½ hour trips from Muskegon to Milwaukee, WI, for pedestrians, cars and motorcycles.

C CELEBRATIONS

<u>Fruitport</u> *Old Fashioned Days:* riverboat cruises, pig roast, parade, circus, ox roast, music, May
<u>Holton</u> *Days:* friends, families, food, fun, July
<u>Muskegon Heights</u> *Festival:* music, food, June
<u>Muskegon</u> *Snowfest:* soup and chili contest, euchre, broomball, cornhole, kidsfest, beer tent, Jan.
...*Rock the Coast:* ride the rides during the day and enjoy Christian music at night at Michigan's Adventure Amusement Park, May

...*Bike Time:* motorcycles, music, food, July
...*LST Movies on Deck:* classic movies on a classic ship, July-Aug.; see 61M
...*Miss Michigan Pageant:* June
...*Multicultural Beach Festival:* celebrates the land, lakes, diversity and culture; promotes healthy lifestyles, sustainability, economic development, diversity, lifelong learning, Aug.
...*Unity Christian Music Festival:* music, prayer, Aug.
...*Breakwater Festival:* music, Frisbee dog show, family karaoke, bike run, bike show, food, Sept.
...*Michigan Irish Music Festival:* 3 stages, Irish Heritage Sessions, Irish market, beer, Sept.
...*Buster Keaton Society Convention & Film Festival:* experience the silent movie era, Oct.
<u>North Muskegon</u> *Northside Family Fest:* local bands, food, arts & crafts, parade, Aug.
<u>Ravenna</u> *Dog Daze:* classic car cruise in, games, beer tent, live music, July
<u>Whitehall</u> *White Lake's St. Patrick's Day Blarney Bash:* marching bands, music, beer tent, March
...*Maritime Festival:* maritime heritage, Venetian Boat Parade, music, 5K run, art, Aug.
...*White Lake Fall Festival:* farmer's market, local food, hayrides, waiter & waitress contest, Sept.
...*Tellabration: A Tale for Two Cities:* White Lake Area Adult Storytelling Festival featuring Sesquicentennial Storytelling, Nov.
<u>White Lake</u> *Chamber Music Festival:* Aug.
...*Maritime Festival:* sailing regatta, trout pond, shrimp boil, live bands, Aug.

D DEMOGRAPHICS

Population: 172,200 **Persons per sq. mile:** 338
Largest city: Muskegon **Population:** 38,400
Largest township: Muskegon **Population:** 24,000
Largest village: Lakewood Club **Population:** 1,290
Median household income: $38,900
Owner-occupied median house value: $114,000
Persons affiliated with a religious congregation: 35%
Persons below poverty level: 19%
Students receiving school lunch subsidy: 52%

E ENVIRONMENT

Michigan has about 250,000 acres of <u>sand dunes</u>, and they are the largest assemblage of fresh water dunes in the world. Seventy thousand acres are classified as critical sand dune formations and are regulated by the state. The Michigan Legislature states that sand dunes "are a unique, irreplaceable, and fragile resource that provide significant recreational, economic, scientific, geological, scenic, botanical, educational, agricultural and ecological benefits to the people of this state and to people from other states and countries who visit this resource." When visiting any dune area, remember that dune habitats are fragile and easily damaged by human activity. Stay on paths or boardwalks and do not remove any vegetation. [DNRE]

The sugar sand dunes that surround the harbor formed by Muskegon Lake found an unusual use during World War II. They provided the perfect molding medium for heavy metal foundries producing some of the war materials that helped make Michigan the "Arsenal of Democracy." [Michigan.org] See 58Y.

Prentice Drake

F FLORA & FAUNA

Forest & Kim Starr, Starr Environmental

Beach grass has an important stabilizing effect on the constantly changing shifting sands of the sand dunes. Several different varieties send out rhizomes, horizontal underground stems that are actually different from roots, and they help to bind the sand in place. Please stay on the paths when walking on the dunes so you don't damage the grass.

Alice Welch, USDA

The eastern hog-nosed snake is at home on the wooded sand dunes of western Michigan. Although very intimidating in their behavior with hissing and puffing, they are harmless to humans.

G GOVERNMENT

County: ...created: 1859 ...organized: 1859
...originally part of: Ottawa County
Size: 337,000 acres / 509 sq. miles (69 of 83 counties)
The county has 7 cities, 4 villages, 16 townships with 2 as charter townships, 4 unincorporated communities, 2 Census Designated Place and 12 school districts.

County seat: Muskegon

...Homestead property tax: 39 mills

Motto: <u>Montague</u>: *Home of the World's Largest Weather Vane*, see 61V

...<u>Muskegon County</u>: *a Lake Michigan must... for visiting... doing business... or living... experience the lake effect*

...<u>North Muskegon</u>: *Between the Calm Lake Waters*

...<u>Ravenna</u>: *the place to come home to*

...<u>Roosevelt Park</u>: *A proud community*

H HISTORICAL MARKERS 20 of 28

Bluffton Actors' Colony: 1908, over 200 vaudeville performers played here each summer

Buster Keaton: 1895-1966, he was the son of one of the actor's who founded Bluffton Actor's Colony and is recognized as one of the creative geniuses of silent comedy.

Hackley House: 3-story wood-framed building is one of Michigan's most splendid examples of Queen Anne architecture; a symbol of Muskegon

Charles H. Hackley: 1837-1905, made his fortune in lumber; he was a philanthropist who helped build Muskegon into a center of industry.

Hackley-Holt House: 1857, widower Joseph Hackley (father of Charles, above) married Catherine; he died and she married Henry Holt; he died and she moved from the house.

Hume House: 1889, massive Queen Anne style, larger yet less pretentious than the Hackley house

Thomas Hume: 1848-1920, business partner of Charles Hackley; built their houses adjacent to one another and shared a barn

Jean Baptiste Recollect Trading Post: 1812, a French fur-trader believed to be the first white settler in the area

Lakeside: thrived in the late 1800s lumber era with sawmills, wood products, a piano factory, and today with paper mills

Lumbering on White Lake: 1838-1907, 1,400 logs a day were cut into lumber and shipped to Chicago.

Marsh Field: 1916, minor league baseball

Muskegon Business College: 1888, was the Ferris Business College; now part of Baker College

Muskegon Log Booming Company: 1864, logs floating down the Muskegon River were sorted, chained together and pulled by tugboats to the mills.

Muskegon Woman's Club: 1890, for intellectual improvement and development of women; their 1902 building is neo-classical style

Old Indian Cemetery: 1750, Ottawa Indians; in the 1800s both American Indians and whites were buried there

Pinchtown: 1873, pinched between Lakeside and the City of Muskegon; annexed to the city in 1895.

Ruth Thompson: 1887-1970, U.S. Representative in 1950s, she was first Michigan woman in Congress

Torrent House: 1892, 31-room mansion, home of successful entrepreneur, John Torrent

Union Depot: 1895, red brick Richardsonian Romanesque style; now a visitors' center and museum

White Lake Yacht Club: 1906, summer resort; in disrepair by 1925; purchased by Henry Sturtevant and Clarence Pitking who brought national power boat races to White Lake

National Historic Landmark: SS *Milwaukee Clipper* and *USS Silversides* (SS-236), see 61M

National Register of Historic Places: 13 listings

State Historic Sites: 34 listings

I INFORMATION

Chamber of Commerce: Montague & Whitehall, Muskegon, Ravenna

Visitor: Muskegon County Convention and Visitors Bureau, 800-250-9283, visitmuskegon.org

J JOKES

You'll *never* hear a Michiganian say …

…that she loves hot and humid summer days.

…there's no difference between the U.P. and the Lower Peninsula.

…that he doesn't like living in a state whose shape can be identified from space.

…"So what's the big deal about the Great Lakes anyway?"

…that she gets tired of small towns with tree-lined streets, the green of the landscape and the blue of the water.

…that winter is too short and summer is too long.

K KINSMAN

Race		Ancestry	
American Indian: <1%		German: 17%	
Asian: <1%		Dutch: 10%	
Black/African American: 14%		U.S./American: 7%	
Hispanic or Latino: 5%		English: 7%	
Other: 4%		Irish: 7%	
White: 80%		Polish: 6%	

L LIGHTHOUSE OR LANDMARK

White Lake Area Chamber of Commerce

The White River Light was built in 1875 and is located on the channel between White Lake and Lake Michigan. It features cream yellow brick with an octagon-shaped light tower. It is now a museum and the tower is open for a climb to the top.

M MUSEUMS

<u>Holton</u> *Historical Society Museum:* in the township hall that once was the United Methodist Church

<u>Montague</u> *Museum:* local history and artifacts

<u>Muskegon</u> *County Museum of African American History:* a forum for urban/community pride

…Great Lakes Naval Memorial & Museum: historic naval ships, including the *USS Silversides* that is the most decorated WWII submarine sill afloat; *USS LST* 393 Veterans Museum has movies shown on deck; tours, meeting facilities; see 61H

NPCR   NPCR

…Heritage Museum: focus on Heritage Homes and Industrial Heritage

…Lakeshore Museum Center: natural and cultural history center, plus the magnificent 1880s restored Hackley (1890 appearance) & Hume homes (1915 appearance) and their shared (fire) barn; the 1930s Depression era Scolnik House

…Museum of Art: tradition of aesthetic excellence, study and appreciation of visual arts

…S.S. Milwaukee Clipper: refurbished 1904 "Queen of the Great Lakes;" tours in summer; see 61H

<u>Ravenna</u> *Area Historical Museum:* in historic I.O.O.F. (International Order of Odd Fellows) building

<u>White Hall</u> *Caboose Museum:* railroad history of area

…White River Light Station Museum: 1875, you can climb the spiral staircase of the octagonal tower; displays; see 61L

N NATURAL RESOURCES

Elevation: <600 - 900 feet

Physiography: lake border plains, rolling plains, hill lands

Forest type: aspen-birch, oak-hickory, pine

Public/private forests: 48% of county

Legislatively protected sand dunes: 3,500 acres

Water in county: 4% of county
  Lakes: 70
    ...largest: Muskegon Lake
  Rivers: Muskegon (muss KEY gun), White
  Rivers & streams: 390 miles

Great Lakes shoreline: 27 miles of Lake Michigan

NPCR

Growing season, avg.: 156 days (3-4 temp. zones)
  Last freeze, avg.: May 5 – May 20
  First freeze, avg.: Oct. 5 – Oct. 15
Precipitation, annual avg.: rainfall: 31 inches
                          snowfall: 109 inches
Temperature (F), avg.: January: high 29°, low 17°
                        July: high 80°, low 60°
  Annual: >90°: 5 days, **<0°:** 5 days
Tornadoes (1930-2010): 5

O ORIGINS

Casnovia:ᵛ from Latin meaning "new home" ᴿᵒᵐⁱᵍ, or a variation of Casanova for the teenage Morman settler with 4 wives ᵂⁱᵏⁱᵖᵉᵈⁱᵃ; 1850

Fruitport:ᵛ in fruit-growing country and on an inland lake port that leads to Lake Michigan; 1868

Holton:ᵘ Henry Holton was the Muskegon County delegate to the 1867 State Convention; 1871

Lakewood Club:ᵛ among the lakes and woods; 1912

Montague:ᶜ (MONT a gew) town founder, William Montague Ferry; 1855

Muskegon Heights:ᶜ lots platted and sold to raise money to bring in business; 1890

Muskegon:ᶜ,ᶜᵒ (muss KEY gun) from the American Indian word meaning "marshy river;" 1834

North Muskegon:ᶜ north of Muskegon; 1872

Norton Shores:ᶜ Canadian patriot, Col. Amos Norton; 1845 ʷⁱᵏⁱᵖᵉᵈⁱᵃ

Ravenna:ᵛ surveyor came from Ravenna, OH; 1844

Roosevelt Park:ᶜ to honor President Roosevelt; 1946

Twin Lake:ᵘ two lakes then, but now four lakes; 1866

Wabaningo:ᵘ local Ottawa chief; <1883

Whitehall:ᶜ on the White River and White Lake (with white clay in the water); 1859

P PARKS

National: 0 **State:** 4 **County:** 8 **Local:** 57
Number of campsites: 1,900
National: *Manistee National Forest:* 13,000 acres, part of 600,000 acres in 8 counties

State Game Area: *Muskegon:*ʷʷ 9,100 acres
State Linear Trail Park: *Hart-Montague:*ʷʷ 22 miles, paved trail through rural, forested lands
State Park: *Duck Lake:* 725 acres on Lake Michigan, towering sand dunes, woods, swimming, fishing

*...Hoffmaster:*ʷʷ,ʷᵇᵃ 1,200 acres on Lake Michigan with 3 miles of shoreline, Gillette Sand Dune Visitor Center, dune climb stairway with deck, camping, trails, sunsets, interpretive programs

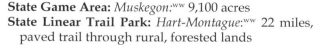

E. GENEVIEVE GILLETTE VISITOR CENTER P.J. HOFFMASTER STATE PARK

Ryan Fox

Prentice Drake

*...Muskegon:*ʷʷ 1,200 acres on Lake Michigan, 2 miles of shoreline, winter luge run, Michigan State Park Explorer Program, trails, camping

County: *Pioneer Park:* 125 acres on Lake Michigan, camping, swimming, sports, near downtown
Other: *Muskegon Lake Nature Preserve:* on a converted dumpsite; Al Bell (wetland) Trail, Outdoor Classroom, Wilder River Walk & Observation Deck
...The West Michigan Parks and Recreation Inventory: see 3P

Q QUOTE FROM THE LOCALS

"Whatever the season, you feel the lake effect the moment you arrive. It's in the way the sun shimmers on the water, the snow falls gently on an upturned palm, and in that impossible happy look on your children's faces. It's the feeling you get in Muskegon County. Here, the beaches are as endless as the possibilities for relaxation and exploration. And the fun isn't limited by time of day or time of year.

"When you're ready to hit the beach, the options are as vast as the sun-kissed horizon. Spend the day in the sun. Wade or paddle in the water. Bike, hike and enjoy...the wilderness. The shoreline stopper is a performance we call 'sunset,' one you can catch every night on our shores." ᵛⁱˢⁱᵗᵐᵘˢᵏᵉᵍᵒⁿ.ᵒʳᵍ

NPCR

R RECREATION & SPORTS

Auto racing: *Thunderbird Raceway:* 1/3-mile, high bank dirt oval track
Golf courses: 15
Great Lakes marinas: 28   **Boat slips:** 2,200

The Muskegon Channel

Hiking/skiing/mountain biking trails: 40 miles
Off-road vehicle trails: 75 miles
Public access sites: 11
Public recreational land: 7% of county
Rail-trail: (15 miles) Hart-Montague, Musketawa
Recreational harbors: Muskegon, Whitehall
State/federal wild/scenic/natural river: 20 miles of the White River
State-funded snowmobile trails: 40 miles
Muskegon Lumberjacks: play ice hockey in the USHL at LC Walker Arena

Muskegon Winter Sports Complex: ice rinks, ice trail rink, luge, wheeled luge, Nordic ski trails

Musketawa Trail: a National Recreation Trail, 25 miles from Marne to Muskegon; paved, all seasons
Ravenna Motor Park: kart racing

S STATE OF MICHIGAN

The Department of Environmental Quality is responsible for monitoring <u>aquatic invasive species</u> in the Great Lakes. "Nonindigenous species, also commonly referred to as nuisance, non-native, exotic invasive and alien species, are species that did not originate in the Great Lakes ecosystem and have been introduced either intentionally or accidentally. Over 160 species have been introduced into the Great Lakes basin since the 1800s. These non-native species threaten the diversity and abundance of native species as well as the ecological and economic stability of systems dependent on the lakes. Without co-evolved parasites and predators, some nonindigenous aquatic species ...displace native populations...as well as threaten public health, add to pollution,

contaminate drinking water and negatively impact water-based tourism. This biological form of pollution has altered the ecosystem more than pollution by chemical contaminants ever has." DEQ

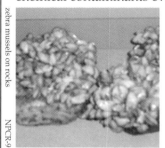

zebra mussels on rocks

NPCR-9

T TRAVEL

Airport: Muskegon County
Bus: Greyhound
Circle Tour: Lake Michigan via US-31
Distance to Lansing: 100 miles
Ferry: *Lake Express* to Milwaukee, WI
Historic Harbortowns: *Muskegon:* Great Lakes Naval Memorial & Museum – *USS Silversides*, Lake Express
Main roads: I-96, US-31, M-37, M-46, M-120
Memorial Highways: I-96, *AmVets MH:* see 19T
...US-31, *Blue Star MH:* see 3T
...US-31, *Moses J. Jones Parkway:* the Reverend (1898-1989) was much loved and very influential in Muskegon.
...M-120, *Veteran's Memorial Causeway*
Scenic Drive: Duck Lake State Park to Muskegon State Park via Scenic Drive

U UNIVERSITIES & COLLEGES

Baker College of Muskegon: see 25U
Muskegon Community College: est. 1926, 5,000 students. ...well rounded education...to provide students the tools, incentives and knowledge required to get a great start on their career path and to build critical job skills. MCCAA, Jayhawks

V VARIETY

White Lake Area Chamber of Commerce

Whitehall Products, the world's premier maker of weathervanes, built the 48' tall World's Largest Weathervane in Montague on White Lake. The ship on top is the *Ella Ellenwood*, whose homeport was White Lake. In 1901, the ship was destroyed in a storm in Wisconsin. The following spring part of her nameplate was found in White Lake. The ship "had come home!"

W WANDERLUST

Cultural: West Michigan Concert WINDS, West Michigan Symphony

Fall colors: early October

Lighthouses, other: *Muskegon South Breakwater, Muskegon South Pierhead:* 1902, both owned by Michigan Lighthouse Conservancy; see 16E

Live theater: Frauenthal Center, Howmet Playhouse, Muskegon Civic Theatre

Planetarium: Carr-Fles at Muskegon Community College

Shopping mall: The Lakes Mall

Walking tour: *Bluffton Walking Tour:* celebrate Buster Keaton; Downtown Muskegon

Wineries: *Bardic Wells Meadery:* Michigan's first meadery (meads are made with fermented honey)

...*Clay Avenue Cellars:* housed in a historic building and also selling items from local artists; wines are made from a wide variety of Michigan fruits, not just grapes

...*Lake Effect Winery:* fruit and berry wines

Blue Lake Fine Arts Camp

Blue Lake Fine Arts Camp: with a 1,300 acre campus, it provides summer school arts education in music, art, dance and drama for over 5,000 gifted elementary to high school students; evening performances open to the public

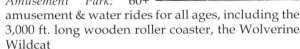

Heritage Landing: on the Muskegon Lake waterfront, it is a converted brown field that has been developed to host large celebrations

NPCR

Michigan's Adventure Amusement Park: 60+ amusement & water rides for all ages, including the 3,000 ft. long wooden roller coaster, the Wolverine Wildcat

Monet Gardens of Muskegon: vacant lot transformed into a lovely park inspired by French Monet Gardens

Port City Princess: cruise on Lake Michigan and Muskegon Lake

There are many quaint Bed & Breakfasts in this area.

X X-TRA STUFF

Commercial port: Muskegon

County fair: *Muskegon County Fair Assoc.:* July

Famous people: ...*Entertainment*: Iggy Pop, Harry Morgan

...*Sports*: Todd Herremans, Earl Morral, Ron Johnson, Nate McLouth, Mark Grimmette

...*Other*: Jim Baker

Hospitals: Hackley, Mercy, Muskegon General

Large employers: Shape Corp. (makes aircraft & aerospace products), Mercy Hospital, Hackley Hospital, County of Muskegon, Herman Miller (makes office furniture), L-3 Communications Corp. (makes truck & tank parts)

Muskegon County is the birthplace of two Miss Americas from the 1960s, Nancy Fleming and Vonda Kay Van Dyke.

FYI: The U.S. Coast Guard has as its mission the safety, security and stewardship of America's maritime interests. The Ninth District is the Guardian of the Great Lakes with 42 Coast Guard Stations in the Great Lakes, 20 of which are in Michigan, including Muskegon. They are concerned with maritime safety, security and stewardship by protecting maritime economy and environment, defending maritime borders, and saving those in peril. They maintain 9 cutters whose primary job is ice breaking, but may also include such things as search and rescue, public affairs and law enforcement. There are 6,000 enlisted and civilian personnel who work in the Ninth District.

Y   YESTERYEAR

Memories of December in Michigan, circa 1940s,
        by Barbara Royston Pardee
Games in the snow, ice on the pond froze,
and a snowman with a funny carrot nose.
    Throwing snowballs back and forth;
    cold winds blow, geese still go north.
Children, be sure to put up your hood;
the rules we should heed, just to be good.
    Uncles and Aunts would come for a time,
    with dishes of food and warm hugs on their mind.
Grandma's pumpkin pie sure smelled good to me.
Food, family, games, that's the way it should be.
    Perhaps we'd have a tree to decorate pretty,
    wreaths with red bows and popcorn a plenty.
Stockings to hang for some goodies, who knows
if Santa will come with his jolly HO HO HO's.
    Lots of things have come and went,
    lots of money and time we have spent.
School plays, Christmas songs we all sang,
and then we would hear the church bell that rang.
    Calling us to come and celebrate Christ's birth
    for God to bring His compassionate love here to earth.
Let us rejoice and be glad, the future is now,
and in thanksgiving before Christ in love let us bow!

NPCR

Z   ZOO & ANIMAL PLACES

Petting zoo: Lewis Farm Market
Watchable Wildlife Viewing Areas:ww see 61P
Whitehouse Whitetails: breeding ranch and hunt preserve

From BIBLIOGRAPHY & NOTES...
   F FAUNA: *(MI H&T)* indicates that Michigan allows Hunting and Trapping of this animal with the proper training, permits, licensing and within the season.

A AGRICULTURE

Land in farms: 24% of county
Number of farms: 950
Size of average farm: 140 acres
Market value of all products: #21 of 83 counties
Crops: ...most acres: forage
...highest $ sales: vegetables
Livestock: ...largest number: cattle & calves
...highest $ sales: milk & dairy products
Among the top Michigan counties:
- #1- deer, onions, spinach, other vegetables
- #2- buckwheat, carrots, cut Christmas trees, goats for milk

Dairy, food and meat processing plants: 17
State ranking for harvested trees: #24 of 83 counties
FYI: Over 25% of Michigan's <u>onion</u> crop is grown here in Newaygo County. Onions are primarily grown on muck soil – old swampland containing a lot of organic material. With only 190 onion growers in the state, this county's 4,500 acres of onions producing 94 million pounds are considered a "minor" crop when compared to other vegetables.

But it is no *minor* matter when your cook runs out of onions. Onions are a *major* ingredient in many of our favorite dishes.
selectmichigan.org, Michigan.gov

Michigan Farm Bureau

Michigan grows a variety of yellow onions, including Yellow Sweet Spanish, Vidalia, Walla Walla and red onions, too.

B BRIDGE OR BOAT

NPCR

White Cloud Railroad Trestle Bridge, built in 1875 over the White River, is one of the last wooden railroad trestle bridges in Michigan that is still used by trains. This is the bridge that is on the City of White Cloud's city seal.

C CELEBRATIONS

<u>Bitely</u> *Homecoming:* July

NPCR

<u>Fremont</u> *National Baby Food Festival:* Kids Expo, family SPA-Tacular Day, parades, sports events, baby food cook-off, corporate Olympics, baby photo contest, bed race, Familypalooza, July

...Harvest Festival: parade, pumpkin bowling, Taste of Fremont, farmer's market, recipe contests, Oct.
<u>Grant</u> *Frontier Festival:* kids' activities, car show, antique pedal tractor pull, tamale eating contest, horseshoes, chili cook-off, parade, Aug.
<u>Newaygo</u> *Winterfest:* chili cook-off, cardboard sled race, euchre, wine tasting, lake plunge, Jan.
...Troutfest: blessing of the poles, fishing contest, fish fry, minnow eating contest, April
...Equinox: An Adventure for All Ages, with all proceeds going to polio research; kayak, canoeing, hike the North Country Trail, biking, kids camp, high ropes course, bluegrass concert, stargazing, Sept.
...Logging Festival: lumberjack & chainsaw carving contest, bingo, parade, arts & crafts, Sept.

D DEMOGRAPHICS

Population: 48,500   **Persons per sq. mile:** 58
Largest city: Fremont   **Population:** 4,080
Largest township: Brooks   **Population:** 3,510
Largest village: Hesperia (partial) **Population:** 340
Median household income: $39,000
Owner-occupied median house value: $116,000
Persons affiliated with a religious congregation: 33%
Persons below poverty level: 19%
Students receiving school lunch subsidy: 47%

E ENVIRONMENT

Owned and managed by the U.S. Forest Service, the <u>Loda Lake Wildflower Sanctuary</u>[wba] offers a .5-mile and a 1.5-mile moderately flat self-guided walking loop through oak-maple woodlands, alongside a stream and floodplain, through old pine plantations, and on a boardwalk through a shrub swamp and emergent wetland. A printed guide is available at the trailhead that describes the 39 numbered viewing stations. Experience the beauty.

F FLORA & FAUNA

Alice Welch, USDA

The common weed burdock was the inspiration for the invention of hook-and loop fasteners like Velcro®. The flower has bristles with hooked tips; when they dry, the little brown burrs stick (dock) to anything that passes by.

Alice Welch, USDA

Chinook salmon, also called king salmon, are often over 3' long and can weigh up to 40 lbs. They live in the Great Lakes and, in the fall, return to inland rivers like the Muskegon River to lay their eggs. Two weeks after this happens, they die.

G GOVERNMENT

County: ...created: 1840 **...organized:** 1851
...originally part of: Kent, Muskegon, Oceana Counties
Size: 552,000 acres / 842 sq. miles (17 of 83 counties)
The county has 4 cities, 1 village, 24 townships, 4 unincorporated communities and 8 school districts.

Ryan Fox

NPCR

County seat: White Cloud
...Homestead property tax: 47 mills
Motto: <u>Fremont</u>: *NOW AND ALWAYS – A Fine City •
A Great Community*
...<u>Fremont</u> Area Chamber: *The Baby Food Capital of the World;* see 62Y
...<u>Grant</u>: *HISTORIC PASTS & Pro-mising Tomorrows*
...<u>Newaygo</u> Area Chamber: *Newaygo Naturally*
...<u>Newaygo County</u> Convention and Visitors Bureau: *Come lose yourself in the moment…*
...<u>White Cloud</u>: *Where the North begins and Pure Waters flow*

H HISTORICAL MARKERS 3 of 3

NPCR

Croton Hydroelectric Plant: 1907, the latest advances in electric power generation and transmission; people came from all over the world to tour the plant.

Hardy Hydroelectric Plant: 1931, with the advance-ments of fossil fuel steam generating plants, this was the last conventional hydroelectric plant built by Consumers Power Company. See 62L.
Hydroelectric Power: harnessing water to produce electricity helped Michigan become a premier in-dustrial state.
National Register of Historic Places: 3 listings
State Historic Sites: 16 listings

I INFORMATION

Chamber of Commerce: Fremont, Newaygo, White Cloud
Visitor: Newaygo County Convention and Visitors Bureau, 877-500-2570, newaygocountytourism.com

J JOKES

Michiganians don't have accents, so we say, but we do say a few things in our very own way. So if you want to talk like us, say…
...“sub” sandwich, not hoagies, baguettes or heroes.
...“tempachur” for temperature.
...“wacha gonna' do” for “what are you going to do.”

…"you guys" when speaking to two or more people, including women.
…"sherbert" for sherbet.
…"thang que" for thank you.

K KINSMAN

Race
American Indian: <1%
Asian: <1%
Black/African American: 1%
Hispanic or Latino: 6%
Other: 3%
White: 94%

Ancestry
German: 20%
Dutch: 14%
U.S./American: 12%
English: 9%
Irish: 8%
Polish: 5%

L LIGHTHOUSE OR LANDMARK

Joan Kokx

Built in 1931 and still owned by Consumers Energy, the Hardy Dam on the Muskegon River is the largest earthen dam east of the Mississippi and the third largest in the world. Besides providing electricity, its backwaters provide excellent recreational activities.

M MUSEUMS

<u>Newago</u> *Newaygo County Museum:* rotating displays celebrate rich lumbering history and strong pioneering spirit

N NATURAL RESOURCES

Elevation: 600 – 1,100 feet
Physiography: rolling plains, hilly uplands

Forest type: oak-hickory, elm-ash-cottonwood
Public/private forests: 60% of county

Water in county: 2% of county
  Lakes: 120   **...largest:** Hardy Dam Pond
  Rivers: Muskegon, Pere Marquette, Rogue, White
  Rivers & streams: 480 miles

Growing season, avg.: 128 days (3 temp. zones)
  Last freeze, avg.: May 20 – May 30
  First freeze, avg.: Sept. 20 – Sept. 30
Precipitation, annual avg.: rainfall: 32 inches
                     snowfall: 71 inches
Temperature (F), avg.: January: high 28°, low 11°
                 July: high 82°, low 56°
  Annual: >90°: 8 days, **<0°:** 16 days
Tornadoes (1930-2010): 15

FYI: There is probably no other place in the whole U.S. that has developed through four (4) distinct geographical changes in 100 years. Once (1) treeless and covered with sand stabilizing native grasses, the <u>Big Prairie</u> was about 1,000 acres. Similar to what happened in Oklahoma 50 years later in the Dust Bowl, the (2) prairie was plowed up to become farmland in the mid-1800s. But it was sandy land and when the drought years came, and with no native grasses to hold the sand in place, the winds did their thing. The winds moved the sand around, piling up 2'-6' in some places and removing it in other places down to the gravel sub-surface. By 1900 it was considered a (3) desert. In the 1920s local people began planting pine trees to help control the erosion and protect the local cemetery. The Civilian Conservation Corps of the 1930s did a great deal of (4) tree planting to help restore the area. Big Prairie is now part of the Manistee National Forest in Big Prairie Township. On the map it is called the Big Prairie Desert. Now, the Big Prairie Desert is neither a prairie nor a desert.

O ORIGINS

<u>Bitely</u>:[u] town founders, Steven and Jerome Bitely; 1889
<u>Bridgeton</u>:[u] bridge across the Muskegon River; 1849
<u>Croton</u>:[u] local topography reminded the town founder of Croton Water Works in NY; 1840
<u>Fremont</u>:[c] Civil War Gen. John C. Fremont; 1884
<u>Grant</u>:[c] Civil War Gen. Ulysses S. Grant; 1882
<u>Hesperia</u>:[v] resembles a garden; 1856
<u>Newaygo</u>:[c,co] Chippewa Chief Naw-wa-goo; 1836
<u>White Cloud</u>:[c] origin unknown, possibly after a cloud in the sky or Chief White Cloud; 1871

From BIBLIOGRAPHY & NOTES…

N NATURAL RESOURCES: Growing Season: Each temperature zone is a 5 day period.

P PARKS

National: 7   **State:** 1
County: 9   **Local:** 20
Number of campsites: 2,400

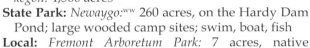

Prentice Drake

National: *Manistee National Forest:*[wv] 109,000 acres, part of 600,000 acres in 8 counties

State Game Area: *Muskegon:* 4,500 acres

State Park: *Newaygo:*[ww] 260 acres, on the Hardy Dam Pond; large wooded camp sites; swim, boat, fish

Local: *Fremont Arboretum Park:* 7 acres, native Michigan trees, shrubs, wildflowers; serene space

Ryan Fox

...Grant Water Tower Park: restored water tower is the last historic wooden water tower in the state; Chessie System Caboose, picnic tables

Other: *Sailors Virgin Pine Forest:* owned by James Sailors, one of few remaining virgin pine stands in Michigan; like forests were in 1800

...The West Michigan Parks and Recreation Inventory: see 3P

Q QUOTE FROM THE LOCALS

"Just think– 356 miles of rivers teeming with fish. Generations convene on the Muskegon, White, Pere Marquette and Rogue Rivers from September to April to witness and be part of one of the greatest natural migrations in the country. Since the planting of Chinook salmon and Steelhead in the 1970s, the rivers through Newaygo County host the annual upriver spawning phenomenon with renowned notoriety.

"From Newaygo to the Croton Dam, a 12-mile stretch, wanders a river credited as a World-Class Fishery in both width and quality. Pack your own tackle and head out or learn from the best on a charter trip with one of the local professional guide services. Add to the salmon and steelhead an abundance of Brown and Rainbow Trout, and you have found what others have come from across the globe for–one of the Top Ten Destination Fisheries in the United States– the Muskegon River." newaygonaturally.com

R RECREATION & SPORTS

Blue Ribbon Trout Streams: Pere Marquette River- Little South Branch, White River
Golf courses: 5
Hiking/skiing/mountain biking trails: 60 miles
North Country National Scenic Trail: yes
Off-road vehicle trails: 60 miles
Public access sites: 20
Public recreational land: 21% of county
State/federal wild/scenic/natural river: 90 miles of the White River
State-funded snowmobile trails: 10 miles
The Muskegon River is an excellent source for steelhead fishing in the spring and salmon fishing in the fall.
Newaygo is the home to the U.S. Canoe & Kayak National Championship every August.

S STATE OF MICHIGAN

Donna Dewhurst, USFWS

Since 1997, the White-Tailed Deer has been the State Game Mammal. It was designated as such after a successful lobbying effort by some fourth graders from the City of Zeeland.

In 1800, it was estimated that there were 200,000 deer in Michigan, and by 1900 they were almost extinct. In 2000, the DNR estimated a statewide herd of almost 2 million animals that have no natural enemies except hunters and automobiles. They are adaptable and prolific animals with keen survival instincts and have thrived due to human intervention.

In the early 1800s a male deer (called a buck) carcass sold for $1.00. Thus originated the slang term for one dollar being called a buck.

White-Tailed Deer do over $200,000,000 in damage to forest and agriculture crops every year.

Hunting season for bow and firearms is in the fall. See 57S, 68S. State of Michigan

T TRAVEL

Airport: Fremont Municipal, White Cloud
County road names: ...**north/south**: named Avenues
...**east/west**: numbered Streets and Roads
Distance to Lansing: 110 miles
Main roads: M-20, M-37, M-82, M-120
Memorial Highways: M-82, Korean War Veterans MH, see 59T

U UNIVERSITIES & COLLEGES

None

V VARIETY

John Kokx

A local artist painted this mural on the North Central Co-op in Fremont. Titled "Farmlandscape," it is part of a public art walking tour that is being developed by the Downtown Development Authority.

W WANDERLUST

Agri-tourism: *Heritage Farms Market:* many fruits & veggies, eggs, bakery, maze, hayrides, tours.
...*Magicland Farms:* they only sell their own home-grown products, from strawberries through pumpkins
Cultural: Grant Fine Arts Center
Fall colors: early October
Live theater: Dogwood Performing Arts Center
Flowing Well Park: this mineral water spring in White Cloud has been flowing since 1882 when a settler was drilling for water and dynamited the rock.
West Michigan's Longest Yard Sale: on M-37 from Grant to Bitely, last weekend in June

X X-TRA STUFF

County fair: *Newaygo Co. Agricultural Fair Assoc.:* to provide educational experiences and fun, Aug.
Famous people: ...*Entertainment*: Ryan Clark, Jack Nitzsche
...*Sports*: Joe Berger, Bert Zagers
Hospitals: Spectrum Health / Gerber Memorial
Large employers: Dura Operating (makes industrial controls), Newaygo County General Hospital, Magna Donnelly (makes motor vehicle parts), Wal-Mart, Grant Public Schools, Bolthouse Farms (vegetable & melons, food preparations and canned fruits), Gerber Products (baby food & baby clothing)

Y YESTERYEAR

Fremont is the home of <u>Gerber Products</u>, the world's first and largest baby food manufacturing plant. In 1927, Daniel Gerber owned a fruit and vegetable canning company. His wife, at the suggestion of their pediatrician, began making hand-strained food for their seven-month-old daughter, Sally. The baby and her Dad both liked the end  results, so he started doing research at his canning company. In 1928, Gerber introduced strained peas, prunes, carrots and spinach and beef vegetable soup. It was an instant success. Six months later the business went national.

Joan Kokx

The adorable baby that is part of the Gerber logo was the winner of a 1928 contest for Gerber's baby food advertising campaign. It was a charcoal sketch of  baby Ann Turner Cook submitted by her neighbor and artist Dorothy Hope Smith.

NPCR

Gerber Products are still known world wide for their baby food. Today they have developed the *Start Healthy Stay Healthy*™ food choices based on the developmental stage of the child from baby through preschool.

Z ZOO & ANIMAL PLACES

Watchable Wildlife Viewing Areas:ww see 62P
Heritage Garden & Wildlife Ranch: deer, buffalo, peacocks

A AGRICULTURE

Land in farms: 6% of county
Number of farms: 590
Size of average farm: 55 acres
Market value of all products: #51 of 83 counties
Crops: ...most acres: forage crops
...highest $ sales: nursery, greenhouse, floriculture
Livestock: ...largest number: pheasants
...highest $ sales: other animals
Among the top Michigan counties:
- #1- sale of horses
- #2- rabbits
- #3- number of horses, pheasants

Dairy, food & meat processing plants: 86
State ranking for harvested trees: #44 of 83 counties
FYI: Oakland County is the #1 Michigan county for income produced from the sale of horses and ponies

and is #3 in the state with over 3,000 horses. State-wide there are 15,000 farms with a total of over 100,000 horses. Horses eat grass, hay and grain (their favorite is oats), drink 10-12 gallons of water daily and need outdoor space in which to run and graze.

There are over 300 breeds of horses in the world today that are used for sport, work, entertainment, therapy and warfare. Here's a list a terms that you'll need to know about horses:
- *Foal:* any horse under one year of age
- *Yearling:* any horse between one and two years old
- *Colt:* a male horse under the age of four
- *Filly:* a female horse under the age of four
- *Mare:* a female horse four years and older
- *Stallion:* a non-castrated male horse four years old and older
- *Gelding:* a castrated male horse of any age
- *Pony:* certain breeds that at maturity are under 58 inches ^MDA, wikipedia

By-products of horses include drugs for hormone replacement therapy (i.e. Premarin = *pregnant mares' urine*), bows for string instruments, and leather for boots and baseballs.

B BRIDGE OR BOAT

Larea Kremhelmer

This is one of seven bridges that span the wetlands of Wolverine Lake and are part of the nature trails of the resort community Hidden Paradise.

C CELEBRATIONS

<u>Auburn Hills</u> *Summerfest:* food, cars, June
<u>Birmingham</u> *Annual Village Fair:* May
<u>Clarkston</u> *Beer University:* 2-3 times a year
...*Taste of Clarkston:* outdoors, food & fun, Sept.
<u>Farmington</u> *Area Founders Festival:* rich cultural heritage, kids' activities, parade, July
<u>Holly</u> *Michigan Renaissance Festival:* medieval fantasy faire, costumed performers, Aug.-Sept.
<u>Milford</u> *Memories Summer Festival:* Aug.
<u>Orchard Lake</u> *Fine Art Show:* top 100 in U.S., July

nancy@downtownrochestermi.com

<u>Rochester</u> *Fire & Ice Sculpture Fest:* world-class carvers, Feb.

nancy@downtownrochestermi.com

...*Heritage Fest:* vintage baseball, antique fire trucks, car show, Civil War Re-enactments, May

...*Arts and Apples Fest:* a top 30 festival in U.S., Sept.

<u>Royal Oak</u> *Arts, Beats, & Eats Festival:* art, music, food, Sept.
...*Clay, Glass, & Metal Show:* artists, June
<u>South Lyon</u> *Pumpkinfest:* parade, games, arts, Oct.
<u>Southfield</u> *Taste Fest:* Oct.
<u>Sylvan Lake</u> *Home & Garden Tour:* award-winning, June

D DEMOGRAPHICS

Population: 1,202,400   **Persons per sq. mile:** 1,378
Largest city: Troy   **Population:** 80,980
  2nd largest city: Farmington Hills Population: 79,700
  3rd largest city: Southfield   Population: 71,700
  4th largest city: Rochester Hills Population: 71,000
Largest township: Waterford   **Population:** 74,700
  2nd largest twp.: West Bloomfield Population: 64,700
  3rd largest twp.: Bloomfield   Population: 41,000
  4th largest twp.: Commerce   Population: 35,900
Largest village: Milford   **Population:** 6,180
Median household income: $62,600 (county, #1/MI)
  Troy: $77,500
  Farmington Hills: $67,500
  Southfield: $51,800
  Rochester Hills: $74,900
Owner-occupied median house value: $215,000 (#3/MI)
Persons affiliated with a religious congregation: 48%
Persons below poverty level: 10% (#81/MI)
Students receiving school lunch subsidy: 20%
FYI: According to the 2010 Census, Lake Angelus is
  the smallest *city* in the state with 290 people and
  Milford is the *largest* village in the state with 6,180
  people.

E ENVIRONMENT

Since 1972, the Clinton River Watershed Council
has been dedicated to protecting, enhancing and
celebrating the Clinton River, its watershed and
Lake St. Clair. It provides programs and services
in watershed management, stormwater education,
Stream Leaders, Adopt-A-Stream, and has a stormwater information clearinghouse and the Clinton
River Coldwater Conservation Project. A watershed
is the land that drains into a body of water. It is where
all the rain and snow goes. There are over 1,000 miles
of streams in the 760 square miles that drain into the
Clinton River that then drains into Lake St. Clair. Clinton
River Watershed Council

> **Bold typeface:** this indicates that this heading
> may be repeated in every chapter, providing
> that the information about the heading is
> applicable to the county.

F FLORA & FAUNA

Laura Perlick, USFWS

Holly once grew wild and was abundant in this area
since most holly species do well in moist soils. With
its glossy leaves and red berries, this evergreen is attractive all year. The berries are a food source for birds.

Alice Welch, USDA

The eastern Massasauga rattlesnake, also knows as
the Michigan rattlesnake, is the smallest (2'-3') and
least toxic of all U.S. rattlesnakes. It is Michigan's
only poisonous snake. It is shy and sluggish and
avoids human confrontation. If you see one, just leave
it alone; don't try to kill it. They are found throughout
the Lower Peninsula.

G GOVERNMENT

County: ...created: 1819 **...organized:** 1820
...originally part of: Wayne County
Size: 581,000 acres / 873 sq. miles (15 of 83 counties)
The county has 31 cities, 10 villages, 21 townships
  with 18 as charter townships and 28 school districts.

Larea Kremhelmer

NPCR

County seat: Pontiac

...Homestead property tax: 36 mills

Motto: <u>Auburn Hills</u>: *Honoring the Past. Building the Future*

...<u>Bloomfield Hills</u>: *A gracious residential community with rolling hills, trees, water and large home sites*

...<u>Clarkston</u> Area Chamber: *Progressive Living, Timeless Setting*

...<u>Clawson</u>: *Little City with a Big Heart*

...<u>Hazel Park</u>: *The Friendly City*

...<u>Holly</u>: *Proud Of Our Past, Confident In Our Future*

...<u>Huntington Woods</u>: *City of Homes*

...<u>Keego Harbor</u>: *Heart of the Lakes*

...<u>Lathrup Village</u>: *Beautiful Homes and Great Neighbors*

...<u>Northville</u>: *Historically Distinctive*

...<u>Southfield</u>: *the center of it all*

...<u>Sylvan Lake</u>: *The Prettiest City in The State of Michigan*

...<u>White Lake Township</u>: *Your Four Seasons Playground*

...<u>Wixom</u>: *A Crossroads Community with Character*

H HISTORICAL MARKERS 19 of 124

First Quaker Meeting: 1831, Quakers established the city of Farmington, a school; were anti-slavery

The Academy of the Sacred Heart: 1851, started in Detroit, then moved to Bloomfield Hills

Barn Church: in 1928 a massive 1912 barn was converted to a church; they removed the silo and added a steeple.

Battle Alley: 1880, so many drunken brawls!

Botsford Inn: 1836, oldest inn in Michigan still providing food and lodging

Chief Pontiac: 1720-1769, a friend of the French, he led attacks against the British

Clinton-Kalamazoo Canal: 1837, plans to cross southern Michigan and link Lake St. Clair to Lake Michigan never materialized; they ran out of money, then came the trains that took over the transportation trade.

Congregation and Temple Beth El: Michigan's oldest Jewish organization, by German immigrants; the new Reform synagogue represents the meeting tents of the ancient Israelites

Larea Kremhelmer

Detroit Finnish Co-operative Summer Camp: 1925, Finns of the area wanted a culture camp for kids.

Detroit Zoological Park: 1928, progressive design of free-roaming outdoor habitats

Harry Frink House: 1850, reflects the national craze for octagon buildings

Lawrence Institute of Technology: 1932, by the Lawrence brothers for applied engineering; pioneered evening classes and quarter semesters

Michigan State Historical Preservation Office

Michigan's First Tri-Level Intersection: 1956, at Woodward and Eight Mile

"Pine Grove": 1845, planted in native Michigan Pines; now the home of Oakland Co. Historical Foundation

Roseland Park Mausoleum: 1914, largest in U.S. at that time; European classic style with 1,300 crypts

S.S. Kresge Co.: 1919, by Sebastion Sparing Kresge, an innovative, careful manager; K-Mart was started in 1962; world headquarters here in 1972

Saginaw Trail: an American Indian trail from Detroit through Pontiac to Saginaw; original path still visible near the John Almon Starr House; most of original trail is now Woodward Ave. and Dixie Hwy.

Larea Kremhelmer

Western Knitting Mills: 1896-1939, made wool socks, gloves, mittens, cloth

Witch's Hat Depot: 1909, Queen Anne style with a front that has a rounded and conical shaped roof (looks like a witch hat); now a museum

Monument: *Michigan Fallen Heroes Memorial:* the only memorial in the State of Michigan that honors both law enforcement and fire fighters who have lost their lives in the line of duty

Larea Kremhelmer

...*The Polar Bears:* 1930, a white marble monument to the Michigan men who fought in Russia in 1918

National Historic Landmark: Cranbrook (see 63M, 63X)

National Register of Historic Places: 70 listings

State Historic Sites: 227 listings

I INFORMATION

Chamber of Commerce: Auburn Hills, Berkley, Birmingham-Bloomfield Hills, Chaldean American, Clarkston, Clawson, Farmington/Farmington Hills, Ferndale, Holly, *Huron Lakes:* Commerce, Highland, Milford, White Lake; *Lakes Area:* Commerce Twp., Union Lake, Walled Lake, Waterford, Wolverine Lake, White Lake, Wixom; Lake Orion, Madison Heights, Novi, Oakland County, Orion, Ortonville, Oxford, Pontiac, Rochester, Royal Oak, South Lyon, Southfield, Troy, West Bloomfield

Visitor: Detroit Metro Convention and Visitors Bureau, 800-DETROIT, visitdetroit.com …destinationOakland.com

J JOKES

Teenage Rebellion 101: Ten Ways to Drive Your Rich Parents Crazy
1. Wear clothes that don't fit, are out of style and are inappropriate for the season.
2. Buy those clothes at thrift stores, not the mall.
3. Insist on swimming at public pools, not the country club.
4. Have a hairstyle that doesn't need a hair stylist.
5. Refuse to have dental work done.
6. Take public transportation instead of having your own car.
7. Refuse to take an allowance.
8. Get a job and give half your money to charity.
9. Study hard and work your way through college.
10. Make friends with people who are not in your social class.

P.S. Don't you wish you had rich parents to drive crazy?

K KINSMAN

Race	
American Indian: <1%	
Asian: 6%	
Black/African American: 14%	
Hispanic or Latino: 3%	
Other: 3%	
White: 77%	

Ancestry	
German: 14%	
Irish: 9%	
English: 9%	
Polish: 8%	
Italian: 6%	
U.S./American: 5%	

L LIGHTHOUSE OR LANDMARK

Larea Krembehlmer

The world headquarters of Chrysler is in Auburn Hills. The company was started in 1925 by Walter Chrysler and is now the 16th largest automaker in the world. Prior to 2009 it was Chrysler Corporation and since then it is Chrysler Group LLC.

M MUSEUMS

NOTE: *HM = Historical Museum; Mus. = Museum*

<u>Auburn Hills</u> *Walter P Chrysler HM:*[1,000] automotive history learned and explored; all things Chrysler

<u>Berkley</u> *HM:* memorabilia, in an old fire hall

<u>Birmingham</u> *HM and Park:* 1822 and 1928 homes in History Plaza, linked to Historic Park

<u>Bloomfield</u> *Cranbrook House:* a 1908 Albert Kahn (see 81Y) designed mansion that used the finest artisans and craftsmen; campus also includes Cranbrook Academy of Art, Cranbrook Art Museum and Cranbrook Institute of Science

Michigan State Historic Preservation Office

<u>Clarkston</u> *Heritage Museum:* in the Independence Twp. Library

<u>Clawson</u> *HM:* 1920s furnishings, in a 3-story house

<u>Commerce</u> *Byers Homestead:* 1825 farm, outbuildling

Farmington Hills *Holocaust Memorial Center:*[1,000] illuminating the past, enlightening the future

Joshua Nowicki

...Marvin's Marvelous Mechanical Museum: historical and modern arcade machines, sideshow wonders, fortunetellers, automatons and other curiosities

...Pine Grove HM: former estate of Gov. Moses Wisner; one-room school, research

Ferndale *HM:* info on each house in the city

Franklin *HM*

Holly *Hadley House Museum*

...Historical Museum

Lake Orion *Art Center:* building community via art

...Scripps Mus.: 1927 Norman Revival mansion

Milford *HM:* printed book of local history

Novi *Old Township Hall Museum*

Orchard Lake *Mus.:* Greater W. Bloomfield His. Soc.

Ortonville *Historical Society Museum:* in an old mill

Oxford *Northeast Oakland HM:* in a bank building

Michigan State Historic Preservation Office

Rochester *Meadow Brook Hall & Gardens:*[1,000] 110 rooms, 88,000 sq. foot Tudor-revival style mansion, 4th largest historic house museum in U.S.

Rochester Hills *Museum at Van Hoosen Farm:* interprets, preserves, collects

Royal Oak *Orson Starr House:* maker of cowbells

South Lyon *Historic Village:* includes the Caboose, Freight House, Washburn School, Little Village Chapel, gazebo

Larea Kremhelmer

Southfield *HM /Burgh Historical Park*

Troy *HM & Village:* hands-on learning, 10 buildings

White Lake *Twp. HM*

...Kelly Fisk Farm

Wixom *Wire House/Gibson Farm:* in an 1850 house

N NATURAL RESOURCES

Elevation: 600 – 1,100 feet

Physiography: hilly uplands, rolling plains, lake-border plains

Forest type: oak-hickory, maple-beech

Public/private forests: 24% of county

National Natural Landmark: *Haven Hill State Natural Area:* 700 acres, contains all southern Michigan principal forest types

NPCR

Water in county: 4% of county

Lakes: 360 (#1/MI)

...largest: Cass Lake (#9/depth/MI)

Rivers: Clinton, Huron (headwaters), Shiawasee (headwaters)

Rivers & streams: 470 miles

Growing season, avg.: 163 days (2 temp. zones)

Last freeze, avg.: May 5 – May 10

First freeze, avg.: Oct. 20 – Oct. 30

Precipitation, annual avg.: rainfall: 29 inches **snowfall:** 35 inches

Temperature (F), avg.: January: high 30°, low 15° **July:** high 84°, low 61°

Annual: >90°: 11 days, **<0°:** 7 days

Tornadoes (1930-2010): 30

O ORIGINS

Auburn Hills:[c] first settler from Auburn, NY; 1821

Berkley:[c] a road and school of the same name; 1923

Beverly Hills:[v] several subdivisions known as the Beverly Hills subdivisions; 1959

Bingham Farms:[v] original farm owners were the Binghams; 1833

Birmingham:[c] man wanted the city to be an industrial center like Birmingham, England; 1818

Bloomfield Hills:[c] after Bloomfield Twp.; 1819

Brandon:[ct,t] after Brandon Twp.; 1835

Clarkston:[c] the Clark brothers platted the town; 1840

Clawson:[c] local grocer, John Lawson; a postal clerical error made it Clawson; 1822

Commerce:[ct] hope for a future business center; 1825

Davisburg:[u] settled by Cornelius Davis and sons; 1836

Drayton Plains:^u mill owner from England called his English mill the Drayton Mill; 1835

Farmington/Hills:^c settlers from Farmington, NY; 1824

Fenton:^c legend is that two men had a fight; Mr. Fenton won; Mr. LeRoy lost and the main street was named after him; 1834

Ferndale:^c many ferns in the area; 1917

Franklin:^v probably after Benjamin Franklin; 1824

Groveland:^u originally Fairfield; 1829

Hazel Park:^c a lot of hazelnut bushes in area; 1869

Highland:^{ct} high elevation; 1835

Holly:^v wild holly grew in the area; 1830

Huntington Woods:^c wooded area where small game was hunted; 1824

Independence:^{ct} settler from Independence, NJ; 1826

Keego Harbor:^c a small fish; an inland lake turned into a harbor by connecting two lakes; 1902

Lake Angelus:^c village was probably founded by a group of religious men; 1920s

Lake Orion:^{v,ct} (OR ee un) originally Canandaigua City, but later townsmen wanted something shorter; Orion was such a lovely name; 1819

Lathrup Village:^c (LAY thrup) founded and developed by Louise Lathrup and her husband; 1926

Leonard:^v founded by Leonard Rowland; 1882

Lyon:^{ct} state legislator, Lucius Lyon; 1832

Madison Heights:^c President James Madison; 1818^{madison-heights.org}

Milford:^v providing valuable waterpower; 1827

Northville:^c north of Plymouth; 1825

Novi:^c No. VI, the sixth stop on the plank road from Detroit to Lansing is a great story, but the township was named in 1832 and the plank road was built in the 1850s. In Latin, Novi means new, as in giving some a fresh start in life; 1825.

Oakland:^{c,co} oaks were the major forest cover; 1823

Oak Park:^c from the Oak Park subdivision; 1914

Orchard Lake:^c American Indians called the area Apple Place; 1873

Ortonville:^v dam & sawmill builder, Amos Orton; 1848

Oxford:^{v,ct} settlers had ox teams; 1832

Pleasant Ridge:^c from the local Ridge Road; 1913

Pontiac:^c after local Ottawa Chief Pontiac; 1818

Rochester/Hills:^c settlers from Rochester, NY; 1817

Rose:^u farmer David Rose; 1830s

Royal Oak:^{c,ct} a huge oak tree reminded Gov. Lewis Cass of a Scottish story about a royal oak tree; 1819

Southfield:^c south fields of Bloomfield Twp.; 1823

South Lyon:^c in the south part of Lyon Twp.; 1832

Sylvan Lake:^c from Sylvan Twp.; 1830

Troy:^c many settlers from Troy, NY; 1822

Union Lake:^u named after the local lake; 1834

Walled Lake:^c places along the lakeshore had the appearance of natural or man-made walls; 1825

Waterford:^{ct} a lot of water in the area; 1819

White Lake:^t clear and beautiful water; 1830

Wixom:^c platted by Willard Wixom; 1830

Wolverine Lake:^v after the State of Michigan nickname [in many European languages wolverine means glutton]; 1918

P PARKS

National: 0   **State:** 8   **County:** 13   **Local:** 85
Number of campsites: 3,750
State Game Area: Holly, Horseshoe Lake
State Park: *Dodge #4:* 139 acres, on Cass Lake
…*Seven Lakes:* 1,400 acres, forests, lakes, 5 trails

State Recreation Area:
Bald Mountain: 4,600 acres, steep and rugged, trout streams, wild game

Larea Krembelner

…*Highland:*^{wv} 5,900 acres, forest, marshes, lakes, rolling hills, trails, camping, hunting, dog trail

…*Holly:* 7,800 acres, woodlands, fields, lake, camping, trails

…*Ortonville:* 5,400 acres, high wooded hills, horse trail and campground, swimming, fishing

…*Pontiac Lake:* 3,700 acres, marshes, ponds, forests, lakes, hunting, fishing, horse trails, bike trails

NPCR

…*Proud Lake:* 4,700 acres, on the Huron River, diverse habitat, 20 miles of trails, River Hawk Lodge

State Wildlife Area: (450 acres) Davisburg

County: The county has 13 parks on 4,000 acres, with 60 miles of trails, including 2 water parks, 2 nature centers, 5 golf courses, for everything from water activities to hunting to horse trails to dog parks to cross-country skiing.

…*Independence Oaks:*^{ww,wv} 1,100 acres, headwaters of the Clinton River, varied habitat, trails

…*The Fridge Toboggan Run:* Winter Thrill Ride, refrigerated, 55 ft. drop, 1,000 ft. run at 30 MPH

Nature Center: *Lloyd Strange Outdoor Education Center:*^{wv} 100 acres, marsh, meadows, forests, rolling uplands, trails

…*Seven Ponds Nature Center:*^{wv} lakes, ponds, marshes, swamps, prairie, woodlands, trails

Other: *Haven Hill State Natural Area:*^{wba} see 63N

...*Huron-Clinton Metropolitan Authority:* see 47P; included in this county:

- *Kensington Metropark:*ww 4,500 acres, Kent Lake, nature center, farm center, golf, fishing

Larea Kremhelmer

- *Indian Springs Metropark:*ww 2,200 acres, what SE Michigan used to look like, Environmental Discovery Center, diverse habitats

Q QUOTE FROM THE LOCALS

"Oakland County offers thousands [Sic] of beautiful lakes, scenic parkland, first-rate educational institutions, internationally-renowned entertainment venues and top-of-the-line medical facilities. It all adds to a quality of life that enhances Oakland County's status as one of America's premier locations in which to live, work, play and raise a family.

"Oakland County has an extensive collection of malls and shopping centers ranging from quaint local centers to multiple floor malls found in major cities. Our quaint downtowns ["Main Street" see 63V] offer strolling opportunities, with local boutiques, restaurants and cafes, art galleries and more.

"With so much to do, from our cultural heritage to automotive and industrial history, to entertainment, culture and nightlife – you're sure to find exciting options." destinationoakland.com

R RECREATION & SPORTS

Auto racing: *Waterford Hills Road Racing:* 1.4 mile track, 12 turns; real people, real cars, real racing
Golf courses: 56 (#1/MI)
Hiking/skiing/mountain biking trails: 205 miles (#4/MI)

Larea Kremhelmer

Horse racing: *Hazel Park Raceway:* the largest horse racing facility in Michigan

Public access sites: 36 (#2/MI)
Public recreational land: 6% of county

Rail-trail: (160 miles - #1/MI) Addison Oaks, Bald Mountain, Clinton R., Highland RA, Holly RA, Huron Valley Paint Creek, Novi Tree Farm, Polly Ann, Pontiac Lake, Stoney Creek MP, W. Bloomfield
Catalpa Oaks: county park, sports field
Detroit Pistons: est. 1941; National Basketball Association, play at the Palace of Auburn Hills; NBA Championships- 1989, 1990, 2004
Oakland County Cruisers: independent professional baseball, Frontier League
Onyx Rochester Ice Arena: hockey, skating, all ages
Paint Creek Trailway: the first rail-trail in Michigan

Palace of Auburn Hills: seating for 22,000, home of the Detroit Pistons; also site of many other sporting events, music concerts and live theatre

Palace Sports & Entertainment

Pine Knob Ski & Snowboard Resort: so close to so many people; 17 runs, 300 ft. vertical drop

Larea Kremhelmer

Pontiac Silverdome: former home of the Detroit Lions and Detroit Pistons; seating for 80,000; closed in 2006; reopened in 2010 as a general events venue

Velodrome at Bloomer Park: NAS-TRACK bike racing, 44° banking, 200 meters

S STATE OF MICHIGAN

Absolute Michigan is "All Michigan, All the Time," a private promotion endeavor by a Michigan company for Michigan residents and visitors. Their area of expertise is providing an online site that features *free links* to other online sites about Michigan or something in Michigan. Michigan is their home and they work every day to make Absolute Michigan a rich resource that promotes the state of Michigan as a place to visit, celebrates the natural beauty that the state is blessed with, and highlights the businesses, organizations, communities and events that make Michigan what it is. And most importantly, they celebrate what makes Michigan one of the best places in the world to live your life with the people you love.

There are nine categories that a customer can choose

from to access the Michigan information they need:

1. *Arts & Entertainment:* bands, entertainers & labels; artists & galleries; festivals, attractions & events; museums & collections; organizations; performance & dance; photography & film; publications; venues

2. *Business:* advertising, marketing & public relations; business services; computers & technology; finance; graphic design & printing; health & medical; industry & manufacturing; jobs & employment; lawyers & legal services; telecommunications & ISPs; web design & media production; wedding & event services

3. *Community:* area information; Chambers of Commerce; churches & religious organizations; community & nonprofit organizations; environment & environmental organizations; government; history & libraries; schools & education

4. *Food:* breweries & wineries; cafes, delis & coffeehouses; casual & family restaurants; catering; dining guides & culinary tours; ethnic restaurants; fine dining restaurants; Michigan grown; natural and vegetarian restaurants; recipes

5. *Homes:* builders, contractors & architects; furniture & appliances; home décor & interior design; improvement, repair & services; landscaping & gardens; mortgage & real estate services; real estate & development; rentals

6. *Lodging:* bed & breakfasts; cabins, cottages & rental homes; destinations; hotels & motels; rental companies; resorts; tours & travel companies

7. *Media:* blogs & forums; books & magazines; movies; newspapers; podcast & radio; technology & internet media; television & video

8. *Sports:* animals; attractions; boating, diving & beaches; camping & RV's; fitness; golf & golf courses; hiking & biking; hobbies; hunting & fishing; motorcycles, snowmobiles & ATVs; offbeat; parks; skiing; sports

9. *Shopping:* antiques & auctions; beauty & clothing; beer, wine & beverages; books, music & video; cars, trucks & other vehicles; food, health & nutrition; hobbies, toys & games; home & garden; jewelry & gifts; online and catalogs; sporting goods ^{absolutemichigan.com}

T TRAVEL

Airports: Oakland International, Oakland-Troy
Amtrak: Birmingham, Pontiac, Royal Oak
Bus: Greyhound, Suburban Mobility Authority for Regional Transportation (SMART)
County road names: see 44T
Distance to Lansing: 70 miles

Heritage Route: *Recreation:* M-1, A Cruise through Time, 28 miles, Woodward Ave., from Detroit to Pontiac; includes arts, education, medical districts, music, neighborhoods, quaint downtowns, industrial giants; an All-American Road

NPCR

…*Recreation:* M-15, Pathway to Family Fun, see 9T
Main roads: I-75 Chrysler, I-96, I-275, I-696 Ruther, US-10, US-102, M-1, M-14, M-24, M-59, M-159
Memorial Highways: I-75, American Legion MH, see 6T
…I-75, Walter P. Chrysler Freeway, see 82T
…I-96, AmVets MH, see 19T
…I-275, Philip A. Hart MH, see 58T
…I-696, Walter P. Reuther Highway: he (1907-1970) was President of the UAW (United Auto Workers) from 1946 to 1970.
…M-5, Keith Deacon MH: he (1927-1996) was a resident of Farmington Hills who worked tirelessly for the improvement of the community, including roads (especially M-5 and the Grand River interchange) and economic development.
…M-10, Adler MH: Rabbi Morris Adler (1906-1966) was pastor of Shaarey Zedek, one of the largest congregations in the world; he also was active in community affairs.
…M-10, Holocaust MH: during WWII from 1939 to 1945, 6 million Jews and other "undesirables" were murdered by the Germans; the highway reminds us that intolerance of diversity is the road to destruction but liberty and justice is for all. ^{holocaustcenter.org} See 63M.
…M-59, Vietnam Veterans MH, see 47T
…M-59, Veterans Memorial Freeway
…M-102, Columbus MH, see 50T
Scenic Drive: Bay City to Ortonville via M-15
FYI: Over the years, US-24 has been called, in part or as a whole, proposed, promoted or legalized: Clara Barton Memorial Hwy., Dixie Hwy., Telegraph Rd. and Victory Memorial Hwy. ^{Barnett}

U UNIVERSITIES & COLLEGES

Baker College of Auburn Hills: see 25U

Central Bible College: est. 1962, 60 students. The Assemblies of God offer multiple opportunities for the training of ministers and missionaries.

Cranbrook Academy of Art: est. 1932, 60 students. Known as the cradle of American modernism, it is now a graduate school and a world leader in art, architecture and design.

Thomas M. Cooley Law School: see 33U

ITT Technical Institute: see 25U

Lawrence Technological University: est. 1932, 4,500 students. It is a preeminent private university producing leaders with an entrepreneurial spirit and global view. Intramural only, Blue Devils

Michigan Jewish Institute: est. 1994, 680 students. It is uniquely positioned to provide career-oriented academic studies in a warm and intimate learning environment that adheres to the highest ethical standards and religious traditions of Judaism.

Oakland Community College: est. 1964, 47,000 students. The largest community college in Michigan; 5 campuses; it has the state's largest English as a Second Language, Nursing and Workforce Development programs. M-TEC. MCCAA, Raiders

Oakland University: est. 1957, 18,000 students. It has excellent and relevant instruction, high-quality research and scholarship, responsive and effective public and community service, student development activities. Summit League, Golden Grizzlies

Rochester College: est. 1959, 1,000 students. It is a vigorous liberal arts education within a Christian community for a life of study and service; Church of Christ. USCAA, Warriors

SS Cyril and Methodius Seminary: est. 1885, 100 students. It has a Roman Catholic Polish tradition, training both priest and lay leaders.

Siena Heights University: see 46U

St. Mary's College of Ave Maria University: est. 1885, 300 students. Part of the Orchard Lake campus of Madonna University. See 82U

University of Phoenix: see 25U

Walsh College: est. 1922, 4,000 students. It has a practical blend of business theory and real-world application... for successful... professionals in a complex global environment, offering business and related technology programs. Advanced degrees too.

V VARIETY

Larea Krenhelmer

"Main Street® Oakland County, a partner with the National Trust's Main Street Center, which is a program of the National Trust for Historic Preservation, is an economic development program specifically targeted to provide technical assistance to the 30 traditional downtowns in the county. Their mission is to emphasize economic growth within the context of historic preservation." Downtown Ferndale was the 2010 Great American Main Street Awards national award winner for "transforming itself from a lost cause...to one of Michigan's top communities, known for its diversity, creative class, progressive attitude and rapid rate of change." oakgov.com

W WANDERLUST

Agri-tourism: <u>Farms</u> *Candy Cane CHRISTmas Trees*

...*Cook's Dairy Farm:* tours, ice cream

...*Farmer's Market:* Auburn Hill, Birmingham, Rochester, Lake Orion, Novi, Southfield, Wixom

...*Kensington Metropark Farm Center:* U-pick, hayrides, tours

...*Middleton Berry:* raspberry, strawberry, tomatoes

...*Mitchell Farm & Greenhouses:* pumpkins, hayrides

...*Yule Love It Lavender:* organic, tours

<u>Orchards</u> *Ashton:* cider, farm-produced products

...*Diehl's:* cider, apples, corn maze, pumpkins, tours

...*Erwin:* cider, apples, raspberries, cherries, maze

...*Franklin Cider Mill:* since 1837, wagon rides, gourds

...*Long Family:* cider, apples, asparagus, strawberries

...*Yates:* cider, apples, bakery, pumpkins

Brewery: (#1/MI) Bastone, Big Rock Chop and Brewhouse, Black Lotus Brewing Company, CJ's Brewing Company, Copper Canyon Brewery, King Brewing Co., Lily's Seafood and Brewery, Rochester Mills Beer Co., Royal Oak Brewery, Woodward Ave. Brewers

Cultural: Birmingham Bloomfield Symphony Orchestra, Rochester Symphony Orchestra

Fall colors: middle October

Live theater: Avon Players Backstage, Birmingham Village Players, Clarkston Village Players, Lakeland Players, Mt. Zion Theatre Company, Jewish Ensemble Theatre

Music theatres:

Palace Sports & Entertainment

...*DTE Energy Music Theater:* seating for 15,000, amphitheater, formerly Pine Knob Music Theatre

Palace Sports & Entertainment

...*Meadow Brook:* Michigan's largest producing professional theatre

MotorCities National Heritage Area: yes

Planetarium: McMath at Cranbrook Institute of Science; Vollbrecht

Shopping malls: Great Lakes Shopping Outlets, Oakland, Olde World Canterbury Village, Somerset Collection, Twelve Oaks

Walking tours: Clarkston

Art Institute of Michigan: culinary, design, fashion, media arts, general studies

Birmingham Bloomfield Art Center: promote the appreciation, understanding, practice of the arts

Commerce Village Cemetery: 1834 pioneer, has a great variety of monuments and headstones

National Shrine of the Little Flower: 1925, named after St. Terese of Lisieux; tours

Paint Creek Center for the Arts: participate in and appreciate the arts

Tollgate Farm & Gardens: part of Michigan State University Tollgate Education Center

Sandi Rosa

Woodward Dream Cruise: many communities bordering Woodward Ave. (M-1) are part of the metro Detroit 16-mile long cruise in August; it is the largest classic car cruise in the U.S. with 40,000 cars and 1 million spectators.

X **X-TRA STUFF**

County Fair: *4-H Fair Assoc.:* free circus daily, racing pigs, Miracle of Birth Barn, July

Famous people: ...*Entertainment:* Tim Allen, Alice Cooper, Eminem, Laura Innes, Christine Lahti, Tony Lucca, Stone Phillips, Robin Williams, David Spade, Noel Stookey

...*Politics:* George and Mitt Romney

...*Sports:* Ernie Harwell, Steve Yzerman

...*Other:* John Dodge, Jeffery Figer, Meg Oliver, Dr. Sanjay Gupta

Hospitals: Wm. Beaumont (2), Botsford, Crittenton, Henry Ford Kingswood, Huron Valley-Sinai, Michigan Orthopaedic Speciality, North Oakland, Oaklawn Regional, POH, Providence, Select Speciality, St. John Oaklawn, St. John Providence Park, St. Joseph Mercy, Straith for Special Surgery

Large employers: General Motors, Chrysler, Beaumont Hospital, Electronic Data Systems, Delphi Automotive Systems, U.S. Postal Service, SBC Ameritech, U.S. Government, St. John Health System, Eagle Ottawa (leather tanning), Blue Cross Blue Shield of Michigan

NPCR

Automation Alley: with its headquarters in Troy, it is Michigan's largest technology business association. With 1,000 members in Genesee, Livingston, Macomb, Monroe, Oakland, St. Clair, Washtenaw and Wayne counties, this non-profit organization fosters a collaborative culture that focuses on workforce and business initiatives that drive the economic development and growth in southeast Michigan.

Detroit Country Day School: top college preparatory

An early 1800s report stated that much of Oakland County was worthless swamp and would never be good for agriculture or anything else. But obviously the report was wrong. Many of the communities on the lakes developed into resorts and wealthy people left Detroit and built their mansions here.

Oakland County is among the four wealthiest counties in the U.S. that have populations of over one million people.

The Cranbrook Educational Community sits on 319 beautiful and enchanted acres, and consists of the Art Museum, Academy of Art (graduate school), Christ Church, House and Gardens (mansion, open to public), Institute of Science (museum) and Kingswood School (high school).

NPCR

Y   YESTERYEAR

Prior to statehood in 1837, Michigan was surveyed and divided into townships that were eventually organized into counties. An important feature in this survey process was the establishment of a starting point whereby all measurements would be standard from that reference point. The north to south line is the meridian. The Michigan meridian runs from Defiance, OH, to Sault St. Marie, MI.

The line from east to west is the baseline. The Michigan baseline in southern Lower Michigan divides the second and third tier of counties from Detroit to South Haven. The baseline between second tier Wayne County and third tier Oakland County is now a road called Eight Mile Road.

In the movie *8 Mile*, that road represented the sociological difference between economically depressed Detroit and economically prosperous Oakland County. In reality, 8 Mile Rd. is the boundary of more than a dozen individual communities, from poor to middle class to wealthy. See 33P, 60Y.

Z   ZOO & ANIMAL PLACES

Petting zoo: Kensington Metropark Farm Center
Watchable Wildlife Viewing Areas:ww West Bloomfield Woods Nature Preserve; see 63P

Larea Kremhelmer

Zoo: Detroit Zoo: 125 acres, celebrating and saving wildlife; 280 species with 3,300 animals; tours, galleries; the largest paid family attraction in Michigan with more than one million visitors annually; see 63H

A AGRICULTURE

Land in farms: 38% of county
Number of farms: 650
Size of average farm: 190 acres
Market value of all products: #27 of 83 counties
Crops: ...**most acres**: corn
...**highest $ sales**: fruits
Livestock: ...**largest number**: hogs & pigs
...**highest $ sales**: hogs & pigs
Among the top Michigan counties:
- #1- asparagus, carrots, peaches, pears, acres of tart cherries, rye for grain, winter squash
- #2- all vegetables, summer squash, Christmas trees, short rotation woody crops
- #3- goat milk, pumpkins
- #4- apples

Dairy, food and meat processing plants: 60
State ranking for harvested trees: #46 of 83 counties

FYI: Three hundred Michigan farms harvest about 11,000 acres of asparagus each year for a value of $15 million dollars, making the state the #3 asparagus producer in the U.S. Unlike asparagus from other states, each Mich-

Michigan Farm Bureau

igan asparagus spear is hand-snapped above the ground, which gives a more tender and flavorful product. Under ideal conditions, asparagus can grow 10" in a 24-hour period. When choosing fresh asparagus, the larger the diameter, the better the quality. Each spear of this delightful spring treat has only 4 calories. Almost 75% of the state's asparagus crop is grown here in Oceana County.
asparagus.com, Michigan.gov

Each asparagus plant (a crown) will send up spears for 6-7 weeks during the spring and early summer and will produce for about 15 years before needing to be replaced.

From BIBLIOGRAPHY & NOTES...

D DEMOGRAPHICS: All numbers given are for the county unless otherwise noted.

B BRIDGE OR BOAT

Ken Nye

Whether it is sailing the saltwater oceans around the world or the freshwater "oceans" of any of the Great Lakes, all sailboats need wind. The average wind speed on the Great Lakes in Michigan in July is 7-9 mph, the same as Florida. Before ships and boats were required to be registered and have identification numbers, they had names. Naming ships is a tradition that is still practiced today. This 1985 Endeavour 42' is named *Traumerie*, from a German word meaning "day dreaming."

C CELEBRATIONS

Hart *Fridays in Hart:* variety of musical concerts
Oceana County *National Asparagus Festival:* Green Spear-ited Fun, parade, crafts, asparagus food show, farm tours, poker-run, May
Rothbury *Rodeo & Pig Roast:* every Saturday night of the summer at Double JJ Resort
...*Music Festival:* jam band music, promoting sustainability and the environment, June
Silver Lake *Apple & BBQ Cook-off Festival:* Kansas City BBQ, fresh apples, apple pie contest, auto & truck show, dune buggy show & swap meet, Sept.

D DEMOGRAPHICS

Population: 26,600   **Persons per sq. mile**: 49
Largest city: Hart   **Population**: 2,130
Largest township: Grant   **Population**: 2,490
Largest village: Shelby   **Population**: 270
Median household income: $37,700
Owner-occupied median house value: $115,000
Persons affiliated with a religious congregation: 32%
Persons below poverty level: 21%
Students receiving school lunch subsidy: 60% (#2/MI)

E ENVIRONMENT

Ducks Unlimited is the world's largest and most effective private waterfowl and wetlands conservation organization. Their mission is to conserve, restore, and manage wetlands and associated habitats for North America's waterfowl, thereby benefiting other wildlife and people as well. Their vision is sufficient wetlands to fill the skies with waterfowl today, tomorrow and forever. With over 700,000 members in North America and influence on 60 million acres, they partner with private individuals, landowners, agencies, scientific communities and other entities to achieve their goal.

In 2011, Michigan had 27,000 DU members who raised over $1.3 million for their conservation efforts. Over the years they have conserved 56,000+ acres statewide and spent $23 million in the process. In this county, they have conserved over 1,000 acres. ducks.org

F FLORA & FAUNA

L.L. Barry, USA

Butter & eggs, a wild weed flower, is so named because of their bi-color resembling that of butter and egg yolks. It is prolific and can crowd out other vegetation. It is also known as yellow toadflax, wild snapdragon, flax weed and Jacob's ladder.

Michigan Farm Bureau

The Mallard Duck (*MI H&T*) is the most recognized waterfowl in the world and is the most common duck species of the Northern Hemisphere. They are an important game bird; loss of habitat is the greatest threat to their long-term survival. See 64E.

G GOVERNMENT

County: ...created: 1831 **...organized:** 1851
...originally part of: Hart County
Size: 349,000 acres/ 540 sq. miles (64 of 83 counties)
The county has 1 city, 6 villages, 12 townships, 3 unincorporated communities and 5 school districts.

NPCR

NPCR

County seat: Hart
...Homestead property tax: 38 mills
Motto: Hart: *Focused on the Hart of Oceana County*
...Pentwater Chamber: *Picture yourself here, in any season.*
...Shelby: *Where the North Begins*
...Silver Lake Sand Dunes Area: *Think Dunes*

H HISTORICAL MARKERS 2 of 5

Graveyard of Ships: the 20 miles between Little Point Sable at Silver Lake and Big Point Sable north of Ludington took nearly 70 ships to their grave between 1848 and 1986.
Veterans' Day Storm: a severe storm on November 11, 1940, destroyed 3 ships and claimed 59 seamen; it was the deadliest day in history on Lake Michigan.
National Register of Historic Places: 7 listings
State Historic Sites: 8 listings

I INFORMATION

Chamber of Commerce: Hesperia, 231-854-3695, hesperiachamberofcommerce.org
…Pentwater, 231-869-4150, pentwater.org
…Silver Lake Sand Dunes Area, 800-870-9786, thinkdunes.com

J JOKES

You might be a Michigan farmer's wife if…
…quality time with your husband means a flashlight in one hand and a wrench in the other.
…the leaky barn roof gets fixed before the leaky house roof.
…you can mend a pair of pants *and* the fence that ripped them, too.
…you call the implement dealer and he recognizes your voice.
…you've spent all day driving around during harvest season trying to find that one part needed to fix that darn old combine.
…you've spent all day in line at the elevator just to unload your corn.
…your mailbox is attached to a piece of old farm machinery.
…taking lunch to the men in the field is as close as you get to a picnic.
…you love your life.

K KINSMAN

Race
American Indian: 1%
Asian: <1%
Black/African American: <1%
Hispanic or Latino: 14%
Other: 8%
White: 90%

Ancestry
German: 22%
U.S./American: 10%
English: 9%
Dutch: 9%
Irish: 8%
Polish: 4%

L LIGHTHOUSE OR LANDMARK

Built in 1874, the Little Sable Point Light Station is 107' tall with red brick walls that are 2'-5' thick. Sitting on a beautiful stretch of beach in Silver Lake State Park, it is open for tours.

M MUSEUMS

Hart *Historic District:* church, one-room schoolhouse, log cabin, house, mill, windmill

N NATURAL RESOURCES

Elevation: <600 – 900 feet
Physiography: rolling plains, lake-border plains

Forest type: maple-birch-beech-hemlock, oak-hickory, elm-ash-cottonwood
Public/private forests: 54% of county
Legislatively protected sand dunes: 4,700 acres

Water in county: 1% of county
  Lakes: 70
    …largest: Silver Lake
  Rivers: Pentwater, Pere Marquette, White
  Rivers & streams: 225 miles
Great Lakes shoreline: 27 miles of Lake Michigan

Growing season, avg.: 142 days (2 temp. zones)
  Last freeze, avg.: May 20 – May 25
  First freeze, avg.: Sept. 30 – Oct. 5
Precipitation, annual avg.: rainfall: 34 inches
        snowfall: 99 inches

OCEANA COUNTY 64

Temperature (F), avg.: January: high 29°, low 16°
July: high 81°, low 58°
Annual: >90°: 5 days, **<0°:** 7 days
Tornadoes (1930-2010): 5

O ORIGINS

Grant:[t] Gen. Ulysses S. Grant; 1851
Hart:[c] pioneer settler, Wellington Hart; 1856
Hesperia:[v] resembles a garden; 1856
Mears:[u] sawmill owner, Charles Mears; 1873
New Era:[v] town founder came from Erie, PA; 1870
Oceana:[co] a long shoreline, like an ocean

Pentwater:[v] small opening of Pentwater Lake into Lake Michigan,
therefore it had pent-up water, OR
possibly "paint water" from the
dark color of Pentwater Lake; 1849

NPCR

Rothbury:[v] named in 1879, origins
unknown; 1865
Shelby:[v] Gen. Isaac Shelby of the
War of 1812; 1866
Stoney Lake:[u] after the lake of the same name; 1837
Walkerville:[v] land owner, Fayette Walker; 1883

P PARKS

National: 2 **State:** 5 **County:** 8 **Local:** 13
Number of campsites: 2,800
National: *Manistee National*
Forest: 53,000 acres, part
of 600,000 acres in 8
counties

State Game Area: (2,400
acres) Pentwater River

NPCR

State Linear Trail Park:
Hart-Montague:[ww,wba] 22
miles, paved trail through
rural, forested lands

NPCR

State Park: *Charles Mears:*
on Lake Michigan, 50
acres, commonly called
Pentwater; a large, ex-
cellent beach with fine
sand; climb the dunes

...*Silver Lake:* 2,900 acres,
on Silver Lake and Lake
Michigan (4 miles of
shoreline), home to the
only sand dunes east of
Utah that allow vehicle
traffic; mature forests too;
trails, ORV beach with
restrictions; see 64Q, 64V

Prentice Drake

Other: Walkinshaw Wetlands Nature Preserve

Q QUOTE FROM THE LOCALS

"The Silver Lake Sand
Dunes are a natural
phenomenon that attract
more than a million visitors
each year. Sand, sun, and
fun await you at the Silver
Lake Sand Dunes nestled
between the shores of Lake
Michigan and Silver Lake
in Oceana County. The
magnificent dunes are divided into three sections. The
northern area is reserved for off-road vehicles where
you can test your vehicle and your sand driving skill.
Whether you rent or take your own vehicle, this is a
thrill you've got to experience.

NPCR

"The center region is for hiking, walking, or simply
enjoying the beaches of Lake Michigan and Silver Lake.
"The southern end is home to Mac Woods Dune
Rides. No other area in Michigan allows vehicle
access to the dunes." thinkdunes.com See 64V.

R RECREATION & SPORTS

Auto racing: *West Michigan 'Silver Lake' Sand Dragway:*
300' of sand and clay track, racing ATVs, dune
buggies and all the way up to top fuel dragsters
...*Winston Speedway:* 3/8-mile semi banked clay oval
track
Golf courses: 6
Great Lakes marinas: 7 **Boat slips:** 300
Hiking/skiing/mountain biking trails: 30 miles
Horse racing: harness racing during fair week
Off-road vehicle trails: 40 miles
Public access sites: 5
Public recreational land: 17% of county
Rail-trail: (25 miles) Hart-Montague

Recreational harbor: Pentwater
State/federal wild/scenic/natural river: 90 miles of the White River
State-funded snowmobile trails: 40 miles
Double JJ Ranch, Waterpark and Golf Resort: horseback trails, indoor & outdoor waterparks, championship golf, weddings, meetings
Mt. Baldy Hill Climb: race 100' up the sand dunes

S STATE OF MICHIGAN

Pure Michigan® is Michigan's Official Travel and Tourism Site on the Internet (at michigan.org) and the sponsor of those wonderful TV ads and billboards. It also has printed material available. The website features Michigan-based tourism businesses that desire to be a part of their database and at no cost to the business. There are seven categories that a customer can choose from to access the information they want:

1. *Cities or Regions:* over 1,000 cities are listed in alphabetical order along with 7 regions in the state
2. *Places to Stay:* bed & breakfasts; cabins & cottages; campgrounds; condos & rentals; historic inns; hotels & motels; resorts
3. *Outdoor Activities:* golf including courses, resorts and schools; paddlesports including canoeing and kayaking; snow sports including cross-country skiing, dog sledding, downhill skiing, snowboarding and snowmobiling; beaches; biking; boating; campgrounds; fishing; hiking; hunting; nature & parks; Off-road vehicles; and rentals
4. *Things to Do:* attractions including amusement parks, kids activities, lighthouses, racetracks, water parks, farms & mills, historic sites, museums, tours and wineries; casinos; dining including breweries, casual dining, dinner cruises & trains and fine dining; entertainment venues including convention & civic centers, fairgrounds, nightlife, performing arts and sports arenas; road trips including city tours, fall color tours, foodie tours, heritage tours, maritime tours and wine trails; shopping including antique & flea markets, art galleries & crafts, farm markets and malls & shops
5. *Events:* antiques, crafts & collectibles; cultural & heritage; exhibits & shows; fairs & festivals; holiday; and sports
6. *Deals:* attractions; cultural & heritage; promotions; dining; fall; family; fishing; golf; holiday; romantic; shopping; snow sports; spa; and sports

7. *Featured Destinations:* the 26 "hot spots" of things to see and do in Michigan

NPCR

T TRAVEL

Airport: Oceana County
Circle Tour: Lake Michigan via US-31
County road names: ...north/south: Avenues
      ...east/west: Roads
Distance to Lansing: 140 miles
Main roads: M-20, M-120, US-31
Memorial Highways: US-31, *Blue Star MH:* see 3T
...US-31, *Pere Marquette HM:* see 53T
FYI: Over the years, US-31 has been called, in part or as a whole, proposed, promoted or legalized: Blue & Gray Trail, Blue Star Memorial Hwy., Cairn Hwy., Dixie Hwy., Dunes Hwy., Grand Traverse Memorial Hwy., Great Lakes Automobile Route, Hamilton Way, LaSalle Trail, Michigamme Trail, Michigan Pike, Michigan Trail, Pere Marquette Memorial Hwy., Saint Joseph Valley Parkway and West Michigan Pike. Barnett

U UNIVERSITIES & COLLEGES

None

V VARIETY

Mac Wood's Dune Rides

Mac Wood's Dune Rides gives you a 7-mile trip up and over, down and around the Silver Lake Sand Dunes on Lake Michigan. See 64Q.

W WANDERLUST

Agri-tourism: *Cherry Point Farm and Market:* fruit & veggies, bakery, fish boils, labyrinth, festivals

...*Country Dairy Family Farm:* Moo School, tours, wagon rides, bottling plant, farm store and deli, show barn, milk, cheese, ice cream

...*Fox Barn Market & Winery:* asparagus, cherries, sweet corn, peaches, pears, apples, pumpkins, specialty products featuring asparagus and cherries, fruit wines

...*Lewis Farm Market:* an Agritainment destination; apples, cherries, strawberries, corn maze, bakery, tours, many activities throughout the year

...*Rennhack Orchards Market:* apples, asparagus, cherries, sweet corn, other fruits & veggies

Fall colors: early October

Wineries: *Fox Barn:* market and winery, an agricultural marketplace; fruit wines

Bygone Basics: learn to do home canning, make jams & jellies, churn butter and bake from "scratch"

Sand Dune Rides: you can rent a dune buggy and drive yourself around the dunes; see 64Q.

Shelby Gemstone Factory: they make more varieties of synthetic and imitation gems than anyone else in the world; factory showroom, tours

X X-TRA STUFF

County fair: *Oceans County Agriculture Society:* Aug.

Hospitals: Lakeshore Community, Hackley Lakeshore

Large employers: Peterson Farms (fresh, frozen, cold pack fruits), Kurdziel Iron (makes gray iron castings), Gray (make maraschino cherries, chocolate and cocoa products), Carlton Creek Ironworks (iron foundry), New Era Canning (canned fruits), Oceana County Medical Care (skilled nursing), Hart Public Schools

Y YESTERYEAR

It is estimated that there have been 5,000 ships lost in the storms of the Great Lakes. Many have been commemorated in songs. Here's just one. [Anderson]

"On the eighteenth in the morning –
And what I saw is true –
The ice upon our riggin' froze,
And the cold winds fiercely blew.
    But no one thought that in two short hours
    That very afternoon
    Some would be froze and some be drowned –
    The *Antelope* was doomed!
The cold increased, the tempest raged,
The huge seas loud did roar;
With our canvas gone, both anchors out,
We were drifting toward the shore! . . .
    We drifted with each pounding sea,
    And then we struck stern on;
    Our mainm'st by the deck was broke,
    Our mizzenm'st was gone!
The huge seas raked her fore and aft,
And then she swung broadside,
And three men overboard were swept
Into that raging tide!
    Our captain tried to swim ashore,
    Our precious lives to save,
    But by his bold endeavor
    He was lost beneath the waves.
And only one of that gallant crew
Was in life once more to stand:
And for miles and miles the *Antelope*
Lined the shores of Michigan."

Z ZOO & ANIMAL PLACES

Petting zoo: Lewis Farm Market
Watchable Wildlife Viewing Areas:[ww] see 64P
Rainbow Ranch: horse rides and lessons, pony rides, hay, carriage and sleigh rides

A AGRICULTURE

Land in farms: 17% of county
Number of farms: 320
Size of average farm: 190 acres
Market value of all products: #44 of 83 counties
Crops: ...most acres: forage land
...highest $ sales: grains: corn, soybeans, wheat
Livestock: ...largest number: cattle & calves
...highest $ sales: milk & dairy products
Dairy, food and meat processing plants: 4
State ranking for harvested trees: #35 of 83 counties
FYI: <u>What is a farm?</u> A farm is "any establishment from which $1,000 or more of agricultural products were sold or would normally be sold during the year." This includes family farms, institutional farms, experimental and research farms, American Indian reservations and places where the entire acreage is enrolled in a government program (i.e., conservation, wetlands). It does not include industrial, public and grazing association land.

In 2007, there were over 56,000 farms in Michigan, with over 10 million acres in these farms; 78% of that land was cropland. The average farm was 180 acres. Nearly 35,000 of Michigan farms had sales of less than $10,000 while 8,000 had sales of more than $100,000.

In the U.S. in 1900, there were over 6 million farms averaging less than 200 acres each, totaling less than 1.2 billion acres. In 2000, there were just over 2 million farms averaging 500 acres each, totaling 1 billion acres. National Agricultural Statistics Service

B BRIDGE OR BOAT

This pedestrian covered bridge crosses the West Branch of the Rifle River in Irons Park.

C CELEBRATIONS

<u>West Branch</u> *Fabulous Fridays:* a different event each Friday, Memorial Day to Labor Day
...*Summer Music Series:* June-Aug.

...*Pioneer Power Antique Tractor & Gas Engine Club Show & Flea Market:* July

...*Heritage Days:* parade, voyageur encampment, July
...*Heritage Fine Art Show:* Michigan artists, July

...*Victorian Art Fair:* Aug.

...*Lamb & Wool Festival:* all things sheep, spinning, looms, classes, Sept.

...*Quilt Show & Raffle:* Oct.

D DEMOGRAPHICS

Population: 21,700   **Persons per sq. mile:** 39
Largest city: West Branch   **Population:** 2,140
Largest township: Mills   **Population:** 4,300
Largest village: Prescott   **Population:** 270
Median household income: $32,600
Owner-occupied median house value: $108,000
Persons affiliated with a religious congregation: 34%
Persons below poverty level: 19%
Students receiving school lunch subsidy: 50%

E ENVIRONMENT

The native <u>trumpeter swan</u> has been reintroduced to wetlands in the Lower Peninsula and the eastern Upper Peninsula of Michigan. All wild swans are protected in Michigan. The trumpeter swan, the

world's largest waterfowl, is 4′ long with a 7′ wingspan and can weigh 25-35 pounds. They are all white. Once abundant and then nearly extinct in Michigan, the Trumpeter Swan Restoration Program has been successful in increasing their population. You can help this magnificent swan by:

▪Learning the difference between swans and snow geese and *not* shooting the swan.

▪Reporting observations of marked swans that have wing tags, neck collars, or leg bands.

▪Reporting any harassment of trumpeter swans.

▪Reporting any trumpeter swan nesting sites.

These magnificent birds may be seen on many of the lakes in the Rifle River Recreation Area. Michigan .gov/dnr

Dr. Thomas G. Barnes, USFWS

F FLORA & FAUNA

Dr. Thomas G. Barnes, USFWS

The 40″ tall cardinal flower can be seen in the spring along the trails in the Rifle River Recreation Area since it likes moist soils. It was probably named after the garment of a Roman Catholic Cardinal, as they are both the same brilliant red color. Historically, this plant was used for teas, medicine and as a smoking and chewing tobacco substitute.

Rick L. Hansen, USFWS

The blue racer snake lives in both dry and wetland environments and can grow to be 4′-6′ in length. Although they may bite if cornered or grabbed, they are not poisonous.

G GOVERNMENT

Sonya Plude

NPCR

County: ...created: 1840 **...organized:** 1875
...originally part of: Saginaw, Branch Counties
Size: 368,000 acres / 564 sq. miles (52 of 83 counties)
The county has 2 cities, 1 village, 14 townships, 1 unincorporated community, 1 Census Designated Place and 2 school districts.
County seat: West Branch
...Homestead property tax: 37 mills
Motto: <u>West Branch</u> Area Chamber: *Ogemaw County, A Four Seasons Destination*

H HISTORICAL MARKERS 3 of 5

Cleveland Park Pavilion: 1930, automobile pioneer Harry Jewett donated land and funds to develop an open-air kitchen and dining hall.
The Big Fire: 1910, destroyed 30 wood frame buildings in the commercial district of Rose City; only two concrete buildings survived

Rose Township District No. 5 School: in the 1903-1904 school year there were 98 children in this two-room school; it was used as a school until 1963.

Michigan State Historic Preservation Office

State Historic Sites: 4 listings

I INFORMATION

Chamber of Commerce: Prescott, Rose City-Lupton
Visitor: West Branch Visitors Bureau, 800-755-9091, visitwestbranch.com

J JOKES

You may be a freshman at a local community college if…
…you spend more time partying than studying.
…diversity now means other kids of different races and from other countries, not just the Swedish kids from the next town.
…your mother told you studying was your most important priority at school. But you're no mamma's boy; you don't have to do what she says.
…you look down your nose at your high school classmates who are wasting their money at a four-year college.
…you couldn't get into a four-year college.
…living at home wasn't your first choice, but the other alternatives are too expensive.
…you're grateful for the opportunity just to get a college education.

K KINSMAN

Race
American Indian: <1%
Asian: <1%
Black/African American: <1%
Hispanic or Latino: 1%
Other: 2%
White: 97%

Ancestry
German: 29%
U.S./American: 12%
English: 10%
Irish: 9%
French: 7%
Polish: 7%

L LIGHTHOUSE OR LANDMARK

Wendi Richardson, Concerned Racers Club

This county is off-road-vehicle friendly with an extensive trail system and a county ordinance that permits ORVs on streets and highways.

M MUSEUMS

<u>West Branch</u> *The Antique Village at the Ogemaw County Fair:* only open during fair week in Aug.; includes the Church in the Woods, Village Press, Knight Cabin, Withey School, Trapper's Cabin, General Store, Ogemaw State Forest Bunkhouse, Robinson Cabin, Bean's Blacksmith Shop, Bessemer Single Piston Engine & Oil Field Display, Edward E. Evans Memorial Garden, Priddy Barn and many things to touch and see and do

Karen Miller

…*Ogemaw County Historical Museum:* preserving history of Ogemaw county and its families

N NATURAL RESOURCES

Elevation: 700 – 1,300 feet
Physiography: hill-lands

Forest type: aspen-birch, maple-beech-hemlock, oak-hickory
Public/private forests: 62% of county

Water in county: 1% of county
   Lakes: 120   …**largest:** Lake Ogemaw
   Rivers: AuGres (aw GRAY), Rifle, Tittabawassee (tit a ba WAH see)
   Rivers & streams: 380 miles

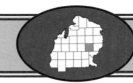

Growing season, avg.: 126 days (2-3 temp. zones)
  Last freeze, avg.: May 20 – May 30
  First freeze, avg.: Sept. 15 – Sept. 20
Precipitation, annual avg.:
  rainfall: 29 inches
  snowfall: 57 inches
Temperature (F), avg.:
  January: high 26°, low 9°
  July: high 81°, low 55°

  Annual: >90°: 6 days,
  <0°: 21 days

Tornadoes (1930-2010): 14

NPCR

O ORIGINS

Lupton:[u] the Lupton family from Ohio; 1880
Ogemaw:[co] (OH ga maw) the American Indian word
  for chief
Prescott:[v] C.H. Prescott owned the local railroad; 1879
Rose City:[c] the Rose family came from NY; 1875
West Branch:[c] west branch of the Rifle River; 1971

P PARKS

National: 2 **State:** 5 **County:** 5 **Local:** 8
Number of campsites: 1,400
National: *Huron National Forest:* 20,000 acres,
  established in 1909 on former "logged out" lands
  that are once again beautiful forests
State Forest: (72,000 acres) AuSable, Ogemaw
...Campground: 1   **...Pathway:** 15 miles
State Recreation Area: *Rifle River:*[ww] 4,300 acres of
  wilderness; camping, fishing, biking, birding
Local: *Irons Park*

Q QUOTE FROM THE LOCALS

"A visit to Ogemaw County is one that your family will remember for many years to come. Enjoy Ogemaw Hills, Rifle River Valley and traverse the many nature trails that will provide you with hours of entertainment. During your visit here you will become enthralled with the enchanting beauty that this region holds for you.

"Ogemaw County is an ideal place to spend a day, a long weekend or an entire vacation. Everything you can imagine is here for your enjoyment. We offer many great scenic adventures that will make

NPCR

your stay seem like a fairy tale. Canoeing, trout fishing and swimming are just a few of the many recreational activities that you will find in this vast four-season playground." [wbacc.com]

R RECREATION & SPORTS

Golf courses: 5
Hiking/skiing/mountain biking trails:
  40 miles

Off-road vehicle trails: 120 miles

NPCR

Public access sites: 28
Public recreational land: 27% of county
Rail-trail: (10 miles) Rifle River Recreation Area
State-funded snowmobile trails: 50 miles
State recreational public access sites: 28
State/federal wild/scenic/natural river: 90 miles of
  the Rifle River
Ogemaw Hills Pathway: 15 miles of winding trails
  through the AuSable State Forest; hike, bike, ski

S STATE OF MICHIGAN

Eric Engbreston, USFWS

Since 1965, the brook trout has been the State Fish. Found in many lakes and streams, it is highly prized by sportsmen for its good flavor.

T TRAVEL

Airport: West Branch Community
Distance to Lansing: 140 miles
Main roads: I-75, M-30, M-33, M-55
Memorial Highways: I-75, *American Legion M H:* see 6T
...M-33, *Veterans Memorial Drive*

U UNIVERSITIES & COLLEGES

Baker College of West Branch: see 25U
Kirkland Community College in West Branch: see 72U

V VARIETY

Brianna Brewer, West Branch Chamber of Commerce

NPCR

The beauty of this region lies in the wide variety of hills, lakes and streams.

W WANDERLUST

Fall colors: late September to early October
Shopping malls: Tanger Outlet Center
Wineries: *Rose Valley Winery:* locally grown winter hardy grapes, wine tasting, grape theme gift shop
…*Valley Mist Vineyards:* specialize in Estate-Bottled Wines

X X-TRA STUFF

Karen Miller

County fair: *Ogemaw County Agricultural Society*: located in the middle of 200 acres, it has been said it is the most beautiful fairgrounds in Michigan

Hospitals: West Branch Regional Medical Center
Large employers: West Branch Regional Medical Center, West Branch-Rose City Schools, Wal-Mart, Tanger Outlet Center, Bortz Health Care, Sandvik Hard Materials (makes pipes & fittings, metal cutting machine tools, etc.), Taylor Building Products (makes metal door, sash & trim)

Y YESTERYEAR

In the late 1800s, the forests of northern Michigan provided the U.S. with much needed lumber to help meet the building needs of a growing U.S. economy. Consequently, it left hundreds of thousands of Michigan acres with cutover and burned over lands. Sometimes farmers moved onto some of this land to finish clearing it and to begin farming. However, in many areas the soil that made good forests did not make good farmland. Many of these farms were eventually abandoned and/or reverted to the state for non-payment of taxes. So the state of Michigan was stuck with "worthless and abandoned land" throughout the state.

In the early 1900s, the State of Michigan established the State Forest system and began the long-term task of redeveloping this once rich but now worthless land. When you look at a map of state forests, you will notice that each forest is not a contiguous body of land, but may be scattered out over a wide area. This is because the land that reverted back to the state came in individual parcels. These parcels were then incorporated into the state forests. There are 3 state forests in the Upper Peninsula (Copper Country, Escanaba River, Lake Superior) and 3 in the Lower Peninsula (Mackinaw, Pere Marquette, AuSable).

Today the State Forests of Michigan are a gem that is available to all who want to appreciate nature at its best. There are over 145 Michigan State Forest Campgrounds and each one is located on a river or a lake to provide you with excellent fishing and boating opportunities. Camping is rustic with vault toilets and hand pumps for water.

There are over 60 State Forest Campgrounds that have Pathways designed for hiking, biking, skiing, horseback riding and just watching nature at its glorious Michigan best. All trails are well marked.
Michigan.gov

NPCR

NPCR

NPCR

Z ZOO & ANIMAL PLACES

Watchable Wildlife Viewing Areas:ww see 65P
A scenic overlook from Lodge Hill in the Rifle River Recreation Area will delight viewers with a bird's eye view of the area's loons and trumpeter swans.
Ogemaw County Nature Park: feed the white-tailed deer.

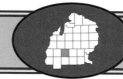
A AGRICULTURE

Land in farms: 33% of county
Number of farms: 830
Size of average farm: 150 acres
Market value of all products: #45 of 83 counties
Crops: ...most acres: forage
...highest $ sales: hay
Livestock: ...largest number: cattle & calves
...highest $ sales: milk & dairy products
Among the top Michigan counties:
- #1- alfalfa, number of beef cattle
- #2- forage crops, hay, wild hay
- #3- goats for milk

Dairy, food and meat processing plants: 17
State ranking for harvested trees: #37 of 83 counties
FYI: There are over 7,880 farms in Michigan raising 110,000 head of <u>beef cattle</u> in 82 of the 83 counties in the state. This county has the most beef cattle at 3,700 animals. An animal goes to market when it is 14-16 months old and weighs 1,000 to 1,300 pounds. Fifty percent of that weight is used as meat (yummm, think steak, roasts and hamburgers), and 48% is used in the manufacturing of soap, shampoo, cosmetics, photographic film, many medicines, sports equipment, shoes, footballs and many, many other items. Because cattle can eat almost anything, they are able to consume many by-products from other food products that would otherwise be wasted. In addition, they can be raised on lands that are not suitable for crop production. USDA, Michigan Farm Bureau

B BRIDGE OR BOAT

Suzie Williams

The Reed City Covered Bridge over the Hersey River is part of the White Pines Linear Trail State Park.

C CELEBRATIONS

<u>Evart</u> *Summer Musicale Series:* includes Folk Festival and Dulcimer FunFest, plus others, June – Aug.
...Woodcarvers Roundup: June
<u>Marion</u> *Old Fashioned Days:* yearly themes, vintage power & machinery, music, pig roast, Aug.
<u>Reed City</u> *Great American Crossroads Celebration:* parades, games, food, music, Aug.
...Music & Art in the Park: June-Aug.

D DEMOGRAPHICS

Population: 23,500 **Persons per sq. mile**: 42
Largest city: Reed City **Population**: 2,430
Largest township: Hersey **Population**: 1,600
Largest village: Marion **Population**: 870
Median household income: $34,800
Owner-occupied median house value: $103,000
Persons affiliated with a religious congregation: 33%
Persons below poverty level: 19%
Students receiving school lunch subsidy: 50%

E ENVIRONMENT

<u>Artesian wells</u> are found in areas that have porous stone, such as limestone or sandstone, which then hold the water in underground aquifers. The water in the aquifers comes from rain or melting snow and percolates down through the porous rock providing cleansing of the water. In certain spots where the underground pressure has built up between the layers of rock, the water will be pushed up naturally

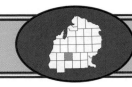
to the surface and flow freely without having to drill a well to bring the water up mechanically or by hand. Osceola County has clusters of artesian wells that form the beginnings of small streams. It is not uncommon for a House for Sale advertisement in this area to mention that there is an artesian well on the property.

F FLORA & FAUNA

Steve Hillebrand/USFWS

The orange hawkweed, often called the devils paintbrush, is a small flower (<1") with a big impact. It's a prolific spreader, invading urban sites, meadows, hay fields, roadsides, gravel pits and forests. It competes for space, light and soil nutrients with more desirable plants and usually wins.

Steve Hillebrand/USFWS

Feral swine, or free-range hogs and pigs, described as prolific and vicious, pose a real threat to crops, domestic animals and the natural environment. They are escapees from hunting preserves and possibly farms. Michigan allows hunting of this nuisance species at any time.

G GOVERNMENT

County: ...created: 1840 **...organized:** 1869
...originally part of: Mason, Newaygo, Mecosta Counties
Size: 367,000 acres / 566 sq. miles (50 of 83 counties)
The county has 2 cities, 4 villages, 16 townships, 1 unincorporated community and 4 school districts.

Ryan Fox

NPCR

County seat: Reed City
...Homestead property tax: 40 mills
Motto: <u>Evart</u>: *Your Inland Oasis Awaits*
...<u>Evart</u> Area Chamber: *Michigan's Best Kept All Season Recreational Secret*
...<u>LeRoy</u> Area Chamber: *Year Round Playground*
...<u>Marion</u> Area Chamber: *Home of Real Water – Artesian Wells*
...<u>Reed City</u>: *Crossroads; Rail Trail Capitol of Michigan*
...<u>Reed City</u> Chamber: *Your crossroads community on the path of progress*

H HISTORICAL MARKERS 3 of 7

Joseph W. Guyton: (1889-1918) the first U.S. soldier killed in WWI in Germany
Founding of Marion: 1875, the Clarks (Marion was the wife) had a general store, a sawmill that produced siding, shingles, flooring, moldings and barrels; they donated land for a park.
"Unto a New Land:" in the late 1800s, hundreds of Swedes came to this area to build the railroad, log the forest and work in the sawmills.
State Historic Sites: 6 listings

I INFORMATION

Chamber of Commerce: Evart, 231-734-9799, evartareachamberofcommerce.com
...Marion, marionmichigan.com

...Reed City, 231-832-5431, reedcity.org

NPCR

J JOKES

You might be a Michiganian if...

...you've ever mowed the grass in your winter coat, hat and gloves.

...you've ever been snow skiing in shorts.

...you ever wore a wet suit while water skiing.

...you ride your bicycle in any kind of weather, hot or cold, wet or dry.

...almost everyone you know owns a hunting gun, or two, or three, or four.

...you measure distance in minutes.

...you know you don't have to go to Florida to go scuba diving in clear blue water.

...you can 'hear' the sun 'sizzle' as it sinks into Lake Michigan

...it is hard to get used to salt water burning your eyes and mouth since you're used to swimming in fresh water.

K KINSMAN

Race
American Indian: <1%
Asian: <1%
Black/African American: <1%
Hispanic or Latino: 1%
Other: 2%
White: 97%

Ancestry
German: 26%
English: 12%
U.S./American: 11%
Irish: 9%
Dutch: 6%
Polish: 5%

L LIGHTHOUSE OR LANDMARK

Suzie Williamas

The Reed City Depot, a reconstruction of the original depot, is open 24 hours a day as a rest area for users of the local White Pine Trail (north and south) and Pere Marquette State Linear Trail Parks (east and west). See 67P, 67R.

M MUSEUMS

Reed City *Old Rugged Cross Historical Museum:* displays of Dr. George Bennard, author of the 1913 song "The Old Rugged Cross;" area history

Tustin *Pine River Area Museum:* nice local history

Suzie Williamas

N NATURAL RESOURCES

Elevation: 900 – 1,700 feet
Physiography: hill uplands, upland plains

Forest type: aspen-birch, maple-beech-hemlock, pine-oak
Public/private forests: 51% of county

Water in county: 1% of county
 Lakes: 85 ...**largest:** Rose Lake
 Rivers: Hersey, Middle Branch, Muskegon (muss KEY gun), Pine
 Rivers & streams: 300 miles

Growing season, avg.: 126 days (2-3 temp. zones)
 Last freeze, avg.: May 20 – May 30
 First freeze, avg.: Sept. 20 – Sept. 25
Precipitation, annual avg.: rainfall: 32 inches
                snowfall: 71 inches
Temperature (F), avg.: January: high 28°, low 11°
                July: high 82°, low 56°
 Annual: >90°: 8 days, **<0°:** 16 days
Tornadoes (1930-2010): 13

NPCR

O ORIGINS

Evart:[c] misspelling of settler Oliver Everts' name; 1870
Hersey:[v] trapper, Nathan Hersey; 1843
Le Roy:[v] federal land agent, LeRoy Carr; 1871
Marion:[v] Marion Clark, wife of village founder; 1880
Osceola:[co] (ah see OH la) American Indian chief; 1869
Reed City:[c] town founder, James Reed; 1870
Tustin:[v] medical missionary, Dr. J.P. Tustin, was sent to Sweden to recruit laborers for the railroad; 1872

P PARKS

National: 0 **State:** 3
County: 2 **Local:** 9
Number of campsites: 1,350

State Forest: (18,000 acres)
Pere Marquette
...**Campground:** 1
...**Pathway:** 9 miles

State Linear Trail Park: *Fred Meijer White Pine:* 93 miles north & south from Cadillac to Grand Rapids
County: *Crittenden:* 10 acres, on Big Lake, camping, lake activities
...*Rose Lake:* 48 acres, camping, large, beautiful sandy beach, lake activities, mini-golf
Other: *SpringHill Camps:* Christian camp and retreats ministry; year-round activities

Q QUOTE FROM THE LOCALS

"The geography of west central Michigan is a blend of hills, forests and quiet farmland punctuated by sparkling rivers and lakes. There is an abundance of diverse wildlife in the region including bald eagles, which nest along the Muskegon River. Osceola County has one of the largest whitetail deer populations in the state. For anglers, the Muskegon River offers excellent bass fishing. Besides fishing and hunting, the Rails to Trails program converted the former railroad bed to a beautiful trail that is favored by walkers, joggers, runners, bikers and snowmobilers." evart.org

R RECREATION & SPORTS

Auto racing: *Michigan Motorsports Park*
Blue Ribbon Trout Streams: Middle Branch River, Pine River
Golf courses: 3

Hiking/skiing/mountain biking trails: 80 miles
Off-road vehicle trails: 20 miles
Public access sites: 19
Public recreational land: 5% of county
Rail-trail: *Pere Marquette:* 84 miles west and east from Baldwin to Midland

...*Fred Meijer White Pine Trail:* used for bikes in the summer and snowmobiles in the winter; see 67P

S STATE OF MICHIGAN

Michigan has:
- 83 counties
- 1,245 civil and charter townships (134 duplicate names)
- 1,339 cities and villages (3 duplicate names)
- 57 intermediate school districts
- 514 public school districts
- 13 named peninsulas
- 183 named bays on the Great Lakes and connecting waters (11 duplicate names)
- 348 named islands in the Great Lakes and connecting waters Schaetzl

T TRAVEL

Airport: Evart Municipal
Bus: Indian Trails
County road names:
...**north/south:** numbered Avenues
...**east/west:** numbered Mile Roads
Distance to Lansing: 120 miles
Main roads: US-131, US-10, M-61, M-66, M-115
Memorial Highway: M-66, *Green Arrow Route:* see 8T
FYI: Over the years, US-131 has been called, in part or as a whole, proposed, promoted or legalized: Central Michigan International Hwy., Colgrove Hwy., Gold Star Memorial Hwy., James Whitcomb Riley Memorial Hwy., Mackinaw Trail, Michigan Trail, Sidney Ouwinga Memorial Bypass and Underground Railroad Memorial Hwy. Barnett

U UNIVERSITIES & COLLEGES

None

V VARIETY

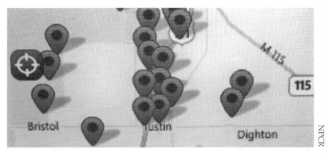

NPCR

Geocaching is a high-tech treasure hunting game played throughout the world by adventure seekers equipped with GPS (global positioning system) devices. The basic idea is to locate containers hidden outdoors, called geocaches, and then share your experience online. Geocaching is enjoyed by people of all age groups who have a strong sense of community and support for the environment.

The goal of the Michigan Geocaching Organization is to promote the sport of geochaching, promote an appreciation of the outdoors, and promote good environmental stewardship through cooperative efforts with Michigan geocachers and land management officials. This activity gets people out-of-doors with a purpose and goal: walking in our parks and open lands, enjoying the great outdoors and having fun doing an outdoor activity for the whole family.

There are over 1.2 million geocache sites worldwide and several thousand in Michigan, including Grove Hill (elevation 1702 ft). in Osceola County, which may be the highest point in the Lower Peninsula. mi-geocaching.org, geocaching.com

W WANDERLUST

Cultural: *Osceloa League for Arts and Humanities:* to promote and inspire creative and cultural experiences for all ages

Fall colors: early October

NPCR

Kettunen Center: a full service conference and retreat facility owned and operated the Michigan 4-H Foundation to train leaders and students; 160 acres of rolling hills and forests, it is "The NATURAL place"

Ryan Fox

NPCR

Osceola County Quilt Trail: part of the National Quilt Barn Trail, it has painted quilt blocks on barns and other notable structures.

X X-TRA STUFF

County fair: *Osceola County 4-H & FFA Fair:* Aug.
Hospitals: Spectrum-Reed City Hospital
Large employers: Ventra (auto supplier), General Mills Yoplait, Spectrum-Reed City Hospital, Osceola County, Liberty Dairy (bottles milk, makes cheese), Reed City Public Schools, Hydaker-Wheatlake Co. (manages substation transmissions), Pine River Area Schools, Evart Public Schools, Krafttube (tube fabrications), Marion Public Schools
Eagle Village: provides evaluation and treatment in a residential and Christian setting for victims of abuse and neglect
Osceola County is a leading gas and oil producer.

Y YESTERYEAR

Lumbering was an important part of the early years (circa 1875) of Osceola County. Timber was only cut in the winter; the logs were stacked up to 30' feet high on bobsleds. As cattlemen branded their cattle, lumberjacks branded each end of the cut trees. The bobsleds were then moved via animals (oxen, mules, horses) to the banks of a stream or river. In the spring when the ice melted and the rivers flooded, the logs were released into the water to be carried downstream, a process called "booming." This was a difficult and hazardous job done by the rivermen who were considered to be the toughest men in the lumber business. The logs had to be kept moving downstream.

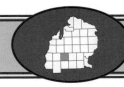
The rivermen had to try and prevent logjams; and when they inevitably occurred, it was their job to wrestle the giant logs into submission and get them moving again.

NPCR-2

NPCR-5

NPCR-5

When the logs reached the mouth of the river where the sawmills were, they were captured, sorted by brand and bundled together into rafts until they could be processed by the sawmills. Dunbar

Ryan Fox

Today, machinery has replaced the dangerous job of cutting trees by hand and transporting the logs using animals and rivers.

Z ZOO & ANIMAL PLACES

NPCR

With forests covering over 50% of the county, it is certain that wildlife abounds in this county.

From BIBLIOGRAPHY & NOTES...

L LIGHTHOUSE or LANDMARK: When you see "this," you know you're in *this* county!

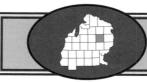
A AGRICULTURE

Land in farms: 5% of county
Number of farms: 135
Size of average farm: 130 acres
Market value of all products: #66 of 83 counties
Crops: ...most acres: forage
...highest $ sales: hay
Livestock: ...largest number: cattle & calves
...highest $ sales: milk & dairy products
Dairy, food and meat processing plants: 11
State ranking for harvested trees: #23 of 83 counties
FYI: The <u>Michigan Department of Agriculture and Rural Development</u> (MDARD) states:

- Underneath all is the land. And the land is more than just dirt. Soil is one of the basic components we depend on to grow food and wood-based products, and use as recreational areas. It is not an unlimited resource. It can be destroyed. With proper management it is a renewable resource that must be protected.

- The primary responsibility of the MDARD is assuring the safety and wholesomeness of Michigan's food supply. It regularly inspects the food supply at each step in the food chain, from the farm to the store.

- All receipts must include the name and address of the responsible party, the name or identity of the product bought or sold, the "net" weight, volume or count, the unit price and the total price.

- Firewood is to be sold by the cord, half cord, or quarter cord and never by the face cord. A cord is 128 cubic feet or 4'x4'x8'.

- Each American farmer provides food for 154 people at home and abroad. Farmers and ranchers comprise less than 2% of the U.S. population.

- One in six jobs in America is related to the food and fiber grown by America's farmers and ranchers.

- The MDARD has lesson plans for teachers on various food items, insects, rain, soils, weights and measures, pizza, cooking and more, which can be found on the MDARD website.

- To avoid the risk of food poisoning, your refrigerator should run at 40° F, just cold enough to keep the milk and lettuce from freezing. The freezer should be kept at 0°F.

- To prevent the spread of disease in the home, wash hands in hot, soapy water before preparing food and after using the bathroom, changing diapers and handling pets.

- See 33A.

B BRIDGE or BOAT

Garland Lodge and Resort

This 92' land bridge over CR-489, Red Oak Rd., is part of the Garland Golf Course of the Garland Resort.

C CELEBRATIONS

<u>Comins</u> *Michigan Magazine Craft Show:* bringing together their many supporters from around the state, June

<u>Fairview</u> *Northern Michigan Relief Sale & Quilt Auction*: Mennonite churches raise money for aid relief work around the world, Aug.

<u>Mio</u> *AuSable Valley Nor-East'r Association of Folk Music and Art Festival:* creative and performance art in northeast Michigan will blow you away, June

D DEMOGRAPHICS

Population: 8,600   **Persons per sq. mile:** 15
Largest city: Mio[CDP]   **Population:** 1,830
Largest township: Big Creek **Population:** 2,830
Median household income: $32,900
Owner-occupied median house value: $97,400
Persons affiliated with a religious congregation: 45%
Persons below poverty level: 21%
Students receiving school lunch subsidy: 56%
FYI: Forty-nine percent (4,300) of all housing units in this county are vacation, seasonal, or occasional homes. [US Census]

E ENVIRONMENT

The <u>Michigan Wild Turkey Hunters Association</u> is the only hunting organization, together with the Michigan Conservation Foundation, that supports the public lands hunter. The <u>National Wild Turkey Federation</u> supports the conservation of the Wild Turkey and the preservation of the turkey hunting tradition. Since 1985, over $100 million dollars has been spent on over 10,000 projects benefiting the Wild Turkey. This includes areas of education, equipment, habitat enhancement, hunting heritage fund, hunter safety, land acquisition, research, restoration and rewards.

The JAKES program, Juniors Acquiring Knowledge, Ethics and Sportsmanship, is dedicated to informing, educating and involving youth in wildlife conservation and the wise stewardship of our natural resources. nwtf.org, mwtfa.net See 68F.

F FLORA & FAUNA

The jack pine ecosystem of the Huron National Forest is amazingly productive and biologically diverse, providing a home for numerous plants and animals. It has dense stands of relatively young trees interspersed with small grass and sedge openings.

Discovering Michigan County by County is the only book where all counties are treated equal. Every county has a story to tell. There's no other book or online site like it!

Wild Turkeys *(MI H&T)* are up to 4' long from beak to tail. They eat insects and grasses in the summer and the fruits and nuts of vines, brush and trees in the winter. See 68E.

G GOVERNMENT

County: ...created: 1840 **...organized:** 1881
...originally part of: Cheboygan, Alpena, Alcona Counties
Size: 366,000 acres / 565 sq. miles (51 of 83 counties)
The county has 6 townships, 5 unincorporated communities, 1 Census Designated Place and 2 school districts.

Oscoda County Courthouse: 1889, while other counties were building elaborate structures, Oscoda wanted a modest wood frame structure. This courthouse is still in use today.
County seat: Mio
...Homestead property tax: (Mentor Twp). 21 mills
Motto: <u>Fairview</u>: *Wild Turkey Capital of Michigan*
...<u>Oscoda</u> Convention and Visitors Bureau: *Oscoda. naturally.*

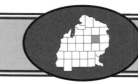

H HISTORICAL MARKERS 1 of 2

Mio Hydroelectric Plant: Built in 1916 by Consumers Power Company, it was the first plant to have a conduit spillway where the water goes through concrete passageways at the foundation of the plant, rather than having the water spill over the top. Michigan's extensive water resources were used to power electric generating equipment and thus helped Michigan become an industrial giant.

National Register of Historic Places: 1 listing
State Historic Sites: 1 listing

I INFORMATION

Chamber of Commerce: Oscoda County
Visitor: Oscoda Area Convention and Visitors Bureau, 877-8-oscoda

J JOKES

You may be a Michigan tightwad if…
…you always order off the dollar menu at fast-food restaurants.
…almost everything you own was purchased at the best store in town, the local thrift store.
…the only way your kids will ever go to college is if you move to Kalamazoo.

…you don't like paying a heating bill, so you heat with the free wood from the state forest and you cut it yourself.

…you'd never pay to get into a state park.

K KINSMAN

Race
American Indian: <1%
Asian: <1%
Black/African American: <1%
Hispanic or Latino: <1%
Other: 2%
White: 98%

Ancestry
German: 30%
U.S./American: 13%
English: 10%
Polish: 8%
French: 7%
Irish: 6%

L LIGHTHOUSE OR LANDMARK

US Forest Service, Philip W. Huber

The Jack Pine Wildlife Viewing Tour starts in Mio and is a 58-mile auto loop tour through the Huron National Forest that is maintained by the DNR. You may see bald eagles, beavers, bluebirds, grouse, herons, Kirkland's warbler, river otters, wild turkeys and many other possibilities. There are 12 well-marked stops and each has an informative interpretive panel. The panoramic views of the Au Sable River Valley are beautiful. Maps are available at the U.S. Forest Service in Mio.

M MUSEUMS

Comins *Michigan Magazine Museum:* a celebration of Michigan and her people; hundreds of displays spotlighting the many talented and enterprising people of Michigan; see 68X
Fairview *Steiner's Museum:* pioneer artifacts

N NATURAL RESOURCES

Elevation: 900 - 1,400 feet
Physiography: hill-lands, plains

Forest type: pine-oak, aspen-birch, maple-beech-hemlock
Public/private forests: 87% of county (#3/MI)
FYI: Of the 15 forest types in Michigan, 9 are primarily known as softwood forests that make up only 25% of the forests in Michigan. Many of these are conifers (cone producing), some are evergreens, some are deciduous, and some have a mix of soft and hardwoods. The most common trees in these softwood forests are balm-of-Gilead, balsam fir, black cherry, black spruce, cedar, jack pine, northern red oak, paper birch, quaking aspen, red maple, red pine, Scotch pine, tamarack, white pine and white spruce. Michigan Forests Forever

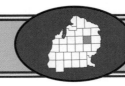
Water in county: <1% of county
  Lakes: 70   **...largest:** Mio Pond Dam
  Rivers: Au Sable (aw SAHBle)
  Rivers & streams: 220 miles

Growing season, avg.: 113 days (2 temp. zones)
  Last freeze, avg.: May 25 – May 30
  First freeze, avg.: September 15 – September 20
Precipitation, annual avg.: **rainfall:** 27 inches (#83/MI)
                            snowfall: 69 inches
Temperature (F), avg.: January: high 27°, low 8°
                        July: high 81°, low 54°
  Annual: >90°: 7 days, **<0°:** 28 days
Tornadoes (1930-2010): 7
FYI: Mio holds the state record for the hottest day
  recorded temperature, 112°F, in July, 1936.

O ORIGINS

Comins:[u] town founder, Colige Comins; 1890s
Fairview:[u] probably pleasant to observe; 1883
Luzerne:[u] first settler was from Luzerne, PA; 1881
Mio:[u] (MY oh) Mioe was the wife of a town founder;
  1881
Oscoda:[co] (ahs CODE a) from American Indian words
  meaning "pebbly stones" and "prairie"

P PARKS

National: 5   **State:** 4
  County: 2   **Local:** 5
Number of campsites: 480

National: *Huron-National Forest:* 300,000 acres in 5 counties; est. in 1909 on former "logged out" lands that are once again lush forests; see 68Y

NPCR

State Forest: (56,000 acres) Oscoda
...Campgrounds: 4
County: *Oscoda:* 90 acres, largest park in county, on
  Au Sable River; camping, fishing, trails

Q QUOTE FROM THE LOCALS

"We are very proud of where we live and work. Oscoda County is known for its natural beauty, friendly people and strong community spirit. Located within the Huron National Forest, deep in the heart of the AuSable River Valley, our location is excellent for both tourism and business. Life here is simple and good! We enjoy our four seasons of recreational activities due to our beautiful lakes, rushing rivers, abundant wildlife and unpolluted forests. And our county, unlike most of Michigan's Lower Peninsula, still has ample room for its people to put down roots and grow! With a terrific school system, outstanding natural resources and dependable government services, Oscoda County offers rural living at it's very finest!" Oscoda County's Official website

R RECREATION & SPORTS

Blue Ribbon Trout Streams: AuSable River, Big
  Creek-Middle, West & East Branches
Golf courses: 6
Hiking/skiing/mountain biking trails: 80 miles
MI Shore-to-Shore (horse) **Riding & Hiking Trail:** yes
... Luzerne is the crossroads for the north trail and
  the east/west trail of this 500-mile equestrian and
  walking trail between Empire on Lake Michigan
  and Oscoda on Lake Huron.

NPCR

Off-road vehicle trails: 250 miles (#1/MI)
Public access sites: 10

Public recreational land: 57% of county

Rail-trail: (40 miles) Huron Forest Snowmobile Trails
State/federal wild/scenic/natural river: 130 miles (#4/MI) of the Au Sable River
State-funded snowmobile trails: 130 miles

Mio Mud Bog & Drags: 4 wheel drive club, May

First Dam Canoe Race: Michigan Canoe Racing Association, Aug.

Wendi Richardson, Concerned Racers Club

ATV/ORVs may use all Oscoda County roads, but not the Forest Service roads, and have a 20 MPH speed limit.

NPCR

S STATE of MICHIGAN

On an average day in Michigan, a car hits a deer once every 8 minutes and most of those deer end up as <u>roadkill</u>. And that doesn't count the opossums, squirrels, raccoons, snakes, and domestic cats and dogs either. It's not a pretty sight and in the summer it can smell bad too. With state and county road budgets squeezed as flat as the roadkill, most of those agencies are no longer doing removal and disposal of the carcass. It's up to Mother Nature to do the clean-up. The crows, beetles and other insects all do their part to continue the cycle of life. In the essence of environmental recycling, it takes about two weeks for a carcass to decompose.

Oscoda County had the lowest number of reported car-deer accidents in 2009, only 154. But that means that one in every 55 residents hit a deer. The highest number of car-deer accidents was in Kent County with 2,164, averaging one in 280 residents hitting a deer. ^{mlive.com}

T TRAVEL

Airports: Oscoda County
Distance to Lansing: 160 miles
Main roads: M-33, M-72
Memorial Highway: M-33, *Veteran's Memorial Drive*
Scenic drive: see 68L

U UNIVERSITIES & COLLEGES

None

> *From BIBLIOGRAPHY & NOTES...*
>
> **W WANDERLUST:** We always recommend you call ahead to check on the operating status of any venue!!! Check the Internet for contact information or call the Visitor Information listed in *I INFORMATION* in the chapter.

V VARIETY

Garland Lodge and Resort

The beautifully crafted main lodge of the Garland Resort is the largest log building east of the Mississippi River. With four championship golf courses, indoor and outdoors pools, fly-fishing lessons and trap shooting among a long list of activities, there is always something to do for everyone on their 3,000 acres of unspoiled wilderness.

W WANDERLUST

Fall colors: late September – early October

Michigan AuSable Valley Railroad: ¼ scale railroad, steam locomotive and diesel engine, 1½ miles of track, 22 attractions including a tunnel and trestles overlooking the valley, train station

Jessie Jakubik

Our Lady of the Woods Catholic Shrine: a shrine-grotto featuring 4 old-world and 2 new-world Marian shrines

X X-TRA STUFF

County Fair: *Oscoda County Fair and Great Lakes Forestry* Exposition: July
Large employers: AuSable Valley Nursing Home, Garland (golf course, hotel), Kneeland Industries (makes machine tool reamers), Cooper-Standard Automotive (makes vehicle parts, pipes & fittings), Mio AuSable School District
Camp Barakel, a non-denominational Christian camp, is located in this county.
Michigan Magazine is a TV show on the RFD TV network that produces shows about Michigan. Local people, local businesses, local talent and local products are featured in every show. See 68M.

Y YESTERYEAR

NPCR

The forests of northern Michigan are rich in history. In the late 1800s logging was at its peak and these virgin forests were quickly cut and cleared. The result was that land was ugly, the topsoil was thin and no wanted these unusable lands. In 1909, the Huron National Forest was established. Working hand-in-hand with Michigan Department of Natural Resources and other partners, the U.S. Forest Service has planted trees on the "lands that nobody wanted," and these lands are now healthy forests. So once again there are vast forests in Northern Michigan, and they provide recreation opportunities for visitors, habitat for fish and wildlife and resources for local industry.
US Forest Service

Z ZOO & ANIMAL PLACES

Watchable Wildlife Viewing Areas:ww AuSable River, Luzerne Boardwalk, Jack Pine Wildlife Viewing Tour; see 68P
Karefree Ranch: horseback rides, wagon & hay rides

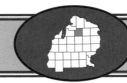
A AGRICULTURE

Land in farms: 10% of county
Number of farms: 180
Size of average farm: 185 acres
Market value of all products: #68 of 83 counties
Crops: ...most acres: forage
...highest $ sales: potatoes
Livestock: ...largest number: cattle & calves
...highest $ sales: cattle & calves
Dairy, food and meat processing plants: 13
State ranking for harvested trees: #18 of 83 counties
FYI: In 2007, Michigan ranked 20th in the nation for all agricultural exports, with ⅓ of the state's annual harvest being exported. There are 15,000 state residents employed directly in the export process. The top 5 commodities that account for almost 80% of the Michigan's agricultural exports are:

- soybeans and products
- feed grains and products
- nursery and greenhouse products
- fruits and preparations
- vegetables and preparations

Michigan ranked 5th nationwide for fruit exports and 9th for vegetable exports. The total value of Michigan exports in 2007 was $1.2 billion and in 2012 it had grown to $1.75 billion. Over 90% of the exports went to Canada, Mexico and Japan, with the balance going to South Korea, China and Taiwan. USDA, NASS, MDA

B BRIDGE OR BOAT

A kayak trip on the AuSable River can be as short as 7 miles or as long as 170 miles, all the way to Lake Huron.

C CELEBRATIONS

Gaylord *Alpenfest:* parades, Alpine foods, yodeling contest, world's largest coffee break, July

...*Friday Night Concert Series Under the Pavilion:* variety of musical venues, Aug.
...*Michaywé Arts & Craft Fair:* at this four-season recreational and residential community, Aug.
...*Old US-27 Motor Tour:* 6-day classic car tour from Coldwater to Cheboygan with 8 stops in between, Aug.

D DEMOGRAPHICS

Population: 24,200　　**Persons per sq. mile:** 47
Largest city: Gaylord　　**Population:** 3,650
Largest township: Bagley　　**Population:** 5,890
Largest village: Vanderbilt　**Population:** 560
Median household income: $42,800
Owner-occupied median house value: $122,000
Persons affiliated with a religious congregation: 46%
Persons below poverty level: 13%
Students receiving school lunch subsidy: 39%

E ENVIRONMENT

The Otsego Wildlife Legacy Society (OWLS) raises funds for the sole purpose of conservation through education, preservation, application and restoration. These funds are then available to those whose projects will enhance the quality and understanding of the natural habitat in Otsego County. Projects have included fruit trees for wildlife, blue bird houses, tree planting, wildlife food plots, I-75 beautification project, duck nests, river studies, fishing derby, children's garden, archery in the schools and many more. otsegoowls.com

Look for those 4' tall OWLpine Bears throughout downtown Gaylord. Each bear has been purchased and decorated by a local business as a fundraiser for the Otsego Wildlife Legacy Society.

F FLORA & FAUNA

Dr. Thomas G. Barnes/USFWS

Trailing arbutus, also called Mayflower or ground laurel, is a spring flower that grows well in the acid soil of the pinewoods in this area.

USFWS

Nesting platforms are provided for Ospreys in areas that flood. Ospreys can plunge completely underwater to snag a fish and then can lift themselves vertically into the air.

G GOVERNMENT

County: ...created: 1840 **...organized:** 1875
...originally part of: Michillimackinac County
Size: 337,000 acres / 515 sq. miles (68 of 83 counties)
The county has 1 city, 1 village, 9 townships, 8 unincorporated communities and 3 school districts.

NPCR

ESTABLISHED 1875

NPCR

...**Homestead property tax:** 39 mills
Motto: Gaylord: *Alpine Village*
...Gaylord Area Convention and Tourism Bureau: *Spectacular Seasons. Endless Reasons!*
...Vanderbilt: *Gateway to the Pigeon River Country State Forest*
...Waters: *The Peaceful Alternative*

H HISTORICAL MARKERS 2 of 4

Otsego County: was first named Okkuddo in 1840, but changed to Otsego three years later; it was settled in the 1860s when lumbering began.
St. Mary's Catholic Church: the 1900 neo-gothic church building is now the Mount Carmel Center, a performing arts center.
National Register of Historic Places: 1 listing
State Historic Sites: 3 listings

I INFORMATION

Chamber of Commerce: Gaylord/Otsego
Visitor: Gaylord Area Convention and Tourism Bureau, 800-345-8621, gaylordmichigan.net

J JOKES

You know your unemployment benefits just ran out when…
…you mark your calendar for how often you can sell your blood plasma.
…hunting and fishing are a necessity and not a recreation. That's why you live here.
…that stuff at the "dollar store" always looked good, and then it looked better and better, and now it looks like it's the best you can do.
…you finally realize that now is the time to sign up for some job skills training.
…Mom and Dad called and said you and the kids can move in with them in their two-bedroom condo in Florida. Hmmmmm.

K KINSMAN

Race	Ancestry
American Indian: <1%	German: 22%
Asian: <1%	Polish: 18%
Black/African American: <1%	Irish: 10%
Hispanic or Latino: 1%	English: 10%
Other: 2%	U.S./American: 9%
White: 97%	French: 4%

L LIGHTHOUSE OR LANDMARK

Pam Duczkowski

Gaylord is known as the Alpine Village and this theme is most noticeable in the architecture of many of the buildings here. See 69Y.

M MUSEUMS

Pam Duczkowski

Gaylord *Otsego County Historical Museum:* in a 1910 cigar factory building with a tin ceiling; displays

N NATURAL RESOURCES

Elevation: 900 – 1,500 feet
Physiography: hill lands, plains

Forest type: maple-beech-hemlock, aspen-birch, elm-as-cottonwood, oak-hickory
Public/private forests: 71% of county

Water in county: 2% of county
   Lakes: 110 ...**largest:** Otsego Lake
   Rivers: headwaters for the AuSable (aw SABle), Black, Manistee, Pigeon and Sturgeon Rivers
   Rivers & streams: 200 miles

Growing season, avg.: 112 days (4 temp. zones)

Last freeze, avg.: June 5 – June 25
First freeze, avg.: Aug. 25 – Sept. 15
Precipitation, annual avg.: rainfall: 34 inches
                          snowfall: 145 inches
Temperature (F), avg.: January: high 25°, low 10°
                       July: high 80°, low 55°
   Annual: >90°: 6 days, **<0°:** 28 days
Tornadoes (1930-2010): 2

O ORIGINS

<u>Arbutus Beach</u>:[u] surrounding woodlands were covered with trailing arbutus, see 69F
<u>Elmira</u>:[u] named after Elmira Township; 1877
<u>Gaylord</u>:[c] railroad attorney, A.S. Gaylord; <1874
<u>Johannesburg</u>:[u] the Johannesburg Manufacturing Company sawmill was named after the company president's sister, Johanna; 1901
<u>Oak Grove</u>:[u] grove of oak trees
<u>Otsego Lake</u>:[co,u] (ott SEE go) possibly from an American Indian word meaning "water that is beautiful and clear" and/or "a meeting place" and/or after Otsego County, NY; 1840
<u>Sparr</u>:[u] early settler and minister, Philip Sparr; 1873
<u>Vanderbilt</u>:[v] the Cornelius Vanderbilt family of NY owned this land; 1875
<u>Waters</u>:[u] area of many lakes; 1873

P PARKS

National: 0   **State:** 8
County: 4   **Local:** 11
Number of campsites: 1,200

NPCR

State Forest: *Pigeon River Country:*[ww] 93,000 acres, called the Big Wild, part of 118,000 acres in Cheboygan, Otsego and Montmorency counties

FYI: The *Pigeon River State Forest* is the home of the only free ranging elk herd in the Midwest. Several elk viewing sites are available or you can just drive through the state forest. See 60L.
...**Campground:** 6   **Pathway:** 110 miles
State Park: *Otsego Lake:* 62 acres, developed by the Civilian Conservation Corps in 1934, ½ mile of beach, swim, boat, fish

County: Ironton Springs, Otsego Lake, Wah Wah Soo

NPCR

Local: *Gaylord's City Elk Park:* 108 acres, viewing areas for the public to see the elk

Q QUOTE FROM THE LOCALS

Prentice Drake

"Located in the exact center of Northern Michigan, Gaylord is unique because of its stunning surroundings, Up North ambience and easy commuting access. Known as Michigan's Alpine Village, …a recreation seeker's paradise, … with 21 championship caliber golf courses, it is America's Golf Mecca, …in the center of the Snow Belt, it offers something for everyone." Gaylordmichigan.not/visitors guide

R RECREATION & SPORTS

Pam Duczkowski

Blue Ribbon Trout Streams: AuSable River-North Branch, Black River, Pigeon River, Sturgeon River

Golf courses: 16

Hiking/skiing/mountain biking trails: 160 miles includes the paved North Central State Trail from Gaylord to Mackinaw City

Off-road vehicle trails: 22 miles

Public access sites: 19

Public recreational land: 30% of county

Rail-trail: (70 miles) Big Bear, Midland to Mackinac, North Central, Shingle Mill

State/federal wild/scenic/natural river: 66 miles of the Pigeon and Upper Manistee Rivers

State-funded snowmobile trails: 40 miles

Otsego County Sportsplex: pool, ice rink, many other activities

Snowmobile trails: popular trails include south to Kalkaska along the Blue Bear Trail, west to East Jordan via the scenic Jordan Valley Trail, east to Lewiston along the North Branch Trail and as far north as the Mackinac Bridge along the Indian River Trail.

Jenna Miller

S STATE OF MICHIGAN

Michigan has a multi-level Driver's License system.

The *Graduated Driver License* for those less than 18 years of age includes these requirements:

…*Level 1*: a. at least 14 years 9 months old

  b. complete Segment 1 of a driver education program (24 hours in class, 6 hours behind the wheel with a driving instructor, 4 hours observation in driver's training vehicle)

  c. responsible adult signature on application.

…*Level 2*: a. at least 16 years old

  b. complete Segment 2 of a driver education program

  c. responsible adult certifies at least 50 hours behind-the-wheel driving experience

  d. have a Level 1 license for at least 6 months

  e. pass a driving skills test

  f. have no convictions or civil infractions, license suspensions, or at-fault crashes

…*Level 3*: a. at least 17 years old

  b. drive for at least six months at Level 2

  c. have 12 months of violation-free driving

In addition to the regular driver's license and Commercial Driver's License (CDL), Michigan offers:

- *Chauffer License:* required for persons driving smaller commercial vehicles that carry property or drive vehicles that carry passengers

- *Moped License:* for those at least 15 years old who do not have another license

- *Motorcycle Endorsement:* must have a valid driver's license and pass a written and road skills' test for motorcycles

- *Farmer Endorsement:* for those involved in farming activities

- *Recreational Double "R" Endorsement:* a pickup truck pulling a fifth wheel trailer with a second trailer attached to the rear of the fifth wheel trailer

- *Enhanced Driver's License:* allows Michigan residents to re-enter the U.S. by land or sea from Canada, Mexico, Bermuda or the Caribbean, without the need to show additional identity or citizenship documents at the border ^{Michigan.gov}

T TRAVEL

Airports: Otsego County
Bus: Indian Trails
Distance to Lansing: 170 miles
Main roads: I-75, US-127, M-32
Memorial Highway: I-75, *American Legion MH:* see 6T
Scenic drive: elk viewing, see 69P

U UNIVERSITIES & COLLEGES

Grace Baptist College: est. 2003, 120 students. This school is fundamental in both its beliefs and behavior and whose objective is to lead students into complete surrender to God's will for their lives.

The M-Tech Center at Kirkland-Gaylord: School specializes in construction and manufacturing technology in a unique, flexible and student-friendly manner.

University Center at Gaylord: provides classroom space for Central Michigan University, Davenport College, Ferris State University, Lake Superior State University, Madonna University, North Central Michigan College, Spring Arbor University

V VARIETY

Michigan Farm Bureau

Treetops Resort is known as "Michigan's Most Spectacular Resort." Among its many activities and amenities are 5 golf courses, the Rick Smith Golf Academy, 23 ski runs, a terrain park and lodging for everyone. It sets on the highest elevation in the area.

W WANDERLUST

Brewery: Big Buck Brewery & Steakhouse
Cultural: Gaylord Area Council for the Arts
Fall colors: late September to early October
Driving tour: map available at the Otsego County Historical Museum for the 10 stops that introduce you to county history
Walking tour: a map is available at the Otsego County Historical Museum for the 14 stops in downtown Gaylord. The Gaylord Motor Car Company was started in 1910 and produced the Gaylord Model 30. The Gaylord Car Factory is a stop on the walking tour.

Brandie Slough

Call of the Wild Bavarian Falls Park: displays of deer, elk, moose, bears, etc.; Michigan fur trading history, gift shop

Local outdoor activities that you can do when you are here: bike, canoe, view the elk, fall color tours, fish, golf, hike, ride horseback, hunt, hunt mushrooms, ski cross-country, ski downhill, take a sleigh ride, snowmobile, snowshoe

X X-TRA STUFF

County Fair: *Otsego County Fair Assoc.:* since 1881, now utilizing the Civilian Conservation Corp buildings from the 1930s, Aug.

NPCR

Hospital: Otsego Memorial
Large employers: Gaylord Community Schools, Treetops Sylvan Resort, Otsego Memorial Hospital, Wal-Mart, Cooper-Standard Automotive (makes auto parts), Quicksilver Resources (gas & oil field exploration)
Gaylord is on the 45th parallel, halfway between the North Pole and the Equator, and is in the center of the tip of the mitten.

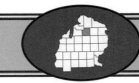
Y YESTERYEAR

One of the first things you notice when you drive toward downtown Gaylord is that many buildings have the look of a Swiss Village. This Alpine idea began in the 1930s when one businessman built a complex of buildings in the Swiss Chalet style of

NPCR

architecture. Beginning in the 1960s, and with the encouragement of the Chamber of Commerce, other building owners began to remodel their storefronts and slowly Gaylord became the Alpine Village. Even the government buildings, local churches, industries, schools, houses and local ski resorts have embraced the Alpine motif theme. Gaylord has a sister city in Pontresina, Switzerland. See 69L. Otsego County Historical Society

Z ZOO & ANIMAL PLACES

Watchable Wildlife Viewing Areas:[ww] Pigeon River
 Country Elk Range; see 69P
Gaylord's City Elk Park: see 69P

To order additional copies of this book, go to discovermichigancountybycounty.com. Books are shipped the following business day.

A AGRICULTURE

Land in farms: 46% of county
Number of farms: 1,450
Size of average farm: 120 acres
Market value of all products: #2 of 83 counties
Crops: ...most acres: corn
...highest $ sales: nursery, greenhouse, floriculture
Livestock: ...largest number: layers
...highest $ sales: poultry & eggs
Among the top Michigan counties:

- #1- ducks, geese, goat milk, greenhouse tomatoes, nursery stock, radishes, sorghum for silage, turkeys
- #2- all floriculture, all goats, angora goats, bedding plants, blueberries, greenhouse veggies & herbs, laying hens, onions, pheasants, rabbits & pelts
- #3- apples, celery, goat meat, other vegetables
- #5- hogs & pigs
- #9- dairy cows

Dairy, food and meat processing plants: 55
State ranking for harvested trees: #51 of 83 counties
FYI: Michigan has the 5th largest <u>nursery and landscape</u> industry in the nation and Ottawa County is the #1 county in the state for these products and services. With over 800 farms and $130,000,000 in sales statewide, nursery stock and perennial plants are shipped to 35 states, Mexico and Canada.

The nursery and greenhouse industry is the fastest growing segment of U.S. agriculture. The Michigan Nursery and Landscape Association has over 8,000 members and represents 15 different segments of the green industry including garden centers, greenhouse production, growers, golf course design and maintenance, interior scapes, irrigation, landscape contractors, landscape design, landscape management, nursery production, suppliers, turf management and arborists. Green is good! mnla.org, MDA

Michigan Farm Bureau

Dr. Robert Schutzki, Michigan State University, Department of Horticulture

B BRIDGE OR BOAT

NPCR

The Holland Princess is a 65' Victorian style paddle-wheel riverboat that offers cruises on Lake Macatawa and Lake Michigan.

C CELEBRATIONS

Mary Willcome

<u>Coopersville</u> *Summerfest:* Del Shannon (see 13H), car show, tractor show, sock hop, quilts & their stories, Aug.

<u>Grand Haven</u> *Coast Guard Festival:* honoring the Coast Guard; fireworks, ship tours, parades, Aug.

...Salmon Festival: learn about and celebrate the region's coastal waterways during the fall harvest and salmon migration; fish boil, wine tasting, Sept.

<u>Holland</u> *Downtown Street Performer Series:* summer

Mary Willcome

...Tulip Time Festival:[1,000] celebration of Dutch heritage and culture; 3 parades, Dutch attractions and food, tulips in bloom, tulip tours, Dutch market place, Historic Dutch Trade Fair, klompen dancing, quilt show, concerts, May

Civil War Muster: at Van Raalte Farm, Sept.
<u>Hudsonville</u> *Sounds of Summer Concert Series:* various music styles, 8 weeks June-Aug.

<u>Spring Lake</u> *Wooden Boat Show:* June

<u>Zeeland</u> *Pumpkinfest:* celebrates Michigan with kid-friendly free and low-cost events, Oct.

Mary Willcome

D DEMOGRAPHICS

Population: 264,000   **Persons per sq. mile:** 466
Largest city: Holland (partial)   **Population:** 26,000
Largest township: Georgetown   **Population:** 47,000
Largest village: Spring Lake   **Population:** 2,320
Median household income: $52,000
Owner-occupied median house value: $162,000
Persons affiliated with a religious congregation: 56%
Persons below poverty level: 10% (#81/MI)
Students receiving school lunch subsidy: 28%

E ENVIRONMENT

"<u>Green infrastructure</u> is an approach to wet weather management that is cost-effective, sustainable and environmentally friendly. Green infrastructure management approaches and [uses] technologies [that] infiltrate, evapotranspire, capture and reuse storm water to maintain or restore natural hydrologies. At the largest scale, the preservation and restoration of natural landscape features (such as forests, flood plains and wetlands) are critical components of green storm water infrastructure. By protecting these ecologically sensitive areas, communities can improve water quality while providing wildlife habitat and opportunities for outdoor recreation. On a small scale, green infrastructure practices include rain gardens, porous pavement, green roofs, infiltration planters, trees and tree boxes, and rainwater harvesting for non-potable uses such as toilet flushing and landscape irrigation." cfpub.epa.gov

Rainwater runoff is a serious issue for the communities in Ottawa County and any up-river county as well.

F FLORA & FAUNA

Michigan Farm Bureau

Tulips may not be a wild flower, but they are the most famous flower in Ottawa County. Nationally, there are over 1,700 varieties of tulip bulbs and 80% of what the U.S. uses are imported from the Netherlands. These iconic bright and bold beautiful flowers are planted alongside Holland's main thoroughfares as well as in home gardens. In the 1600s in the Netherlands, tulips were in such demand that they were traded on the Dutch stock exchange as well as used as a form of currency.

James Harding

The northern spring peeper, the most abundant singing frog in Michigan, is known for its unique call that sounds like the peep of a chick. Frogs like these hibernate in the winter by producing an anti-freeze-type substance in their cells that prevents the cells from freezing. Although small (around 1") they are very vocal in the late winter and early spring when the weather is still cold. Their call is recognized as a sign of the coming spring.

G GOVERNMENT

County: ...created: 1831 **...organized:** 1837
...originally part of: Kent County
Size: 389,000 acres / 566 sq. miles (49 of 83 counties)
The county has 6 cities, 1 village, 17 townships with 8 as charter townships, 17 unincorporated communities and 9 school districts.

Mary Willcome

Mary Willcome

County seat: Grand Haven
...Homestead property tax: 34 mills
Motto: <u>Allendale</u>: *A great place to dine, live, learn, grow, worship, stay, work, relax, shop, visit, play, retire*
...<u>Coopersville</u> Area Chamber: *Coopersville is a great place to Live, Work & Play*
...<u>Ferrysburg</u>: *the Ottawa Peninsula*
...<u>Grand Haven</u>: *Coast Guard City, USA; see 61X*
...<u>Holland</u>: on the city seal, written in the Dutch language: *Unity creates power. God be praised by us.*
...<u>Hudsonville</u>: *Good People. Good Living; Michigan's Salad Bowl*
...<u>Spring Lake</u>: *Where Nature Smiles for Seven Miles*
...<u>Tallmadge Charter Twp.</u>: *Gateway to Ottawa County*
...<u>Zeeland</u>: *Feel the Zeel*

H HISTORICAL MARKERS 31 of 51

Blendon Landing: on the Grand River, a former mid-1800s logging community that has been excavated for archeological study by Grand Valley State University

The Cappon House: 1874, Italianate home built for Holland's first mayor and successful businessman; now the Netherlands Museum

Michigan State Historic Preservation Office

Central Park Chapel: 1903, know as Saint's Rest because of the number of clergy who vacationed in the area

DeWitt School: 1891, one-room, a single teacher taught from 25 to 40 students by holding one ten-minute session per subject for each of the 8 grades
Dutch in Michigan: in 1847 Rev. Albertus Van Raalte, from Holland, Netherlands, founded the city of Holland; within four years Graafschap, Zeeland, Vriesland and Overisel were established
1869 Vriesland Reformed Church: the congregation was organized in Freisland, Netherlands, in 1846.
First Reformed Church: 1866, the Dutch immigrant community was founded upon a resolute faith in Almighty God.
First United Methodist Church: 1861, helped the Dutch immigrants and was the first English-speaking church in Holland
Grand Haven: • 1830: trading post run by Rix Robinson
• 1834: Rev. Ferry came to help develop the town
• 1837: more than 200 inhabitants
• 1840s: Dutch immigration begins
• 1870s: lumber boom; population was 6,000
• 1890s: health resort popular for magnetic mineral spring

Grand Trunk Depot: 1870-1955, passenger service from Detroit to Grand Haven; now a museum

Mary Willcome

Highland Park Association: 1886, a resort community in the dunes and hardwood forests, with grand houses that are still standing today
Holland Harbor: 1850s, due to lack of government funding for harbor development, the Dutch settlers dug the channel between Lake Macatawa and Lake Michigan themselves, thus spurring business and resort expansion.

Holland Harbor Lighthouse: 1907, called Big Red, it has a gabled roof that reflects Dutch influence; it is on the south pier in Holland State Park.

Holland Post Office: 1915, Neoclassical Indiana limestone building; now the Holland Museum
Hope Church: Reformed Church in America: 1854, 7 years after arriving in America, Dutch settlers establish a preaching mission that later would become Hope Church and Hope College.

Hope College: 1866, the college's name, seal and motto are from Rev. Van Raalte who said, "This is my Anchor of Hope for this people in the future."

Interurban Depot: 1902-1928, electric railroad; see 70Y

Jenison Museum: 1900, in a 10-room mansion built to honor the Jenison twins

Marigold Lodge: 1913, Prairie School style; Egbert Gold, industrialist & inventor, had over 100 patents

The Netherlands Museum: 1889, became museum in 1940 to interpret the rich heritage of the founders and the dynamic epic of this community

New Groningen: 1847, established as an industrial town; the Veneklasen brickyard provided bricks for many buildings that still stand today

Ninth Street Christian Reformed Church: 1856, Greek Revival style, referred to as the Pillar Church; the copper rooster on the belfry, symbolizing Peter's denial and pride, is commonly found on Calvinist churches in the Netherlands. Dutch immigrant ideals in America were freedom of religion, purity of doctrine, and a Christian education for their children in home, school and church.

Ottawa Beach: 1880s, well-preserved example of the summer cottage resorts that developed along the Lake Michigan shore

Shipwrecks and the Coast Guard: 1929, after 4 ships and 77 men were lost, Congress funded 6 more Great Lake Coast Guard cutters

Michigan State Historic Preservation Office

Third Reformed Church: 1874, carpenter's Gothic style; in 1872 it established a $30,000 endowment fund for Hope College

Van Raalte Farm: land purchased in 1847 for $2.32 an acre; home built in 1873

Van Vleck Hall: 1858, built for the Holland Academy that later became Hope College in 1866

Mary Willcome

Veneklasen Brick: 1849-1920s, architectural bricks that were cream-colored and set against contrasting red brick backgrounds; this distinctive polychromatic brickwork carried on masonry traditions from the Netherlands

Waukazoo Woods: 1833, an Ottawa Indian village on Black Lake, now called Lake Macatawa (mack a TAW wa), with Chief Waukazoo, a prophet and orator

Winsor McCay: 1867-1934, of Spring Lake, was an early cartoon animator who was the "most brilliant cartoon pen on the whole American scene;" the Winsor McCay Award is one of highest honors given in the animation industry

National Register of Historic Places: 21 listings
State Historic Sites: 64 listings

I INFORMATION

Chamber of Commerce: Allendale, Coopersville, Grand Haven-Spring Lake-Ferrysburg, Holland, Hudsonville, Jenison, Zeeland

Visitor: Grand Haven Area Convention and Visitors Bureau, 800-303-4092, visitgrandhaven.com

…Holland Area Convention and Visitors Bureau, 800-506-1299, holland.org

J JOKES

You might be a Dutchman if…

…klompen dancing was a physical education class in high school.

…all your kids are towheads.

…the shortest girl on your basketball team is 6'2."

…you wonder what's up with Don Quixote.

…you absolutely love or absolutely hate blue Delft.

…you have a top rated work ethic.

…Hope, Calvin and Central are the alma mater of all your closet friends.

NPCR

…you always get teased about being tight, but you know you're actually frugal.

…you know that VanderMolen means "from the mill."

…you know the real purpose of the windmills in the Netherlands.

…the families on your block are the Van Dyks, the Van Elks, the Koenings, the VanderMolens, the Hoekstras, the Breedvelds and the Boonzayers.

NPCR

…you know "Yer not much if yer not Dutch."

…you actually know why the real Dutch wore wooden shoes.

…tulips remind you of your first kiss.
…you sweep the street in front of your house.
'Wooden shoe' rather be Dutch?

K KINSMAN

Race
American Indian: <1%
Asian: 3%
Black/African American: 1%
Hispanic or Latino: 7%
Other: 3%
White: 90%

Ancestry
Dutch: 37% (#1/MI)
German: 15%
English: 6%
Irish: 6%
U.S./American: 5%
Polish: 4%

L LIGHTHOUSE OR LANDMARK

Sara Simmons. Photo courtesy of the Holland Museum

DeZwaan windmill[1,000] at Windmill Island Gardens is the only authentic Dutch windmill operating in the U.S. Tours are available.

M MUSEUMS

Allendale *Knowlton House Museum & the 1940s -1960s Museum:* preserving and promoting

Coopersville *Area Historical Society:* in the Interurban Railway Substation building, electric train cars, drug store, sawmill and home of the Del Shannon Memorial (see 9Y, 13H)

Jim Budzynski

…*Farm Museum:* interactive celebration of agriculture

Grand Haven *Tri-Cities Historical Museum:* in the Grand Trunk Railroad Depot and Akeley Building; American Indians, pioneers, lumberjacks, changing exhibits

Holland *Museum:* Dutch history & religious foundation, Lake Michigan maritime history, shipwrecks, resorts, agriculture, manufacturing, community service and old world art

Sara Simmons. Photo courtesy of the Holland Museum

…*Cappon House Museum:* a wealthy Dutchman
…*Settlers House Museum:* 1867, working class man
Jenison *Historical Association:* in the restored 1900s Husband-Hanchett-Tiffany House

Mary Willcome

Zeeland *Dekker Huis / Zeeland Historical Museum:* a community known for designer clocks (Howard Miller Co). and furniture (Herman Miller Co).

N NATURAL RESOURCES

Elevation: <600 - 900 feet
Physiography: hill-lands, lake border plains

Forest type: maple-beech, oak-hickory, pine-aspen
Public/private forests: 2% of county (#82/MI)
Legislatively protected sand dunes: 3,800 acres

Water in county: 2% of county
 Lakes: 40 …**largest:** Lake Macatawa (mack a TAW wa)
 Rivers: Bass, Grand, Macatawa (mack a TAW wa), Pigeon
 Rivers & streams: 310 miles
Great Lakes shoreline: 25 miles of Lake Michigan

NPCR

Growing season, avg.: 173 days (#3/MI) (2-3 temp. zones)
 Last freeze, avg.: May 5 – May 10
 First freeze, avg.: Oct. 5 – Oct. 15
Precipitation, annual avg.: rainfall: 31 inches
  snowfall: 75 inches
Temperature (F), avg.: January: high 31°, low 19°
  July: high 79°, low 62°

Annual: >90°: 3 days,
<0°: 3 days (#82/MI)

Prentice Drake

Tornadoes (1930-2010): 21

O ORIGINS

<u>Allendale</u>:[v,ct] in honor of Cap. Hannibal Allen, son of Revolutionary War hero, Ethan Allen; 1842

<u>Coopersville</u>:[c] sawmill owner, Ben Cooper; 1845

<u>Drenth</u>:[u] early settlers from the province of Drenth, Netherlands; 1847

<u>Eastmanville</u>:[u] village platter, Dr. Tim Eastman; 1835

<u>Ferrysburg</u>:[c] platted by the Ferry brothers; 1850

<u>Grand Haven</u>:[c,ct] located at the mouth of the Grand River; 1833

<u>Holland</u>:[c,ct] early settlers from the province of Holland, Netherlands; 1847

<u>Hudsonville</u>:[c] first postmaster, Homer Hudson and storekeeper, Horace Hudson; 1826

<u>Jamestown</u>:[ct] 4 of the first 12 voters had the first name of James; 1843

<u>Jenison</u>:[u] town founder, mill owners and twin brothers, Lumand and Lucius Jenison; 1864

<u>Marne</u>:[u] originally named Berlin by German settlers, but changed to Marne after WWI to honor soldiers who died in the Battle of the Marne [France]; 1839

<u>Ottawa</u>:[co] the Ottawa Indians lived in this area

<u>Polkton</u>:[ct] to honor President James Polk; 1845

<u>Spring Lake</u>:[v] on the shore of Spring Lake; 1837

<u>Tallmadge</u>:[ct] pioneer settler, Mr. Tallmadge; 1835

<u>Zeeland</u>:[c,ct] settlers from the province of Zeeland, Netherlands; 1847

P PARKS

National: 0   **State:** 3
County: 33   **Local:** 35

Number of campsites: 2,100

State Game Area: Blendon Twp., Grand Haven, Olive Twp., Ottawa County

NPCR

State Park: *Grand Haven:* 48 acres of beach sand on Lake Michigan and the Grand River; pier and lighthouse, camping, swimming, beach volleyball

NPCR

…*Holland:* 140 acres on Lake Michigan and Lake Macatawa; dune walk stairway, camping, fishing

…*Hoffmaster:* partial, see 61P

State Recreation Area: *Bass River:* 1,700 acres of open land & mature hardwoods; horse trails, boating, mountain biking, hiking

State Underwater Preserve: *Southwest Michigan:* see 3P

County: *North Ottawa Dunes:* 500 acres of wooded dunes, 185' elevation change

…*Riley Trails:* 300 acres, partially on former landfill, rolling terrain, pine plantations, trails

…*Tunnel Park:* 22 acres, wooden tunnel through sand dunes to Lake Michigan, dune climb, stairway

Local: *Hudsonville Nature Center:* rare combination of vegetation and landforms – mixed hardwood forest, sand prairie, mesic prairie, moraines, wetlands, flowing creek

…*Mulligan's Hollow Ski Hill:* city park with lighted ice rink, downhill ski and snowboarding area, cross-country trails

…*Rosy Mound Natural Area:* a classic Great Lakes dune system including high wooded dunes, foredunes, beach and a dune blowout; stairs up and down the dunes, dune boardwalk trail

Other: *Degraff Nature Center:* 18 acres in the city of Holland; nature close to home

Q QUOTE FROM THE LOCALS

"It's both easy to see and hard to imagine that Holland, Michigan, has its roots in the most solemn aspects of Dutch culture. Much of the religious conviction remains as does the traditional Dutch architecture and ambiance. But like its pioneers, Holland has reinvented itself without letting go of its

heritage… Long-time residents can't imagine living anywhere else; newcomers wonder why they didn't move here sooner. …Our visitors delight in the vast array of recreational activities, visual and performing arts, Dutch attractions, magnificent beaches and an award-winning downtown with exceptional shops, galleries and eateries. There's even a snowmelt system that keeps the downtown streets and sidewalks dry in winter." Holland.org

R RECREATION & SPORTS

Auto racing: *Berlin Raceway:* $7/16$-mile paved oval, premier short track
Golf courses: 13
Great Lakes marinas: 40   **Boat slips:** 3,500 (#5/MI)
Hiking/skiing/mountain biking trails: 25 miles
Horse racing: during county fair week
Public access sites: 15
Public recreational land: <1% of county
Rail-trail: (30 miles) Bass River, Grand Haven Boardwalk, Lakeside Trail, Lakeshore Connector
Recreational harbor: Grand Haven Municipal Marina, Holland Harbor of Refuge

Watersports available along Lake Michigan and the inland lakes include charter fishing, skim boarding, surfing, tubing, water skiing, personal watercraft, kayaking, windsurfing, kiteboarding, paddleboarding and scuba diving.

NPCR

Holland Blast: International Basketball League; plays at Holland Civic Center

S STATE OF MICHIGAN

Michigan encourages its residents to donate $10 to the Department of Natural Resources when renewing their license plates. In turn, that enrolls them in the Michigan Recreation Passport program that allows free entry into all 98 state parks and recreation areas, 133 state forest campgrounds and over 1,000 boat launches. The fee will help preserve nearly 1,000 miles of hiking, riding and skiing trails as well as provide a sustainable funding source for state parks. The annual Vehicle Registration says Recreation Passport on the top and the license plate renewal tab has a "P" on it to indicate a participating vehicle. In addition, merchants throughout the state are offering a program called Passport Perks that give Passport owners discounts (or perks) at their businesses. Michigan.gov

Mary Willcome

T TRAVEL

Airport: Tulip City, Memorial Airpark, Ottawa Executive, Riverview, Park Twp.
Amtrak: Holland
Bus: Cardinal, Indian Trails, Harbor Trolley & Transit, Macatawa Area Express
Circle Tour: Lake Michigan via Lake Shore Drive
County road names:
   …north/south: numbered Avenues
   …east/west: named Streets & Roads
Distance to Lansing: 90 miles
Historic Harbortowns: Holland Harbor Lighthouse, Holland Museum, Tri-Cities Historical Museum
Main roads: I-96, I-196, US-31, M-6, M-21, M-45
Memorial Highways: I-96, *AmVets MH*: see 19T
…I-196, *Gerald R. Ford Freeway*: see 41T
…US-31, *Blue Star MH*: see 3T
…M-6, *Paul B. Henry Freeway*: he (1942-1993) was a well-respected Calvin college professor, state and U.S. politician who served the area well
FYI: Michigan has two American Indian Trails that are now modern roads:
   • US-12, a Sauk trail from Lake Michigan to the Detroit River, now called Michigan Ave.
   • US-16, the Grand River Trail (once called Grand River Ave). that ran from the Detroit River to the point where the Grand River turns from flowing north to flowing west in Ionia County, and then, still following the river, over to Lake Michigan at Grand Haven; now roughly I-96.

U UNIVERSITIES & COLLEGES

Grand Rapids Community College, *Lakeshore Campus:* M-TEC
Grand Valley State University: est. 1960, 26,000 students. Their mission is educating students to shape their lives, their professions, and their societies. The

university contributes to the enrichment of society through excellent teaching, active scholarship, and public service. GLIAC, Lakers

Hope College: est. 1866, 3,200 students. Affiliated with the Reformed Church in America, it is an exceptional undergraduate liberal arts college that provides excellent professional and pre-professional programs. MIAA, Flying Dutchmen

Western Theological Seminary: est. 1885, 230 students. In covenant with the Reformed Church in America, it equips men and women for Christ-centered, biblically based, theologically integrated, culturally sensitive and mission-oriented Christian leadership.

V VARIETY

Whether it's here at Holland State Park or any other place on Lake Michigan, take time to enjoy one of the simple pleasures of the Lake. And it's free, too.

W WANDERLUST

Agri-tourism: *A & L Farm Market:* blueberries and their products; many veggies in the Community Supported Agriculture program

...*Blueberry Heritage Farm:* "The Berry Bunch Farm Market," organic, cranberries, cherries, jams, maple syrup

...*Critter Barn:* educational farm that teaches about food sources, fiber, dairy, composting, animal care

...*DeLange's Redberry Farm:* strawberry, raspberry

...*Gavin Orchards:* U-pick, apples, cherries, peaches

...*Grassfields:* organic milk, beef, poultry, pork, lamb, eggs, cheese; tours

...*Farm Markets:* Grand Valley State University

...*Moelker Orchards & Farm Market:* Centennial Farm, apples, peaches, cherries, tours, wagon rides, cider, sweet corn, pumpkins

...*Post Family Farm:* bakery, cherries, festivals, pumpkins and beautiful facilities for rent

...*Woodland Berry Farms:* blueberries, raspberries, strawberries

Brewery: New Holland Brew Co.-Production, New Holland Brewing Company Pub, Old Boys' Brewhouse

Cultural: DePree Art Center and Gallery, Holland Area Arts Council, West Shore Symphony Orchestra

Fall colors: early October

Lighthouse, other: *Grand Haven Lighthouse:* 1839, 2 lighthouses on the same pier; walk the pier

...*Holland Harbor:* see 70H

Live theater: Knickerbocker Theatre

Shopping mall: Holland Outlet Center, Westshore

Coopersville & Marne Railway: ride aboard restored vintage passenger cars

DeKlomp Wooden Shoe & Delft Factory:[1,000] see wooden shoes being made and the only authentic blue and white delftware made in the USA; gifts, food

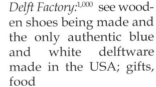

Dutch Village:[1,000] Holland, circa 1800s, with authentic Dutch architecture, canals, windmills, gardens; wooden shoe slide, klompen dancers

Escanaba Park: was established as a memorial to the sailors of the Coast Guard Cutter Escanaba that was sunk during WWII. Grand Haven was declared "Coast Guard City USA" by a 1998 Act of Congress.

Musical Fountain: Grand Haven, world's largest, plays 20-minute shows daily at sunset in the summer

The Grand Haven Boardwalk: 2.5 miles along the Grand River harbor and Lake Michigan past marinas, beaches, shops; beautiful sunsets

NPCR

Statues in Downtown Holland: 13 statues and fountains; walking guide available

Veldheer Tulip Gardens:[1,000] 5 million tulips, 50,000 daffodils, 10,000 hyacinths, 10,000 crocuses

Wind Dancer Schooner Charters: sail the 63' double gaff-rigged schooner; hands-on if you want

X X-TRA STUFF

Commercial port: Grand Haven, Holland

County fair: the only county in Michigan with three 4-H Fairs: Ottawa County Fair Assoc. in Holland, the Berlin Fair in Marne, and the Hudsonville Fair

Famous people: ...*Entertainment*: Chuck "Del Shannon" Westover

...*Other*: Ed Cole

Hospitals: Holland Community, Zeeland Community

Large employers: Magna Electronics (auto parts), Haworth International (makes office furniture), Herman Miller (makes office furniture), Zeeland Chemicals, Holland Community Hospital, Johnson Controls Interiors (makes vehicle parts), Sara Lee (meat processing), Ottawa County, Holland Public Schools, Grand Valley State University

Grand Valley State University has *The Grantmaking School*, the first university-based program for teaching the techniques and ethics of grantmaking specifically to foundation program officers.

Singing Sands: only on the beaches of Lake Michigan can you hear your footprints in the sand talk back to you

The Heinz pickle cannery in Holland is the world's largest pickle factory.

NPCR

Y YESTERYEAR

Started in 1955, the Michigan <u>Historical Markers</u> Program is a collaborative effort of the Michigan Historical Commission, the Michigan History Foundation and Eastern Michigan University Historic Preservation Program (the largest program of its kind in the U.S). These green markers help the local residents tell the story of what they think is important about their area. The $2,000-$3,000 cost for each marker is the responsibility of individuals or communities who make the request for the marker. In 2010, there were 1,630 markers statewide with requests for 20-30 new ones each year.

Mary Willcome

There is a wonderful website, michmarkers.com, which lists by county or by topic, all the historical markers in the state with their complete text, pictures and a map of their location. That website was used extensively for the *H HISTORICAL MARKERS* part of this book. Although the summary of each marker in this book has been reduced to a mere 2-4 lines, the entire text is full of rich details. michigan.gov, michmarkers.com

Z ZOO & ANIMAL PLACES

Petting zoo: *Critter Barn:* dedicated to educating children about animals, farming food and fiber sources, and ag-science careers; hands-on fun

Watchable Wildlife Viewing Areas:[ww] De Graaf Nature Center, Harbor Island, Kitchel-Linquist Dunes Preserve

Teusink's Pony Farm: hayrides, sleigh rides, pony rides, fun-on-the-farm activities

A AGRICULTURE

Land in farms: 17% of county
Number of farms: 290
Size of average farm: 250 acres
Market value of all products: #54 of 83 counties
Crops: ...most acres: forage
...highest $ sales: grains: oats, corn, soybeans, wheat
Livestock: ...largest number: cattle & calves
...highest $ sales: milk and dairy products
Among the top Michigan counties:
• #1- acres of oats
Dairy, food and meat processing plants: 10
State ranking for harvested trees: #20 of 83 counties

FYI: There is production of oats in 82 of the 83 counties in the state with around 55,000 acres producing 3,000,000 bushels. Presque Isle has more acres than any other county with over 4,000 acres. Oats are popular as a healthy breakfast food because of their high protein content (highest of any cereal grain) and cholesterol-lowering properties. The most common use for oats, though, is as food for livestock such as cattle, chickens and horses. Oats can tolerate cool and wet weather, can be planted in the fall or the spring and then harvested in late summer. ^{MDA, Wikipedia}

B BRIDGE OR BOAT

The Presque Isle Harbor of Refuge offers shelter for many boats during foul weather on Lake Huron and a secure home for many others during the summer.

C CELEBRATIONS

<u>Onaway</u> *Tractor Show:* July
<u>Posen</u> *Potato Festival:* Budweiser Clydesdales, polka pavilion, motocross, bump-n-run, Sept.

<u>Presque Isle</u> *Wooden Boat Show:* love those antiques, June

<u>Rogers City</u> *Double Handled Sailing Challenge:* June
...Great Lakes Lighthouse Festival: Oct.
...Nautical Festival: Aug.
...Salmon Tournament: Aug.

D DEMOGRAPHICS

Population: 13,400 **Persons per sq. mile:** 20
Largest city: Rogers City **Population:** 2,830
Largest township: Presque Isle **Population:** 1,660
Largest village: Posen **Population:** 230
Median household income: $36,500
Owner-occupied median house value: $110,000
Persons affiliated with a religious congregation: 65%
Persons below poverty level: 14%
Students receiving school lunch subsidy: 47%

E ENVIRONMENT

The <u>Michigan Karst Conservancy</u> is dedicated to the preservation of examples of Michigan's karst areas. Karst terrains are characterized by caves, steep valleys, sinkholes and a general lack of surface streams because

the drainage is underground. A consequence of this is not only a very interesting landscape with unusual habitats for plants and animals, but special problems in water supply, waste disposal, construction and other land uses. There are spectacular sinkholes and earth cracks here in northeast Michigan, including Presque Isle County. caves.org/converancy/mkc

F FLORA & FAUNA

William Radke, USFWS

The dried, prickly heads of the teasel plant (3'-5' tall) are a common sight along roadside ditches in the winter and spring. An invasive species, it can crowd out all native plants.

Time Bowman, USFWS

The snipe is a wading bird whose long bill is used to secure its food from the water. "Going on a snipe hunt" is an initiation for new campers who are told to do various odd things to catch a snipe. In reality, the snipe is difficult to catch and a "sniper" has to be an excellent shot in order to shoot one.

G GOVERNMENT

County: ...created: 1840 **...organized:** 1871
...originally part of: Mackinac County
Size: 441,000 acres / 660 sq. miles (31 of 83 counties)
The county has 2 cities, 2 villages, 14 townships, 5 unincorporated communities and 3 school districts.

Jessie Jakubik

NPCR

County seat: Rogers City
...Homestead property tax: 36 mills
Motto: Onaway: *Sturgeon Capital of Michigan*
...Onaway Chamber: *Live, Work & Play in Onaway*
...Posen: *Home of the Potato Festival*
...Rogers City: *The Nautical City*

H HISTORICAL MARKERS 10 of 13

Bearinger Union School: 1919, after the log school burned, they built this one from fieldstone.

Jessie Jakubik

Burnham's Landing: 1850s+, lumberman, businessman and Great Lakes shipper, Frederick Burnham, helped develop this area

Elowsky Mill: 1870, milling operations for flour, shingle, siding, planning and lathe

Forty Mile Point Lighthouse: 1896, so that mariners would always be within sight of at least one light

Graveyard of Ships: as of 2006, there were 1,200 recorded wrecks in Lake Huron

Lake Huron: 1615, the first white men called it the Freshwater Sea.

The Metz Fire: 1908, the raging fires that swept through the pine forests left hundreds homeless, with many deaths. See 71Y.

Old Presque Isle Lighthouse: 1840, built on one of Lake Huron's safest harbors of refuge; see 71M, 71W

Presque Isle Electric Cooperative Monument: 1937, part of the New Deal's Rural Electrification Administration to bring electricity to rural America

World's Largest Limestone Quarry: since 1910, the high quality limestone has been used in steel, chemicals and cement, and is easily shipped on Lake Huron. See 71X.

National Register of Historic Places: 8 listings

State Historic Sites: 13 listings

I INFORMATION

Chamber of Commerce: Onaway

Visitor: Presque Isle County Visitor Information Service, 989-734-8446, presqueislemi.org

J JOKES

Michiganians don't have accents, so we say, but we do say a few things in our very own way. So if you want to talk like us, say…

…"kinny-gar-in" or "kinner-gar-in" for kindergarten.

…"Porch Yeurn" for Port Huron.

…"brussel sprouts" for Brussels sprouts.

…"worsh" for wash, for those of us with southern backgrounds.

…"Canadian geese" for Canada geese. That's what we get for living so close to the real Canadians.

…"ma-chure" for mature.

…"da-troi" for Detroit.

K KINSMAN

Race

American Indian: <1%

Asian: <1%

Black/African American: <1%

Hispanic or Latino: <1%

Other: 1%

White: 98%

Ancestry

German: 28%

Polish: 27% (#1/MI)

English: 8%

U.S./American: 6%

French: 6%

French Canadian: 3%

From BIBLIOGRAPHY & NOTES…

H HISTORICAL MARKERS: At the discretion of the author, not all historical markers have been included.

L LIGHTHOUSE OR LANDMARK

NPCR

The 1896 Forty Mile Point Lighthouse is still operational today. The lighthouse, grounds and outbuildings have been restored and are open to the public.

M MUSEUMS

<u>Onaway</u> *Historical Museum:* in a restored 1909 historic courthouse; displays of old steering wheels

<u>Presque Isle</u> *County Historical Museum:* in the 1914 Bradley House; 1920s furnishings, American Indian artifacts, displays of farming, lumbering, shipping

NPCR

…*New Presque Isle Lighthouse Park & Museum:* built in 1870, tallest tower open to the public on the Great Lakes; 3 historic buildings; displays of local history and light-keepers lives

NPCR

…*Old Presque Isle Lighthouse:* built in 1840, one of the oldest surviving lighthouses on the Great Lakes; open to the public; climb the tower, blow the foghorn, examine artifacts, get picture taken in punishment stocks; open to the public

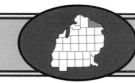
Rogers City *Great Lakes Lore Maritime Museum:* stories, uniforms, tools, furniture, foul weather gear, lifeboats; home of the Great Lakes Maritime Hall of Fame

N NATURAL RESOURCES

Elevation: <600 - 900 feet
Physiography: lake border plains, rolling plains

Forest type: aspen-birch, maple-beech-hemlock, pine-oak
Public/private forests: 71% of county

Water in county: 5% of county
Lakes: 60   **...largest:** Grand Lake
  Rivers: Black, Rainey, Ocqueoc (AH key ock), Swan, Trout
  Rivers & streams: 300 miles
  Waterfall: 1
Great Lakes shoreline: 70 miles of Lake Huron

NPCR

Growing season, avg.: 129 days (5 temp. zones)
  Last freeze, avg.: May 10 – June 5
  First freeze, avg.: September 10 – October 10
Precipitation, annual avg.: rainfall: 30 inches
                        snowfall: 90 inches
Temperature (F), avg.: January: high 27°, low 10°
                  July: high 81°, low 55°
  Annual: >90°: 8 days, **<0°:** 22 days
Tornadoes (1930-2010): 8

O ORIGINS

Hawks:[u] railraod president, James Hawks; 1895
Manitou Beach:[u] Manitou is an American Indian word for "the great spirit, good or bad;" 1834
Metz:[u] after Metz, Germany; 1889
Millersburg:[v] village founder, C.R. Miller; 1897
Onaway:[c] an American Indian maiden in Longfellow's "The Song of Hiawatha;" 1882
Posen:[v] after the province of Poznan in Poland; 1870
Presque Isle:[u,co] (presk eel) French for "almost an island;" 1860
Rogers City:[c] landowner, William Rogers; 1868

P PARKS

National: 0   **State:** 5   **County:** 3   **Local:** 6
Number of campsites: 540
State Forest: Alpena, Black Lake (total 80,000 acres)
...Campground: 5   **...Pathway:** 40 miles

State Park: *PH Hoeft:* 300 acres, 1 mile beach on Lake Huron, wooded, camping, CCC shelter
...*Onaway:* 160 acres, on Black Lake, virgin white pines, rugged and beautiful, trails
...*Thompson's Harbor:* 5,100 acres, 7 miles of Lake Huron shoreline, undeveloped, 2 rustic cabins
County: *Presque Isle Range Light Park:* New and Old Presque Isle lighthouses with towers to climb, museums, picnic, woods, trails, beaches, beautiful scenery; see 71M
...*Volger Conservation Area:* 270 acres, trails along the Trout River, forests, cedar thickets, marshes

Q QUOTE FROM THE LOCALS

"Michigan is known by snowmobilers nationwide for its unique combination of abundant and dependable snow, exciting terrain and extensive trail network. More than 6,100 miles of designated snowmobile trails are located throughout the state in six state forests, three national forests and many acres of privately owned lands. Michigan is one of only three states that offers a large system of interconnected snowmobile trails. Approximately 50% of the snowmobile trail system is located on Private lands, 20% Federal, 25% State and 5% other Public. More than 100 grooming tractors are used by 6 DNR offices and by more than 60 grant sponsors to groom the 6,100-mile trail system."
onawaychamber.com

NPCR

R RECREATION & SPORTS

Auto racing: *Onaway Motor Speedway:* ¼-smile semibanked track and a motocross track
Blue Ribbon Trout Streams: Black River, Canada Creek
Golf courses: 1
Great Lakes marinas: 4   **Boat slips:** 260
Hiking/skiing/mountain biking trails: 50 miles
MI Shore-to-Shore (horse) **Riding & Hiking Trail:** yes
Off-road vehicle trails: 30 miles
Public access sites: 20
Public recreational land: 20% of county
Rail-trail: (50 miles) Alpena to Cheboygan Trail, Huron Sunrise
Recreational harbors: Hammond Bay State Harbor, Presque Isle State Harbor, Rogers City Marina

State-funded snowmobile trails: 40 miles

Bummers Roost ORV Trail: 17 miles, part of a 73-mile trail in Presque Isle and Cheboygan counties

Huron Sunrise Trail: 10 miles along Lake Huron to Hoeft State Park, paved with beautiful scenery

S STATE OF MICHIGAN

Of the 38,000 miles of rivers and streams in Michigan, 12,500 are classified as trout streams. Over 850 miles of these premier top-quality streams are classified by the DNR as <u>Blue Ribbon Trout Streams</u>. The Black River and Canada Creek in Presque Isle County have this designation. These streams are the best of the best for trout fishing. They support excellent stocks of wild resident trout; are able to permit fly casting yet are shallow enough to wade; have good insect life and fly hatches; have excellent water quality and provide fishermen with an exciting fishing experience. Michigan DNR If a county has any Blue Ribbon Trout Streams, it is listed in *R RECREATION & SPORTS*.

NPCR

T TRAVEL

Airports: Goetz County, Presque Isle County

Bus: Indian Trails, Straits Regional Ride

Circle Tour: Lake Huron via US-23

Distance to Lansing: 240 miles

Heritage Route: *Recreational:* Sunrise Side Coastal Highway; see 6T

Lights of Northern Lake Huron Tour: Forty Mile Point Lighthouse, Great Lakes Lore Maritime Museum, Harbor View, New Presque Isle Lighthouse Park and Museum, Old Presque Isle Lighthouse, Presque Isle County Museum, Presque Isle Range Light Park

Main roads: US-23. M-33, M-65, M-68, M-211

Memorial Highway: US-23, *United Spanish War Veterans MH:* see 1T

U UNIVERSITIES & COLLEGES

None

V VARIETY

National Park Service

Even foggy days along the Lake Huron coastline have their own beauty with a touch of the mystique.

W WANDERLUST

Agri-tourism: *Knaebe's Mmmunchy Krunchy Apple Farm:* eclectic old barn, cider, donuts, pies

Fall colors: late September to early October

Lighthouses, other: *Presque Isle Front and Rear Range Lights:* two lights that mark the entrance to the harbor

Sink Holes: over 2,500 sinkholes in the area around Shupac Lake (also a sink hole) have been formed as water has dissolved the underlying bedrock

Jessie Jakubik

Ocqueoc Waterfall: the largest waterfall in the Lower Peninsula; two falls on the Ocqueoc (AH key ock) River that flows south to north; swim, fish, hike; paths along the river

X X-TRA STUFF

Commercial ports: Calcite, Stoneport

County fair: *Presque Isle County Fair Association:* tractor pull, heavy horse pull, mud bog, June

Hospital: Rogers City Rehabilitation

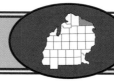
Large employers: Carmeuse Lime & Stone (limestone mining, processing), Cadillac Products (paper mill, makes plastic items), LaFarge Quarry, Rogers City Area Schools, Tendercare (nursing home)

Live Theater: Rogers City Community Theatre

Onaway is the Sturgeon Capitol of Michigan due to its proximity to Black Lake, historically a spawning area for sturgeon.

Jessie Jakubik

Port of Calcite is the world's largest open pit limestone quarry and the world's largest limestone processing plant.

Y YESTERYEAR

The year of 1908 was the "perfect storm" for a major fire disaster. It rained less that year than any other year in the previous 50 years. What rain did come, it came early in the season and produced an unusually hardy crop of ground cover in the forest. And then that summer it was very hot and dry. Early frosts killed the vegetation but the hot weather returned and dried it out even more. On a very normal day in October the smoke started rolling into the town of Metz. Many families loaded their children and some belongings onto a rescue train. On the way out of town that train was caught in a flaming inferno, derailed, and many people burned to death right there in the train. It was reported that the wall of fire propelled by gale force winds was at least 5 miles wide as it raced across the county to Lake Huron. It is amazing that only 25 people lost their lives. But hundreds were scarred physically and mentally for life. The Metz Fire of 1908 was the most destructive forest fire in the history of modern Michigan. [Nagel]

Z ZOO & ANIMAL PLACES

Watchable Wildlife Viewing Areas:[ww] Nettie Bay Lodge

A AGRICULTURE

Land in farms: 1% of county
Number of farms: 55
Size of average farm: 90 acres
Market value of all products: #81 of 83 counties
Crops: ...most acres: forage
...highest $ sales: other crops and hay
Livestock: ...most acres: cattle & calves
...highest $ sales: cattle & calves
Among the top Michigan counties:
• #3- herbs
State ranking for harvested trees: #30 of 83 counties
FYI: Michigan's Top 20 Crops in Cash Receipts, 2007
Percent of $5.7 billion total (numbers are rounded)
   • 26% dairy products
   • 15% corn
   • 11% floriculture & nursery
   • 9% soybeans
   • 6% cattle
   • 4% hogs
   • 3% each: wheat, blueberries, eggs
   • 2% each: sugarbeets, apples, potatoes, hay, dry beans, turkeys
   • 1% each: tart cherries, cucumbers for pickles
   • <1% each: grapes, fresh tomatoes, snap beans ᴺᴬˢˢ

B BRIDGE OR BOAT

Canoeing the Muskegon and AuSable Rivers offers a moderate current with a depth of around 4'. The scenery is spectacular through this area of unspoiled wilderness.

C CELEBRATIONS

<u>Houghton Lake</u> *Tip Up Town USA:* ice fishing, polar bear dip, parade, snowmobiles, Jan.; see 72L

...Historical Round-Up: July
<u>Roscommon</u> *Kirtland's Warbler Festival:* on the campus of Kirtland Community College; field trips to bird viewing sites, nature tours & walks, art show, music, food, May
...Arts Festival: juried, Michigan artists, July
...Michigan Firemen's Memorial Festival: thousands come to honor fallen heroes; fire safety, fire vendors, memorial service, parade, Sept.
<u>St. Helen</u> *BBQ Rib Cookoff & Pig Roast:* May
...Bluegill Festival: some say bluegills are the best-tasting pan-fried fish ever, July

D DEMOGRAPHICS

Population: 24,400   **Persons per sq. mile:** 47
Largest township: Denton   **Population:** 5,560
Largest village: Roscommon   **Population:** 1,080
Median household income: $33,300
Owner-occupied median house value: $111,000
Persons affiliated with a religious congregation: 32%
Persons below poverty level: 23% (#3/MI)
Students receiving school lunch subsidy: 53%
FYI: There are more vacation, seasonal or occasional homes (11,200) in this county than in any other Michigan county, representing 49% of all housing units. ᵁˢ ᶜᵉⁿˢᵘˢ

E ENVIRONMENT

As you're driving through the state in the spring, you may see many unsightly egg masses (up to 1,500 eggs per each ¾" long egg cluster) on tree trunks and branches or any other sheltered location. These gypsy month eggs hatch into caterpillars in the spring. From then until late June they begin eating

their way through their favorite trees. When a healthy tree is stripped of more that 50% of its leaves for two years in a row, it weakens and becomes susceptible to disease and could die. If it was already under stress from other factors like drought, one year of defoliation could kill the tree. This county controls its environmental pests by sponsoring a <u>Gypsy Month Suppression Program</u> using a variety of hands-on inspections, physical removal, natural enemies and sprays that only affect the gypsy moth. Roscommoncounty.net

F FLORA & FAUNA

Alice Welch, USDA

Northern white cedar is the predominant tree in National Natural Landmark Dead Stream Swamp as US-27 passes through it north of Houghton; see 72N.

Katherine Wittemore, USFWS

The Bald Eagle, our national emblem, is found in almost all Michigan counties in the winter, but they build their nests "up north." They need to be near bodies of water in order to hunt for fish, their favorite food. Look for their large nests of sticks (sometimes up to 10' deep and 20' across) in the tallest tress in the area. Just north of Mile Marker 197 on US-127, look to the east to see the Bald Eagles' nests high up in the trees. This eagle is no longer on the endangered species list but is still classified as a threatened species.

G GOVERNMENT

County: ...created: 1840 **...organized:** 1875
...originally part of: Cheboygan, Midland Counties
Size: 37,100 acres / 521 sq. miles (67 of 83 counties)
The county has 1 village, 11 townships, 5 unincorporated communities, 3 Census Designated Place and 2 school districts.

Sonya Novatny

NPCR

County seat: Roscommon
...Homestead property tax: 38 mills
Motto: <u>Houghton Lake</u> Chamber: *Tip-Up Town USA; Enjoy Michigan's Other Great Lake*
...<u>Houghton Lake</u> Area Tourism and Convention Bureau: *Michigan's Other Great Lakes*
...<u>Roscommon</u>: *A Proud American Community*
...<u>St. Helen</u> Chamber: *Four Seasons of Fun*

H HISTORICAL MARKERS 3 of 3

Gerrish: 1880, residents met at a logging camp to elect officers for their newly formed township
Pioneer House: 1870s, a hotel that attracted visitors from around the country; still a motel today
Terney House: 1887, this Queen Anne-style house with white oak parquet flooring and ornate paneling, was built by a lumber baron
Monument: *Fireman's Memorial:* see 72V
National Register of Historic Places: 1 listing
State Historic Sites: 4 listings

I INFORMATION

Chamber of Commerce: Higgins Lake-Roscommon, Houghton Lake, St. Helen
Visitor: Houghton Lake Area Tourism and Convention Bureau, 800-676-5330, visithoughtonlake.com

J JOKES

Michigan Truisms:
1. If you don't like the weather, don't worry, this afternoon it will change.
2. The true Michiganian doesn't care how cold it is, as long as the sun is shining.
3. Who needs sunshine anyway?
4. When traveling in the tropics, never say to a native, "Yeah, we're from Michigan. You know, the state that looks like a mitten." They're from the tropics. They don't know what a mitten is.
5. When you live in Michigan, you already live here in the state where out-of-state travelers come to for their vacations. So where do Michiganians go on vacation?
6. It may be 85° in August, some maples are starting to turn red and the black walnut trees are losing their leaves, and you *know* in your bones that winter is just around the corner.

K KINSMAN

Race
American Indian: <1%
Asian: <1%
Black/African American: <1%
Hispanic or Latino: 1%
Other: 1%
White: 97%

Ancestry
German: 24%
English: 13%
Irish: 10%
Polish: 9%
U.S./American: 9%
French: 7%

L LIGHTHOUSE OR LANDMARK

Thomas Reznich, Houghton Lake Resorter

The "tip-up" of Tip-Up Town USA (City of Houghton Lake) refers to the method used to catch fish when ice fishing. Instead of using a fishing pole, a tip-up is used. First, an auger is used to drill a hole (appx. 6"-10" wide) in the ice. The tip-up, with both its horizontal and vertical arms, is placed on top of the hole. The fishing line, complete with bobber and fishhook, is attached to the vertical arm of the tip-up and placed in the water through the hole in the ice. Above the ice, a flag on a spring is secured in the 'down' position on the horizontal arm. When a fish bites the hook, the flag springs up notifying the ice fisherman that there is a fish on the line. The fish is brought in by pulling the fishing line in by hand (hand reeling), instead of reeling it in as is done when using a rod and reel.

Here in Roscommon County you can ice fish for crappie, bluegill, large and smallmouth bass, northern pike, pike and walleye on frozen Houghton Lake, Higgins Lake and Lake St. Helen.

M MUSEUMS

Houghton Lake *Historical Village:* 11 restored buildings from the 1800s

Roscommon *AuSable River Center:* exhibits that highlight the river and its great past

...Civilian Conservation Corps Museum: between 1933 and 1942, 100,000 young men planted 484 million trees, spent 140,000 days fighting forest fires, constructed 7,000 miles of truck trail, 504 bridges and 222 buildings. See 48Y. It is part of the Michigan Historical Museum System.

Nicole Sevrey

...Gilmore Boarding House (1880s) *& Richardson School-house* (1914): period displays

...Kirtland House: art collection and displays

N NATURAL RESOURCES

Elevation: 1,000 – 1,300 feet
Physiography: upland plains, hill lands

Forest type: aspen-birch, oak-hickory, spruce-fir

Ellen Vanderwaal

Public/private forests: 70% of county

National Natural Landmark: *Dead Stream Swamp:* 12,000 acres, northern white cedar swamp, the climax in bog forest development

Water in county: 10% of county
Lakes: 60
   ...largest: Houghton Lake (#1/MI)
Rivers: Cut, Muskegon (muss KEY gun), South Branch of the AuSable (aw SAHBle), Tittabawassee (tit a ba WAH see)
Rivers & streams: 200 miles

NPCR

Growing season, avg.: 126 days (2 temp. zones)
  Last freeze, avg.: May 25 – May 30
  First freeze, avg.: Sept. 15 – Sept. 20
Precipitation, annual avg.: rainfall: 29 inches
                     snowfall: 57 inches
Temperature (F), avg.: January: high 26°, low 9°
                 July: high 81°, low 55°
  Annual: >90°: 6 days, **<0°:** 21 days
Tornadoes (1930-2010): 8

O ORIGINS

<u>Higgins Lake:</u>[u] early topographer, Sylvester Higgins; 1902
<u>Houghton Lake:</u>[u] (HOE ton) pioneer state geologist, Douglas Houghton; 1852
<u>Houghton Lake Heights:</u>[u] originally just The Heights, due to its high elevation; 1883
<u>Lyon Manor:</u>[u] local developer, Charles Lyon; 1910
<u>Prudenville:</u>[u] village founder, John Pruden; 1875
<u>Roscommon:</u>[v,co] a county in Ireland; 1845
<u>St. Helen:</u>[u] from St. Helen's Lake; 1872

P PARKS

National: 0 **State:** 3 **County:** 0 **Local:** 8
Number of campsites: 1,600

State Forest: (195,000 acres) AuSable (includes Dead Stream Swamp, see 72N), Houghton

...Campground: 1
...Pathway: 14 miles
State Game Area: Backus Creek

NPCR

State Park: *North Higgins Lake:* 430 acres

...*South Higgins Lake:*[ww] 1,000 acres, 1 mile of shoreline, boating, great fishing, trails

State Wilderness Area: *George Mason Wilderness Retreat:* 4,500 acres, a gift from Mr. Mason; game reserve, no camping, no mountain biking, 11 miles of prime trout fishing streams
State Wildlife Area: Houghton Lake Wildlife Research Area
Local: *Margaret Gahagan Preserve:* 10 acres, mature white and red pine forest & swamps, trails

NPCR

Q QUOTE FROM THE LOCALS

"They're not exactly the Great Lakes, but they're some pretty darned good ones. In fact, folks in these parts like to call them 'Michigan's other Great Lakes:' Houghton Lake, Higgins Lake, and Lake St. Helen. Fun, sun and adventure abound here amid the relaxing atmosphere of our quaint, relaxing villages.

"Enjoy pristine beauty and friendly surroundings of the Houghton Lake-area, which includes Michigan's largest inland lake at more than 22,000 surface acres and offers great boating fun and world-class walleye, northern pike and bass fishing. And all that gorgeous water is surrounded by several thousand more acres of magnificent state forest. Besides enjoying the water and woods, you can hike, bike, golf, snowmobile, ORV, hunt, boat, canoe and fish your way to one of the most enjoyable times you will ever have.

"Want to relax? The area features myriad shopping and dining opportunities, too!" Houghton Lake Area Tourism

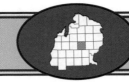
R RECREATION & SPORTS

Blue Ribbon Trout Streams: AuSable River-South Branch
Golf courses: 6
Groomed cross-country trails: 200 miles
Hiking/skiing/mountain biking trails: 65 miles
Off-road vehicle trails: 190 miles (#2/MI)
Public access sites: 8
Public recreational land: 55% of county
Rail-trail: (40 miles) Midland to Mackinac
State/federal wild/scenic/natural river: 39 miles of the South Branch of the AuSable River
State-funded snowmobile trails: 110 miles
Cross Country Ski Headquarters: the only Official Salomon Race Center in Lower Michigan; the largest Atomic Race center in the eastern Great Lakes region; lessons, equipment & clothing sales
Cross-country skiing: over 50 miles of groomed trails
Hanson Hills: 1,000 acres, winter/summer sports park, ski, ice skate, ski boarding, tubing
Michigan Snowshoe Center: sales, rentals, trails

S STATE OF MICHIGAN

According to this information from the Department of Natural Resources, Michigan has 24,997 lakes.

Number of Inland Lakes	Size (acres)
13,105	1 to 3
7,392	3 to 10
3,409	10 to 30
723	100 to 300
273	300 to 1,000
67	1,000 to 3,000
18	3,000 to 10,000
10	10,000 or larger

Houghton Lake is the largest inland lake in Michigan with more than 22,000 acres (over 35 sq. miles).

Often you read that Michigan has over 11,000 inland lakes. What this really means is that Michigan has almost 12,000 lakes (actually 11,892) that are over 3 acres each.

T TRAVEL

Airport: Roscommon County, Roscommon Conservation
Bus: Greyhound, Roscommon County Transit Authority
Distance to Lansing: 140 miles
Main roads: I-75, US-27, M-55, M-18
Memorial Highway: I-75, *American Legion MH:* see 6T

U UNIVERSITIES & COLLEGES

Kirtland Community College: est. 1966, 2,000 students. With their campus in the forest, they provide open access to education as well as cultural opportunities, to enrich the lives of the people in Northern Michigan; M-TEC; home of the Kirtland Warbler's Festival. MCCAA, Firebirds

V VARIETY

The Fireman's Memorial monument is dedicated to all fire fighters who have died in the line of duty.

A Firemen's Prayer
*When I am called to duty, God,
Wherever flames may rage
Give me the strength to save some life,
Whatever be the age.
Help me embrace a little child
Before it is too late;
Or save an older person from
The horror of that fate.
Enable me to be alert,
And hear the weakest shout,
And quickly and efficiently
To put the fire out.
I want to fill my calling and
To give the best in me;
To guard my every neighbor and
Protect his property.
And if according to your will
I have to give my life;
Please bless with your protecting hand
My children and my wife.*
firemensmemorial.org

W WANDERLUST

Cultural: Summer Gazebo Concerts in Markey Township and Roscommon

Fall colors: late September to early October

Live theater: *Kirtland Center for the Performing Arts:* many different types of entertainment

…*Houghton Lake Historical Playhouse:* restored, home to many events

…*Pines Theatre:* 1941, 450-seat Log Cabin Chalet that looks like a hunter's cabin

X X-TRA STUFF

County fair: *Roscommon County Fair Board:* Aug.

Famous people: …*Entertainment*: Charlton Heston

Large employers: Kirtland Community College, Lear Corp (auto parts supplier), ROOC (job training), Randy's Restaurant, Wal-Mart, International Health Care, Catts Realty (Glen's Market/retail groceries), Home Depot

Ralph A. MacMullan Conference Center: this is an ideal setting for any group that needs to have an environmental, conservation or natural resource program on the agenda; it is run by the DNR

Y YESTERYEAR

Michiganian vs. Michigander

By the way, we are Michiganians, a word originally devised for the purpose of describing people from Michigan. Michigander was a facetious expression used in a speech in Congress by Rep. Abraham Lincoln in 1848. Lincoln was opposing the nomination of Lewis Cass (from Michigan) as the Democratic presidential candidate, and accused the Democrats of "dovetailing on to the Great Michigander." The exact definition of a Michigander is unclear in that statement (although it is obviously derogatory), but the mental picture is quite graphic. Who wants to be described as a male goose anyway? Certainly not anyone who lives is Roscommon County or in all of Michigan, for that matter. So forget the old goose and go with the modern term of Michiganian.

Z ZOO & ANIMAL PLACES

Petting zoo: *Cindy Lou's Petting Zoo:* feed the exotic and domestic animals, gift shop

Watchable Wildlife Viewing Areas: ʷʷ Backus Lake, Dead Stream Flooding, Houghton Lake Flats-South Unit, Marl Lake, Wakerly Lake

Discovering Michigan County by County is the only book where all counties are treated equal. Every county has a story to tell. There's no other book or online site like it!

A AGRICULTURE

Land in farms: 62% of county
Number of farms: 1,530
Size of average farm: 210 acres
Market value of all products: #13 of 83 counties
Crops: ...most acres: corn
...highest $ sales: grains: corn, soybeans, wheat, dry edible beans
Livestock: ...largest number: cattle & calves
...highest $ sales: milk & dairy products
Among the top Michigan counties:
- #1- corn for grain, cucumbers & pickles, pigeon or squibb
- #3- soybeans
- #4- sugarbeets
- #5- wheat
- #7- vegetables

Dairy, food and meat processing plants: 21
State ranking for harvested trees: #71 of 83 counties
AgBioResearch Centers (MSU): *Saginaw Valley Research and Extension Center:* focuses on dry beans and sugarbeets to help keep Michigan as a top producer of these products

FYI: Michigan farmers plant over 40,000 acres of <u>cucumbers</u> each year. Michigan is the #1 state in the U.S. for pickling cucumbers and Saginaw County is the #1 Michigan county with almost 6,000 acres. A pickling cucumber

is usually around 4" long and has warts, and the slicing cucumber for eating fresh is around 10" long and has smooth skin. Cucumbers that are sold fresh are hand picked.

Technically the cucumber is considered a fruit because it has an enclosed seed and develops from a flower. But culturally it is considered a vegetable because it is not sweet like a fruit. The average American eats 9 pounds of pickles a year.

Only cucumber pickles are called "pickles." Other foods can be *pickled* using the same process of salt brine, vinegar and flavorings, but those are called a pickled food. MDA

B BRIDGE OR BOAT

The Bavarian Belle Riverboat offers a 1-hour tour cruise along the Cass River in Frankenmuth.

C CELEBRATIONS

<u>Chesaning</u> *Mid-Michigan Old Gas Tractor Association Show:* Aug.
...*Showboat:* annual variety show, July
<u>Frankenmuth</u> *Zehnder's Snowfest:* fun winter event
...*Bavarian Easter Celebration:* April-May
...*Bringin' Back the 80's:* retro bands & apparel, April
...*World Expo of Beer:* sample 150+ beers from around the world, music, May

...*Bark, Bike & Balloons:* includes the Dog Bowl, the nation's largest Olympic style event for dogs; Tour De Frankenmuth, a road race and tour of Michigan's Thumb; and Balloons Over Bavaria, a hot air balloon championship and balloon glow; May
...*Bavarian Festival:* parades, German food, beer, June

381

...*Summer Music Fest:* polka, Polish, German & Solvenian ethnic style music, Aug.

...*Auto Fest:* over 2,000 cars, Sept.

...*Oktoberfest:* German festival, Oct.

Saginaw *Jazz of Jefferson:* along historic Jefferson Ave., music, food, activities, fun, June

Courtesy of Frankenmuth COC

...*Friday Night Live Concert Series:* different musical style every week, July-Aug.

...*Spirit Ice Blast:* celebrate Saginaw with the hockey team, activities, music, beer, Feb.

Courtesy of Frankenmuth COC

D DEMOGRAPHICS

Population: 200,000   **Persons per sq. mile:** 247
Largest city: Saginaw   **Population:** 51,500
Largest township: Saginaw   **Population:** 40,800
Largest village: Chesaning   **Population:** 2,400
Median household income: $39,400
Owner-occupied median house value: $110,000
Persons affiliated with a religious congregation: 49%
Persons below poverty level: 22% (#4/MI)
Students receiving school lunch subsidy: 48%

E ENVIRONMENT

Saginaw Bay Watershed is the largest watershed in Michigan and includes all or part of 22 counties with about 7,000 miles of rivers and streams that eventually drain into Saginaw Bay. It is America's largest contiguous freshwater coastal wetland system and the home to large populations of waterfowl, birds and more than 90 fish species. In addition to supplying water to the wildlife, residents rely on the watershed for recreation, irrigation, electrical power generation, industrial processes and drinking water.

saginawbayrcd.com/watershed

F FLORA & FAUNA

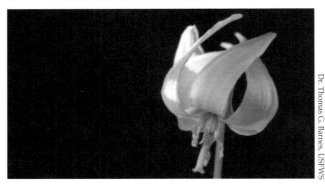

Dr. Thomas G. Barnes, USFWS

The trout lily is an early messenger of spring in the woodlands. It is so named because its mottled leaves resemble the coloring of brook trout.

Alice Welch, USDA

The mosquito is an insect pest that breeds in standing water. The female needs a blood meal for development of her eggs. Saginaw County has a Mosquito Abate Commission to remove breeding areas where possible, to control egg hatches and to provide a quality environment for man and animals.

G GOVERNMENT

County: ...created: 1822 ...organized: 1835
...originally part of: Oakland County
Size: 522,000 acres / 809 sq. miles (21 of 83 counties)
The county has 3 cities, 5 villages, 27 townships with 3 as charter townships, 45 unincorporated communities, 9 Census Designated Place and 14 school districts.

From BIBLIOGRAPHY & NOTES...

G GOVERNMENT: Size: land and land-based water acres; does not include Great Lake waters, unless otherwise stated.

Teresa Crook

NPCR

County seat: Saginaw

...Homestead property tax: 44 mills

Motto: <u>Birch Run</u> Chamber: *Gateway to the Saginaw Valley*

...<u>Frankenmuth</u> Chamber: *Michigan's Little Bavaria*

...<u>St. Charles</u>: *Gateway to the Shiawassee Flats*

H HISTORICAL MARKERS 22 of 30

Bliss Park: 1903, a beautiful Victorian garden on land donated by Michigan Gov. Aaron Bliss

Burt Opera House: 1891, a community effort to build, it is a community building for the township, vaudeville shows, weddings, fairs

Coal Mine No. 8: mined coal from 1917-1931; in 1919 a miner earned 60-75¢ per ton

The Cushway House: 1844, Greek revival style; built on site of old Fort Saginaw, it is the oldest surviving residence in Saginaw County; it was moved twice

Benjamin & Adelaide Cushway: 1810-1881, formerly Cauchois, French Canadians from Detroit; for over 30 years he was the official blacksmith to the Chippewa Indians and stood up for their rights

First Congregational Church, Saginaw: 1867, Romanesque Revival style with Tiffany stained glass windows

Karen Stoneman

Saint Lorenz Evangelical Lutheran Church: the first log church was built in 1846 as a German Lutheran colony; the third church, a brick Gothic Revival style, was built in 1880.

Frankenmuth Bavarian Inn: the Zehnder family emigrated from Germany in the 1840s; in the 1950s they redecorated their restaurant in a fantasy Bavarian motif, serving all-you-can-eat family-style chicken dinners.

George Nason House: 1880s, Georgian Revival style, now elegant dining of the Chesaning Heritage House

Michigan State Historic Preservation Office

Gugel Bridge: 1904, part of the Detroit to Saginaw Turnpike; closed in 1979, moved and restored in 2004 as a pedestrian bridge

Hess School: 1925, handsome red brick schoolhouse

Michigan State Historic Preservation Office

Hoyt Library: 1890, Richardsonian Romanesque style, a gift from New Yorker Jesse Hoyt who had real estate and lumber interests in the area

Leamington Stewart House: 1896, Queen Anne style, from a house plan book that said the house could be built for $5,250

Michigan's German Settlers: 1845, fifteen German immigrants founded Frankenmuth; German settlers contributed greatly to the state's cultural heritage

Saginaw Club: 1890, building was a monument to "enterprise, sagacity, and liberality"

Karen Stoneman

Saginaw Oil Industry: in 1925 Michigan's first oil field was discovered in this county; by 2000, Michigan oil and gas exploration and production was in 63 counties and produced one-fifth of the petroleum energy the state consumed. See 51S.

Michigan State Historic Preservation Office

Saginaw Post Office: 1898, French Chateau style built with Bedford limestone, remodeled with additions in 1930s; it is now the Castle Museum; see 73M

Saginaw Valley Coal: produced 1890s–1940s.

Saginaw Valley Lumbering Era: 1830s – 1890s, Michigan produced more lumber than any other state and the Saginaw Valley was the leading producer of lumber in the state

Saint Michael Catholic Parish: 1854, there were German Catholics from Bavaria in this area

St. Paul's Episcopal Mission: 1873, Gothic Revival-inspired style built by Scottish, Irish and English immigrants; owned by Taymouth Twp. since 1920

Schroeder House: 1896, 1½ story log home, now part of the Hartley Outdoor Education Center

Theodore Roethke: 1908-1963, Pulitzer Prize winning poet with two National Book Awards; he grew up in Saginaw where the family greenhouses inspired many of his poems

National Register of Historic Places: 40 listings
State Historic Sites: 71 listings

I INFORMATION

Chamber of Commerce: Birch Run, Bridgeport, Chesaning, Frankenmuth, Saginaw, St. Charles
Visitor: Great Lakes Bay Regional Convention and Visitors Bureau, 800-444-9979, visitgreatlakesbay.org

J JOKES

You may be a golfer in Michigan if…
…your country club closed down.
…you're sorry you named your oldest son Tiger, so you plan to name your next son Lion.
…the long winter layover gives you an excuse for your score.
…your son would rather play video games than golf.
…your golfing buddies are beginning to look as old as you remember your Dad.
…you're thankful you don't have to go out of state for top rated golf courses.
…you only wish you could afford to play on them.
…you're looking forward to the new 12-hole courses.

K KINSMAN

Race		Ancestry	
American Indian: <1%		Other: 52%	
Asian: 1%		German: 16%	
Black/African American: 19%		Irish: 5%	
Hispanic or Latino: 8%		Polish: 5%	
Other: 3%		English: 5%	
White: 75%		French: 5%	

L LIGHTHOUSE or LANDMARK

Bronner's CHRISTmas Wonderland is the world's largest Christmas store and a top Michigan tourist destination. Their billboard advertisements can be seen throughout the state and the Midwest.

M MUSEUMS

<u>Bridgeport</u> *Historical Museum and Village:* 6 buildings include museum, school, house, fire hall
<u>Chesaning</u> *Area Historical Museum:* in an 1800s church
<u>Frankenmuth</u> *Historical Museum:* stories of the City

…*Michigan's Own Military and Space Museum:* Michigan in the 7 foreign wars and space program

<u>Saginaw</u> *Art Museum:* to provide *Art for All* through education, collection and preservation of art; see 73H

…*Castle Museum of Saginaw County History:* built in 1898 in a massive French Renaissance Revival style post office, the building is now home to over 100,000 pieces of local history, lumbering, archaeology, auto manufacturing, model railroad; see 73H

...*Catholic Heritage Museum:* at the Diocese of Saginaw

...*Mid-Michigan Children's Museum:* hands-on and interactive

Teresa Crook

Geoffe Haney

...*Marshall M. Fredericks Sculpture Museum:* on the SVSU campus; impressive monumental figurative sculpture, changing exhibits, 20 bronzes around campus

...*Railway Museum:* in a 1907 passenger depot

St. Charles *Historical Museum:* American Indian, logging, coal mining, Civil War veterans

Teresa Crook

N NATURAL RESOURCES

Elevation: 600 - 800 feet
Physiography: lake-border plains

Forest type: maple-beech, elm-ash-cottonwood, aspen-birch
Public/private forests: 19% of county

Water in county: <1% of county
Lakes: 0 (the only county with no lakes)
FYI: Although there are no natural lakes in this county, the Saginaw River Watershed is the largest in the state and provides an abundance of water activities.
Rivers: Bad, Cass, Flint, Saginaw, Shiawassee (shy a WAH see), Tittabawassee (tit a ba WAH see)
Rivers & streams: 590 miles

NPCR

Growing season, avg.: 163 days (2 temp. zones)
Last freeze, avg.: May 10 – May 15

First freeze, avg.: Oct. 5 – Oct. 10
Precipitation, annual avg.: rainfall: 30 inches
                                          snowfall: 46 inches
Temperature (F), avg.: January: high 27°, low 14°
                                     July: high 82°, low 60°
Annual: >90°: 10 days, **<0°:** 9 days
Tornadoes (1930-2010): 22

O ORIGINS

Birch Run: [v] named after Birch Run Creek; 1852
Bridgeport: [ct] many bridges cross the Cass River; 1836
Buena Vista: [ct] in honor of Gen. Zachary Taylor's victory over Santa Ana in the Mexican War; 1832
Burt:[u] Saginaw business, civic leader and philanthropist, Wellington Burt [michmarkers.com]; 1889
Chesaning: [v] (CHESS a ning) American Indian for "big rock place;" 1839
Crow Island: on the Crow Island Road [wikipedia]; 1882
Frankenmuth: [c] (FRANK en mooth) founded as a German Lutheran community to minister to the American Indians; Franconia is a district in Bavaria, and *muth* is German for courage; 1845
Freeland:[u] tavern owner, Mammy Freeland; 1867
Hemlock:[u] large hemlock trees in this area; 1865
Merrill:[v] railroad man, N.W. Merrill, helped the residents after the 1881 fire; 1872
Oakley: [v] an uncle of an early resident, Judge Oakley of New York; 1842
Saginaw: [c,co,ct] from American Indian origin, either meaning "the place where the Sauk lived" [Romig] or "an opening to Lake Huron" [wikipedia]; 1816
St. Charles: [v] first storeowner Charles Kimberly was so fastidious the local people called him Saint Charles; 1852
Shields: [u] the Shield brothers from Ireland; 1842 [wikipedia]
Zilwaukee: [c] the Johnson brothers, sawmill owners, purposely named it to sound like Milwaukee so German immigrants might get confused and come here instead; 1848

From BIBLIOGRAPHY & NOTES...

O ORIGINS:
[c] = current city
[co] = current county
[ct] = current charter township
[t] = current township
[u] = current unincorporated place
[v] = current village

P PARKS

National: 1   **State:** 3   **County:** 4   **Local:** 45
Number of campsites: 800

NPCR

National Wildlife Refuge: *Shiawassee:*[ww] 9,000 acres, part of the Saginaw River Watershed and know as The Flats; documented 265 bird species; it is an U.S. Important Bird Area for its global significance to migratory waterfowl

State Game Area: Crow Island, Gratiot-Saginaw, Shiawassee River, 15,000 acres

Karen Stoneman

IMERMAN MEMORIAL PARK

County: *Haithco Recreation Area:* 40 acres on a man-made lake; paddleboats, kayaks, fishing

…Imerman Memorial Park: on the Tittabawasee River; trails, sports, picnic

Other: *Green Point Environmental Learning Center:* 76 acres, 2.5 miles of trails, programs, exhibits; in the Shiawassee National Wildlife Refuge
…Hartley Outdoor Nature Center: day trips and over night residential outdoor education
…Price Nature Center: 186 acres, 3 miles of trails

Q QUOTE FROM THE LOCALS

"Saginaw County has long been known for its productive agricultural lands, lively culture, solid manufacturing base and bountiful natural resources. We offer a rich and diverse quality of life enhanced and defined by the unique character of our five major communities: Saginaw, Saginaw Township, Birch Run, Chesaning and Frankenmuth. The county's… system of waterways and woodlands as well as a wealth of nature preserves, trails and facilities support Saginaw's love of green spaces and outdoor opportunities." saginawchamber.org

NPCR

R RECREATION & SPORTS

Auto racing: *Dixie Motor Speedway:* ¼ mi. asphalt oval
Golf courses: 15
Hiking/skiing/mountain biking trails: 25 miles
Public access sites: 8
Public recreational land: 5% of county
Rail-trail: (20 miles) Harger Line, Saginaw Valley
Apple Mountain Resort: golf in the summer and ski in the winter
Saginaw Spirit: Ontario Hockey League, play at the Dow Event Center
Saginaw Sting: Continental Indoor Football League, play at the Dow Event Center

S STATE OF MICHIGAN

Michigan's <u>safety belt law</u> allows police officers to stop a motorist solely for not wearing a safety belt in the front seat of a vehicle. The law requires all children under the age of 8 to be properly restrained in an approved child safety seat or booster seat, unless they are over 4'9" tall. The law also allows police officers to stop a motorist if a child age 4 through 15 is not properly restrained, no matter where they are riding in the vehicle. Michigan.gov

T TRAVEL

Airport: MBS International Airport, Browne International Airport, Zehnder Field
Bus: Bay Metro Transit, Indian Trails, Midland Transit, Saginaw Transit Authority Regional Services (STARS)
Distance to Lansing: 70 miles
Heritage Route: *Recreation:* M-15, Pathway to Family Fun, see 9T
Main roads: I-75, I-675, US-10, US-23, M-13, M-46, M-47, M-52, M-54, M-57, M-58, M-81, M-83, M-84
Memorial Highways: I-75, *American Legion MH:* see 6T
…I-75 & US-23, Roberts-Linton Hwy: around 1910, William Linton and Rolla Roberts were instrumental in the dredging of the Saginaw River in order to deepen the channel
…I-75 & US-23, Veterans of WWI MH
Scenic Drive: Bay City to Ortonville via M-15
FYI: The Saginaw Trail was originally a Sauk Indian foot trail that ran from Detroit to Saginaw and went through Oakland and Genesee counties. It was first developed as the Saginaw Turnpike beginning

in 1818. Following the trail today is to get an introduction into Michigan history. There are many different roads along the way - some interstates and some two-lane state roads.

U UNIVERSITIES & COLLEGES

Davenport University: see 13U

Saginaw Valley State University: est. 1963, 10,000 students. The most affordable public university in Michigan, SVSU creates opportunities for individuals to achieve intellectual and personal development through academic, professional and cultural programs. GLIAC, Cardinals

V VARIETY

Courtesy Archives of Michigan

"Northern Michigan's timber was part of a vast band of forests that began far to the east in Canada's Maritime Provinces and swept westward through New England, the St. Lawrence Valley, New York, Pennsylvania, and on to Michigan, Wisconsin, and Minnesota. Of the forests' variety of trees, white pine was the most highly prized by lumbermen. Cedar was cut to make shingles and hemlock was sometimes taken because tanners used its bark, but white pine dominated the lumber industry. Saginaw Valley was Michigan's leading lumber producer in the 1800s."
May, Michigan

W WANDERLUST

Agri-tourism: *Johnson's Giant Pumpkins:* U-pick, cider, bakery, corn maze, tours, catapult demos, rope making

…*Leaman's Green Applebarn:* centennial farm, apples, bakery, tours, wagon rides, U-pick

…*Russell Blueberry Farm & Nursery:* blueberry items like ice cream, pies, muffins; U-pick

Cultural: Saginaw Bay Symphony Orchestra, Saginaw Choral Society, Saginaw Valley Concert Association

Fall colors: early October

Lighthouse, other: *Gravelly Shoal Light:* 1939, in the Saginaw Bay to help keep boats away from the shallow shoals

Live theater: Frankenmuth Center Stage at the Bronner Performing Arts Center, Pit and Balcony Theatre (Michigan's oldest community theatre), SVSU Theatre, Temple Theatre

MotorCities National Heritage Area: yes

Shopping mall: *Fashion Square Mall:* 110 stores

…*Prime Outlets at Birch Run:* 130 stores

Andersen Enrichment Center & Lucille E. Andersen Memorial Rose Garden: formal gardens, meeting & banquet rooms

Teresa Crook

Bronner's CHRISTmas Wonderland: see 73L

Teresa Crook

Fantasy Carriage Tours: tour Frankenmuth

Japanese Cultural Center and Tea House: on 3 acres, gardens, walking paths, tea ceremony

Johnny Panther Quests Adventure Trips: scenic boat tours through "Michigan's Everglades," the Shiawassee National Wildlife Refuge

Junction Valley Railroad: the largest quarter size railroad in the world, 2-mile train ride

NPCR

Lager Mill Beer Store & Brewing Museum

Michigan Cruise & Snooze Charters: high performance airboat, cruiser or pontoon boat

Old Saginaw City: 12 block area with turn-of-century homes and businesses

The Dow Events Center: home to Wendler Arena, Heritage Theater and Unity Hall

Teresa Crook

Zehnder's of Frankenmuth: world famous chicken dinners, golf course, hotel, indoor waterpark, host of unique retail shops

at the place they would call Frankenmuth. This mission colony in the wilderness, with their loyalty to the Lutheran church, their German heritage and language, was the beginning of Michigan's Little Bavaria. Frankenmuth.org

Courtesy of Frankenmuth COC

X X-TRA STUFF

County fair: *Saginaw County Agricultural Soc.:* Aug
Famous people: ... *Entertainment:* Stevie Wonder ...*Sports:* Serena and Vanessa Williams
Hospitals: Covenant Medical Center, Mid-Michigan Medical Center, Saginaw Community Hospital, St. Mary's Medical Center, Select Specialty Hospital
Large employers: Delphi (makes motor vehicle parts), General Motors, Covenant Medical Center, St. Mary's Medical Center, AT & T, Dow Corning, Frankenmuth Bavarian Inn

Teresa Crook

Star of the West Milling Co.: the largest food-grade cereal bran manufacturer in the U.S.; headquarters in Frankenmuth with 10 other locations in Michigan, plus a few more in NY, OH, IN, ND

Y YESTERYEAR

In 1845, a group of 15 colonists from Bavaria, after a harrowing 7-week trip across the Atlantic, finally arrived in New York. They had faced severe weather, a drunken sea captain, violent storms and seasickness, a collision with a sand bank and then a trawler, a damp and overcrowded ship, stale food and smallpox. From there to Michigan it took another 9 weeks. They traveled by several steamboats (one of which had to be pulled 15 miles up the Saginaw River) and a train which collided with another train. Pushing an oxcart full of their belongings, they walked the last 12 miles through forest, thickets and swamps to finally arrive

Z ZOO & ANIMAL PLACES

Petting zoo: *Grandpa Tiny's Farm:* a working historical and petting farm

Watchable Wildlife Viewing Areas:ᵂᵂ see 73P

Teresa Crook

NPCR

Zoo: *The Children's Zoo at Celebration Square:* 8 acres, 150 animals, butterflies, train, carousel, gardens

...*Wilderness Trails Zoo:* 56 acres, 200 animals
Frankenmuth Riding Stables: ride through the woods and by the stream
Shiawassee National Wildlife Refuge: see 73P

From BIBLIOGRAPHY & NOTES...

W WANDERLUST: We always recommend you call ahead to check on the operating status of any venue!!! Check the Internet for contact information or call the Visitor Information listed in *I INFORMATION* in the chapter.

A AGRICULTURE

Land in farms: 68% of county
Number of farms: 1,500
Size of average farm: 270 acres
Market value of all products: #4 of 83 counties
Crops: ...most acres: soybeans
...highest $ sales: grains: corn, soybeans, wheat
Livestock: ...largest number: cattle & calves
...highest $ sales: milk & dairy products
Among the top Michigan counties:
- #1- acres of soybeans, cattle operations, dairy farms, pheasants
- #2- alfalfa, all animal operations, organic production, wheat
- #3- barley, forage, milk cows, sugar beets
- #4- hay, oats for grain
- #5- colonies of bees

Dairy, food and meat processing plants: 15
State ranking for harvested trees: #79 of 83 counties
FYI: The farmers in this county plant the most acres of Michigan's over 2 million acres of <u>soybeans</u> that produce 76,000,000 bushels of soybeans. This fascinating and edible seed has been called "The Miracle Seed" because it can be used for human food, consumer and industrial products, and livestock feed. A 60 pound bushel of soybeans can produce 10 pounds of soybean oil and 90% of that oil is used in foods such as salad dressings, baking mixes and candy. The oil is also used in soy inks, plastics, biodiesel fuels and biodegradable products. The popular edamame is an immature whole soybean pod that has been boiled in water with various condiments and served whole. ^{MDA}

B BRIDGE OR BOAT

Denise Mazei

The 1905 swinging bridge over the Black River in Croswell is the only suspension footbridge in Michigan. The sign on one side says "Be Good to Your Mother-in-Law."

C CELEBRATIONS

<u>Croswell</u> *Swinging Bridge Festival:* a salute to agriculture, cardboard boat races, zucchini races, sugar beet launch & catapult, corn roast, Aug.
<u>Deckerville</u> *Homecoming:* good times, good friends, horseshoes, pet parade, mud volleyball, Aug.
<u>Lexington</u> *Bach Festival:* Sept.
...Fine Arts Streets Fair: Aug.
...Thumbfest: traditional music festival, Aug.
<u>Peck</u> *Hunter's Round-up:* Oct.
<u>Port Sanilac</u> *Bark Shanty Festival:* bark shanty race, fireman's demonstration and breakfast, boat show, watermelon eating, ugly dogs, sand castles, July
...Civil War Days: trials, tribulations, triumphs, re-enactments, educational, enjoyable, Aug.
...Antique Boat Show: wooden vessels, races, Aug.

<u>Sandusky</u> *Michigan's Original Country Christmas Lighted Farm Implement Parade*: hockey, fruitcake toss, human sled dog races, chili, Dec.

Wm. Dixon

D DEMOGRAPHICS

Population: 43,100   **Persons per sq. mile:** 45
Largest city: Sandusky   **Population:** 2,680
Largest township: Worth   **Population:** 3,900
Largest village: Lexington   **Population:** 1,180
Median household income: $39,000

Owner-occupied median house value: $120,000
Persons affiliated with a religious congregation: 37%
Persons below poverty level: 17%
Students receiving school lunch subsidy: 44%

E ENVIRONMENT

"Founded in 1997, Project GREEEN (Generating Research and Extension to meet Economic and Environmental Needs), is Michigan's plant agriculture initiative at Michigan State University. It is a cooperative effort by plant-based commodities and businesses in cooperation with the Michigan Agriculture Experiment Station, Michigan State University Extension and the Michigan Department of Agriculture to advance Michigan's economy through its plant-based agriculture. Its mission is to develop research and educational programs in response to industry needs, ensure and improve food safety, and protect and preserve the quality of the environment." Project GREEEN

F FLORA & FAUNA

Alice Welch, USDA

Goat's beard, or wild spirea, is a large wildflower (5' tall & 4' wide) that blooms is late summer and through the fall. It has been domesticated and can be planted in shade gardens.

Alice Welch, USDA

The insect earwig (1" long) is no more common in the ear of humans than other insects. They can live almost anywhere undercover and eat both other insects and plants, sometime doing damage to crops with their pincers. They fall into the category of "creepy crawlers."

G GOVERNMENT

County: ...created: 1822 **...organized:** 1849
...originally part of: Oakland, St. Clair, Lapeer Counties
Size: 617,000 acres / 964 sq. miles (11 of 83 counties)
The county has 4 cities, 9 villages, 26 townships and 7 school districts.

Denise Mazei

NPCR

County seat: Sandusky
...Homestead property tax: 42 mills
Motto: Marlette: *Heart of the Thumb*
...Port Sanilac: *Your Great Lakes Getaway - Our Bright Lights are the Stars & Sunrise*
...Sandusky: *A City of Today, with Memories of Yesterday*

H HISTORICAL MARKERS 9 of 14

Brown City Banner: 1891, a newspaper whose motto was "Our Community is our Hive. The Rights of the People, our Queen."

Flint and Pere Marquette Depot: 1890, local residents raised money to help build the tracks in order to lure the railroad to Marlette.

Great Storm of 1913: Nov. 1913, a total of 235 seaman and 10 ships were lost on the Great Lakes; 178 crewmen and 8 ships lost on Lake Huron alone

Loop Harrison House: 1870s, this 20-room Second Empire style mansion is now part of the Sanilac County Historic Village & Museum.

Michigan State Historic Preservation Office

Marlette District Library: 1921, the second to last in the U.S. to receive a Carnegie library grant; there were 53 Carnegie libraries in Michigan

Masonic and Town Hall: 1884, fanciful Late Victorian brickwork; foundation had 3-foot-thick walls to provide refuge from forest fires.

Matthews Farm: 1852, typical plank-frame construction of Canadian immigrants

Methodist Episcopal Church: 1902, Neo-gothic style, by the same architect who designed Marlette High School and the Sanilac County Courthouse

Old Town Hall & Masonic Lodge: 1876, Italianate style, village owned the first two floors and the Masons owned the third floor

National Register of Historic Places: 11 listings

State Historic Sites: 30 listings

I INFORMATION

Chamber of Commerce: Croswell-Lexington, Freeland, Sandusky

Visitor: Sanilac Tourism Association, 810-648-5550, sanilaccounty.org

J JOKES

A Week's Worth of Reasons to Move Back to Michigan

- Monday: We've got more fresh water than any other place on earth.
- Tuesday: Housing prices are really low.
- Wednesday: We've got fresh water for drinking, fishing, swimming, boating and irrigating.
- Thursday: Our fresh farm food is outstanding.
- Friday: Our license plates have said we are the Water Wonderland state, the Water-Winter Wonderland state and the Great Lakes State. License plates rock.

NPCR

- Saturday: We have four distinct seasons that are not equal in length.
- Sunday: Did you know that we have an abundance of good, clean water? PTL

K KINSMAN

Race

American Indian: <1%

Asian: <1%

Black/African American: <1%

Hispanic or Latino: 3%

Other: 1%

White: 97%

Ancestry

German: 29%

English: 12%

U.S./American: 10%

Polish: 10%

French: 3%

Scottish: 3%

L LIGHTHOUSE OR LANDMARK

Courtesy Archives of Michigan

These 300 to 1,000 year-old Sanilac Petroglyphs rock carvings were discovered after the 1881 forest fire. They portray the ancient woodland people who once lived in this area. These are the only prehistoric rock carvings ever found in Michigan. The park, on 240 acres on the Little Cass River, is part of the Michigan Historical Museum System.

M MUSEUMS

Carsonville *International Harvestor Collection:* tractors, trucks, toys, advertising

Deckerville *Historical Museum:* American Indian artifacts, items from local farms and businesses

Marlette *Historical Depot Museum:* appointment only

Port Sanilac *Sanilac County Historic Village & Museum:* 10 acres, 9 Victorian, Edwardian and vintage buildings; includes the Loop Harrison house, schoolhouse, general store, church, Barn Theatre, dairy shrine, log cabin, beautiful gardens, shipwreck info

Beth Motz

N NATURAL RESOURCES

Elevation: <600 - 900 feet
Physiography: rolling plains, lake-border plains

Soil: Loam
  Depth: 8"-12"
  Color: dark gray, brown, or black
  Type: light to heavy; compact, sticky and impervious [very poorly drained] when wet, very hard when dry
  Details: surface is mostly level with some low knolls, swells and depressions

  Agriculture: when properly drained and cultivated, can yield good crops of corn, oats, wheat, hay and sugar beets

NOTE: soil types are not limited to any one county.

Forest type: elm-ash-cottonwood, aspen-birch, maple-beech
Public/private forests: 13% of county

Water in county: 0% of county
  Lakes: 1   **...largest:** no name
  Rivers: Black, Elk, Little Cass,
  Rivers & streams: 1,000 miles

Great Lakes peninsula: Thumb
Great Lakes shoreline: 41 miles of Lake Huron

Growing season, avg.: 147 days (3-4 temp. zones)
  Last freeze, avg.: May 5 – May 15
  First freeze, avg.: Oct. 5 – Oct. 20
Precipitation, annual avg.: rainfall: 28 inches
                         snowfall: 54 inches
Temperature (F), avg.: January: high 29°, low 14°
                       July: high 82°, low 58°
  Annual: >90°: 10 days, **<0°:** 8 days
Tornadoes (1930-2010): 16

O ORIGINS

Applegate:[v] leader of the party which opened the southern road into Oregon, Jesse Applegate; 1856
Brown City:[c] town founders, Robert & John Brown; 1879
Carsonville:[v] businessman, Arthur Carson; 1853
Croswell:[c] Michigan Gov. Charles Croswell; 1845
Deckerville:[v] lumberman, Charles Decker; 1865

Forestville:[v] heavily timbered area; 1853
Lexington:[v] Civil War Battle of Lexington; 1838
Marlette:[c] maiden name of two Irish settlers who carved their name Marlett on a log; 1854
Melvin:[v] 1862
Minden City:[v] town founder from Minden, Germany; 1855
Peck:[v] 1862
Port Sanilac:[v] originally Bark Shanty, but renamed after the county; 1840
Sandusky:[c] town founder from Sandusky, Ohio; 1870
Sanilac:[co] (SAN ill lack) Wyandot Chief Sannilac [wikipedia]

P PARKS

National: 0 **State:** 5 **County:** 4 **Local:** 11
Number of campsites: 1,100

State Game Area: Minden City, Sanilac, 8,200 acres

State Historic State Park: *Sanilac Petroglyphs:* see 74L
State Underwater Preserve: *Sanilac Shores:* 163 square miles, 16 sunken ships from 1856 – 1920 includes wooden steamers, steel freighters, wooden schooners, tugboats and a canaler

County: *Evergreen:* 68 acres, on Cass River, camping, handicapped accessible, trails
…*Forester:* 68 acres, on Lake Huron, camping, rustic cabins, fish, swim, trails
…*Lexington Park:* 27 acres, on Lake Huron, swim, day use only, scenic wooden bridge
…*Delaware Park:* 111 acres, on Lake Huron, swim, fish, trails, day use only
Other: *Minden Bog:* part of Minden SGA, a 5,000 acre wetland that once may have been 30 square miles; beautiful, remote, rugged; beavers, animal trails

Q QUOTE FROM THE LOCALS

"At a glance of the map of the lower peninsula of Michigan, one sees an outline that resembles a left-handed mitten, placed palm down, with the thumb projecting into the blue waters of Lake Huron. As a result, the area lying between Lake Huron and Saginaw Bay has become known as the Thumb.

"Thinking in terms of the geography of Michigan, the Thumb may be called a …geographic region…

that includes Huron, Lapeer, Sanilac, St. Clair and Tuscola counties. The Thumb, like all of Michigan, is a product of the Ice Age …as glaciers advanced and retreated five times… spreading rich top soil over much of the surface." Schults

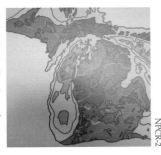

NPCR-2

R RECREATION & SPORTS

Golf courses: 8
Great Lakes marinas: 3   **Boat slips:** 270
Hiking/skiing/mountain biking trails: 1 mile
Horse racing: harness racing at Croswell Fair, June
Michigan Heritage Water Trail:
    Tip of the Thumb
Public access sites: 4
Public recreational land: 14% of county

Recreational harbors: Lexington State Harbor, Port Sanilac Harbor of Refuge

Flat Track Motorcycle Races: June, Aug, Sept.

NPCR

S STATE OF MICHIGAN

According to the Michigan Department of Community Health, on an <u>average day in 2007</u> there occurred in Michigan…

- 343 live births: including 29 low birth weight babies and 6 sets of twins
- 156 marriages
- 95 divorces
- 237 deaths: including 3 infants, 3 suicides, 4 due to kidney disease, 7 due to Alzheimer's, 10 due to accidents, 13 due to strokes, 24 due to diabetes complications, 55 due to cancer and 66 due to heart disease

T TRAVEL

Bus: Thumb Area Transit
Circle Tour: Lake Huron via M-25
Distance to Lansing: 120 miles
Main roads: M-19, M-25, M-46, M-53, M-90
Memorial Highway: M-53, *Earle MH:* see 44T
Scenic Drive: Port Huron to Tawas City via M-25

U UNIVERSITIES & COLLEGES

None

V VARIETY

Paul Jackson

Paul Jackson

Milk and dairy products are the #1 agricultural commodity in Michigan and Sanilac County has more dairy farms than any other county. See 30A.

W WANDERLUST

Agri-tourism: *Bechtel Greenhouse & Produce:* bedding plants, hanging baskets, fresh produce
Cultural: Lexington Fine Arts Council: satisfying the increasing cultural taste of the Thumb Blue Water community by producing musical, visual and other fine arts programming
Fall colors: mid October
Lighthouse, other: Port Sanilac light station is operated by the U.S. Coast Guard and is not open to the public
Live theater: Barn Theatre, Lexington Music Theatre,
Wineries: *Blue Water Winery:* Think Globally, Drink Locally

Six Gun Territory: wild west town theme park, pan for gold, make rope, go to jail, saloon, chuck wagon, livery stable, general store, wagon rides

jackie@sixgunterritory.com

X X-TRA STUFF

County fair: *Croswell Agricultural Society:* June
…*Sanilac County 4-H Agricultural Society:* diversity of animals and commodities in 4-H events, July

Hospitals: Deckerville General, Marlette Community, McKenzie Memorial

Large employers: Marlette Regional Hospital, Cros-Lex Community Schools, Trelleborg YSH (makes rubber products), Numatics (makes pneumatic tools), Grupo Antolin Michigan (makes vehicle parts), Dott Industries (makes plastic items), Huron (makes screw machine products)

Don't forget to check the *BIBLIOGRAPHY & NOTES* at the back of the book for explanations and additional information.

Y YESTERYEAR

The great and devastating <u>fire of 1871</u> was decades in the making. When Michigan became a state in the 1830s, speculators moved in and bought up huge tracks of land. They sold the forested land to the lumbermen who came in to harvest the pine forests. After that, the farmers moved in to continue to clear and then cultivate the land. Inherent in clearing the land was getting rid of the tree limbs left over from logging millions of trees and the resulting tree stumps. Therefore, fires were constantly simmering all over the area. It had been a very hot and dry summer and fall that year and smoldering fires were everywhere. A severe windstorm from the west hit the area and turned the entire territory into a flaming inferno that consumed every living person, animal, tree and plant in its path. This fire in Huron and Sanilac Counties and surrounding areas was the same day as the Great Chicago Fire and the Peshtigo Fire Storm. See 55Y. Neva Dumond

Z ZOO & ANIMAL PLACES

Petting zoo: *Six Gun Territory-Wild West Town:* see 74W ...*Summer Wind Farms Sanctuary:* 140 acres, 200 animals in a licensed sanctuary for exotic birds, animals and reptiles; tours

Shayna Tondreau

Shayna Tondreau

...*Whispering Pines Animal Kingdom:* wildlife educational programs & guided farm tours, 50 species of animals

A AGRICULTURE

Land in farms: 65% of county
Number of farms: 1,100
Size of average farm: 210 acres
Market value of all products: #25 of 83 counties
Crops: ...most acres: soybeans
...highest $ sales: grains: soybeans, corn, wheat
Livestock: ...largest number: cattle & calves
...highest $ sales: milk & dairy products
Among the top Michigan counties:
• #1- field & seed grass crops, all nuts, red clover
Dairy, food and meat processing plants: 13
State ranking for harvested trees: #76 of 83 counties

FYI: Field and seed grass crops provide the basic food for domestic and wild animals around the world. In Michigan, the following crops are grown for animal feed and also as harvested seeds that will be planted elsewhere:

Alice Welch, USDA

• *Alfalfa:* a highly nutritious legume that is used for forage, hay, silage and honey production
• *Birdsfoot trefoil:* a legume primarily suited for grass-legume pastures
• *Crimson and Red clover*: popular legumes grown for forage and wildlife feed providing useful energy, protein and fiber for the animals, and soil improvement for the land
• *Ryegrass:* used in pastures mixed with other grasses and as a cover crop to increase soil fertility, reduce soil erosion from water run-off, manage weeds, disease and pests, and improve wildlife habitat
• *Timothy*: a very leafy bunchgrass used for pasture in rotational grazing, hay, silage and erosion control
• *Vetch:* a legume with over 150 varieties, it provides forage opportunities (stays green under the snow and begins growing very early in the spring) not present in other forage crops.
   NOTE: A legume is a plant that produces seedpods that have to be opened in order to get out the seed, which is the edible part of the plant.

B BRIDGE OR BOAT

Shiawassee County Convention & Visitors Bureau

The Heritage Bridge is a footbridge in Owosso that connects the downtown business area to Curwood Castle Park. It is part of the James S. Miner River Walk that runs from Corunna to Owosso.

C CELEBRATIONS

<u>Durand</u> *Railroad Days:* pays tribute to railroad heritage, May

<u>Morrice</u> *Homecoming Festival:* parade, races, June

Courtesy of Durand Union Station

Courtesy of Shiawassee County Convention & Visitors Bureau

<u>Owosso</u> *Curwood Festival:* river events, talent show, children's parade, pet show, writing contest, June; see 76H, 76V

...*Summerfest:* concerts all summer long at the Mitchell Amphitheater
<u>Perry</u>*Fest:* craft show, car show, talent show, pedal pushers, battle of the bands, 5K walk/run, Sept.

D DEMOGRAPHICS

Population: 70,600   **Persons per sq. mile:** 131
Largest city: Owosso   **Population:** 15,200
Largest township: Owosso **Population:** 4,820
Largest village: Morrice **Population:** 930
Median household income: $42,900
Owner-occupied median house value: $134,000
Persons affiliated with a religious congregation: 39%
Persons below poverty level: 14%
Students receiving school lunch subsidy: 30%

E ENVIRONMENT

Project Food, Land & People strives to develop citizen understanding about the connections between agriculture, the environment and people. The Pre-K-12 classroom materials provide integrated content in food and nutrition, natural resources, conservation, farming and consumer choices. They were written by experts in education, agriculture, environmental sciences, natural resources, conservation, materials development and training, and provide curriculum support through workshops. It is crucial to understand the relationship between food, land and people to maintain a viable agricultural system, a sustainable environment and a healthy society. foodlandpeople.org

F FLORA & FAUNA

Alice Welch, USDA

Bedstraw needs to stay in the wild because it can take over a garden. It is so named because the flower stems (2' long) were used to stuff mattress in the old days because they did not disintegrate when they dried out.

Brian Hanse, USFWS

Common garter snakes have three light stripes running the length of their body that can be black, brown, gray or olive. They are welcome in the garden to help control slugs and insects and are considered harmless to humans.

G GOVERNMENT

County: ...created: 1822 **...organized:** 1837
...originally part of: Oakland, Genesee Counties
Size: 346,000 acres / 539 sq. miles (65 of 83 counties)
The county has 5 cities, 5 villages, 16 townships with 2 as charter townships, 23 unincorporated communities and 10 school districts.

Shiawassee County Convention & Visitors Bureau

Shiawassee County Courthouse: 1904, elegant clock tower and columned facade
County seat: Corunna
...Homestead property tax: 39 mills
Motto: Corunna: *City of History   City of Growth*
...Durand: *Railroad City, USA*
...Morrice: *A Community on the GROW / A Nice Place to Live*
...Owosso: *where tomorrow meets today...*
...Shiawassee County Convention and Visitors Bureau: *Great Things are Happening in Shiawassee County*

H HISTORICAL MARKERS

Birthplace of Thomas Edmund Dewey: 1902-1971, he prosecuted organized crime in NY, was 3-time NY governor, 2-time Republican presidential nominee
Byron Cemetery: 1837, an interesting variety of internments and grave markers; American Indians lived here prior to it becoming a cemetery
Corunna Public Schools: 1842, the teacher received the unprecedented salary of $2.50 per week and the privilege of boarding 'round in the community.
Curwood Castle: James Curwood, 1878-1927, was a successful adventure novelist and conservationist whose stories were made into movies; his castle, built in 1922, was his writing studio. See 76C, 76V.

Durand Railroad History: Durand became the railroad center for the Grand Trunk and the Ann Arbor railroads; around 1900, there were 35 passenger trains, 100 freight trains and 3,000 passengers who used the depot each day.

Laura Hamlin

Durand Union Station: this 239' long granite and cut stone building was once one of the largest stations in small towns in the U.S.; in 1970 the last regularly scheduled passenger train in the U.S. to be pulled by a steam locomotive left this station; it is now an Amtrak stop. See 76M.

Ellen May Tower: 1868-1898, a nurse who died in the Spanish-American War, she was the first woman in Michigan to have a military funeral

Frederick Carl Frieske: 1874-1939, an award winning French Impressionist painter

Hugh McCurdy: 1829-1908, Grand Master of the Knights Templar of the U.S. and founder of First National Bank of Corunna; gave 34 acres for a park

Knaggs Bridge Area: archaeological evidence indicates men lived in this area before the time of Christ.

Michigan's First Coal Mine: a large vein of coal was mined from 1839 until after WWII

Old Perry Centre: 1877, the railroad wouldn't build a sidetrack to their town, so residents bought their own materials and built their own sidetrack and depot in one weekend.

National Register of Historic Places: 41 listings
State Historic Sites: 69 listings

I INFORMATION

Chamber of Commerce: Durand, Morrice, Perry, Shiawassee Regional
Visitor: Shiawassee County Convention and Visitors Bureau, 989-723-1199, shiawassee.org

J JOKES

You'd like to move to a "big city" in Michigan, but…
…you can't sell your house.
…you'd have to quit your current job in order to take a better paying job.
…you like to see the stars at night.
…you don't really care about all the cultural events in the "big city," you like the ones you already have.
…commuting 1 hour to drive 20 miles to work is more than you can tolerate.
…you'd miss seeing the forests and the crops going in and coming out.
…you'd be too far away from your favorite hunting and fishing spots.
…anyway, it's where your in-laws live.

K KINSMAN

Race		Ancestry	
American Indian: <1%		German: 25%	
Asian: <1%		English: 14%	
Black/African American: <1%		U.S./American: 14%	
Hispanic or Latino: 2%		Irish: 10%	
Other: 2%		Polish: 4%	
White: 95%		French: 4%	

L LIGHTHOUSE or LANDMARK

Shiawassee County Convention & Visitors Bureau

Shiawassee County is the epicenter of railroading history in Michigan. Pictured above is the steam locomotive Pere Marquette 1225, the "real" Polar Express. Train excursions are available.

M MUSEUMS

<u>Corunna</u> *Historical Village:* 1900s one-room school, homes, cabin, windmill, church, caboose, tinsmith

<u>Durand</u> *Michigan Railroad History Museum:* in the historic Durand Union Station; library, archives, changing displays, model of Durand yards; see 76L

Laura Hamlin

Owosso *Curwood Castle:* see also 76V, 76H

...*DeVries Historic Carriage and Sleigh Museum:* 25 restored vehicles, visitors' center

...*Steam Railroading Institute:* steam and diesel locomotives, passenger cars, rolling stock, a variety of riding opportunities

Perry *Historical Society Museum / Calkins-MacQueen House:* history of Perry, Morrice and Shaftsburg area; Mastodon bones found in 2001; see 76S

Shiawassee *County Historical Museum:* collect and preserve facts, reminiscences and objects

Shiawassee County Convention & Visitors Bureau

N NATURAL RESOURCES

Elevation: 700 - 900 feet
Physiography: rolling plains

Forest type: maple-beech, oak-hickory
Public/private forests: 1% of county

Water in county: <1% of county
Lakes: 30   ...**largest:** Manitou
Rivers: Looking Glass, Maple, Shiawassee (shy a WAH see)
Rivers & streams: 310 miles

NPCR

Growing season, avg.: 144 days (2 temp. zones)
Last freeze, avg.: May 5 – May 10
First freeze, avg.: Oct. 5 – Oct. 10
Precipitation, annual avg.: rainfall: 29 inches
                        snowfall: 41 inches
Temperature (F), avg.: January: high 29°, low 14°
                 July: high 82°, low 59°
   Annual: >90°: 9 days, <0°: 11 days
Tornadoes (1930-2010): 32

O ORIGINS

Bancroft:[v] origin unknown; 1824 michmarkers.com
Caledonia:[ct] probably from Caledonia, NY; 1838
Corunna:[c] village founder came from Corunna, Spain; 1832
Durand:[c] Congressman George Durand; 1836
Laingsburg:[c] village founder and tavern-keeper, Peter Laing; 1836
Lennon:[v] village founder, Peter Lennon; <1880

Morrice:[v] the Morris brothers from Scotland; 1836
New Lothrop:[v] William Lothrop gave bells for the Methodist Church; 1836
Owosso:[c,ct] (oh Wah so) Objiway Chief Wasso; 1833
Perry:[c] naval hero, Oliver Hazard Perry; 1850
Shiawassee:[co] (shy a WAH see) American Indian word for "river that twists about"
Vernon:[v] Geo. Washington's home, Mt. Vernon; 1833

P PARKS

National: 0   **State:** 1   **County:** 7   **Local:** 25
Number of campsites: 1,500
State Wildlife Area: *Rose Lake,* 900 acres; see 76Z
Other: *DeVries Nature Conservancy:* 136 acres, 4+ miles of trails through farmland, forest, restored prairie and floodplain on the Shiawassee River; plus educational workshops, kids programs, facilities

Laura Hamlin

Laura Hamlin

Q QUOTE FROM THE LOCALS

"No matter the season, Shiawassee County has something fun for everyone! Enjoy a canoe trip down the river, take a hike on our wooded trails, or partake in some shopping in one of our quaint downtowns. Take in a race in our outdoor speedway; relax while listening to an outdoor concert, or try your luck in catching the perfect fish. During the winter months, you can enjoy a cross-country ski trip, try some downhill sledding or snow shoeing, explore our arts center and museums or just take in the beautiful sights. Shiawassee County is fun for the whole family" shiawassee.org

R RECREATION & SPORTS

Auto racing: *Owosso Speedway:* 3/8-mile high-banked paved oval track
Golf courses: 7
Public recreational land: <1% of county
Bass fishing on the Shiawassee River is a popular activity in this county.

S STATE OF MICHIGAN

NPCR-9

NPCR

Since 2002, the Mastodon has been the State Fossil. Fossils of this prehistoric mammal (14,000 – 11,000 years ago) have been found in more than 250 locations in the state, all in the southern half of the Lower Peninsula. The Mastodon, a giant browsing megaherbivore, ate tree leaves and shrubs and thrived in Michigan's woodlands. The almost complete skeleton of the female Owosso Mastodon is on display in the University of Michigan's Museum of Natural History (above). Along with the male Mastodon, they are the only Mastodon pair in the U.S.

T TRAVEL

Airport: Owosso Community
Amtrak: Durand
Bus: Indian Trails, Shiawassee Area Transportation Agency
Distance to Lansing: 30 miles
Main roads: I-69, M-13, M-21, M-52, M-71
Memorial Highway: M-21, *PFC Harold R. Cooley WWII Marine Corps League MH*: he died on Guam in 1944

U UNIVERSITIES & COLLEGES

Baker College of Owosso: see 25U

If you have comments, suggestions, corrections or updates, please email these to: info@discovermichigancountybycounty.com And thanks for reading this book and taking time to share your thoughts!

V VARIETY

Laura Hamlin

Curwood Castle is a 1922 replica of a Norman château that was the writing studio of writer James Curwood. It is now a museum; see 76H, 76M.

W WANDERLUST

Agri-tourism: *Country Corn Maze:* 4 mazes to challenge all skill levels; pumpkins, corn

Cultural: Shiawassee Arts Center

Fall colors: early October
Live theatre: Owosso Community Players Studio Theatre

NPCR

Laura Hamlin

MotorCities National Heritage Area: yes

Walking tour: Miner Bicycle River Walk, 5-miles along the Shiawassee River

...Owosso is home to the second largest number of historical homes in the state; maps available

King Kone Ice Cream: stop and enjoy, just for fun

North Pole Express: take a magical winter train ride from Owosso to "Santa's Village" in Chesaning's "North Pole, USA" every December

Laura Hamlin

X X-TRA STUFF

County fair: *Shiawassee County Agricultural Society:* the fairgrounds come alive with 4-H and FFA projects, agricultural and commercial displays, amusement rides and family entertainment, Aug.

Famous people: *...Other:* James Curwood, George Hoddy

...Politics: Thomas Dewey

...Sports: Brad Van Pelt

Hospitals: Memorial

Large employers: Memorial Hospital, Owosso Public Schools, Meijer, Machine Tool & Gear (makes vehicle parts), Shiawassee County Government, Shiawassee County Mental Health Clinic, Perry Public Schools

Morrice is the center of population in the state of Michigan.

Laura Hamlin

Since 1910, Owosso has been the headquarters of the Indian Trails Bus Line serving all of Michigan with connections to Chicago, the east shore of Wisconsin and Minneapolis, MN.

Since 1866, Owosso has been the home of the Woodard Furniture Company that today makes quality handcrafted wrought iron furniture.

Y YESTERYEAR

<u>The Wallace Circus Train Wreck</u>

In August, 1903, two circus trains, 22 cars and 16 cars in length, were on their way from Charlotte to Lapeer. The first train had stopped for another train on the track, but workers were not able to communicate with the second train in time and it ran into the rear of the first train. There were 23 deaths in the accident; most were performers who were in a sleeper car at the

Courtesy of Durand Union Station

end of the first train. The second train contained the animals and at least three camels, an elephant and a performing dog were killed also. This train wreck is a featured exhibit at the Durand Union Station – Michigan Railroad History Museum. durandstation.org

Z ZOO & ANIMAL PLACES

NPCR

Rose Lake State *Wildlife* Area: diversity of habitats; song birds, Sandhill Cranes, Great Blue Herons, American Bitterns

From BIBLIOGRAPHY & NOTES...

F FAUNA: *(MI H&T)* indicates that Michigan allows Hunting and Trapping of this animal with the proper training, permits, licensing and within the season.

A AGRICULTURE

Land in farms: 33% of county
Number of farms: 1,100
Size of average farm: 150 acres
Market value of all products: #38 of 83 counties
Crops: ...most acres: soybeans
...highest $ sales: grains: corn, soybeans, wheat
Livestock: ...largest number: cattle & calves
...highest $ sales: milk & dairy products
Among the top Michigan counties:
- #1- beets, garlic, head lettuce, mustard greens, pumpkins
- #2- herbs
- #3- wild hay

Dairy, food and meat processing plants: 9
State ranking for harvested trees: #55 of 83 counties
FYI: Pumpkins are a food, a holiday decoration and a seasonal activity all in one. What would Halloween be without a jack-o-lantern and what would Thanksgiving be without pumpkin pie? Many families enjoy a trip to the pumpkin patch in the fall to pick their own pumpkins. There are over a thousand farms in Michigan growing nearly 7,000 acres of pumpkins. St. Clair County is the largest grower with 13% of the acreage. MDA

B BRIDGE OR BOAT

The Blue Water Bridge over the St. Clair River connects Port Huron with Sarnia, Ontario, Canada. This international twin-span bridge consists of the 1938 westbound cantilever truss bridge that is esthetically tied to the 1997 eastbound continuous tied arch bridge.

C CELEBRATIONS

<u>Marine City</u> *Music & Arts Festival:* all types of music, quilt show, talent competitions, raffles, July
<u>Port Huron</u> *IceFest:* ice carving exhibition, Jan.
...*CelticFest:* Irish-American festivities, music, Maid of Erin Pageant, parade, March

...*Feast of the Ste. Claire:* a living re-enactment of 18th century life of American Indians, French explorers, British traders, American revolutionaries, May

...*Mackinac Race Activities:* Port Huron to Mackinac Island Sailboat Race, pre-race activities, July

...*Antique & Classic Auto Weekend:* July

...*Antique & Classic Boat Show:* July
<u>Richmond</u> *Good Ole Days Festival:* one of Michigan's Best Small Town Festivals, Sept.
<u>St. Clair</u> *Winter White Out:* I'm from Michigan and I can party in any weather! Jan.

...*Art Fair:* fine juried art along the river, June

...*Riverfest & Offshore Power-boat Race:* free music & fun all weekend long, July

...*Classic Car Show:* July

...*Vintage Weekend:* antiques and antique boats, July

...Whistles on the Water: the largest steam engine event in North America and possibly the world, this equipment produces both high volume and high quality steam, Sept.

Daniel Lockwood

Photo provided by: The Yale Expositor

<u>Yale</u> *Bologna Festival:* Big Bologna Parade, fried bologna sandwiches, bologna hotdogs, bologna royalty, outhouse race, July

D DEMOGRAPHICS

Population: 163,000
Largest city: Port Huron
Largest township: Fort Gratiot
Largest village: Capac
Median household income: $45,800
Owner-occupied median house value: $156,000
Persons affiliated with a religious congregation: 43%
Persons below poverty level: 14%
Students receiving school lunch subsidy: 32%

Persons per sq. mile: 225
Population: 30,200
Population: 11,100
Population: 1,890

E ENVIRONMENT

<u>St. Clair Flats</u> is the largest fresh water delta in North America. It is a large coastal marsh that provides critical habitat for migratory waterfowl, wading birds, sport and forage fish, muskrats and other aquatic species. At the southern mouth of the St. Clair River in Lake St. Clair, dozens of small islands and almost all of the larger Dickson Island and half of Harsens Island are included in The Flats. It also provides water recreation and hunting opportunities for many families.

From BIBLIOGRAPHY & NOTES...
C CELEBRATIONS: Usually only those events of 2 or more days in length have been included.

F FLORA & FAUNA

Alice Welch, USDA

Chara, also known as stonewart, muskgrass or skunkweed, is a pondweed form of algae living below water level. It has a musky odor (muskgrass or skunkweed) and usually becomes encrusted with hard minerals (stonewart) like lime and calcium. It is a beneficial species since it filters the water and therefore helps keep the water clear; but when there is too much of it, it can impede water flow.

Alice Welch, USDA

The pumpkinseed sunfish is a real prize for anglers fishing in the St. Clair Flats who want a good tasting small fish that is low in fat and high in protein. Children love this fish since they readily bite on worms on the hook and put up a good fight on the line when reeling it in.

G GOVERNMENT

County: ...**created:** 1820 ...**organized:** 1821
...**originally part of:** Wayne County
Size: 481,000 acres / 724 sq. miles (24 of 83 counties)
The county has 7 cities, 2 villages, 24 townships with 3 as charter townships, 6 unincorporated communities and 9 school districts.

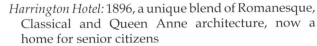

NPCR

NPCR

County seat: Port Huron

...Homestead property tax: 37 mills

Motto: Algonac: *Yours to Discover; The Pickerel Capitol of the World; Venice of Michigan*

...Blue Water Area Convention and Visitors Bureau: *Discover the BLUE... shores of eastern Michigan*

...Marine City Chamber: *We're closer than you think.*

...Marysville: *A great place to visit, a better place to live*

...Memphis Chamber: *A Pleasant Place to Live*

...Port Huron: *Maritime Capital of the Great Lakes*

...St. Clair On The River Downtown Development: *a getaway from the everyday*

H HISTORICAL MARKERS 21 of 44

Almont Society of the New Church: 1851, Scottish immigrants built this chapel

C.H. Wills & Co.: built 14,000 Wills Ste. Claire cars from 1921-1926

Colony Tower: 1825, a 136' water tower built to look like a lighthouse

Davidson House: 1890, Queen Anne style

Diamond Crystal Salt Co.: 1866, the St. Clair Rock Salt Co. changed its name when the new Alberger process resulted in exceptionally high purity levels.

EC Williams House: 1890, an early and rare duplex

East China Fractional School District No. 2: 1873, handsome red brick building, now a museum

Michigan State Historic Preservation Office

First Congregational Church: 1879, the 66' red brick clock tower with four back-lighted clock faces can even be seen from Canada

First International Tunnel: 1891, the first-in-the-world international submarine railway tunnel

Greenwood Cemetery: 1856, reminiscent of Victorian era perpetual care lawn cemeteries

Harrington Hotel: 1896, a unique blend of Romanesque, Classical and Queen Anne architecture, now a home for senior citizens

Harsen House: 1800, owned by the family that owned the entire island

Huron Lightship: 1921, the last Coast Guard lightship on the Great Lakes 1940-1970; see 77M

Marine City: 1800s, city was one of the largest shipbuilding centers in the Great Lakes area

Newport Academy: 1845-1865, private education for area children; now Marine City Library

Port Huron Public Library: 1902, a grand, Beaux-Arts-style building built from money from Andrew Carnegie; now the Port Huron Museum of Arts and History

Michigan State Historic Preservation Office

St. Clair Inn: 1926, Neo-Tudor style modeled after English country inns

St. Mary's Church: 1865, the bricks were hand formed and hauled to the site by the women of the church.

Stewart Farm: 1849, grandson of the first settler on Harsens Island in the 1780s, Aura Stewart wrote about his life on the island in the 1820s.

Michigan State Historic Preservation Office

NPCR

Tom Edison at Grand Trunk: as a 12-year-old he sold newspapers and confections on the Port Huron-Detroit run; he was so successful that he was able to support himself and hired two other boys to service other trains to Detroit. See 77Y.

Water Speed Capital: in the 1920s, Algonac was the home to speed race winning *Miss Americas* racing boats; starting in the 1930s, the Chris Craft Corporation became one of the world's largest builders of power pleasure boats.

National Historic Landmark: Lightship *No. 103,* St. Clair River Tunnel; see 77M

Michigan State Historic Preservation Office

National Register of Historic Places: 25 listings
State Historic Sites: 44 listings

I INFORMATION

Chamber of Commerce: Algonac, Marine City, Marysville, Memphis, Port Huron, St. Clair, Yale
Visitor: Blue Water Area Convention and Visitors Bureau, 800-852-4242, bluewater.org

J JOKES

You'll *never* hear a Michiganian say…
…they consider Canada a "foreign" country.
…green or blue? I just can't remember whether it's Michigan or Michigan State. But I definitely know my community college colors.
…oh hum, clear blue water. Big deal!
…boats, boats, boats everywhere! I get so tired of seeing boats on big lakes, boats on small lakes and boats on the Great Lakes.
…summer is so long and time goes by so slow.
…that they wished they lived in a state where they couldn't have basements.

K KINSMAN

Race
American Indian: <1%
Asian: <1%
Black/African American: 2%
Hispanic or Latino: 2%
Other: 2%
White: 92%

Ancestry
German: 26%
Polish: 10%
Irish: 10%
English: 9%
U.S./American: 8%
French: 5%

L LIGHTHOUSE OR LANDMARK

NPCR

Built in 1829, the Fort Gratiot Lighthouse is the oldest lighthouse in Michigan. At 85' tall, it is at the mouth of the St. Clair River and Lake Huron and still provides an important service to all boats and ships passing through this area. The buildings are being restored. See 77M.

M MUSEUMS

Algonac/Clay Twp. *Historical Society Community Museum:* models of pleasure boats built in Algonac
Capac *Community Museum:* in the restored Grand Trunk depot; home of the (1923) 40' Kempf Model City train
Goodles *Historical Village:* home to the Farm Museum Barn, Murphy/Ryan Farmhouse and Lynn Township School
Marine City *Captain David Lester Historical Residence:* tours available
…*Pride and Heritage Museum:* an 1847 schoolhouse; maritime, lifestyle, business/commercial galleries
Marysville *Wills Ste. Claire Auto Museum:* from 1921-1926, produced cars that were sleek, stylish, perfection, unique, timeless and valuable
Port Huron *Museum:* five museums include:

- *Carnegie Center:* 1904 former library, now home for the history of the Blue Water Area

Brian Blaz

- *Huron Lightship:* used as a lighthouse where a lighthouse was impractical, tours available; see 77H

- *Thomas Edison Depot Museum:* Edison did work here; displays about his life
- *USCGC Bramble:* 1944 Coast Guard Cutter; groups can stay overnight

- *Fort Gratiot Lighthouse:* currently closed but raising money for restoration; see 77L

...*Great Lakes Maritime Center:* watch the river traffic, fish, maritime artifacts, underwater cameras

Ralph W. Polovich, Acheson Venture, LLC

...*Knowlton's Ice Museum:* artifacts used in cutting, harvesting, storing, selling and use of natural ice

Richmond *Area Historical & Genealogical Society*

St. Clair *Historical Museum:* in a historic church, shipbuilding, lumbering, salt production, more

N NATURAL RESOURCES

Elevation: <600 - 900 feet
Physiography: lake border plains, rolling plains

Forest type: maple-beech, oak-hickory, aspen-birch
Public/private forests: 17% of county

Water in county: 2% of county
  Bay: Anchor Bay of Lake St. Clair
  Lakes: 20   **...largest:** a no-name lake
  Rivers: Belle, Black, St. Clair, Pine
  Rivers & streams: 960 miles (#5/MI)

Great Lakes islands: 34
Great Lakes shoreline: 164 miles of Lake Huron

Growing season, avg.: 170 days (#4/MI) (4 temp. zones)
Last freeze, avg.: April 25 – May 10
First freeze, avg.: Oct. 5 – Oct. 20
Precipitation, annual avg.: rainfall: 31 inches
                        snowfall: 42 inches
Temperature (F), avg.: January: high 30°, low 17°
                  July: high 82°, low 62°
  Annual: >90°: 13 days, **<0°:** 5 days
Tornadoes (1930-2010): 22

O ORIGINS

Algonac:[c] (AL ga nack) a word coined by Henry Schoolcraft from the Algonquin Indian; 1805
Capac:[v] Peruvian emperor, Huayna Ccapac; 1857
China:[ct] from China, Maine, that was named after a man's favorite hymn [Charter Township of China]
Emmett:[v] Irish poet, Robert Emmett; 1856

Fort Gratiot:[ct] (GRASS shut) engineer in charge of building the fort, Charles Gratiot; 1814
Goodells:[u] named for John Goodell; 1840
Marine City:[c] where the Belle River meets the St. Clair River; 1820
Marysville:[c] Mary Mills, wife of sawmill owner; 1843
Memphis:[c] after Memphis, Egypt, and means "a place of good abode;" 1834
Port Huron:[c,ct] originally Fort Gratiot; 1790
St. Clair:[c,co] first explorer entered the lake on the feast day of Ste. Clare; later the name was changed to St. Clair to honor first American governor of the Northwest Territory, Gen. Arthur St. Clair; 1818
Yale:[c] in honor of Yale University; 1851

P PARKS

National: 0 **State:** 5 **County:** 1 **Local:** 24
Number of campsites: 1,400
State Game Area: Port Huron, 6,100 acres
State Park: *Algonac:*[wba] 1,450 acres on St. Clair River, international freighter watching, lake plain prairies, oak savannas, summer & winter camping, hunting

...*Lake Port:* 565 acres on Lake Huron, two separate units, camping, swimming, picnics

Daniel Lockwood

State Recreation Area: *St. John's Marsh:* largest surviving wetlands in southern Michigan, rich in wildlife; educational trails
State Wildlife Area: *St. Clair Flats:* the largest fresh water delta in North America, 7,800 acres; a recreation paradise close to large population areas; see 77E
Other: Prairies & Savanna Natural Area[wba]

Q QUOTE FROM THE LOCALS

"Along the eastern shores of Michigan lies a collection of communities that are boastful about the color blue. 140 miles of shoreline unite the quaint towns of Algonac, Clay, Marine City, St. Clair, Port Huron, Lexington, Port Sanilac, Harbor Beach and Port Austin. These charming communities, forming what is called the Blue Water Area, invite you to discover the natural spirit that brings them all together. . .true blue water. The Blue Water Area is perched on the edges of Lake Huron and the St. Clair River. With admirable depths,

the waterways show off incredible colors of cobalt, turquoise and sparkling sapphire. The stunning hues restore a sense of freshness and tranquility that can get lost in the current of every day life. Green parks, boardwalks and wide beaches bordering the shorelines entice visitors and locals to lounge along the water and breathe in the natural beauty." bluewater.org See 77V.

R RECREATION & SPORTS

Golf courses: 9
Great Lakes marinas: 64

Boat slips: 4,500 (#4/MI)

Hiking/skiing/mountain biking trails: 8 miles
Public access sites: 12
Public recreational land: 2% of county
Rail-trail: (120 miles) Wadhams to Avoca
Recreational harbors: Charles Moore Harbor, Port Huron Marina

Jim Fisher

Port Huron Predators: plays football in the Continental Indoor Football League at Mc Morran Place

Welkin Vintage Base Ball Club: 1860 style; a gentleman's game with no gloves

Bridge to Bay Trail: 54-mile paved trail includes boardwalks, river trails, tail trails, lakeshore paths, natural areas, past lighthouses and museums

St. Clair Blue Water Ramble Bicycle Tour: a one-day ride, 30, 45, 65 or 100 miles

The Port Huron area has been named the #1 fly-fishing destination in the world by *American Angler Magazine.*

Grace Grogan

S STATE OF MICHIGAN

Lighthouses have been called American Castles and Michigan has over 100 of them, with 26 open to the public, more than any other state. Some of these lights still function as they were intended – to provide navigational signals for lake vessels at critical spots to help prevent the ships from running aground into shallow water or shoals. All of Michigan's navigational lights have been automated and are now the responsibility of the U.S. Coast Guard. Since the Coast Guard is not in the historic preservation business, many of the associated lighthouses have been abandoned.

The mission of the non-profit Michigan Lighthouse Conservancy is to promote the preservation of Michigan's lighthouses and life-saving station structures along with the artifacts associated with them. Each abandoned lighthouse needs a caretaker to preserve it. Some are now museums, private homes, schools or bed & breakfast inns. michiganlights.com

T TRAVEL

Airport: St. Clair County International Airport
Amtrak: Port Huron
Bus: Blue Water Area Transit
Circle Tour: Lake Huron via US 25
County road names: see 44T
Distance to Lansing: 120 miles
Ferry: Champion Auto Ferry to Harsens Island
…to Russell Island
…to Walpole Island, an authentic Canadian Indian Reservation
…Bluewater Ferry to Sombra, Ontario, Canada
Main roads: I-94, I-69, M-19, M-25, M-29, M-154
Memorial Highways: I-69, *DeWayne T. Williams MH:* he (1949-1968) served in Vietnam and was the only Michigan Marine to receive the Medal of Honor; he fell on a grenade to save others
…I-69, *Veterans Memorial*
…I-94, *James O'Hare:* see 50T
Michigan Welcome Center: I-94 in Port Huron
Scenic Drive: Port Huron to Tawas City via M-25
FYI: Over the years, US-25 (now US-75 and US-94 to Port Huron) has been called, in part or as a whole, proposed, promoted or legalized: Blue Water Hwy., Clara Barton Memorial Hwy., Dix Ave., Fort St./Rd. and Rogers Memorial Hwy. Barnett

U UNIVERSITIES & COLLEGES

St. Clair County Community College: est. 1923, 8,000 students. SC4 strives to be a leader in our community's renaissance by establishing dynamic partnerships and focused programs that are the top choice for students; M-TEC. MCCAA, Skippers

V VARIETY

NPCR

There is a reason this area is called the Blue Water Area. You can see cobalt, turquoise and sparkling sapphire in the color of these beautiful waters. See 77Q

W WANDERLUST

Agri-tourism: *Blueberry Ridge Farm:* U-pick, honey …*Marvin's Gardens:* U-pick, raspberries, pumpkins
Brewery: Quay Street Brewing Co.
Cultural: International Symphony Orchestra of Port Huron and Sarnia, Lexington Music Theatre Co.
Fall colors: early October
Lighthouse, other: Peche Island Lighthouse
Live theater: Algonac Community Theater, Port Huron Civic Theatre, Richmond Community Theatre, St. Clair Theatre Guild
Shopping mall: Birchwood, Port Huron Factory Shops Outlet
Walking tour: Olde Town Historic Neighborhood; …Marine City Nautical Mile and history of shipping …Marine City Architectural and Maritime Artifacts self-guided tours
Wineries: *Blue Water Winery and Vineyards & Old Town Hall Winery:* "Think Globally, Drink Locally!"
Train watching spot: from the Amtrak station you can see trains going in and out of the St. Clair River tunnel to Canada
While you're here in Blue Water Country, you can take a sportfishing, fly fishing, Chinook or bass fishing charter boat trip, go diving or take a scenic cruise, or just watch the Great Lakes ships go by.

Daniel Lockwood

The City of St. Clair has the longest fresh water boardwalk in the world.

X X-TRA STUFF

County fair: *St. Clair County Agricultural Society:* provides a valuable educational and entertaining experience for all those who attend by recognizing the accomplishments of the county youth through a wide variety of 4-H projects, Aug.
Famous people: …*Other*: Preston Thomas Tucker
Hospitals: Mercy Health, Port Huron, St. Clair Community, St. John River
Large employers: Port Huron Area School District, Port Huron Hospital, Detroit Edison (utilities), SEMCO Energy (natural gas), County of St. Clair, Mercy Health Hospital, U.S. Coast Guard, Visiocorp (makes glass products), International Automotive, St. Clair Community College

Daniel Lockwood

Algonac is the birthplace of Chris Crafts Boats and the former home of Gar Wood.

The St. Clair River carries more freighter traffic than the Suez and Panama Canals combined.

Y YESTERYEAR

Thomas Edison (1847-1931) moved with his family from Ohio to Port Huron when he was seven years old. He was a curious child who asked many questions (too many, according to his teacher) and as a 9-year-old he loved doing experiments from a chemistry book. When he was 12, he took a job with the Grand Trunk Railway selling newspapers, candy, sandwiches and peanuts on the train from Port Huron to Detroit. He even printed a newspaper, the first ever to be printed on a moving train. One day he saved the life of a young boy and the grateful father taught him how to tap messages on the telegraph key. From the time he left Michigan at age 16 to age 21, his main occupation was as a telegraph operator. Edison went on to patent over 1,000 inventions in his lifetime, including the electric light and the phonograph. worldbook See 77H.

Z ZOO & ANIMAL PLACES

…*Powder Puff Pacas:* alpacas, tailored tours

A AGRICULTURE

Land in farms: 65% of county
Number of farms: 1,030
Size of average farm: 210 acres
Market value of all products: #16 of 83 counties
Crops: ...most acres: corn
...highest $ sales: grains: corn, soybeans
Livestock: ...largest number: chickens for meat
...highest $ sales: milk & dairy products
Among the top Michigan counties:
- #1- seed corn production; see 78V
- #2- broiler chickens, potatoes, snap beans, sorghum for silage
- #3- all vegetables
- #5- corn for grain

Dairy, food and meat processing plants: 10
State ranking for harvested trees: #72 of 83 counties
FYI: St. Joseph County ranks third in the state for <u>vegetable</u> production with over 10,000 acres. Nationally, Michigan ranks 5th in the production of fresh vegetables and 9th in the production of vegetables for processing, producing 764,000 tons of almost 50 different vegetables. Of the 2,900 farms that grow vegetables in Michigan, the most acreage is devoted to cucumbers, snap beans, asparagus, sweet corn, carrots and squash, in that order. Some cucumbers, all tomatoes, asparagus and squash are hand picked.

The best place to get fresh vegetables is from your own garden. But if you're not a gardener, then make friends with the local farmers who attend the Farmers Markets or who sell directly from their farms. And if that's not possible, then for optimum nutrition choose fresh vegetables at the grocery store, then frozen veggies and make canned vegetable your last choice.

Michiganvegetablecouncil.org, USDA

Paul Jackson

From BIBLIOGRAPHY & NOTES...

All USDA numbers, in all categories, are rounded.

B BRIDGE OR BOAT

Michigan State Historic Preservation Office

MDOT Historic Bridge: built in 1887 of the finest white pine available, the Langley Bridge over the St. Joseph River in Lockport Twp. is 282' long, making it the longest remaining covered bridge in Michigan. The name honors a local pioneer family. It is still open to lighter weight vehicle traffic less than 7' in height.

C CELEBRATIONS

<u>Centerville</u> *Covered Bridge Days:* talent show, fireworks, parade, classic car show, June
<u>Colon</u> *Magic Festival:* everything magic, magic shows, lectures, tours, dealer showroom, July

Sturgis Journal

<u>Mendon</u> *Riverfest:* lip synch, Riverfest Idol, canoe race/swamp, duck race, millionaire club, Aug.

<u>Sturgis</u> *Ribs on the Runway:* July
<u>Three Rivers</u> *Water Festival:* parade, blue grass band, pie sales, ox roast, classic car show, June

D DEMOGRAPHICS

Population: 61,300	**Persons per sq. mile:** 122
Largest city: Sturgis	**Population:** 11,000
Largest township: Lockport	**Population:** 3,720
Largest village: Constantine	**Population:** 2,080

Median household income: $43,400
Owner-occupied median house value: $156,000
Persons affiliated with a religious congregation: 35%
Persons below poverty level: 17%
Students receiving school lunch subsidy: 47%

E ENVIRONMENT

At one time <u>prairies</u> covered about 150 square miles (96,000 acres) in the three southern tiers of Michigan counties. Prairies are eco-systems dominated by native grasses and wildflowers. In the past, prairies were kept healthy by frequent fires which cleared out the underbrush and stimulated the prairie plants. Less than 1% of the native prairies remain due to conversion to agriculture or having grown into forests due to the absence of wild fires. The preservation and replanting of prairies is just as important to the health

of the environment as is protecting wetlands. Many plants and animals depend on this environment for their survival. Prairie restoration is a long process that includes planting selected seeds, mowing, burning and weeding out invasive species. michiganwildlife. org, DNR

Alice Welch, USDA

F FLORA & FAUNA

NPCR-9

The prickly pear cactus can be found in West Michigan in dry sandy prairies, savannas and dunes. Though less than 12" in height with 2"-3" pads, their bristles have a hooked tip that clings tightly to whatever comes in contact with them.

Michigan Farm Bureau

There are 114 dragonfly species in Michigan and all live in or near fresh water. Often called "mosquito hawks," they feed on mosquitoes, midges, black flies and other small insects. They are some of the fastest, and prettiest, insects in the world.

G GOVERNMENT

County: ...created: 1829 **...organized:** 1829
...originally part of: Wayne County
Size: 332,000 acres / 504 sq. miles (72 of 83 counties)
The county has 2 cities, 6 villages, 16 townships 1 unincorporated community and 10 school districts.

Sarah Pion

NPCR

The St. Joseph County Courthouse, built in 1900, is the Romanesque Revival design that creates a commodious, well-lighted, solid building that echoes the justice and stability it represents.
County seat: Centreville
...Homestead property tax: 37 mills
Motto: <u>Colon</u>: *Magic Capital of the World*
...<u>Constantine</u>: *Seed Corn Capital of the World*!
...<u>Mendon</u>: *On the St. Joseph River*
...<u>River Country TC</u>: *For Family, Four Seasons, For Fun!*
...<u>Sturgis</u>: *Where Success is a Habit*

H HISTORICAL MARKERS 10 of 18

Chief Wahbememe Burial Site: a friend of the white settlers, he died in 1830 after running 150 miles from Detroit to warn the settlers in White Pigeon about an impending attack; in 1909 White Pigeon residents dedicated this giant, engraved boulder in his honor; see 78O

Angie Walton

Colon: Magic Capital of the World, began with the mail order Abbott Magic Novelty Company in 1933; see 78L

Harry Blackstone: 1885-1965, the world famous magician, lived in Colon

rszwed0312@aol.com

Three Rivers Historic District: well preserved Victorian streetscapes

Mottville Bridge: 1922, over the St. Joseph River, 270-foot long, triple-span reinforced concrete camelback bridge; now used for foot traffic only

Old Three Rivers Public Library: 1904, a Carnegie grant library, with mosaic skylight and Grecian columns in the entrance room

Sturges-Young Auditorium: 1955, Modernist design, local people gave money to spur construction

Sue Sillman House: 1870s, originally a blacksmith shop and residence; Ms. Sillman (d. 1945) was the Three Rivers librarian and historian for 42 years

Three Rivers: originally a favorite camping site for the American Indians; with the intersection of 3 rivers, it was a major inland shipping spot

U.S. Land Office: after the American Indians lost their lands to the U.S. in 1821, the government built this land office in 1831, selling 260,000 acres by 1834 for $1.25 an acre; it is the oldest remaining land office in Michigan

National Register of Historic Places: 15 listings
State Historic Sites: 32 listings

River County Tourism Council of St. Joseph County Michigan

I INFORMATION

Chamber of Commerce: Burr Oak, Sturgis, Three Rivers
Visitor: River Country Tourism Council, 800-447-2821, rivercountry.com

J JOKES

You know it's hot and sunny in Michigan when…
…the asphalt squishes under your feet.
…people are begging for a cloudy day.
…the morning glories refuse to open.
…the water hose cracks and gets rubbery.
…teenagers aren't wearing black.
…thoughts of winter are refreshing.
…it's just like Florida and people stay inside all day just to get out of the heat.

K KINSMAN

Race	Ancestry
American Indian: <1%	German: 29%
Asian: <1%	U.S./American: 15%
Black/African American: 3%	English: 10%
Hispanic or Latino: 7%	Irish: 8%
Other: 3%	Dutch: 5%
White: 88%	Polish: 4%

L LIGHTHOUSE OR LANDMARK

Sara Trattles

Abbott's Magic Manufacturing Company is the world's largest producer of magic paraphernalia. With 50,000 sq. feet of factory space, a retail store, an extensive online store, magic shows and conventions, Abbott's is also the world's top innovator in magical apparatus. This also means that Colon is the Magic Capital of the World. See 78H, 78M.

ⅿ MUSEUMS

Centerville *St. Joseph County Historical Society:* includes the U.S. Land Office Museum, Old Klesner Hotel Museum, preserving other historical sites

Colon *Historical Museum:* magic artifacts & displays

Constantine *Gov. John Barry Historical Society Museum:* in his local home

Nottawa *Stone School:* 1870, one room

Sturgis *Historical Society:* in the 1893 New York Central Railroad Depot

Three Rivers *W.R. Monroe:* traveling exhibits of national renown on science, history, culture

White Pigeon *Land Office:* part of the St. Joseph County Historical Society

Ⅳ NATURAL RESOURCES

Elevation: 700 - 900 feet
Physiography: rolling plains

Forest type: oak-hickory, maple-beech
Public/private forests: 20% of county

Water in county: 3% of county
  Lakes: 90
    ...largest: Lake Templane
  Rivers: Fawn, Prairie, Rocky, St. Joseph, Portage
  Rivers & streams: 290 miles

Growing season, avg.: 146 days (1-2 temp. zones)
  Last freeze, avg.: May 10
  First freeze, avg.: Oct. 5 – Oct. 10
Precipitation, annual avg.: rainfall: 34 inches
      snowfall: 46 inches
Temperature (F), avg.: January: high 31°, low 15°
      July: high 84°, low 60°
  Annual: >90°: 15 days, <0°: 9 days
Tornadoes (1930-2010): 12

NPCR

Ⓞ ORIGINS

Burr Oak:[v] many bur oak trees in the area; 1835

Centreville:[v] in the center of the county; 1831

Colon:[v,t] "...the lake and the river correspond exactly to the shape of a colon," the punctuation mark; 1832

Constantine:[v,t] in honor of Constantine the Great; 1828

Lockport:[t] early settlers' canal and water-power projects; 1836

Mendon:[v,t] early settlers from Mendon, MA, and Mendon, NY; 1829

Nottawa:[u,t] first settler was Wm. Nottram; American Indians were known as Nottawa-Seepes; 1836

St. Joseph:[co] named after the St. Joseph River which was named by French missionaries; see 78Y

Sturgis:[c,t] first settler, Judge John Sturgis; 1827

Three Rivers:[c] where the St. Joseph, Rocky and Portage Rivers meet; 1830

White Pigeon:[v,t] English translation of American Indian name to Chief White Pigeon, who gave his life to save the settlement; see 78H; 1827

Ⓟ PARKS

National: 0 **State:** 3 **County:** 7 **Local:** 16
Number of campsites: 1,800

State Game Area: (2,200 acres) Fabius Lake, Leidy Lake, Three Rivers

NPCR

County: *Cede Lake:* 50 acres, camping, swimming, fishing, boat rentals, hiking trails

...*Meyer Broadway:* 150 acres, trails, natural areas, rolling hills, woodlands, paved trail, sand volleyball, disc golf, tubing hills

...*Nottawa Park:* 12 acres, free public beach, boat launch, fishing, camping

...*Rawson's King Mill Park:* restored mill, trails, fishing, islands, wedding spot

Angie Walton

Ⓠ QUOTE FROM THE LOCALS

"There are a million and one reasons to visit River Country in St. Joseph County, MI. River Country in Southwestern Michigan offers a variety of sights and activities for all. Southwestern Michigan's River Country features six distinct rivers for your adventurous spirit. St. Joseph County, MI, is the place to go for a relaxing weekend of history, wine tasting, shopping and dining. St. Joseph County in Southwestern Michigan has beautiful parks, peaceful bed and breakfast inns and offers some of the best golf in the

state. Make your plans now to visit and experience the hidden treasures that can only be found in River Country of Southwestern Michigan!" ^{rivercountry.com}

R RECREATION & SPORTS

Auto racing: *Mottville Speedway:* ¼-mile, asphalt low banked oval track
Golf courses: 5
Horse racing: harness racing during fair week, Sept.

Michigan Heritage Water Trail: River Country

Public access sites: 18
Public recreational land: <1% of county

River County Tourism Council of St. Joseph County Michigan

S STATE OF MICHIGAN

Local planning commissioners and zoning boards of appeals are often called upon to make important decisions to guide the growth and development of their communities. Issues surrounding land use planning and regulation, and the tools and techniques available within Michigan to address them, have become increasingly complex. The Michigan State University Extension <u>Citizen Planner Program</u> was developed to address the basic, ongoing education needs of citizens appointed to serve on local land use planning bodies. The Citizen Planner Program's objective is to equip volunteer community leaders with the technical knowledge and leadership skills needed to perform their duties more effectively and responsibly. ^{citizenplanner.msu.edu}

T TRAVEL

Airport: Three Rivers
Bus: Greyhound
Distance to Lansing: 90 miles
Heritage Route: *Historic: US-12 Heritage Trail*, see 11T
Main roads: US-12, US-131, M-60, M-66, M-86, M-103, M-216
Memorial Highways: US-12, *Iron Brigade MH*: see 12T
…US-12, *Pulaski MH*: see 11T
FYI: US-131, St. Joseph County to Petoskey, and US-31, Petoskey to the Straits, has been called the Mackinac Trail.

U UNIVERSITIES & COLLEGES

Glen Oaks Community College: est. 1965, 1,400 students. Their philosophy is that an education is not only a privilege but also a right. Each and every person is entitled to the opportunity to develop his or her greatest potential. MCCAA, Vikings

V VARIETY

Terry Krull *Terry Krull*

Constantine is the Seed Corn Capital of the World and St. Joe County is the #1 seed corn county. Constantine and St. Joseph County produce over 10% of the nation's Seed Corn and the surrounding counties add another 10%. Seed corn production is a very controlled, seasonal, labor-intensive crop requiring hundreds of youth to detassel the corn plants. As a necessity of these very controlled growing conditions, this county has more acres under irrigation than any other county in the state. The young man in the picture is standing on an irrigator in a cornfield.

W WANDERLUST

Agri-tourism: *Corey Lake Orchards:* apples, strawberries, grapes, corn, tomatoes, U-pick
…*Nottawa Fruit Farm:* strawberries, blueberries, asparagus, corn, raspberries, bakery, wagon rides
Brewery: Fantail Brewing Company
Cultural: *Krasl Art Center:* where imagination and art fill your senses
Fall colors: middle October
Live theater: Riviera, Three Rivers Community Players
Amish Meander: there are 33 shops and stops on the tour; maps available from River Country Tourism Council

River Country Bus or Self-Guided Tours: step-on guide bus tours or get a map and drive yourself for these tours: Amish, Art, Bed & Breakfast Sight-Seeing, Bird Watching, Garden, Girlfriends Getaway, Historic Water Trails, Historical, Little Bit of Everything, Peddle, Shopaholics, Sports, Wine, Winter Wonderland

The area is home to several religious and spiritual centers including the Apple Farm Community, EarthSong Peace/Sound Chamber, The Fen Sanctuary for Women, GilChrist, The Hermitage and St. Gregory's Abbey.

X X-TRA STUFF

County fair: *St. Joseph County Grange Fair Association:* Sept.

Kelsey Maystead

Famous people: *…Entertainment:* Harry Blackstone Jr., Charles Collingwood, Verne Troyer *…Sports:* Matt Thornton

Hospitals: Sturgis, Three Rivers

Large employers: Morgan Olson (makes truck bodies), American Axle & Manufacturing, Three Rivers Health, Abbott Laboratories (makes baby food, food preparations), Wal-Mart, Oak Burr Tool (makes dies & tools), Meijer, Three Rivers Community Schools, Summit Polymers (makes thermoformed plastic products)

Y YESTERYEAR

"St. Joseph derives its name from the river which bisects the county, named by La Salle for the patron saint of New France. The region was occupied in prehistoric times by the "Mound Builders," and later, the Potawatomi and Miami Tribes. Pioneers were drawn to the area by the fertile prairie lands, which were well suited for agriculture. …Logging helped improve the land for agriculture and the first crop to be sown was wheat. Harvested crops were shipped via the St. Joseph River.

"Many historic trails and river trails cross here! These trails were used for centuries by Native American tribes, by the French adventurer LaSalle and the French trappers, by the English, and some now form the routes of our busiest highways. The Heritage Water Trail charts the course of these travelers along the mighty St. Joseph River." rivercountry.com

Z ZOO & ANIMAL PLACES

NPCR

Petting zoo: *Skidmore Park:* part of the Three Rivers Park system

Diamond D Ranch: horseback riding through woods and across streams

From the INDEX…

1,000 This notation indicates that the noted item is on the *1,000 Places To See Before You Die* list (and book of the same name) by Patricia Schultz.

A AGRICULTURE

Land in farms: 66% of county
Number of farms: 1,370
Size of average farm: 250 acres
Market value of all products: #12 of 83 counties
Crops: ...most acres: corn
...highest $ sales: grain: corn, soybeans, dry beans, wheat
Livestock: ...largest number: cattle & calves
...highest $ sales: milk & dairy products
Among the top Michigan counties:
- #1- daikon, emmer & spelt, horses sold, organic farms, other poultry
- #2- dry edible beans, sugarbeets
- #3- wheat
- #4- cucumbers & pickles, corn for grain

Dairy, food and meat processing plants: 12
State ranking for harvested trees: #78 of 83 counties
AgBioResearch Centers (MSU): *Saginaw Valley Research and Extension Center:* focuses on dry beans and sugarbeets to help keep Michigan as a top producer of these products
FYI: The U.S. is the world leader in <u>dry bean</u> production and Michigan grows more beans than any other state in the U.S. This county produces 20% of the state's beans. Dry beans are low in fat because, unlike soybeans, they have no oil in them. Over half of the Michigan dry bean crop of azuki, black turtle, cranberry, dark red kidney, great northern, light kidney, navy, pinto, small white and yellow eye beans, is exported. Navy beans make up 70% of the Michigan bean crop. See 79X.

Beans have the second highest source of protein (meat is first) and have more fiber than any other unprocessed food. The average American eats over 6 pounds a year of this highly nutritious food. Don't forget that as a protein, beans are a meat substitute and can substantially stretch your food dollar. Always eat beans with a grain product to make a complete protein meal. Cultures around the world know this and that is why bean soup and corn bread or refried beans and corn tortillas go so well together. ^{MDA,} Michigan Bean Commision

B BRIDGE OR BOAT

Elizabeth Metz

The pedestrian Chippewa Bridge in Chippewa Landing Park in Caro crosses over the Cass River with connecting trails throughout the park. There is even a Labor Day Bridge Walk.

C CELEBRATIONS

<u>Caro</u> *Cars, Crafts & Bikes:* June

Thumb Area Tourism Council, Inc.

...150 Winter Fest & Snowmobile Races: ice carving, horse-drawn wagon rides, fireworks; variety of snowmobile races at the Fairgrounds

<u>Fairgrove</u> *Michigan Bean Festival:* Bean Queen, tractor pull, bean creations contest, off-road demolition derby, parade, free bean soup, homemade pie, Sept.

<u>Mayville</u> *Sunflower Festival:* bump & run, garden tractor pull, parade, fireworks, saloon, July

<u>Tuscola County</u> *Pumpkin Festival:* sells over 4,000 pumpkin pies; bean soup give-away, parade, Pumpkin Festival Royal Court of giant pumpkins, decorating contests, arts & craft show, Oct.

Thumb Area Tourism Council, Inc.

D DEMOGRAPHICS

Population: 55,700   **Persons per sq. mile:** 69
Largest city: Caro   **Population:** 3,240
Largest township: Vassar   **Population:** 4,090
Largest village: Cass City   **Population:** 2,430
Median household income: $38,900
Owner-occupied median house value: $117,000
Persons affiliated with a religious congregation: 43%
Persons below poverty level: 16%
Students receiving school lunch subsidy: 41%

E ENVIRONMENT

Some cities in Michigan have <u>floodplain</u> regulations. A floodplain is the area adjacent to a river, creek, lake, stream, or other open waterway that is subject to flooding when there is significant rain. The City of Vassar has such regulations because of its proximity to the Cass River. The city allows building within a 100-year floodplain providing the lowest floor elevation of the building is at least one foot above the 100-year floodplain plan. In addition, there are special floodplain provisions in the building, electrical, mechanical and plumbing codes. There are also flood-proofing standards for some remodeling projects for homes and businesses. cityofvassar.org

F FLORA & FAUNA

Elizabeth Motz

In the 1800s, cork pine, the finest variety of white pine trees, grew along the Cass River. It was called cork pine because when it was cut and put into the river, it floated high in the water like a cork. In those days, the trees were 150' tall and 36"-48" in diameter. The wood was light and strong and easy to work with.

USFWS

Yellow perch have the distinction of being the most frequently caught game fish in Michigan. This delicious fish, 4"-10" in length, is found in all the Great Lakes and is particularly abundant in the Saginaw Bay.

G GOVERNMENT

County: ...created: 1840   **...organized:** 1850
...originally part of: Saginaw County
Size: 523,000 acres / 813 sq. miles (20 of 83 counties)
The county has 2 cities, 9 villages, 23 townships with 1 as a charter township, 24 unincorporated communities and 9 school districts.

Michigan State Historic Preservation Office

The Tuscola County Courthouse, built in 1933, is Art Deco style and is faced with Indiana limestone.
County seat: Caro
...Homestead property tax: 42 mills
Motto: <u>Caro</u> Chamber: *Growing ...to serve you better*
...<u>Cass City</u>: *each step in the right direction*
...<u>Reese</u>: *Gateway to the Thumb: come grow with us*
...<u>Unionville</u>: *The Gateway to the Thumb*
...<u>Vassar</u>: *The Cork Pine City; see 79F*

H HISTORICAL MARKERS 8 of 21

Frakenhilf: 1849, this German settlement became Richville for the fertile farmlands of the area.
Indian Dave: 1803-1909, the last Chippewa Indian to live traditionally in Tuscola County

Peninsular Sugar Refining Company: 1898, after the trees had been logged and the land cleared, it was found that the soil and climate were just right for growing sugarbeets; the state legislature offered a bounty of 1¢ per pound of sugar produced for farmers to start growing sugarbeets.

State Reward Road #1: 1905, the first mile of road improvements that met state standards was given state aid of $500 for the $985 project.

Trinity Episcopal Church: 1880, board and batten Gothic Revival design

Tuscola County Advertiser: award-winning newspaper publishing since 1868

Vassar's Logging Era: named after the man who founded Vassar College; after logging came agriculture and manufacturing

Watrous General Store: 1860s, Aaron Watrous built this store, now the museum of the Watrousville-Caro Area Historical Society

National Register of Historic Places: 13 listings

State Historic Sites: 49 listings

I INFORMATION

Chamber of Commerce: Caro, Cass City, Reese, Vassar

Visitor: Thumb Area Tourism Council, 989-672-0323, thumbtourism.org

J JOKES

You might be a Michigan farmer's son if…

…you learned to drive the tractor before the car.

…helping at the birth of foals, calves, lambs and piglets is doing what comes naturally.

…everything you ever learned about leadership you learned through FFA [formerly Future Farmers of America].

…your idea of a family vacation is to go camping at the county fairgrounds during fair week so you can be close to your animals.

…you've been a 4-H member all your life.

…you think the silly refrain "Beans, beans, the musical fruit…" is bad for business.

…"sowing your wild oats" sounds like just another chore around the farm Dad wants you to do.

K KINSMAN

Race	Ancestry
American Indian: <1%	German: 34%
Asian: <1%	English: 10%
Black/African American: 1%	Polish: 8%
Hispanic or Latino: 3%	U.S./American: 8%
Other: 2%	Irish: 8%
White: 96%	French: 6%

L LIGHTHOUSE OR LANDMARK

The Thumb Octagon Barn was built in 1924. It has 8 sides, each 42 feet long and 24 feet high, giving it 8,600 square feet on the floor and 5,700 square feet in the loft. Since 1995, it has been under restoration and is now the Thumb Octagon Barn Agricultural Museum. You'll find it just east of Gagetown. Tours are available.

M MUSEUMS

<u>Caro</u> *Roadhouse Museum:* in a building that was probably built in 1859

…*Watrousville Museum:* the last 1864 Lincoln Flag Pole in the U.S.; providing local history

<u>Gagetown</u> *Thumb Octagon Barn Agricultural Museum:* see 79L

<u>Kingston</u> *Depot*

Mayville *Area Museum:* in an old railroad depot, regional artifacts, furnished log cabin, one-room school house

NPCR

N NATURAL RESOURCES

Elevation: <600 - 900 feet
Physiography: lake-border plains, rolling plains

Forest type: maple-beech-hemlock, aspen-birch, elm-ash-cottonwood
Public/private forests: 22% of county

Water in county: <1% of county
  Bay: Saginaw
  Lakes: 20   **...largest:** Fish Point
  Rivers: Cass, Quanicassee (kwahn icka SEE)
  Rivers & streams: 180 miles

Great Lakes peninsula: Thumb
Great Lakes shoreline: 20 miles of Lake Huron

Growing season, avg.: 122 days (4 temp. zones)
  Last freeze, avg.: May 5 – May 20
  First freeze, avg.: Sept. 30 – Oct. 15
Precipitation, annual avg.: rainfall: 28 inches
                    snowfall: 37 inches
Temperature (F), avg.: January: high 29°, low 13°
                    July: high 84°, low 57°
  Annual: >90°: 15 days, **<0°:** 14 days
Tornadoes (1930-2010): 17

O ORIGINS

Akron:[v] after Akron, OH; 1854
Caro:[c] after Cairo, Egypt; 1847
Cass City:[v] territorial governor, Lewis Cass; 1851
Fairgrove:[v] a grove of trees; 1837
Gagetown:[v] mill and storeowner, Joseph Gage; 1869
Kingston:[v] first settler, Alanson King; 1857
Mayville:[v] unknown origin; 1860
Millington:[v] from the early mills along the creek; 1857
Reese:[v] Mr. Reese got the railroad through here; 1865
Tuscola:[co] probably a name invented by Henry Schoolcraft from root words that may mean "level lands" [wikipedia]

Unionville:[v] first settler from Union, OH; 1854
Vassar:[c] Matthew Vassar was a relative of one of the town founders; 1849; see 79H
Watrousville: mill owner, village platter and first postmaster, Aaron Watrous; 1851

P PARKS

National: 0   **State:** 8   **County:** 2   **Local:** 15
Number of campsites: 180
State Game Areas: (26,000 acres) Cass City, Deford, Gagetown, Murphy Lake, Tuscola, Vassar.

State Wildlife Area: *Fish Point:*[ww] 3,000 acres, called "Chesapeake of the Midwest" due to migratory birds; observation tower, wildlife viewing trails

Elizabeth Motz

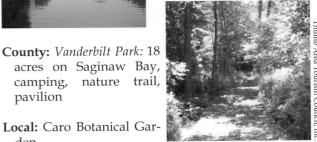

Thumb Area Tourism Council, Inc.

...*Quanicassee:*[ww] (kwahn icka SEE) on Saginaw Bay at the mouth of the Quanicassee River

County: *Vanderbilt Park:* 18 acres on Saginaw Bay, camping, nature trail, pavilion

Thumb Area Tourism Council, Inc.

Local: Caro Botanical Garden
...*Cass City Recreational Park:* 82 acres, urban park

Q QUOTE FROM THE LOCALS

"Wildly famous for its cork pine and fertile farmland, the area has served all of its inhabitants well through time. Today, it's one of the country's most productive and valuable sources of dry beans and sugarbeets. So what attracts people to Caro? Its location is right on M-81. Despite its rural surroundings, Caro is only 30 minutes from Saginaw, 45 minutes from Flint and well under two hours from Detroit. Caro is truly in a strategic location for businesses looking to expand

their operations to a less expensive location, yet one that offers direct routes to the major industrial centers of Michigan. Lake Huron surrounds the peninsula that Caro is located on and many fine fishing spots can be found in the area. Caro maintains and prides itself in having a small town feeling and friendly atmosphere and low crime rates, compared to its larger neighbors and a slower pace of life – a Norman Rockwell feel, but with the modern amenities." carochamber.org

R RECREATION & SPORTS

Golf courses: 7
Great Lakes marinas: 4   **Boat slips:** 260
Hiking/skiing/mountain biking trails: 3 miles
Horse racing: harness racing during fair week, July
Michigan Heritage Water Trail: Tip of the Thumb
Public access sites: 7
Public recreational land: 6% of county
Rail-trail: (5 miles) Southern Links

NPCR

S STATE OF MICHIGAN

In 1937, *My Michigan* was designated as the official State Song. But just because it was official didn't make it memorable. Even in 2000, the people in the state government who are supposed to know about these things were confused. That song is under copyright and cannot be printed here or anywhere. What the people remember and like is *Michigan, My Michigan*, sung to the tune of *O Tannenbaum*. There have been three versions: 1862, 1886 and 1902. Wikipedia says the 1902 version is the most popular. So this is the official "unofficial state song of Michigan." DNRE, Wikipedia

A song to thee, fair State of mine,
    Michigan, my Michigan.
But greater song than this is thine,
    Michigan, my Michigan.
The thunder of the inland sea,
The whisper of the towering tree,
United in one grand symphony,
    Michigan, my Michigan.
        I sing a song of all the best-
            Michigan, my Michigan.
        I sing a State with riches blessed-

Michigan, my Michigan.
Thy mines unmask a hidden store,
But richer thy historic lore,
More great the love thy builders bore,
    Michigan, my Michigan.
Glow fair the bosom of thy lakes,
    Michigan, my Michigan.
What melody each river makes,
    Michigan, my Michigan.
As to thy lake thy rivers tend,
Thy exiled ones still to thee send,
Devotion that shall never end,
    Michigan, my Michigan.
        Rich in wealth that makes a State,
            Michigan, my Michigan.
        Great in the things that make men great,
            Michigan, my Michigan.
        Eager the voice the sounds thy claim,
        Under the golden roll of Fame,
        Willing the hand that writes the name,
            Michigan, my Michigan.

NPCR

T TRAVEL

Airport: Tuscola Area Airport Authority
Circle Tour: Lake Huron via M-25
Distance to Lansing: 90 miles
Heritage Route: *Recreation:* M-15, Pathway to Family Fun, see 9T
Main roads: M-15, M-24, M-25, M-46, M-81, M-138
Memorial Highways: M-81, Veterans of Foreign Wars
Scenic Drive: Port Huron to Tawas City via M-25 …Bay City to Ortonville via M-15

U UNIVERSITIES & COLLEGES

None

Don't forget to check the *BIBLIOGRAPHY & NOTES* at the back of the book for explanations and additional information.

V VARIETY

SENATE NAVY BEAN SOUP

This traditional soup has been on the lunch menu every day on Capitol Hill in Washington, D.C., in both the House and Senate restaurants for over 100 years.

Soak 1 lb. (2 cups) of dry Navy Beans in 6 cups of water for 8 hours or overnight in the refrigerator. Drain and rinse.

In large stockpot add: 8 cups cold water
 the soaked Navy Beans
 1½ lbs. ham hocks or meaty ham bone

Slowly bring to boil and simmer (covered) for 1 hour.

Stir in: 1 c. chopped onion
 2 garlic cloves, minced
 1 c. chopped celery
 2/3 c. instant potato flakes or 1½ c. mashed potatoes
 ¼ c. fresh parsley, chopped
 1 tsp. pepper
 1 tsp. nutmeg
 1 tsp. oregano
 1 tsp. basil
 1 bay leaf

Simmer (covered) until tender.

Remove bone and trim off ham. Put ham back in soup. Remove bay leaf.

Makes 3 quarts or 12, 1-cup servings. Michigan Bean Commission

W WANDERLUST

Fall colors: early October

X X-TRA STUFF

County fair: *Tuscola County Fair Assoc.:* July

Famous people: ...*Politics:* Murray Van Wagoner
...*Sports:* Heidi Androl, Leland Stanford "Larry" MacPhail, Sr.
...*Other:* Brewster Shaw

Hospitals: Caro Community, Hills & Dales General

Large employers: Tuscola County, Michigan Department of Community Health, Wolverine Human Services (consulting), Wal-Mart, Grede Foundries (iron castings), TI Group Automotive Systems (tests auto equipment)

Caro is the home of the first ethanol plant in Michigan.

FYI: At the end of the 1800s, navy beans were raised entirely by hand labor with one farmer planting one to five acres. The seed was unreliable, no fertilizer was used, and rain and insects were always an unknown factor. The beans were harvested either by pulling them up by hand, cutting them off with a sharp hoe, or cutting them off with a sickle. They were then taken to the barn where they were threshed during the winter. Some farmers used flails, while others let horses walk over them to break the pods so the seeds could be removed. In 1908, a mechanical harvester was invented and after that a special bean thresher. In 1899 Tuscola County produced 72,000 bushels of beans and 20 years later produced 355,000 bushels. The 2007 harvest was 3 million bushels. See 79A. Gerard Schultz (V), USDA

Y YESTERYEAR

"When the first white settlers came to the Thumb, it was still a dark, almost impenetrable forest wilderness with numerous swamps and with water courses clogged with logs and brush. The land was covered with a dense growth of white pine, oak, hemlock, maple, cedar, beech and a variety of other trees. Some of the best Michigan pine was found in this area. Here the tall, magnificent pine forest was from 100 to 300 years old. Here white pine trees were 125 to 170 feet tall with trunks two to five feet in diameter. In some places the forest was so dense that it completely obscured the sun. At other places the wind had at one time felled all the trees that were spread over the ground in confusion. Many windfalls were seven or eight feet high and were covered with moss nearly a foot in thickness." In 1820 Gov. Lewis Cass said that this area would never be of any importance and it was not worth the expense of surveying it. Gerard Schultz (V)

NPCR

NPCR

Z ZOO & ANIMAL PLACES

Watchable Wildlife Viewing Areas:ww see 79P

A AGRICULTURE

Land in farms: 46% of county
Number of farms: 1,200
Size of average farm: 150 acres
Market value of all products: #9 of 83 counties
Crops: ...most acres: corn
...highest $ sales: grains: corn, soybeans
Livestock: ...largest number: hogs & pigs
...highest $ sales: milk & dairy products
Among the top Michigan counties:
- #1- acres of all berries, bell peppers, blueberries, cranberries, cauliflower, other greenhouse vegetables & herbs, sorghum for grain, watercress
- #2- grapes, nuts, strawberries
- #3- greenhouse tomatoes, sales of vegetables

Dairy, food and meat processing plants: 32
State ranking for harvested trees: #51 of 83 counties

FYI: Van Buren County farmers grow black-berries, <u>blueberries</u> (tame and wild), cranberries, currants, raspberries and strawberries. They are the #1 blueberry county (8,600 acres) in the #1 blueberry state (21,800 acres) that grows one-third of all the blueberries in the U.S. Half the crop is eaten fresh and the other half is processed. Blueberries need sandy, acidic soil, cool weather and irrigation to do well. The blueberry-harvesting season is mid-July to late September, so blueberries are readily available in farm markets throughout the area. All berries that are sold fresh are hand picked. MDA, USDA, Michigan Blueberries Asso.

Michigan Farm Bureau

<u>Cranberries</u> have similar soil needs to blueberries so they do well in southwest Michigan, although there

Bob DeGrandchamp

are cranberry farms in the U.P. too. Total acreage is only about 300 acres. Some cranberry fields are flooded to harvest the berries that will be made into cranberry sauce. But to sell the cranberries fresh they have to be harvested dry.

B BRIDGE OR BOAT

Sarah J. Pion

The Black River Covered Bridge is on the Kal-Haven Trail just 1 mile from the end of the trail in South Haven. It is 120' feet long and was built in 1988 by the Michigan Civilian Conservation Corps.

C CELEBRATIONS

NPCR

<u>Bangor</u> *Apple Harvest Festival:* parade, car show, golf, bike ride, quilt show, arts & crafts fair, Sept.

<u>Hartford</u> *Strawberry Festival:* parade, car and motorcycle show, strawberry bake-off, strawberry pie eating contest, music, food, arts & crafts, June

<u>Paw Paw</u> *Wine & Harvest Festival:* "A Grape Time for Everyone;" wine tours and tasting, grape stomp, car show, midway, fireworks, Sept.

Abbey Dorr

Abbey Dorr

<u>South Haven</u> *National Blueberry Festival:* Highbush Blueberry Capital, blueberry pancakes & bakeoff, parade, fish boil dinner, art shows, pageants, Aug.

D DEMOGRAPHICS

Population: 76,300   **Persons per sq. mile:** 125
Largest city: South Haven (partial) **Population:** 4,400
Largest township: Antwerp   **Population:** 8,200
Largest village: Paw Paw   **Population:** 3,530
Median household income: $41,700
Owner-occupied median house value: $125,000
Persons affiliated with a religious congregation: 31%
Persons below poverty level: 17%
Students receiving school lunch subsidy: 47%

E ENVIRONMENT

The World's Water
- 97.5% of the water on Earth is salty.
- 2.5% of the water on Earth is fresh.
- about two-thirds of the fresh water is frozen
- about one-third of the fresh water is liquid surface water and groundwater [.008 of the world's water]

The Great Lakes contain 20% of the Earth's fresh, unfrozen water. Is it no wonder that taking care of this valuable resource has to be a top priority, not only here in Van Buren County and Michigan, but it must be a world-wide priority too. National Geographic

Desalination is the process where salt and other chemicals are removed from saline water (oceans) and made suitable for human consumption and crop irrigation. There are various processes used around the world in 14,000 desalination plants, but all methods are rather expensive and limited in capacity. Some day technology may provide the answer to limited fresh water supplies, but in the meantime, conservation and re-use of fresh water is the best answer to a freshwater shortage in some parts of the world.

F FLORA & FAUNA

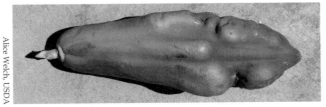

The pawpaw fruit is in the tropical custard apple family and resembles a short, fat banana and grows in this area. Its flavor is a combination of banana, mango and pineapple tastes.

The Cooper's hawk is somewhat common in southern Michigan and likes to live near forests. You may see them along roads, next to clearings and near stream or lake edges.

G GOVERNMENT

County: ...**created:** 1829 ...**organized:** 1837
...**originally part of:** Cass County
Size: 399,000 acres / 611 sq. miles (35 of 83 counties)
The county has 4 cities, 7 villages, 18 townships with 1 as a charter township and 12 school districts.

County seat: Paw Paw
...**Homestead property tax:** 48 mills
Motto: Decatur: *Live, Work and Play in Decatur, a Friendly Community*
...Hartford: *Working Together*
...Mattawan: *Rural living at its best*
...Paw Paw: *Uncork Paw Paw – A Village to Discover: Friendly, Familiar, Nearby*

H HISTORICAL MARKERS 12 of 20

Covert Library: 1871, this general store was the first commercial building in town; it is now the library
Decatur Township Hall: 1901, Georgian Revival brick and stone structure; now houses a museum
Hamilton Grange Hall: 1875, hosted elections, rallies, school programs, church services, funerals, lectures, parties; now Hamilton Township Hall

Haven Peaches: developed by Michigan State University from 1924–1963, 8 yellow-fleshed freestone varieties were selected from 21,000 crossbred seedlings. One of them, the Red Haven peach, is now the most widely planted freestone peach variety in the world.

HAVEN PEACHES

The Haven peach varieties were developed here by Michigan State University's South Haven Experiment Station, under the direction of Professor Stanley Johnston. From 1924 to 1963, eight yellow-fleshed freestone varieties were selected from more than 21,000 cross-bred seedlings. They were named Halehaven, Kalhaven, Redhaven, Fairhaven, Sunhaven, Richhaven, Glohaven, and Cresthaven. Redhaven was

Abbey Dorr

Houppert Winery: successful 1900s winery burned in 1940, was rebuilt, but never recovered financially; building is now a community center and museum.

Liberty Hyde Bailey: (1858-1954) the world-famous botanist and horticulturist was born in South Haven when it was a wilderness; he established the nation's first horticultural laboratory at Michigan State University. See 80M.

Paw Paw Public Library: 1920, a Carnegie grant library; now a community center

Scott Club: 1892, a clubhouse for a ladies' reading circle and literary and antiquarian societies; sandstone Queen Anne style

Territorial Road: sometimes the Dodge Tavern in Paw Paw was so crowded that some weary travelers "offered a dollar for a post to lean on."

Van Buren County: • 1829: platted and named for one of Andrew Jackson's cabinet members
  • 1830s: early settlers came for the lumber
  • 1837: Paw Paw chosen as county seat
  • 1860s: thriving fruit industry
  • 1903: monumental Classic Revival county courthouse was dedicated

NPCR

Van Buren County Poorhouse: 1884, home for the indigent and mentally retarded; able-bodied residents worked on the farm; now the County Historical Museum; see 80M

Warner Wine Haus: 1898, was a city waterworks station, now restored and remodeled as a tourist and education center

National Register of Historic Places: 6 listings
State Historic Sites: 29 listings

I INFORMATION

Chamber of Commerce: Decatur, Paw Paw, South Haven
Visitor: South Haven/Van Buren County Convention & Visitors Bureau, 800-SO-HAVEN, southhaven.org
…Southwestern Michigan Tourist Council, 269-925-7540, swmich.org

J JOKES

It's a good day at the beach in Michigan when…
…the water is warm enough for an adult to go swimming.
…you forgot your sweatshirt, but it didn't make any difference.
…you found a parking spot.
…the sand didn't burn your feet.
…sitting on the beach reminds you of your last Caribbean vacation.
…it's September, it's still warm and there are no crowds.
…the black flies, the bees and the alewives decided to stay home.
…the 'shock value' of the water is tolerable.
…you know all water is warm, "once you get used to it."
…you brought your own "portable shade units."
…you stuck it out all day and the sunset was beautiful.

NPCR

NPCR

K KINSMAN

Race
American Indian: <1%
Asian: <1%
Black/African American: 5%
Hispanic or Latino: 10%
Other: 4%
White: 88%

Ancestry
German: 20%
U.S./American: 10%
Irish: 9%
English: 9%
Dutch: 8%
Polish: 5%

L LIGHTHOUSE OR LANDMARK

South Haven Visitors Bureau

The South Haven Light was built in 1872 on the south pier and still welcomes boats as they come into the harbor of the Black River. Visitors are welcome for a stroll on the pier in any weather conditions except high winds and high waves. Lives have been lost when unsuspecting visitors were swept off the pier.

M MUSEUMS

Bangor *Don Cleveland Antique Auto Museum:* autos, tools, tractors, horse-drawn carriages

…*Foster Trophy Collection:* get up close and personal with (stuffed) exotic animals

Bloomingdale *Depot Museum:* oil, rail, lumber, local heritage, old iron toys, miniature train display

Covert *Historical Museum:* preserving the past for the future, education and enjoyment

South Haven *Historical Association of South Haven:* in the Hartman School building; archives, programs, publications

…*Liberty Hyde Bailey Museum:* America's Father of Modern Horticulture; the museum is on the farm where he was raised (now in downtown South Haven); the farm served as an open-air scientific arboretum that was the beginning of his work in botany, education, environmentalism and horticulture; see 80H

Liberty Hyde Bailey Museum

City of South Haven

…*Michigan Flywheelers Museum:* dedicated to the restoration and preservation of antique gas and steam engines

…*Michigan Maritime Museum:* commemorates the rich maritime heritage of the Great Lakes State

Van Buren County *Historical Society:* in the 1884 county poorhouse; includes one-room school, general store, period products; see 80H

N NATURAL RESOURCES

Elevation: <600 - 900 feet
Physiography: hill-lands

Soil: Fine Sandy Loam
 Depth: 9-12"
 Color: brownish gray
 Type: very fine sandy loam, homogenous texture
 Details: surface is lightly undulating with rolling drainage that varies with local topography
 Sub-soil: brown or yellow fine sand up to 24" deep overlying clay; no gravel in soil or sub soil
 Agriculture: very good for apples, pears and grapes, and also beans, potatoes and beets
 NOTE: soil types are not limited to any one county.

Forest type: oak-hickory, maple-beech
Public/private forests: 31% of county
Legislatively protected sand dunes: 1,850 acres

Water in county: 2% of county
 Lakes: 120   **…largest:** Saddle
 Rivers: Black, Paw Paw
 Rivers & streams: 320 miles

Great Lakes shoreline: 13 miles of Lake Michigan (#36 of 36 counties with Great Lake shorelines)

Growing season, avg.: 168 days (#4/MI) (2-3 temp. zones)
    Last freeze, avg.: May 5 – May 10
    First freeze, avg.: Oct. 5 – Oct. 15
Precipitation, annual avg.: rainfall: 35 inches
                  snowfall: 60 inches
Temperature (F), avg.: January: high 32°, low 18°
              July: high 79°, low 61°
    Annual: >90°: 4 days, **<0°:** 4 days
Tornadoes (1930-2010): 19

O ORIGINS

Bangor:[c,t] after Bangor, Maine; 1837
Bloomingdale:[v,t] a blooming valley; 1855
Breedsville:[v] first settler and sawmill builder, Silas Breed; 1835
Decatur:[v,t] in honor of naval hero, Stephen Decatur; 1847
Gobles:[c] first hotel builder, John Gobles; 1865
Hartford:[c,t] first settler wanted it named after Hartland, NY, but there was already a Hartland, MI; 1837
Lawrence:[v,t] named after the township; 1835
Lawton:[v] Nathan Lawton gave 10 acres to get a railroad station built on his land; 1848
Mattawan:[v] after Mattawan, NY; 1845
Paw Paw:[v] the paw paw fruit growing on the banks of the Paw Paw River; 1832
South Haven:[c,ct] south of Grand Haven; 1831
Van Buren:[co] Martin Van Buren, Secretary of State and later Vice President under President Andrew Jackson

P PARKS

National: 0 **State:** 5 **County:** 1 **Local:** 16
Number of campsites: 1,900
State Game Area: Keeler
State Linear Park: *Kal-Haven Trail:*[ww] a 34-mile, old rail trail between Kalamazoo and South Haven
…*Van Buren Trail State Park:* 14-mile multi-use trail between South Haven and Hartford

Abbey Dorr   NPCR

State Park: *Van Buren:* 400 acres, high sand dunes and a 1-mile sandy beach on Lake Michigan, camping
State Underwater Preserve: *Southwest Michigan:* see 3P
County: *North Point Conservation Area:* 17 acres, on Lake Michigan, forested critical dunes, wetlands

Other: *Algrid Barvicks Dunes Nature Sanctuary:* 40 acres, moving dune covered by luxuriant ferns, oaks, jack pine, pin and sand cherries

Jeptha Lake Fen Preserve: 49 acres, spring-fed fen with high quality wetlands, wet forest, flowers
Ross Preserve: 1,400 acres, coastal plain marsh, sand dunes, wooded inland dunes, wetlands, small lakes, northern hardwood forest, Nature Center
Sarett Nature Center: 5 miles of trails, special programs

Q QUOTE FROM THE LOCALS

"Van Buren County is known as the fruit basket of Michigan. The growing season opens with asparagus harvest in May and closes in the fall with apples and grapes. The Lawton, Porter and Paw Paw area is the grape capital of the County with each accommodating the fruit processors and wineries. Bangor, Bloomingdale, Hartford and Lawrence grow premium peaches and apples; Keeler has extensive strawberry beds, Hamilton produces acres of pickling cucumbers and the large blueberry plantations are located in Columbia and Geneva.

"Though …it is known as an agricultural county, suburbia is invading its borders. Population increases [show] the East side is the growth area and the County's location on the Lake Michigan shoreline indicates the trend of increased tourism." [vbco.org]

R RECREATION & SPORTS

Auto racing: *Ginger Man Raceway:* 1.9-mile road course with 11 turns
…*Hartford Motor Speedway:* ½-mile oval clay track
Golf courses: 7
Great Lakes marinas: 25
  Boat slips: 1,000

Hiking/skiing/mountain biking trails: 30 miles

Michigan Heritage Water Trail: Bangor/South Haven
Public access sites: 28
Public recreational land: <1% of county
Rail-trail: (30 miles) Kal-Haven Trail Sesquicentennial State Park, Van Buren Trail State Park
Recreational harbor: South Haven Marina
State-funded snowmobile trails: 30 miles
Timber Ridge: skiing, snowboarding, tubing, lessons
Deerlick Creek Park & Beach: a designated trout and smelt dipping stream

NPCR

S STATE OF MICHIGAN

Paul Jackson

Since 1897, the Apple Blossom, the beautiful and fragrant springtime flower of the apple tree, has been the State Flower. It reminds us of the important part apples are to our health and our economy.

T TRAVEL

Airport: South Haven Regional
Amtrak: Bangor
Bus: Indian Trails
Circle Tour: Lake Michigan via US 31
County road names:
  …**north/south:** numbered Streets
  …**east/west:** numbered Avenues
Distance to Lansing: 85 miles
Historic Harbortowns: Michigan Maritime Museum
Heritage Route: *Historic: US-12 Heritage Trail,* see 11T
Main roads: US-31, I-94, I-196, M-40, M-43, M-51, M-140, M-152
Memorial Highways: US-31, *Blue Star MH:* see 3T
Scenic Drive: *Dunes Parkway:* along Blue Star Highway in Covert Township

U UNIVERSITIES & COLLEGES

None

V VARIETY

City of South Haven

The beach at South Haven is a wonderful way to spend a summer day. The fine sand, the summer sun, the pier, the water and waves, Lake Michigan as far as the eye can see, the boats and the boardwalk into town all add to the ambience of a delightful day at the beach. Don't forget your suntan lotion!

W WANDERLUST

Agri-tourism: *Apple-A-Day Farm:* U-pick, large variety of apples, cherries
…*Barden's Farm Market:* strawberries, sweet corn, cut flowers, beans, peppers, hanging baskets
…*Big Dan's U-pick 'em & Farm Market:* apples, cider, peaches, pumpkins, squash, wagon rides
…*Gene The Pumpkin Man:* pumpkins, pumpkin butter, pumpkin honey, Indian corn, straw
…*Krohne's Last Stand:* asparagus, strawberries
…*Leduc Blueberries:* more delicious blueberries

...Schultz Fruitridge Farms: U-pick, apples, cider, asparagus, grapes, honey, peaches, fruit salsas

...True Blue Farms: blueberries, of course!

Brewery: Old Hat Brewery & Grill

Cultural: South Haven Center for the Arts

Fall colors: middle October

Live theater: Foundry Hall, Our Town Players, Paw Paw Village Players

Walking tour: *South Haven Harborwalk:* self-guided tour of 12 interpretive historical markers along the Black River

Abbey Dorr

Wineries: *St. Julian Wine Company:* Michigan's oldest and largest winery

...Warner Vineyards: Wine Haus, wine tasting, champagnes, juices

Blueberry Store: everything blueberries, all the time

Blue Coast Artists: travel the scenic Blue Star Hwy. and back roads between South Haven and Saugatuck to experience behind-the-scenes look at working artists in their studios

Abbey Dorr

Lakeshore Harvest Country: a trail of farms, farm markets, quilt trail; bet. between Saugatuck & South Haven

X X-TRA STUFF

County fair: *Van Buren County Youth Fair Association:* July

Famous people: *...Entertainment*: Edgar Bergen & Charlie McCarthy

...Sports: Jason Babin, Noah Herron

Hospitals: Lakeview Community, South Haven Community

Large employers: MPI Research (commercial physical research), Lakeview Continuing Care (skilled nursing), Entergy Nuclear Palisades (nuclear power plant), Coca-Cola (fruit juices), AFL Automotive (makes auto parts), Lakeview Community Hospital, Welch Foods (food processor-juice, frozen fruits & vegetables)

Y YESTERYEAR

The Michigan One-Room Schoolhouse Association has in their database a listing of over 7,000 <u>one-room</u> <u>schoolhouses</u> in Michigan. Van Buren County alone had almost 200 schools. Today fewer than 2,000 schoolhouses remain throughout the state and most of these have been converted to private residences although some are antique shops and art galleries. Many one-room schoolhouses can be found in the Historic Villages that are common throughout the state. There are 120 schools that are used as museums or offer 'Day in a One-Room School' programs.

Many schools were still functional in the 1950s and 1960s, but today statewide, there are only about 20 active one-room schools.

The architectural style of these schools and the materials used to build them vary widely depending on the skills of the local people who did the construction and the available natural resources. But what they had in common is generally they

NPCR-2

were one room, with one teacher for first grade through eighth grade. Fifty students in a school were not uncommon. Typically, the teacher may have spent 10 minutes per subject, per grade, per day. Students helped each other learn. Recitation was important, as books and paper were limited in most schools.

The teacher and the students did all the chores needed to keep the school operational. Things like cleaning the building, keeping the fire going and the stove working properly, obtaining water by pumping it, drawing it from the well, or hauling it from the stream and cleaning the outhouse (if there was one), were daily activities.

As you travel around the state, be on the lookout for these symbols of yesteryear. Generally they are almost square, are somewhat taller than a traditional house, may have an enclosed entryway or a bell house on the roof, and the building usually sits closer to the road than other residential homes. They really are everywhere in rural Michigan if you know what you are looking for.

NPCR

NPCR

NPCR

NPCR

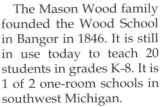

Van Buren Regional Genealogical Society

The Mason Wood family founded the Wood School in Bangor in 1846. It is still in use today to teach 20 students in grades K-8. It is 1 of 2 one-room schools in southwest Michigan.

The Van Buren District Library houses the Bess Britton Michigan One-Room Schoolhouse Collection on the history of about 4,500 Michigan historic rural schoolhouses. The Clarke Historical Library at Central Michigan University has information and displays on the teachers, the experiences of the students, a typical school day, the buildings themselves and books used in the schools.

Z ZOO & ANIMAL PLACES

Watchable Wildlife Viewing Areas:[ww] see 80P

Abbey Dorr

Abbey Dorr

Wolf Lake State Fish Hatchery: At any time over 1 million fish fingerlings in over 40 indoor and outdoor tanks can be seen as they grow for the purpose of stocking Michigan rivers and lakes; this includes steelhead trout, Chinook salmon, lake sturgeon, walleye, northern pike, channel catfish and northern muskellunge. The Visitors Center features exhibits on the importance of lakes and wetlands to the Great Lakes, fisheries' history, commercial fishing, lake sturgeon rehabilitation and offers tours of the hatchery.

Noelle Trese

Noelle Trese

Noelle Trese

Noelle Trese

427

A AGRICULTURE

Land in farms: 36% of county
Number of farms: 1,300
Size of average farm: 130 acres
Market value of all products: #29 of 83 counties
Crops: ...most acres: corn for grain
...highest $ sales: grains: corn, soybeans, wheat
Livestock: ...largest number: cattle & calves
...highest $ sales: milk & dairy products
Among the top Michigan counties:
- #1- greenhouse vegetables & herbs, llamas, number of horses & ponies, sale of sheep & goats, snow peas, vegetable transplants
- #2- acres of cut flowers, sale of horses
- #4- nursery stock

Dairy, food & meat processing plants: 48
State ranking for harvested trees: #61 of 83 counties
FYI: There are around 2,200 <u>sheep</u> operations in Michigan, raising 82,000 animals with 20,000 going to market each year. Over 70,000 sheep are shorn and produc about 6 pounds of wool each. Sheep have a herd mentality and are equal to cattle in intelligence. Washtenaw County is the leading sheep producing county in Michigan.

There are 28,000 <u>goats</u> in the state with 10,000 being milked every day; 1,000 are raised for their wool (angora and mohair goats) and 17,000 are being raised for their meat. Curious and intelligent animals, they explore their environment with their upper lips and tongue by "nibbling" on whatever catches their interest; and sometimes they eat it too.

The almost 4,000 <u>llamas</u> and <u>alpacas</u> in the state are primarily raised as pets and for their exceptional wool. The owners of these animals have active associations for breeding and showing, wool yarn making and weaving and textile production. They are popular at petting zoos and county fairs and are much beloved by their owners. ^{MDA, wikipedia}

Sheep — Michigan Farm Bureau

Goat — Michigan Farm Bureau

Llama — Paul Jackson

Alpaca — Stacey Choate

B BRIDGE OR BOAT

MDOT Photo and Video Unit

MDOT Historic Bridge: Built in 1942, the highway bridge at Wiard Rd. and NB US-12 is one of four bridges comprising the Willow Run Tri-level Grade Separation Historic District. It was designed to bring in workers from Detroit to build the B-24 airplanes during WWII. It is on the National Register of Historic Places.

C CELEBRATIONS

<u>Ann Arbor</u> ...*Film Festival:* oldest of its kind, March
...*Folk Festival:* storytelling, songwriting, music, Jan.
...*Hash Bash:* yep, just what it says, April
...*Book Festival:* bookstore crawl, May
...*Shakespeare in the Arb:* change location from scene to scene, June
...*African-American Downtown Festival:* June
...*Taste of Ann Arbor:* sample food, music, June

Courtesy of www.visitannarbor.org

...*Summer Festival:* variety-type shows, June-July

Courtesy of www.visitannarbor.org

...*Art Fairs:*^{1,000} four juried art fairs draw 500,000 people, July

...*Rolling Sculpture Car Show:* 400+ exotic, antique, classic and concept cars, July
<u>Chelsea</u> *Summerfest:* art, food, music, cars, July
<u>Dexter</u> *Daze:* clowns, music, parade, good food, Aug.
<u>Manchester</u> *Chicken Broil:* 12,000 meals, July
...*Riverfolk Music & Arts Festival:* jam camp, songwriters, concerts, workshops, Aug.
...*Oktoberfest:* parade, bed race, car show, Oct.

Milan *Bluegrass Festival:* Aug.
Saline *Celtic Festival:* Highland activities, July
Ypsilanti *Show & Shine Street Rods:* May
…*Michigan Brewers Guild Summer Beer Festival:* 300+ beers from 50+ Michigan breweries, July
…*Michigan Roots Jamboree:* outdoor music and art festival, food, activities, camping, Aug.

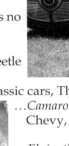

Ypsilanti Area Convention & Visitors Bureau

…*Orphan Car:* car makes no longer made, Sept.

…*Vintage Volkswagen:* beetle mania, June
…*Depot Town Cruise:* classic cars, Thurs., June-Sept.

Ypsilanti Area Convention & Visitors Bureau

…*Camaro:* celebrate the Chevy, July

…*Elvis:* the king has been spotted in Ypsi too, July

…*Summer Beer:* Michigan Brewers Guild, July
…*Fire Truck Muster:* vintage fire trucks, Aug.
…*Heritage Festival:* historic tours, Civil War Camp, Aug.
…*Thunder Over Michigan:* air show, war birds, Aug.
…*Antique Truck Show:* all kinds of trucks, Oct.

D DEMOGRAPHICS

Population: 344,800
Largest city: Ann Arbor
Largest township: Ypsilanti
Largest village: Dexter
Median household income: $54,900 (#3/MI))
Owner-occupied median house value: $223,000 (#2/MI)
Persons affiliated with a religious congregation: 33%
Persons below poverty level: 14%
Students receiving school lunch subsidy: 25%

Persons per sq. mile: 486
Population: 114,000
Population: 53,400
Population: 4,070

From the INDEX…

[1,000] This notation indicates that the noted item is on the *1,000 Places To See Before You Die* list (and book of the same name) by Patricia Schultz.

E ENVIRONMENT

The Legacy Land Conservancy works to protect and preserve the forests, prairies, farms, wetlands and waters in Southern Michigan. It was among the first conservancy nationwide to be awarded accreditation by the Land Trust Accreditation Commission. Now with over 3,500 acres under protection in over 50 parcels, including 5 nature preserves, its goal is to protect – for today and forever - 25,000 acres in the next 20 years. Their high priority areas include the natural areas in and around the Waterloo-Pinckney-Sharonville arc, farmland in southwest Washtenaw County and land critical to protecting the water resources. Local lands are protected to preserve what is unique about a region for all time, to support the economic health of a community, to protect the environment, to take advantage of unique tax incentives and to leave a gift for future generations to come. legacylandconservancy.org

F FLORA & FAUNA

Alice Welch, USDA

A lot of people have a love/hate relationship with their black walnut trees. They either love or hate the strong tasting nuts, and for sure they hate the labor-intensive process of extracting the nuts from their husk and shell. They're the last tree to get their leaves in the summer and the first to lose them in the fall. Commercially, part of the nut can be processed and used as a natural dye, and the shell is used for abrasive cleaning, cosmetics and water filtration. The roots produce a toxic substance that prohibits growth by some plants. But the wood is beautiful and highly desirable for furniture.

DNR, David Kenyon

Although the <u>wolverine</u> is the <u>State of Michigan's nickname</u> and the U of M mascot, there is no hard evidence that the animal ever lived in Michigan. However, many wolverine pelts from Canada were shipped out of Upper Peninsula trading posts in the 1600 and 1700s, giving Michigan the reputation of being a wolverine state. UPDATE: In 2004 the first wolverine ever verified as living in the wild in Michigan was discovered in Sanilac County. How it got there is unknown. It died in 2010 and is now on display at the visitor center at Bay City State Recreation Area.

G GOVERNMENT

County: ...created: 1822 **...organized:** 1826
...originally part of: Wayne, Oakland Counties
Size: 463,000 acres / 710 sq. miles (26 of 83 counties)
The county has 5 cities, 3 villages, 21 townships with 6 as charter townships, 5 unincorporated communities, 1 Census Designated Place and 10 school districts.

Kenny E. Siler

Kenny E. Siler

County seat: Ann Arbor
...Homestead property tax: 46 mills
Motto: <u>Ann Arbor</u> Convention and Visitors Bureau: *Doing LIFE Different*
...<u>Dexter</u> Area Chamber: *Live ·Work ·Play ·Prosper*
...<u>Manchester</u>: *The spirit of community, a sense of pride*
...<u>Saline</u>: *One of America's Best Places to Live, Work and Play*

H HISTORICAL MARKERS 9 of 53

Antislavery Society: 1836, established Michigan's first antislavery newspaper

Blacksmith Shop: built in 8 days in 1877 and used as a blacksmith shop until 1952; now owned by Manchester Historical Society; it is one of the last operational main-street shops of its kind

Kathleen A. Siler

Cleary College: 1883, started as Cleary's School of Penmanship with two students
Dexter Depot: passenger service 1841-1953; original landscape plantings came from railroad greenhouses
Eastern Michigan College: 1849, as Michigan State Normal School, a teacher's college; now EMU
Elijah McCoy: (1843-1929), son of former slaves, he held more than 40 patents for the lubrication of motors in trains, boats and factory machines. Assurances of authentic McCoy lubricating devices are believed to be the origin the phrase "the real McCoy."
Michigan Becomes a State: 1836, to end the boundary dispute with Ohio, Michigan delegates met here and agreed to give the strip of land to Ohio, and receive most of the U.P. as a consolation. Only then was Michigan is allowed to join the Union.

Kathleen A. Siler

Michigan's First Jewish Cemetery: 1848, now re-intered elsewhere

Michigan's Interurbans: 1890 -1929, original mass transit [electric trains] from Ypsilanti to Ann Arbor

University of Michigan: 1837, founded as the University of Michigania with 7 students, 2 faculty
Willow Run: • 1941-1953: at the time it was the largest manufacturing plant under one roof; Albert Kahn designed, Ford Motor Company built, it was the "Arsenal of Democracy" during WWII, with 42,000 employees building 8,700 B-24 bombers.
• After WWII, Kaiser-Frazer built 740,000 cars.
• After 1953: cargo airport, General Motors site, home of Yankee Air Museum
National Register of Historic Places: 74 listings
State Historic Sites: 140 listings

I INFORMATION

Chamber of Commerce: Ann Arbor-Ypsilanti, Chelsea, Dexter, Manchester, Milan, Saline

Visitor: Ann Arbor Convention and Visitors Bureau, 800-888-9487, visitannarbor.org

...Ypsilanti Area Convention and Visitors Bureau, 734-483-4444, Ypsilanti.org

J JOKES

You might be a graduate student at Michigan if…

...you look forward to taking time off to do laundry.

...you feel guilty if you recreate.

...you always "talk shop" at a frat party.

...you have never been to a frat party.

...your office and your home have the same décor: none, except for the dust.

...you wish you knew more Americans so you could improve your English.

...you thought "home" was wonderful, but now Papa will be very disappointed that you want to stay in America.

K KINSMAN

Race
American Indian: <1%
Asian: 8%
Black/African American: 13%
Hispanic or Latino: 4%
Other: 4%
White: 75%

Ancestry
German: 17%
English: 9%
Irish: 8%
Polish: 5%
U.S./American: 5%
Italian: 4%

L LIGHTHOUSE OR LANDMARK

Shaina Lamb

The Michigan Stadium of the University of Michigan, affectionately called The Big House, is the largest stadium in the U.S., seating around 110,000 people for a football game. Each home football game generates about $2.2 million for the local economy.

M MUSEUMS

Ann Arbor *African American Cultural & Historical Museum:* a museum of community history; tour area Underground Railroad sites

...*Cobblestone Farm:* rural 1800s exhibits

...*Gallery One:* challenging & thought-provoking

...*Gerald R. Ford Presidential Library:* his materials

...*Hands-On:* 250+ interactive exhibits

...*Kempf House:* an 1890s German-American family

...*Washtenaw County Historical Society Museum on Main Street:* 1830s historic home

WCHS, Ann Arbor, MI

Ypsilanti Area Convention & Visitors Bureau

...University of Michigan
- *Art:* Africa, America, Asia, Europe, Mid-east
- *Exhibit Museum of Natural History & Planetarium:* Michigan's largest collection of dinosaurs
- *Kelsey Museum of Archaeology:* ancient and medieval objects from the Near East
- *Sindecuse Museum of Dentistry:* 11,000 items
- *Sterns Musical Collection:* 2,000+ instruments

Chelsea *Area Historical Society Museum:* in an 1880s restored train depot

...*Eddy Discovery Center:* the world of geology, see 81P

Dexter *Area Historical Society & Museum:* local

Manchester *John B. Swainson Room & John Schneider Blacksmith Shop:* Swainson was a former Michigan governor from Manchester; blacksmith demonstrations are still available

Milan *Hack House:* 1880s stick-style Victorian home

Saline *Railroad Depot:* depot, caboose, track path

...*Rentschler Farm:* early 1900s, extensive exhibits

...*Weber-Blaess School:* 1860s one-room school

Ypsilanti *Automotive Heritage Collection & Miller Motors Hudson:* Ypsilanti has lots of auto history

Ypsilanti Area Convention & Visitors Bureau

...*Firehouse Museum:* 10,000 sq. ft. of exhibit space; preservation of fire-fighting history and the promotion of fire safety

...*Historical Museum:* in an 1860s Italianate mansion

Ypsilanti Area Convention & Visitors Bureau

N NATURAL RESOURCES

Elevation: 700 – 1,100 feet
Physiography: rolling plains, hill uplands, lake-border plains.

Forest type: oak-hickory, elm-ash-cottonwood, maple-beech
Public/private forests: 18% of county

Water in county: 2% of county
   Lakes: 120   **...largest:** Ford Lake
   Rivers: Huron, Raisin, Saline
   Rivers & streams: 370 miles

Growing season, avg.: 174 days (#2/MI) (3 temp. zones)
Last freeze, avg.: April 30 – May 10
First freeze, avg.: Oct. 10 – Oct. 20
Precipitation, annual avg.: rainfall: 30 inches
                        snowfall: 36 inches
                        Temperature (F), avg.:
                        January: high 31°, low 17°
                        July: high 84°, low 52°

NPCR

                        Annual: >90°: 11 days
                               <0°: 6 days

Tornadoes (1930-2010): 29

O ORIGINS

<u>Ann Arbor:</u>[c,ct] the wives of the first two settlers were both named Ann; the area had many natural tree groves or arbors; 1823
<u>Augusta:</u>[ct] early settler from Augusta, NY; 1836[local info]
<u>Barton Hills:</u>[v] Barton Hills Country Club; 1920s
<u>Chelsea:</u>[c] (CHEL see) Chelsea, MA, was the former home of the man who got a railroad station built here; 1848
<u>Dexter:</u>[v] first settler Judge Samuel Dexter; 1824

<u>Manchester:</u>[v] early settlers came from Manchester Township, Ontario County, NY; 1833
<u>Milan:</u>[c] formerly called Tolanville, Farmersville and Woodward's Mill; 1836
<u>Pittsfield:</u>[ct] Prime Min. of England, William Pitt; 1831
<u>Saline:</u>[c] the salt springs of the Saline River; 1832
<u>Superior:</u>[ct] the best town around; 1823
<u>Washtenaw:</u>[co] American Indian word meaning "far country," asin far from Detroit
<u>Willow Run:</u>[u] a small stream through the willow trees
<u>York:</u>[ct] settlers from New York; 1830
<u>Ypsilanti:</u>[c,ct] (ip sill ANT ee) the Greek war hero of independence, Gen. Demetrius Ypsilanti; 1809

P PARKS

National: 0 **State:** 6 **County:** 9 **Local:** 69
Number of campsites: 1,100
State Game Area: 4 areas
State Recreation Area: *Pinckney:* 11,000 acres, 40 miles of multi-use trails and horse trails offer backcountry experience; boating, swimming, chain of excellent fishing lakes

...*Waterloo:* 20,000 acres, largest park in the Lower Peninsula, 4 campgrounds, 11 fishing lakes, 47 miles of hiking trails, horse and bike trails, swimming; the <u>Eddy Discovery Center</u> introduces visitors to the fascinating world of geology and to the diverse natural habitats that are found within Waterloo SRA

Kathleen A. Siler

County: *County Farm:* 141 acres, formerly housed a poorhouse, insane asylum, hospital (all razed); now is an exercise trail, nature area, gardens
...*Independence Lake:* beach, boats, fishing, trails

...*Parker Mill:* 26 acres, 1873 operable mill, trails
...*Rolling Hills:* 363 acres, water park, wave pool, lazy river ride; fishing, trails, winter activities

...*Sharon Mills:* 6 acres, 1835 mill, museum

Kathleen A. Siler

County Preserves: *Brauer:* 187 acres, diverse habitat includes southern forest & swamp

…*Burns-Stokes:* 29 acres along the Huron River

…*Devine:* 137 acres, wetlands, woods, trails

…*Kosch-Headwaters:* of Fowler Creek

…*Leonard:* 237 acres protect 1 mile of River Raisin shoreline, diverse and rich landscape

…*Osborne Mill:* natural area, limited trails

…*Park Lyndon:* wetlands, trails

Other Preserves: Ervin-Stucki, Goodrich, Lefurge Woods, Miller, Squiers

U of M: *Matthaei Botanical Gardens and Nichols Arboretum:* gardens, trails, exhibits, art, library

Laura L. Stidham

Other: *Huron-Clinton Metropolitan Authority:* see 47P; included in this county:
- *Delhi Metropark:* 53 acres, Huron River, canoes
- *Dexter-Huron Metorpark:* 122 wooded acres
- *Hudson Mills:* 1,500 acres, golf, fish, bike, boat

…*Leslie Science and Nature Center:* 50 acres of fields, prairies, forest and pond; camps, raptors, rentals

FYI: "Washtenaw County's Natural Areas Preservation Program (NAPP) purchases unique natural areas to ensure their preservation for the benefit of all County residents – plants, animals, and people! The Washtenaw County Parks & Recreation Commission manages the program, identifying and caring for the lands with special ecological, recreational, and educational benefits." ewashtenaw.org This is why there are so many preserves in this county.

Q QUOTE FROM THE LOCALS

"The Ann Arbor area is the state's rare jewel: a small, friendly town with big city sophistication; a world-class educational and high-tech research center nestled in a peaceful rural setting; a close-knit community of charming neighborhoods with a rich mix of cultures.

"Although geographically small, the area is perhaps most renowned for its cultural offerings.

From exclusive art exhibits to performances by jazz legends, there are abundant opportunities to enjoy arts and culture. More than 30 independent bookstores, dozens of unique galleries, and a variety of top-notch museums - including the newly-renovated University of Michigan Museum of Art – are all within the downtown limits.

"The Ann Arbor area also offers a bounty of recreational activities for those looking to golf, hike, or cycle, and three metroparks are within a short drive of the city center.

"In the warmer months, the area offers an array of street festivals and outdoor fairs. In the fall, football Saturdays are more than just events – they are experiences, as more than 100,000 people fill "The Big House" to watch the Wolverines. In the winter, holiday light festivals and the Ann Arbor Folk Festival are always crowd pleasers." visitannarbor.org

R RECREATION & SPORTS

Auto racing: *Milan International Dragway:* ¼-mile IHRA sanctioned, 75 races a year; seats 14,000

Golf courses: 30

Hiking/skiing/mountain biking trails: 75 miles

Public access sites: 18

Public recreational land: 4% of county

Rail-trail: (40 miles) Border to Border, Gallup Park, Olsen Park, Pinckney RA

State/federal wild/scenic/natural river: 20 miles of the Huron River offering kayaking and canoeing

Meri Lou Murray Recreation Center: 51,000 sq. ft., fitness, recreation, pool, track

S STATE OF MICHIGAN

"Cultural Economic Development means leveraging our creative talent and cultural assets to spur economic growth and community prosperity. The cultural sector is a critical contributor to Michigan's economy because it creates jobs, strengthens a community's tax base, attracts and retains people to live and work in Michigan. It influences business development and expansion decision, inspires downtown revitalization and historic preservation, builds community identity and pride of place, promotes diversity, and stimulates the growth of creative enterprise. There is strong reason to believe that the cultural sector will, in fact, have an even more important role in the 'new economy' characterized by technology, innovation and creativity." Ann Arbor is a leader in Cultural Tourism. Michigan.gov/ced

T TRAVEL

Airports: Ann Arbor Municipal
Amtrak: Ann Arbor
Bus: Greyhound; Ann Arbor Transportation Authority (AATA; voted the #1 transit authority in the country)
Distance to Lansing: 60 miles
Heritage Route: *Historic: US-12 Heritage Trail*, see 11T
Main roads: I-94, US-12, US-23, M-14, M-52, M-153
Memorial Highways: US-23, United Spanish War Veterans MH, see 1T
…US-12, Iron Brigade, see 12T
…US-12, Pulaski MH, see 14T

Scenic drive: Huron River Drive between Ann Arbor and Dexter

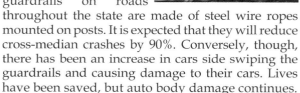

FYI: The new median cable guardrails on roads throughout the state are made of steel wire ropes mounted on posts. It is expected that they will reduce cross-median crashes by 90%. Conversely, though, there has been an increase in cars side swiping the guardrails and causing damage to their cars. Lives have been saved, but auto body damage continues.

U UNIVERSITIES & COLLEGES

Cleary University: est. 1883, 1,000 students. It is committed to teaching the American free market economic system, ethical business practices and leadership skills; multiple campuses and 100 online degrees
Concordia College: est. 1963, 1,100 students. Part of the Concordia University system of the Lutheran Church-Missouri Synod, it offers a faith-based liberal arts education. WHAC, Cardinals
Thomas M. Cooley Law School: see 33U
Eastern Michigan University: est. 1849, 23,000 students. Motto: Education First. It has an emphasis on people, education, community engagement, service and excellence; your success and well-being, academically, professionally, personally. MAC, Eagles
University of Michigan: est. 1817, 41,000 students. Motto: Art, Science, Truth. Internationally renowned for high educational standards, research, health care, diversity, community involvement, endowments, campus life, sports. Big 10, Wolverines
University of Phoenix: see 25U
Washtenaw Community College: est. 1974, 17,000 students. An accessible and affordable education with comprehensive training and transfer agreements with EMU and U of M. Club sports, Warriors

V VARIETY

www.visitannarbor.org

Whether you're a student, a resident, or a visitor, there is always a variety of activities and opportunities available for you to choose from in downtown Ann Arbor. It is a city alive with vitality.

W WANDERLUST

Agri-tourism: *Alber's Orchard:* cider, apples
…*Donahee Farms:* U-pick, strawberries, tomatoes
…*Farmers' Market:* Ann Arbor, Chelsea, Dexter, Downtown Ypsilanti, Manchester, Saline
…*Fusilier Family Farm & Greenhouse:* working farm, tours, corn maze, greenhouse, veggies year-round
…*Obstbaun Orchards:* apples, cherries, wagon rides
…*Plymouth Orchards & Cider Mill:* tours, wagon rides, pumpkins, apples, bakery
…*Rowe's:* largest U-pick strawberry farm in MI
…*Wasem Fruit Farm:* U-pick, apples, cherries, cider, blueberries, bakery, tours
…*Wiard's Orchard & Country Fairs:* cider mill, pies
Brewery: Arbor Brewing Company Pub & Eatery, Arbor Brewing Company-Corner Brewery, Grizzly Peak Brewing Co., Jolly Pumpkin Artisan Ales
Cultural: Ann Arbor Symphony Orchestra, The Encore Musical Theatre, Michigan Theater, The New Theatre Project, Performance Network, Power Center for the Performing Arts, Purple Rose Theatre, Rackham Auditorium, The Ark, U of M Hill Auditorium, Ypsilanti Symphony Orchestra
Fall colors: middle October
Live theater: Ann Arbor Civic, Back Stage, Michigan, Purple Rose Theater (founded by Jeff Daniels), Riverside Art Center, Trueblood, U of M University Productions, Wild Swan
MotorCities National Heritage Area: yes
Planetarium: Exhibit Museum, University of Michigan
Shopping malls: Arbor-land, Briarwood
Walking tours: EMU, U of M, Ypsilanti
Ann Arbor Antiques Market: in Saline

Chelsea Milling Co.: tour the Jiffy Mix factory

Motawi Tileworks: art studio creates unique handmade tiles; tours available

Kathleen A. Siler

Washtenaw County Heritage Tours: four distinct themed driving routes through the cities, villages and rural areas

Don't miss Depot Town in Ypsilanti, a historic district and center of many activities.

See the Bixby Marionettes on display at the Saline District Library.

X X-TRA STUFF

County Fair: *Chelsea Community Fair:* 2010 #1 festival in SE Michigan, a special place for both the young and the old; to enjoy where generations of the farming community get together one last time before the summer's end; Aug.

…*Manchester Community Fair:* Michigan's Biggest Little Fair, July

…*Milan Community Fair:* parade, cruise night, fireworks, baby contest, entertainment, June

Famous people: …*Entertainment:* Jeff Daniels, Iggy Pop

…*Politics:* Royal Samuel Copeland

…*Sports:* Lisa Bonder, Bobby Korecky

…*Other:* William Hewlett, Tom Monaghan, Ted Heusel

Hospitals: Chelsea, Forest Health, Select Speciality, St. Joseph Mercy, University of Michigan, Veterans Affairs

Large employers: University of Michigan, U of M Health Centers, General Motors, Automotive Holding Components, Regents of the University of Michigan (public relations), Ford Motor Co., Eastern Michigan University, Veterans Healthcare System

The buildings in Milan have a wide variety of architectural styles.

Saline has been voted one of best places to live in the U.S. It is also the home to two outstanding high-school-age fiddle groups.

The old Ann Arbor Bus Depot, built in 1940, is a beautiful example of the Art Deco Streamline Moderne style.

NPCR

Ypsilanti Area Convention & Visitors Bureau

Ypsilanti Water Tower: built in 1890 for $21,000, 147 ft. high, with a 250,000 gallon steel tank and sits at the highest point in the city; it held water and provided electricity; it was voted by *Cabinet Magazine* as the "most phallic" building in the world

Y YESTERYEAR

Albert Kahn (1869-1942) was an architect whose innovative industrial buildings helped Michigan become a great manufacturing center. He opened his own architectural firm in 1896, just when Detroit was emerging as the automobile center of America. He designed factories for Packard Motor Car Co., Ford Motor Co., including the Ford River Rouge Plant, several for Chrysler Corp. and the first General Motors Building in Detroit. He pioneered the use of reinforcing rods in concrete, natural lighting and standard materials for more economical construction.

His work was not limited to factories. He designed 17 buildings on the campus of the University of Michigan including Hill Auditorium, Hatcher Graduate Library, Clements Library and Burton Tower. His designs also included many "mansion" homes, especially for his friends in the automobile industry. In all, he designed over 1,000 buildings around the world and left a beautiful legacy for all of us to enjoy.

NPCR

Z ZOO & ANIMAL PLACES

Petting zoo: *Domino's (Pizza):* 25 acres, educational, group events

…*Fusilier Family Farm:* see 81W

Ann Arbor Alpacas: open farm days

Spring Valley Trout Farm: spring-fed, pollution-free pond stocked with farm-raised catfish or trout

A AGRICULTURE

Land in farms: 4% of county
Number of farms: 310
Size of average farm: 60 acres
Market value of all products: #47 of 83 counties
Crops: ...most acres: soybeans
...highest $ sales: floriculture
Livestock: ...largest number: laying chickens
...highest $ sales: poultry & eggs
Among the top Michigan counties:
• #1- aquatic plants, collards, indoor foliage plants, sales of cut flowers
• #3- acres of potted flowering plants, sod, watermelons
• #5- ducks
• #7- sale of floriculture
Dairy, food & meat processing plants: 182
State ranking of harvested trees: #82 of 83 counties
FYI: On any Saturday, 45,000 people come to shop for fresh fruit and vegetables directly from the farmer, meat from the butcher, flowers and plants of every description, plus products from around the world, at Detroit's Eastern Market. Established in 1841, and now occupying over 43 acres, it is the hub of the wholesale fresh food market in the state. It is the largest open-air wholesale/retail market of its kind in the U.S. Macomb and Monroe Counties are among the state's leaders in vegetable production and both are adjacent to Wayne County. Open six

days a week, it has over 125 food vendors plus over 100 restaurants and specialty stores. It hosts many special events during the year such as the Annual Flower Day and the World's Largest Fruit Cocktail, featuring fresh fruit.

Eastern Market Corporation

NPCR

NPCR

B BRIDGE OR BOAT

Mike Wenkel

The Ambassador Bridge is North America's #1 international crossing with more than 10,000 commercial vehicles a day. Built in 1929 and privately owned, it spans the Detroit River, connecting Detroit with Windsor, Ontario, Canada. There is some talk in Michigan about building a second bridge in order to more effectively handle the large volume of traffic. Both the current owner and the State of Michigan and Canada have proposed their own plans.

C CELEBRATIONS

Belleville *Sumpter Country Fest:* rural, rodeo, May
...*National Strawberry Festival:* June
Canton *Liberty Fest:* June
Dearborn *Arab International Festival:* June
...*Motor Muster:* 1930 - 1970s vehicles, June
...*Homecoming Festival:* Aug.
...*Festival of Trees:* funds raised are for Children's Hospital of Michigan, Nov.
Dearborn Heights *Spirit Festival:* June
Detroit *Movement: Detroit's Electronic Music Festival:* emphasizes the progressive qualities of the culture surrounding electronic music, May

...*Detroit Riverdays Festival:* celebrating Detroit's maritime, ecological and culinary culture, June

...*Chrysler/Jeep APBA Gold Cup:* boat races on the Detroit River, July
...*Detroit Jazz Festival:* largest free jazz festival in North America, Sept.

Venupix

...*America's Thanksgiving Parade:* televised, a "real" parade, not a parade that promotes other entertainment venues, Nov.

<u>Grosse Ile</u> *Island Festival:* June

<u>Hamtramck</u> *Labor Day Polish Festival:* Sept.

<u>Livonia</u> *Spree:* six-day birthday bash, June

<u>Northville</u> *Art in the Sun:* June

Northville Chamber of Commerce

...*Victorian Festival:* Sept.

<u>Plymouth</u> *Ice Festival:* the oldest, largest ice-carving event in North America with world-class competition, Jan.

...*Art in the Park:* Michigan's 2nd largest art fair, July

...*Fall Festival:* raises money for non-profits, Sept.

<u>Romulus</u> *Pumpkin Festival:* Sept.

<u>Taylor</u> *City Summer Festival:* July

<u>Trenton</u> *Mid-Summer Festival:* July

<u>Wayne</u> *Wheelfest:* Aug.

<u>Westland</u> *Festival:* June

...*Patriot's Celebration:* Sept.

D DEMOGRAPHICS

Population: 1,820,600   **Persons per sq. mile:** 2,964

NPCR

Largest city: Detroit
Population: 714,000

2nd largest city: Dearborn
   Population: 98,200
3rd largest city: Livonia
   Population: 96,900
4th largest city: Westland
   Population: 84,100
5th largest city: Taylor   Population: 63,100
Largest township: Canton   **Population:** 90,200
2nd largest twp.: Redford   Population: 48,400
3rd largest twp.: Brownstown Population: 30,600
4th largest twp.: Van Buren   Population: 28,800
5th largest twp.: Northville Population: 28,500
Median household income: $38,300 (county)
   Detroit: $29,500
   Dearborn: $44,600
   Livonia: $63,000
   Westland: $46,300
   Taylor: $42,900
Owner-occupied median house value: $125,000

Persons affiliated with a religious congregation: 38%
Persons below poverty level: 24% (#2/MI)
Students receiving school lunch subsidy: 53%

FYI: In statistics, <u>median</u> is the middle number. It means that 50% of household incomes or house values are above the median and 50% are below the median.

E ENVIRONMENT

Once one of the most polluted rivers in the U.S., the 126-mile <u>Rouge River</u>, also known as the River Rouge, is now healthy enough to support fish and other wild life as well as provide recreational opportunities for area citizens. A collaborative effort between the Federal EPA, state and local governments, and private organizations have made the massive cleanup a blue print for success that is recognized around the world. msnbc.msn.com

F FLORA & FAUNA

Alice Welch, USDA

Pussytoes, so named because the cluster of flowers resembles the bottom of the cat's paws, are a plain and common weed that grows where it may be too dry and the soil too poor for more desirable plants.

Mike Wenkel

The ring-bill gull, commonly called a seagull, is also known as the "fast-food gull" because, as omnivores, they will eat almost anything from fish and insects to rodents and garbage. They are around 20" long and have a wingspan that is almost 48." They are summer residents only north of a line roughly from Detroit to Holland. But south of that line and including around Lake Erie, is the only place in the U.S where these birds have a year-round home.

FYI: Although not native to Michigan, the most famous "fauna" in Wayne County *and* Michigan are the Detroit *Tigers* and the Detroit *Lions*. See 74Z, 82R.

G GOVERNMENT

County: ...created: 1815 **...organized:** 1815
...originally part of: the Original County
Size: 406,000 acres / 614 sq. miles (34 of 83 counties)
The county has 34 cities, 9 townships with 9 as charter townships and 41 public school districts.

County seat: Detroit
...Homestead property tax: 67 mills
Motto: <u>Belleville</u>: *Quality Living*
...<u>Brownstown Twp.</u>: *Where The Future Looks Brighter*
...<u>Dearborn Heights</u>: *City with a Future*
...<u>Gibraltar</u>: *...the Venice of Michigan*
...<u>Hamtramck</u>: *A touch of THE WORLD in America*
...<u>Highland Park</u>: *Return to Excellence*
...<u>Livonia</u>: *People Come First*
...<u>Melvindale</u>: *Little city with a BIG heart*
...<u>Northville</u>: *Historically Distinctive*
...<u>Romulus</u>: *The Sky's The Limit*
...<u>Southgate</u>: *Celebrate the Dream*
...<u>Taylor</u>: *made for you*
...<u>Westland</u>: *An All American City*

H HISTORICAL MARKERS 34 of 220

Am. Academy of Pediatrics: 1930, at Harper Hospital
Am.'s First Bessemer Steel Mill: 1854, Wyandotte
Birth of Kiwanis: 1915, their principle is "We build"
Birthplace of Ford Automobile: 1892, Henry Ford began experiments with motorized vehicles
Birthplace of Model T: 1913, mass production, moving assembly line; by 1925, Ford Motor Company was building 9,000 cars a day
Birthplace of Dr. Ralph J. Bunche: 1904-1971, Under-secretary General of United Nations
Chicago Road: 1830, the Great Sauk Trail between Detroit and Chicago; now US-12 & Michigan Ave.

Chrysler Corp.: 1925, W.P. Chrysler bought out 130 auto companies to form Chrysler Corporation
David Buick/Buick Motor Co.: 1900, developed the overhead valve engine
Dearborn Hills Golf Club: 1922, Michigan's first public golf course

Dearborn Inn: 1931, world's first airport hotel

The Detroit Free Press: 1831, Michigan's oldest daily newspaper; 1853, state's first Sunday newspaper
The Detroit News: by 1973, it had the largest evening circulation in America
The Edison Institute: 1929, built by Henry Ford to honor Thomas Edison; contains Greenfield Village, Henry Ford Museum and the Greenfield Village Schools
Fair Lane Manor: fifty-six room mansion, home of Henry Ford from 1915-1950; named for the road in Ireland where his father was born; see 82H/ National Historic Landmark
First Mile of Concrete Highway in the world: 1909, Woodward Ave. between Six and Seven Mile Rd.

Fisher Building: 1928, called Detroit's largest art object, with outside metallic trim that is solid bronze; the Fisher Brothers developed the closed automobile [Body by Fisher]

Ford Motor Company: 1903, to manufacture and sell motor cars; first product was the Model A
Ford Rouge Plant: 1917, by mid-1920, it was the largest manufacturing center in the world

Fordson High School: 1928, designed in Neo-Tudor style to look like sixteenth century English universities and manor houses

Fort Pontchartrain: 1701, was the first name of the area that became Detroit; named after Count Jerome de Pontchartrain, French Minister of Marine

Fort Wayne: 1840, built to protect from U.S. from British invasion from Canada

Germantown: lured by the State of Michigan recruiting pamphlets, Germans began coming to Detroit [and Michigan] in the 1830s.

Indian Village: late 1800s to early 1900s, 300 distinct and unique homes; present day significant neighborhoods

Mariner's Church: 1842, for Great Lakes seaman

Merrill-Palmer Institute: 1919, devoted to improving the quality of parenting through study, research and working with children

Michigan Alkali Co.: 1893, soda ash for making glass

Motown: 1959-1972, the sweet Motown Sound of pop music

Packard Motor Car: 1903, prestigious luxury cars

Ransom E. Olds: 1899, founded Olds Motor Works that later became Oldsmobile Co.

Shrine Circus: 1906, nation's first Shrine Circus

Stroh Brewery: 1850, German light lager beer

Tiger Stadium: 1901-1999, where the Detroit Tigers played baseball; it was called Bennett Park, Navin Field, Briggs Stadium, finally Tiger Stadium [and now it is no more; it was demolished in 2009]

University of Michigania: 1817-1837, now U of M

Monument: *Bagley Memorial Fountain:* John J. Bagley was a leader in police activities in Detroit and Governor of Michigan from 1873-1877

…*Hurlbut Memorial Gate:* 132' long x 50' high, it honors Chauncey Hurlbut (1803-1885), the "father" of the public waterworks system in Detroit

…*Joe Louis Fist:* 1914-1981, he was the Heavyweight Boxing Champion of the World from 1937-1949; affectionately called the Brown Bomber; the 24'x24'x11' sculpture was installed in Detroit in 1986

…*Michigan Soldiers' and Sailors' Monument:* in honor of those killed in the Civil War

…*Spirit of Detroit:* the man holds symbols for God and all human relationships; the inscription from 2 Corinthians 3:17 says, "Now the Lord is that Spirit: and where the Spirit of the Lord is, there is liberty."

National Historic Landmarks: Columbia (steamer), Edison Institute (The Henry Ford Museum and Greenfield Village), Fair Lane (see below), Fisher and New Center Buildings, Ford River Rouge Complex, Ford Piquette Ave. Plant, Fox Theatre Building, General Motors Building (the first one), Guardian Building, Highland Park Ford Plant, Parke-Davis Research Laboratory, Pewabic Pottery

…*Fair Lane Estate:*[1,000] the home of Henry and Clara Ford, shows the details that Ford himself designed into the home; on 72 acres of natural landscaping, 1914; not open to the public. See 82H above.

National Register of Historic Places: 302 listings
State Historic Sites: 512 listings

I   INFORMATION

Chamber of Commerce: Allen Park, American Arab, Belleville, Canton, Dearborn, Dearborn Heights, Detroit, Garden City, Hamtramck, Highland Park, Inkster, Lincoln Park, Livonia, Northville, Plymouth, Redford Twp., Romulus, Southern Wayne County, Wayne, Westland

Visitor: Detroit Metro Convention and Visitors Bureau, 800-DETROIT, visitdetroit.com

J JOKES

You may be an Old Detroiter if…

…you saw the Lions and the Tigers play at Briggs Stadium.

…you know Kresge's and Woolworth's were real "dime" stores.

NPCR-7

…you took a moonlight cruise to Bob-lo Island.

…you took the train to Lansing to visit the Capitol.

…you had your picture taken with the "real" Santa Clause at Muirheads Department Store.

…you rode the elevator at Hudson's with the white-gloved elevator operator.

…you remember Buffalo Bob, Howdy Doody, Clarabel the Clown, Phineas T. Bluster and Princess Summer-Fall-Winter-Spring.

…you visited the Wonder Bread Bakery and took home a mini loaf of bread.

…Motown music is still your favorite.

…you rode the bus to downtown Detroit to go Christmas shopping at JL Hudson's.

…you grew up and grew old with Ernie Harwell as the voice of summer.

…you remember Black Bart and "Which way did he go? Which way did he go? He went for Faaaaygo!"

…you remember Twin Pines Dairy and Milky the Clown.

…you remember the Vernor's bottling plant on Woodward Ave., with a bearded troll as their logo.

…you went to "all-night" gospel sings at the Masonic Temple.

…you never heard the term "Doo-wop" until it was used on the local PBS TV station during fund-raising events. Now you know you're getting old.

K KINSMAN

Race	
American Indian: <1%	
Asian: 3%	
Black/African American: 41%	
Hispanic or Latino: 5%	
Other: 3%	
White: 50%	

Ancestry	
Other: 66%	
German: 9%	
Polish: 8%	
Irish: 6%	
English: 4%	
Italian: 4%	
U.S./American: 3%	

L LIGHTHOUSE OR LANDMARK

Mike Wenkel

The Ford Motor Company World Headquarters is in Dearborn. The company was started in 1903 by Henry Ford and in 2010 it was the 2nd largest U.S. automaker and 5th largest in the world. See 82Y.

General Motors, LLC 2011

General Motors World Headquarters is in downtown Detroit in the Renaissance Center. Started in 1908 as General Motors Corporation, it is now General Motors Company as of 2009. It is the world's largest automaker and has been for over 78 years. See 25Y.

M MUSEUMS

<u>Belleville</u> *Area Museum:* small replicas of historical buildings

…*Yankee Air Museum:* tells the WWII story of Michigan aviation and the "Arsenal of Democracy"

<u>Canton Twp.</u> *Historical Mus.:* 1884 one-room school

<u>Dearborn</u> *Automotive Hall of Fame:*[1,000] the highest place of honor in the international vehicle industry

...*Historical Museum:* 1833 arsenal, Dearbornville

...*Arab American National Mus.:* the only one in U.S.

...*Arab Folk Heritage:* tours, traditional performances

...*Greenfield Village:* 90 acres of the living history experience at its very best

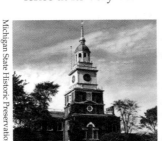

NPCR

Michigan State Historic Preservation Office

...*Henry Ford Museum:*[1,000] celebrating Genius at Work!

Detroit *Black Holocaust Museum:* slavery artifacts

...*Carver/Curtis Museum:* honoring the work of Dr. George Washington Carver

...*Children's Museum* of Detroit Public Schools

...*Dossin Great Lakes Museum:* Belle Isle, shipping and maritime history

...*Graystone International Jazz Mus.:* jazz artifacts

...*Great Lakes Indian Mus.:* at Historic Fort Wayne

...*Historic Fort Wayne:* 1840, five point star design

...*Historical Mus:* includes history of auto production

...*Institute of Arts:*[1,000] exhibitions, education, research; one of the nation's greatest museums

NPCR

...*International Gospel Music Hall of Fame:* expose, promote and celebrate the Gospel through music

...*International Institute:* ethnic enrichment, vast collection of ethnic and cultural artifacts

...*Mbad African Beads Mus.:* cultural African relics

...*MI Sports Hall of Fame:* the best of the greatest

...*Model T Automotive Heritage Complex:* the 1904 birthplace of the Model T

...*Motown Historical Museum:*[1,000] Motown music; to preserve, educate, motivate

Mike Wenkel

NPCR

...*Museum of African American History:*[1,000] extensive displays

...*Museum of Contemporary Art:* 22,000 sq. ft.

...*National Mus. of the Tuskegee Airman:* at Historic Fort Wayne; WWII African-American soldiers

...*Pewabic Pottery:* 1907 building is a National Historic Landmark, Arts & Craft movement, displays

...*Science Center:* creative exploration for the family

Livonia *Greenmead Museum & Historical Village:* agricultural history of early Michigan

Grosse Ile *Historical Society:* 1871, 1906 buildings, artifacts

Grosse Pointe *Historical Society*: local history brought to life

Grosse Pointe Shores *Edsel & Eleanor Ford House:* he was the son of Henry Ford; his Albert Kahn designed home is impressive yet unpretentious; it is open for tours

Michigan State Historic Preservation Office

Elizabeth K. Kerstens

Lincoln Park *Historical Museum:* "a perfect gem of a museum"

Northville *Mill Race Historic Village:* 1900s era living

Plymouth *Historical Mus.:* Henry Ford village industry

Trenton *Historical Museum:* Victorian artifacts

Wyandotte *Museum:* Queen Ann home, restored

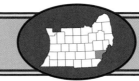
N NATURAL RESOURCES

Elevation: <600-800 feet
Physiography: fairly flat

Forest type: oak-hickory, elm-ash-cottonwood, maple-beech
Public/private forests: 9% of county

Water in county: 3% of county
    Lakes: 35   **...largest:** Belleville Lake
    Rivers: Detroit, Ecorse, Huron, Rouge
    Rivers & streams: 390 miles

Great Lakes islands: Belle Isle, Grosse Ile
Great Lakes shoreline: 75 miles of the Detroit River between Lake St. Clair (not a Great Lake) and Lake Erie

Avg. sunshine: January: 36%   July: 70%
Growing season, avg.: 166 days (#6/MI) (3 temp. zones)
    Last freeze, avg.: April 25 - May 5
    First freeze, avg.: Oct. 25 – Nov. 5
Precipitation, annual avg.:
    rainfall: 32 inches
    snowfall: 39 inches
Temperature (F), avg.:
    January: high 31°, low 16°
    July: high 84°, low 60°

    Annual: >90°: 16 days
    (#3/MI), **<0°:** 6 days

Kelly Turner

Tornadoes (1930-2010): 38 (#2/MI))

NPCR-2

FYI: There is a salt reservoir from ancient oceans one mile below the surface of southeastern Michigan with enough salt to supply the whole world for a million years. It is still being mined today for road salt.

O ORIGINS

Allen Park:[c] lawyer & lumberman Lewis Allen; 1926
Belle Isle: the daughter of Gov. Lewis Cass, Isabella Cass; 1868
Belleville:[c] French for "beautiful town;" 1826
Brownstown:[ct] according to legend, Adam Brown, age 8, was captured and raised by American Indians; 1812

Canton:[ct] province in China; 1834
Dearborn[c]**/Heights:**[c] War of 1812 Gen. Henry Dearborn; 1795
Detroit:[c] (de-TROYT) French word for "strait," a river connecting Lake Erie and Lake St. Clair; 1701
Ecorse:[c] French for "bark;" American Indians used birch bark for canoes and wigwams; 1795
Flat Rock:[c] smooth rock bed of the Huron River; 1821
Garden City:[c] home lots large enough to have vegetable gardens; 1921
Gibraltar:[c] the Gibraltar & Flat Rock Co. was trying to build a canal to connect Lake Erie with Lake Michigan; 1811
Grosse Ile:[t] (gross eel) means "large island;" 1851
Grosse Point:[c] made up of 5 communities: Cities of GP, GP Farms, GP Park, GP Shores, GP Woods; large point of land into Lake St. Clair; 1800s
Hamtramck:[c] (ham TRAM ick) Col. J. Hamtramck, under Gen. Anthony Wayne; 1798
Harper Woods:[c] hospital founder Walter Harper, wooded area; 1850
Highland Park:[c] settler built home on high lands; 1818
Huron:[ct] Huron River runs through the township; 1833
Inkster:[c] sawmill owner Robert Inkster; 1825
Lincoln Park:[c] from the many subdivisions with Lincoln in their name; 1921
Livonia:[c] settlers from Livonia, NY; 1832
Melvindale:[c] Melvin Wilkinson built affordable homes for Ford workers; 1870
New Boston:[v] after Boston, MA; 1820
Northville:[c,ct] north of Plymouth; 1831
Plymouth:[c,ct] early settlers were descendants of the Pilgrim Fathers; 1825
Redford:[ct] Rouge Ford, an American Indian crossing place of the River Rouge; 1818
River Rouge:[c] French, means "river red," for the muddy red clay in the water; 1700s
Riverview:[c] view of the Detroit River; 1906
Rockwood:[c] formerly Huron Station; 1834
Romulus:[c] settled by a family from Romulus, NY; 1827
Southgate:[c] named in 1955 for being the south entrance to the metro Detroit area; 1795
Sumpter:[t] misspelling of Revolutionary War hero Gen. Thomas Sumter; 1835
Taylor:[c] Mexican War Gen. Zachary Taylor; 1830
Trenton:[c] limestone strata beneath the town; 1834
Van Buren:[ct] V.P. of U.S., Martin Van Buren; 1834
Wayne:[c,co] American General "Mad" Anthony Wayne, evicted British from Northwest Territory; 1796
Westland:[c] west of Detroit; from the JL Hudson Westland Shopping Center; 1966
Woodhaven:[c] a six square mile village; 1961
Wyandotte:[c] (Y an dot) American Indians of the area, means "peninsula people;" 1818

P PARKS

National: 1 **State:** 5 **County:** 6 **Local:** 127
Number of campsites: 0
State Game Area: *Pointe Mouillee*[ww] (moo yay)*:* 4,000 acres on Lake Erie; it is one of the largest fresh water restoration projects in the world
State Park: *Maybury:* 1,000 acres, meadows, forests, 6-mile trail, 11-mile horse trail, fishing, on a former state hospital site; operated by the Northville Community Foundation
...Tri-Centennial SP & Harbor: 31 acres of green space on the Detroit River in downtown Detroit; Michigan's first urban state park; fishing, boat slips

NPCR

...William G. Milliken SP & Harbor: on the Detroit River; has a scaled down replica of the Tawas Point Light in Iosco County
State Wildlife Area: (500 acres) Brownstone Prairie
County: *Crosswinds Marsh Wetland:* Interpretive Preserve
...Oakwoods Nature Study Area: 400 acres, canoe paths on Huron River, forest and meadow trails
...Wayne County Parks System: 5000+ acres, parks, open spaces, rivers and lakes, wetlands & forests
...William P. Holliday Forest & Wildlife Preserve: 550 acres, Tonquish Creek watershed in its natural state; thickets, woods, wetlands, meadows

Mike Wenkel

Local: *Belle Isle:* 982 acres, the largest island park in the U.S.; athletic complex, aquarium, beach, carillon tower, casino building, coast guard station, conservatory, Detroit Yacht Club, Dossin Museum, fishing piers, golf course, greenhouse, harbor masters office, Livingston Memorial Lighthouse, McArthur Bridge, nature center, nature zoo, rock sculptures, playscape, Remick Music Shell, Scott Fountain
Other: *Detroit River International Wildlife Refuge:* a joint effort of the U.S. and Canada, with 48 miles along the Detroit River and Lake Erie to provide save refuge for millions of migratory birds
...Huron-Clinton Metropolitan Authority: see 47P; included in this county:

Holly Clegg

- *Lake Erie Metropark:*[ww] 1,600 acres, swimming pool, Marshlands Museum and Nature Center, hawk-watching site, watch the lake freighters

- *Lower Huron Metropark:* 1,200 acres on the Huron River, mature woodlands, aquatic center, golf, outdoor ice rinks, sports facilities

Holly Clegg

- *Oakwoods Metropark:* 1,800 acres, scenic woods, nature center, trails, nature study area, horse trails, Monarch butterfly waystation (see 21E)

- *Willow Metropark:* 1,500 acres, mature woodlands, fish or canoe the Huron River or Washago Pond, golf, skatepark, sledding

Q QUOTE FROM THE LOCALS

"Get to know this vibrant city by touring The D [Detroit] during your visit. ...in The D, where urban decay is being buffed away by innovation and opportunity, there's so much more to see beyond the bus window. ... D-troit has distinctive cultural institutions and museums, three newly expanded casinos, a transformed riverfront, new hotels, stadiums, theater, entertainment, symphony and the arts." visitdetroit.com

- *Audio Tours:* (audio, scripts and maps are available online, for FREE) Downtown Detroit History and Architecture Tour; Midtown Detroit Highlights Tour; Downtown Detroit Entertainment Tour; The Dearborn Inn; Woodward Avenue Action Association – Automobile Heritage; Woodward Avenue Association – Woodward Avenue Public Act

- *Behind-the-Scenes Tours:* Ford Field; Historic Elmwood Cemetery; Morley Candy Makers; Stahl's Famous Original Bakery; Westview Orchards & Cider Mill of Romeo
- *Bike, Segway and Kayak Tours:* Wheelhouse Detroit; Inside Detroit; Riverside Kayak Connection
- *Brew Tours:* Motor City Brew Tours

- *Cruises:* Detroit Princess Riverboat; Diamond Jack's River Tours; Infinity & Ovation Yacht Charters

- *DTOURS:* Houses of Worship, African American Heritage, Cultural Heritage, bus tours
- *Walking Tours:* Action Tours; Culinary Escapes; Detroit Tour Connections; Detroit Urban Adventures (The D You Must See and Detroit's Rise, Fall & Renewal); Feet on the Street (history, art, architecture, fun, food, music, Prohibition Jazz tour); Inside Detroit (walking tour, Segway tours, bus tours of different parts of the city); Michigan Millennium Metro Tours; The Original Touring Company (safe & secure, walking or riding) visitdetroit.com

R RECREATION & SPORTS

Auto racing: *Flat Rock Speedway:* ¼-mile oval asphalt track with Figure 8

Golf courses: 40+ (#3/MI)

Mike Wenkel

Great Lakes marinas: 72
Boat slips: 6,000 (#2/MI) FYI: The Detroit Boat Club is the oldest (1839) sport rowing club in the U.S. and the Detroit Yacht Club is the largest yacht club in the U.S.

Hiking/skiing/mountain biking trails: 84 miles
Horse racing: *Northville Downs:* the road to the Kentucky Derby starts here; it also has harness racing, charity poker
Public access sites: 9
Public recreational land: 2% of county
Rail-trail: (6 miles) Conner Creek Greenway, Dequinder Cut Greenway, Southwestern Detroit Greenway

Recreational harbors: Detroit Erma Henderson Park, Elizabeth Park Marina, Lake Erie Metropark Harbor of Refuge, William G. Milliken State Park and Harbor, St. Clair Shores Harbor of Refuge
Detroit Hoops: play basketball in the American Basketball Association

Detroit Lions: est. 1934, National Football League, play at Ford Field; Championships - 1935, 1952, 1953, 1957

Detroit Pistons: see 63R

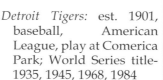

Detroit Redwings: est. 1926, National Hockey League, play at Joe Lewis Arena; Stanley Cup winner- 1936, 1937, 1943, 1950, 1952, 1954, 1955, 1997, 1998, 2002, 2008

Detroit Shock: see 63R

Detroit Tigers: est. 1901, baseball, American League, play at Comerica Park; World Series title- 1935, 1945, 1968, 1984

S STATE OF MICHIGAN

"It is important that Michigan be a part of the largest and most comprehensive national study of child health ever mounted…that will lead to new ways of treating and preventing disease and new public health programs in Michigan. The University Research Corridor conducting this monumental project involving more than 100,000 children consists of Wayne State University (Detroit), University of Michigan (Ann Arbor), Michigan State University (East Lansing), Children's Hospital of Michigan, Henry Ford Health System, Michigan Department of Community Health, and Wayne County and City of Detroit health departments." urcmich.org/news

T TRAVEL

Airports: Detroit Metro-Wayne County (DTW), Detroit City, Larson Airpark, Grosse Ile, Willow Run

FYI: The nation's first regularly scheduled air passage service began operation between Detroit and Grand Rapids in 1926.

Mike Wenkel

Amtrak: Dearborn, Detroit

Bus: Greyhound; Detroit DOT; Suburban Mobility Authority for Regional Transportation (SMART)

County road names: see 44T

Detroit-Windsor Tunnel: 1930, 5,160 feet long; the first vehicular international sub-aqueous border crossing in the world

Distance to Lansing: 80 miles

Ferry: Detroit-Windsor Truck Ferry, for oversized trucks hauling hazardous materials

Heritage Route: *Historic:* <u>US-12 Heritage Trail</u>, see 11T

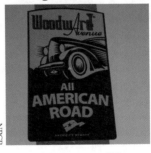

NPCR

…*Recreation:* M-1, A Cruise through Time, 28 miles, Woodward Ave., from Detroit to Pontiac; includes arts, education, medical districts, music, neighborhoods, quaint downtowns, industrial giants; an All-American Road

Main highways: *History of their names:*

…*I-75:* <u>north of downtown Detroit</u>, *Walter P. Chrysler Freeway*: founder of Chrysler Corporation in 1925

…*I-75:* <u>south of downtown Detroit</u>, *Fisher Freeway*, seven brothers started Fisher Body in 1908

…*I-94:* <u>Detroit and north</u>, *Edsel Ford Expressway*, son of Henry Ford

…*I-94:* <u>west of Detroit</u>, *Detroit Industrial Expressway*, to get WWII workers to defense plants; formerly Willow Run Expressway

…*I-96:* *John C. Lodge Freeway*, Detroit's most respected statesman, honored citizen, 1900-1950

…*I-96:* *Jeffries Expressway*, Edward Jeffries, beloved mayor of Detroit who promoted a network of expressways in the 1940s

…*M-39:* *Southfield Expressway* (from Southfield Twp., Oakland Co).

Note: in the 1980s Michigan abandoned the use of proper/historic names for the highways and now uses only the designated trunkline and number.

Memorial Highways: I-75, *American Legion MH*: see 6T

…I-75, *Walter P. Chrysler Freeway*: founder of Chrysler Corporation in 1925

…I-75 & M-8, *Charles J. Rogers Interchange*: owner of a Detroit excavation company involved in building the first freeways in Michigan

…I-96, *AmVets MH*: see 19T

…I-96, in the city of Detroit, *Rosa Parks Memorial Hwy.*: civil rights icon; formerly the Jeffries Expw.

NPCR-2

…I-275, *Disabled American Veterans MH*

…I-275, *Phillip A. Hart MH*: see 58T

…US-12, *Iron Brigade MH*: see 12T

…US-12, *Pulaski MH*: see 11T

…US-24, *10th Mountain Division MH*: to honor those who served in mountain warfare in WWII

…M-53, *Earle MH*: see 44T

…M-85, *Matt McNeely Blvd.*: served in the Michigan House of Representatives from 1964-1986; he was the first African-American to be Speaker Pro-Tem

…M-125, *Clara Barton MH*: see 58T

FYI: Over the years, I-275 has been called, in part or as a whole, proposed, promoted or legalized: Disabled American Veterans Memorial Hwy. and Philip A. Hart Memorial Hwy. [Barnett]

From Detroit, it is 550 miles north to Houghton (in the U.P.).; 540 miles south to Nashville, TN; 520 miles east to Washington, DC; and 530 miles southwest to St. Louis, MO.

U UNIVERSITIES & COLLEGES

Baker College: see 25U

College for Creative Studies: est. 1906, 1,200 students. A national leader in arts education, they educate visual artists and designers who understand the social, cultural and international dimensions of the arts. Peacocks

Davenport University: see 13U

Detroit Baptist Theological Seminary: est. 1974, 75 students. It exists to prepare men for the New Testament gospel ministry, emphasizing expository preaching based on a study of the Scripture in the original language.

Dorsey Business School: est. 1934. It prepares students for promising career opportunities, technologies and certifications for the medical, business, legal and computer fields.

Ecumenical Theological Seminary: est. 1980, 220 students. Within an urban setting, provides education for ministry that is grounded in the Christian tradition while welcoming interfaith dialogue…to integrate theology…with social responsibility.

Henry Ford Community College: est. 1938, 20,000 students. A comprehensive CC with a diverse student population… who measure success by the success of the students in a democratic, diverse, and… technological nation; M-TEC. ECC, Hawks

ITT Technical Institute: see 25U

Lewis College of Business: est. 1939, 300 students. The oldest and only historically Black, private college in Detroit, offering associate degrees; it has educated over 20,000 students in its first fifty years.

Madonna University: est. 1937, 5,000 students. A liberal arts, independent Catholic, Franciscan…to instill in its students Christian humanistic values, intellectual inquiry, a respect for diversity, and a commitment to serve. WHAC, Crusaders

Marygrove College: est. 1946, 1,900 students. Sponsored by the Sister, Servants of the Immaculate Heart of Mary, Liberal arts…foster Christian values… to professional competence…; USCAA, Mustang

Michigan School of Professional Psychology: est. 1980, 100 students. Offers master and doctoral degrees for a humanistic model of psychotherapy.

Michigan Theological University: est. 1994, 200 students. It is a graduate level institution that seeks to train students to be theologically prepared and spiritually mature leaders who will serve the church community in Michigan and worldwide.

Sacred Heart Major Seminary: est. 1924, 400 students. It is a Catholic, educational ecclesiastical community proclaiming the Truth, who is Jesus Christ…to prepare candidates for the priesthood, and lay women and men for ministerial leadership.

Schoolcraft College: est. 1961, 9,000 students. As a community-based college, a student can spend the first two years at SC at $1/3$ the yearly cost of a four-year university, then transfer to get a Bachelor's degree; Livonia and Garden City campuses. MCCAA, Ocelots

University of Detroit Mercy: est. 1887, 1941, 1990, 6,000 students. It is ranked by *U.S. News and World Report* in the Top 25 Midwest master's university, and one of only 15 Midwest "Great Schools at Great Prices." HL, Titans

University of Michigan-Dearborn: est. 1959, 8,500 students. Distinguished by its commitment to providing excellent educational opportunities, it is responsive to the needs of southeastern Michigan. NAIA, Wolves

University of Phoenix: see 25U

Wayne County Community College: est. 1967, 13,000 students. Five state-of-the-art campuses in the county; 80% of students are part-timers; mission is to prepare students for the workplace or for a transfer to advance degree programs.

Wayne State University: est. 1933, 1956, 33,000 students. A national research university with an urban teaching and service mission…that also serves the needs of a nontraditional student population that is racially and ethnically diverse, commuting, working, and raising families. GLIAC, Warriors

V VARIETY

Mike Wenkel

Throughout southeast Michigan are many "Coney Island" restaurants, each one with a slight variation of the same theme. Start with a grilled Michigan-made hot dog with natural casings (preferably a Koegel Vienna), add a beanless all-meat chili, chopped onion and yellow mustard. Round out the meal with Michigan-made Better Made potato chips and a Faygo soft drink or Stroh's beer. The Coney Island dog was invented in Jackson, MI, in 1914 and the name pays homage to the birthplace of the first hot dog. By the way, Michigan has the highest hot dog standards in the U.S. by requiring 100% meat and not allowing innards and other "parts."

W WANDERLUST

Agri-tourism: *Detroit Eastern Market:* see 82A

…*Farm Markets:* Dearborn Farmers & Artisans Market, East Warren Avenue Farmers' Market

…*Three Cedars Farm:* apples, pumpkins, activities, U-pick, Christmas trees, corn maze, country store

Brewery: Atwater Block Brewery, Detroit Beer Company, Fort Street Brewery, Motor City Brewing Works

Casinos: *Greektown, Motor City* and the *MGM Grand* are the only non-American Indian casinos in Michigan

Cultural: *Detroit Symphony Orchestra,* since 1914

...*Michigan Opera Theater:* music & dance come alive

Fall colors: middle October

Lighthouse, other: *Grosse Ill:* tour, climb

...*Livingstone Memorial:* only light in the U.S. that is made of marble; Albert Kahn Design, art deco/modern style, on Belle Isle

...*Windmill Point:* active

Live theater: Fox

Motor Cities National Heritage Area: Nearly 1,200 auto-related resources in 16 Michigan counties, including Wayne County, have been identified in order to preserve the unique culture and heritage of the development of the automobile. It is a public/private partnership affiliated with the National Park Service and is the largest concentration of auto-related sites, attractions and events in the world.

Planetarium: Children's Museum; Digital Dome; Henry Ford Community College; Wayne State University

Shopping malls: Eastland Center, Fairlane Town Center, Laurel Park Place, Livonia Market Place, Shoppes at Gateway Park, Southgate, Southland Center, Taylortown Trade Center, Westland Center, Wonderland Village

Walking tours: *Detroit Heritage Tours:* Preservation Wayne offers regularly scheduled guided walking tours that are a great way to experience the city's rich architectural heritage and discover the landmarks of Detroit

...*See 82Q*

Ford Motor Company: tour the Rouge Plant with its interactive displays, 10-acre living green roof

Ford-Wyoming Drive-In Theatre: largest in U.S., 9 screens, parking for 2,500 cars

Greektown: Greek food, Trapper's Alley, casinos

North American International Auto Show: Cobo Hall, the excitement is palatable, Jan.

Ride the 740 ft. elevator to the top of the Marriott Renaissance Center in downtown Detroit, the second tallest hotel in North America.

Go online to see The Fabulous Ruins of Detroit Tour @ detroityes.com.

The People Mover: elevated train, downtown Detroit

Underground Railroad Tour: provided by the Detroit First Congregational Church

Uniroyal tire: 80' high, on I-94 in Allen Park

Whitcomb Conservatory: tropical plants, learning labs

X X-TRA STUFF

Commercial port: Detroit on the Detroit River

County fair: *Wayne:* free children's petting zoo, Aug.

Famous people: ...*Entertainers*: Tim Allen, Sonny Bono, Ellen Burstyn, Alice Cooper, Francis Ford Coppola, Aretha Franklin, Bill Haley, Julie Harris, Casey Kasem, Ed McMahon, Dick Martin, Ted Nugent, Wilson Pickett, Gilda Radner, Della Reese, Smokey Robinson, Diana Ross, Steven Seagal, Bob Seger, Tom Selleck, Lily Tomlin, Robert Wagner, Margaret Whiting

...*Politics*: Ralph Bunch, John N. Mitchell

...*Sports*: Ty Cobb, Joe Lewis, "Sugar" Ray Robinson

...*Other*: William Boeing, Henry Ford, Mike Illitch, Charles A. Lindberg

Hospitals: <u>Detroit</u>-Detroit Medical Center includes Children's H. of MI, Receiving, Harper U, Hutzel Women's, Karmanos Cancer, Kresge Eye, MI Orthopedic, Rehab Institute, Sinai-Grace; Henry Ford; John D. Dingell Veterans; Hope; Rehab Inst. of MI; Select Specialty; Riverview; St. John Health System (3); Triumph; United Community

...<u>Dearborn</u>-Oakwood

...<u>Garden City</u>-Garden City

...<u>Grosse Pointe</u>-Beaumont, Grosse Pointe Farms, Henry Ford Cottage

...<u>Lincoln Park</u>-Kindred

...<u>Livonia</u>-St. Mary Mercy

...<u>Northville</u>-Hawthorn

...<u>Taylor</u>-Oakwood

...<u>Trenton</u>-Oakwood Southshore

...<u>Wayne</u>-Oakwood Annapolis

...<u>Westland</u>-Walter P. Reuther Psychiatric

...<u>Wyandotte</u>-Henry Ford, Select Specialty

Large employers: Ford Motor Company, General Motors, St. John Health System, Delta Airlines, City of Detroit, Comerica Bank, Chrysler Group, Wayne State University, Detroit Diesel (makes engines), Oakwood Healthcare, Quicken Loans, Blue Cross Blue Shield of Michigan

Canada lies directly south of the USA at the Detroit-Windsor Tunnel.

Fred Sanders invented the ice cream soda in 1875.

In 1907, over 2,000,000 tons of bituminous coal was mined from southeast Michigan.

In 1879, Detroit telephone customers were first in the nation to be assigned phone numbers.

James Vernor, Detroit pharmacist, invented the world's first carbonated soft drink, Vernor's Ginger Ale, in 1862.

Mail Delivery: the Detroit River is the only place in the world where ships can have their mail delivered directly to the ship while they are still underway. The *J.W. Westcott II* has been providing this service since 1949 and prior to that Captain Westcott started the service in 1874.

Metropolitan Detroit area (Wayne, Oakland and Macomb counties) has the largest concentration of people with Arab heritage outside the Middle East, with over 350,000 people. They own over 3,000 businesses in Michigan. Nationally, they have twice the college degree rate as the American average and over 80% are citizens.

Since the 1910s, Michiganians call soft drinks "pop," because of the sound made when opening a bottle of Detroit-made Faygo pop.

The Detroit River, connecting Lake St. Clair (not a Great Lake) and Lake Erie, is 32 miles long and handles more boat traffic than any river in the U.S.

The world's first traffic light was installed at Woodward and Grand Ave. in 1915.

Wayne County is the #1 county in Michigan for:

...museums, 40.

...historical attractions open to the public.

...dollars spent on pleasure trips.

Wayne County is the #1 county in the USA for:

...the largest annual fireworks display.

...the largest NAACP membership.

...the largest number of registered bowlers.

... the largest free jazz festival.

Wayne county is:

Kathy Boyer

…the potato chips capital of the world and, since 1930, the home of Better Made Potato Chips. Detroiters eat an average of 7 lbs. of chips per year, while the national average is 4 lbs. See 59A.

…the softball capital of the world.

FYI: "The most evident economic assets of Wayne County are its mature status as an industrial center and the presence of numerous multinational corporations, including Ford and General Motors. Although the decline of the auto-based employment has had a negative impact throughout the county and adjacent counties, the county has consistently led the state in economic growth and development. The county is positioning itself to become a national and global center of aviation-oriented business and development, becoming an aerotropolis. With 25,000 acres to develop [at Detroit Metro Airport], this airport complex would bring jobs and expand the tax base as it is established as an international center of world commerce." waynecounty.org

Y YESTERYEAR

Why did Detroit become the Automobile Capital of the World?

1880s: Many men, in both the U.S. and Europe, were experimenting with electric, battery, steam, spring and gasoline engines. Their successes and failures were important lessons in engine development for those who followed.

1890s: Detroit was a national leader in railroad car, stove and marine engine manufacturing, with strong pharmaceutical, tobacco, chemical and shipbuilding companies. Therefore, there were wealthy people with money to invest. This mix of industrial talent and investment capital paved the way for Detroit to become the car capital of the world.

1896: Charles King from Detroit, Ransom E. Olds from Lansing and Henry Ford from Dearborn all successfully developed and operated an internal combustion, gasoline-engine-driven horseless carriage. All were involved in various kinds of national recognition, including scholarly publications. They were respected manufacturers prior to auto development, were highly skilled engine builders and were skilled advertisers. All wanted to develop a lightweight, powerful, reliable vehicle for ordinary use.

1899: Because of the need for developmental capital, skilled labor, suppliers and shipping facilities, Olds moved his Olds Motor Works from Lansing to Detroit.

1901-1903: Olds built 9,175 cars using the assembly line for the first time.

1907: By this time there were 2,700 car-manufacturing companies in Michigan.

1908: Henry Ford introduces the Model T and cuts cost by improving the assembly line. William Durant, from Flint, formed General Motors by buying and combining Buick, Cadillac, Oakland, Oldsmobile and seven other companies. May

General Motors, LLC 2011

2011: a General Motors assembly line (in Eaton County) has come a long way since Ransom Olds and Henry Ford; see 25Y

FYI: "Henry Ford (1863-1947) was an American industrialist, the founder of the Ford Motor Company, …his introduction of the Model T [1908] revolutionized transportation and American industry. He is credited with *"Fordism:* mass production of inexpensive goods coupled with high wages for workers. Ford had a global vision, with consumerism as the key to peace. His intense commitment to systematically lowering costs resulted in many technical and business innovations, including the franchise system…" Wikipedia

Z ZOO & ANIMAL PLACES

Petting zoo: Mayberry State Park; Heritage Park (City of Taylor)

Watchable Wildlife Viewing Areas:ww see 82P

Zoo: *Detroit Zoological Park:* see Oakland County

…*Belle Isle Nature Zoo:* part of the Detroit Zoo

Belle Isle Aquarium: oldest freshwater aquarium in U.S., 1904

Detroit Mounted Police stables: in Palmer Park

A AGRICULTURE

Land in farms: 10% of county
Number of farms: 380
Size of average farm: 105 acres
Market value of all products: #64 of 83 counties
Crops: ...most acres: forage
...highest $ sales: cut Christmas trees
Livestock: ...largest number: cattle
...highest $ sales: cattle
Among the top Michigan counties:
• #3- acres of Christmas trees
• #6- sales of Christmas trees
Dairy, food and meat processing plants: 14
State ranking for harvested trees: #17 of 83 counties

FYI: **State of Michigan**
  Land in farms: 27% of state
  Number of farms: 56,000
  Size of average farm: 180 acres
  Market value of all products: #22 of 50 states
  Crops: ...most acres: corn
  ...highest $ sales: grains, oilseeds, dry beans and
    dry peas
  Livestock: ...largest number: laying hens
  ...highest $ sales: milk & dairy products
  Among the top *states*: see 43A
  Dairy, food and meat processing plants: 1,700+
  State ranking for harvested trees: #5 of 50 states
  AgBioResearch Centers (MSU): 15

B BRIDGE OR BOAT

Four Winns is one of the world's largest manufactures of fiberglass recreational products. Established in Cadillac in 1975 and still manufactured here, the company and their boats have a reputation for innovative design and quality construction.

C CELEBRATIONS

Buckley *Old Steam Engine Show:* Aug.

Cadillac *North American Snow Festival:* polar dip, snowmobiling for everyone, ice fishing, reindeer, parade of lights, queen, music, food, Feb.

...*Upbeat Cadillac:* jazz concerts at the Rotary Pavilion, June, July, Aug.

Manton *Harvest Festival:* lumberjack activities, Sept.

Mesick *Mushroom Festival:* morel hunting contest, horseshoes, horse pull, parade, arts & crafts, May

D DEMOGRAPHICS

Population: 32,700   **Persons per sq. mile:** 58
Largest city: Cadillac   **Population:** 10,400
Largest township: Haring   **Population:** 3,170
Largest village: Buckley   **Population:** 700
Median household income: $38,600
Owner-occupied median house value: $112,000
Persons affiliated with a religious congregation: 41%
Persons below poverty level: 17%
Students receiving school lunch subsidy: 48%

FYI: **State of Michigan**
  Population: 9,883,600   **Persons per sq. mile:** 174
  Largest city: Detroit   **Population:** 713,800
  Largest township: Canton (Wayne County)
                Population: 90,200
  Largest village: Milford (Oakland County)
                Population: 6,180
  Median household income: $45,300
  Owner-occupied median house value: $148,000
  Persons below poverty level: 16%
  Students receiving school lunch subsidy: 37%

E ENVIRONMENT

Carl T. Johnson, Chairman and Commissioner of the Natural Resource Commission for 17 years, founded the Michigan Conservation Foundation in 1982. The goal is to keep Michigan's natural resources and its public lands compatible with all recreational uses while protecting wildlife so that future generations

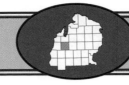
may experience their rightful inheritance. The Johnson Hunting and Fishing Center at Mitchell State Park is named after him. mwthq.net
See 83P, 83V.

F FLORA & FAUNA

Alice Welch, USDA

Morel mushrooms are an elusive yet edible delicacy found in the forests and fields of northern Michigan. All species of these mushrooms have cone-shaped caps, pitted surface, hollow stem and no break between the cap and stem. A warm, moist spring is ideal for the fungi. Mesick is the Mushroom Capital of the United States. For you fungi 'schroomers, pick up your Mushroom Picker's Kit that includes a local treasure map.

James Dowling-Healey/BIOKids

The North American river otter (MI H&T) can tolerate a wide variety of environments and does well here in Michigan. They build their dens on land adjacent to rivers or lakes and then build an underwater tunnel to connect the water and the den.

G GOVERNMENT

County: ...created: 1840 **...organized:** 1869
...originally part of: Manistee County
Size: 369,000 acres / 566 sq. miles (48 of 83 counties)
The county has 2 cities, 3 villages, 16 townships, 7 unincorporated communities and 4 school districts.
County seat: Cadillac

Rick Gleason

NPCR

...Homestead property tax: 42 mills
Motto: Cadillac: *People, Place, Partnerships: The Cadillac Standard*
... Cadillac Area Visitors Bureau: *Your Up North Vacation Travel Destination*

H HISTORICAL MARKERS 8 of 10

Battle of Manton: 1882, Manton was the first county seat and then Cadillac won an election to move it there. In a confrontation, the Cadillac sheriff forcefully removed the county documents from Manton.

Caberfae Ski Resort: 1938, built by the U.S. Forest Service, Civilian Conservation Corps, Cadillac Chamber of Commerce and local volunteers, it was the first winter sports facility that offered a wide variety of winter activities. See 83L.

Cadillac Carnegie Library: 1906, built for $30,000, Classical Revival style building; now home of Wexford Historical Society Museum

Charles T. Mitchell House: 1874, a Second Empire house with ornately carved woodwork and mansard roof was totally renovated in 1926 to a Prairie style house.

NPCR

Clam Lake Canal: 1873, constructed between Big and Little Clam Lake to allow cut timber to get to the mills in Cadillac; now Lakes Mitchell and Cadillac

Cobbs & Mitchell Building: 1907, brick and limestone exterior with an interior of 9 varieties of native Michigan wood; Jonathan Cobbs and William Mitchell were prime movers in the growth of Cadillac and northern Michigan's timber industry

First Wexford County Courthouse: in 1869 the first county seat was in Sherman, then Manton, then in Cadillac in 1882.

Michigan State Historic Preservation Office

Shay Locomotive: 1881, was a smaller, but more powerful engine that could be used to remove the cut trees, even when the ground wasn't frozen; it used vertical pistons and a flexible drive shaft to transfer power via gears to all the wheels. The actual locomotive is on display in City Park, Cadillac. See 83Y

National Register of Historic Places: 7 listings
State Historic Sites: 16 listings

I INFORMATION

Chamber of Commerce: Cadillac, Mesick, Manton
Visitor: Cadillac Area Visitors Bureau, 800-22-LAKES, cadillacmichigan.com

J JOKES

You may be a hunter in Michigan if …
…the mosquitos know your name.
…the critters know how good you can shoot, so they all run and hide whenever you're in the woods.
…your son would rather "Facebook" but your daughter is an ace marksman.
…you like to see the leaves falling like snow.
…you like it when the snow falls at night and stops falling right before daybreak.
…your wife appreciates the lower food bills due to your tenacity in the woods.
…your wife doesn't appreciate the ongoing and never-ending hunting equipment expenses.

…you've patrolled this road and know in your heart that this sign is a joke, but you still keep watching and hoping.

NPCR

K KINSMAN

Race
American Indian: <1%
Asian: <1%
Black/African American: <1%
Hispanic or Latino: 2%
Other: 2%
White: 97%

Ancestry
German: 21%
English: 11%
U.S. / American: 9%
Irish: 9%
Dutch: 6%
Swedish: 5%

FYI: State of Michigan

Race
American Indian: <1%
Asian: 2%
Black/African American: 14%
Hispanic or Latino: 4%
Other: 3%
White: 79%

Ancestry
Other: 25%
German: 20%
Irish: 11%
English: 10%
Polish: 9%
U.S./American: 5%

L LIGHTHOUSE OR LANDMARK

Pete Meyer-Caberfae Ski and Golf Resort

Caberfae Peaks Ski & Golf Resort has 34 downhill ski runs with 6 lifts and 9 holes of challenging golf. See 83H.

M MUSEUMS

Rick Gleason

<u>Cadillac</u> *Wexford County Historical Society & Museum:* to discover, collect and display material of history and culture in the county; in the old Carnegie Library building

<u>Manton</u> *Area Historical Museum:* northern Michigan historical displays, logging

…Veteran's Memorial Museum: artifacts from Civil War, WWI, WWII and peacetime

<u>Mesick</u> *Area Historical Museum:* started as part of the centennial celebration in 1989 to preserve the history of the community

N NATURAL RESOURCES

Elevation: 1,500 feet
Physiography: hilly uplands, plains

NPCR

Forest type: maple-beech-hemlock, pine-oak, aspen-birch
Public/private forests: 76% of county

Water in county: 2% of county
Lakes: 33   **...largest:** Lake Mitchell
FYI: The canal between Lake Mitchell and Lake Cadillac freezes before the lakes do; but once the lakes freeze, the canal thaws!
Rivers: Manistee, Pine
Rivers & streams: 250 miles

Growing season, avg.: 100 days (3 temp. zones)
Last freeze, avg.: May 25 – June 5
First freeze, avg.: Sept. 10 – Sept. 20
Precipitation, annual avg.: rainfall: 31 inches
                                   snowfall: 71 inches
Temperature (F), avg.: January: high 25°, low 10°
                          July: high 79°, low 54°
  Annual: >90°: 5 days, **<0°:** 23 days
Tornadoes (1930-2010): 9

O ORIGINS

<u>Buckley</u>:^v local Buckley & Douglas Lumber Co.; 1905
<u>Cadillac</u>:^c founder of Detroit, Antoine de la Mothe Cadillac; 1872
<u>Harrietta</u>:^v James Ashley combined the names of his father Harry and fiancée, Henriette; 1874
<u>Manton</u>:^c early settler, George Manton; 1872
<u>Mesick</u>:^v sawmill owner, Howard Mesick; 1890
<u>Wexford</u>:^{co} after Wexford County, Ireland

P PARKS

National: 5   **State:** 6   **County:** 1   **Local:** 8
Number of campsites: 1,400

Federal: *Nordhouse Dunes Wilderness Area:* 3,500 acres, a lakeshore dunes ecosystem of 3,700-year-old dunes that are 140' high. It is part of the Ludington Dune Ecosystem that has the largest area of fresh water interdunal ponds in the world.

Rick Gleason

National: *Huron-Manistee National Forest:* 95,000 acres, est. in 1938 on logged-out abandoned lands and partly replanted by the CCC

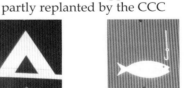

State Forest: (48,000 acres) Pere Marquette
...Campground: 3
State Linear Park: *White Pine Trail:* longest rail-to-trail park in Michigan; 92 miles from Cadillac to Comstock Park in Kent County

State Park: *William Mitchell:*[ww] 330 acres, on the canal between Mitchell and Cadillac lakes, camping, fishing, boating, wildlife, Heritage Trail; home to the Carl T. Johnson Hunting and Fishing Center; see 83V, 83N

NPCR

Q QUOTE FROM THE LOCALS

The Downtown Cadillac Association says, "Take Control of our Local Economy – Buy Local, Buy Michigan!
- Spend $100 in a locally owned business – recirculate up to $73 into the local economy
- Spend $100 in a Michigan-owned business – recirculate up to $43 into the local economy
- Spend $100 online or from a catalog company – recirculate $0 into the local economy.
The choice is yours."

R RECREATION & SPORTS

Blue Ribbon Trout Streams:[1,000] Pine River
Golf courses: 7
Hiking/skiing/mountain biking trails: 55 miles
MI Shore-to-Shore (horse) **Riding & Hiking Trail:** yes
North Country National Scenic Trail: yes
Off-road vehicle trails: 90 miles
Public access sites: 11
Public recreational land: 39% of county
Rail-trail: (8 miles) White Pine
State-funded snowmobile trails: 75 miles
State/federal wild/scenic/ natural river: 10 miles of the Pine River

Cadillac Area Visitors Bureau

Hodenpyle Dam Pond & Man- istee River: slow-moving water for novice kaya- kers and canoeists to those with more experience

Lake Cadillac Bike Path: 7 miles around the lake
Pine River canoeing: fast-moving water for experienced canoeists only
The Cadillac Area Visitors Bureau lists the following outdoor activities for their area: biking, bird watch- ing, boating, camping, canoeing, cross-country skiing, downhill skiing, fall color tours, fishing, geocaching, golfing, hiking, horseback riding, hunting, skateboarding, snowmobiling and tennis.

S STATE OF MICHIGAN

Michigan Facts:
- U.S. ranking, by size: 10th largest (land + water)
- Land: 58,000 square miles
- Length: 456 miles
- Width: 386 miles
- Great Lakes water: 38,575 square miles
- Great Lakes shoreline: 3,286 miles
- Inland water: 1,300 square miles
- Inland lakes: 11,037 (3+ acres)

Top 20 Michigan Municipalities by 2010 Population

Rank	Municipality	County	Population
1	Detroit	Wayne	713,800
2	Grand Rapids	Kent	188,000
3	Warren	Macomb	134,000
4	Sterling Heights	Macomb	130,000
5	Lansing	Ingham	114,000
6	Ann Arbor	Washtenaw	114,000
7	Flint	Genesee	102,000
8	Dearborn	Wayne	98,000
9	Livonia	Wayne	97,000
10	Clinton Charter Twp.	Macomb	97,000
11	Canton Charter Twp.	Wayne	90,000
12	Westland	Wayne	84,000
13	Troy	Oakland	81,000
14	Farmington Hills	Oakland	80,000
15	Macomb Twp.	Macomb	80,000
16	Kalamazoo	Kalamazoo	74,000
17	Shelby Charter Twp.	Macomb	74,000
18	Wyoming	Kent	72,000
19	Southfield	Oakland	72,000
20	Waterford Ch. Twp.	Oakland	72,000

T TRAVEL

Airports: Wexford County
Bus: Indian Trails, Cadillac Wexford Transit Authority
County road names:
  ...north/south: odd number Roads
  ...east/west: even number Roads
Distance to Lansing: 130 miles
Main roads: US-131, M-37, M-42, M-55, M-115
Memorial Highways: US-131 Bypass, *Sydney Ouwinga Memorial Bypass:* he (1927-1991) was a potato farmer and state representative who "was one of the finest, most influential northern Michigan legislators ever" ...M-55, *Gold Star Mothers MH:* see 51T

U UNIVERSITIES & COLLEGES

Baker College: see 25U

V VARIETY

Rick Gleason

The Carl T. Johnson Hunting & Fishing Center presents a fascinating and informative look at the history of hunting and fishing in Michigan. Included are wildlife displays, interactive kiosks and multi-media presentations. There is also a scenic 2-mile Marsh Trail for hiking and wildlife watching. See 83E, 83P.

W WANDERLUST

Fall colors: late September to early October
Walking tours: Keith McKellop Walkway in downtown Cadillac; Pathway around Lake Cadillac; Clam River Greenway

Cadillac Area Visitors Bureau

Sound Garden: interactive musical collaboration of wood and metal; a rustic musical art sculpture that really does make good noise

Caberfae Scenic Overlook: pristine panoramic views
Clam Lake Band: the Ancient and Honorable Clam Lake Dock and Dredge Marching and Chowder Society Silver Cornet Band; for all those grown-ups who can't play in the school band anymore; concerts on Mondays in July and August

X X-TRA STUFF

County fair: *North District Fair Assoc.:* Aug.
Culture: Cadillac Area Artists Association, Cadillac Area Symphony Orchestra, Cadillac Community Chorus, Cadillac Philharmonic Club, Cadillac String Association, Gopherwood Concerts, Northern Michigan Art Guild
Famous people: ...*Politics:* Sid Ouwinga (see 83T) ...*Sports:* Jim Bowman, Paul McMullen, Phil McMullen, Cammy Potter
Hospital: Mercy
Large employers: Four Winns Boats (builds & repairs inboard or outboard motorboats), Meijer, Mercy Hospital, Wal-Mart, Cadillac Casting (makes wheels & parts), Cadillac Rubber & Plastics (makes auto rubber products), Avon Protection Systems (makes gas masks), Lakeview Lutheran Manor (nursing home)
Live theater: Footliters Community Theater

Y YESTERYEAR

"Cadillac was one of few <u>non-river lumbering communities</u> that grew and prospered. The main reason for this was that in 1878, Ephraim Shay perfected his Shay Locomotive (see 83H), which was particularly effective in its ability to climb steep mountain grades effortlessly and to maneuver sharp turns and imperfections in railroad tracks. Until the invention of the Shay Locomotive, horses were used to transport logs, but this process was costly and often dangerous. The lumbering industry was dominant in the 1880-1900s and included many Swedish immigrants." cadillacmighigan.com

Z ZOO & ANIMAL PLACES

Watchable Wildlife Viewing Areas:ww Brandybrook Semiprimitive Area, Manistee River, see 83P

Harrietta State Fish Hatchery: opened in 1901; interpretative area providing information on how watersheds work and how a hatchery operates; rears over 1 million rainbow trout and brown trout annually

NPCR

Carl T. Johnson Hunting and Fishing Center: see 83V

BIBLIOGRAPHY & NOTES, SUBJECT INDEX, INDEX

Bibliography and Indexes refer to the entire state of Michigan.

Information not found in this edition can be located in
*Discovering Michigan County by County: LOWER PENINSULA -
Your A-Z Guide to Each of the 68 Counties in Michigan's Lower Peninsula.*

BIBLIOGRAPHY & NOTES

A AGRICULTURE

All USDA numbers, in all categories, are rounded.

NOTE: (#x/MI) indicates ranking from highest number or percentage (#1) to lowest number or percentage (#83) in Michigan; the significance of either a high or low number depends on the item it describes.

Land in farms: United States Department of Agriculture 2007 Census of Agriculture (USDA CA);

Number of farms: 2007 USDA CA

Size of average farm: 2007 USDA CA

Market value of all products: by state ranking; 2007 USDA CA

Crops ...most acres: 2007 USDA CA

...highest $ sales: by commodity group; 2007 USDA CA, Michigan Department of Agriculture (MDA)

Livestock: ...largest number of: 2007 USDA CA, MDA

...highest $ sales: by commodity group; 2007 USDA CA, MDA

Among the top Michigan counties for
• #x- 2007 USDA CA, MDA

Dairy, food & meat processing plants: MDA

State ranking for harvested trees: Michigan Timber Products Output 2007

AgBioResearch Centers (MSU): Michigan State University

FYI: Sources are cited.

Central Michigan University. Pamphlet: <u>Michigan's GROWING with Michigan's FORESTS</u>, 1996.

B BRIDGE or BOAT

MDOT Historic Bridge: mdot.state.mi.us
• City and county websites
• dalejtravis.com
• discoverboating.com

C CELEBRATIONS

• City and county websites

NOTE #1: Usually only those events of 2 or more days in length and whose information is available on the Web have been included.

NOTE #2: Most Independence Day and Christmas celebrations have not been included since most communities have these events.

NOTE #3: Just of a few of the activities for each celebration have been listed; there are *many* more activities at each event.

D DEMOGRAPHICS

All numbers given are for the county, unless otherwise stated. All numbers are rounded.

NOTE: (#x/MI) indicates ranking from highest number or percentage (#1) to lowest number or percentage (#83) in Michigan; the significance of either a high or low number depends on the item it describes.

Population: 2010 U.S. Census

Persons per sq. mile: 2010 U.S. Census

Largest city: 2010 U.S. Census
  Population: 2010 U.S. Census

Largest township: 2010 U.S. Census
  Population: 2010 U.S. Census

Largest village: 2010 U.S. Census
  Population: 2010 U.S. Census

Median household income: 2009 U.S. Census

Owner-occupied median house value: 2005-2009 U.S. Census

…NOTE: the value of Michigan real estate declined an average of 26% from 2006 to 2011

Persons affiliated with a religious congregation: city-data.com

Persons below poverty level: 2009 U.S. Census

Students receiving school lunch subsidy: MDA 2007

…NOTE: In the 2012-2013 school year, the upper income limit for a family of four was $30,000 for free school meals and $42,600 for reduced school meals. [USDA]

E ENVIRONMENT

Schaetzl, Randall. <u>Michigan Geography and Geology</u>. New York: Custom Publishing, 2009.

Sources are cited.

F FLORA & FAUNA

NOTE: All Flora and Fauna can be found in the county where they are listed and are not limited to that county unless otherwise stated.

• biokids.umich.edu
• carsoncity.k12.mi.us
• Michigan.org
• *(MI H&T)* = Michigan allows Hunting and Trapping of this animal with the proper training, permits, licensing and within the season.
• msuturfweeds.net

Schinkel, Dick. <u>Favorite Wildflowers of the Great Lakes and the Northeastern U.S.</u> Lansing: Thunder Bay Press, 1994.

BIBLIOGRAPHY & NOTES

Smith, Norman F. <u>Michigan Trees Worth Knowing</u>. Hillsdale: Hillsdale Educational Publishers, 1952.

Wells, Diana. <u>100 Flowers and How They Got Their Names</u>. Chapel Hill: Algonquin Books of Chapel Hill, 1997.

G GOVERNMENT

County: ...created: Michigan GenWeb
...organized: Michigan GenWeb
...originally part of: Michigan GenWeb
Size: Michigan State University Extension County Tourism Profile (MSUE CTP); National Association Of Counties (NAOC); number is rounded
...NOTE: land and land-based water acres; does not include Great Lakes waters, unless otherwise stated.
The county has: Michigan Economic Development Corporation Economic Profiler; Wikipedia
County seat: NAOC
...NOTE: Information about a county courthouse is from a Michigan Historical Marker. Not all counties have Historical Markers about their courthouse.
...Homestead property tax: Michigan Property Tax Estimator, 2011, number is rounded; see also 44S.
Motto: city and county websites; also includes slogans, taglines and signs

H HISTORICAL MARKERS

•michmarkers.com
of #: At the discretion of the author, not all historical markers have been included.
Monuments: various sources
National Historic Landmark: michigan.gov
National Register of Historic Places: nr.nps.gov
State Historic Sites: Michigan State Housing Development Authority
• Ella Sharp Museum display
• Flat River Historical Museum display
• Grand Rapids Public Museum display
• Hartwick Pines Logging Museum display
• Michigan Historical Museum display

I INFORMATION

Chamber of Commerce: listed by city
...Chamber of Commerce listing, by city, for all Chambers in Michigan at mich.info/michigan/business/michambers1
...Chamber of Commerce listing, by county, of all Chambers in Michigan at greatlakesonline.com/coc/mi

Visitor: city and county tourism websites
See Also:
...Michigan Travel Bureau: 888-78-GREAT, Michigan.org
...Pure Michigan: Michigan.org
...Upper Peninsula Travel and Recreation Association: "5-Star Wilderness®" 800-562-7134, uptravel.com
...West Michigan Travel Association: 800-442-2084, wmta.org
...Western U.P. Travel & Recreation: westernup.info

J JOKES

NOTE: Just a little bit of humor to make you smile or snicker or, at least, wrinkle your brow and say, "Huh?"
• Various sources

K KINSMEN

Race: 2010 U.S. Census
...NOTE: Race is in **bold** type because the same races repeat in every county.
Ancestry: Most Common First Ancestries, 2000 U.S. Census
...NOTE: The Ancestry listings are *not* in bold type because they are different in every county.
NOTE: Totals may not equal 100% because numbers are rounded and not all races or ancestries are included.

L LIGHTHOUSE OR LANDMARK

When you see "this," you know you're in *this* county!
• Michiganlights.com
• county websites
• local residents

M MUSEUMS

• City and county websites' visitor information
NOTE: *We always recommend you call ahead to check on the operating status of any venue!!!* Check the Internet for contact information or call the Visitor Information listed in *I INFORMATION*.

458

BIBLIOGRAPHY & NOTES

N NATURAL RESOURCES

NOTE: (#x/MI) indicates ranking from highest number or percentage (#1) to lowest number or percentage (#83) in Michigan; the significance of either a high or low number depends on the item it describes.

Elevation: UniversalMap Michigan County Atlas, 1989 (UM MCA)

Physiography: UM MCA

Soil: mighiganfruitbelt.org

…NOTE: Many soils occur throughout the state and are not limited to any one county; every county has multiple soil types. The county where 'Soil' is listed is a good example of that soil type.

Forest type: UM MCA

Public/private forests: Michigan State University Extension County Tourism Profile (MSUE CTP)

Legislatively protected sand dunes: MSUE CTP

National Natural Landmark: wikipedia.org

Water in county: MSUE CTP
  Bay: MDOT map, major bays only
  Lakes: lakeplace.com/lakefinder/mi
    NOTE: Generally, number of lakes includes the larger, named lakes; it *may not* include all lakes.
      Largest: lakeplace.com/lakefinder/mi
  Rivers: UM MCA
  Rivers & streams: MSUE CTP, number is rounded
  Waterfall: geology.com/waterfalls/mich

Great Lakes islands: MDOT map, major islands only

Great Lakes peninsula: mich.gov; named peninsulas only

Great Lakes shoreline: MSUE CTP

Growing season, avg.: days: Michigan Economic Development Corporation Economic Profiler (MEDC EP), 1995
  temp. zones: Sommers, Lawrence M. Atlas of Michigan. Michigan State University Press, 1977.
    …NOTE: each **temp**erature zone is a 5-day period
  Last freeze, avg.: Sommers
  First freeze, avg.: Sommers
Precipitation, annual avg.: rainfall: MEDC EP
                          snowfall: MEDC EP
Temperature (F), avg.: January: MEDC EP
                    July: MEDC EP
  Annual: >90°F: MEDC EP, **<0°F**: MEDC EP
Tornadoes (1930-2010): Sommers; National Oceanic and Atmospheric Administration
NOTE: Some pictures are not specific to the county in which they are shown, but *are* representative of the county's natural environment.

O ORIGINS

Romig, Walter. <u>Michigan Place Names</u>. Grosse Pointe: Walter Romig Publisher, 1986.

Date: earliest known settlers/settlement as stated by Romig

<u>City</u>: this double underline indicates that the city was founded as a railroad stop or was a station on a railroad line in its *very early* years, as stated by Romig

^c = current city
^{co} = current county
^{ct} = current charter township
^t = current township
^u = current unincorporated place
^v = current village

NOTE: All ORIGINS place names are from Romig unless stated otherwise.

NOTE: The county, all cities, villages and charter townships are listed; other localities are listed at the discretion of the author.

[1,000]Schultz, Patricia. <u>1,000 Places To See Before You Die</u>. New York: Workman Publishing, 2007.

P PARKS

All numbers for *acres* are rounded.

National, State, County, Local parks: UniversalMap Michigan County Atlas, 1989

Number of campsites: Michigan State University Extension County Tourism Profile

National: National Park Service

State: Michigan.gov/dnr

County: county websites

Local: city and county websites

Other: varied sources
  ^{ww}=Watchable Wildlife Viewing Area: michigandnr.com
  ^{wba}= Wildflower Blooming Area: michigandnr.com

NOTE: Some pictures are not specific to the county in which they are shown, but *are* representative of the county's natural environment.

Q QUOTE FROM THE LOCALS

Sources cited.

Sunfield History Seekers, <u>Sunfield Town and Country</u>, 1995

R RECREATION & SPORTS

NOTE: (#x/MI) indicates ranking from highest

number or percentage (#1) to lowest number or percentage (#83) in Michigan; the significance of either a high or low number depends on the item it describes.

Auto racing: track websites

Blue Ribbon Trout Streams: tailtstotrout.com

Golf courses: Michigan State University Extension County Tourism Profile (MSUE CTP)

Great Lakes marinas: MSUE CTP
    Boat slips: MSUE CTP

Hiking/skiing/mountain biking trails: MSUE CTP; number rounded

Horse racing: michigangaming.com

Michigan Heritage Water Trail: wmich.edu

North Country National Scenic Trail: northcountry trail.org

Off-road vehicle trails: designated trails; MSU CTP; number is rounded

Public access sites: MSUE CTP

Public recreational land: MSUE CTP

Rail-trail: railstotrails.org; number is rounded

…NOTE: Includes rail and other type trails but may not include *all* trails in the county.

Recreational harbor: michigandnr.com

State/federal wild/scenic/natural river: A river with State of Michigan or U.S. Park Service designation as a wild and/or scenic and/or natural river; mi. gov.dnr; U.S. Park Service; number is rounded.

State funded snowmobile trails: MSUE CTP; number is rounded

NOTE: Some pictures are not specific to the county in which they are shown, but *are* representative of the county's natural environment.

S STATE of MICHIGAN

Reed, Jane Mende. Locks & Ships. Sault Ste. Marie: National Office Products & Printing, Inc., 2010
Sources are cited.
Schaetzl, Randall. Michigan Geography and Geology. New York: Custom Publishing, 2009.

T TRAVEL

Airport: Michigan Economic Development Corporation Economic Profiler (MEDC EP), 1995

Amtrak: amtrak.com

Bus: MEDC EP; city and county websites

Circle Tour: michiganhighways.org

County road names: …north/south: UniversalMap Michigan County Atlas, 1989 (UM MCA)
    …east/west: UM MCA

Distance to Lansing: MEDC EP

Ferry: city and county websites

Great Waters Lake Superior Trail Tour: michigan.org

Historic Harbortowns: michigan.org

Heritage Route: michiganhighways.org

Lights of Northern Lake Huron Tour: michigan.org

Main roads: MEDC EP

Memorial Highways: Michigan.gov

Barnett, LeRoy, Ph.D. A Drive Down Memory Lane: The Named State and Federal Highways of Michigan. Allegan Forest: Priscilla Press, 2004.

Michigan Welcome Center: Michigan Department of Transportation

Northwest Michigan Port of Call Tour: michigan.org

Scenic Drive: allgetaways.com

FYI: Barnett

U UNIVERSITIES & COLLEGES

- Information is from the website of each school.
  Est.: year school was established
  # students: current enrollment; number is rounded
  Athletic Conferences abbreviations:
  Big 10: Big 10, Div. I
  CCHA: Central Collegiate Hockey Association, Div. I
  GLIAC: Great Lakes Intercollegiate Athletic Conference, Div. II
  HL: Horizon League, Div. l
  MAC: Michigan Athletic Conference, Div. I
  MCC: Mid-Central College Conference
  MCCAA: Michigan Community College Athletic Association
  MCHA: Midwest Collegiate Hockey Association, Div. III
  MIAA: Michigan Intercollegiate Athletic Association (the nations oldest athletic conference), Div. III
  NAIA: National Association of Intercollegiate Athletics
  NCCAA: National Christian College Athletic Association
  NCHA: Northern Collegiate Hockey Association, Div. III
  NJCAA: National Junior College Athletic Association
  Summit League: Div. I
  USCAA: United States Collegiate Athletic Association, Div. II
  WHAC: Wolverine-Hoosier Athletic Conference, Div. II
  WIAC: Wisconsin Intercollegiate Athletic Conference, Div. III

BIBLIOGRAPHY & NOTES

V VARIETY

Sources are cited.

May, George S. <u>MICHIGAN, An Illustrated History of The Great Lakes State</u>. Northridge: Windsor Publications, 1987.

Schultz, Gerard. <u>The New History of Michigan's Thumb</u>,1969.

W WANDERLUST

NOTE: *We always recommend you call ahead to check on the operating status of a venue!!!* Check the Internet for contact information or call the Visitor Information listed in *I INFORMATION*.

Agri-tourism: michiganfarmfun.com (2011), farms with websites only

…NOTE: For the complete list of all farms, get the printed book at your local Farm Bureau Office or Michigan Welcome Centers, or go online.

Brewery: michiganbrewersguild.com, 2011

…NOTE: There may be other breweries in the county but only members of the Michigan Brewers Guild are listed here.

Casino: 500nations.com

Cultural: city and county websites' visitor information

Fall colors: UniversalMap Michigan County Atlas

Lighthouse, other: city and county websites' visitor information

NOTE: at the discretion of the author, not all lighthouses or lights have been included.

Live theater: city and county websites' visitor information

MotorCities National Heritage Area: motorcities.org

Planetarium: go-astronomy.com; does not include public school planetariums

Shopping mall: city and county website visitor information

…NOTE: It is assumed that all communities have downtown shopping districts so these are not listed.

Walking tour: city and county websites' visitor information

Wineries: michiganfarmfun.com; city and county websites

NOTE: Some pictures are not specific to the county in which they are shown, but are representative of the county's natural environment.

X X-TRA STUFF

American Indian Community: bjmi.us/maps

Commercial port: Michigan Economic Development Corp. Economic Profiler (MEDC EP), 1995

County fair: Michigan Department of Agriculture; fair websites; local residents

Famous people: michigan.gov; local residents

Hospitals: MEDC EP 1998; updated by local residents

Large employers: MEDC EP 2008; updated by local residents

[1,000]Schultz, Patricia. <u>1,000 Places To See Before You Die</u>. New York: Workman Publishing, 2007.

Y YESTERYEAR

Sources are cited.

Anderson, David D. <u>Michigan: A State Anthology</u>. Detroit: Gale Research Company, 1983.

Baker, John Milnes, A.I.A. <u>American House Styles</u>. New York: W. W. Norton & Company, 1994.

DuMond, Neva. <u>Thumb Diggings</u>. Lexington: NEVA DUMOND, 1962.

Dunbar, Willis. <u>MICHIGAN: A History of the Wolverine State</u>. Grand Rapids: William B. Eerdmans Publishing Company, 1965.

Elliott, Gerald. <u>Grand Rapids, Renaissance on the Grand</u>. Tulsa: Continental Heritage Press, 1982.

Hollands, Hulda T. <u>When Michigan Was New</u>. A. Flanigan Company, 1906.

May, George M. <u>A Most Unique Machine</u>. Grand Rapids: William B. Eerdmans Publishing Company, 1975.

McAlester, Virginia & Lee. <u>A Field Guide to American Houses</u>. New York: Alfred A. Knopf, 1994.

Nagel, Herbert. <u>The Metz Fire of 1908, Presque Isle County, Michigan</u>. Presque Isle County Historical Society, 1979.

Sigsby, Rick. <u>Images of America Gladwin County</u>. Arcadia Publishing, 2008.

- Ella Sharp Museum display
- Flat River Historical Museum display
- Grand Rapids Public Museum display
- Hartwick Pines Logging Museum display
- Michigan Historical Museum display

Z ZOOS & ANIMAL PLACES

Petting zoo: city and county websites' visitor information

[ww]**Watchable Wildlife Viewing Areas:** Michigan Department of Natural Resources

[wba]**Wildflower Blooming Areas:** DNR

Zoo: city and county websites' visitor information

NOTE: Some pictures are not specific to the county in which they are shown, but are representative of the county's natural environment.

SUBJECT INDEX
LETTER CATEGORIES A, B, E, F, L, S, V, Y

Number = the number that corresponds to the alphabetical listing for each *county*, from Alcona County 1 to Wexford County 83

Letter = the alphabetical letter category *within* each county, from A Agriculture to Z Zoo & Animal Places

AGRICULTURE FYI – Crops

AGRICULTURE FYI – Livestock

AGRICULTURE FYI– Organizations

AGRICULTURE FYI - Other

SUBJECT INDEX
LETTER CATEGORIES A, B, E, F, L, S, V, Y

SUBJECT INDEX
LETTER CATEGORIES A, B, E, F, L, S, V, Y

SUBJECT INDEX
LETTER CATEGORIES A, B, E, F, L, S, V, Y

INDEX

Number = the number that corresponds to the alphabetical listing for each *county,* from Alcona County 1 to Wexford County 83

Letter = the alphabetical letter category *within* each county, from A Agriculture to Z Zoo & Animal Places

INDEX includes the *SUBJECT INDEX.*

INDEX

INDEX

INDEX

INDEX

INDEX

About the Author

Prentice Drake

Barbara J. (Mitchell) VanderMolen grew up in Dearborn Heights (Wayne County), graduated from Western Michigan University (Kalamazoo County), and now lives in Charlotte (Eaton County) with her husband, John. They have three adult children and seven grandchildren.

As a "big city girl" who moved to a "rural" area with her husband, who was employed by Michigan Farm Bureau, she developed a broad and unique perspective on the State of Michigan. She was able to experience the agricultural and natural resources' cultures in the state with a wide-eyed wonder, and thought many times, "I never even knew that *that* even existed." Her desire is that you, too, will develop that same appreciation for the beauty of the natural resources, the uniqueness of these natural resources, and the blessing of an agricultural abundance that God has given our wonderful state.

As a 'professional volunteer,' she is very active in her church and community, loves to organize anything, designed her own home, created the small businesses of Give-A-Tree and Day Tripper Tours of Mid-Michigan, and is well known locally for her homemade pies and jam. That's her dog, Charlie Rose, a Cavalier King Charles Spaniel, with her in the picture.

If you have comments, suggestions, corrections or updates, please email these to info@discovermichigancountybycounty.com.

To order additional copies of this book, please visit our website at discovermichigancountybycounty.com.